MAJOR FIGURES OF MODERN AUSTRIAN LITERATURE

STUDIES IN AUSTRIAN LITERATURE, CULTURE, AND THOUGHT

MAJOR FIGURES OF MODERN AUSTRIAN LITERATURE

Edited and with an Introduction
by
Donald G. Daviau

Ariadne Press
Riverside, California

MAJOR FIGURES OF MODERN AUSTRIAN LITERATURE

Table of Contents

MAJOR FIGURES
OF MODERN AUSTRIAN LITERATURE

Edited and introduced by Donald G. Daviau

Preface

Like the previous volume of this series, *Major Figures of Contemporary Austrian Literature,* the present collection of essays is intended to present another generation of outstanding Austrian authors to the English-speaking world. It is felt that these writers have something valuable to say to a wider audience than they can reach in German alone, and hence the rationale for what will be a series of six volumes containing the major authors from approximately 1800 to the present, that is, from Franz Grillparzer, possibly the first consciously Austrian writer, to contemporary figures such as Bernhard and Handke. The series is predicated on the notion that an independent Austrian tradition has existed at least since the age of Grillparzer, justifying the decision to highlight Austrian literature as a unique, independent phenomenon, separate from the German tradition from which it emanated and to which it is still closely related.

The postwar period has witnessed a worldwide interest—one might almost call it a fascination—in Austria and Austrian culture. This extensive popularity has been both scholarly, in the form of numerous books, articles, and symposia devoted to Austrian arts and culture, and popular, in the form of broad public attendance at art exhibits such as the "Vienna 1900" in New York in 1986. Because of this growing awareness of Austria and its cultural contribution, there has been a perceived need to make more information available in English to provide in convenient form the background needed to appreciate the

Austrian literary contributions, to permit understanding this rich tradition in its own terms and to make possible comparisons to the Western European tradition.

In preparing this series the decision was made to proceed from the present to the past rather than to follow the more orthodox procedure of moving chronologically from past to present. Hence the first volume, mentioned above, treats only living authors. The present volume, the second in the series, moves a generation back in time to feature for the most part those authors who had begun to write in the 1930s but only attained widespread prominence in the postwar period. Thus the fifteen major figures presented here are intended to represent the chronological period from roughly 1930 to 1955, the year when Austria became an independent state and when the Vienna Group began heralding a change of literary direction.

The methodological approach of the first volume has been continued here, namely, each of the essays is written by an expert on that particular author and follows a straightforward life and works approach. The contributors were asked to accomplish the extremely difficult task of producing an introductory essay for an English-speaking audience with no presumed background in Austrian or German culture or literature, while at the same time providing sufficient breadth of coverage, depth of analysis, and original insight to make the essays of interest and utility to students and even to specialists in the field. From this and the other volumes in preparation readers can expect to receive a basic introduction to the major Austrian writers along with an understanding of their major works, forms, and themes. In the aggregate these essays will also provide a perception of the dominant literary trends of the period under consideration and ultimately an awareness of the unique features that distinguish Austrian literature and characterize its independent national identity.

ACKNOWLEDGMENTS

I would like to express my appreciation to all those who helped bring this volume to fruition. In addition to the contributors of the individual essays my thanks go to my colleagues who read the manuscript and made valuable suggestions for improvement: Professors Harvey I. Dunkle, Jorun B. Johns, and Richard H. Lawson. I wish also to thank Jean Weiss for preparing the name index, Mary Reyes for typing assistance, and the Research Committee at the University of California, Riverside for financial support.

MAJOR FIGURES
OF MODERN AUSTRIAN LITERATURE

Introduction

Donald G. Daviau

This volume is intended to feature the generation of writers who began their literary careers before World War II but attained full prominence only in the postwar period. Thus, although in terms of strict chronology the writers presented here span virtually the first half of the twentieth century, the introduction will emphasize the historical period extending from 1933, when Hitler was named German Chancellor, to 1955, when Austria regained its status as an independent country. Coincidentally Austrian literature, which had restored its severed link with tradition, was ripe for innovative change at approximately this same time, led initially by H. C. Artmann and the Vienna Group in the mid-1950s and extended and amplified by the Graz Group in the 1960s. Since the period from 1955 to the present has been covered in the introduction to the previous volume, *Major Figures of Contemporary Austrian Literature,*[1] that information will be reduced here to the minimal details necessary to establish the proper context and perspective for the essays to follow.

The authors in the present volume were born at different times and in different places, but they all had a number of shared experiences in common: World War I (1914–1918), the death of Emperor Franz Joseph in 1916, the trauma of the loss of the Monarchy and the reduction of Austria to a small fragment of its former size and power in 1918, the founding of the First Republic on 12 November 1918, the severe inflation and high unemployment rate during the 1920s, the civil uprising and the burning of the Palace of Justice in 1927, the workers' uprising and civil war of 1934, the aborted Nazi *Putsch* and the murder of Chancellor Dollfuss in 1934, the *Anschluß* (annexation) of Austria by Hitler on 11 March 1938, World War II (1939-1945), the experience of exile or inner emigration, and finally the four-power Allied occupation until national autonomy was restored in 1955 and the country was declared a permanently neutral land analogous to Switzerland. Above all Austrian writers all shared a deep and abiding love of their homeland that never wavered or diminished even in exile.

Historically the atmosphere of Austria from 1867 to 1914 had been rather tranquil, reflecting the conservative governing principle of Emperor Franz Joseph's rule: to preserve the *status quo*. Austria has always hovered between the poles of tradition and innovation, but clearly during the era of Franz Joseph there was an attempt to an almost reactionary degree to make tradition the dominant trend, even in the realms of literature and culture, as the strongest bulwark to preserve the country against the problems and the confusions created by a rapidly changing world: the spread of industrialization, technical and scientific advances, and the growing pressures from member states of the Monarchy for greater representation and autonomy. The figure of the Emperor, an archetype of the benevolent lovable grandfather, who reigned longer than any other European monarch (1848-1916), served as a magnificent symbol of stability and steadfastness for his people, creating the impression—some may call it the illusion—of what Stefan Zweig has so aptly termed "the golden age of security." Even though its close ties to Germany had been severed after the Battle of Königgrätz in 1866, and its control over Hungary weakened by the establishment of the Dual Monarchy in 1867, Austria was still a powerful multi-ethnic nation of some fifty million people, extending eastward to include an enclave in Poland and southward to encompass the major seaport of Trieste (that Austria had a navy until the end of World War I is an often overlooked or forgotten fact). On the surface, the Monarchy was seemingly at peace with itself and with the world; although there were always nagging problems with the various territorial states such as Dalmatia (Yugoslavia), Hungary, and Serbia, it had an important and clearly defined role to play in its sphere of influence. A solidly entrenched, well-staffed bureaucracy and a loyal, well-disciplined army seemed to provide solid guarantees for maintaining the country's stability, and there appeared to be no reason why the Monarchy should not continue basking indefinitely in the glitter and glamour of the royal house and the kind protective good will of Franz Joseph.

These conditions at the turn of the century produced a unique environment in which the arts and sciences flourished as rarely before in Austria, lifting the country in the space of a few years to worldwide cultural recognition. With the aura of successful cultural progress created by the Ringstrasse and the buildings adorning it, the writings of Altenberg, Bahr, Hofmannsthal, Kraus, and Schnitzler, the paintings of Klimt and the Secessionists, the buildings of Otto Wagner and Joseph Olbrich, and the artifacts of Josef Hoffmann and the "Wiener Werkstätte" (Vienna Workshop), few Austrians seemed to mind that the country failed to follow the path of England, France, and Germany toward rapid industrialization. The resplendent surface opulence made it easy to conceal the festering political and economic problems and so bedazzled the ruling class as well as the artists and intellectuals that the suppression and repression of any evidence of harsh reality was easily accomplished and became the fashion of the day. To a degree this tendency represented a widely shared desire for escape from reality, but it was not necessarily frivolous. The major authors seriously endorsed the idea that the arts held the key to a prospective better life, so what need had one for industrialization and above all for concern about dreary politics? Moreover, with the conservative Emperor Franz Joseph on the imperial throne, the highly admired and flamboyant "handsome" Karl Lueger ("der schöne Karl") solidly entrenched as the three-time mayor of Vienna, and the daily operations in the far-flung reaches of the Monarchy secure in the hands of a dedicated, if not necessarily efficient, bureaucracy, there seemed to be no need for progress and change and, indeed, little possibility of it.

What was overlooked at the time in Austria, and particularly in Vienna before World War I, was that the image the country projected even to its own citizens was almost pure façade, as Karl Kraus and, in his own way, Freud kept trying to point out. But the artistic surface was so glamorously attractive, the atmosphere it created so warm and comfortable, and the promise of a future of beauty and culture so enticing, that the majority of writers, artists, and intellectuals were caught up in the perception that this idealistic appearance represented all the reality the country needed. There was no widespread clamor for social change despite the harsh economic conditions and poor housing for the working classes even in Vienna and despite signs of deep discontent against Austrian mismanagement in the satellite states, because these unpleasant realities were glossed over by the grandiose cultural façade in which people wanted to believe and which few wanted to see changed. The majority of middle- and upper-class Austrians at the turn of the century were in love with their society exactly as it was, in a way and to a degree not usually found in other countries. For those with talent and/or money life was good and beautiful, and it was easy to avoid anything distasteful as well as any sense of social responsibility.

One shared concern—one that still remains today, although it has now been fairly well resolved—was the question of national identity which arose with the severing of connections with Germany in 1866. The relationship of Austrians to Germany and the development of an independent national identity is an important chapter in itself. Because of Austria's historical origin in the tenth century under the Babenbergs for the express purpose of preventing a Turkish invasion of Germany, a role that the country has performed twice, in the sixteenth and seventeenth centuries, Austria and Austrian thinking was traditionally oriented toward Germany. Only in the late eighteenth century did Austrian literary historians begin to raise the question of a separate Austrian literary tradition. Even after 1866 the dominant sentiment in Austria was to restore the connections with Germany, and the cry for reannexation became the party program for Schönerer and his German National Party. It can be said that the *Anschluß* in 1938 was for many the fulfillment of a goal yearned for since 1866.

Throughout the nineteenth century, but particularly after World War II, Austrians have been preoccupied with such questions as what it means to be Austrian, whether Austria should be regarded as a country separate from Germany, and whether there is an independent Austrian literature *sui generis*. With the founding of the Second Republic in 1955 most of these questions were laid to rest because an independent identity was then established; but the debate still continues, as the number of books, articles, and symposia devoted to these issues attests.[2] At the turn of the century there was a strong feeling, one that became even stronger with time, that the Austrian society represented by Vienna was special and unique. Therefore whatever threatened to break the spell of enchantment, to intrude upon the glorious dream, was simply ignored. One of the great myths perpetuated in the literature about Austria is the notion that an atmosphere of melancholy reigned at the turn of the century, that the young writers and artists, having succumbed to aestheticism, suffered from languor, pessimism, especially cultural pessimism, and a general feeling of lassitude, lacking energy and will. This myth is simply not true. On the contrary Austria was brimming over with young talent in all fields, and, like young people everywhere and always, they believed in themselves, they believed in the future, and they particularly believed in their role in making that future even better and brighter for everyone. The young artists and intellectuals at the turn of the century, all of them energetic, creative, intelligent overachievers, had no reason to suspect an impending end to the Monarchy, which had existed for nearly a thousand years and which seemed, on the basis of the perceivable façade, destined to last another thousand. Certainly there were various cracks and blemishes in the structure, but the foundation looked as secure as ever.

This fallacy about the *fin-de-siècle* mood of decline, perpetuated and exaggerated in the secondary literature about turn-of-the-century Austria, was created retrospectively after the fall of the Monarchy in 1918 and imposed retroactively upon a historical situation. Because the Monarchy did end in 1918, critics, with the advantage of hindsight, have interpreted certain manifestations such as the phenomenon of literary decadence as signs not only indicative of, but also leading to the inevitable decline. In the process the entire early work of Hofmannsthal and Schnitzler was badly misinterpreted and to a large degree remains so even today. Every recent study of *fin-de-siècle* Vienna describes this period as a golden age fatally afflicted with a sense of ennui, despair, and hopelessness, and this idea, repeated by one commentator after another without reference to the primary sources, has taken root as the accepted canon. Yet in fact the situation looks quite different from the perspective of the time. The writings of the authors, artists, and intellectuals, particularly their diaries and letters, provide abundant evidence of positive feelings of optimism, enthusiasm, and progressiveness. The evidence does not support the current myth of a country inevitably doomed to collapse.[3] If one could be exposed to the period around 1900 without the awareness that the Monarchy ended, one would not be led to the conclusion that a sense of pessimism and despair reigned. Rather one would see that these young writers and artists, all gifted with extraordinary talent and brimming with the self-confidence that they were destined to accomplish great things, were filled with glorious hopes for and enormous confidence in the future they would help to create, a future based on a renewed culture that would be meaningful in the everyday life of every citizen and would produce a new sense of humanity and humanitarianism. The arts individually and culture in general were viewed as the key elements in this blueprint for the future, not politics, which was relegated to the background as unimportant beyond the necessary bureaucracy to keep the country functioning.

Reality intruded into this heady atmosphere in June 1914 when the heir apparent, Archduke Franz Ferdinand and his wife were assassinated at Sarajevo. There was no love lost between Franz Joseph and his nephew, whose personal political ambitions did not accord with those of his uncle, but nevertheless the over-confident and arrogant Austrian high command under General Conrad von Hötzendorf persuaded the Emperor to teach the Serbians a lesson from which any other malcontent states could learn. An air of tension hovered over all of Europe at the time, an atmosphere analogous to the pressure built up by sultry weather and requiring a sudden rainstorm to clear the air. The major countries were poised like a row of dominoes, with Austria, Germany, and Italy linked by treaties on one side, and England, France, and Russia on the other. Once one move was made, it set into motion a chain reaction that could not be stopped. The "little action" against Serbia, which was expected to last a few weeks, rapidly escalated into World War I and through political maneuvering at the peace negotiations the end of the Austrian Monarchy forever. By the miscalculation of his advisers Franz Joseph, who had devoted an exemplary Spartan life to the single-minded goal of preserving the Monarchy at all costs, achieved ironically the diametrically opposite result. Mercifully his death in 1916 spared him the ignominy of witnessing the forced resignation of his successor, Emperor Karl I, in November 1918, and the Allied insistence on the breakup of the Monarchy, a demand which was raised only after the war by Woodrow Wilson and his Fourteen Points. Until Wilson had presented his proposal there had been no pressure to disestablish the Monarchy and realign borders in a way maximally unfair to natural geographical boundaries and the ethnic makeup of the population. The declaration of what remained of Austria as the First Republic under the leadership of the Socialists Dr. Otto Bauer and Dr. Karl Renner radically reduced Austria overnight from a major multinational power with a population of some fifty million people and a navy to a small landlocked torso (*Rumpfstaat*) with approximately seven million inhabitants. Thus was created "the state against its will" or "the state that nobody wanted," as Helmut Andics has called it.[4]

Geographically and politically the transformation from Monarchy to Republic was profound; from the standpoint of Austrian literature, art, and culture in general it was as if absolutely nothing had changed. The national transition to a Republic was most remarkable in the sense that the writers took virtually no notice of it. Instead, in keeping with their practice of avoiding politics and their dedication to preserving the beautiful façade, they ignored the new reality in which Austria found itself, including even the new form of government, and continued to glorify the Monarchy. The writers and artists were unwilling to relinquish the wonderful world in which they had been raised and continued to pursue the same themes and interests as before the war. All of the writers in this volume, even if they were very young at the time of the Monarchy, were raised in an atmosphere that reflected a pervasive Habsburg image and influence.

The main reason for the lack of any sudden literary change was that the dominating turn-of-the-century writers such as Hugo von Hofmannsthal, Arthur Schnitzler, Richard Beer-Hofmann, Hermann Bahr, Karl Kraus, Rainer Maria Rilke, and Stefan Zweig continued to produce the same kind of works they had always written. They all appreciated the Austria in which they had been raised, even though they could all be critical of the foibles of the Viennese, and they continued to glorify the greatness of the Austrian tradition in their works. They and all of their colleagues cultivated what Claudio Magris has called the Habsburg myth and perpetuated the Monarchy long after it had ended.[5] Hofmannsthal in his comedy *Der Schwierige* (1918, *The Difficult Man*), his drama *Der Turm* (1927, *The Tower*), and his final opera in collaboration with Richard Strauss, *Arabella* (1929), and Schnitzler in his comedy, *Die Schwestern oder Casanova im Spa* (1921, *The Sisters or Casanova in Spa*), or his drama about the Austrian past, *Der Gang zum Weiher* (1926, *The Walk to the Pond*), were representative of all the established authors. In 1928 and 1929, when Hitler and the Nazi party were using a combination of promises, threats, and beatings to assume political control in Berlin through the polls, Schnitzler and Raoul Auernheimer in Vienna were debating the question of whether or not drama should be written in verse! While it might be expected that the older generation would preserve a tradition under which it had spent most of its life, it is surprising that this attitude could continue unabated throughout the 1930s despite the rapidly changing political climate. In 1938 Joseph Roth, exiled in Paris and the most ardent champion of the past, was still advocating the restoration of the Monarchy. The preservation of the Habsburg myth or, if one prefers, a yearning for tradition as a means of clinging to the happiness and stability of an earlier era will be seen as a recurring theme in almost all of the writers in this volume.

Certainly there were and always had been serious problems in every direction and in every sphere of Austrian life, if one cared to note them, as some of the writers did. Both Bahr and Kraus, though bitter enemies, wrote about political problems. They were joined by Altenberg and Schnitzler among others in reinforcing Freud's attempt to unmask the widespread hypocrisy surrounding sex.[6] But even in the context of this theme the authors attacked different concerns. Kraus fought hard for the rights of prostitutes, including the legal right to the protection of the courts, but at the same time he never considered women equal to men or entitled to the same rights and prerogatives. By contrast Schnitzler came to accept these principles of equality in his later writings. Sex and eroticism as major problems of the early twentieth century were rivaled in thematic importance only by anti-Semitism, which had been growing ever more virulent since the advent of Ritter Georg von Schönerer and his German National Party in the 1880s, with its enormous influence on the university fraternities.[7] The two topics were combined by the young Jewish philosopher Otto Weininger, an arch-misogynist and anti-Semite, whose book *Geschlecht und Charakter* (1903, *Sex and Character*), written at age twenty-two, was followed by his suicide as a result of his self-loathing. The book created a sensation in its time, and it remains a work commanding continued scholarly attention today, both for its intrinsic ideas, even though they are generally repudiated, and for its influence on Weininger's contemporaries.

Anti-Semitism was widespread, and all of the Jewish writers experienced it in varying degrees. Some Jewish authors, for example, Karl Kraus, were themselves anti-Semites, but for the most part they all came from assimilated or at least acculturated families; with their economic status and/or their literary reputations they circulated in the best society and could personally escape most of the ill effects. The writer who confronted the issue of anti-Semitism most directly was Theodor Herzl, a young aesthete whose most fervent early desire resembled that of every talented young man in Vienna: to create a play that would be accepted and performed by the prestigious Burgtheater. While waiting for this breakthrough to success, Herzl worked as the Paris correspondent of the *Neue Freie Presse,* earning a reputation for his essayistic brilliance. In covering the Dreyfus trial in Paris Herzl was struck by the injustice of anti-Semitism and developed his program of Zionism, calling all Jews to return to their homeland in Palestine. The issue was as hotly debated as anti-Semitism itself, for most Austrian Jews considered Austria their country, their homeland for which fathers and sons had fought and died and would do so in World War I.

Nevertheless, Zionism, once launched, became a fact of life that every Jew in Austria had to confront and resolve. Schnitzler, for example, devoted his most important novel, *Der Weg ins Freie* (1908, *The Road to the Open*), to the subject, illuminating the issue from all sides, typically without taking a clear stand. Kraus, on the other hand, was absolutely opposed to Zionism. Regardless of the final position adopted, the issues of anti-Semitism and Zionism caused all of the Jewish writers to rediscover and reassess their bond with Judaism as the twentieth century progressed.

The debate diminished to some degree during World War I, and the writers readjusted to the horrors of four years of military struggle. Some, like Doderer and Trakl, served in the army, with the ordeal causing Trakl's death. But the majority either escaped military service entirely, like Bahr, Beer-Hofmann, and Schnitzler, or performed token services, like Hofmannsthal, who gave some patriotic lectures in Switzerland and Sweden before being excused from duty in 1916. The military obligation of most writers consisted of service in the press department, where Rilke and Zweig served among others. Most of the authors continued to write works that had little to do with the war. One exception was Zweig, who wrote short narratives and the pacifist play *Jeremias* (1917, *Jeremiah*), which inspired an attitude of victory in defeat. The most fanatical opponent of the war, however, was Karl Kraus, whose monumental drama *Die letzten Tage der Menschheit* (1922), *The Last Days of Mankind*), for which he was nominated three times for the Nobel Peace Prize in the 1920s, remains one of the greatest antiwar statements of all times.

During the 1920s Austria, like Germany, first suffered through a debilitating inflation, while staggering under the burden of punitive war retributions. Both factors severely crippled the new government's attempts to establish a democracy. Political factionalism ran rampant in Austria. However, as earlier, the writers for the most part ignored the intensification of political problems in the country and the political debates between the "Black" clerical party of Chancellor Ignaz Seipel and the "Red" party of the Socialists and Social Democrats, each with its own paramilitary organization, the "Heimwehr" or Front Fighters and the "Schutzbund" respectively.[8] Even as major an incident as the riot which led to the burning of the Palace of Justice in 1927 elicited no immediate literary response. A clash between representatives of the two paramilitary groups in the village of Schattendorf not far from Vienna on 30 January 1927 had resulted in the loss of lives and several injuries. The trial in Vienna of the three men who had fired the shots was followed closely, and the verdict of acquittal for the Front Fighters led to a riot of the outraged Socialist workers, who in their anger and frustration set fire to the Palace of Justice. The police overreacted and opened fire on the crowd, killing eighty-nine civilians. Only Karl Kraus among the writers voiced outrage, pillorying the behavior of the police and immortalizing in his famous "Schoberlied" the incompetent and shameful conduct of Police Chief Schober.[9] Not until the passage of time had turned this tragic occurrence into a historical event was it treated in literature, almost a decade later, by Elias Canetti in his novel *Die Blendung* (1935, *Auto-da-fé*), and a generation later by Heimito von Doderer in *Die Dämonen* (1956, *The Demons*). In short, the writers, artists, and intellectuals who set the cultural tone of the nation remained generally aloof from politics during the 1920s and well into the 1930s, just as they had to a large degree ignored World War I. Raoul Auernheimer, a distant cousin of Herzl who worked as the drama critic for the *Neue Freie Presse* from 1908 to 1937, developing into a most perceptive cultural and social commentator with a keen eye for Austrian manners and foibles, accurately captured the prevailing priority system of values:

> In general Viennese society, the ruling as well as the ruled, in those years before the apocalypse, lived a life busily devoted to the beauties and joys of existence, not exactly without a conscience, but with a conscience easily lulled to sleep by the effects of wine. Beauty was everything and politics very little. A guest performance of Caruso, for example, masked Austria's poor relationship with Italy, an appearance of Nijinski with the Russian ballet overshadowed the mobilization of several army corps along the Russian border.[10]

It may be difficult today to understand the glorification of literature and the other arts that prevailed at the turn of the century and endowed this era of the *fin-de-siècle* with the unique and wonderful aura that continues to fascinate the modern-day world. It was not a question of irresponsible writers pursuing solipsistic aestheticism and art for art's sake at the expense of responsible social behavior. These writers believed in serving society and thought they were doing so in their writings by advocating moral and ethical principles among other social values. There are no better literary guides to morality and to the question of what it means to be a human being than the writings of Hofmannsthal and Schnitzler. The generation of 1890 and the one following it continued to believe through World War I and up to the *Anschluß* in 1938 that art was the path to the future and that politics was unimportant. To find success in the theater, particularly in the Burgtheater, was the highest ambition and goal. The Burgtheater served as the recognized forum for fashion and taste, and the public attended to learn the latest in social manners as well as the current fashions in gestures and speech. The Viennese have always preferred reality made palatable by being masked and filtered through art, hence properly aestheticized and diluted. It is no wonder that in such an atmosphere politics was considered simply a dirty business to be ignored at all costs.

There was some attempt in the 1930s to confront the political situation directly in the works of Ferdinand Bruckner, Ödön von Horváth, Jura Soyfer, and Ernst Weiss, but these socialist writers had difficulty in getting their works performed. As harbingers of the coming political disaster they could not make their apprehensions visible when they would have been most relevant. For example, Horváth's unvarnished analysis of pitiless Viennese life, *Geschichten aus dem Wiener Wald* (1931, *Tales from the Vienna Woods*), now recognized as a classic and even made recently into a successful film starring Helmut Qualtinger, the satirist, cabarettist, and author, was considered too unpleasantly realistic for acceptance in its own time, as was his hard-hitting drama unmasking fascism in Austria, *Italienische Nacht* (1931, Italian Night). Jura Soyfer's unsophisticated cabaret-like plays, now published and performed, found few outlets in the 1930s. Similarly, Ferdinand Bruckner, who had fled Austria to settle in Berlin, where he struggled to establish himself as a writer, attempted to confront the political situation in the 1930s. His tendentious political drama, *Rassen* (1933, *Races*), one of the most powerful contemporary indictments of anti-Semitism, vividly depicts the havoc and the tragedy caused by the Nazi introduction of rabid anti-Semitism into the university setting. Less polemical but relevant to these works is Weiss's posthumously published novel *Ich, der Augenzeuge* (1963, *I, the Eyewitness*), which deals with Hitler's recovery from temporary blindness in World War I and the unleashing of his political ambitions, which Hitler feels are a matter of destiny. Of the four only Bruckner survived emigration and exile; Horváth was killed tragically by a falling branch during a rainstorm in Paris in 1938; Soyfer was executed in a concentration camp after the *Anschluß;* and Weiss took his own life in Paris in 1940 when the Germans occupied the city.

Unlike most others in Austria Zweig had early first-hand information about the Nazi threat to writers, for he had been courted by Richard Strauss, who had been searching for a librettist ever since the death of Hofmannsthal. Together Strauss and Zweig produced the opera *Die schweigsame Frau* (1935, *The Silent Woman*), which Strauss was to conduct at the première in Munich. It was planned as a gala event, befitting Strauss's preeminence, until it was discovered that Zweig had written the text. The matter became an affair of state—it was illegal to perform a work by a Jewish writer in Germany—requiring consultation with Hitler, who had been invited and had planned to attend. After negotiation the performance was permitted on 24 June 1935 as a special exception (Hitler was not in the audience), but Strauss, who served as President of the "Reichsmusikkammer" because of his international prestige, had sullied his reputation not only by his collaboration with a Jewish writer, but also by insisting that Zweig's name be listed on the program. Even after this debacle Strauss tried to persuade Zweig to produce other librettos that he could set to music and store away for more propitious times, but Zweig refused. The hot-tempered Bavarian grew incautious and, apparently forgetting that letters crossing the border to Switzerland were being monitored, tried to persuade Zweig to change his mind by candidly expressing his views on the political situation.[11] He was asked to resign as President of the Reichsmusikkammer and was carefully watched, although his services were sought whenever his presence seemed politically advantageous. In view of these actions against him and because of the treatment of Jews in Germany, Zweig had no desire to continue his collaboration with Strauss and wrote no more librettos for him. When his house on the Kapuzinerberg in Salzburg was subjected to a search by the police, Zweig, who lived close to the border as if poised for flight, quickly resolved to leave Austria for more hospitable surroundings, first in Paris, then in England.

Zweig attempted to address the Nazi threat, but in a much lower, less polemical key in keeping with his nature in the historical novel *Triumph und Tragik des Erasmus von Rotterdam* (1934, *Right to Heresy*). Zweig dealt with the issues of tyranny and fascism in an indirect manner, drawing parallels between the age of Erasmus and the present; again his message was not heeded, just as his pacifist play *Jeremias* had been ignored. After Zweig settled in England, he did not feel free to introduce political issues into his writings because he felt that such behavior could prove embarrassing to his host country. Consequently his other major writings of the 1930s, the historical novels *Marie Antoinette* (1932), *Maria Stuart* (1935), *Castellio gegen Calvin* (1936, *Castellio against Calvin*), *Magellan* (1938), and the portraits of Freud and Nietzsche in *Baumeister der Welt* (1936, *Master Builders of the World*) had little relevance to the contemporary political or social scene. *Der begrabene Leuchter* (1937, *The Buried Candelabrum*), however, did show how the anti-Semitism in Germany and Austria had reawakened his ties to Judaism, and his masterful tale *Schachnovelle* (1942, *The Royal Game*), written in safe exile in Petropolis, Brazil, revealed Zweig's pessimism about the fate of the humanistic world threatened by fascism.[12]

Most of the major writers tried to avoid political reality by addressing the past rather than the present. Hermann Broch wrote his outstanding trilogy, *Die Schlafwandler* (1931/1932, *The Sleepwalkers*), treating the decline of values over three generations, and in exile in the United States in 1945, completed his masterpiece *Der Tod des Vergil* (*The Death of Virgil*), debating the issue of a writer's social responsibility. The novel reflects Broch's personal uneasiness about writing an "aesthetic" book at a time of political crisis: the dying Vergil wonders whether he should have written the *Aeneid* rather than addressing some of the more serious questions of his day. But pondering this dilemma is as close as Broch came to the political realities of the 1930s except for the development of his theory of mass psychology. Similarly, Robert Musil devoted the period from 1931 to his death in 1942 in Switzerland, often supported by friends, to working on his monumental but uncompleted novel, *Der Mann ohne Eigenschaften* (1930–1943, *The Man Without Qualities*), which is also set in the Austrian past.

Elias Canetti wrote his major novel, *Die Blendung* (1935, *Auto-de-fé*), about the fate of an Austrian eccentric, against a background that largely ignored current reality beyond the inclusion of the fire at the Palace of Justice. The protagonist lives only for his personal library and disregards everything else. Paradoxically (and prophetically) his behavior results in the destruction by fire of his books and himself. The novel made little impression in Austria and Germany and received its first important critical recognition in France. Only belatedly did it find modest reception in German-speaking countries and in other parts of the world. Despite winning the Nobel prize for literature in 1981 Canetti is still not as widely known and read as he should be, although his works are enjoying increased attention.

Heimito von Doderer, a student of the doubly talented painter and writer Albert Paris Gütersloh, began working on *Die Dämonen* (*The Demons*) in 1931 and completed it in 1956. Like this novel, *Ein Mord den jeder begeht* (1938, *Every Man a Murderer*), the acclaimed *Die Strudelhofstiege* (1951, *The Strudelhof Stairway*), and *Die Wasserfälle von Slunj* (1963, The Waterfalls of Slunj), were all set in Austria of the past. Gütersloh himself, after devoting years to painting, returned to his writing and began in 1935 what he called the historical novel of the present, *Sonne und Mond* (Sun and Moon), completing it in 1962. Others like Franz Theodor Csokor, Fritz von Herzmanovsky-Orlando, Fritz Hochwälder, Joseph Roth, George Saiko, and Franz Werfel all devoted their writings of the 1930s to the Austria of the past. Certainly the phenomenon of Adolf Hitler in Germany, beginning with his failed *Putsch* of 1923 and subsequent trial and imprisonment, was noted without great concern. Neither were the gains made by the National Socialist Party at the polls cause for alarm. As the letters of writers like Stefan Zweig reveal during the 1920s, it was generally believed that Hitler and the Nazis were simply a radical political aberration that would soon spend itself and self-destruct of its own excesses. Typically, Hermann Bahr trivialized the Nazi threat, in a novel entitled *Österreich in Ewigkeit* (1928, Austria in Eternity), revealing that even he, one of the keenest observers of his day in diagnosing contemporary trends and predicting future directions, believed like the majority that there was no serious threat. Only Karl Kraus saw the real danger, but the alarm he sounded in his journal *Die Fackel* had little appreciable effect. Throughout his career Kraus more than any others of his generation had addressed the political problems of his time, but then even he found himself overwhelmed by the monumentality of the Nazi horrors, which so outstripped his imagination that they rendered even his superior intellectual powers impotent to cope with the new political reality. In 1934 he had to plead "Mir fällt zu Hitler nichts ein" ("I can't think of anything to say about Hitler"). However, in actuality he continued to speak out against Hitler and fascism when his journal *Die Fackel* was not censored or confiscated. Despite the rapid political changes in Germany and even after Hitler came officially to power as Chancellor in 1933, there were still many Austrian writers who ignored the jeopardy from Germany right up to the *Anschluß* on 11 March 1938.

The idea of annexation to Germany was not a frightening thought to many Austrians but rather had been a fervent wish ever since the expulsion of Austria from the German Confederation after the Battle of

Königgrätz in 1866. The Germans in Austria had felt a much greater common bond with their neighbors to the northwest than with the non-German-speaking peoples in the various eastern and southern states of the Monarchy. Schönerer, a forerunner of Hitler in the use of anti-Semitism as a political program, attracted a rabid following among university students and farmers in the 1880s, and after World War I the idea of annexation was renewed as a means of helping Austria overcome its severe economic problems. From 1918 on the feeling had persisted that Austria was too small a country to exist on its own. There were a number of *Anschluß* demonstrations between 1925 and 1929, and the idea of *Anschluß* formed almost the single goal of Austrian foreign policy until 1933.[13] In the minds of the people the inflation, followed by financial depression and widespread unemployment in Austria (400,000 in January 1934), was linked to the experiment in democracy forced on Austria by the punitive terms of the Versailles treaty. The perceived economic progress in Germany under Hitler and in Italy under Mussolini revived the call for a stronger form of government in Austria to overcome the country's continued weakness resulting from a government by coalition. Engelbert Dollfuss, a Christian Socialist and a martinet of the Mussolini type, was elected Chancellor on 20 May 1932 to provide the strong proto-fascist kind of leadership modeled on Mussolini. Against this background the Nazi party made consistent gains in Austria as a bulwark against Marxism. Dollfuss, urged by Prince Starhemberg, leader of the "Heimwehr" or Front Fighters, formed a "Vaterländische Front" in May 1933 in an attempt to stem the growth of National Socialism. Apart from trying to control the increasing number of terrorist acts by the National Socialists, Dollfuss was also confronted by the growing militancy of the Social Democrats despite appeals to join forces with Christian Socialists to combat the Nazi party. On 8 February 1934 the discovery of weapons in the Social Democratic party headquarters caused a general search to begin on 12 February. In retaliation the workers called a general strike, and in Linz the police were fired upon. This action started a civil war that spread throughout Austria and brought fighting to the streets of Vienna. After three days of battle the Social Democrats accepted Dollfuss's offer of amnesty and ended the struggle. Nine leaders were executed, but Dr. Otto Bauer and Julius Deutsch fled to Czechoslovakia.

The end of the civil war did not signal an end to the strife in Austria. On 25 July 1934 a Nazi Putsch, led by a small band of Germans who miscalculated the party strength in Austria, attempted to take over the government. Hopes for a popular uprising never materialized, and after three tense days the plot failed. However, in the process Dollfuss was murdered, and the Nazis had succeeded in eliminating a major obstacle to National Socialism in Austria. The immediate result was the decree of the new Chancellor, Kurt Schuschnigg, to ban both the Nazi Party and the Social Democratic Party in Austria, a step that served only to drive the parties underground without weakening them. As Hitler consolidated his power and more people covertly joined the movement, it became necessary to legalize the parties again in 1936. Even the official propaganda newspaper of the German Nazi party, the *Völkischer Beobachter*, could be sold openly on the streets.

Despite his previous favorable attitude toward annexation Schuschnigg resisted the idea initially when Hitler tried to force it on him in 1938. Schuschnigg insisted on calling a plebiscite for 13 March 1938 so that the people could decide their own future. Furious at Schuschnigg's recalcitrance, Hitler summoned him to his headquarters in Berchtesgaden on 11 March 1938 and ordered the plebiscite canceled under threat of invasion. He then proceeded to annex Austria by fiat. The Nazi leaders in Austria had hoped that the matter could be left at that, but when Hitler received the field reports that no resistance was to be expected against troops moving into Austria and that no other countries would move to protect Austria, he suddenly ordered a military and political takeover.

The initial reaction by a large segment of the Austrian public was one of elation and jubilation. Anyone who has ever watched newsreels of those days is familiar with the highways lined with crowds cheering the tanks on their way to Vienna. Underground members of the Nazi Party suddenly surfaced everywhere, and banners obviously stored for the occasion blossomed throughout the city overnight. When Hitler flew to Vienna a few days later to bask in the glory of having conquered a city he had once left as a failure, he required no particular security other than protection from the throngs of people who wished to see him. He was enthusiastically greeted by a quarter of a million people crammed into the Heldenplatz to hear him solidify the ties between the two countries. Hundreds of thousands of additional onlookers and curiosity-seekers lined the Ringstraße. This initial euphoria was short-lived, however. Disillusionment set in rapidly among the Austrians, including the Austrian Nazis, when a month later a German administrative corps moved in as "advisers" and soon assumed control of all operations. The Austrian Nazi leaders had advised against this move and were as dismayed by this decision as nonparty members were. Theaters, for example, were taken over as were all of the publishing houses and the radio stations, so that only approved material could be broadcast, performed, or published. During the next seven years cultural life in Austria was tightly ruled by Nazi policies.

Austrian literature in the 1920s, already seriously affected by the deaths of the *Jung-Wien* writers, suffered the additional loss of those driven into exile. The weakness of this decade is aptly illustrated in a witticism of Hans Weigel, who jested that the literary situation interrupted by the *Anschluß* in 1938 consisted primarily of Lernet and Holenia, a play on the name of the distinguished and highly respected writer, Alexander Lernet-Holenia. The generation that had flourished around the turn of the century and that had brought Austrian literature to its greatest flowering since the days of the Minnesänger (medieval troubadours) such as Walther von der Vogelweide and Der von Kürenberg in the Middle Ages, and since the age of Franz Grillparzer, Johann Nestroy, and Ferdinand Raimund in the first half of the nineteenth century, died out in the early 1930s. Hofmannsthal, one of the greatest Austrian writers of all times, died in 1929, Schnitzler in 1931, Bahr in 1934, and Kraus in 1936. The only major figures from the *Jung-Wien* generation to survive the 1930s were Beer-Hofmann and Salten, and they were both forced into emigration by 1938, like all of the other Jewish writers, artists, and musicians who fled in a new diaspora of the Jews from Austria. This exodus to escape Hitler represented a veritable Who's Who of Austrian culture, including among many others the writers Franz Blei, Felix Braun, Hermann Broch, Max Brod, Ferdinand Bruckner, Franz Theodor Csokor, Albert Drach, Alfred Ehrenstein, Erich Fried, Fritz Hochwälder, Ödön von Horváth, Ernst Lothar, Robert Musil, Robert Neumann, Hertha Pauli, Joseph Roth, Hilde Spiel, Fritz Torberg, Johannes Urzidil, Ernst Waldinger, Hans Weigel, Franz Werfel, Martina Wied, and Stefan Zweig. Egon Friedell (died 1938) and Ernst Weiss (died 1940), who simply could not cope with exile, took their own lives to avoid persecution. Stefan Zweig, who had every reason to live, committed suicide with his wife in Petropolis, Brazil in February 1942, when the Germans looked invincible and he felt that *Die Welt von gestern* (1944, *The World of Yesterday*), which he had eulogized in his posthumously published autobiography and which meant everything to him, would never return and that instead he faced a dismal future world of dictatorships, war, and materialism.

Those who did not leave early enough often had a difficult time arranging their departure and were usually forced to bribe officials for exit visas or attempt to escape over the border without papers at the risk of being turned over to the Austrian or German authorities if caught. Most of the émigrés who waited until the last moment before leaving had an adventurous story to tell of their perilous journey to freedom. Hermann Broch, for example, was arrested and held prisoner, then released just long enough to enable him to escape. Fritz Hochwälder and Hans Weigel slipped over the border into Switzerland illegally, while Raoul Auernheimer returned to Vienna from Zürich, where he had been attending the première of one of his plays, believing that with a German Protestant father he was protected by the Nuremberg laws. Instead he was arrested immediately because he had sent a message of support to Chancellor Schuschnigg, congratulating him for defying Hitler's order against the plebiscite on the question of annexation. Auernheimer was sent to Dachau and obtained his release six months later only through the intervention of the German writer, Emil Ludwig, and the American attaché in Berlin, Prentice Gilbert, a personal friend of Auernheimer's, who had translated two of his plays into English. Auernheimer was allowed to emigrate to the United States with the sum of seventy-five cents in his pocket. Peter Hammerschlag, Paul Kornfeld, and Jura Soyfer were less fortunate: all three died in concentration camps.

The usual escape route for those fleeing into exile was to Prague and from there via Switzerland to Paris or Milan to obtain a visa for England, South America, or the United States. Detailed studies have been written about the history of the émigrés in France, England, and the United States, and in each case the chronicle is a fascinating and important chapter in the life of the exiled writer.[14] A most important aspect of the exile experience is the influence of the émigrés on shaping governmental and popular opinion in their host countries concerning the treatment of Austria by the Allies at the end of the war. In addition to the attempts to organize and help other exiles and to maintain a sense of Austrian presence, the émigrés all faced the question of whether to return to Austria after the war or to remain in their host country, where they had often become citizens.

Those in exile had ample time to contemplate what had happened, what they could have done to prevent it, and when they could have acted. This soul-searching had a major impact on German literature of the postwar era but had less effect in Austria. At the time the writers attempted to ignore the political situation as much as possible until the proclamation of the *Anschluß* caused a panicked flight, but even so the circumstances after 1933 could not be totally ignored. Austrian writers have always needed German publishers and German readers in order to survive, for there have always been many more writers than the country could support by itself.[15] More books of Austrian writers are published in Germany than at home, a situation as true today as at the turn of the century when all of the major writers appeared through the S. Fischer Verlag. To lose the German market was a major setback if one's living depended on one's literary income, for there was no replacement market. A large part of the tragedy of emigration was the necessity of writers to learn to address new audiences and essentially to gain public acceptance for a second time because, for all except the already internationally established authors like Thomas Mann or Bertolt Brecht, their previous reputations counted for little in their new environments. Some, like the authors in this volume, were able to make the transition successfully, while many others were not.

A crisis of conscience occurred with the book burnings in Germany in 1933, which included Austrian authors, and the attacks on the "degenerate" artists of the Bauhaus. These well-publicized spectacles were impossible to ignore: even though the anti-Semitic and anti-intellectual acts were not recognized as dangerous for Austria in a direct way, the repercussions of these political pressures made themselves felt in the sense that every writer had to take a stand on them. As a result the literary scene in Austria became as fragmented and polarized as the political arena, with writers spanning the full range from enthusiastic acceptance of Hitler's cultural policies to unequivocal rejection of them. An early watershed event in this respect was the meeting of the XI Congress of the International P.E.N. Club from 25 to 28 May 1933 in Ragusa (now Dubrovnik), where members of the Austrian delegation lodged an official protest against the book burnings. Since works by writers like Beer-Hofmann, Brod, Schnitzler, Werfel, and Zweig were among those being burned and banned in Germany, the Austrian authors had ample basis for their motion. The German delegation withdrew in protest against the proposed resolution and were joined by Grete Urbanitzky, the founder of the Austrian P.E.N. Club and head of the Austrian delegation, which included the principled Raoul Auernheimer, who supported the motion, and Felix Salten, who refused to do so and departed because he did not want to harm his fellow writers who needed the German market for their livelihood. The matter was subsequently debated at a meeting in Vienna, and a group of twenty-five liberal authors, including Auernheimer, Csokor, Fontana, Kraus, Lothar, Müller, Neumann, and Torberg succeeded in passing a resolution condemning the suppression and persecution of writers in Germany and defending intellectual freedom and the inviolability of human rights. In opposition nine Nazi sympathizers left the meeting and so did others a few months later, including Urbanitzky and Salten, who withdrew from the P.E.N. Club.[16]

The consequences of this stand on principle were serious, for those who supported the resolution found themselves blacklisted in Germany. They could no longer publish or lecture there nor could their plays be performed, a severe economic loss. By contrast, those writers who defended Nazi policies, such as Franz Karl Ginskey, Paula Grogger, Max Mell, Franz Nabl, J. G. Oberkofler, H. H. Ortner, J. F. Perkonig, Karl Schönherr, Ferdinand Schreyvogel, Karl Heinrich Waggerl, and H. Suso Waldeck among others were rewarded for their political support by being favored and promoted in Germany. Thus Austrian writers in the 1930s had to choose between their conscience and their income.[17]

As some of the leading writers began to leave Austria and others were stifled because of their opposition to the Nazi policies, a literary vacuum was formed in Austria that was increasingly filled by those authors favorable, whether out of conviction or opportunism, to the ideas of Hitler's Germany. The Austrian P.E.N. Club had been seriously weakened—in 1936 a new organization, the "Bund der deutschen Schriftsteller Österreichs" (League of German Writers in Austria), had been founded on the model of the "Reichsschrifttumskammer" in Germany "to distinguish between reliable and unreliable writers."[18] Max Mell served as the first president. In 1939 the League became an official branch of the Reichsschrifttumskammer with Karl Hans Strobl as President. Many of the members were privileged writers favored by the state, and several were former P.E.N. Club members—giving this organization with its membership of known Nazi sympathizers a veneer of respectability. A number of these authors received state prizes during the 1930s: Ginskey, Grogger, Mayer, Mell, Oberkofler, Ortner, Perkonig, Schreyvogel, Wenter, and Weinheber. Not only was the literary scene dominated by Nazi influence, but great pressure was also exerted on the publishing firms to enforce the ban on uncooperative anti-Nazi authors through the coercion of economic sanctions. Grete Urbanitzky, who justified her support of Hitler by portraying him as the last bulwark against Bolshevism, urged readers and publishers in Germany to boycott those who had signed the P.E.N. resolution condemning the book burnings. In addition there was pressure within Austria. For example, the respected Zsolnay publishing house, threatened with economic ruin by boycott in Germany, had to shift its loyal Austrian writers to publishers in Switzerland, while the firm was forced to publish Nazi writers in Austria.

One force attempting to defend Austria's interests against the dominance of Nazi-influenced writers was Guido Zernatto (1903–1943), a staunch patriot who divided his talents between literature and politics. In 1929 Zernatto was called by Schuschnigg to become Secretary of the "Heimatblock," a forerunner of the party called the "Heimatschutz," which eventually was transformed into the "Heimwehr" paramilitary organization. Zernatto, a conservative Catholic, was dedicated to the concept of "old Austria," that is, to the traditional Austria that existed prior to the formation in 1918 of the "Republic that nobody wanted." In 1934 he became Vice-President of the "Katholischer Schriftstellerverband" (Catholic Writers' Union) and in 1935 was named Vice-President of the state-operated Austrian Bundesverlag, the leading Austrian publishing house for school texts. He also served as a member of the "Bundeskulturrat" (National Cultural Council) overseeing the cultural activities of the state, with responsibility for formulating cultural policies that supported Schuschnigg's aims. When Prince Starhemberg, the leader of the "Vaterländische Front" became a liability to Schuschnigg because of his support for Mussolini's intervention in Ethiopia, Zernatto was invited to join Schuschnigg's cabinet as Secretary of State. He served in this capacity and headed the "Vaterländische Front" organization until the *Anschluß*. Zernatto was even more adamant than Schuschnigg in his opposition to *Anschluß* and fought for the plebiscite until the last moment. Like so many others on the Nazi list of political enemies, Zernatto had to flee, escaping first to Bratislava and eventually making his way to the United States, where he died in New York in 1943.

Despite all of these conflicts and pressures it was still possible for some to continue to ignore the political realities around them. When, for example, Max Reinhardt resigned as director of the Theater in der Josefstadt, Ernst Lothar, his assistant, assumed his position and, although subject to some anti-Semitic unpleasantness, remained as director until it was almost too late to leave. Reinhardt continued meanwhile to entertain the cultural elite at his villa in Leopoldskron, just as Alma Mahler continued to hold court at her salon, another gathering place of the famous and the fashionable, until the very last moment; she too fled, from Vienna to Prague, virtually on the day of the *Anschluß*. A unique case was that of Carl Zuckmayer, a German writer who only a few days before had acquired Austrian citizenship to seek refuge from Hitler. He now had to emigrate quickly again, first to Zürich and then to the United States.

The writers who remained in Austria after the *Anschluß* had three choices available to them: to endorse the new regime, a course followed by such writers as Richard Billinger, Max Mell, Karl Schönherr, and Josef Weinheber as well as Heimito von Doderer, who was an early enthusiast of the Nazi party and served in the German army but later repudiated the Nazi movement; to write neutral works to maintain one's integrity while trying to avoid giving offense to the Nazi government, the course followed by Gütersloh, Henz, and Lernet-Holenia; or to follow the path of "inner emigration," maintaining public silence while writing manuscripts for later publication, like Otto Basil and Rudolf Kassner, the friend of Hofmannsthal and Rilke, who remained quietly in Vienna throughout the *Anschluß* and the war. Gütersloh was still branded as a decadent artist because of his paintings and was forced to work in a war factory. Lernet-Holenia's defense of Austria, courageous at the time, in such novels as *Beide Sizilien* (1942, Two Sicilies) and *Mars im Widder* (Mars in Aries), published in magazine form in 1941 and then banned until it was published in book form in 1947, was still much too outspoken for the Nazis, and he was silenced. Rudolf Henz, fired from his position as head of the radio network, also refrained from producing any literary works during the occupation and devoted himself to producing and restoring stained-glass windows.

Basil is a noteworthy figure because he played an important role along with Rudolf Henz, Friedrich Torberg, and Hans Weigel in helping to bridge the literary hiatus caused by the *Anschluß*. As an active socialist Basil had developed the journal *Plan* in order to oppose the literary trend that had come to dominate Austrian literature after 1933: provincial literature modeled on the "blood and soil" (*Blut und Boden*) literature in Germany, which combined a strong sense of nationalistic fervor with an almost mystical belief in the strength to be gained from close ties to the land. The aesthetic program of the strongly Catholic "Vaterländische Front," while not to be confused with the Nazi program, was nevertheless also oriented toward a glorification of the healthy full life in the provinces as contrasted to the "decadence" of

Vienna. Thus in general the "official" literary approach sanctioned by the Austrian government appeared not far removed from that of Germany. It was a question of degree more than of kind.

In 1936 Chancellor Schuschnigg appointed Zernatto head of a new organization called "Neues Leben" (New Life) with a broad charter covering leisure-time activities in Austria: culture, athletics, and travel. The following year the organization introduced a cultural journal under the same name, a publication made necessary by the terms of the Non-Intervention Pact Schuschnigg signed with Germany in 1936, restoring the legal status of the National Socialist Party, which had been banned since 1934. Censorship was relaxed in general, and the still illegal Social Democrats were also able to increase their public activities. Hence there was a perceived need to combat such propaganda efforts by stressing the Austrian heritage, traditional Catholic values, and the healthful life of the provinces. One purpose was to arouse Austrian patriotism and to keep Austria independent rather than succumbing to the annexational blandishments of the National Socialists, both in Germany and in Austria. The reception of *Neues Leben* was good and circulation exceeded 300,000 copies, but the attempt came too late. Only the three issues of December 1937 and January and February 1938 appeared before the *Anschluß* ended its publication. As a result of the liberal publication policy after 11 July 1936 Basil, who had been thinking about a journal devoted to the arts since 1935, decided to proceed with the publication. Thus was born *Plan,* a periodical intended to serve as a voice of opposition to the aesthetic policies of both the "Vaterländische Front" and the National Socialists. The journal, devoted to art, architecture, and literature, proclaimed its intention of defending the integrity of the arts: "Our little periodical represents, figuratively speaking, the attempt to allow young and relevant art—i.e., art which is struggling to give sense and expression to the lifestyle of today—to appear before the viewer both as a manifesto and as a forum for debate."[19] Like *Neues Leben,* only the three issues of December 1937 and January and February 1938 were published—of these only the first was actually circulated. The second and third issues, which among other things emphasized workers' literature, were confiscated, and further publication of this socialist periodical was banned. Not a single copy of the last two issues survived. Basil was summoned to appear before the Gestapo in September 1938 and might have been sent to a concentration camp except for the intercession of Weinheber on his behalf. Basil was reduced to keeping a low profile during the war and, like Gütersloh, worked in a factory.

A number of provincial writers in Austria such as Rudolf Hans Bartsch, Richard Billinger, Franz Karl Ginskey, Paula Grogger, Max Mell, Franz Nabl, Hans Sassmann, Karl Schönherr, and Franz Tumler, encouraged by the National Socialist endorsement of *Blut und Boden* literature, produced works emphasizing Germanic heroes and pre-Christian pagan rituals or glorifying the strength deriving from ties to the soil. Two of these authors, Billinger and Mell, had begun with great promise, drawing the favorable attention of Hofmannsthal, who was enthusiastic about their utilization of religious myths. The latter did not live to see how this initial artistic tendency easily developed in the 1930s into works fitting the National Socialist ideology. All of these writers produced works acceptable to the new regime and grew in reputation beyond the level of their true literary significance because of political sponsorship. After the war they for the most part continued to write without suffering any appreciable public or critical reaction because of their earlier opportunism. Though not an exponent of "Heimatkunst," another close friend of Hofmannsthal, Leopold von Andrian, also endorsed Nazism and in 1937 before the *Anschluß* wrote the volume *Österreich im Prisma der Idee: Katechismus der Führenden* (Austria in the Prism of the Idea: Catechism of the Leaders), to endorse National Socialist ideas.

Because the turbulent political situation in Austria during the 1930s adversely affected literary production and because the forced emigration of many of the major writers severely disrupted the normal literary progression, the interlude between the wars remains one of the least researched periods of twentieth-century Austrian literary history. Some excellent studies have recently appeared concerning the situation within Austria[20] and more are in preparation, but the most attention up to now has been devoted to the exiled writers, an obvious choice since generally they were the major literary figures at the time of their departure and remained so even in exile. Also sympathy existed for the exiles rather than for those who stayed and collaborated. The intensive investigation of the 1930s and 1940s currently in progress insures that before long we will have a more accurate overview of the events and activities of this era.[21] Even now it seems clear that no great works of literature emerged from the period 1933-1945 by those writers who elected to follow the Nazi leadership and to write according to party dictates. Those opponents of the new government who stayed in Austria likewise did not find conditions propitious for producing noteworthy works. For the significant Austrian literature of this period one has to look to the writings of the exiles in England, France, the Netherlands, South America, and the United States.

For the writers in exile the first major problem to be faced after achieving some kind of stability in their personal lives and in their living conditions was language. Very few émigré writers learned the language of their host country well enough to write in it, with the exception of several writers in England who did actually produce books in English: Robert Hans-Flesch-Brunnigen, Hermynia zur Mühlen, Robert Neumann, and Salka and Berthold Viertel. Other writers published autobiographies and factual accounts in English: Ilse Barea, Franz Borkenau, Sir George Franckenstein, Willi Frischauer, Bruno Heitig, Hans Peter Kraus, and Oskar Kokoschka.[22] This situation has created an interesting body of work that now falls between two national literatures, not counting either as Austrian works or as part of the English literary tradition. In general in England as in the United States the majority of the authors wrote their works in their native German and then employed a translator to render them into English. Except for Hermann Broch, who found a dedicated translator in Jean Untermayer, none of the other writers were as fortunate as Thomas Mann, whose works were unusually well translated by the dedicated efforts of Katherine Lowe-Porter. Both Broch and Mann knew enough English to be able to work with their translators in polishing the renditions, but most writers had to find translators wherever they could, usually individuals recruited by the publishing house. The primary prerequisite then as now was that they work cheaply, and the results rarely achieved a level above adequate. But the quality of the translations was not the main concern. To be published at all was a major triumph. All of the exiled writers shared a concern about keeping their German style intact, an indication that they all harbored the expectation of being read by German readers again, and usually lived in the hope of returning "home" after the war.

Not only the language problem and the difficulty of presenting their works in translation handicapped the émigré writers. They also had grown accustomed to writing for a known audience, whose shared interests and backgrounds they knew well. Now they faced the dilemma of writing for a totally different audience in a new setting without that shared background. Stefan Zweig, the most translated Austrian author, whose works had appeared regularly in English as well as in many other languages, suffered no loss of reputation and no difficulty or break in the continuity of his production while moving to England, to the

United States, and finally in 1941 to South America. The most cosmo-
politan of all Austrian writers, he had made successful lecture tours
both in the United States and in South America and was very well
known on both continents. His series of historical biographies were all
well accepted by the public in English, and *Marie Antoinette,* his most
popular contribution in this genre, was even included in the abridged
book series of the *Reader's Digest.* Zweig's novella *Brief an eine Unbekannte* was also made into a popular film entitled *Letter to an Unknown Woman,* although Americans do not generally recognize Zweig
as the author of the story that served as the basis of the movie.

Alongside Zweig stood Franz Werfel, whose novel *Das Lied von
Bernadette* (1941, *The Song of Bernadette*) became a bestseller in the
United States and was also made into a successful feature film. The play
Jakobowsky und der Oberst under the title "Me and the Colonel" became a starring vehicle on Broadway and in film for Danny Kaye and
made Werfel possibly the Austrian writer with the most widespread
name identification in the United States after Zweig.

Major success was also achieved by Ernst Lothar, who produced
two novels that became bestsellers and book-club choices, *Die Zeugin*
(1941, *A Woman is Witness*) and *Unter anderer Sonne* (1943, *Beneath
Another Sun*). Other successes included *Der Engel mit der Posaune*
(1944, *The Angel with the Trumpet*), *Die Tür geht auf* (1945, *The Door
Opens*), *Heldenplatz* (1945, *The Prisoner*), and *Die Rückkehr* (1949,
Return to Vienna). After a disappointing beginning of his exile in New
York, where he attempted to found a German-speaking theater together
with Raoul Auernheimer and others, Lothar was successful in obtaining
a teaching position at Colorado College in Colorado Springs, where he
was able to use his experience as a director both in putting on productions of plays and in teaching Austrian dramatic literature to his
students. Lothar was highly influential in creating a favorable image of
Austria in the United States through his sphere of influence as a teacher
and through his lectures and writings. His wife, Adrienne Gessner, was
prominent on the New York stage.

But for every émigré who made the transition to a new country
and a new life successfully, there were many others who found the
adjustment difficult. Felix Braun supported himself meagerly in England, while in the United States Raoul Auernheimer, a close friend of
Lothar, was assisted financially by his son-in-law and daughter who had
settled in California in the late 1920s. The tragedy of Auernheimer's
later years was caused by his inability to produce works that appealed

to an American audience. His literary debut in English translation began auspiciously enough, for in 1938, after his release from the concentration camp at Dachau and his arrival in New York, where he was joined by his wife, he thought to emulate his good friend Stefan Zweig by writing a historical novel. This was a favorite genre of émigré writers because it was a more universal form that could appeal to readers in every country. The historical setting also allowed comment on the political situation by allusion and analogy. Auernheimer tried to publish a direct account of his imprisonment, but it was rejected by publishers on the ground that the book did not describe enough atrocities. When Auernheimer remonstrated that he could not write about anything that he had not personally witnessed, his plea was ignored. He finally found it possible to publish a few excerpts in the weekly magazine *Monitor* but was prevented from presenting Americans with his full text containing the kind of insight that would have been useful in 1939.[23] His full account appeared in print only as part of his autobiography *Das Wirtshaus zur verlorenen Zeit* (The Inn at the Sign of Lost Time), published posthumously in 1948.[24]

Auernheimer's biography *Metternich—Statesman and Lover* (1939, *Metternich—Staatsmann und Kavalier*), his only success in English, was the result of considerable study. Like Hofmannsthal, Auernheimer felt more comfortable in the past than in the present and had devoted himself to the study of Austrian history. His choice of Metternich becomes obvious from the preface, where he compares the Austrian tyrant to Hitler and predicts the fall of the dictator in time. This preface was deleted from the German edition of the book in 1947. In keeping with Auernheimer's personal interests and capabilities the biography presents a psychological portrait focusing on the two major aspects of Metternich's life, the personal and the political. The fact that Metternich the lover rather than the political figure is highlighted makes the book entertaining reading but at the expense of the complexity and depth that would have made it useful to serious students of history. Nevertheless, the book received favorable reviews, and it appeared as if Auernheimer was on his way to successfully adapting to his new environment. However, he was never able to repeat this success, and for the next ten years he labored unstintingly, producing novels, short stories, and movie scripts without success. Neither his friends in Hollywood and New York nor literary agents could find publishers for his manuscripts, and he never published another work in English. His final two major books, a psychological portrait of *Franz Grillparzer: Licht und Schat-*

ten eines Lebens (Franz Grillparzer. Light and Shadows of a Life), and his autobiography *Das Wirtshaus zur verlorenen Zeit,* which ranks alongside Stefan Zweig's *Die Welt von gestern* as one of the best portrayals of their generation, both appeared posthumously in German in Vienna in 1948.

Auernheimer is mentioned at this length not because of his own intrinsic importance but because his fate is representative of the majority of exile writers, most of whom were not major writers on the order of Broch or Werfel, but who nevertheless had been well-known authors with a substantial following in Austria. Auernheimer, for example, a cousin of Theodor Herzl, had moved in the best literary circles in Vienna as a friend of Hofmannsthal and Schnitzler[25] and had pursued a successful career as a drama critic and feuilletonist for the *Neue Freie Presse,* Austria's most prestigious newspaper. All Viennese writers in Vienna knew their position in the literary hierarchy in those days, and all were accepted on their own level.

Auernheimer's difficulties in publishing his works in exile reveal another dilemma of exile authors: what was acceptable for publication? The continuing German-language publishing houses had to be careful to print what they could sell, and American, British, or French publishers were also highly selective for the same economic reasons. Sentiment or former friendships played no role in determining their choices: the market ruled. Propaganda was out, as were accounts of Nazi brutality — until the war broke out, and then they were acceptable. Historical novels were safe, and escape literature, avoiding rather than addressing the political reality, was also a desideratum. Since the publishers had the last word about what they could or would bring out, authors struggling for survival had little choice but to cooperate. The history of publishers during the exile years is an important chapter in itself,[26] as is the history of film.[27] A number of writers were recruited by Hollywood, Werfel and Torberg among them, and a few Austrian directors like Fritz Lang, Otto Preminger, and George Froeschel achieved major careers. Few of the authors succeeded as well, even in Hollywood.

Auernheimer is also representative of the attitude of the émigrés toward Austria while they were in exile. Even though he had spent six months in Dachau, Auernheimer harbored no ill feelings toward Austria. On the contrary, he remained a devoted patriot. One of the greatest achievements of the Austrian exile writers, a factor of great importance for influencing the allied treatment of Austria after the war, was the unified, loyal, and patriotic stance of the émigrés. Almost unanimously the writers in exile exculpated Austria from any responsibility for their fate and went to great lengths in their writings and in their public speeches to create an autonomous identity for Austria, carefully separating it from Germany and from German guilt in causing the war.

Auernheimer wrote a number of essays and gave many talks before a variety of American groups on such topics as "Austria—Not in Germany," "Hitler and Napoleon," and "There Was a Country Named Austria," all designed to create in the minds of the Americans the fact that Austria was a totally separate entity from Germany and that Austrians should not be considered Germans and certainly not Nazis. The exiles generally depicted Austria as the helpless victim of annexation, and they attributed their own fate of being driven into exile to the circumstances caused by the German Nazis and not to their countrymen. This positive image of an Austria occupied against its will prevailed in the minds of the Allies and contributed to the decision to treat Austria differently than Germany after the war. Austrian writers in various parts of the United States, particularly in Los Angeles and New York as well as in England and France, all presented the same message. These individual efforts effectively supplemented the attempts of the émigrés to create larger political groups which could speak with the more powerful voice of unity. An open appeal to President Roosevelt entitled "Für ein freies Österreich" (For a Free Austria) in the French anti-Hitler review *Freies Österreich,* is indicative of the tenor of all these statements: "And yet there is one motto—a single one—to which the entire nation of Austria subscribes, for which, according to the pledge of impartial and objective observers, Monarchists and Republicans, Christians and Jews, Democrats and Socialists will fight and die. This motto is: Down with Hitler! For a free, autonomous, independent Austria!"[28] In the United States *The Austro-American Tribune* was founded similarly to create a sense of group spirit among the Austrian émigrés, but the efforts to create any kind of solidarity were never very successful because of political differences among the individuals and because of the lack of effective leadership. This inability to unify was largely true in England and France as well as in the United States.

Another example of the strong feeling for Austria is the case of Friedrich Torberg, whose novel *Auch das war Wien* (That Too Was Vienna) contributes to the revisionism occurring today about Austria's conduct in the 1930s and particularly at the time of the *Anschluß.* The work, planned as the first part of a trilogy covering the stages of his flight into exile, was written in 1938/1939 and prepared for publication in 1941 while he was in the United States. Yet, although the novel was completed, Torberg refrained from publishing it. His wife released the manuscript after his death in 1984. The novel, which is quite weak – probably one of the reasons Torberg declined to publish it – drew little notice after it appeared, but the film version "38" by director Christoph Gluck was nominated for an Academy Award as the best foreign film of 1987, and has attracted considerable attention, particularly because of its relevance to the current political situation with the election of Kurt Waldheim as President of Austria, even though he has been accused of war crimes and placed on the watch list in the United States. The film and the novel are contributing to the broad revaluation of the reaction of Austria to the *Anschluß* and the amount of resistance to it. Since Torberg did not release the novel, it is apparent that beyond his dissatisfaction with it as a work of art he had changed his mind about the contents, which were written in a period of anger and heightened emotions. In the United States he joined those voices attempting to exculpate Austria from war guilt, and, like the vast majority, he lived for the day when he would be allowed to resume his life in Austria. As soon as it was possible after the war he returned to Vienna to help rebuild and reorganize the literary scene and particularly to combat Communist influences.

In essence, then, the literary scene in Austria during the 1930s was a heterogeneous fragmented period with the major writers attempting to cling to a status quo that had already disappeared in 1918 with the end of the Monarchy and the advent of the First Republic, along with a group of writers following political expediency, and a new generation of writers who had not yet found their voices. There was a tendency among the older writers to continue to perpetuate the Austrian tradition and a general refusal to acknowledge that the age which best suited their temperaments and to which they had attuned their writings was changing before their very eyes. The attempt to preserve a mood of nostalgia created a head-in-the-sand attitude or what Doderer so impressively termed "Apperzeptionsverweigerung" (a refusal to perceive reality) toward politics. In consequence, a reality for which they were not prepared and against which they were defenseless simply overtook the writers and changed or took their lives. Whether earlier recognition of the threat of Nazism could have changed the situation in any way is a moot point, but little was done, as most of the writers abrogated all responsibility to act as a public conscience and to take an active role in leading or guiding the country on the political level. This valuable lesson was not lost on the writers of the postwar period, who from the beginning determined to become more directly involved in the political sphere.

After the war some of the writers actually held to this resolve and produced works confronting the issues of the war, war guilt, and the Holocaust: Ilse Aichinger in the novel *Die grüne Hoffnung* (1946, *Herod's Children*); Paul Celan in the two volumes of poems *Der Sand aus den Urnen* (1948, Sand from the Urns), and *Mohn und Gedächtnis* (1952, Poppy and Remembrance). which included his famous *Todes-fuge* (Death Fugue); Erich Fried in the poems in *Genügung* (1947, Moderateness) and the novel *Ein Soldat und das Mädchen* (1960, A Soldier and the Girl; Fritz Hochwälder in the dramas *Das heilige Experiment* (1947, *Lonely are the Brave*), *Meier Helmbrecht* (1947), and *Der Flüchtling* (1948, The Fugitive); Friedrich Torberg in the novels *Mein ist die Rache* (1943, Revenge is Mine) and *Hier bin ich, mein Vater* (1948, Here I Am, My Father); and Hans Weigel in the satiric novel *Der grüne Stern* (1946, The Green Star). However, the turn to an examination of recent past history was not widespread; and there was no overall reaction to the war on the order of that in Germany for at least two major reasons: 1) The pragmatic Austrians simply preferred to forget the traumatic past and resume their normal lives unencumbered by unpleasant memories, and 2) there was no reason to launch into a full-scale examination of the Nazi era, for, thanks in large part to the efforts of the émigrés, Austrians were not charged with war guilt or with crimes against humanity; thus exonerated, there seemed to be no need to cope with the issues. On the contrary, because of the favorable attitude of the Allies who were disposed to establish an independent Austria, the country was well positioned to begin the task of reconstruction immediately. To be sure, Austria remained under four-power control, but this form of governance was intended primarily as a means of de-Nazifying the country and accelerating its recovery and rebuilding. The nation was divided into four sectors under American, English, French, and Russian control, with Vienna being supervised by all four powers concurrently, each country by turns alternating in command of the city for one week out of each month. This arrangement lasted until 1955 when the Second Republic was formed and Austria was decreed to be an independent country with permanently neutral status. The removal of the occupation forces was made possible by Austria's restoration to financial stability and a capability of functioning largely in terms of its own economy. In addition, it was felt that there was no longer any lingering threat of a revival of Nazism in the country. The conservative People's Party (ÖVP) won eighty-five seats in Parliament at the first election, the Socialists (SPÖ) seventy-six, and the Communists four, and the conservatives continued to dominate at the polls after the state treaty was signed on 15 May 1955. The initial anger at Germany and the mistrust against any lingering Nazi spirit in the country soon dissipated, and it was not long before sensible voices like that of Hans Weigel began calling for the reestablishment of normal ties with their German neighbors.[29]

Like the reconstitution of the government and the economy, the revival of the arts was also given a high priority at the end of the war, commencing almost immediately after the cessation of hostilities in 1945. As in the government the cultural trend tended toward conservatism with the major stress placed on the reestablishment of the broken link with tradition. All writers, both those who had stayed in Austria and those who had been driven into exile, seemed to agree on this approach to the revival of literature and the arts. Those who had stayed in Austria in inner emigration, like Basil, Gütersloh, and Henz, were now able to resume their careers. Even writers who had become Nazi sympathizers during the 1930s and during the war, for the most part simply continued writing without recrimination and were accepted in good standing by the new government and the public. The émigrés who returned from exile likewise resumed their careers where they had left off in the 1930s and often reached the pinnacle of their reputations in the postwar period. Other exiled writers who did not return nevertheless published their works in German for Austrian audiences and in this fashion also contributed to the postwar revival even though they preferred to remain in their host countries.

The initial cultural wave came in the form of literary and cultural journals, which were spawned rapidly and readily in the immediate postwar period and played a major role in reviving tradition and reawakening national pride. They also brought an awareness of the recent literary trends in other countries, information that had been unavailable during the Nazi occupation. The value of these publications was not lost on the Allies, who supplied the newsprint which was otherwise in short supply and in some cases even supplied the financial backing for various publications. Most of the independent publications did not stay in existence long for lack of financial support.

The major postwar journals were *Der Turm, Monatsschrift für* österreichische Kultur (1945-1946), and Otto Basil's revived journal Plan: Literatur, Kunst, Kultur (1945-1947). Others in no particular order of importance include Österreichische Rundschau (1945-1946); Austria. Die Welt im Spiegel Österreichs (1945-1946); Zeitschrift für Kultur und Geistesleben (1946); Die Eule (1946); Lynkeus (1945-1952); Das Silberboot. Zeitschrift für Literatur (1946-1953); Österreichisches Tagebuch. Wochenschrift für Kultur, Politik, Wirtschaft (1946); Wiener Literarisches Echo. Kritische Vierteljahresschrift für Dichtung und Geistesgeschichte (1948-1949); Europäische Rundschau (1946); Wort und Tat. Internationale Monatsschrift (1946-1947); Wort und Wahrheit. Monatsschrift für Religion und Kultur (1949); Die Drau (1950-1952); Von Mensch zu Mensch (1950-1953); Die Silberrose (1951-1953); Publikation (1951-1954); Alpha (1953-1960); Wort in der Zeit (1954-1967).

Der Turm, strongly Catholic in orientation and backed by the People's Party (ÖVP), showed its conservative intent by using St. Stephen's Cathedral as a symbol with which the public could readily identify. In a sense this magnificent Gothic cathedral, one of the oldest in Europe, dating from 1328, was a symbol of Austria itself, one of the country's most recognized and hallowed landmarks. The church was severely damaged by the retreating Germans, and the tiled roof depicting the Habsburg double eagle collapsed from the flames as did the belltower containing the famous bell, the "Pummerin," an important symbol to the Austrians. To rebuild St. Stephen's was an urgent issue in the postwar period. Even people who had virtually nothing donated money to the restoration of the cathedral. The raising of the bell to its proper position in the tower was a major event of the reconstruction period. The journal Der Turm capitalized on all of these connotations in its efforts to help unite the people and boost morale.

To demonstrate its conservative nature and its conciliatory position Der Turm published among its first articles Hofmannsthal's essay "Preusse und Österreicher" (The Prussian and the Austrian) to contrast two distinct types and then appended an appeal for "humanity" toward the Germans. Der Turm lasted only two years but performed an important function in reviving the connections with the past. In this respect the contribution of Lernet-Holenia, "Gruß des Dichters," on 17 October 1945 carried programmatic force: "Indeed, we only need to resume at the point where the dreams of a madman interrupted us; in fact we do not need to look ahead but only back. To state it with complete clarity, there is no necessity for us to flirt with the future and undertake nebulous projects; we are, in our best and most valuable aspects, our past. We only have to remind ourselves that we are our past—and it will become our future."

Otto Basil's *Plan*, which had begun in 1938 as an opposition journal of the left, was considered avant-garde in the postwar period, although it too made the revival of the past and the awareness of foreign developments in the arts a central goal. In his editorial statement "Zum Wiederbeginn" Basil specified as his goals: "To clear away the rubble in the intellectual realm which . . . the fascist dictatorship left behind, to reattach Austria . . . to the rest of Europe and the world, and to awaken Austrian youth . . . to realize its own responsibility in the reconstruction of intellectual life within the country."[30]

Plan was avant-garde in orientation, stressing the interdisciplinary nature of the arts and featuring a European outlook while affirming national Austrian interests. Basil featured Karl Kraus and at the same time rediscovered for its readers the works of Kafka and of French Surrealism, which took root in Vienna in both literature and art under the rubric of fantastic realism.[31] Thus *Plan* looked backward and forward, at home and abroad, simultaneously.

In 1955, *Wort in der Zeit*, edited by Rudolf Henz, followed the same policy of establishing literary connections between old and new Austria, as does its successor, the present-day *Literatur und Kritik*, founded by Henz and edited for ten years by Jeannie Ebner, who was succeeded in April 1979 by the current editor Kurt Klinger when she resigned to her own writing. *Literatur und Kritik*, which celebrated its twentieth anniversary in 1986, enjoys not only the greatest longevity of any postwar periodical, but also the prestige of being one of the leading Austrian journals, rivaled only by *manuscripte*, edited in Graz by Alfred Kolleritsch.

None of the other early journals was as influential as *Der Turm* and *Plan*, primarily because none of them lasted long enough to create a major impact. They ranged the full political spectrum, and all celebrated the renewed opportunity for free speech after seven years of oppression. The possibility of being able to use language in its true meaning again rather than either as propaganda or phraseology was a welcome relief, and the opportunity to publish information about what had been happening in the realm of literature and the arts in other countries during the years of censorship was a heady experience for this generation.

Language emerged again as an important issue among the postwar writers. Language skepticism has a lengthy history in Austria, reaching prominence at the turn of the century in the writings of Hofmannsthal and Schnitzler as well as Mauthner and Wittgenstein. In the postwar period this skepticism took a new form in reaction to the abuse of language as a propaganda tool. The immediate concern was voiced by Ilse Aichinger, who in "Aufruf zum Mißtrauen" (1946, Call to Mistrust), urged her contemporaries to be wary of language as well as of politics, to prevent any possibility of a revival of Nazism or another fascist state.[32] Aichinger, who was one of the major writers concerned with confronting the past, published her statement in an issue of *Plan* entitled "Stimme der Jugend" (7 July 1946, Voice of Youth), which introduced the new generation of young writers. Her appeal touched a responsive chord and was often quoted as well as imitated. For example, the writer and critic Herbert Eisenreich entitled his essay on the Austrian literary tradition "Das schöpferische Mißtrauen" (1962, Creative Mistrust), and Otto Breicha and Gerhard Fritsch entitled an important cultural anthology *Aufforderung zum Mißtrauen. Literatur, Bildende Kunst, Musik in Österreich seit 1945* (1967, Summons to Mistrust. Literature, Visual Arts, Music in Austria since 1945). However, beyond this call to remain alert, to stifle any lingering bacillus of fascism, and except for the few works dealing with the immediate past the dominating political tenor of Austrian literature was conciliatory. Indeed, the emphasis on tradition made it possible to overcome the seven years of the *Anschluß* and the ravages of the war almost as if they had not existed. There was nothing resembling the "Schutt- und Trümmerliteratur" (Literature of the Ruins), the "Heimkehrerliteratur" (Literature of the Returning Soldier), and the stress on *Vergangenheitsbewältigung* (Overcoming the Past) that dominated German postwar literature. Neither was there any concerted movement toward political activism among writers beyond the loosely knit boycott of Brecht, which will be discussed shortly, and no equivalent of "Gruppe 47" (Group 47), the influential organization of writers established in Germany in 1947. Because of the designated status of Austria as a victim rather than an ally of Germany there was no necessity for the writers to dwell on the inhumanity that had transpired in the immediate past nor to insist that their readers confront the issue of war guilt, as Heinrich Böll, Wolfgang Borchert, Günter Grass, Uwe Johnson, Peter Weiss, et al., were doing in Germany.

Austrians could concentrate instead on reestablishing the Austrian cultural tradition. A position paper by the critic Edwin Rollett in 1945 entitled *Österreichische Gegenwartsliteratur. Aufgabe, Lage, Forderung* (Austrian Contemporary Literature. Task, Situation, Challenge), the first major critical statement of the postwar era, provides an excellent survey of the literary scene and of the intellectual concerns of the time. Rollett stressed the need for cooperation between writers, something that Austria has usually lacked, and particularly for greater communication between authors in Vienna and those in the provinces in order to create a unified Austria. Rollett also wished to overcome the notion that only Viennese literature represented Austrian literature, an idea that again goes back to the turn of the century. Finally, he stressed the need for public support of writers if Austria wished to remain a cultural nation. Here too he touched on a theme which had long been a sore point in Austria, where writers have traditionally not been able to support themselves from their writings without German readers. Rollett's recommendations aroused enthusiastic response from governmental and cultural agencies in Austria, which from the very beginning of the postwar period developed programs to support writers through stipends and prizes.

Like Basil's stress in *Plan* on the importance of cultural mediation, reviving ideas which hearkened back to innovations featured by both the writers of the *Jung-Wien* group at the turn of the century and by the members of the Secessionist art group around the art journal *Ver sacrum* (1897), Rollett insisted that Austria must be "weltoffen" (open to the world), receptive to the artistic achievements of other countries, and at the same time make other nations aware of Austrian accomplishments. He concluded with a plea for a responsible press and general freedom of speech without censorship. Overall Rollett's programmatic position paper offered a most practical and conservative plan, but except for the ready receptiveness of the public and of young writers to foreign influences—French, English, and American, particularly Wilder and Hemingway—his ideas stirred little reaction. Even the sensible idea of eliminating the barriers between Vienna and the provinces awakened no response; the situation became even more problematical, as it remains today. A rivalry grew up between older established writers belonging to the P.E.N. Club in Vienna and the new younger authors of the *Forum Stadtpark* in Graz. As a result the Graz writers formed their own independent anti-P.E.N. organization in 1973, the "Grazer Autorenversammlung" (Graz Writers' Association), under the initial leadership of H. C. Artmann.

The divisiveness between writers existed not only between Vienna and the provinces but also developed between the older and younger generations. Since the main thrust of the initial postwar period was to reestablish the link with tradition, writers with known reputations received the initial attention. It was difficult for young writers to break through in the climate of that day. Ilse Aichinger, Ingeborg Bachmann, and Paul Celan, the three brightest young talents on the horizon at that time, first had to gain acceptance by winning prizes from Group 47 in Germany before they could begin to receive serious consideration in Austria. Needing the sanction of German acceptance before finding appreciation in Austria was not a new development but is a long-term feature of Austrian letters.

One who gave strong impetus to young writers and who in general served as a major organizer and catalyst during the postwar development in Vienna was the former caberettist, humorist, and critic, Hans Weigel, who had returned immediately after the war from exile in Switzerland. Even though he is a traditionalist, as his writings confirm, he assumed a leadership role in fostering young writers. In his words "I looked for young Austrian literature and found a generation."[33] This statement is similar to that made by Hermann Bahr (1863–1934) when he returned to Vienna in 1891, discovered the *Jung-Wien* group, and determined to stay in Austria and work for the cultural revival of the country. In many ways Weigel's role in the postwar period resembles that of Bahr. Like Bahr, he set about with determination, enthusiasm, and seemingly unlimited energy to rejuvenate the literary scene. On one occasion he described himself as "the proprietor in Vienna of a one-man writing factory, known throughout the city, which operates on a 24-hour-a-day, 7-day-a-week schedule, producing, as the occasion arises, works of drama, fiction, and journalism."[34] While producing his own works such as the novel *Der grüne Stern* (1946, The Green Star), a humorous satire on Nazism, Weigel gathered the new writers around him—Ilse Aichinger, Ingeborg Bachmann, Paul Celan, and a host of others—encouraged them, helped them to get their manuscripts into print, and worked to mediate their introduction to the public. Weigel published five anthologies of lyric poetry under the title *Stimmen der Gegenwart* (1951–1956, Voices of the Present), as one contribution to gathering and publicizing the new young poets. Concurrently, he published twelve volumes of *Junge österreichische Autoren* (Young Austrian Authors) as well as a volume *Die gute neue Zeit* (The Good New Time) containing twenty-four narrative selections from Schnitzler to the present.

While he promoted the young writers, Weigel remained in the mainstream of the Austrian tradition, as all of his many publications indicate. His volume *Flucht vor der Grösse* (1960, Flight from Greatness) dedicated to Adalbert Stifter and containing essays on six prominent Austrian writers and composers of the nineteenth century — Schubert, Raimund, Nestroy, Grillparzer, Stifter, and Johann Strauss — fits perfectly into the postwar trend to rediscover and reaffirm the Austrian cultural tradition. Weigel discusses but does not answer the question of when Austrian literature begins, a topic that has been a major issue of the postwar period and remains so. He presents evidence for beginning with Grillparzer around 1800, or alternatively with the Middle Ages, but fails to come to any particular conclusion, just as no other critic has been able to resolve the matter. The general theme of the essays is to trace the "Austrian 'fate' of not being recognized . . . of being misunderstood, greatness in flight from itself."[35] Weigel's contribution illustrates the role of cultural mediation that he played to remind Austrians of their unique cultural history. Weigel has still other direct connections to the Austrian tradition through his concern for language and his admiration for earlier Austrian writers mainly concerned with language — as he shows in his books, *Johann Nestroy* (1967) and *Karl Kraus. Oder die Macht der Ohnmacht* (1968, Karl Kraus, or the Power of Powerlessness), Weigel had his literary beginnings in the cabaret scene of the 1930s, and his strength is his use of language, particularly puns, plays on words, paradoxes, sudden unexpected twists of meaning, and humorous anecdotes, of which he seemingly has an inexhaustible supply. Weigel may keep the surface amusing, for he would never want to be accused of boring his readers, but beneath the surface he attempts to emulate Kraus both as a social and cultural critic and above all in his serious concern for the care and well-being of the German language. His volume *Die Leiden der jungen Wörter* (1975, The Sorrows of Young Words), modeled on Kraus's *Die Sprache* (The Language) and dedicated to Kraus, is directed against the corruption of language in any form.

The theater and the opera have always been central cultural institutions in Austria: because of their importance they were reopened as quickly as possible with the aid of the occupation forces, for both the Austrians and the Allied governments recognized their significance for helping to restore the country to normalcy. The obstacles were many, for the theaters had been forced to close on 1 September 1944 when lack of personnel and other deficiencies, including the impossibility of heating the buildings, made it impossible to operate. Some theaters like the Burgtheater and the Opera House were destroyed, sets and costumes were burned, and the former ensembles had scattered. It was a major feat therefore, that only three weeks after the capture of Vienna by the Russians on 1 May 1945, some theater productions and operas could be performed, even while the city was basically in ruin. The efforts of Dr. Victor Matejka, who was put in charge of cultural affairs in the provisional city government of Vienna, were a major factor in this amazing revival, and Ernst Lothar also contributed in an important way. Lothar, whose son-in-law Ernst Haeussermann later became director of the Theater in der Josefstadt, became impatient while waiting to return to Vienna from his exile in the United States. To expedite his return he volunteered for military service, and on 25 May 1946 in the uniform of a United States Army officer he found himself in his native city, charged with the task of "promoting the interests of the American theater and American music in Austria through the medium of his office and of working equally for the rehabilitation of artistic life in Austria."[36] This mandate gave him responsibility for reestablishing and supervising more than twenty-five theaters in Vienna as well as overseeing the Salzburg Festival.

Like Weigel and all of the other exiles who returned early to Vienna, Lothar was dedicated to the Austrian tradition. He had begun his literary career under the influence of Schnitzler, whose prose narratives *Leutnant Gustl* (*Lieutenant Gustl*) and *Fräulein Else* he had adapted successfully for the stage. Grillparzer's motto prefacing Lothar's postwar novel *Der Engel mit der Posaune* (1947, *The Angel with the Trumpet,* 1944) shows how his heart and his art were solidly rooted in the Austrian tradition: "If the Austrians knew Austria better, they would be better Austrians; if the world knew better what Austria is, the world would be better."[37] This novel was made into a film starring Paula Wessely, who had been accused of collaborating with the Nazis but was cleared by the authorities and permitted to perform again. Lothar's attachment to his native country was so strong that his United States citizenship caused him great concern and anguish. When his term of service in Austria was coming to an end, he asked for an extension and then for another in order to prolong his stay as long as possible. Finally, he could not stand the torment of indecision any longer and turned in his American passport, having resolved to remain in Vienna. He described the ambivalence that he suffered and the arguments leading to his decision in the novel *Die Rückkehr* (1948, The Return).

Others who returned were Vicki Baum, Felix Braun, Robert Neumann, Alfred Polgar, Hilde Spiel, and Friedrich Torberg. Spiel too wrote an account of her return in *Rückkehr nach Wien: Tagebuch 1946* (1968, Return to Vienna: Diary 1946), which was intended as a report on the conditions in 1946 when she returned to her native city as a member of the British Occupation Forces and as a foreign correspondent for the journal *The New Statesman* after ten years of living in England.[38] The original English version is dated 29 January to 23 February with only an afterword dated September 1967 to conclude the work shortly before publication in 1968.

When Torberg returned to Vienna in 1951 from exile in the United States, he displayed a changed attitude toward politics, which had not concerned him in his earlier writings. The short story *Mein ist die Rache* (1943, Revenge is Mine) and the novel *Hier bin ich, mein Vater* (Here I Am, My Father), written between 1943 and 1946 and published in 1948, both deal with the Nazi treatment of Jews. Torberg probably ranks only second to Weigel as a critical force in postwar Austria. Like Weigel, he turned out numerous essays, reviews, commentaries, and parodies, and made a major contribution as editor of the monthly review, *Forum,* one of the most important literary journals of the day. Also like Weigel, Torberg was an avowed anti-Communist, and both he and Weigel worked actively to resist the Marxist presence in any form during the cold war.

The most notable example of their efforts was the methodical boycott of Bertolt Brecht that they initiated and maintained from 1945 until 1966. For over twenty years only a few sporadic Brecht performances were staged in Vienna, not because theater directors were unaware of Brecht's literary significance but because of the combined efforts of Weigel, Torberg, and Ernst Haeussermann. All three recognized Brecht's literary talent but opposed him on political grounds. Because of the existing cold war these three returned exiles (Haeussermann, too, had fled to New York during the war) saw no reason to publicize a writer who was espousing a Communist system inimical to the values for which the Second Republic of Austria stood. All three were well aware of Brecht's dramatic talent, but for this very reason they regarded him as all the more dangerous. The few performances that were staged by leftist groups in small theaters called forth a newspaper campaign, and pressures were brought to keep the major theaters from participating. Haeussermann finally relented in 1963 and performed a Brecht play, and by 1966 the boycott ended. Overall the affair is not very instructive about Brecht beyond describing his political ideology, but the episode reveals how the literary establishment functioned in Vienna. Above all it shows the inordinate power wielded by Weigel and Torberg during those critical postwar years. This interlude also demonstrates that postwar critics and writers had learned their lesson well and no longer turned their backs on politics.

While the campaign against Brecht was clearcut and could be waged in terms of principle, whether one agreed with it or not, the de-Nazification of Austrian writers was a more complex matter. According to Heinz Lunzer, the list of authors who had collaborated or cooperated with the Nazis was seventy-three pages long.[40] Yet few of these authors suffered any long-term negative effects. There were extreme cases such as Josef Weinheber (1898-1945), a highly popular gifted poet who committed suicide when he heard that the Russians were advancing into Vienna. Weinheber had cast his lot with the Nazis and from 1936 to 1943 had edited a journal entitled *Der Augarten,* which followed the Nazi literary ideology. Other authors who took part in this journal were Bruno Brehm (1892-1974), Egon Corti (1880-1953), Karl Hans Strobl (1877-1946), and Joseph Wenter (1880-1947). Basil had once listed forty authors who had collaborated, including Billinger, Brehm, Grogger, Hohlbaum, Jelusich, Oberkofler, Ortner, Sacher, Schreyvogel, Tumler, Waggerl, and Weinheber, and he stated his intention to deal with each author individually.[41] However, the plan was not carried out.

An interesting case was that of Paula von Preradović (1897-1951), who had at first gone along with the new fascist regime but subsequently became an anti-Nazi, was arrested, and became a member of the resistance. Her patriotism is reflected in her poem "Land der Berge, Land am Strome," which became the new national anthem of Austria.

Beyond the publishing of lists of names and some articles deploring the conduct of writers like Weinheber, there was surprisingly little hostility toward previous collaborators. The atmosphere in postwar Austria was conciliatory, and few wanted to keep old wounds open by belaboring the past. But the decisions were not always consistent. The literary historian Josef Nadler, for example, was not de-Nazified and never forgiven for having published his *Literaturgeschichte der deutschen Stämme und Landschaften* in a deluxe edition during the war under Nazi sponsorship, and he was subsequently prohibited from teaching, while Heinz Kindermann, a leading professor of theater history, escaped sanction for works favorable to Nazi ideology such as

Die Sendung des Burgtheaters im dritten Reich (1940). Even Nadler was allowed to continue to publish, producing an Austrian literary history, *Literaturgeschichte Österreichs* (1951), and he could be awarded the Stifter medal in 1958 for his scholarly contributions. Unfortunately, Nadler's theory of literary history, attributing the makeup of an artist to his regional and ethnic origins, smacked so much of the blood and soil theories of Nazism that people could not accept him. He is still ignored today, one of the very few Austrians from that period who has not been reclaimed, even though his theory, which was advanced well before Hitler's racial propaganda, has never been disproved but only dismissed. Academics still refuse to recognize any of his positive accomplishments but dwell on this one theory, which remains to be tested on its own merits apart from any relationship to Nazism. Nadler's rediscovery of the importance of the Baroque to Austria in the third volume of his literary history in 1918, for example, deserves more credit than it has received to date.[42]

On the whole, the eagerness of the Austrian government and of the literary establishment to reestablish ties with tradition overcame all considerations of punitive action. There were simply too many authors involved to be able to enforce any kind of ban if the desire to revitalize the Austrian literary scene was to be carried out. Publishers played an important role in the decision to overlook the past, because with a limited amount of paper at their disposal they were unwilling to take risks with young new authors. They preferred to publish authors who already had name identification. Other contributing factors were the public's desire to forget the past and the attitude of those who did not feel at all repentant about the past and agreed with the actions of these authors. Because of the difficult economic conditions in postwar Austria the government established a system of literary prizes and stipends, rewarding performance as a means of reestablishing the pool of authors and reviving Austrian identity as a nation of writers. Even here no discrimination was made between those writers driven into exile or otherwise penalized and those who collaborated with the Nazis. The majority of prizes went to former Nazi sympathizers who had benefited in the prewar era from collaboration with the Austrofascists and the National Socialists: Blass, Fussenegger, Ginskey, Grogger, Hohlbaum, Keller, List, Mell, Nabl, and Zerzer, many of whom were among the seventy-one authors who contributed to the *Bekenntnisbuch österreichischer Dichter* (1938, Book of Allegiance of Austrian Poets).[43]

Conspicuously absent was any attempt to use such prizes as a means of attracting exile writers back to Austria. Only after a period of time was there recognition of the exiled writers who decided for one reason or another to stay in their host countries, including Broch in the United States, Fried in England, and Hochwälder in Switzerland. This enlightened program of state and city prizes, stipends, and awards has in time become so extensive that not a single postwar author of any stature has failed to receive multiple awards. While merit and reputation are central considerations, the main purpose is to help the large number of writers continue in their chosen profession in a country that has a far greater proportion of authors for its size than any other.

The conscious effort to support Austrian writers worked hand in hand with the decision to establish an identity for Austria, as distinct from Germany. If there had been a question about Austrian identity earlier, after the establishment of the Second Republic there was no longer any doubt about the political autonomy of Austria. The hegemony of the Germans in Austria had been broken, and the nostalgia over the former union with Germany, which had existed ever since 1866, no longer prevailed. Austrians of the early postwar period were now proud to live in Austria and to be identified with Austria without any further yearning for attachment to Germany or to any other outside government. If the First Republic had been "the state that nobody wanted," the Second Republic could be called by contrast "the state that everyone wanted." The general tenor of the postwar period up to 1955 can be characterized as positive and moderate. Extremes were avoided: neither idealism nor nihilism is in evidence. Because of the circumstances people were very conscious of the present, but at the same time they drew upon the strength of the past tradition, which served as a unifying bond during that period of great stress. One of the notable publishing ventures, which was intended to foster an awareness of the past and its continued relevance, was the series of Austrian writers published by the Stiasny Press, an undertaking made possible by a generous government subsidy. The books, printed in small affordable paperback editions, contained complete works and excerpts along with a chronology and an introduction to put the author and his writings in perspective. The series ran to more than a hundred volumes before financial mismanagement caused its demise.

The first major postwar turning point was virtually coincidental with the founding of the Second Republic, as if literary and artistic innovation could begin to occur only in an atmosphere of political security. Gerhard Fritsch's novel *Moos auf den Steinen* (1956, Moss on the Stones) heralded the first signs of a call for literary change in Austria and for a general change of attitude away from the past and toward the future. The novel, which uses the central symbol of the care of a castle to preserve it for the future, was well received for the wrong reasons: readers accepted the book within the context of the ongoing nostalgia for the past, while in reality it marked the transition to the new youth movement which had been growing slowly throughout the 1950s and came to full prominence in 1958 when H. C. Artmann published his inordinately successful volume in dialect *Med ana schwoazzn dintn* (With Black Ink).

One who helped bring about this success was Heimito von Doderer, an established author who perhaps reached greater importance in Austria than any other writer on the postwar scene. Doderer was the last Austrian novelist who attempted to create the polyhistoric novel, the all-encompassing narrative that created its own world and drew the reader into it. Indeed, some works that pass for novels today are glorified novellas printed in large type to make them appear longer than they actually are.

Although Doderer preferred the Austrian past, he was not opposed to encouraging the new young writers to assert themselves and allow their voices to be heard. He was particularly impressed by the writings of the "Wiener Gruppe" (Vienna Group), consisting of Achleitner, Artmann, Bayer, Rühm, and Wiener. Since these writers could not find an outlet for their works in any other form, Doderer offered to release his space in the *Wiener Kurier* to them so that they could begin to gain recognition. When the newspaper refused to accede to his request, Doderer resigned in protest.

This gesture of Doderer and the popular response to Artmann's volume in 1958—also for the wrong reason: the public mistook the dialect works as part of the nostalgic wave—marked the irreversible turning point in the postwar scene. Having reestablished the connection with Austrian tradition for some dozen years and having it solidly entrenched in the major novels and dramas of the postwar period, the young generation could now begin to react against this tradition to assert its own voice in terms of its own new forms. The postwar situation makes an interesting contrast to the turn of the century. In the late nineteenth century the *Jung-Wien* writers reacted against the literary tradition and introduced a period of innovation, only to return later in life to the camp of tradition.[44] In the postwar period the effort had to be made first to reestablish the broken tradition, so that the young writers could turn to innovation in reaction against it. A generation later these same writers, like Peter Handke and Thomas Bernhard, in emulation of the *Jung-Wien* writers also returned to tradition, indeed, to the Austrian tradition of the nineteenth century, particularly in the rediscovery of Stifter, who has become the measure of contemporary prose writing.

The parallels with the turn of the century show that, as has always been the case, innovation and tradition have continued to succeed each other in Austrian literature, when they are not actually running side-by-side in tandem. These tendencies are clearly seen in the authors who now came to the fore and emerged as the major figures of the contemporary generation.

Notes

1. Donald G. Daviau, ed., *Major Figures of Contemporary Austrian Literature* (New York, Bern: Peter Lang, 1987), pp. 1–33. The authors included are: Ilse Aichinger, H. C. Artmann, Wolfgang Bauer, Thomas Bernhard, Elias Canetti, Jeannie Ebner, Erich Fried, Barbara Frischmuth, Peter Handke, Franz Innerhofer, Ernst Jandl, Gert Jonke, Friederike Mayröcker, Gerhard Roth, and Peter Turrini.

2. For a variety of views on this subject and a comprehensive bibliography containing more than four hundred titles see "Perspectives on the Question of Austrian Literature," Special Issue of *Modern Austrian Literature*, Vol. 17, Nos. 3/4 (1984).

3. On this point see Joachim Remak, "The Healthy Invalid: How Doomed the Habsburg Empire?" *The Journal of Modern History*, 41 (1969), 242 ff.

4. Cf. Helmut Andics, *Der Staat, den keiner wollte. Österreich 1918-1943* (Wien: Molden, 1968).

5. Claudio Magris, *Der habsburgische Mythos in der österreichischen Literatur* (Salzburg: Otto Müller, 1966).

6. Cf. Nike Wagner, *Geist und Geschlecht. Karl Kraus und die Erotik der Wiener Moderne* (Frankfurt am Main: Suhrkamp, 1982).

7. Cf. Andrew G. Whiteside, *The Socialism of Fools* (Berkeley, Los Angeles, London: University of California Press, 1975).

8. For a detailed account of Austrian politics from 1918 to 1928, see Charles A. Gulick, *Austria: From Habsburg to Hitler*, 2 vols.

(Berkeley and Los Angeles: University of California Press, 1948). For the 15 July riot see pp. 725-746.

9. Cf. Harry Zohn, "Karl Kraus and the Events of July 1927," *Modern Austrian Literature,* Vol. 12, No. 2 (1979), 81-92.

10. Raoul Auernheimer, *Das Wirtshaus zur verlorenen Zeit* (Wien: Ullstein, 1948), p. 112. My translation, D.G.D.

11. Edward E. Lowinsky, "Foreword," in *A Confidential Matter. The letters of Richard Strauss and Stefan Zweig 1931-1935* (Berkeley: University of California Press, 1977), p. xxiii.

12. Cf. Donald G. Daviau and Harvey I. Dunkle, "Stefan Zweig's *Schachnovelle," Monatshefte,* 65 (Winter 1973), 370-384.

13. Bruce Pauley, *Hitler and the Forgotten Nazis. A History of Austrian National Socialism* (Chapel Hill: The University of North Carolina Press, 1981), p. 10.

14. See Sylvia M. Patsch, *Österreichische Schriftsteller im Exil in Grossbritannien* (Wien, München: Brandstätter, 1985); Hans Wurgner, ed., *Österreichische Exilliteratur in den Niederlanden 1934-1940* (Amsterdam: Rodoni, 1986); Ulrich Weinzierl, ed., *Österreicher im Exil. Frankreich 1938-1945. Eine Dokumentation* (Wien: Österreichischer Bundesverlag, 1986); John Spalek and Joseph Strelka, eds., *Deutsche Exilliteratur, Kalifornien.* 2 vols. (Bern und München: Francke, 1976).

15 Cf. Wolfgang Kudrnofsky, "Österreichische Literatur—zu viel Mann für ein kleines Boot," *Zur Lage des österreichischen Schriftstellers:* Tiraden, Tatsachen, Tendenzen (Wien: Europa Verlag, 1973).

16. For a detailed account including the names of all of the writers involved, see Hilde Spiel, ed., *Die zeitgenössische Literatur Österreichs* (Zürich und München: Kindler, 1976), pp. 19-23. See also Klaus Amann, "Vorgeschichten. Kontinuitäten in der österreichischen Literatur von den dreißiger zu den fünfziger Jahren," *Literatur der Nachkriegszeit und der 50er Jahre in Österreich,* eds. Friedbert Aspetsberger, Norbert Frei, and Hubert Lengauer (Wien: Österreichischer Bundesverlag, 1984), pp. 48-50.

17. On the economic plight of writers see Friedbert Aspetsberger, *Literarisches Leben im Austrofaschismus* (Königstein/Ts.: Hain, 1980), pp. 53-56.

18. Klaus Amann, "Vorgeschichten," p. 53. (See note 16.)

19. Ruth Gross, *Plan and the Austrian Rebirth* (Columbia, South Carolina: Camden House, 1982), p. 24.

20. In addition to Friedbert Aspetsberger, *Literarisches Leben im Austrofaschismus* (note 17), see Klaus Amann and Albert Berger, eds., *Österreichische Literatur der dreißiger Jahre* (Wien: Böhlau, 1985), and Anson Rabenbach, ed., *The Austrian Socialist Experiment: Social Democracy and Austromarxism (1918-1934)* (Boulder and London: Westview Press, 1985).

21. Apparently, six symposia are scheduled on topics bearing on these two decades: Austrian Studies Center at the University of Minneapolis; Ohio State University; the Oxford Polytechnic Institute, England; the P.E.N. Club, Vienna, Austria; the University of California, Riverside; and the University of Innsbruck. Undoubtedly there will be still other conferences.

22. For further details on these writers see Sylvia Patsch, *Österreichische Schriftsteller im Exil in Grossbritannien.*

23. Raoul Auernheimer, "Inside Barbed Wire," *The Christian Science Monitor*, 26 September 1942; "Mark Twain and the Gestapo," *The Christian Science Monitor*, 10 October 1942.

24. Raoul Auernheimer, *Das Wirthaus zur verlorenen Zeit* (Wien: Ullstein, 1958).

25. Donald G. Daviau and Jorun B. Johns, eds., *The Correspondence of Arthur Schnitzler and Raoul Auernheimer* (Chapel Hill: The University of North Carolina Press, 1972); D.G.D., "The Correspondence of Hugo von Hofmannsthal and Raoul Auernheimer," *Modern Austrian Literature*, Vol. 7, Nos. 3/4 (1974), 209-307.

26. See Murray G. Hall, *Österreichische Verlagsgeschichte 1918-1938*, 2 vols. (Wien: Böhlau, 1985); M.G.H., "Buchhandel und Verlag der dreißiger Jahre im Spiegel von Innen- und Außenpolitik," in: Klaus Amann and Albert Berger, eds., *Österreichische Literatur der dreißiger Jahre*, pp. 164-177; and Wulf Koepke, "Die Exilschriftsteller und der amerikanische Buchmarkt," in *Deutsche Exilliteratur seit 1933*, Vol. I, Kalifornien, edited by John M. Spalek and Joseph Strelka (Bern und München: Francke, 1976), pp. 117-134.

27. See Erna M. Moore, "Exile in Hollywood," in *Deutsche Exilliteratur seit 1933*, Vol. I, Kalifornien, pp. 21-39.

28. *Freies Österreich*, Jg. 3, Heft I (Mai 1940), 4-5.

29. Hans Weigel, "Das verhängte Fenster," *Plan*, No. 5 (March-April 1946), 397 ff.

30. Quoted from Ruth Gross, *Plan and the Austrian Rebirth*, p. 41.

31. "Fantastic Realism," sometimes called "Magic Realism" refers to

literature in which a realistic surface through incidents, occurrences, or gestures provides entrée to the subconscious instincts and drives of the characters. The writings of Broch, Gütersloh, Kafka, and Saiko are considered major representatives of this narrative technique.

32. Ilse Aichinger, "Aufruf zum Mißtrauen," *Plan,* 7 July 1946, p. 588.
33. Hans Weigel, "Es begann mit Ilse Aichinger," in Otto Breicha and Gerhard Fritsch, eds., *Aufforderung zum Mißtrauen,* p. 28.
34. Quoted in Katharina Wilson and Robert Harrison, eds., *Ad Absurdum: A Hans Weigel Potpourri* (Columbia, South Carolina: Camden House, 1987), p. 13.
35. Hans Weigel, *Flucht vor der Größe* (Wien: Morawa, 1960), p. 13.
36. Ernst Lothar, *Das Wunder des Überlebens* (Wien: Zsolnay, 1961), p. 227.
37. Ernst Lothar, *Der Engel mit der Posaune* (Wien: Zsolnay, 1963), Preface.
38. Cf. Peter Pabisch, "Hilde Spiels *Rückkehr nach Wien* – eine besondere Thematik der Exilliteratur," in *Exil: Wirkung und Wertung,* eds. Donald G. Daviau and Ludwig M. Fischer (Columbia, South Carolina: Camden House, 1985), pp. 173–184.
39. Kurt Palm, *Vom Boykott zur Anerkennung. Brecht und Österreich* (Wien: Locker, 1983).
40. Heinz Lunzer, "Der literarische Markt 1945 bis 1955," *Literatur der Nachkriegszeit und der 50er Jahre in Österreich* (Wien: Bundesverlag, 1984), p. 38.
41. Otto Basil, "Vom österreichischen Parnass," *Plan,* 72–76. Cf. also Klaus Amann, "Vorgeschichten," *Literatur der Nachkriegszeit und der 50er Jahre in Österreich,* p. 56.
42. See George C. Schoolfield, "Nadler, Hofmannsthal und 'Barock,'" and Donald G. Daviau, "Hermann Bahr, Josef Nadler und das Barock," in *Vierteljahresschrift des Adalbert-Stifter-Instituts,* Vol. 35, Nos. 3/4 (1986), 157-170 and 171-190, respectively.
43. Cf. Klaus Amann, "Vorgeschichten," p. 47. (See note 16).
44. Cf. Donald G. Daviau, "Das junge und das jüngste Wien," in *Österreichische Gegenwart. Die moderne Literatur und ihr Verhältnis zur Tradition,* ed. Wolfgang Paulsen (Bern und München: Francke, 1980), pp. 81–114.

Ingeborg Bachmann

Beth Bjorklund

Ingeborg Bachmann has the dubious distinction of being regarded as a "poetic princess" or the "first lady" of a new literary generation. She may be that but she is also much more, and such appellations are unfortunate to the extent that a virtual myth has arisen around the figure that uncritically confounds personality and artistic work. In 1954 *Der Spiegel,* West Germany's leading news magazine, published a cover article on Bachmann, thus solidifying her meteoric rise to prominence.[1] Despite Bachmann's frequent protests against a mere culinary enjoyment of her work, public interest in the personality of this sensuous yet intellectual cosmopolite persisted until her untimely death in 1973, which elicited a further spate of speculative journalism. More than most writers Bachmann lived in the eye of the public, which created its own image of her. In an attempt to dismantle the myth, the present essay will disregard the popular misconceptions and focus instead on Bachmann's work and the changing reception it has received during the past three decades. The shift in reception has to do in part with changes in the intellectual climate of the times and in part with the developmental nature of Bachmann's oeuvre, which includes the poetry and radio plays of the 1950s, the short stories of the early 1960s, the novels published in the early 1970s, and numerous essays during the entire period.[2] In accordance with this development the leading interpretations have been existential-philosophical, sociopolitical, and feministic. A strong undercurrent throughout is the problem of language, which this essay will focus on in particular.

Ingeborg Bachmann was born in 1926 as the daughter of a schoolteacher in Klagenfurt, the capital of Austria's southernmost province of Carinthia. After 1945 she studied philosophy, German literature, and psychology at the universities of Innsbruck, Graz, and Vienna. In 1950

she received the Ph.D. degree at the University of Vienna with a dissertation entitled "Die kritische Aufnahme der Existentialphilosophie
Martin Heideggers" (The Critical Reception of Martin Heidegger's Existential Philosophy), which constituted an attack on Heideggerian metaphysics. A more important spiritual mentor for her was Wittgenstein, in
whose works she saw an alternative to the alleged impasse of Western
philosophy. After working briefly at a radio station in Vienna she lived
for the last twenty years of her life, from 1953 to 1973, as a free-lance
writer. Rome was her principal place of abode, but she also lived intermittently in Munich, Zurich, and Berlin. She traveled widely, not only
to Paris and London but also to Egypt and Poland, and in 1955 she
visited the United States at the invitation of Harvard University. She
made her literary debut in Germany at the meeting of contemporary
writers known as the "Group 47" in 1952, and in the following year
she returned to win the coveted prize of the group. She was awarded
many of the important literary prizes of her time, including the Great
Austrian State Prize in 1968. In the 1950s she was associated, both
personally and professionally, with poets of the postwar generation
such as Paul Celan, Günter Eich, and Ilse Aichinger, and in later years
she came to be associated with writers such as Max Frisch, Uwe Johnson, and Christa Wolf, all of whom wrote about Bachmann in their own
works.[3] There are many autobiographical references in Bachmann's
writings, which are often set in her native Austria or in other places
where she lived or visited. For Bachmann, however, it was never simply
a matter of merely naming reality but rather of transforming it through
the poetic word, and her abiding concern with language is what transforms personal biography into world literature.

Bachmann's first volume of poetry, *Die gestundete Zeit* (1953,
Borrowed Time), won immediate acclaim upon its publication, for the
moral engagement and the provocative commentary on current times
struck a dominant chord in postwar Germany. Her second and final
volume of poetry, *Anrufung des großen Bären* (1956, Invocation
of the Great Bear), contains temporal as well as mythical references and
demonstrates an increasing concern for language and the poetic process.
Most of the poems are in free rhythm, and they were regarded as a
happy fusion of traditional and modern elements. Bachmann's poetic
vision presents extravagant pictorial evocations of the existential
themes of time and consciousness, with poetry functioning as a summons to lucid wakefulness and moral sensitivity. The presence of an
ineluctable past serves as a signal of an approaching end, and a recurring

motif is that of departure, flight, and farewell. Expansive, glowing panoramas of European culture are juxtaposed with mock imperatives and terse, magic formulas of warning and promise. It is a highly musical language in which spellbinding rhythms and delicate sound patterns stand in contrast to ominous, furioso impulses, with both forces serving to underscore the bold emotive imagery. The tension between hope and despair, fantasy and skepticism, jubilation and anguish is expressed in alternating tones of hymnic pathos and laconic irony. The poems are both panegyric and elegiac as the poet both radiantly and somberly confronts the presence of the past in the modern world. The "fall" is a common metaphor for truth sullied by speech, to which the counter-balance is "flight" as restoration to a state of truth in perfect language. The dialectic results in an unflinching look at utopia, whereby the existence of limits is recognized but the gaze remains fixed on a purity of language as entailed in a purity of being. Communication, however, reveals itself to be impossible, and a barren, benumbed sense of inarticulate isolation leads to a questioning of the adequacy and efficacy of the poetic word.

"Die gestundete Zeit" (Borrowed Time; I, 37), the title poem in Bachmann's first volume, stands as a warning signal dramatizing a central theme of the book: the end of time and the necessity of departure. The metaphor is taken from the financial world, and time, conceived literally as "borrowed" or "on loan" and also "measured" into hourly segments, is about to be recalled. The metaphor is an ingenious one and suggests that whereas payment had been deferred, the end of that respite is now appearing as a threat on the horizon. The speaker addresses a "you," which includes also the self, and the images of the marsh landscape—dogs, fish, and flowers—are also caught up in the urgency of departure. Repetition of the opening image at the end of the first stanza intensifies the panic sense of time running out. In contrast to the harsh onset the second stanza presents rhythmic and erotic images of the beloved as she sinks in the amorphous sand dunes of the northern sea coast, engulfed by and yielding to the process of the poem, and there is no time to mourn the loss of a loved one or cling to familiar elements of warmth and comfort. The urgency is underscored by the repetition of images from the first stanza in imperative rather than declarative form as a command to dissolve all ties and prepare for departure: "Don't look around. / Tie your shoe. / Chase the dogs back. / Throw the fish into the sea. / Put out the lupins!" The last line in the poem, repeating the first in a sort of pincer construction, gives an epigrammatic explanation for the stern orders: "Harder days are coming," implying that the individual too must become "harder."

The dominant metaphors are visual, and sight is both the cause and the effect of the action. As the self begins to see, it becomes aware of transitoriness, and this consciousness leads to true sight and insight. Several years later in the second volume the poet echoed the lines in a different tone, almost a palinode: "O borrowed time, time loaned to us! / What I forgot has touched me deeply" (I, 85). The emphasis in the later work is not on the end of time, but on the value of the time allowed to us, which can be redeemed in memory and in vision. In contrast to the metaphysical concern of the second volume, the moral engagement of the first becomes more evident, and the reader is admonished to accept departure, death, and the end without illusion. The theme occurs in another poem in which a leaf/heart analogy, a genitive metaphor typical of the period, explicitly sounds the warning to avoid attachment to the temporal: "Fall down, heart, from the tree of time" (I, 31). Poetry, in this case, functions as a call to lucid wakefulness: "Pay attention that you stay awake" (I, 40).

The scene in several poems is Germany's immediate past and the postwar conditions of denazification, reconstruction, economic miracle, remilitarization, and the Cold War. The poems are a command in "the aftermath of horror" (I, 54) to reject the self-righteous contentment and comfortable satisfactions of blind acquiescence. Bachmann's poetry has a unique double perspective, looking both backwards and forwards in time, and it is as relevant today as it was in the 1950s: "War is no longer declared, / it's simply continued. The unheard-of / has become commonplace," from the poem significantly entitled "Alle Tage" (Every Day; I, 46) with its characteristically Brechtian tone. The problem of German history is graphically portrayed in surrealistic images in "Früher Mittag" (Early Noon; I, 44–45):

> Where Germany's sky blackens the earth
> its beheaded angel seeks a grave for hatred
> and passes you the plate of its heart.

Beauty is used against itself as this passage is followed by quotations from poems by Goethe and Müller set to music by Schubert. The juxtaposition of these treasures from the German cultural heritage with images of Nazi war crimes illustrates the morass to which the so-called humanistic tradition has led. The dominant metaphor in the above-cited stanza is then repeated in reverse:

> Where Germany's earth blackens the sky
> the cloud searches for words and fills the crater with silence
> before the summer hears it in the pouring rain.

The consequence of horror for the poet is silence, which has a positive effect as a mystical condition preceding a breakthrough of truth when "hope alone cowers blinded in light." Silence results in purifying rain and leads to the final image: "The unspeakable, softly spoken, walks the land: / It is already noon." From suffering and silence, darkness and death, a different kind of language can emerge, "softly spoken," but nonetheless a true speech that has power to bring about the climax and turning point suggested by the title "Früher Mittag."

"Nachtflug" (Night Flight; I, 52) shows modern society on a precarious course, headed for a crash landing. The presence of an unresolved past is evident both in social conditions and in individual consciousness, as guilt comes back to haunt the poet: "Who lived there? Whose hands were pure? / Who shone in the darkness, ghost among ghosts?" Guilt is, of course, not limited to Nazi Germany but is rather a condition for membership in the human race. The questions are, however, too painful to deal with, and modern society tries instead to repress them by focusing on the materialistic values of consumerism. The vulgar sunsets of tourism are parodied in "Herbstmanöver" (Autumn Maneuver; I, 36) while in "the cellar of the heart" the self goes sleepless. "Reklame" (Advertisement; I, 114), a poem from the second volume, gives dramatic presentation to current hi-tech consumer consciousness:

> Where shall we go
> *don't worry don't worry*
> when it gets dark and it gets cold
> *don't worry*
> but
> *with music*
> . . . .
> but what will happen
> *it's all for the best*
> when deadly silence
>
> sets in

The important questions in life are interrupted by pat pseudo-answers (in italics). These slogans bombarding the speaker—from television, loudspeakers, or neon signs, for example—not only give no true answers but they even prevent one from posing the questions. The modern memento mori—its theological implications replaced by moral reflections—is made especially poignant by its juxtaposition with social satire.

A veiled type of memento mori is present in numerous poems of farewell and departure, a journey out or a crossing over to an as yet unspecified goal. The topic of temporality is sounded again and again, and it would be interesting in this regard to compare Bachmann's poetry with that of her Austrian predecessor Hofmannsthal. Rilke's *Sonette an Orpheus* (Sonnets to Orpheus) are a probable reference point for Bachmann's variation of the Orphic myth, which opens with the following analogy: "Like Orpheus I play / death on the strings of life" (I, 32). The center section of the poem develops the dialectics of beauty and death, song and silence, light and dark, as the poet reflects on the distance. Whereas Rilke's Orpheus is "one called to sing praise" of life from the other side of the grave (*Sonette an Orpheus;* I, 7), Bachmann's speaker, on this side and aware of the finality of death, knows only how "to say dark things," as indicated by the title of the poem, "Dunkles zu sagen." But Bachmann's Orpheus, like his legendary predecessor, undergoes a transformation in consciousness and reappears in metamorphosed form to re-establish identity in an antithetical final stanza: "But like Orpheus I know / life on the side of death." An ambivalent relation to beauty is suggested in this poem and others. Whereas beauty is a powerfully attractive force, rather than "succumbing" to beauty the poet unites it with existential insight. In a deromanticized negation of negation the poem dialectically achieves a synthesis and transcendence of antinomies.

Many of the central themes are brought together in the final poem of the volume, a major work entitled "Große Landschaft bei Wien" (Great Landscape near Vienna; I, 59-61). A wide panoramic view presents sheer vastness of time and place and illustrates also Bachmann's approach to terrain, whereby history and geography become mythical and metaphysical. The modern elegy opens with an invocation:

> Spirits of the plain, spirits of the swelling stream,
> Summoned to our end, do not stop outside the city!

If the landscape of great beauty and cultural heritage was to have provided a haven, it now engenders a "giddy limes-feeling" near the edge of Roman civilization both spacially and temporally where "Asia's breath is beyond." In powerful imagery the poet evokes the greatness of a past that has now been reduced to crumbling ruins devoid of meaning: "Two thousand years are over, and nothing remains." The decline of the Austrian Empire has been sung before with sweet sadness, and in taking up this common theme the poet is self-consciously traditional, adapting the elegiac mood to modern mentality. The moral imperative, indispensable in Bachmann's first volume, points in this case toward her development in the second volume:

> Dream that you are pure, raise your hand to the oath,
> dream your race that conquers you, dream
> . . . .
> What divides you is yourself. Flow away,
> come back knowingly in a new farewell form.

The admonition to "dream," repeated three times, is a challenge to a new level of consciousness, a vision of purity and perfection that is developed in the later poetry. The elegy closes with recognition of those who faced the end knowingly and willfully, "with a sharper ear for the fall"—Bachmann's theme in *Die gestundete Zeit*.

Anrufung des großen Bären (Invocation of the Great Bear) shows an increased concern with language and the poetic act as such, often set in a mythological or metaphysical framework. The wellknown title poem (I, 95) develops a cosmology and a theology to present an eschatological vision of the end of the world. The titular bear is united with the stellar constellation of the Ursa Major (also known as the Big Dipper or the Great Bear), and this combined force stands threateningly in the "shaggy night" sky with its "star eyes" and "star claws." Man— bravely or foolhardily—challenges the creature, and, as if in response, the perspective changes to that of the bear. The world, seen from this transcendent position, is a mere pine cone that he contemptuously rolls with his paws from creation to destruction, with Biblical allusions to the Fall of the Angels and the Last Judgment. There is a productive tension within the central image, and the bear is throughout both a predatory natural animal and a powerful supernatural force (or a present-day technological analogue thereof). The poem is structured around this extended metaphor, and its effectiveness derives from the fact that all statements have a double meaning.

The opening selection in the volume, "Das Spiel ist aus" (The Game Is Over; I, 82-83), also deals with the end of time and the certainty of loss, in this case the end of an illusionary idyll; but it also introduces the principles of memory and vision, which add an important dimension to the poetry in this volume. The protagonists are children who lead the reader into an imaginary world of fairy tale, which, although not without its dangers and fears, is nonetheless a realm of hope and desire. It is also the domain of language, as topicalized in the children's game: "Only he who still knows the word of the almadine fairy / on the golden bridge has won." The magic word has been lost, but redemption is nevertheless possible: "The children's king with the key to the kingdom in his mouth / will fetch us, and we shall sing." Language is both the container and the contained, and the poem thus refers also to itself. Past memory and future vision are preserved in the present poetic song, which survives even though the beautiful illusion is over. Many of these themes recur, and for the sake of exposition the following survey will view the topics of love, poetry, and language, with special consideration of the two major cycles.

Love is a central topic in Bachmann's work, but it is most often conceived as separation, departure, and distance from the loved one, who is an alien being. In "Nebelland" (Fogland; I, 105-106) the oppressive landscape of fog, clouds, winter, and night stands as the controlling metaphor and serves to hinder speech, deaden feeling, and limit perception. The "beloved" persistently puts off her "lover," the speaker, by changing form among the animals of the wood, the trees of the forest, and the fish of the waters; when he falls on the field she throws him a bone in mockery. In seeming contrast to the metaphors from nature but actually synonymous with them are subsequent images of faithlessness in the modern city, where "she finds words for everyone. / But I don't understand that language." Communication proves to be impossible in the wasteland of the modern ice age, and the joy of love is supplanted by a benumbed, inarticulate sense of desolation.

In contrast to the bleak northern landscape, two of the four sections of the book are devoted to poems about the Mediterranean south. Bachmann thematized the contrast in poems such as "Nord und Süd" (North and South; I, 125), although neither geographical region is unambiguously positive or negative. In "Das erstgeborene Land" (The First-Born Land; I, 119-120) the speaker is born anew, and through the experience of pain he or she comes to see both beauty and cruelty in a clear light: "I was awakened to seeing." One of Bachmann's most widely anthologized poems is her hymn "An die Sonne" (To the Sun; I, 136-137), which has a place in the tradition of panegyric literature since classical antiquity. Jubilantly assertive landscapes evoke a conception of unusual beauty that leads to the seemingly spontaneous exclamation: "Nothing more beautiful under the sun than to be under the sun." The irony comes in the last line when the magnificent scene is undercut by the fact that the speaker is revealed to be blind. On another level, however, the experiential quality is not diminished but enhanced by the twist, since, as Oedipus knew, blindness is the condition for the true sight of insight.

Just as nature is "redeemed" as inner vision in the heliotropic hymn, so also love is transformed into art in other poems of the Italianate south. Physical love is presented as a concrete reality in all its sensuality; but it is at the same time raised to a higher power by consciousness, and erotic love and poetic creativity are inextricably intertwined. This is paradigmatically illustrated by the important cycle of fifteen poems entitled "Lieder auf der Flucht" (Songs in Flight; I, 138-147), which portrays a flight from and to the self, from suffering to poetry. Love is a reality but only as memory, for the speaker has at the outset already experienced the end of the love relationship and is in flight from the ensuing coldness and despair. The introductory section (poems I-IV) presents the desolation of the speaker alone in Naples in the winter when ice coats the city of passion and the volcano lies dormant. After a call for release (V) the central section of the cycle (VI-VIII) recalls the intensity of the love experience, symbolized by summer, tropical luxuriance, and hot lava. With bold imagery the poet portrays the ecstasy of physical union, and the openness of expression conveys a sense of the perfection of love. The climax is followed by spontaneous expression in poetry, already suggesting the connection, as well as the problem: "Ravaged by kisses / the earth, / the sea and the sky. / Encircled by my words."

Separation follows, and the poet is plagued by guilt, self-consciousness, and despair (IX-XII), which is the temporal point portrayed by the bleak nature imagery in the opening section. Pain and suffering are unrelieved and seemingly unrelievable and one is reminded of Rilke's query: "Shouldn't these oldest of sufferings finally / become fruitful for us?" (*Duineser Elegien* / Duino Elegies, I). The turning point is prepared for by repetition of ambivalence: "I am still guilty. . . . I am not guilty" (XIII). Salvation comes in the final section of the cycle (XIV-XV) as the pain is transformed into poetry, as Rilke also said: "Only the song over the land / hallows and praises" (*Sonette an Orpheus* / Sonnets to Orpheus; I, 19). Correspondences here and elsewhere are not meant to suggest that Bachmann's work is derivative, for there are also significant differences from Rilke; yet they have a similar conception of the power of poetry. The final poem in Bachmann's cycle—and in the book—gives definitive expression to the verbal transcendence of song:

> Love has a triumph and death has one,
> time and the time thereafter.
> We have none.
>
> Around us only the sinking of stars. Splendor and silence.
> Yet the song over the dust thereafter
> will transcend us.

Love's victory is even more temporary than death's, and only the poetry that springs from the experience of love has immortality. The work is a cycle in both structure and theme, and it reflects on its own existence and on the redemption of experience in the present instance of poetry.

Poetic creativity is at the center of the poem "Mein Vogel" (My Bird; I, 96-97), which is set in a northern forest landscape of solitude. The nocturnal visits of the bird are the modern equivalent of the traditional visitation of the muse, and the bird, an owl, is a Greek emblem of wisdom and watchfulness, sacred to Athena. Like the bear in the title poem of this volume, the bird retains its natural characteristics but is at the same time developed into an extended structural metaphor for inspiration, whereby its feather becomes the poet's "weapon" (pen), and its veil serves as the form in which art conveys truth and beauty indirectly. In contrast to the rationality of the preliminary phase, the central act of creation is described in sensual and erotic terms, demonstrating Bachmann's characteristic dichotomy of intellect and emotion:

> Even when my skin burns
> in the needle dance under the tree
> and the hip-high bush
> tempts me with its spicy leaves,
> when the locks of my hair shoot up
> and sway and long for moisture,

then the dust of the stars
falls precisely on my head.
. . . .
When I stay inflamed as I am
and loved by the fire,
until the resin streams from the trunks . . .

The irrationality of poetic frenzy is equated with the heat of sexual excitement, and the climax is symbolized by a cosmic connection, after which the poem emerges like resin from the trees. The highly suggestive nature of the poem derives from its ability to operate simultaneously on several different levels; it stands as a modern statement on artistic creativity.

The poet's medium is, of course, language, and reflection on the nature of language—what it can or cannot do—occupies a central place in the lyric. "Rede und Nachrede" (Word and Afterword, or in a free translation, Word and Anti-Word; I, 116–117) employs parallel and oppositional structures to dramatize the antithetical effects of true and false use of language. The poem opens with the "word that sows the dragon," from which emerge strong images of dissonance, violence, and decay that threaten to take over the world. To combat the evil the speaker implores language itself for a true expression: "Word, be with us / in gentle patience / and impatience." After a structurally central discursive section that demonstrates the false language of (in-)human society, the imploration recurs: "Word, be of us, / free-minded, clear, beautiful." The word has transcendental power, and the threatening animals recede. Pure language is powerful because it expresses truth, as presented in the poem "Was wahr ist" (What Is True; I, 118), and one is reminded of the divine logos of the Gospel of St. John. The closing plea to the "Word" resembles a prayer to a supernatural force: "Come, favor of sound and breath, / strengthen this mouth . . . Come and don't fail, / since we are at war with so much evil. . . . My Word, deliver me!" Bachmann later became skeptical of this idealistic conception of language, and the few poems that she wrote after this volume show an increasing mistrust of language. Her concern with the problem of language could be traced from early poems such as "Holz und Späne" (Wood and Chips; I, 40–41) to mature poems such as "Scherbenhügel" (Heap of Fragments; I, 111) to late works such as "Exil" (I, 153), "Ihr Worte" (You Words; I, 162–163), and "Keine Delikatessen" (No Delicacies; I, 172–173), which appeared in 1968 as the last poem she published. Dissillusionment is, however, a later development, and the two published volumes of poetry are based on a conception of the incarnate Word.

To the imperative at the end of the first volume, "Dream that you are pure" (see p. 55), Bachmann responded in the second volume with a visionary view of pure language. This utopian conception is present in many poems and particularly in a major work entitled "Von einem Land, einem Fluß und den Seen" (Of a Land, a River, and the Lakes; I, 84–94). It is a cycle consisting of ten poems, each with seven four-line stanzas in iambic pentameter, thus displaying a tight formal construction. It is set in an imaginary world of legend and fairy tale, reminiscent of "Das Spiel ist aus" (see p. 56), and through memory and vision it recalls and projects a form of utopia. The opening scene shows the protagonist fearlessly embarking on a journey to experience the world. It is an odyssey in memory that goes backward in time through the idyllic life of a village to a primeval time upon entry into a new land. The "land" metaphor in the title of the poem suggests its proximity to other "land" poems such as "Landnahme" (Claiming the Land; I, 98), "Nebelland," "Das erstgeborene Land," and "Große Landschaft bei Wien," and once again the hero, together with his companion, experiences mythic and paradisiacal conditions. Through the Fall, however, man lost the original correspondence between word and thing, and borders were drawn that are primarily language borders as symbolized by the Tower of Babel. Man, however, retains a conception of unsullied language: "A word? We have preserved it well in our mouths," like the children's king in "Das Spiel ist aus," and it will one day be realized when through our consciousness of separation the gap is overcome and the original unity restored.

The central section V deals with these borders and the disparity between language and being:

> We, however, want to speak about borders,
> and even if borders still pass through every word:
> we shall transcend them by our longing for home
> and then stand in harmony with every place.

The two central terms, "word" and "place," form a rhyme pair in German (*Wort/Ort*) which is unfortunately lost in translation. This vision of utopia stands at the center of the poem—and as the goal of the poet's long-term preoccupation with the themes of "departure" and "journey." The narrative line returns to life in the village, but in section VIII the speaker of the poem offers a "theoretical" commentary, given in parenthesis, on the scene that has been projected. It is admittedly fictional: "Did I not invent them, these lakes / and this river?" Yet it is "redeemed" by human consciousness and attains a higher level of reality: "In the destruction of the most beautiful countries / we are the ones that internalize it as dream." Despite other differences the transformation reminds one again of Rilke: "Earth, isn't this what you want: to arise within us, *invisible?*" (*Duineser Elegien,* IX). The vision of perfection exists in language, which is equated with being:

> Where is law, where order? Where do leaf and tree
> and stone appear to us totally comprehensible?
> They are present in beautiful language,
> in pure being.

In terms of past memory and future vision the cycle presents a utopian vision that unites all aspects of life—language, love, truth, and poetry—in a conception of perfection. This vision of utopia is a main characteristic of *Anrufung des großen Bären* and is developed also in the later prose.

Apart from some isolated poems published in magazines, Bachmann did not write poetry after 1956, her "thirtieth year" (portrayed as a time of crisis in her short story by that title). Critics have speculated about a language crisis, perhaps analogous to that expressed by Hofmannsthal in "Ein Brief" (the so-called "Chandos" letter). In any case it is evident that the shift from poetry to prose is connected with a process of increasing intellectualization. The concept of the absolute—in love, language, truth, or freedom—evident in the poetry becomes particularly prominent in the prose works. Together with this desire for the ideal and as a built-in corrective to it is the notion of limits, as Bachmann expressed it in an essay that has been taken as a type of credo:

> In everything that we do, think, and feel, we sometimes want to go to the ultimate. We have the desire to transcend the limits that are set. . . . It is clear that we must remain within the given order. But within these limits we direct our gaze to the perfect, the impossible, the unattainable, be it in love, freedom, or any important dimension. In the interplay of the impossible with the possible we expand our horizons (IV, 276).

The tension between hope and despair generated by the yearning for perfection is resolved only in understanding that "utopia is not a goal but a direction" (IV, 27).

Bachmann delivered a series of lectures on contemporary literature at the University of Frankfurt in 1956–1960 when she occupied the newly created Chair for Poetics. A central thesis in the lectures as well as in other essays she published is the utopian nature of literature, illustrated with frequent reference to the works of Robert Musil. Bachmann was also strongly attracted to the writings of Wittgenstein, and her starting point was the famous closing statement of the *Tractatus logico-philosophicus* (7.1): "What we cannot speak about we must consign to silence."[4] She accepts Wittgenstein's premise concerning the limits of language; but she interprets Wittgenstein's silence not as the negative silence of skepticism but rather the positive silence of mysticism with reference to passages such as the following: "There are, indeed, things that cannot be put into words. They make themselves manifest. They are what is mystical" (*Tractatus* 6.522). It is this "desperate concern with the inexpressible" (IV, 13) that most engaged her interest. Wittgenstein's aphorism, "The limits of my language mean the limits of my world" (*Tractatus* 5.6), is the governing principle for her inquiry into what language is and what it can or cannot do.

Language in relation to the inexpressible and also language and music are important questions in her choice of works for adaptation and translation. Bachmann wrote the "Monolog des Fürsten Myschkin" (Prince Myshkin's Monologue, published together with *Die gestundete Zeit* in 1953) for Hans Werner Henze's ballet pantomime *Der Idiot* (The Idiot), an adaptation of Dostoyevsky's work. This was followed by several further collaborations with Henze. Bachmann's adaptation of Kleist's play *Prinz Friedrich von Homburg* (1960, Prince Friedrich of Homburg) as an opera libretto illustrates her central concern of impossible demands made on an imperfect world, and she also wrote the libretto for Henze's comic opera *Der junge Lord* (1965, The Young Lord) after a story by the nineteenth-century German writer Wilhelm Hauff. Bachmann's translations include a selection of poetry by Giuseppe Ungaretti and Thomas Wolfe's *Mannerhouse*.

More important are two radio plays, "Die Zikaden" (1955, The Cicadas) and "Der gute Gott von Manhattan" (1958, The Good God of Manhattan), a highly successful radio play on the theme of unconditional love and its contradiction to reality. The inherent pathos of the topic is offset by the ironic framework of a court trial in which the "offense" (in a double sense) is retrospectively brought to light. The defendant, the God of Manhattan, tries to justify to the judge his assassination attempt on the two students, Jan and Jennifer, whose love affair is an affront against law and order. Love for them is an all-consuming passion with potential power to subvert the world. As they move higher and higher in the hotel to an ever loftier love-making, the world recedes, time stands still, and the old order is left behind. The lovers' "transgression" is that of transcendence, which is incompatible with the mundane world. The work is thus also about Orpheus and Eurydice, Tristan and Isolde, Romeo and Juliet, Abelard and Héloïse, and Francesca and Paolo, to whom the chipmunks make ironic reference (I, 294). Shakespeare expressed it as follows in *Romeo and Juliet* (III, v. 9–11):

> These violent delights have violent ends,
> And in their triumph die; like fire and powder,
> Which, as they kiss, consume.

This love worries the God, for in its absolute demands it calls his world into question. He is the God not of perfection but of contingency, and his is the ordinary world of rationality and practicality. The conventional "law of the world" is pitted against the contravening "leap into freedom" as the lovers commit a kind of ontological adultery. Jennifer dies, but Jan survives, thus forfeiting his chance for a modern love-death, and the distinction between the sexes points towards Bachmann's later focus on women's love. The God is "good" because he preserves the order of the world from such dangerous extremes; yet can the destruction of transcendence be called "good"? The judge remains silent, neither indicting nor acquitting the God, since finally judge and defendant are one, secretly admiring the absolute lovers. The work operates on many levels, both ironic and mythic, and it is ultimately open-ended as both an apotheosis and an indictment of absolute love. If Bachmann makes a mockery of all demands that are less than immoderate she does so in order to insist on the utopian nature of literature, a force that is grounded in the real but directed toward the ideal.

Bachmann's collection of seven short stories was published in 1961 under the title of *Das dreißigste Jahr* (The Thirtieth Year). The protagonists are all fanatical absolutists seeking an ideal, and each comes to a point of crisis entailing a break with the past and, less tangibly portrayed, a breakthrough to a new order. It is a spirited attack on the "givens" of this world, and the inner conflicts of the characters are very much also those of the author. The theme of language is central in the reaction against the limitations of society and in the utopian desire for a new world. The protagonist in each case comes to experience the limits of thought and language and to recognize the inexpressibility of the ideal. Reflection often takes precedence over action in the narrative flow as Bachmann attempts to construct a psychological basis for philosophical questions.

The title story opens with an existential arrest reminiscent of the opening scene in Kafka's *Der Prozeß* (The Trial):"When a person enters his thirtieth year people will not stop calling him young. But he himself, although he can discover no changes in himself, becomes unsure" (II, 94). The protagonist—nameless and thus everyone—enters a year of crisis, and the experience is narrated in powerful scenes of departure and destruction on the one hand and visions of renewal and perfection on the other. The "hero" is a Bachmannian absolutist, as revealed by an incident in the Austrian National Library when "he was on the point of understanding something relating to everything and the ultimate" (II, 107), only to be struck down by the realization that he had reached the limits. Language plays a central role in the striving, and "he would have liked to come back with another language that would have been capable of expressing the secret he had discovered" (II, 108). The antagonist is personified in the figure of Moll, the Molls that one meets everywhere, those creatures of compromise and masters of *Gaunersprache* (literally "thieves' cant"). The term is an important one, and Bachmann uses it to connote the language of lies, the slick phrases, the overworked clichés, hypocrisy, and opportunism on which societal power is based. As a recurring element in Bachmann's work the critique is directed against uncritical mindlessness.

The dominant theme of the story is the end of an old order "with nothing to hold onto anymore" (II, 112). Individual perspective is expanded as images of Hapsburg Austria and Old Vienna appear momentarily before they go under, and "some drank the cup of hemlock unconditionally" (II, 127). Rejecting the old world, the protagonist envisions a "new order," and indictment of the old is as resolute as yearning for the new: "We cling so tenaciously to habits from fear of thinking without tables of prohibitions and commandments, from fear of freedom. Men do not love freedom. . . . The freedom I mean: the permission . . . to recreate and rearrange the world. The permission to dissolve all forms starting with moral forms so that all others can dissolve" (II, 131). The hero (or anti-hero) comes, however, to see the impossibility of the demand and echoes the Wittgensteinian insight: "No new world without a new language" (II, 132). Bachmann's criticism seems to be double-edged, just as it was in "Der gute Gott von Manhattan." She reserves her special scorn for the Molls of this world and the conventional moralists in their self-satisfied mediocrity. Yet there is also an attack on idealism, and the protagonist is associated with Lucifer as a "creature that had risen too high" (II, 108). Furthermore, the hero survives the crisis by recognizing the unattainability of the ideal and accepting the limitations of reality. Transcendence remains, however, in the form of desire and vision, and it is this tension between imprisonment and liberation, between the undesirable relative and the unattainable absolute that gives this story and others their cutting edge. The objection might be raised that to wish an impossibility is sentimental or at best juvenile; but that misses the point, for the power is in the presentation, and in this Bachmann succeeds very convincingly.

"Alles" (Everything) is the totalitarian title of a paradigmatic fable that lays claim to a perfect language encompassing nothing less than everything. The crisis takes place in the mind of the father-narrator who after the death of his child makes a despairing attempt to analyze the situation. As in several other works, the narrative stance of retrospection removes the external suspense to focus on the inner tension. The birth of a child leads to a radical break with the past and a total reorientation around the future of the child, who is potentially the new Adam if the old order of moralities and teleologies of language can be kept from him. Utopia is conceived as a problem of language and the lost unity of language, thought, and being:

> And suddenly I knew it is all a question of language and not
> merely of this one language of ours that was created with
> others in Babel to confuse the world. For underneath it there
> smolders another language that extends to gestures and looks,
> the unwinding of thoughts and the passage of feelings, and in
> it is all our misfortune. It was all a question of whether I could
> preserve the child from our language until he had established a
> new one and could introduce a new era (II, 143).

Biblical allusions in this story and others are prominent as the father ponders the guilt incurred by the Fall and infecting all of existence.

The father's hopes are predictably frustrated as he sees the child learning the processes of socialization and conforming to a world that he himself rejects. He comes to question the possibility of his assault on reality: "But where is this island from which a new human being can found a new world? ... One doesn't believe it possible but there is no way out for us" (II, 147-148). He had wanted too much, flown too high, as he retrospectively perceives: "I had expected that this child, because he was a child—yes, I had expected him to redeem the world. It sounds monstrous" (II, 149). One might say that the protagonist here as elsewhere is enriched by the loss of an illusion; but there is here as elsewhere also a note of bitter irony and exhausted resignation (capitulation?) in the concluding self-admonition: "Don't go too far. First learn to walk forward" (II, 158).

The story entitled "Ein Wildermuth" (A Wildermuth) explores the search for the absolute in the realm of truth, as indicated by the opening programmatic statement: "A Wildermuth always chooses the truth" (II, 214). The proper name "Wildermuth" literally means "wild courage," and the High Court Judge is initially taken aback by the coincidence of his own name with that of the accused. He is thus prompted to pursue an ever-receding truth to the point of his own breakdown —an involuntary inarticulate cry in the courtroom, with which the story begins and unfolds retrospectively. The case had seemed simple and unambiguous in conventional legal terms; but "truth" in the absolute sense in which Wildermuth seeks it has little to do with convention and leads instead to an infinite regression. The trial assumes Kafkaesque proportions as greater precision of evidence paradoxically leads to greater uncertainty of truth: "Truth—a goal that recedes as we approach it," as Bachmann wrote in an essay (IV, 276). The judge symbolically murders his father, a patron of simple truth, just as his namesake, the accused, has allegedly also committed patricide, and thus both Wildermuths, each in his own way, transgress against the rules of society. The judge, unable to answer the question of truth but equally unable to silence it, ends as a broken man for whom truth is inexpressible or expressed at best in an inarticulate cry.

The female water spirit in "Undine geht" (Undine Goes) belongs by definition to the speechless realm beyond conventional society. Bachmann's embodiment of the myth in lyrical prose successfully portrays the contrast between the security-prisons of society and the vulnerable freedom of the realm beyond. Most memorable is Undine's opening address, skillfully interweaving the social and the mythical: "You humans! You monsters! You monsters named Hans! Bearing this name that I can never forget" (II, 253). Men are drawn to Undine by their own unacknowledged yearning for the absolute, and they are on the brink of her silent world; but in the end they retreat from following the nymph's "cry for the end," a call for freedom from all bonds. Men or mankind are portrayed as betraying their own better knowledge by renouncing truth and remaining within conventional forms. The fable has been regarded as a turning point between Bachmann's short stories and her later prose works, in which women are presented as having a greater proclivity for love than men. Yet that remains incipient at this point, and the story has a more general significance, as expressed by the author: "Undine is not a woman, not even a human being, but rather, to speak with Büchner, 'Art, oh, art.' And the author, in this case myself, stands on the side of those who are called Hans."[5] We, the "Hanses" and the "Molls," are those caught up in the world with its conventions and clichés and who thus avoid the deadly contact with the absolute.

The second and final volume of short stories, *Simultan* (1972, Simultaneous), was published one year after the novel *Malina* (1971, Malina) and shares many of the same themes and some of the same characters as the novelistic works. The protagonists are exclusively women portrayed at various ages and in different occupations and interpersonal relations, and the five stories can be regarded as a type of cycle in their focus on the different facets of female consciousness. The first and last stories, Bachmann's best, form a frame with the common theme of a successful career woman. Nadja in "Simultan" is a professional translator, and Elisabeth in "Drei Wege zum See" (Three Paths to the Lake) is an international journalist. The protagonists of the other three stories live in a much more restricted world. Beatrix in "Probleme, Probleme" (Problems, Problems) is a young woman who spends her time either sleeping or in a beauty salon to escape a world she rejects. Somewhat analogously, Miranda in "Ihr glücklichen Augen" (You Wondrous Eyes) uses her extreme shortsightedness as a defense mechanism to avoid seeing reality. The elderly Mrs. Jordan in "Das Gebell" (The Barking) suffers from ingratitude and mistreatment on the part of her son, a famous psychiatrist; her sole contact with the world is her daughter-in-law, Franziska (who appears later as the protagonist in the novel *Der Fall Franza*). The men in the stories remain in the background and generally represent convention and conformity, whereas the women are all individually characterized as complex personages. Relations between the sexes are in no case happy or lasting, and love as something intense and exclusive does not exist. Common to all is a sense of isolation, inauthenticity, and lack of meaningful relations. For this portrayal of the social and psychological situation of women in modern times Bachmann chose a much more realistic and mimetic mode of narration than is present in her other works.

"Simultan," the title of the leading story as well as the volume, refers to, among other things, Nadja's profession as a simultaneous translator of six languages. Language is indeed a central theme in the story, although here it is seen in its social context rather than in the philosophical context of Bachmann's earlier work. "Simultan" refers not least of all to the mode of narration in which inner monologue, narrated monologue, and direct and indirect discourse are seamlessly interwoven while phrases from foreign languages characterize the consciousness of the leading figure. Nadja is a highly skilled, highly paid, up-to-date woman, independent, confident, and urbane. Having achieved the professional status previously reserved for men, she is subject to the same emotional pressures and dehumanizing consequences. Simultaneous and multilingual translation has turned her into a language machine no longer capable of authentic self-expression. For Nadja language consists of codified signals that control the speaker more than the speaker controlling them, and the cliché-ridden speech paradigmatically illustrates Bachmann's concern with the loss of self in a mechanized society. To relax from the stress of the job Nadja takes a trip with a newly formed acquaintance, Mr. Frankel, and this event forms the sketchy plot. Language stands in the way of communication as they talk past each other in simultaneous monologues, neither being capable of anything but small talk. Nadja, however, becomes increasingly aware of her situation, both past and present, and this leads to a turning point. On the cliffs high above the ocean she sees a stone crucifix, and through this intense experience she gains insight into the meaning of life. Thereafter she is unable to translate a passage from the Bible, a positive sign in contrast to her previous routine operations. But she can cry, previously an impossibility, and her speechlessness seems more authentic than all the talk that otherwise formed the substance of her life. The religious-mystical experience points beyond language habits to the silent realm of the inexpressible.

Elisabeth in the concluding story is, like Nadja, highly aware of the language of lies used in her profession, in this case, photojournalism.

The focus is however more on personal relations, and as she reviews her life of the past fifty years she finds that her relationships with men have been largely unsatisfactory and meaningless. She proposes isolation of the sexes, not as a solution but as a temporary necessity: "Men and women should keep a distance and not have anything to do with one another until each has found a way out of the confusion, disturbance, and noncorrespondence of any relationship" (II, 450). This negative assessment of the relationship between the sexes concludes the work that Bachmann published within her lifetime. The causes and consequences of such a position are explored more fully in the novels.

Todesarten (Modes of Dying) is the title Bachmann projected for her novelistic trilogy, of which only the first book was completed and published in 1971 under the title of *Malina*. The other two parts, *Der Fall Franza* (The Case of Franza) and *Requiem für Fanny Goldmann* (Requiem for Fanny Goldmann), were published posthumously in unfinished form in the collected edition. *Todesarten* represents a cycle of crime stories, instances of bloodless murder, as each of the three female protagonists is forced to recognize to the point of despair the lethal truth of her role and her relationships. Although *Malina* was a best seller, it met with widespread disapproval by the critics, many of whom found it to be melodramatic, sentimental, and toying with a false profundity. In recent years it has received more favorable attention, particularly from feminist critics. Although the emphasis on women's concerns came as a surprise to many readers, in retrospect it is evident that the book represents a sum of previous prose works, since the familiar themes of love, language, and society are taken up and further developed.

There is no plot to the novel, at least not in any conventional sense; it is rather the presentation of an emotional inner world. The central figure is a first-person female narrator, by profession a writer. External similarities between narrator and author raise the question of self-portraiture, to which Bachmann responded with ironic distance: "Certainly an autobiography, but not in the traditional sense. A spiritual, imaginary autobiography" (*Interviews*, p. 73). The work narrates the thoughts, experiences, memories, dreams, and wishes of the central figure as she reflects on her existential situation as woman and writer. One of the most striking features of the book is its reduction to a single consciousness, that of the introspective self. The world presented is totally subjective, even solipsistic, one might say, since there is no relativizing perspective. Furthermore, all events are narrated in the present tense, and thus the I-figure does not even have the distance to her experiences that the time of the past tense would lend. These intentional limitations of person and time give rise to the narcissistic, hysterical quality that critics have noted. There is little discursiveness to the text, and episodes correspond more to momentary constellations. The mode of presentation, designated as "erratic monologues" (III, 101), is indicative of personality, as the central figure reveals the self in speaking and writing.

In contrast to the fluidity of the narrated material Bachmann gave the novel a tight formal construction, and one can speak of a musical composition principle. A musical phrase from Schönberg's *Pierrot lunaire* with poems by Albert Giraud sets the tone at the beginning and recurs near the end: "O fragrance old from days of yore" (III, 15 and 319). There are correspondences between Bachmann's and Schönberg's works in the tripartite structure, the theme of a sensitive artist and lover, and recurring images of desire and beauty as well as crime and punishment. Bachmann also adapted Schönberg's *Sprechstimme,* a type of spoken recitative, for the final dialogues in which she uses musical terminology to denote vocal inflections. The repeated occurrence of key phrases and motifs is an integral formal principle, and only upon repeated readings does the extent of the tightly woven network become apparent. In contrast to the self-styled "convulsive" dialogues a lyrical and highly rhythmical language is used to convey the utopian visions. The immediacy of the content is thus thoroughly governed by the distancing sovereignty of form.

The novel is structured in the form of a triptych consisting of three chapters with a preamble. The introductory section lists the dramatis personae (the I-figure, Ivan, and Malina) and gives the time (today) and the place (Vienna). The format is reminiscent of a theater program and serves to remind readers that they are in the world of art. The simplicity of the designations is suspicious in view of Bachmann's panic sense of impermanence and frenetic search for location, and the empiricism is subsequently undercut by the narration. Time is suspended while material from the past, both personal and mythic, is drawn into the present. Place expands in the imagination to distant lands and contracts in reality to the self in her domicile. Character too is a questionable category, for in contrast to the strong central consciousness, both of the male figures, Ivan and Malina, remain shadowy and visible only from the perspective of the I-figure. The first and last chapters depict the I between these two men, and the middle chapter is devoted to another male figure, the father.

The plot, if indeed such exists, consists of something as hackneyed as a love story, but one presented in a highly nontraditional way. The first chapter, entitled "Happy with Ivan," describes the beginning, duration, and end of the narrator's intense relationship with her neighbor Ivan. It systematically and almost clinically explores the dynamics of desire ranging from the heights of euphoria and ecstasy to the depths of doubt and despair. Ivan is associated, if more in wishful thinking than in reality, with the world of emotions, unreflective spontaneity, and joy of life. As the I-figure recognizes that her love is not and cannot be requited to the extent that she offers it, she becomes increasingly despondent and isolated. Although complete dissolution of the relationship does not occur until the end of the novel, the outcome becomes clear in the final episode of the first chapter, in which the narrator visits acquaintances in lieu of a vacation with Ivan and experiences a breakdown.

Concrete episodes are related, such as the activities with Ivan's children; but the more fundamental topic is the phenomenon of love itself. Woman's love is presented as intense, exclusive, and unconditional, in contrast to the limited emotional life of the man, which lacks this capacity for love. Bachmann commented on the topic as follows: "The question for me is not the role of women but rather the phenomenon of love—how one loves. This woman [in the novel] loves so extraordinarily that nothing on the other side can correspond to it. ... Love is a work of art, and I don't think that many people can achieve it" (*Interviews*, 109). A conception of absolute love is developed as the most important and powerful force in the world, and it is underscored by allusions to the love of Isolde and by quotations from Wagner's opera. One is also reminded of Bachmann's radio play, "Der gute Gott von Manhattan" in which unconditional love is presented as a force that would explode the everyday world. But this inwardness cannot be integrated with life, and people (that is, women) who are ruled by emotion do not survive in the real world. Jennifer, Undine, and the I-figure stand in contrast to their male counterparts, Jan, Hans, and Ivan. The women die because of the intensity of their love; the men survive because of their emotional moderation. Like Undine the narrator in the novel notes that she and Ivan do not speak the same language (III, 36 and 86), and she comes to a harsh generalization: "One could say that the entire attitude of men toward women is sick" (III, 269).

Interwoven with the theme of human relationships is the search
for security in language. The acquaintances that the narrator visits in
the fateful final scene are the Altenwyls, figures that Bachmann adapted from Hofmannsthal's drama *Der Schwierige* (*The Difficult Man*),
and which she uses to present a satire of Austrian aristocratic society.
An important point of contact between the two works is the problem
of speech and communication, which is central to Hofmannsthal's protagonist and also to Bachmann's I-figure, not only in her profession as a
writer but also in her personal situation. The various forms of communication—letters, phone calls, interviews, and books—occupy a central
place in the chapter, and contact becomes increasingly distorted as the
I-figure becomes more and more distraught. The irony of the narrator
(self-irony of the author?) is evident as she takes common figures of
speech literally, whereby they become absurd—or only then meaningful—and fiction arises from a negation of the givens. Self-deprecating
humor and also fragmentation of perspective emerge in scenes in which
the narrator, always in a state of "extreme fear and greatest haste"
(III, 12), recasts a letter in many different versions but does not mail
any of them. The narrator's private secretary serves as mediator to
society, and after her departure only the telephone functions as an
umbilical cord to the outside world. To the charge of having described a
narrow world, Bachmann responded as follows: "For me it is not
isolated. What actually does it mean to describe a society, the consciousness of an age? It certainly does not mean repetition of the
sentences that society speaks. Rather, society must be portrayed
differently. . . . The sickness of the world and the sickness of this person [in the novel] is the sickness of our time" (*Interviews,* 71–72).

In the second chapter, entitled "The Third Man," Ivan's dominance is replaced by that of a father figure dominating the female child.
Grotesque and surrealistic dreams and hallucinations graphically depict
the obsessive sense of murderousness of a father intent on destroying
the identity of the daughter and robbing her of speech. This "third"
man (besides Ivan and Malina) is as father, the first man in a child's life,
and the chapter presents previously excluded material from the narrator's earlier life. One could say that the father is the chief antagonist,
for he instilled in the child the dependence and dominance relations
that were repressed, only to emerge later in distorted form, in some
ways perhaps causing the disturbances depicted in the preceding chapter. Whereas eroticism is virtually absent from the first and last chapters, it is portrayed in this central chapter in lurid scenes of incest, rape,

and violation of the individual. Bachmann, like Freud, demonstrates that dream images portray the eros of violence more effectively than any rational description could.

Rather than being a psychoanalytic interpretation of a personalized father of childhood, the chapter portrays the figure as an embodiment of all forms of brutality and torture in patriarchal society. The father is fascist dictator, czar, inquisitor, gas chamber attendant, theater director, and absolute authority. The images often recall Nazi terrorism, and the depiction contains many allusions to Germany's past. Bachmann skillfully interweaves phrases from Celan's famous poem "Todesfuge" (Fugue of Death) dealing with persecution of the Jews; women, in Bachmann's text, are identified with Jews, and both are seen as victims of authoritarian male aggression. The phrase "cemetery of the murdered daughters" (III, 175) recurs as a leitmotif throughout the chapter and is taken up also in the other novels of the cycle. Whereas the identification of personal and political history may seem overextended, Bachmann insists on the warlike conditions that obtain in interpersonal relations. A central dialogue between Malina and the narrator concerns the topic of war and peace (III, 185):

> Malina: There is no war and peace.
>   I: How am I ever supposed to find peace. I want peace.
> Malina: There is no peace, not even in you.
>   I: Don't say that, not today. You are terrible.
> Malina: It is war. And you are war. You yourself.
>   I: Not me.
> Malina: We all are, you too.

Bachmann commented as follows: "I don't want to write about war. That is too simple. Anyone can write about war, and war is always terrible. But to write about peace, about that which we call peace but is really war ... [that is the real challenge]. War, actual warfare, is only the explosion of the war that is [called] peace" (*Interviews*, 70).

In stark contrast to this graphic portrayal of negativity, the author offers futuristic visions of a perfect society in the form of a fairy tale. It was prefigured at the beginning of the novel by the phrase from Schönberg's *Pierrot lunaire* suggesting archaic reminiscences. The narrator began writing the story entitled "The Secrets of the Princess of Kagran" early in the first chapter upon the request of Ivan, and it is continued intermittently throughout in sections identifiable on the page by italic print. The I-figure clearly identifies with the princess and, just as demonized images of Ivan occur in the dream section, idealized images of Ivan occur in the fairy tale. The designation "legend" indicates its proximity to the sacred, and the utopian fragments portray the power of absolute love. It culminates in reiterations of the prophetic faith, "The day will come" (III, 121 and passim) for the return of a golden age of love, harmony, and unity, but it is later problematized by negation, "The day will not come" (III, 303). The path to perfection is not without trials, as indicated by the French variation of the family and place name, "Chagre" (related to "chagrin" meaning sorrow or affliction, perhaps with an analogy to Klagenfurt). The princess lives in a hostile society, but she experiences perfect love in the meeting with the prince; she dies a love-death, but there is a promise of reunification "in twenty centuries" (III, 69). The mythic, cosmic images of redemption remind the reader of Novalis; Bachmann also interlaces the passages with phrases from Celan's poem "Corona." The social and metaphysical conjuration of love is intended as the feminine counterpart to the loveless world of men, and spiritual transcendence is juxtaposed to brutal nightmare.

The apocalyptic title of the third and last chapter, "Of Final Things," leads one to expect resolution of the antinomies. In uniting the themes of personal identity, language, and love, it is one of the most puzzling parts of the novel and has led to various interpretations. Malina becomes increasingly prominent in this chapter, and he is in the end the sole survivor, who also gives his name to the novel. He was presented earlier as a dry and dispassionate figure, the long-term companion of the narrator with whom she lives and who functions as the glue that holds her together. This has led some critics to speak of a triangular relationship of the woman between two men, but a more convincing interpretation sees Malina as a part of the narrator's self, an alter ego. The I-figure speaks on occasion of a "double life" (III, 105 and 284) and questions the unity of the self: "Am I a woman or something diamorphic?" (III, 278). She analyzes her situation as follows: "Ivan and I: the converging world. Malina and I, because we are one, the diverging world" (III, 126). The polarity becomes explicit in the episode of her horoscope reading, which reveals the image not of one person but of two: "the masculine and the feminine, intellect and emotion, productivity and self-destruction" (III, 248). When questioned, Bachmann characterized the Malina figure as a "Doppelgänger," a "double," and stated that Ivan is probably also a kind of double or even triple (*Inter-*

views, 74 and 87-88). The characters with whom the narrator comes in contact are thus real and abstract at the same time and represent confrontation with different and complementary parts of the self. Critics speak of a disintegration of character as the boundaries between subject and object are dissolved. Ivan can be regarded as a means for presenting the principle of love, the subjective part of the self, and Malina as the embodiment of intellect and rationality, the part of the self that conforms to the reality principle. Thus the narrator can say, "I lived in Ivan and I die in Malina" (II, 335). Personal identity and unity of character are thus undermined and torn apart by the opposing forces.

The structure of the final chapter consists largely of dialogues between the narrator and her fictional counterpart Malina presented in the form of a musical parlando. The high degree of stylization in these dialogues of the Malina chapter stands in contrast to the fluidity of the monologues in the Ivan chapter. The topic of conversation is largely writing, which is presented as a process for healing the wounds inflicted by society and as a means of gaining power over the imperfect world by the creation of a pure realm. Whereas the narrator at the beginning of the novel had observed that "survival was in the way of insight" (III, 223), at the end it is seen as the opposite, thus emphasizing the polarity and mutual exclusivity of feeling and intellect. The loving woman in contradiction to herself is immured in grief and desolation and disappears into a crack in the wall. The last words of the work, "It was murder" (III, 337) are presumably spoken by Malina, the self-preservative drive in the self. They remind the reader once again of the symbolic level of the narrative. The "murder" is a suicide, the death of the feminine, emotional part of the self, as subjectivity ceases and a new level of consciousness takes over. What this means for the problem of writing remains open to interpretation, and critics differ radically. Witte represents a consensus when he interprets the event as the death of writing together with the death of love. Steiger, in contrast, understands it as the birth of writing and a sublimation of love, constructing a poetics of the three chapters as a process of 1) intense experience, 2) conscious distancing, and 3) inspiration for writing. Marsch sees it as a change in the kind of writing; he reads the novel as an autobiographical account of the author's development from the emotionality and imagination of poetry to the rationality and intellectuality of prose. Although the novel is intentionally and intriguingly ambiguous on some of the central questions, unambiguous is its portrayal of absolute love and the irreconcilability of that love with the given world.

Der Fall Franza was the first novel of the trilogy to be written, and in some ways it is the most bitter in its strident accusation of men. Although it was intended as the third and final novel of the cycle *Todesarten,* the editors of the complete edition placed it in second position because of its relative completeness. The novel again portrays the crimes (explicitly designated as "Verbrechen") against women when a woman's unconditional love is exploited and betrayed. The protagonist, Franza, is familiar to the reader from the story "Das Gebell" in *Simultan.* At that earlier stage of her life she had accepted her role of dependence, suffering, and sacrifice in her marriage to the famous psychiatrist Professor Dr. Jordan. The novel opens at a later stage when she is psychically disturbed and gravely ill as a result of mistreatment by her estranged husband. She characterizes him as one who "didn't like women and always needed them to have an object for his hatred" (III, 409). Franza finds in retrospect that "he took all my possessions. My laughter, my tenderness, my joy, my sympathy, my helpfulness, my animality, my radiance" (III, 413). Fleeing from the defilement of her marriage, she implores her brother, a geologist, to take her along on a research tour to Africa. The novel is in part written from the narrative perspective of the brother, to whom she appears insane.

The trip to Africa is also a flight from Western civilization. Personal and political history are merged as Franza's fate is linked with minorities and other exploited groups who have no rights in society; analogies are drawn to African women, Jews, and Australian aborigines. Franza finds no place of exile, and thus she implores a former SS doctor living in Egypt for the final solution of euthanasia. Franza employs the sociopolitical term "fascism" to designate personal behavior (III, 403). Bachmann commented as follows on the usage: "Fascism does not begin with the first bombs that are dropped, it does not begin with the terrorism that one can write about in the newspaper. It begins rather in the relationships between individuals. Fascism is the primary characteristic of the relation between a man and a woman, and I have attempted to show that in this society there is always war" (*Interviews,* 144). In the last chapter, "The Egyptian Darkness," Franza comes face to face in the desert with the burning vision of the patriarchal constellation of husband-father-God, the horrible monster beneath the smooth surface of society. When at the end she falls victim to a sexual assault, she finds it is an extension of her marriage, for her husband too had systematically killed her. Thus Bachmann, as she states in the prologue to the novel, "offers a demonstration that still today many people do not merely die but are murdered" (III, 342).

The final novel of the planned trilogy, *Requiem für Fanny Goldmann,* was not completed beyond a fragmentary stage. It is however clear that the theme is again the exploitation of women. The protagonist is an actress whose lover uses her and betrays her for the sake of his own career. The three novels thus read like variations on a single theme, "modes of dying."

It has been said that a writer has only one main topic, one basic question of life that continually recurs in different forms. To find such a unity in Bachmann's work is a challenge, for it is more obviously marked by discontinuity and change—from poetry to prose and, to use general terms, from existentialism to feminism. In retrospect, however, it is also possible to see constant elements and abiding concerns that remain throughout, however much they evolved. Language is certainly one such pervasive topic, although the focus shifted from the philosophical and ontological underpinnings of language in poetry to its social and political use or misuse in the late prose works. In either domain there is a concern with authentic speech as the sine qua non of both art and morality. Love between the sexes is also a constant topic, and it led to a focus on the nature of female sensibility. Often coupled with the problematics of love is the dichotomy of intellect and emotion, which runs throughout from early poems such as "Im Zwielicht" (At Twilight) to late prose such as *Malina.* The desiderata of a pure language, perfect love, complete knowledge, and unlimited freedom can be subsumed under the notion of "utopia," which I would suggest as the central topic of Bachmann's work. The author herself frequently used the term to characterize her concept of the absolute, and a yearning for the absolute pervades the oeuvre, giving rise to the tension between an unacceptable real world and an impossible ideal. Although the utopian goal is recognized as unattainable, it nevertheless determines the direction of human striving. Utopia has, of course, many different facets, and in accordance with Bachmann's own development of the theme, critics have stressed different dimensions of her work from the philosophical to the sociopolitical to the feminist. It was her poetry that initially catapulted the author to fame in the 1950s, and posterity will probably judge the poetry to be her most lasting achievement. Although critics are sharply divided over the aesthetic value of her late prose, it is undeniable that with their focus on women her works struck the tenor of the times in the 1970s. Bachmann's writings are strong enough to support many and varied interpretations, and she emerges as a leading—if highly controversial—contemporary writer in the Western world.

Notes

1. Klaus Wagner, "Bachmann: Stenogramm der Zeit," *Der Spiegel,* 18 August 1954, pp. 26-29.

2. A relatively complete edition of Bachmann's works makes them readily available: Ingeborg Bachmann, *Werke,* eds. Christine Koschel, Inge von Weidenbaum, and Clemens Münster, 4 vols. (München: Piper, 1978). References to quotations from this edition are given in the essay with the Roman numeral indicating the volume and the Arabic numeral the page. All translations are my own unless otherwise noted.

3. Uwe Johnson, *Eine Reise nach Klagenfurt* (Frankfurt: Suhrkamp, 1974); Max Frisch, *Montauk* (Frankfurt: Suhrkamp, 1975); Christa Wolf, "Die zumutbare Wahrheit—Prosa der Ingeborg Bachmann," in C. W., *Lesen und Schreiben* (Berlin: Aufbau, 1971), pp. 87-102.

4. English translations of quotations from Wittgenstein are taken from the following volume: Ludwig Wittgenstein, *Tractatus logico-philosophicus,* trans. D. F. Pears and B. F. McGuinness (London: Routledge & Kegan Paul, 1961). Hereafter the work is identified as *Tractatus* with reference to paragraph number given in the text.

5. *Ingeborg Bachmann: Wir müssen wahre Sätze finden. Gespräche und Interviews,* eds. Christine Koschel and Inge von Weidenbaum (München: Piper, 1983), p. 46. Hereafter the work is identified as *Interviews* with references given in the text. There are theoretical problems in using such material, since a categorical difference exists between poetic and discursive statements. With this understanding I shall continue to refer to the interviews as a shorthand guide to interpretation.

Bibliography

I.   Works by Ingeborg Bachmann in German

Die gestundete Zeit. Frankfurt am Main: Frankfurter Verlagsanstalt, 1953.
Anrufung des großen Bären. München: Piper, 1956.
Der gute Gott von Manhattan. München: Piper, 1958.
Das dreißigste Jahr. München: Piper, 1961.
Malina. Frankfurt am Main: Suhrkamp, 1971.
Simultan. München: Piper, 1972.
These and other works are collected in *Werke. In 4 Bänden,* eds. Christine Koschel, Inge von Weidenbaum, and Clemens Münster. München: Piper, 1978.
Wir müssen wahre Sätze finden. Gespräche und Interviews, eds. Christine Koschel and Inge von Weidenbaum. München: Piper, 1983.
Die kritische Aufnahme der Existentialphilosophie Martin Heideggers, ed. Robert Pichl. München: Piper, 1985.

II.   Works in English Translation

The Thirtieth Year, trans. Michael Bullock. London: Andre Deutsch, 1964.
In a Storm of Roses: Selected Poems of Ingeborg Bachmann, trans. Mark Anderson. Princeton: Princeton University Press, 1986.

III.   Secondary Works in English

Achberger, Karen. "Ingeborg Bachmann's 'Homburg' Libretto: Kleist between Humanism and Existentialism." *Modern Austrian Literature* 12, Nos. 3/4 (1979), 305–316.
Casey, T. J. "The Collected Works of Ingeborg Bachmann." *German Life and Letters* 34 (1981), 315–336.
Demetz, Peter. "Ingeborg Bachmann," in P. D., *Postwar German Literature.* New York: Pegasus, 1970, pp. 75–78.
Dierick, Augustinus P. "Eros and Logos in Ingeborg Bachmann's *Simultan.*" *German Life and Letters* 35 (1981), 73–84.
Lennox, Sara. "In the Cemetery of the Murdered Daughters: Ingeborg

Bachmann's *Malina.*" *Studies in 20th Century Literature* 5 (1980), 75-105.

Von der Lühe, Irmela. "'I without Guarantees'—Ingeborg Bachmann's Frankfurt Lectures on Poetics." *New German Critique* 27 (1982), 32-55.

Lyon, James K. "The Poetry of Ingeborg Bachmann: A Primeval Impulse in the Modern Wasteland." *German Life and Letters* 17 (1964), 206-215.

Modern Austrian Literature. Special Ingeborg Bachmann Issue, 18, Nos. 3-4 (1985).

"Murky labyrinths," *Times Literary Supplement,* 14 January 1972, p. 31.

"New women, old-time men," *Times Literary Supplement,* 20 February 1964, p. 141.

"Out of contact," *Times Literary Supplement,* 5 January 1973, p. 5.

Schlotthaus, Werner. "Ingeborg Bachmann's Poem 'Mein Vogel': An Analysis of Modern Poetic Metaphor." *Modern Language Quarterly* 22 (1961), 181-191.

Schoolfield, George C. "Ingeborg Bachmann," in *Essays on Contemporary German Literature,* ed. Brian Keith-Smith. London: O. Wolff, 1966, pp. 187-212.

IV.   Major Studies in German

Aichinger, Ingrid. "'Im Widerspiel des Möglichen mit dem Unmöglichen': Das Werk der österreichischen Dichterin Ingeborg Bachmann." *Österreich in Geschichte und Literatur* 12 (1968), 207-227.

Bareiss, Otto, and Frauke Ohloff. *Ingeborg Bachmann: Eine Bibliographie.* München: Piper, 1978.

Bender, Wolfgang. "Ingeborg Bachmann," in *Deutsche Literatur seit 1945,* ed. Dietrich Weber. Stuttgart: Kröner, 1968, pp. 504-523.

Blau, Anna Britta. "Der lyrische Sprecher in den Gedichten der Ingeborg Bachmann." *Studia Neophilologica* 52 (1980), 355-371.

Deschner, Karlheinz. "Ingeborg Bachmann," in K. D., *Talente—Dichter—Dilettanten.* Wiesbaden: Limes, 1964, pp. 71-124.

Doppler, Alfred. "Anrufung der Sprache," in A. D., *Wirklichkeit im Spiegel der Sprache.* Wien: Europa, 1975, pp. 197-206.

Doppler, Alfred. "Die Sprachauffassung Ingeborg Bachmanns." *Neophilologus* 47 (1963), 277-285.

Eifler, Margret. "Ingeborg Bachmann: *Malina.*" *Modern Austrian Literature* 12, Nos. 3/4 (1979), 373-391.

Hapkemeyer, Andreas. *Die Sprachthematik in der Prosa Ingeborg Bachmanns. Todesarten und Sprachformen.* Bern: Lang, 1982.

———, ed. *Ingeborg Bachmann: Bilder aus ihrem Leben.* München: Piper, 1983.

Hirschenauer, Rupert, and Albrecht Weber, eds. *Interpretationen zu Ingeborg Bachmann.* München: Oldenbourg, 1976.

Hoffmann, Gerhard. "Sternenmetaphorik im modernen deutschen Gedicht und Ingeborg Bachmanns 'Anrufung des großen Bären.'" *Germanisch-Romanische Monatsschrift* 14 (1964), 198-208.

Holschuh, Albrecht. "Utopismus im Werk Ingeborg Bachmanns: Eine thematische Untersuchung." Dissertation, Princeton, 1964.

Holthusen, Hans Egon. "Kämpfender Sprachgeist," in H.E.H., *Das Schöne und das Wahre.* München: Piper, 1958, pp. 246-276.

Ingeborg Bachmann. Eine Einführung. München: Piper, 1963.

Jurgensen, Manfred. *Ingeborg Bachmann: Die neue Sprache.* Bern: Lang, 1981.

———. "Ingeborg Bachmann," in M. J., *Deutsche Frauenautoren der Gegenwart.* Bern: Francke, 1983, pp. 23-52.

Marsch, Edgar. "Ingeborg Bachmann," in *Deutsche Dichter der Gegenwart,* ed. Benno von Wiese. Berlin: Schmidt, 1973, pp. 515-527.

Mauch, Gudrun B. "Ingeborg Bachmanns Erzählband *Simultan.*" *Modern Austrian Literature* 12, Nos. 3/4 (1979), 273-304.

Mechtenberg, Theo. *Utopie als ästhetische Kategorie: Eine Untersuchung der Lyrik Ingeborg Bachmanns.* Stuttgart: Heinz, 1978.

Oelmann, Ute Maria. *Deutsche poetologische Lyrik nach 1945: Ingeborg Bachmann, Günter Eich, Paul Celan.* Stuttgart: Heinz, 1983.

Pausch, Holger. *Ingeborg Bachmann.* Berlin: Colloquium, 1975.

Pichl, Robert. "Voraussetzungen und Problemhorizont der gegenwärtigen Ingeborg-Bachmann-Forschung." *Jahrbuch der Grillparzer-Gesellschaft* 14 (1980), 77-93.

Probst, Gerhard F. "Mein Name sei Malina—Nachdenken über Ingeborg Bachmann." *Modern Austrian Literature* 11, No. 1 (1978), 103-119.

———. "Zur Symbolik und Kompositionstechnik bei Ingeborg Bachmann." *Modern Austrian Literature* 3, No. 3 (1970), 19-35.

Seidel, Heide. "Ingeborg Bachmann und Ludwig Wittgenstein." *Zeit-schrift für deutsche Philologie* 98 (1979), 267-282.

Steiger, Robert. *Malina: Versuch einer Interpretation des Romans von Ingeborg Bachmann.* Heidelberg: Winter, 1978.

Summerfield, Ellen. *Ingeborg Bachmann: Die Auflösung der Figur in ihrem Roman 'Malina.'* Bonn: Bouvier, 1976.

———. "Verzicht auf den Mann," in *Die Frau als Heldin und Autorin,* ed. Wolfgang Paulsen. Bern: Francke, 1979, pp. 211-226.

text + kritik 6 (1980).

text + kritik, Sonderband (1984).

Weber, Norbert. "Ingeborg Bachmann: Simultan," in N. W., *Das gesell-schaftlich Vermittelte der Romane österreichischer Schriftsteller seit 1970.* Bern: Lang, 1980, pp. 110-133.

Witte, Bernd. "Ingeborg Bachmann," in *Kritisches Lexikon zur deutsch-sprachigen Gegenwartsliteratur,* ed. Heinz L. Arnold. München: text + kritik, 1981, loose-leaf.

Addendum:

Höller, Hans, ed. *Der dunkle Schatten, dem ich schon seit Anfang folge.* Wien: Löcker, 1982.

———. *Ingeborg Bachmann: Das Werk.* Frankfurt: Athenäum, 1987.

Hermann Broch

Joseph P. Strelka

It was not an idyllic home into which Hermann Broch was born on 1 November 1886 in Vienna. His father, a hard working upstart, was already the owner of a spinning mill in the village of Teesdorf (Lower Austria). He had married a beautiful lady of old money, but a vain woman with whom he did not harmonize well. Hence his mother went away from time to time, and little Hermann found himself alone, especially during vacations, in the small resort town of Baden,[1] halfway between the residence of his parents in the first district of Vienna and the village of Teesdorf, where their factory was located.

To observe the social graces the young boy had to learn to play the piano. Between such "duties" and boredom food played an important role. Since his father had decided at birth that his first son was to become a spinner, he soon started to use Hermann as a trouble-shooter and pacifier when he had made morally questionable business deals. Because of this role the young Hermann Broch soon developed an almost neurotic and messianic fervor for salvation and against injustice.

His mother fixation, which also had developed very early, showed when the twenty-five-year-old Broch addressed a letter to his mother as "père de famille"[2] and also in an eight-line poem which the thirty-two-year-old Broch wrote for his two-year-older wife addressing her as "mother."[3] This deliberately childish and clumsy poem revealed no trace of the greatness of the writer who later stated that "aristocrats have a family history, while Jewish families like his own have a history of neurosis." He spoke of a "hell of kindhearted shabbiness" regarding his early family life.[4]

Broch received a technically oriented education, attending the college for textile technology in Mühlhausen. As a graduation present he was given a two-month tour through the United States, which took him from New York City to the South. He bought some cotton in Memphis and New Orleans for his father's mills, and he visited the "International Cotton Growers, Buyers and Spinners Conference" in Atlanta.[5]

Shortly after his return from the United States Broch met Franziska ("Fanny") von Rothermann, fell in love with her, and married her against the wishes of both families. At this time he dressed like a dandy, converted to Catholicism for social and not religious reasons, and as a "game" wrote a chapter of a questionable novel. His fiancée and seven of her sisters and friends each wrote additional chapters. During the same period Broch became a reserve officer in the Austrian army, as an obedient son of his father, who was loyal to the Hapsburg Monarchy. Only after he made lieutenant and returned home did he marry Fanny in 1909.

Broch started work as director of the spinning mill in Teesdorf and lived there without a salary. Financial quarrels started to ruin his relationship with his father and also with his wife.[6] In his growing isolation and loneliness Broch returned to science and philosophy. He started to lead a double life. During the day he ran the spinning mill. At night he poured over his books. He enrolled at the University of Vienna and took courses in mathematics and philosophy. His most famous and influential teacher at this time was Ludwig Boltzmann,[7] a follower of Ernst Mach. He was a founder of modern statistical physics and, like Mach, a representative of the strict method of thought in mathematics and its application to other disciplines such as philosophy and psychology.

Broch also started to visit the Viennese literary cafés, "Café Central" and "Café Museum," where one could meet Karl Kraus, Franz Blei, Alfred Polgar, Robert Musil, and Franz Werfel. He befriended painters like Albert Paris Gütersloh and Georg Kirsta, and he read Otto Weininger.[8] Later on he started to study Schopenhauer and Kant systematically. He read the church fathers and began to learn Hebrew in order to read the "Sohar." Like very few others he clearly recognized the era before the outbreak of World War I as an ending period and a time of termination. This prophetic second sight supposedly triggered his first serious literary production, an unusually long poem composed of alternating verse and prose passages entitled "Cantos."[9]

During World War I Broch was in charge of a Red Cross convalescent home for wounded soldiers.[10] The war plunged him into increasing depression and confirmed his ideas of a European breakdown.

In his capacity as a representative of the Austrian union of industrial producers after the war he was involved in settling labor disputes and in helping to ease the general unemployment crisis. Because of his social awareness and devotion Teesdorf, the site of the Broch mills, was the first village in the state to have electricity and to establish a cooperative grocery store for the workers.

After the war he also started to undergo psychoanalytic treatment. Although it was not totally successful, causing him to speak of "unresolved remnants," he claimed that he had to thank psychoanalysis for his real life and his ability to write.[11] Probably of no less help was his involvement with the beautiful, charming, and highly intellectual lady Ea von Allesch, the center of a circle of artists. Broch rented an apartment for her in Vienna and occasionally lived there with her.

His first serious publications appeared in the journal *Der Brenner* in 1913. He condensed his aesthetic convictions into a sonnet and his Kantian convictions of moral obligations in an essay entitled "Ethik."[12] Broch's first story, a parody of Expressionism, was written for *Summa,* a journal published by his friend Franz Blei. In his later philosophical essays he contrasted the thoughts of Kant and Husserl as real philosophers against the ideas of early positivism and materialism. He also planned but never wrote a book on the theory of values.

After several years of silence he met Anja Herzog in 1927, the same year in which he sold the family mills just one year before the worst economic crisis hit Austria. Anja was a native of Slovakia who combined tender loving care with a kind of analytical treatment of Broch. In her house Broch wrote most of his first great novel, the *Schlafwandler* trilogy.[13] At the same time he resumed his studies at the University of Vienna, taking classes in mathematics, physics, philosophy, and psychology.

Broch reworked the first two volumes of the trilogy slightly and the third volume drastically. He did so partly for aesthetic reasons under the influence of Joyce's novel *Ulysses.* These aesthetic reasons, however, were augmented by his desire to give a general analysis of his time, to influence the understanding and political views of his readers by fighting the increasing danger of totalitarianism.

Die Schlafwandler, published in three volumes (1931–1932, *The Sleepwalkers,* 1932) does not take a particular or even aggressive stand on daily politics, but as a "polyhistorical novel" it gives an overall view of the entire development of economic, social, political, and philosophical events in Germany in three stages: 1888 (*Pasenow or the Romanti-*

cist), 1903 (*Esch the Anarchist*), and 1918 (*Huguenau or the Realist*) and with it what Broch called the "decay of values."

In this broad and complex historical overview, in which the total breakdown in World War I appears to be exemplified, the danger of rising fascism in particular and totalitarianism in general is seen as a symptom and consequence of this development towards the decay of values. The novels Broch wrote were created out of no less an intention than to serve as an antidote for the deep-reaching sickness of the time. By analyzing the roots of this decay the novel was to provide cognition. Beyond this analytical cognition of evil Broch wanted to demonstrate the decay of society by presenting a view of the totality of the human condition in its broadest human universality.

His novel, like art in general, has, according to Broch, a social significance on a metaphysical level. He does not advocate a specific metaphysical system but wants the reader to realize the metaphysical dimensions of experience in general (the self in the Jungian sense, God, the divine powers) in order to enable him to transcend the narrow materialistic limits of the external appearance of "reality."

Thus Broch's characters have to come to terms with the irrational, which is misconceived in a one-sided and limited romantic way by Joachim von Pasenow in the first novel of the trilogy; in an even more dangerous and limited way by Esch in the strange and unreal dream world of his view of the universe as a bookkeeping journal in the second novel; and which is virtually unrecognized by Huguenau in his constant hopeless nihilism in the third novel.

In such a way the protagonist of the first volume, Joachim von Pasenow, reduces the real totality of being and of the world to a narrow fictional viewpoint of the prejudiced outlook of the Prussian officer whose uniform becomes the empty façade of an "order" that excludes most important parts of life and many human beings including Ruzena, a barmaid for whom Pasenow feels real love. Representing a most important social and historical viewpoint of the year 1888 in Germany Pasenow is followed by another sleepwalker daydreaming away within the narrow confines of another reduction of the real totality of life and the world. The protagonist of the second volume stands for a widespread chimera representing the period around 1903, half a generation later than the first volume. After having been fired from his job without justification Esch develops the complex of seeing social injustices everywhere. The world in his view looks like one big playground of social injustice as seen from the limited perspective of a narrow-minded accountant who discovers "bookkeeping" mistakes in life wherever he looks. On the one hand he adopts unreal utopian ideas: on the other he "finds" his reduced solution to his problems in a substitute satisfaction on the sexual level.

The third and last protagonist, Huguenau, representing the total decay of values and breakdown of order, stands for ideas expressed widely another half generation later in the year 1918, which coincides with the breakdown of the old European order. Coming from Alsace and therefore during World War I belonging neither to France nor to Germany, he stresses the negative qualities of such an in-between position rather than the positive possibilities; thus he becomes the sleepwalking victim of a total relativity of values which enforces his innate tendency to live out his ruthless egotistic ambitions. He becomes the coldest and most cynical inhuman creature. Consequently, Pasenow finally becomes insane; Esch, like a fanatical anarchist, ends up murdured; and Huguenau, the most radical and lowest of all, finishes as a murderer.

However, Broch attempted much more than to narrate life stories of typical characters exemplifying a given time. He tried to show that the limitation of the totality of the life and world to the reduced value system of the officers' caste, of the anarchists, and of the ruthless businessman not only leads to a reductionist perspective and outlook, but will also necessarily proceed to the second step of taking the respective limited value system as absolute. He thereby opposes all of the other reductionist value systems, causing a total decay of values and providing the ideal breeding ground for totalitarianism, within which one of these narrow and limited systems finally suppresses and undoes all the others. In this context the "fourth" part of the trilogy, the Epilogue, is of utmost significance because here Broch counters the decay of values of the real world with a fictional philosophical synthesis of all single systems and perspectives of even total opposites in order to achieve a spiritual synthesis embracing the rational and the irrational and providing a totality or true total view of life and world vis-à-vis the reductionist view of any totalitarianism.

The claim to portray such a totality in literary terms is more easily made than executed. Broch was very much aware of this fact and tried to approach the problem from all possible angles extending from lyrical-irrational vision to rational-theoretical reflection and analysis of theory expressed in essay form. He knew that the difficulty lay at least as much in the form and structure, in the "how" of the presentation as it did in the "what." Out of this inner necessity he developed, especially in the third volume of the trilogy, the structure of novel writing which combines the usual narrative with lyrical passages on the one hand and with abstract essays of analytical cognition on the other. Many years later in a totally different context Broch described the function and meaning of the Joycean style and structure which I once labeled "neo-symbolist":

> But although the artist's problem seems to be mainly technical, his real impulse goes beyond this—it goes to the universe; and the true piece of art, even though it be the shortest lyric, must always embrace the totality of the world, must be counterweight and the mirror of that universe. This is felt by every true artist but is creatively realized only by the artist of old age. The other, who remains bound to his conventional vocabulary, seduced by the known richness of its content—a Franz Hals or a Thomas Wolfe—though he may enlarge his art more and more, reaching a boundless abundance, is never able to achieve his real goal: one cannot capture the universe by snaring its atoms one by one; one can capture it only by showing its basic and essential principles, its basic, and one might even say, its mathematical structure. And here the abstractism of such ultimate principles joins hands with the abstractism of the technical problem. . . .[14]

And Broch continues:

> The artist who has reached such a point is beyond art. He still produces art, but all the minor and specific problems, with which art in its worldly phase usually deals, have lost interest for him; he is interested neither in the beauty of art, nor in the effect which it produces on the public: although more the artist than any other, his attitude approximates that of the scientist, with whom he shares the concern for expressing the universe; however, since he remains an artist, his abstractism is not that of science but—surprisingly enough—very near to that of a myth.

Under myth Broch understands nothing less than the archetype of "every phenomenal cognition of which the human mind is capable."[15]

After the publication of *Die Schlafwandler*, which Wladimir

Weidle in his review called the "apocalypse du temps présent"[16] and which had brought Broch literary recognition, he started to lecture on literary topics in Vienna in the literary section of the "Volkshochschule Leopoldstadt," directed by Ernst Schönwiese[17] as well as in other organizational frameworks like the then famous "Kulturbund." He started to attend the so-called "Blei-Kreis" in the Café Herrenhof once a week. To this circle, named after Broch's friend, the writer and critic Franz Blei, belonged Robert Musil, Albert Gütersloh, Ernst Schönwiese, Ernst Polak-Schwenk, the husband of Kafka's Milena, and others.[18]

After hurriedly finishing another small and less significant novel *Die unbekannte Größe* (1933, *The Unknown Quantity,* 1935), he started to work on another large novel, the so-called "Berg-Roman" (mountain novel). Broch's intensive wish to influence the dangerous political developments through his novel writing had grown so important to him that he wrote to his friend and publisher Daniel Brody: "I am possessed by a burning ambition still to intervene in this world, just because it has become so monstrous, and it almost seems to me, as if in this urge a metaphysical obligation has announced itself" (7 June 1935). In this "Berg-Roman" he tried to exemplify in the miniature model of a small Tyrolean Alpine village how the unleashing of mass hysteria in a time of decaying values leads to injustice, enslavement, and murder.

From 1935 to 1937 Broch lived alone in the small Tyrolean village of Mösern and worked on this novel. In 1938 he was working on it in Alt-Aussee when Hitler took over Austria. Broch was arrested and confined for three weeks in the local prison in the county court of Alt-Aussee. Then he was released to go to Vienna. Only by good luck was he able to escape new arrests there and, recognizing his jeopardy, Broch tried everything to secure a visa to escape into exile as soon as possible. First he had to fight for the return of his passport from the Gestapo and then for a visa to emigrate to a foreign country. According to a letter from his publisher Daniel Brody, not only his English translators, Edwin and Willa Muir, but also his English publisher as well as English writers like James Joyce, Aldous Huxley, and especially Stephan Hudson vouched for him.[19] After some bureaucratic complications he received his visa and flew on 29 July 1938 from Vienna to London. Broch's efforts to obtain a Danish, French, or Swiss visa remained unsuccessful.[20] In London Broch stayed first with Stephan Hudson and later with the Muirs, only to leave two months later on board the "Statendam" for the United States, where he arrived on

10 October 1938, never to return to his homeland.

First he lived in a miserable apartment on Amsterdam Avenue in New York City, then for a short time with Henry S. Canby, editor of the *Saturday Review,* in a small town in Connecticut. Another three months were spent at the artists' colony "Yaddo" in Saratoga Springs. From Yaddo he went to Princeton, where he lived for a month in Albert Einstein's house while Einstein was on vacation. Then he rented an inexpensive room in Princeton and finally was introduced by Einstein to the philosopher, Erich von Kahler, also an exile and a friend of Thomas Mann. Broch moved into Kahler's house and stayed there from 1942 to 1949.[21]

The experiences of exile strengthened Broch's humanistic commitment even more. He wrote one of the greatest aesthetic masterpieces ever produced on the topic of whether it is ethically permissible in a time of totalitarian endangerment and crisis to devote one's life to creating literature. In *Der Tod des Vergil* (1945, *The Death of Virgil*) the dying Roman poet in an interior monologue covering his last eighteen hours of life wants to burn the great work of his lifetime, the *Aeneid,* because it deals with only the cognition of life. To be a great work of art it would have to deal with death, thus covering the entire necessary totality of the human condition. Three dream-like figures rising from the depths of Virgil's deepest unconscious in his fever visions make him aware of the insufficient cognition of his work. This lack of cognition coincides with the neglected love in his life: the young boy Lysanias stands for Virgil's own childhood and at the same time as a guide to the world of death; Plotia for his sweetheart whom he had left many years before; and a slave symbolizes the compassionate love of social commitment, which Virgil never knew. At the same time this stands for the modern slavery found in totalitarian states with their concentration camps.

Again Broch presented his own view of the universal totality of the human condition against the reductionist and partial view with which Emperor Augustus and modern totalitarians perceive reality. This universal totality can be subdivided into three different kinds of special totalities: first, the totality of the many intellectual currents and movements of the Roman Empire as it was undergoing a period of crisis and transition comparable to ours; second, the totality of the hero Virgil's life and times, past and future, captured as an entirety through one simultaneous point in the present, namely, the eighteen hours; and third, the totality of man. According to Broch's theory, this totality may be grasped by encompassing the entire range of the possibilities of human experience from the physical and emotional through the moral to the metaphysical ones.

This totality of life, which the novel is supposed to cover and to express, corresponds to the formal structure. Broch shaped *Der Tod des Vergil* as an entirety by employing the structural pattern of a symphony. The novel's four main parts correspond to the four movements of a symphony. They further relate to each other in their motific and denotative qualities as well as in their structural and formal qualities. As in the closed and unified musical structure of a symphony the structure of the entire novel is reflected in its parts, and as in musical variation the motifs unfold in recurrences. Finally, Broch uses the narrative means and the microcosmic views of the dying Virgil to achieve the totality of a complete cosmogony.

There is even one more aspect which makes this novel aim at universal totality; it is not merely a historical novel giving an exact picture of Roman thought and problems at the time of Virgil. It summarizes in some way the basic ideas of the entire ancient world about life, art, and literature, while focusing on the special time of crisis and transition Virgil experienced and presenting it in such a general and symbolic way that it refers to *our* time of crisis and transition no less than to Virgil's. During World War II Broch's publisher, then in exile in Mexico City, wrote to Broch, then in exile in Princeton:

> You are right. Virgil has to appear now or never, since just so many young Americans are about to see the countries from where the entire thing only becomes understandable. It was Virgil, to be sure, who was the father of Western culture (the mother was the synagogue), and the center of this culture in its beginning was in the Greek parts of Italy. Rome was only the warehouse in which everything was stored and offered. Even admitting that Virgil was only one of the chairmen of the board of distribution which obtained the commodities from the Phoenician-Egyptian-Greek manufacturers, like Plato, Philo, Hermes Trismegistus, it was he, Virgil, who drew up the best prospectus for the merchandise and who was able to attract most of the buyers (23 August 1943).[22]

Again and again Broch's *Der Tod des Vergil* has been placed beside Joyce's *Ulysses* in terms of such technical parallels as the description of a single day and night in the life of one man, the use of the inner monologue, etc. It has also been noted that Broch had attempted to publish his first novel with the same publisher who had brought out the German version of *Ulysses.*

Broch certainly held the highest opinion of Joyce, and it is probable that only Kafka enjoyed a loftier position in his critical pantheon. He also wrote a very interesting analysis of *Ulysses,*[23] but he definitely did not aspire to follow Joyce on the path blazed by *Ulysses.* There is also no doubt that Broch's relationship to Joyce changed with the passage of time and that his admiration of 1930 later developed into almost complete independence.

While there are many similarities between Broch's *Der Tod des Vergil* and Joyce's *Ulysses,* there are also a great number of differences, and critics have fixed resolutely upon either one side or the other. In both novels the technique of presentation becomes to some extent a part of the novel's content, and in this fashion the author's formative hand becomes apparent. Both novels have broken with the usual narrative tradition of looking at an action and describing it from a distance. The narrator-observer becomes part of the narration, not directly as an acting character but indirectly through his function as narrator. The style of both novels is translucent; both novels expand the possibilities of language and widen the limits of expression; both are characterized by an intertwining and concatenation of symbols created to establish a sense of simultaneity; and both employ musical forms.

A difference arises, however, as soon as one examines the kind of musical forms employed and their respective functions. Joyce fragments words themselves into quarter and eighth notes. He uses auditory particles in a pointillistic manner to establish a radical degree of reality and develops them further in symbolic series that lead into the last realms of dream and ancient myth. Broch may occasionally employ similar means, but his primary endeavor is the utilization of music-like motifs and motivistic symbolism in order to apply a symphonic compositional form complete with four movements to his novel. His goal is to achieve a wholeness like that of a symphony. He does this because he wishes to realize this totality, a concept in which Joyce simply does not believe.

The differences between the two novels are not merely a function of dissimilar plots: Joyce describes an average day of an average person, while Broch describes the most unusual day, the dying day, of a most unusual person, one of the world's greatest writers. The difference lies instead in the contrast between Joyce's use of external means, inner monologue notwithstanding, and his distance from totality and myth as opposed to Broch's realization of the mythical realm. Broch once even called *Ulysses* essentially positivistic[24] and contrasted it to his own novel, which he claimed was neither "pointillistic" nor "analytical."[25] He admitted, however, that in *Ulysses* he found for the first time a kind of novel that surpasses the usual novel, a kind of literature that surpasses literature, and there is little doubt that in *Der Tod des Vergil* Broch was striving for the same goal.[26] Falling behind the aesthetic level of *Ulysses,* Broch's *Der Tod des Vergil* attempts at the same time to transmit cognitive and ethical values to a much greater extent than Joyce's novel does. The reader of the book becomes aware of all of Virgil's thoughts, feelings, and visions concentrated and recapitulated at the very end of his life as he dies. The entire novel is in fact nothing but one gigantic inner monologue treating the poet's last eighteen hours. This explains to some degree why there is not much of a plot.

There is nonetheless the skeleton of a plot: the dying Roman poet, sailing on a ship of the imperial fleet of Caesar Augustus, disembarks in the harbor of Brundisium, is carried to the imperial palace, and receives as visitors real people as well as imaginary people projected by his own mind or, perhaps better, aroused from deep levels of his own subconscious. These visionary visitors are, as already mentioned, the young boy Lysanias, Plotia Hieria, and a nameless slave. Among the real visitors are a physician, two friends of Virgil, Plotius Tucca, Lucius Varius, and finally the most important one of all, Caesar Augustus.

Dialogues take place between Virgil's consciousness and the imaginary figures representing his own subconscious: they are an inner monologue of Virgil, turned by this technique into apparent dialogues. One of the main problems is revealed in the great discussion between Virgil, the greatest living poet of his time, and Caesar Augustus, the emperor who ruled the then-known world. This new version of a Platonic dialogue leads into Broch's innermost philosophy of art. The topic is nothing less than the being or non-being of literature and its value and function for humanity. Like Broch on a peak of the contemporary crisis and transition, facing the reality of the catastrophes of World War II, his dying Virgil, facing the truth of death, starts to doubt the value of his great work, the *Aeneid,* here representing literature as such, and wishes to have it destroyed.

Caesar Augustus first wants to save the poem for not entirely unselfish reasons: he is glorified in it. Broch was, however, an aesthetically sensitive person. He was more than that, namely, a great writer forced by his innermost being to express himself in terms of literature. At the same time he was close to guilt complexes because he had come to doubt that anyone was justified in writing literature at such times of crisis. Broch lets his figure Virgil articulate what he did not achieve in his poem but what literature had to be in order to have a right to exist and to have a true function for humanity.

At the end of the dialogue Caesar Augustus succeeds, but not because his reasoning convinced Virgil that his ideas about literature and about having failed were wrong. Augustus succeeds for entirely different reasons. Caesar Augustus, the ruler of the Roman Empire, supposedly a god, loses dignity as well as his grand gestures and phrases completely. Outraged about Virgil's adamant will to destroy the *Aeneid,* Augustus starts to rave, which makes him human and truthful. He seriously begins to doubt Virgil's friendship and provokes his feelings severely. Finally, however, it becomes clear that changing Virgil's mind would and indeed did create a second of real love, love in reality. Even though aware of how much more important for the dying poet a second of real love was than all the great words of his poem, a work containing an essential part of the time and effort of his life, one may doubt that this second of love was the only reason for Virgil's changing his mind and saving the poem.

There is to be sure a second reason. Augustus, even while ameliorating the lot of the Roman slaves, thought it was necessary for economic reasons as well as for the welfare of the empire to limit by law the widespread emancipation of the slaves. Now, after having given the poem to Augustus, Virgil asks for a favor in return: Caesar's permission required by law to let Virgil's slaves go free. These were not personal servants but rather farm workers on Virgil's estate, which was managed by his stepbrother.

The messages of Broch's *Der Tod des Vergil* reach even further. There are passages in which it becomes apparent that Broch tried to achieve, and thought that he might have achieved, exactly what Virgil accuses himself of having failed to do. These thoughts are expressed especially clearly when Broch lets his Virgil explain his, Broch's, theory of literature.

First of all, literature surpasses the possibilities of abstract thought. It consists of images and symbols created by the writer's imagination, and it corresponds to the most essential powers of human life. The human psyche does not think in terms of abstract reflections or logical conclusions but in images. Human life is thus "image-graced and image-cursed; it could comprehend itself only through images, the images were not to be banished, they had been with us since the herd-beginning, they were anterior to and mightier than our thinking, they were timeless, containing past and future, they were twofold dream-memory and they were more powerful than we."[27]

Broch's dying Virgil is afraid of having failed to create genuine metaphors, the real poetic images for which Broch strives and which his Virgil describes to Caesar Augustus in the following words: "Oh, Augustus, to recognize the celestial in the terrestrial and by the virtue of that recognition to bring it to earthly shape as a formed work or a formed word, or even as a formed deed, this is the essence of the true symbol . . ." (*Der Tod des Vergil*, 355).

This kind of true symbol can embrace the entire man and touch upon the entire man, not merely his intellectual reflections. For this reason it is so important for Virgil, as it was for Broch, to encompass in his literary work the totality of human existence, which means not only life, but also death. There is no question that Broch's firm intention was to achieve the goal of creating such true symbols. There is no doubt that he was thinking about himself at least as much as about Virgil when he let his Virgil reflect upon the occupation of a writer, of a poet:

> For the sake of the all-embracing might of this goal he had long, yes too long, searched for his own vocation; for the sake of his always known yet never known goal, dissatisfied with every profession, he had prematurely broken away from each one, unable to find peace in any, either in the calling of a medical man, a mathematician, astrologer, philosophical scholar or teacher: the demanding but unrealized vision of knowledge, the grave recognizable image of death had stood perpetually before his eyes, and no vocation measured up to that, as none exists that is not exclusively subserviated to the knowledge of life, none with the exception of that one to which he had finally been driven and which is called poetry, the strangest of all human occupations, the only one dedicated to the knowledge of death (81).

Literature is, thus, among other things, a special form of knowledge or perception and of human self-understanding. Virgil's own perception is:

> discovering itself and turned towards itself,
> as if for the first time,
> begins to comprehend
> the necessity inherent in the universe, the necessity of
> every occurrence,
> as the necessity of his own soul . . . , (99)

which is floating over the abyss of nothingness, open and threatening, and over the blindness of man.

Literature for Broch, on the one hand, does not exist for the sake of literature and even less for the sake of literary theory; and, on the other hand, neither is it identical with a specific political or ideological message. It is indivisibly connected with a basic human commitment which he called in *Der Tod des Vergil* "the one duty, earthly duty, the duty of helpfulness, the duty of awakening" (132).

Literature has, as Broch pronounces through his Virgil, its definite limitations, the most important of which is that it cannot enable people to experience the true realization of rebirth which Virgil undergoes in the process of his dying. In this sense Virgil claims "that the writer is not really alive" (382). Literature can describe essential knowledge but not provide its essential achievement. Nevertheless, literature can express the real, the essential knowledge or perception by pointing toward it. The novel distinguishes expressively between two basic different kinds of perception; Virgil and Augustus each represent opposite kinds of perception and thus have problems communicating: Virgil spells out the difficulty when he says: ". . . superficial perception may be increasing, while the kernel of perception may be shrinking" (352).

It is of the greatest importance that this "kernel of perception" should be increasing, and here literature can do its share. As Broch and his Virgil see it, life can indeed be grasped only in metaphor, and metaphor can express itself only in metaphor: "The chain of metaphors was endless and death alone was without metaphor, death to which the chain reached, as though death, even though lying outside it, were its last link . . ." (357).

One of the major questions raised in *Der Tod des Vergil* is whether it is ethical in a time of a totalitarian crisis to write literature. This was a very serious issue for Broch. He practiced what he preached by devoting a great amount of his time before and after World War II to a basic and universal investigation of contemporary philosophy, mass hysteria, and the dangerous relativism of the different contemporary theories of value to create together with an analytical diagnosis of the totalitarian sickness of our times an antidote that was at least theoretically compelling.

He was planning to write a book on the theory of politics and then a three-volume work on mass psychology. The three most significant and original concepts in this regard were in the field of the philosophy of history, his theory of historical "Fehlsituationen" (failing situations), in the field of sociology his detailed theory of totalitarianism, and in the field of philosophy of law his notion of a "human right" as "earthly absolute." Broch could not finish these two books; his unfinished fragments have been published posthumously.[28] He had to interrupt his theoretical writings too often and too long because of accidents and sickness, because of helping friends and acquaintances, because of his correspondence, and because of the work on his last novels.

Broch moved as "poet in residence" to the Saybrook College of Yale University in New Haven, Connecticut in the spring of 1949.[29] When he received the galley proofs of several of his old stories which were to appear as a volume of his collected novellas, he disliked them so much that he decided to write a number of new stories in order to round out the entire collection into a novel. Thus *Die Schuldlosen* (1950, *The Guiltless*) came into existence.[30] Its main theme is the guiltless guilt of passivity or rather the lack of activity of people who fail to fulfill their human duties when other human beings are persecuted, enslaved, or murdered. At the same time it reveals the paramount sin of any totalitarianism, namely, the spiritual reduction of the absolute and infinite to the finite as well as the projection of the finite into the absolute and infinite.

As he had done in his former novels, Broch decided to portray a totality here, especially the totality of the guiltless guilty, whom he labels "Spießer" (petty bourgeois). His protagonist, Andreas, meets another guiltless guilty person of the same type named Zacharias, as different as they might look on the surface. The names Andreas and Zacharias, from A to Z, point to the intention of embracing totality. While Zacharias's guilt is more (but not only) political, Andreas's guilt is more personal. The entire novel unfolds in pairs of stories which in a certain way complement each other like opposite poles: stories I and XI, II and X, III and IX, IV and VIII, and V and VII are built around the middle axis of story VI "Eine leichte Enttäuschung" (A Slight Disappointment). While this technique of composition represents the outer bond of coherence, there are of course also inner elements like motives and symbols creating a deeper-reaching unity.

Like *Die Schlafwandler,* the novel unfolds in three stages: 1913, 1923, and 1933, the year in which Hitler came to power in Germany. The protagonist is Andreas, a young Dutchman, who is therefore "neutral" and guiltless-guilty. He moves into a German town, becomes guilty of the suicide of a young girl, tries to escape with his elderly landlady and mother-substitute to an idyllic life in the country, and finally, after inner purification—he has a "dialogue" with his own conscience personified as an old beekeeper who resembles the grandfather of the dead girl—he takes his own life.

In a metaphysical way the entire novel unfolds from its introduction, which is entitled "The Parable of the Voice" and is shaped like one of Martin Buber's Hassidic tales. Broch tries to include all layers of human nature and of life from the animal level to the metaphysical, thus embracing a totality in another way. The end of the novel focuses on the revival of the little spark of the absolute that everyone carries within himself and preaches awakening as in *Der Tod des Vergil.*

Persuaded by the publisher Alfred Knopf, Broch finally started to write the last and by far the most ambitious version of his "Berg-Roman"[31] but could finish only the first four chapters of it. He died of a heart attack in his apartment in New Haven in 1951. However, the novel became a masterpiece of literary adaptation when Felix Stössinger combined the different chapters of the three versions into a unified novel which appeared under the title *Der Versucher* (1953, *The Spell,* 1986). Unfortunately the English version is based on only the extremely poor first draft of the novel which Broch never wanted to see published.

Before he was persuaded to take up again the old manuscript of the novel, Broch complained in a letter: "Certainly, the mountain novel is still on the program since it is already half finished. But I am scared of it, because if I attempt to finish it I shall enter into an unbounded task since it has to become a book that can stand next to Virgil . . ."[32] When he finally sat down to write the third version of the novel, he truly accomplished what can be considered the peak and masterpiece of his literary achievements. The fictional storyteller of the novel is the figure of a country doctor who describes how a stranger moves into the village and changes certain aspects of social life drastically by establishing a kind of local fascism. The "totality" of the description could be achieved much more easily in terms of a miniature model of a small

Alpine village than in using an entire country as an example.

The anti-hero Marius Ratti preaches a kind of modern rationalizing of pagan mythology combined with what he calls "male knowledge." In both cases his approach boils down to a reductionism which in spite of its mythological overtones limits all thought to an acceptance of the "earth" as matter and as finite. The positive counter figure of the novel is old "Mother Gisson" (Gisson being an anagram for Gnosis), who stands for the expansion of the finite to the infinite and for the message of love. Marius turns out to be victorious in the short range by successfully disturbing the villagers' harmony with the great rhythm of nature and the natural law. Broch applied the insights and results of his studies in mass psychology to the entire development and to the different reactions of the villagers. But there is no doubt that in the long run Marius will disappear. His hatred stands against love, his message of fear against the force of comfort, his rationalization of myth against real myth, his awakening of greed for the finite against the awakening to insight into the unchanging rhythm of nature, the images of which stand for the infinite. Although Mother Gisson's daughter is killed in an outburst of mass hysteria during a strange attempt to revive atavistic customs, the hope rests with the unborn child of a simple girl, who will outlive and outgrow all the insanity.

The psychological as well as the ideological mechanism of totalitarianism, its power of lying and use of greediness and opportunism, is analyzed and revealed in a masterly way. The non-Austrian features of the "Italian" Marius Ratti parallel the non-Austrian features of German fascism, and the petty flexible scoundrel Wenzel represents the cleverness of public relations' make-believe, which glorifies the narrow-minded Marius into a superman and turns every word into its opposite. The Hungarian Calvinist Wetchy represents the "different" minority within the village such as the Jews. What Marius and his followers intended to be omnipotent strength is revealed as insecurity and weakness. On the other hand, the reader might detect within the most fleeting appearances and images of nature the deepest possible unchanging meaning and the symbolic reference to the infinite which reduces all the efforts and successes of Marius to plain silliness.

Among Broch's poems there are some great ones, many of which were put into his lyrical novels. Of his few attempts as a playwright only *Die Entsühnung,* published for the first time in a radio-play version by Ernst Schönwiese in 1961, stands out.

Exile forced Hermann Broch to his last, almost superhuman

attitude of responsibility and to his theoretical studies of cognition in the fields of philosophy of law and philosophy of history, in value theory and mass psychology, which he considered the most important and most promising contribution a single individual and writer could make to the improvement of human life in our time, which he felt was endangered in so many ways. To some degree what Broch had once written about Tolstoy was true of himself:

> ... Tolstoy's radicalism was not content with this artistic approach to myth; in contrast to Goethe and Beethoven, who were in spite of their human greatness preponderantly artists, Tolstoy was striving for more: he was striving for the complete abstractness of a new theogony. For the style of old age, which he achieved in time, had a goal other than the Homeric one, a goal nearer to Hesiod and Solon than to Homer, and to the merging of myth and art. With a zeal akin to that of Savonarola he aspired to radical finalities and so withdrew from art altogether to construct his own ethical universe.[33]

Although it was not supposed to be a "theogony," the "ethical universe" Broch constructed bears the title "mass psychology" and covers much more than one usually expects to find in a compendium of this discipline. This "ethical universe" or "mass psychology" has so far found fewer readers and had less effect than his philosophy of the history of the decay of values. He had developed the latter before his mass psychology and later combined the two. This lack of effect is on the one hand the result of the coy, difficult, and theoretical character of this mass psychology: except for Freud and Le Bon there existed, according to Broch, almost nothing theoretical, a statement which characterizes his own work.[34] On the other hand, as Broch himself judged the topic and problems of mass psychology in general, "the danger which is planted within a mass . . . [is] just less palpable than the danger of an atomic bomb."[35] These difficulties make involvement with his mass psychology less encouraging and profitable than the examination of almost any other aspect of Broch's work. The central position of his mass psychology, however, the immense significance of this topic not only in its theoretical implications, but also in its practical importance for human existence makes it worthwhile to risk trying to understand and elucidate it.

A first glance at his mass psychology clearly shows the inner unity of his entire work, and one can see how the knowledge of his mass psychology can help to deepen the understanding of his novels: it is equally true that a familiarity with his novels can facilitate the appreciation of his mass psychology. This overall unity of Broch's entire work leads to the first problem in attempting to analyze his mass psychology, namely, the methodological foundation needed to approach the special means and methods of Broch's mass psychology. In order to clarify and to limit the field of his investigation and the aims of his topic, he had constructed a theoretical model. Such a model ought to represent, according to Broch, the maximum of a probability value, which means—and that was always a matter of intuition—it has to come as close as possible to the reality of the specific situation or problem being commanded. At the same time there is the implied expectation that the ongoing scholarly investigations will continuously rectify and sometimes even change entirely the model's initial structure.[36]

In Broch's mass psychology the heuristic sparks and the intuitive ideas are combined with a process of scholarly verification in order to grasp reality. In a similar way the creating of his novels combines his personal experience of social and historical reality with his intuitive vision and imagination. The only difference, which is of utmost importance from the viewpoint of literature, is the fact that the mass psychology consists of condensed abstract thoughts, while the novels, using Broch's term, are "written." By that he means that the novels are dominated by aesthetic and artistic principles of presentation and expression. However, according to Broch, the novels too are directed toward reality and always in search of reality.[37]

Lützeler suggested that his theory of mass psychosis differs from other mass psychologies on three points. First, he proposes the concept of a "state of twilight" in the individual mind that is the precondition of mass psychotic reactions in the individual. Second, he joins his theory of values and his theory of history to the mass psychology. And third, he offers a concept of the conversion of the masses to democracy as the centerpiece of his book.[38] This need not only be elaborated in some detail, but must also be supplemented to a considerable extent.

First of all, it must be understood that Broch's mass psychology, its fragmented, diverse, and uncompleted character notwithstanding, is the work of a single mind. It is not an eclectic collection but a true synthesis, and it makes sense that Broch does not refer to the thinkers that influenced him and that he foregoes the scholarly clutter of notes and bibliographical references. Given the outward state of Broch's work on mass psychology, it is hardly surprising that Paul Reiwald's standard work on the subject found a much wider scholarly audience than Broch's would have. Reiwald's book consists of nothing but a summary of the essential contributions to mass psychology from the various disciplines.[39]

Nevertheless, a book similar in concept to Broch's *Massenwahntheorie* could reach an audience of specialists as well as the intelligentsia at large. Ortega y Gasset's *Revolt of the Masses* had already demonstrated this. Many of the notes in Ortega's book may as well have been part of the text, and hardly more than a half dozen refer to the works of other authors. Why, one may ask, did Broch's book not enjoy a similar success?

One basic reason is that Broch's book is more than twice as long and was written in a much more condensed, demanding style. It embraces more than the facts of mass psychology in the narrower sense, expanding into the fields of epistemology, philosophy of law, the theory of values, philosophy of history, comparative religion, and even anthropology. This synthetic structure with its intention to comprehend a totality makes it a book more difficult than, for instance, a book of the sort that Hedley Cantril had written. Cantril was the director of the project on mass psychology within which Broch received his grant from the Rockefeller Foundation. By limiting himself to empirical analyses Cantril was assured of a much greater impact within the scholarly establishment than the academic outsider Broch.[40]

From the perspective of his attempt to create an encompassing model of mass psychology Broch complained that his task was unmanageable.[41] His observation is true not only for the author but for the reader as well. Yet its very magnitude remains one of the project's greatnesses.

Like the contributions of depth psychologists Freud, Adler, and Jung to the study of mass psychology, and different from almost anyone else, Broch put the "individual soul" at the center of his project. No matter what external events in mass life may be in question, Broch seeks them out within the soul of the individual. According to him, no mass phenomenon, however single-minded it may appear, justifies the solecism of a "mass soul." Mass soul and mass consciousness are simply expressions of convenience.[42]

This appeal to the individual soul simultaneously establishes personal responsibility as a basic premise in Broch's thought. It is connected for him to a new and special concept of human rights, which turns out to be the true foundation of Broch's mass psychology. He deduces it from a so-called "earthly absolute" without which, as Broch has asserted, his entire project would be no more than useless babble.[43] From this perspective Paul Michael Lützeler's edition of the *Massenpsychologie* supersedes that of Wolfgang Rothe because Lützeler includes these seminal reflections in his version.[44]

Even this relatively brief and certainly essential aspect of Broch's work—the elaboration of a new concept of human rights—has had little or no impact. When I once attempted to interpret this vital center of Broch's mass psychology for an audience of specialists, i.e. in the *Newsletter of the Austrian League of Human Rights,* it gained little attention.[45] In one important way Broch's concept of human rights differs from other such concepts, and his mass psychology differs from its counterparts in like fashion: in both undertakings, and in his novels as well, Broch aims at a comprehension of totality that embraces the entire human being and comprises all levels of human existence from the animal up to the metaphysical. More recent mass psychologies not only exclude the therapeutic moment that should follow the diagnosis but they also limit themselves to an abstract scaffold of structural characteristics and statistics. They include hopelessly superficial behavioristic theories and at best address some ethnological parallels. Yet they leave important parts of the entire problem virtually untouched and unresolved. This failure may correspond to a contemporary pseudo-scientistic trend that eagerly takes on the appearance but not the substance of serious investigation. In any event it remains unsatisfactory[46]

The entire problem might best be clarified through a comparison to Goethe's work in the natural sciences. After Goethe's death, for example, the great nineteenth-century physicist Hermann von Helmholtz pointed out the tautological nature of Goethe's theory of the "Urpflanze." A century later one critic observed: "Even if one grants that Goethe's theory is untenable, Helmholtz's criticism makes no sense either, but only shows how unbridgeable is the gulf between Goethe's vision and what can be comprehended through the mental operations of modern science. The two can never meet, and polemic becomes an intellectual fidgeting about in strictly separated and closed compartments."[47]

At first glance it might be surprising that Goethe accuses modern physics of "subjectivism." What he meant to express was his view that the emancipation of an individual discipline from the whole obstructs the man's attempt to grasp the world in its totality. Broch too criticized the compartmentalization of modern thought for similar reasons. However, Erich Heller found also in the modern physicist Werner Heisenberg an "echo of Goethe's voice" when he wrote: "The dangers threatening modern science cannot be averted by more and more experimenting, for our complicated experiments have no longer to do with nature in her own right, but with nature changed and transformed by our own cognitive activity."[48]

The two principles shared by Goethe and Broch are the need to comprehend the totality and the need to search for and find values. Both points are missing in more recent psychologies of Elias Canetti and Erich Fromm. The second principle has a certain similarity to Goethe's scientific writing, especially to his theory of color. In opposition to Helmholtz a contemporary physicist has asserted:

> With this view we have come to the conclusion that one may ... count colors to the outside world, as Goethe in his theory of colors would have wanted it. Therefore we must ask: Is it thinkable that the "quality of color" (and then, of course, numerous other qualities) exists outside of ourselves and our science yet does not acknowledge it because it is initially limited to quantities? Or do we have to imagine that the world around us consists only of measurable facts and that all qualities are bound to living beings with sense perceptions? A sound reason for it would be hard to give, though this is the position held by science.[49]

Perhaps it was no accident that neither scientist nor a scholar of law but the poet Dante originated the concept "human right." Broch does not seem to have known this fact, although there is no doubt that he received ideas from outside. There are borrowings from Kant and especially from Husserl, and Ortega y Gasset concluded his mass psychology by proposing that the main problem of the age is to be sought in the widespread belief that we can enjoy every right without the burden of any duty.[50] A similar concept finds elaboration in Broch's version of mass psychology when he complements or even "replaces," as he put it in a letter to Hannah Arendt, his "Bill of Rights" with a "Bill of Duties."[51]

Regardless of whatever correspondences may be present, Broch's attempt to found a new concept is highly original. He anchors his theory of human rights in a "Logos-existence" that exists beyond the merely empirical and beyond chance.[52]

How does Broch portray the development of a group of individuals who either sink into or avoid mass psychosis? For him it is a question of understanding culture in terms of the rational regulation of irrational needs: "The scale of these needs extends from the metaphysical realm to those instinctive urges that are lived out initially in our fellow man and thus ultimately in the collective."[53] From the perspective of this view the normal healthy human being can follow two routes:

> 1. The path of enriching the irrational, and this path is in general manifest as irrational values of culture. For it is precisely the culture that endows the self on precondition of the individual self's intact rational consciousness, culture's own contribution of irrationality. It does so through its ethically bound patterns of community, its cultic ties, and not lastly through the artistic-aesthetic shaping of life (*Daseinsformung*). The endowment of irrationality is needed not only for immediate satisfaction of irrational needs and drives, but also for their cultural transformation to feelings of community and togetherness.
>
> 2. The path of impoverishing the rational, (which can of course also be the a priori presence of impoverished rationality). This path is taken mostly when the individual becomes incapable or is incapable of rational reactions and control. This incapacity is often accompanied by the fear of personal madness, which is not infrequently associated with the loss of ethical rationality. Instinct supplants deficient rationality with attitudes shared by the largest possible number of individuals in the same group. In this way the manifold replication of an instinctive mode of behavior generates a kind of cosmetic ethic, i.e., phony justification for living out unchecked instincts. If a large number of individuals forfeit their rationality for the same cause, and if they then share a like instinctive behavior, we can then rightfully speak of mass psychosis (*Massenwahn*), especially in cases—as is characteristic of man's nature and his bad conscience—where pseudo-rational justifications are adduced in order to 'rationalize' irrational-instinctive behavior (*Massenwahntheorie*, 14–15).

Although these two paths have persisted throughout history, they rarely exist in the pure abstract-paradigmatic form that Broch offers in the above definitions. An intermingling of the two forms inevitably occurs and can lead to changing the one into the other. Broch himself gave examples of such developments. His first example warns that "irrational enrichment" can so overpower the individual soul that it ends in religious madness and reverts into "rational impoverishment." On the other hand, the phenomena of mass psychosis can also fall under the sway of rationality and lead to an irrational enrichment of the newly intact consciousness-self (*Bewußtseins-Ich*). Broch refers here to "the continuation of primitive magic religions within the spheres of higher consciousness, working the antique mysteries into systems of belief that have become Apollonian; indeed, almost the entire genesis of religion can serve as an example" (15).

If Broch's phenomenological constitution of the two alternatives should still seem complex in spite of his examples, then his verification of them at a psychological level should help to clarify his position. Each human being, suggests Broch, tries to incorporate into himself values in order to overcome the loneliness of the self and in order to make the world more valuable to himself. There are many different ways of such ego-extension: intoxication, possession of power, force or love for one's fellow man, extension of knowledge, and identification with the non-self. Broch emphasizes that the defense of negative aspects as such, of the fear of worthlessness, indeed, of the fear of fear, goes hand in hand with such "positive" ego-extensions. To assuage fear is for Broch the meaning of security in culture and the totality of values. Here too in the psychological realm of extending the ego and overcoming fear we find the two basic ways by which the self can develop out of its formal state into the supra-individual: 1) "the path of irrational enrichment that leads to value experience of the type 'I am the world,'" and 2) "the path of rational impoverishment typified especially by values of the type 'I have the world'" (17).

The archetypal contrast can hardly be described more simply and precisely: "I am the world" and "I have the world." The first represents the genuine, true, and positive way of extending the ego that leads ultimately to an overcoming of ego. In an ecstatic solitude the individual surpasses the reality of the collective and becomes solely the object of an ethical reality. The I-have-the-world mode represents false extension of ego. It assuages the fear only by possession and subjugation, even at the cost of its own submission to collective madness.

Those who succumb to the second path live in a twilight realm partly as willing, partly as joyous victims of historical events and cyclical spiritual developments. Broch analyzes this twilight of the human mind within the mass in the first two chapters of the *Massenwahntheorie*. Here he discusses the connections, interrelationships, and functions that make up the whole of most other mass psychologies. The earlier expressions of this condition are well known to the readers of Broch's novels. In addition to being afflicted by the much-discussed "disintegration of value" the protagonists of *Die Schlafwandler* live and move in this twilight condition.

Times had been bad enough when Broch was writing *Die Schlafwandler* (1928–1931), but the subsequent decades that produced his theory of mass psychology were even worse. Consequently, the outlook expressed in it is more pessimistic. It seems to suggest sometimes that the human race is condemned to swing forever between two poles of insanity, "between the insane system of an autonomous hypertrophy of values on one side and relativistically maimed values on the other" (273). The negative message has displeased Broch's readers and therefore left his work without great effect. The modern scission of values that has driven man into totalitarian self-enslavement is perhaps the inevitable moment in a cycle, an insane moment from which there is no escape, and which must decay utterly before renewal is possible.

Two types of leader correspond to the two paths: one is the true religious savior anticipated by Broch's Virgil. Broch anticipates a coming era in the same way that his Virgil does. But there is also the figure of the demonic demagogue to lead the masses on the path of archaic-infantile ecstasies. Marius Ratti of *The Spell* belongs to this category (*Massenwahntheorie*, 300–301).

Broch called the third large section of his study "The Struggle against Mass Psychosis. A Psychology of Politics." In contrast to most similar works he introduces a therapeutic turn. He assigns to democracies the task of carrying out the struggle, even if he shows little optimism about their power to do so. A reflection that addresses the "present moment," probably 1941, remains valid after half a century: "The question of fighting mass psychosis, resolution to the great work of conversion, resolution to dispel the world's demons again, however difficult and complex the task may be, constitutes the touchstone of the will to life and to the power of the life of democracy at the present moment" (342).

He tried to develop a "theory of conversion," and in a letter he even called such a conversion the actual theme of his studies in mass psychology (343–358). The theory's main points that can be mentioned in this context are the "devaluation of victory," the unmasking of empty phrases, and faith in the simple powers of conscience. Broch introduces here his concept of human rights, anchored in the absolute and resembling Husserl's notion of eidetic formations. From the perspective of human rights his exhortation to conversion amounts to a conversion to humanity that would be best realized in a totalized democracy, "because democracy is anti-enslavement, and in fact can be defined as such."

Yet because democracy, suggests Broch, is itself susceptible to totalitarianism, it must be supplemented through the power of a religiosity that renews faith. Even the renewal of ethics is contingent upon this supplement, for an authentic ethic must begin by joining man to the absolute. From this conjunction, "from [man's] presentiment of the immutability of his basic physical and spiritual structure, from the dimly foreseen mystical unalterability of the structure of his consciousness, he accepts the mandate of being human, the ineluctable impetus to create religion" (531).

Democracy cannot achieve such a development by force, but it can prepare the way. It will do so automatically, for democracy has as its aim the realization of the ethical ideal that all humankind is equal before the law—and before God. Democracy aims not at this or that codified morality but at the ethical as such. There exists basically no other democratic aim. Broch even goes so far in his opposition to the secular quasi-religions of totalitarian ideology as to say that democratic man is the worldly version of truly religious man.

The democratic man, who can even harness the power of technology for his benefit, can also pit against ideologies and "political religions" another specifically democratic concept: the idea of decency. In his concept of decency Broch finds the two basic elements of democratic attitudes united, "first of all that of dispassionate, sober rationality, and secondly that of the innermost equality of all that bears a human countenance" (532).

In spite of his insight into the difficulties mitigating against a successful struggle against mass psychosis Broch remains confident and perhaps even optimistic "because [the coming ethic-centered value] is a human necessity" (533). Yet this confidence belongs only to the "Massenwahntheorie" proper; his private comments often express misgivings. In a letter of 1946 he writes:

Whoever approaches the humanly impossible task of humane politics anew (practically a madman) always has to start *ab ovo*, i.e., he has to go back to logical and dialectical foundations. This is exactly what I am trying to do in my mass psychology as well as in the political book that has to come before it. Even though I am aware of the enormous fundamental difficulties on the one hand, and of my own inadequacies on the other — everybody has them — I am sticking with the task. For if there are firmly structured theories of inhumanity, then there can, should, ought to be also a no less firmly structured theory of the humane ... ,[54]

To make known, to realize, to live this unique theory of the humane depends upon each one of us.

Notes

1. Karin Mack and Wolfgang Hofer, *Spiegelungen. Denkbilder zur Biographie Brochs* (Wien: Sonderzahl, 1984), pp. 19-21 and 24-25.
2. Ibid., p. 47.
3. Ibid., p. 56.
4. Manfred Durzak, *Hermann Broch* (Reinbek bei Hamburg: Rowohlt, 1966), p. 11.
5. Ibid., p. 37.
6. Paul Michael Lützeler, *Hermann Broch* (Frankfurt am Main: Suhrkamp, 1985), p. 53.
7. Manfred Durzak, *Hermann Broch*, p. 39.
8. Ibid., p. 42.
9. Ibid., p. 45.
10. Paul Michael Lützeler, *Hermann Broch*, p. 61.
11. Ibid., pp. 102-103.
12. Manfred Durzak, *Hermann Broch*, pp. 51-52. Cf. Joseph Strelka, "Hermann Broch's Jugendessays," *Wiener Zeitung*, No. 252, 28 October 1956.
13. Paul Michael Lützeler, *Hermann Broch*, p. 105.
14. Hermann Broch, *Dichten und Erkennen* (Zürich, 1955), p. 251.
15. Ibid., pp. 251 and 253.
16. Wladimir Weidlé, *Les Somnabules de M. Hermann Broch: Apocalypse du présent Le Mois* 18 (1-7 June 1932), 198-203.

110   Joseph P. Strelka

17.   Ernst Schönwiese, "Zentrum Zirkusgasse 1935," *Die Pestsäule* 8 (1973), 704–710.

18.   The "Blei-circle" goes back to 1917, when Gina Kaus and Paul Schrecker were important participants.

19.   *Hermann Broch – Daniel Brody. Briefwechsel 1930–1951*, eds., Bertold Hack and Marietta Kleiss (Frankfurt am Main: Buchhändler Vereinigung, 1971), letter no. 410 and note 410 A.

20.   Paul Michael Lützeler, *Hermann Broch*, pp. 227–232.

21.   Manfred Durzak, *Hermann Broch*, pp. 114–120.

22.   *Hermann Broch – Daniel Brody. Briefwechsel 1930–1951*, pp. 183–210.

23.   Hermann Broch, *Dichten und Erkennen*, pp. 183–210. An English translation appeared in the *James Joyce Yearbook* (Paris, 1949), pp. 68–108.

24.   Hermann Broch, *Erkennen und Handeln* (Zürich, 1955), p. 160.

25.   Herman Broch, *Briefe* II (Frankfurt am Main: Suhrkamp, 1981), p. 359.

26.   Hermann Broch, *Briefe* III (Frankfurt am Main: Suhrkamp, 1981), p. 265.

27.   Hermann Broch, *The Death of Virgil*, trans. Jean Starr Untermeyer (New York: Grosset & Dunlap, 1965), p. 76.

28.   Hermann Broch, *Massenpsychologie*, ed. Wolfgang Rothe (Zürich: Rhein, 1959). *Hermann Broch, Massenwahntheorie*, ed. Paul Michael Lützeler (Frankfurt am Main: Suhrkamp, 1979).

29.   Manfred Durzak, *Hermann Broch*, p. 138.

30.   Hermann Broch, *Briefe* III, p. 327.

31.   Ibid., p. 362.

32.   Ibid., p. 27.

33.   Hermann Broch, *Dichten und Erkennen*, p. 258.

34.   Hermann Broch, *Briefe* II, p. 339.

35.   Hermann Broch, *Briefe* III, p. 101.

36.   Hermann Broch, *Massenwahntheorie*, p. 2.

37.   Hermann Broch, *Briefe* III, p. 14.

38.   Paul Michael Lützeler's "Editorische Notiz" in his edition of Broch's *Massenwahntheorie. Beiträge zu einer Psychologie der Politik. Kommentierte Werkausgabe*, henceforth cited as *KW*, 12, pp. 580–581.

39.   Paul Reiwald, *Vom Geist der Massen. Handbuch der Massenpsychologie* (Zürich: Pan, 1946).

40.   Hedley Cantril, *The Psychology of Social Movements* (New York: J. Wiley & Sons, 1941).

41. Hermann Broch, *Briefe. KW* 13, no. 2, p. 339.
42. Hermann Broch, *Massenwahntheorie. KW* 12, p. 15.
43. Hermann Broch, *Briefe. KW* 13, no. 2, p. 35.
44. Hermann Broch, *Massenwahntheorie.* "Zeitgenössische Entwicklung und die Bekehrung zur Humanität. Demokratie versus Totalitärstaat." *KW* 12, pp. 510-554. Cf. Hermann Broch, *Massenpsychologie,* ed. Wolfgang Rothe (Zürich: Rhein, 1959).
45. Joseph Strelka, "Harmann Broch und das Menschenrecht," *Menschenrecht* 9, no. 5 (October 1956), 8-10.
46. Cf. the similar problem within the field of literary criticism as portrayed by René Wellek in his "Science, Pseudoscience, and Intuition in Recent Criticism," in R. W., *The Attack on Literature* (Chapel Hill: University of North Carolina Press, 1982), pp. 78-86.
47. Erich Heller, *The Disinherited Mind* (Cleveland and New York: Meridian Books, 1959), p. 12.
48. Ibid., p. 33.
49. Walter Heidler, *Der Mensch und die naturwissenschaftliche Erkenntnis* (1961), cited here according to Heinrich O. Proskauer's preface to J. W. Goethe, *Farbenlehre* 1 (Stuttgart, 1979), pp. 9-10. (My translations, J.S.).
50. Jose Ortega y Gasset, *Revolt of the Masses* (New York: Norton, 1932), pp. 201-202.
51. Hermann Broch, *Briefe. KW* 13, no. 3, p. 337.
52. Cf. ibid., p. 338.
53. Hermann Broch, *Massenwahntheorie. KW* 12, p. 14. (My translation, J.S.)
54. Hermann Broch, *Briefe. KW* 13, no. 3, pp. 350-351.

Bibliography

I. Works by Hermann Broch in German

Die Schlafwandler. Novel. München, Zürich: Rhein, 1931-1932.
Die unbekannte Größe. Novel. Berlin: S. Fischer, 1933.
James Joyce und die Gegenwart. Speech. Wien, Leipzig, Zürich: Reichner, 1936.
Der Tod des Vergil. Novel. New York: Pantheon , 1945.
Die Schuldlosen. Novel in eleven stories. Zürich: Rhein, 1950.

Der Versucher. Novel. Zürich: Rhein, 1953.
Die Entsühnung. Radio-play version of a drama. Zürich: Rhein, 1961.
Hofmannsthal und seine Zeit. A Study. München: Piper, 1964.
Zur Universitätsreform. Essays. Frankfurt am Main: Suhrkamp, 1969.
Gedanken zur Politik. Essays. Frankfurt am Main: Suhrkamp, 1970.
Hermann Broch–Daniel Brody. Briefwechsel 1930-1951. Frankfurt am Main: Buchhändler-Vereinigung, 1970.
Menschenrecht und Demokratie. Essays about politics. Frankfurt am Main: Suhrkamp, 1971.
Briefe über Deutschland. Letters. Frankfurt am Main: Suhrkamp, 1986.

Collected Works

Gesammelte Werke in zehn Bänden. Zürich: Rhein, 1953-1961.
Kommentierte Werkausgabe in dreizehn Bänden (respectively fünfzehn Bänden) Frankfurt am Main: Suhrkamp, 1974-81 (sometimes quoted as thirteen volumes, sometimes as fifteen volumes, depending on whether the "Briefe" are counted as three parts of one volume or as three separate volumes).

Bibliographies and Sources of Material

Klaus W. Jonas unter Mitarbeit von Herta Schwarz. Bibliographie Hermann Broch, 1913-1970. In *Hermann Broch–Daniel Brody. Briefwechsel 1930-1951.* Frankfurt am Main: Buchhändler Vereinigung, 1970. Sp. 1083-1168.
Klaus W. Jonas. Bibliographie der Sekundärliteratur zu Hermann Broch. In *Hermann Broch,* ed. Paul Michael Lützeler. Frankfurt am Main: Suhrkamp, 1986, pp. 331-357.
Erica Doctorow and Madeleine Hogan. *Catalog of the exhibition "Hermann Broch: Poet and Prophet"* held at the Swirbul Library, Adelphi University, Garden City, New York, 26 February-26 April 1970.
Christa Sammons. "Hermann Broch Archive. Yale University Library." In *Modern Austrian Literature* 5, nos. 3/4 (1972), 18-69.
Karin Mack und Wolfgang Hofer, eds., *Spiegelungen.* Denkbilder zur Biographie Brochs. Wien: Sonderzahl, 1985. Materials and sources of the "Hermann Broch Museum" in Teesdorf, Lower Austria.

II. Works in English Translation (Only First Editions)

The Sleepwalkers, trans. Willa and Edwin Muir. London: Secker, 1932.
The Unknown Quantity, trans. Willa and Edwin Muir. London: Collins, 1935.
The Death of Virgil, trans. Jean Starr Untermeyer. New York: Pantheon, 1945.
Short Stories, ed. Eric W. Herd. London: Oxford University Press, 1966.
The Spell, trans. H. F. Broch de Rothermann. New York: Farrar and Strauss, 1986.

III. Secondary Works in English

Arendt, Hannah. "The Achievement of Hermann Broch." *Kenyon Review* 11 (1949), 476–483.
Cohn, Dorrit Claire. *The Sleepwalkers*. Elucidations of Hermann Broch's Trilogy. The Hague: Mouton, 1966.
Daviau, Donald G., ed., Special Hermann Broch issue of *Modern Austrian Literature* XIII, no. 4 (1980), 1–235.
Enright, D. J. "Seeking the Undiscoverable," in *Man Is an Onion*. London: Chatto & Windus, 1972, pp. 74–77.
Horrocks, David. "The Novels as History: Hermann Broch's Trilogy 'Die Schlafwandler,'" in *Weimar Germany. Writers and Politics*. Edinburgh: Academy Press, 1982, pp. 38–52.
Mueller, Randolph R. "Waiting for the Logos," in *Celebration of Life*. New York: Sheed & Ward, 1972, pp. 251–272.
Simpson, Malcolm R. *The Novels of Hermann Broch*. Bern, Frankfurt, Las Vegas: Peter Lang, 1977.
Weigand, Hermann J. "Broch's Death of Virgil." *Publication of the Modern Language Association* 62, no. 2 (1947), 525–554
White, John J. "Hermann Broch," in *Mythology in the Modern Novel*. Princeton: Princeton University Press, 1971, pp. 156–166 and 199–211.
Ziolkowski, Theodore. *Hermann Broch*. New York: Columbia University Press, 1964.
———. "Hermann Broch, 'The Sleepwalkers,'" in *Dimensions of the Modern Novel*. Princeton: Princeton University Press, 1969, pp. 138–180.

114   Joseph P. Strelka

IV. Major Studies in German

Durzak, Manfred. *Hermann Broch.* Reinbek bei Hamburg: Rowohlt, 1966.
———. *Hermann Broch. Dichter und Erkenntnis.* Stuttgart, Berlin, Köln, Mainz: Kohlhammer, 1978.
———. *Hermann Broch. Der Dichter und seine Zeit.* Stuttgart, Berlin, Köln, Mainz: Kohlhammer, 1968.
Kahler, Erich. *Die Philosophie von Hermann Broch.* Tübingen: Mohr, 1962.
———, ed. *Dichter wider Willen.* Zürich: Rhein, 1958.
Kreutzer, Leo. *Erkenntnistheorie und Prophetie.* Hermann Broch's Roman trilogie 'Die Schlafwandler.' Tübingen: Max Niemeyer, 1966.
Lützeler, Paul Michael. *Hermann Broch.* Eine Biographie. Frankfurt am Main: Suhrkamp, 1985.
Steinecke, Hartmut. *Hermann Broch und der polyhistorische Roman.* Bonn: Bouvier, 1968.
Strelka, Joseph, ed. *Broch heute.* Bern, München: Francke, 1976.
Thieberger, Richard, ed. *Hermann Broch und seine Zeit.* Bern, Frankfurt am Main: Peter Lang, 1980.

Christine Busta*

Marilyn Scott

One of the first voices heard immediately after World War II was that of the Austrian poet Christine Busta. At a time when her contemporary poets were questioning the validity of language as expression Busta chose traditional poetic elements to create form amidst the chaos of the period. Radical experimentation was absent from her poetry at that time. Today, however, Busta's work occupies a position between tradition and experimentation in Austrian literature. Her increasing economy of verbal means and the directness of her voice produce a form of modernity in keeping with the most recent developments of contemporary poetry. But Christine Busta holds on to a strong religious tradition in a more and more secularized and uncertain world. In fact, in each of her volumes of poetry a constant number of poems consists of direct prayers to God, new interpretations of biblical settings and liturgical feasts, vignettes devoted to humble and lowly creatures (not only humans, but also animals, flowers, and plants, even minerals) in a vein that harks back to St. Francis's brotherly love for God's whole creation. It is no accident that in her poem "Steckbrief . . . Für meine Freunde" (A Wanted Poster . . . for My Friends), she formulates the third and last stanza in this way:

> I love God from my heart. But if the devil trips me,
> then I stumble blindly thanks to his wily hoof
> And I hold fast to the roots of the sunflower;
> Brother Francis planted it there for my eternal life.[1]

The appellation "Brother" expresses the relationship between the saint and all living creatures, but it also underscores the special affinity that Busta feels for St. Francis.

Her graceful blending of the modern and the traditional has brought Christine Busta a large audience both in Austria and abroad. The multiple printings of her books alone are unusual for a poet today, and she is one of the few Western writers published in East Germany.[2] Despite the undeniably broad appeal of her work critical evaluation of Busta's poetry has been slow in coming. Critics have tended to see in her early poetry the influences of her mentor, Josef Weinheber, or to group her with her countrywoman, Christine Lavant, because of the religious symbolism they share. However, she has grown beyond the former in both language and poetic form, and her themes are more universal than those of Lavant. Busta's work stands apart from any fashions or trends in literature. While it speaks to the problems confronting modern man, it conveys a timelessness as well. As Rudolf Henz remarked in his "Laudatio für Christine Busta" when she received the "Großer österreichischer Staatspreis" in 1969, "We sense in her poems a humanity that draws its power from Christian values, a language that is appropriate to our modern ears and yet reaches deeply into the great poetic tradition."[3] In addition to this coveted award her eight volumes of poetry appearing since 1951 have won many other prestigious prizes.[4] The spirit in which Busta accepted her awards is evidence of the humility and reserve that typifies both the poet and her work: "We cannot receive anything in this world that is not taken away from another or at least denied to him."[5] This is a recurring motif in Busta's poetry: There is an economy of good in this world. Whoever takes or even only receives too much takes away from someone else and ipso facto upsets the balance of justice. Conversely and in a profound human sense (one could call it a radical Christian communism) it is man's duty to share willingly and to sacrifice the "good" he or she has received and to help all other creatures, especially the "lowly," so that they are recognized in their true worth (as seen by God) and receive some part of this "good." The poet Busta sees herself in many ways as the person who gives them their due in poetry. The characteristic modesty underlying all of Busta's poetry is the source both of her sensitivity towards all creatures and of the poetic impulse itself, as she expresses it in an early poem: "Humility opens up the universe to me / and gives it countenance" (*Regenbaum,* 40).

Busta's large readership testifies to the fact that she finds enthusiastic response in the audience she addresses so directly and compassionately. Poetry is for her the transformation of the familiar and the immediate into the transcendent. She poses disturbing questions concerning the place of mankind on this planet and our relationship to God and to our fellow man and all creatures, but she does not offer answers that are simple or clichéd. The poet describes her writing as personal communication with the reader and compares the poetic process to telling a friend about a walk she has taken: while one cannot relate every detail of the woods and path, by bringing back a single leaf the poet can conjure up the entire landscape.[6] This connection from person to person is the essence of her poetry. For Busta poetry is a summary of the state of her life. Her report may be playful, ironic, reassuring, compassionate, or even despairing, but Busta never loses sight of the importance of communication. This personal voice grows out of her own life experiences. As she writes in her poem, "Kurz-biographie" (A Short Biography): "I grew up in narrowness and need, / but I had enough to marvel at / before they taught me to complain. / I draw upon this (wonder) even today for survival" (*Wappen,* 110).

Born on 23 April 1915, Busta grew up in bitter poverty in a state of isolation imposed by her unwed mother. Her mother had to struggle hard to support herself and her child, yet the shame she felt at the circumstances of their life kept her and her daughter estranged from family and neighbors. Busta characterizes herself as an early "latchkey child," and in her sketch "The Colors of My Childhood" she describes the predominant atmosphere alone in her childhood apartment as "gray."[7]

She enlivened her days, even as a very small child, by listening to sounds of life outside the apartment in the narrow dark courtyards of the apartment house in suburban Vienna's fifteenth district. From fragments overheard in the milieu of the "poor and the poorest people" her rich imagination created entire scenes, making sense of a world she could not see. She fantasized family, friends, and playmates: they were her early audience. Her fantasy was fed as well by the radio and by the stories told to her by her mother—Bible stories and fairy tales, the religious and folklore fables of our culture that she transforms in her later poetry. Her childhood situation outside the mainstream of neighborhood and family life created an early empathy with the marginal or forgotten figures who are the subject of so much of her work.

Her evolution and emergence as a poet suggest that she shared the national experience of the 1930s and 1940s very directly. She knows the dark side of life as well. Indeed, she was motivated to write by a series of personal crises. At key times in her life she lost connection with the people close to her and was forced to overcome her natural

modesty and speak out to an audience. Busta had written poetry even
as a schoolgirl. When she was fourteen, her ailing mother lost her job
and was never able to earn a regular income again. Busta assumed the
task of supporting the family. Nevertheless, she managed to graduate
from the Gymnasium in 1933 and to begin her studies of English and
German at the University of Vienna, where she continued to write
poetry. The financial burden of her mother's care coupled with the
pressures of her studies proved to be too much. Busta suffered a nervous collapse shortly before her examinations at the university. After
she left her studies, she worked at a variety of jobs, as an assistant
teacher, as a translator, and after the war in a hotel for British personnel.

Busta did not burst upon the literary scene but rather worked in
silence until her first small volume of poetry, *Jahr um Jahr* (Year after
Year), was published privately in 1950.[8] Although she had gained some
attention as an eighteen-year-old in 1933 when she read her poetry on
the radio, she had withdrawn to anonymity immediately afterward. In
1945 she was discovered again, this time by Josef Weinheber. Despite
his encouragement Busta felt that a poetic voice required more maturity and life experience: "I had the feeling more personal maturity,
more knowledge of life, more experience and suffering were necessary
in order to write the way I had wanted to. In addition the times were
too heroic for my taste."[9]

Finally the poet emerged by her own decision in 1946: her
experiences during the war pressed her to speak out. In 1942, the
second year of their marriage, her husband, the musician Maximilian
Dimt, had been inducted into the army. He was reported missing on the
Russian front in 1944 and never returned. The pain of that loss is
expressed directly in the poem, "Am Kammerfenster eines Verscholle-
nen" (At the Chamber Window of One Who Is Missing) (*Regenbaum*,
26). The last line in the poem cites "the terrible commitment to life"
and continues, "It cannot wait." Busta finds evidence of this adherence
to life in the inexorable bearing cycle of the fruit trees she sees from
her window. The grave crisis of outliving one who was to be her life's
partner is explicable only in terms of this natural cycle: ultimately one
must commit oneself fully to life despite the sacrifices it demands.[10]

After the war Busta also experienced further personal isolation
when her closest friend was deported to Germany. At this time Busta
published her first poem in the newspaper *Die Furche* under the name
of Dimt. She seems to have been able to overcome her inhibitions about

writing whenever her need for communication became great enough: "In oppressing isolation, my husband missing, my best friend absent, my friends scattered to the winds—I started to write again."[11]

In 1947 she sent a selection of seven poems to *Plan,* the first literary journal to be published in Austria after the war and the forum for virtually all postwar literature. Her loneliness gave Busta a voice.

> It was first of all the need to express myself . . . to begin to speak with a "Thou" . . . From the beginning there was no possibility for me to come to an art-for-art's sake perspective. My fascination with language as a means of communication, and the discovery that all that I possess comes to me through language, probably caused me to write.[12]

In the same year Busta won first prize for her legend "Das Fisch-wunder" (The Miracle of the Fish) in a contest sponsored by *Die Furche.* When in 1950 the "Förderungspreis für Lyrik zum österreichi-schen Staatspreis" was again awarded after thirteen years it was given jointly to Christine Busta and Frank Kiesling. Other awards followed rapidly.[13]

In 1959 the poet identified an important theme in her work as "the transformation of fear, horror, and guilt into joy, love, and re-demption."[14] Certainly the concept of transformation is central to her 1951 work, *Der Regenbaum* (The Raintree). The first poem, "Die Verwandlung" (Transformation), describes human existence as gray and dismal, lost in the roots of the raintree. Nevertheless, the transforma-tion promised by the title takes place as the golden sunbird flies to God, carrying a twig of the tree heavenward. The poet's role as patient listener is a common one for Busta: from deep within the branches of the tree she asks "Do I still sing? The tree alone is singing." The meta-morphosis from the concrete-visual to the fundamental-spiritual may occur in this early poetry without the active involvement of the poet. For Busta everything we see, hear, or know through our senses gives testimony of a higher order. Man's physical presence as well as his accomplishments symbolize a meaning in life that is known through direct experience.

Transformation of this kind informs much of the poetry in the book's four sections: "Der Wanderer" (The Traveler), "Das andere Schaf" (The Other Sheep), "Largo," and "Mondsichel am Horizont" (Crescent Moon on the Horizon). Man's physical environment at its most humble, birds, trees, a sunflower, even the found objects in a little boy's pockets, is thus elevated in stature (*Regenbaum*, 28).

The poet sheltered within the raintree is an image of childlike harmony with her natural surroundings. Yet human existence is always problematical with Busta. The first section of *Der Regenbaum*, "Der Wanderer," introduces the image of *homo viator* that Busta will develop throughout her work. While she confirms the underlying order in life, man is nevertheless uprooted, a vagabond who may never find a resting place ("Vagabundenlied" [Song of the Vagabonds], *Regenbaum*, 33). The poet concludes: "Everything good on this earth / Is yours only for a short stay, / You can be called home again only / When you have suffered greatly" (*Regenbaum*, 44).

The themes of guilt, justice, and Christian redemption preoccupy the poet here. Busta's religion, a simple belief in humanity and devotion to her fellow man, is reminiscent of the "Sermon on the Mount": "All that counts on judgment day is what you do for your brother" (66). Many of the poems in the section "Das andere Schaf" are based directly upon scriptural readings: often the poet retells biblical stories from a new perspective to make them more appropriate for the modern audience. She directs her compassionate interest to the marginal figures, the publican, the cock, a small dog, the "other" sheep.

Like the slow solemn movement of a musical composition that the title evokes the poems in "Largo" deal with the darker themes of personal loss, loneliness, death, and the passage of time. The poet believes that poetry transforms and gives meaning to the troubled side of man's existence. In "Das Gedicht" (The Poem, *Regenbaum*, 75) Busta states that words and images stand as guardians before a sterner kingdom of reality. Aware of the abyss below, people fear looking beneath the surface of words. Indeed, as long as Busta's faith in the power of language remains strong, she is able to complete the transformation she undertakes at the beginning of the book and to find her way back to the confirmation of Christian fellowship. But this process is not without difficulty. The last section, "Mondsichel am Horizont," explores man's spiritual inheritance and finds it meager indeed. The final poem of the work, "Besitz des Menschen" (The Possessions of Man), underlines the distinction that she perceives between mankind and a nature that is eternally free from our burden of responsibility: "What is left for us? To our heads the stars, unapproachable and strange, / Under our feet the dead, the wild childlike grass / And in our hearts guilt, restlessly alive" (*Regenbaum*, 127). This three-line poem places man precisely between an aloof firmament and an earth that in a compressed cycle of decay and fertility both receives the dead and produces wild grass. Man stands with his guilt between heaven and earth and is estranged from both realms. The stars are unapproachable, but there is no place for us in the earth either, for we are unlike the dead, who are free from human guilt. While Busta equates the vital grass with mankind by calling it "childlike," she also suggests with this adjective a state of innocence now lost to man.

In a commentary to her poem "In der Morgendämmerung" (At Dawn, *Scheune,* 41) the poet elaborates on the concept of human guilt in the modern age as responsibility for the welfare of the entire race. She states that our circumstance is much like that of past generations who also lived in troubled times, but unlike that of our forebears: our existence is questionable not only because of our natural ignorance, but also because of the powers mankind now holds—and abuses—to destroy civilization and, indeed, the planet itself. She continues in a tone of warning: "Only our estrangement is fated, not our guilt. Wherever man earns the name man, and he has earned it only out of the spirit of humanity and not out of his material nature—natura non constritatur—, he remains responsible, even in lost outposts."[15]

Lampe und Delphin (1955, Lamp and Dolphin) continues the theme of man as traveler, as the journey becomes a return to a lost spirituality, "homecoming to an alien interior" (*Lampe,* 5). With Christian and classical symbols for the transcendent, the poet reassures us that, no matter how great the estrangement from our origins, ultimately we will reach our goal: "At the long-obscured walls / we grope blindly toward the signs / And recognize with timid hands / once again the lamp and the dolphin."[16] In the first part the objects Busta chooses to represent life on this planet are mostly familiar and on the whole comforting: fruits, bread, baskets (*Lampe,* 22–23). Once more against these symbols of harmony and community, however, our own dwelling place is uncertain as we are called "squatters of the earth . . . refuse" (*Lampe,* 9).

The poet's role in the metamorphosis implied by the title "Magische Gegenwart" (Magical Presence) is that of the observer of nature and guide to its hidden meanings. Like a visionary the poet refers parts of our external reality back to their mythic origins. She identifies through archetypal memory with the mosquito petrified in ancient times within a drop of amber, a spirit heard now only by God (*Lampe,* 52). Such voices in nature are manifest in every part, although silent and unseen by others. The sense of an unbroken connection to the natural surroundings is expressed in the poem "Blick in den August-himmel" (Look into the August Heaven). Here birds flying across the blue sky create an ideogram in their formation. For whom is the message intended? For the sunflower? For our souls? Perhaps for both, although the message will ultimately be inexplicable: "Restless writing created by the flight of birds, snuffed by the wind" (*Lampe,* 57).

The strength of meaning radiating from each natural object is considered in the section "Die Botschaft" (The Message). Here the poet questions the function of language and concludes that words are not the primary form-giving principle. Meaning and form lie both within the objects of nature themselves and in the silent gestures of affection from one person to another. She feels that true communication does not depend upon the conventions of ordinary language and looks instead for a silent happiness that she often recalls from earlier times. Busta identifies man freed from the constraints of language with birds, who are capable of pure experience (*Lampe,* 38, 81):

> Today as the sharp mountain wind
> thrusts us arm in arm before it,
> I recognized you once again by a quickened heartbeat.
> Halting speech was torn from our mouths
> and we flew once again,
> suddenly in our throats the sound
> of pure mindless joy (38).

This message of silence has implications as well for the numerous poems of this section concerning the scripture and liturgical feasts. The poet develops the biblical allusion in the term "Botschaft" (message, tidings) just as the titles of certain poems and their cyclical chronology constitute a direct reference to the life of Christ: "Aufzeichnungen eines Fremden über Golgatha" (Notes of a Stranger on Golgotha), "Vor der Krippe" (Before the Manger), "Die drei Weisen singen vor Herodes" (The Three Wise Men Sing before Herod), "Der taube Hirte" (The Deaf Shepherd), "Drei Stimmen am Ostermorgen" (Three Voices on Easter Morning), "Spruch auf ein Wegkreuz" (Text on a Wayside Crucifix), and finally, "Der Traum vom Jüngsten Gericht" (The Dream of the Last Judgment). Once again there are the questionings and reinterpretations of biblical stories that are familiar from the second part of *Der Regen-*

baum, "Das andere Schaf." Here the tidings we are supposed to receive are not always audible to us, "the citizens of Babel," and may even be obscured by our efforts to interpret them: "Now the Word stands mangled and warped: / our flesh was a frail seal, / our spirit only a blind mirror . . ." (*Lampe,* 64).

Certainly Busta's sense of the difficulties inherent in language leads to a conclusion that contradicts Stefan George's assumption: "Nothing may exist where the word is lacking."[17] Rather, Busta the listener perceives the signals from nature despite her inability to express them: "Some words are soundless / but there is always something eying / you out of the silence" (*Lampe,* 61). The words "songless" and "soundless" explain the new proselike style of this work, a style that is developed further in Busta's later poetry. The poems are less musical with little inversion and less rhyme. Her stanzas diminish from verses to sentences:

> Long is the grass of oblivion
> Who grazes at night on the hills?
> Ghostly sound of the wind,
> the golden bodies of heaven.
> But the grape spurs stand
> immobile as ever" (46).

In the final section, "Auch wenn es Nacht ist" (Even at Night), the poet attempts to establish a source of joy and fellowship within the bleakest moments of personal doubt. For Busta linguistic and religious concerns are often bound together; hence it becomes the function of the poetic word to remind us of our shared humanity. While the poems in "Die Botschaft" focused on Busta's reinterpretation of the New Testament stories of Christ's birth and sacrifice, here the poet turns her playful and speculative attention to a fairy tale retold at the request of a young friend. She concludes her conciliatory retelling of the tale with evident satisfaction: "Only now are our fairy tales fairy tales" (83).

Busta's language in both *Lampe und Delphin* and *Der Regenbaum* is less self-conscious and less intricate than in her later poetry. The simple folk-song stanza is much in evidence formally with its clearly structured four-line stanzas and its alternating rhythms. In these first two works melodious words and images chosen from daily life often evoke the sounds of the rich tradition of Austrian folk poetry, of nearly forgotten children's rhymes that invite recitation, and even of the

German poet Matthias Claudius, whose joyful descriptions of nature
find an echo in such poems as "Heimweh nach dem Sommer" (Longing
for Summer, *Regenbaum,* 78).

At times the simple poetic language and form coupled with the
straightforward statement of the poet's religious convictions are directly reminiscent of the poets of the seventeenth century: "God is no
ecstasy to which we give ourselves weakly. He is a lord. He demands
service and deed" (*Regenbaum,* 60). Many of the poems, particularly in
Der Regenbaum, recall formally the neoclassicism of the Austrian poet
Josef Weinheber with their use of the ode and the hymn and their pre-
dominance of longer, metrically regular lines and strongly marked
rhyme schemes.[18] The musicality of language in Busta's early poetry
tends towards a massing of images for the sake of sound alone and at
the sacrifice of that direct personal statement that is so characteristic
of the poet's mature voice. The poet's love of metaphor continues to be
strongly felt in *Lampe und Delphin,* where no poem is free from metaphor and some poems contain such complex imagery that the reader
may become lost in the sheer vastness of the construct. "Der Traum
vom Turm" (The Dream of the Tower, 89) serves as one example of the
poet's fulsome imagery.

The title of Busta's collection of poetry, *Die Scheune der Vögel*
(1958, The Hayloft of the Birds), recalls the symbols of bird and nest-
ing place frequently encountered in her poetry. Signifying security and
harmony, the image depicts the poet's preoccupation with "a seclusion
that I never knew."[19] In her poetry the bird in its nest often represents
spiritual redemption. Here the *Scheune* is the physical world in its
many manifestations. It is a temporary shelter for the human soul
symbolized by the bird. The barn is described in the first poem of the
volume: the season is spring; the doors of a barn unused over the winter
have been thrown open to the fresh air. Some dust-covered remnant of
last fall's harvest still hangs from the rafters. Other faint reminders of
the past are the smells of resin, the sun, and the fermenting wine (5).
The poem conveys a sense of passing time as one pauses to contemplate
the work place before taking up the tasks once more. The last two lines
of the poem suggest that the work ahead will be not of an earthly but
of a spiritual nature. As in nearly all of Busta's poetry the simple natural elements are featured in this highly visual poem.

This moment of silent reverie leads the poet to the series of impressions of present and past times in different cultures that comprise
the first of five sections in the work. Appropriately entitled "Funde"

(Findings), the poems are like poetic excavations that grow out of the poet's reconsideration of a familiar world in light of history and cultures. This resonance comes in the first poem from an analogy between the contemporary life and ancient times signified by an Egyptian wall painting. While the figures in the wall painting retain for eternity their symbolic connection to both the spiritual and the poetic realms, modern man no longer finds a home on his own planet. The fish and bird, symbols of spirituality, are unrecognizable to us, and we have become grotesque reflections of our civilization's most awesome accomplishment, the atom bomb. By recalling Hiroshima (9) the poet refers to recent history, which had been absent from her earlier poetry. In this work specific citations grow from a sense of obligation to be more responsive to the ethical and political mandates of the day. Thus, for example, the second section of the work, "Chronik" (Chronicle), is primarily the poet's response to the 1956 Hungarian uprising. Here "Der andere Herodes" (The Other Herod) is quite unlike her earlier Bible stories that brought marginal figures back into the fold. The poet suggests chillingly that this Herod is only one of many who abuse power in society. "Dornröschen" (Sleeping Beauty) represents the poet's desire to write "a political poem with entirely lyrical means . . . a metaphor for freedom."[20]

This section is remarkable for its radical departure from the familiar order of time and space in Busta's poetic world; an awareness of "die Asche" (the ashes) intrudes upon the poet to threaten disruption of the very cosmos: "I know that the terrible ashes rain on our star, / and many ashes also fall into our hearts. // Death is near, the breath of life leaves gently . . ." (41). The word "Asche" (ashes) appears frequently in the poet's work to represent man's self-destruction. She defines the "cosmic dust" that fills our environment as a deadly pollutant of our own creation: "It is not industrial smoke that afflicts us most strongly. What takes away our breath are the ashes of Auschwitz and Hiroshima . . . this ash is a metaphor for blameful death, for all human blame . . ."[21]

Composed of thirty-nine poems, "Phasen" (Phases), the long center section of the work, continues to develop the theme of time by representing the seasons of the year often through religious symbolism; the second poem, "Weihnachten der ersten Liebe" (Christmas of First Love), introduces the winter setting, while subsequent titles take the reader through spring ("April," 55), summer ("Ende August vor einem Bahnhof" [End of August in Front of the Train Station], 69), autumn ("Herbstspuk" [Autumn Ghost], 70), and winter ("Brief zum Jahresende" [Letter at Year's End], 77) to a completion of the natural cycle. The seasonal imagery is brought together effectively in "Der alte Fischer" (The Old Fisherman):

> Testing, he filters the water of the stream.
> He holds Time in a net:
> morning, noon, evening,
> the fateful signs of the year: the flotsam of springtime,
> a rack filled with hay thrown by a summer storm,
> the discarded autumn fruits (83).

In an early review of *Der Regenbaum* and *Lampe und Delphin* Wolfram Mauser correctly cited the thematic consistency that distinguished Busta's poetry in the two volumes. "Heilen, Trösten und Helfen," (Healing, Comforting, and Helping), he found, "stehen im Mittelpunkt von Bustas Schaffen"[22] (stand in the center of Busta's work). In this later work that positive transformation of the human condition is attained only with much greater difficulty, as the poems in Section Four indicate. To some extent the reader finds the whimsical childlike handling of familiar Bible fables anticipated by the title of the section, "Biblische Kindheit" (Biblical Childhood, *Scheune,* 89, 93, 101). Busta clearly knows the comforts of traditional belief, yet she is not timid even here about confronting the guilt, isolation, and anxiety that she sees as part of our lives. The religious symbolism in several of these poems is strikingly personal: the wet winter snow that appears to the poet as a renewed *Wasserzeichen* (water symbol) for baptism (90) or the poet's description in "Der weiße und der braune Heiland" (The White and the Brown Savior) of the latter as the warm loaf of country bread remembered from her childhood, the *panis quotidianus* of the Lord's Prayer (103).

The title of the final section,, "Flaschenpost," suggests an intensified concern by the poet for her audience. Unlike the more passive role of the poet/listener in *Der Regenbaum* the poet is concerned here to establish a connection with her audience. Poetry is a message sent off in a bottle. The poet's task completed, she can only hope that the message will be taken up, read, and understood. Will there be someone to receive the leaf that the poet brings back from her walk? This question engages Busta deeply. Since the theme of this part of the work is both linguistic and spiritual regeneration, the uncertain dialogue suggested by "Flaschenpost" addresses the difficult communication between man and man, and man and God as well.

In *Die Scheune der Vögel* Busta's poetry begins to show the formal reduction that will continue to predominate in her later work.[23] Like messages in a bottle the poems are much abbreviated, pared down to their most essential utterances. Gone entirely is the massing of images in favor of one central image; absent also is the radically inverted word order of some of her earlier poetry. Many of the poems are now unrhymed; they are much more the direct personal statements of the poet.

The title of Busta's collection of poetry, *Unterwegs zu älteren Feuern* (1965, *On the Way to Older Fires*), brings a different perspective to the motif of man the traveler with the suggestion of departure once again. Equally important in the title are the journey itself, symbolic of a new beginning and the destination, man's lost cultural traditions. Throughout the work there are optimistic signs that mankind has lost neither the inherent relationship with its spiritual past nor the ability to use poetic language: "In us primeval heavens / create themselves anew and radiate light, / and so we are still fulfilling / the message of the first light" (*Unterwegs,* 72).

Parallel with this more positive perception of man's spiritual inheritance is Busta's belief in the power of her own creative function. The time for passive contemplation is past; the poet must take an active role and speak out on the fundamental issues affecting mankind, as she exhorts her fellow poets to do in a poem entitled "Ihr müßt deutlicher werden (Zu einem Aufruf an die Dichter wider die Atombombe)" (You Must Become Clearer [For an Appeal to the Poets against the Atom Bomb], *Unterwegs,* 44). Through the ages symbolic language has been incapable of changing the course of history, but nevertheless Busta makes a plea for poets to engage themselves in the salvation of our endangered civilization. Each of the four stanzas in the poem begins with the line "Before there was the bomb" and proceeds to cite the conveyors of meaning that existed in the past: "the voice of Sinai," "the voices of the birds," "the whispering of love," "the voices of the children." Appreciation and understanding of religion, nature, love, and children are lost to modern civilization; these aspects of human experience are therefore not represented in contemporary language, which is too abstract to include the strands of earlier tradition. In order to write meaningful poetry today poets must be aware of the possibilities for expression beyond the written word that are part of our cultural heritage. Despite such considerations the potential of the poet is great indeed: her function has become "to bring back home to the heart / the beautiful vulnerable world" (50).

The involvement of the poet in the process of transformation has become much more than that of interpreter of spiritual meaning for her fellow man. In this work the poet transforms visible reality into poetry and is herself transformed in the process. Her three-line poem, "Epitaph," suggests the way in which the poet's sanctuary in nature as depicted in *Der Regenbaum* has now become a personal metamorphosis within nature and extends even beyond death: "Nothing can silence! / Throw earth into my mouth, / and I will sing you grass . . ." (*Unterwegs*, 67).

The schism seen in the previous work between guilt-burdened man and an indifferent nature is symbolically resolved as the poet's voice becomes not conventional language but the perceived utterances of nature itself, the sound of rain or the beating of birds' wings (86). The poet finds the most intimate form of communication in a wordless language.

"Epitaph" cited above is an excellent example of the far simpler and more elliptical form of Busta's poetry in *Unterwegs*.[24] Largely absent now are the many descriptive adjectives and the predominant musicality of her earlier work. The direct expression of this more nominal style grows from the greater personal involvement of the poet; this poetry is truly experienced, not created intellectually.[25] The majority of poems in this collection are in free verse, only a few have traditional form and diction, and the work itself is not structured around formal subsections. The frequency of the one- and two-line poems in the collection shows Busta's fascination with haiku and the "brief small moment of tension and surprise" in that form.[26] In *Unterwegs* the formal economy goes so far that in two poems (50, 72) the title is integrated into the poem optically. Busta uses and expands this technique again in her later collections (see below). At this time she began to paint, and the reader senses in the visual quality of the imagery and the plasticity of form the eye of the artist. Busta recalls that, like Albrecht Dürer, who adjusted his art to the subject matter, she attempted to find within each image its most appropriate form of expression.[27]

The contradiction in the title *Salzgärten* (1975, *Salt Gardens*), is developed in one of the last poems in the collection, where the poet describes a phoenix flower blooming from a salt flat (81). Such objects are symbolic of the human paradox: whenever life seems to promise least, comfort miraculously appears. The hope of resurrection or re-birth that underlies Busta's portrayal of man's increasingly doubtful existence is the inspiration for this volume dedicated to Busta's mother, who died the year before *Salzgärten* appeared. In this collection of exceedingly personal poems, the predominant themes are isolation, suffering, loneliness, and the passage of time. Our situation is bleak indeed, yet we can learn from the fragile wild flowers growing on the barren rock high up in the mountains. Assaulted by the icy wind, receiving scant nourishment from the soil below, endangered even by falling stars, the tiny plants nevertheless flourish (*Salzgärten,* 68).

It is poetry that once more offers the poet a way out of her iso-lation; accordingly, many of the poems are dedicated to her friends and fellow poets. Nevertheless, the reader senses most strongly in this work the frustration of the poet, for whom language and other forms of artistic expression are merely "narrow steps over the abyss" (73). As Leonard Retiz has carefully documented, Busta's crisis of language is closely linked with her existential despair.[28] Her language expresses her skepticism about terms traditionally employed to articulate concepts of Christian beliefs. The poet rejects the language of religious orthodoxy because it has become trivialized:

> The bread and the Word
> have become small change,
> squandering the myths, the utopias.
> We pray for
> the daily trash can (33).

The old myths are dead for us and ready to be discarded; in the poem "Dürre" (Drought), most probably inspired by the droughts and mass starvation in northern Africa during the late 1960s and early 1970s (the poem refers specifically to that geographical area, "[die] Sahelzone"), the poet creates a bleak parody of the biblical quotation, "The Word has become flesh" (John I:14). In a drought "God is the water. / God is the bread, / and the Word / has become bone" (39). For the poet any attempt to find a return to spiritual meaning through regeneration of poetic language is an arduous process: "Language . . . is not spoken, / it is suffered."(8) for there is no new script for her experiences. The language we know cannot make sense of a world in which all values have become questionable. In the poem just cited, "Die Sprache"

(Language), the poet does not reject entirely the presence of myths in modern language, but she says that they are petrified in history and tradition. Because language is overburdened with layers of usage through time, it is difficult for one to be original today. Language has provided us with the bridge from one person to the next, however, and the poem ends more optimistically with a reference to children.

While Busta's early poetry represented the thoughtful imposition of form upon the multiplicity of her experience, here language does not reshape; it simply registers the existence of objects. A process of reduction now leads the poet to record without interpretation. The language and form of the poetry no longer express the earlier process of transformation precisely; Busta uses few significant metaphors, few adjectives, and little connective syntax. While the general condition of the world in *Salzgärten* lacks clarity and legibility, flashes of insight do still occur, and the larger reality becomes transformed by what the objects express about themselves as they stand in isolation: "Misery says misery / and snow nothing more than snow. / A dagger of ice slashes our tongues" (36). In this manner a single slowly spoken word may become a poem in itself: "Say: / Grass stigma. / Say it slowly. / You speak / a finished / poem (79). The role of the poet is now that of dynamic listener, for "We are concerned with the unheard that wants to be *heard* in the encounter of love and suffering between matter and spirit."[29] The italicized use of the verb "hear" suggests a parallel between the natural world demanding articulation from the poet and the Christian asking God for an answer to his prayers. Poetry as service is suggested, since the poet is only one of many "listening posts in the service of the unheard."[30] The poet ends this slender volume with the humble but ironical suggestion that we unravel the entanglement of the written word entirely and send the printed page back to its origins in the forest. Only the spoken word is important, she concludes, since it alone provides the crucial link from man to man and the promise of immortality as well (*Salzgärten,* 15, 92). Appropriate to the new emphasis on the spoken word are the formal characteristics of the poetry in *Salzgärten.* Only one poem in the volume is rhymed (46); the others achieve the naturalness of simple speech. The frequent use of titles integrated into the text also suggests more attention to aural effect than to the appearance of the printed text.

The poet feels that her collection of poetry of 1981, *Wenn du das Wappen der Liebe malst* ... (If You Paint the Escutcheon of Love ...), originated entirely from the spoken word and is therefore the most accessible of her works.[31] Her exhortation (5) to include the humble thistle on the escutcheon of love underscores the poet's compassionate acceptance of all aspects of nature, even the traits generally forgotten or having negative associations. A coat of arms, an identifying feature in knightly battle, suggests that love in all of its manifestations is an experience to be pursued energetically, not passively acquired. Busta's late poetry is imbued with sympathetic understanding of the great difficulties that beset human life. It is a blessing and a curse that we, unlike other creatures, suffer "the terrible freedom / of our choice between good and evil" (31). The tone of the poetry is intimate, conciliatory, even playful as the poet once again retells fairy tales for the modern audience. Busta's epigrammatic lines, "Sätze für Freunde" (Statements for Friends), suggests one-half of a humorous loving dialogue with her friends; a significant line is "LIFE IS PROVOCATION / God's compassion for nothingness" (106). Busta states that her poetry is intended to reach out to her audience comfortingly: "Sometimes a poem / is a shy hand, / that reaches out in the darkness / to a neighbor" (*Wappen,* 8). Poetry can be like a mother's voice that reassures a child not with reason but with the sound of words. Therefore not the content but the sound of poetry is crucial (9). The regeneration of language occurs as each word is lifted out of the linguistic structure of common usage and hence out of clichéd meaning to be examined by itself: in some poems entire stanzas consist of only four or five loosely related words or of a single statement such as the beautifully spare poem, "I would like to learn / from the sunflower / how I turn my face / to You" (7). The integration of title into poem, begun in *Unterwegs* and expanded in *Salzgärten,* is used here in eleven of the poems.

The poet contrasts her work, a process of reduction, with that of her grandfather, a stone carver. While her grandfather carried his stone from the silent forest in order to transform it into an object that conveys meaning, or "speaks" to his society, Busta performs the opposite task. She reduces the cacophony of social language to the preverbal state: "Silence, the first-born word" (109).

Busta's discovery that the essence of poetry is silence validates her development as a poet and the increasing economy of verbal means she employs. In the minimal poems of the mature Busta each word in the poem becomes the bearer of great meaning. In fact, the poet feels that each name for an object is also a cipher for the history of the world; it therefore remains for her only to speak the unadorned words in order to reveal the significant relationships inherent in them:

> Every word means itself
> and at the same time means another.
> Anemone—the flower,
> Anemone—the child.
> All words are ciphers.
>
> Even to say stone or crystal
> is to speak of the history of the universe (*Wappen,* 10).

In contrast to the image in the earlier works of man, the traveler who seeks a return to the nest, in this collection Busta presents an image of the migratory bird leaving the abandoned nest far behind. In "Zugvögel" (Migratory Birds), the poet asks four key questions concerning the eventual destination of the birds, the safety of their passage, and their nests (27). Once again the poet portrays the uncertainty of our existence: none of the questions she poses in the poem is answered.

Given the existential questioning that characterizes the body of the poet's work, it may be surprising that she has also written highly acclaimed children's poetry treating quite different themes. Christine Busta has stated that to enjoy her poetry a reader must understand both its playfulness and the importance of reading it aloud, and her two books of poetry for children grow directly out of this enjoyment of language.[32] The poet feels that her most lasting contribution may be her poetry for children. She wrote for children because "I wanted to find a melodic form that would please parents when they read aloud and would enthrall children through rhyme and content."[33] Busta's language in these books is exuberant with lively rhymes, strong metrical patterns, and—out of sheer pleasure in their sounds—tongue twisters and nonsensical listings of words. The poetry corresponds beautifully to the colorful and amusing illustrations by Johannes Grüger for *Die Sternenmühle* (1959, The Mill of Stars) and Hilde Leiter for *Die Zauberin Frau Zappelzeh* (1979, Mrs. Zappelzeh the Magician). Busta's spontaneous use of language itself generates intimacy with God in a reassuringly safe world which she creates, for these poems are Busta's acknowledgement of the greater yearning she senses in life: "For everything seeks redemption in song."[34] The joy that Busta finds in the world of children she creates is by no means absent in her other poetry, where she acknowledges the ambiguities and uncertainties of life while reaffirming man's basic goodness and the underlying order of the universe.

Busta's popularity with today's audience says as much about the concerns of the contemporary reader of poetry as it does about the quality of her expression and the beauty of her language. The appeal of her poetry lies in its directness, compassion, and ethical engagement. Busta speaks to the fundamental anxieties of the modern reader in a way that identifies her with Hans Naumann's category of "ethical writer." Writing about Franz Werfel sixty years ago, Naumann made the distinction between the ethical and the aesthetic writer with their different kinds of appeal: "Every time demands its poet and may be happy when it finds him, and if there are times when only the aesthetic measure is necessary, there are also times that demand only the ethical measure."[35] After the nadir following World War II and the skepticism about language that ensued, poetry to be relevant had to be morally and ethically, if not politically, engaging. Busta's poetry continues to answer these needs today.

While the poet's loving response to the visual details of the natural world recalls the Austrian writer Adalbert Stifter's "sanftes Gesetz" (gentle law), where what is known to the point of greatest familiarity appears to us suddenly in a new light, the concept of transformation underlying her poetry and giving it its remarkable thematic unity also reaches back to her lyrical forebears, Trakl and Rilke.[36] Her writings are characterized by a creative spirituality, a loving affinity with inanimate objects, and a compassion for all living things. In the future she will continue to inspire the imagination of her readers by making comprehensible for them the language of nature that one may sense but not fully grasp, "Because the things around us are very often strange enough. One doesn't have to make them stranger than they are."[37]

Notes

1. From *Scheune der Vögel: Gedichte,* p. 99. In all further references to the poet's works an abbreviated form of the title will appear with a page number: *Scheune der Vögel* (*Scheune*); *Der Regenbaum: Gedichte* (*Regenbaum*); *Lampe und Delphin: Gedichte* (*Lampe*); *Unterwegs zu älteren Feuern: Gedichte* (*Unterwegs*); *Salzgärten: Gedichte* (*Salzgärten*).
2. *Der Regenengel: Gedichte und Erzählungen: Eine Auswahl* (Leipzig, 1978).

3. Rudolf Henz, "Laudatio für Christine Busta," *Literatur und Kritik,* 43 (March 1970), 130.

4. Among the poet's many awards are the Österreichischer Förderungspreis für Lyrik, 1950 and 1961; George-Trakl-Preis, 1954; Österreichischer Staatspreis für Kinderliteratur, 1959; Jugendbuch-Preis der Stadt Wien, 1959; Preis der Christian Andersen-Stiftung, 1960; Annette von Droste-Hülshoff-Preis der Stadt Meersburg, 1963; Großer Preis für Literatur der Stadt Wien, 1964; Anton Wildgans-Preis der österreichischen Industrie, 1976; Ehrenmedaille der Stadt Wien in Gold, 1980; Charles Péguy-Preis, 1981; Österreichisches Ehrenzeichen für Wissenschaft und Kunst, 1981; Eichendorff-Preis, 1982.

5. Christine Busta, "Dankrede," *Literatur und Kritik* 43 (March 1970), 133-134.

6. From an interview with the poet by Franz Richard Reiter in "Weltverbundenheit durch Lyrik," *Die Presse* (Wien, 13/14 September 1980), no page.

7. Christine Busta, *Das andere Schaf* (Graz, Wien: Stiasny, 1959), p. 32.

8. Containing early poems, this volume was a printing for friends and employees of the Herder Verlag, Vienna. The first edition of *Der Regenbaum* also appeared with this firm; all other collections, including the second edition of *Der Regenbaum,* have been published by Otto Müller Verlag, Salzburg.

9. From an interview with the poet by Renate Doppler in "Lebensversuche," *Welt der Frau* (Linz, December 1975), pp. 11-12.

10. This is only one example of a poem dedicated to the poet's husband. "Fußwaschung" (Washing of Feet, *Wappen,* 92) concludes *In memoriam M.D.* If Maximilian Dimt is meant here, there is an extraordinary parallelism with Christ and with Saint John.

11. Renate Doppler, "Lebensversuche," p. 11.

12. Franz Richard Reiter, "Weltverbundenheit durch Lyrik," no page.

13. See note 3 above. From 1950 to 1975, when she retired, Busta found financial security in her position as Head Librarian at the "Städtische Bücherei" in Vienna while continuing to devote time to her poetry.

14. From a letter quoted by Victor Suchy in his introduction to *Das andere Schaf,* p. 31.

15. In *Doppelinterpretationen,* ed., Hilde Domin (Frankfurt am Main,

Bonn: Athenäum, 1966), pp. 114-115. See also the commentary
by Paul Böckmann on the same poem, pp. 116-119.

16. See Leonard Retiz's discussion of the archetypes lamp and dolphin in this poem in "Faith and Language in a Lyric Cycle by
Christine Busta," *Modern Austrian Literature* 12, nos. 3/4
(1979), 347-372.

17. "kein ding sei wo das wort gebricht." From "Das Wort," *Das neue
Reich,* 1928.

18. Christine Busta discusses with Victor Suchy the importance of
her personal contact with Weinheber in a taped interview of 24
June 1968, no. 191, at the Dokumentationsstelle für neuere
österreichische Literatur in Vienna.

19. From an interview with Frau Busta in Stuttgart, 7 October 1982.

20. Fritz Weilandt, "Das lyrische Werk von Christine Busta," *Formen
der Lyrik in der österreichischen Gegenwartsliteratur,* ed., Wendelin Schmidt-Dengler (Wien: Österreichischer Bundesverlag, 1981),
p. 83.

21. Christine Busta, in *Doppelinterpretationen,* p. 114 ff.

22. Wolfgang Mauser, in *Rivista di Letterature Moderne e Comparate*
IX, no. 4 (1956), 312.

23. In 1959 Gerhard Fritsch traced the growing reduction in the form
of Busta's poetry to "laconic power" and cited her language as
the perfect example of the development to absolute lyrical expression. Fritsch, "Die Welt ist schön und schrecklich (Bemerkungen zu den Gedichten Christine Bustas)," *Welt in der Zeit,* no. 2
(February 1959), 4.

24. See Kurt Adel, "Christine Busta, Lyrik," *Österreich in Geschichte
und Literatur* 20 (1976), 182-206, for an investigation by com-
puter of this development to simpler forms in Busta's poetry.

25. Wolfgang Mauser calls Busta's poetry "erlebt, und nicht erdacht,"
Rivista di Letterature Moderne e Comparate, p. 313.

26. From an interview with Frau Busta in Stuttgart, 7 October 1982.

27. 7 October 1982 interview. Also in the *Neue Kronen-Zeitung*
(Wien, 8 April 1976), no page, the poet remarked, "My school
was the fine arts—I tried to translate the quality of a woodcut
into language."

28. Leonard Retiz, "Faith and Language in a Lyric Cycle by Christine
Busta," p. 370.

29. Christine Busta, "Dankrede," pp. 133-134.

30. Ibid.

31.   The poet has commented, "I have tried to surround language from all sides. One writes about communication, but (often) it doesn't succeed." (Interview, 7 October 1982).

32.   "For me a poem must unnegotiably be spoken. I hear it when I write." (Suchy interview, Tape no. 191).

33.   Quoted by Max Mayr in "Die Sternenmüllerin," *Kleine Zeitung* (Graz, 11 November 1975), no page.

34.   From "Einem jungen Cellospieler" (To a Young Cello Player): "Unknowingly you learn wisdom, and play yourself into / the eternal mystery. / For everything seeks redemption in song." *Unveröffentlichte Gedichte* (Wien: Direktion und Lehrkörper der Höheren Graphischen Bundes-Lehr- und Versuchsanstalt Wien VII, Weihnachten 1965).

35.   Hans Naumann, *Die Deutsche Dichtung der Gegenwart 1885–1924* (Stuttgart: J. B. Metzlersche Verlagsbuchhandlung, 1924), p. 364.

36.   Adalbert Stifter (1805–1868) formulated his concept for the "gentle law" in the prologue to his collection of short stories, *Bunte Steine* (1853). He sees in all manifestations of nature the universal "law of love" that sustains mankind and guides it.

37.   Franz Richard Reiter, "Weltverbundenheit durch Lyrik," no page.

Bibliography

I. Works by Christine Busta in German

Jahr um Jahr: Gedichte. Wien: Herder, 1950.

Der Regenbaum: Gedichte. [1]Wien: Herder, 1951; [2]Salzburg: Otto Müller, 1977.

Die bethlehemitische Legende. Salzburg: Otto Müller, 1954.

Lampe und Delphin: Gedichte. Salzburg: Otto Müller, 1955; [3]1966.

Die Scheune der Vögel: Gedichte. Salzburg: Otto Müller, 1958; [2]1968.

Die Sternenmühle, Gedichte für Kinder und ihre Freunde. Illustrated by Johannes Grüger. Salzburg: Otto Müller, 1959; [5]1974. With a recording.

Das andere Schaf. Selected and introduced by Victor Suchy. Graz, Wien: Stiasny, 1959; [2]1961.

Unterwegs zu älteren Feuern: Gedichte. Salzburg: Otto Müller, 1965; [2]1978.

Unveröffentlichte Gedichte. Wien: Direktion und Lehrkörper der Höheren Graphischen Bundes-Lehr- und Versuchsanstalt Wien VII, Weihnachten 1965.

Salzgärten: Gedichte. Salzburg: Otto Müller, 1975; [2] 1979.

Die Zauberin Frau Zappelzeh, Gereimtes und Ungereimtes für Kinder und ihre Freunde. Illustrated by Hilde Leiter. Salzburg: Otto Müller, 1979.

Wenn du das Wappen der Liebe malst: Gedichte. Salzburg: Otto Müller, 1981.

Inmitten aller Vergänglichkeit: Gedichte. Salzburg: Otto Müller, 1985.

II. Works in English Translation

German Poetry 1910-1975, trans. and ed. Michael Hamburger. New York: Urizen, 1976.

Anthology of Modern German Literature, ed. Adolf Opel. London: Oswald Wolff, 1981.

Austrian Poetry Today: Österreichsche Lyrik heute, eds. and trans. Milne Holton and Herbert Kuhner. New York: Schocken, 1985.

III. Secondary Works in English

Best, Alan. "The Innovator in a Suspect World," *Modern Austrian Writing,* eds. Alan Best and Hans Wolfschütz. London and Totowa, New Jersey: Oswald Wolff and Barnes & Noble, 1980, pp. 128- 141.

Blumenthal, Bernhardt G. "Imagery in Christine Busta's Writings." *Seminar* XIII, no. 2 (1977), 111-116.

Last, Rex. "Paul Celan and the Metaphorical Poets." *Modern Austrian Writing,* eds. Alan Best and Hans Wolfschütz, pp. 142-155.

Miller, J. W. "Christine Busta: Contemporary Austrian Religious Poet." *Studies in Language and Literature,* ed. Charles Nelson. Richmond: Department of Foreign Languages, Eastern Kentucky University, 1976, pp. 391-400.

Retiz, Leonard. "Faith and Language in a Lyric Cycle by Christine Busta."*Modern Austrian Literature* 12, nos. 3/4 (1979), 347-372.

Scott, Marilyn. "Venice/Vineta as a Metaphor in the Poetry of Christine Busta." *Modern Austrian Literature* 18, no. 1 (1985), 83–94.

Scott, Marilyn and Petrus Tax. "Christine Busta and *das Kinderlied:* An Exploration." *Modern Language Notes* 101, no. 3 (1986), 629–658.

IV. Major Studies in German

Adel, Kurt. "Christine Busta, Lyrik: Untersuchung auf statistischer Grundlage." *Österreich in Geschichte und Literatur* 20 (1976), 182–206.

Fassel, Horst. "Zerreißprobe des Natürlichen." *Literatur und Kritik* 122, pp. 103–109.

Haubrichs, Wolfgang. "'Funde' Interpretation eines Gedichtes von Christine Busta." *Saarbrücker Beiträge zur Ästhetik,* eds. Rudolf Malter and Alois Brandstetter. Saarbrücken: Kommissionsverlag Buchhandlung der Saarbrücker Zeitung, 1966, pp. 79–86.

Strutz, Johann. "Krippensermon für unsere Zeit. Über einige Probleme der Lyrik Christine Bustas." *Literatur und Kritik,*nos. 165/166 (1982), 3–15.

Suchy, Victor. Introduction to *Das andere Schaf.* Graz, Wien: Stiasny Bd. 43, 1959.

Weilandt, F. "Das lyrische Werk von Christine Busta." *Formen der Lyrik in der österreichischen Gegenwartsliteratur,* ed. Wendelin Schmidt-Dengler. Wien: Österreichischer Bundesverlag, 1981, pp. 70–94.

*After this article went to press, Christine Busta published one more collection of poetry, *Inmitten aller Vergänglichkeit.* Unfortunately, it was her last: Frau Busta died 3 December 1987 in Vienna.

Paul Celan

Michael Winkler

Many thoughtful readers of modern German literature consider Paul Celan the most innovative poet of the postwar era, perhaps even of this century. Nearly all critical discussion of his work agrees that his artistic achievement stands beyond doubt and controversy. Earlier reactions of impatience and belligerent uncertainty have almost unanimously yielded to at least cautious sympathy. Most often the reaction to Celan's poetry has become one of profound respect for the accomplishment of a radically inventive and meticulously precise use of language. His abiding fame will certainly continue to grow much like the influence of all enduring poetry: with slow and subtle but inescapable force.

But to this day his true stature remains clouded by his image, which is characterized by an aura of sanctified suffering. For it was the expectation of many of Celan's readers that his poetry (and even his life) might somehow serve as a representative sacrifice which could take the place of their own atonement. Celan had no intention of satisfying this kind of expectation, and he refused to accept any public role, most of all that of poetic redeemer. He reacted to these imputations not in the disputatious style of self-righteous disclaimers but with subtle reminders in his verse that true poetry has different purposes. At first he did so with gentle, almost didactic pleas; toward the end of his life with depair and sarcastic anger.

Celan was well aware of the fact that much of his poetry resists spontaneous understanding; and he knew that even his most scrupulous readers found it difficult, if not impossible, to overcome the obstacles he himself had put in the way of ready comprehension. He therefore appealed to those who asked him for help that they read his poems again and again until their meaning becomes apparent. He never ac-

ceded to any request for an exemplary interpretation, and he declined
to provide, aside from a few factual hints, any information about the
intent and background of his poems; he did, however, give many helpful suggestions in the poems themselves about their significations.
Surprising as it may seem, Celan was also keenly interested to find out
how other people responded to his verse, and he was disturbed when he
found a review that was careless or unjust. His relationship with his
readers, especially with professional critics, was a problematical one,
because he often thought himself misunderstood and misappropriated,
a fear that became almost an obsession in his last years. The following
untitled poem, which was included in the last section of the posthumous volume *Schneepart* (1971, Snow Part)[1] expresses this concern
with characteristic force. It may speak for many others:

> AND STRENGTH AND PAIN
> and what pushed me
> and drove me and kept me:
>
> Jubilee-Leap-
> Years,
>
> Fir trees swaying, once,
>
> the poaching conviction growing wildly
> that this ought to be said some other
> way.

The poem evokes a carefully balanced alternation between what provides strength and what causes pain, suggesting a dual impetus of
repulsion and impulsion, of drive and hindrance. This incentive is
sustained by the prospect of the jubilee-year, which marks a time of
joyous fulfillment and new beginnings. As the culmination of seven
sabbatical periods it happens only once every fifty years. This may
seem so distant a future as never to be attainable. But at the same time
fifty years would have been Celan's age when the poem was published.
He did not reach that special time of satisfaction and renewal; yet the
assurance that he was working to attain that moment, that "free" day
which a leap-year grants, gave him purpose and support. So too did the
remembrance of a past associated with an extremely concise and
polyvalent image of fir trees swaying in the wind, which recalls the
language of German poetic and philosophical idealism ("Fichte"),
and which brings to mind the intoxication ("Rausch") that has always

been a part of this tradition. It alludes also to the motif of the darkling forest in Romantic poetry and most prominently to Goethe's "Wandrers Nachtlied" (Wanderer's Evensong) with its promise of safety and eternal rest. Because of the very structure and temper of the poem, however, it is altogether necessary to include in one's recollective associations the subtle though unspoken reminder that Buchenwald (literally: beechwood forest) is the contradictory companion of "Fichtenrausch," as is also in its turn the Bukovina ("Buchenland") of Celan's youth. None of these elements is part of any direct (biographical, causal, or ideological) relationship. They are invoked as the substance of ever-present memory in a poem which looks backward and ahead and which expresses in its conclusion a barely controllable feeling of anger, an emphatic rage, but about what?

It is symptomatic that many commentators read the concluding lines as an admission of very serious self-doubts and as a form of self-refutation. Their understanding of the poem indicates, almost with a sigh of relief, that Celan himself had become convinced his poetry was a failure. If proof be needed, however, the poem itself is sufficient evidence to dispel that notion, suggesting instead that the reader who expects Celan to express himself in a less demanding language is at fault.

In refusing facile appropriation—at the risk of being dismissed as unintelligible—Celan also seeks to protect himself from the response of commodious assent. Often enough he does so by retreating into a privacy of expression that is most sensitively alert to and suspicious of any other use of language. In this way he leaves behind virtually all linguistic conventions, all agreements of syntax and semantic signification, all traditions of metaphorical reference, connotation, and implicit suggestion. What emerges from this descent, as it were, or return to the very roots of language is neither the spontaneous and dreamlike utterance of surrealistic sound-image associations nor a paradoxical plea for the higher truth of silence. It is rather the arduous process of exploratory reordering, which begins with the smallest particles of words and with fragments of minimal meaning. Celan's poetry reassembles individual words with all their possible nuances to establish new constellations that point to possible, though as yet utopian, forms of community. His language is in search of reality and must transform and absorb what exists into its domain. For Celan this continual task was not merely a thematic concern about which he wrote poems in a secretive, lyrical language; it had become rather a process that informs the very impetus and direction in much of his work, and as such it is directly expressed as poetry. This process required no less than the creation of a new language in German, paradoxically speaking: a *lingua Adamica* for the future. Its vocabulary is chosen with scrupulous care and through its combinations has evolved to a large extent into an idiom both of neologisms and of etymologies that are traced back to their original meanings. Its key words with all their semantic shadings and densities are not only retained as points of orientation throughout his *oeuvre,* thus establishing a firm sense of stability; they also are reexamined constantly to affirm their validity ever anew. As a result Celan's poetry provides its own network of ciphers, topoi, and symbolic images, which attest to the expanding continuity and to the flexible constancy of his writing.

This apparent absorption in the intricacies of language as a self-constructed "hermetic" code, which seems excessive even for a modernist *poeta doctus,* has given rise to a curious accusation. It is the charge that Celan was attracted by the intellectual challenge inherent in an existentialist aesthetic of absolutist poetry more than he was committed to the poetic evocation of experienced reality, that he relinquished much of the world in order to capture words. His answer to this suspicion that his poetry shared the solipsism of meta-art was neither to insist on the subjective authenticity of private experience nor to allow the language of art as a medium of encounter and dialogue to withdraw into the purity of silence. "May we, as now happens so often, assume that art is something preexistent, something absolutely to be presupposed; should we, to put it quite specifically, above all—let us say—accept Mallarmé's premises and follow them to their logical conclusions?"[2] We should not! For the poem, though it shows a strong inclination "to succumb to muteness," sustains its precarious ability to speak "by expressing through its singular and immediate presence the distinct character of its time. It is the objective recording of personal experience." And what then would be its images? "That which once, once and again, and only now and only here, has been perceived and is to be perceived. And the poem would therefore be the place where all tropes and metaphors want to be shown their own absurdity."[3]

This *reductio ad absurdum* is an ambivalent process. It demonstrates through counterexample how inadequate all mimetic imagery is to the task of poetry after Hitler, Stalin, and Hiroshima. It also shows that the perversions of this era, which defy any return to the traditions of logical discourse, require a paradoxical structure of image and syntax. For only through paradox does the reality of non-sense become transparent as the absurd, as "the majesty of the absurd," which "testifies to the presence of the human" and which "is known by one of its names as—poetry."[4] This characterization of poetry as an exemplary instance of the absurd appears in the form and context of a poetological statement. More appropriately though it should be read as part of a poetic projection, for Celan does not give an analytical definition here. On the contrary, he used the terminology of a then popular tradition of existentialism to confront or perhaps simply to allude to its ideological tenets—not to indicate that he had made them his own.

Such an identification, for example with Camus's analysis of the myth of Sisyphus, appeared all the more plausible, since many of the poems that Celan wrote toward the end of the 1950s contain religious motifs and make use of imagery traditionally associated with Judeo-Christian devotion. They are often cast in the rhythm of an elegiac lament for the nonexistence of God, and they seek to find language that would make a *deus absconditus* accessible again. This approach persuaded many of his readers that Celan was not so much a poet as a God-seeker with the religious fervor of an existentialist mystic, and that his poetry was like the visionary annunciation of sacred text. Celan abhorred the role of ontological *vates* with its implications of profundity and surrogate torment. He considered it a grave misunderstanding to assume that he had taken it upon himself to suffer for Germany. His reaction, however, eschewed the form of public disclaimer or corrective polemic, which in turn should not suggest that he had come to accept Heidegger's stance of silence. He responded only in poetry, for example in the following masterpiece of sublime sarcasm:[5]

> LAVISH ANNOUNCEMENT
> in a crypt where
> we are swaying,
> our gas flags aflutter,
>
> we're surrounded here
> by the odor
> of sanctity, y'know.
>
> Igniferous
> clouds from beyond
> emanate from our pores, densely,

> every second case of
> tooth
> decay brings forth
> an indestructible anthem.
>
> That farthing's worth of twilight that you threw in,
> come on, down the hatch with it.

The poem repudiates especially the inclination to attach an aura of sanctity to the holocaust victims and survivors. It expresses an attitude of unmitigated scorn directed against the presumptuous solace that their existence is destined for an unusual degree of metaphysical dignity and poetic elevation. For this purpose Celan imitates the tone of colloquial joviality with satiric precision, fully cognizant at the same time that the overwhelming show of "cordiality" that is extended to the dead of the gas chambers will tolerate no oppositional exception. That small measure of resistance, which throws the different "light of ambivalence" on what appears to be perfectly clear, is constantly invited to give up its contradictions and be absorbed by the "comforts" of majority opinion.

Celan was an incessant reader and a person of both extensive and concentrated learning, familiar not only with contemporary thought in many disciplines but also with many different cultural traditions and literatures, especially those of Europe. But he did not devise a poetic language in order to articulate any specific philosophical doctrine or any systematic convictions. The truth of his images is rather that of an uncompromising search for evidence of human goodness and honesty. This form of truth has learned how to live with the realization that beyond this fundamental verity there is only the irreducible multivalence of implications. This position suggests anything but the trite apology that there are no straightforward answers and simple solutions. It asserts its self-identity at the ultimate risk of self-negation and rejects whatever support any invitation to complicity may offer:[6]

> STANDING, in the shadow
> of the wounds' memorial in the air.
>
> Standing-for-nobody-and-nothing.
> Unrecognized,
> for yourself
> alone.

With all that has room in it,
even without
language.

Overshadowed by the reality of the concentration camp crematoria, which has left, as it were, a permanent scar in the air, the poem (and its persona) speaks for itself because it stands for nothing but itself. There is no need for further discussion, which implies also that the less talk there is about the "unspeakable" the better. But the poem does not stand in isolation. It refers back to an earlier poem, and through this allusion it evokes a modern poetic tradition or, perhaps more specifically, its popular reception. The poem "Psalm" in the volume *Die Niemandsrose* (1963, Noman's Rose) had spoken of the "nothing-, / the noman's rose."[7] This rose is a flower that against all logical expectation owes its imaginary existence to a desperately searching desire for and remembrance of beauty. It blooms as a flower of beauty wrested from evil, not as a *fleur du mal,* and it praises paradoxically that Noman who grants no rebirth to that Nothing which "we" (the singers of this psalm) were, are, and will continue to be. This most precarious coexistence of beauty and the irredeemable finiteness of death also recalls Rilke's epitaph.[8] In a gesture of "pure contradiction" its rose expresses the fervent desire to be and takes pleasure in being nothing but itself. In doing so it contradicts our tendency to construct an analogy between petals and eyelids and to postulate a metaphorical correspondence between them and sleep as a figure of speech for death. For this reason it should not come as a surprise that Celan's "Psalm" (along with a number of similar poems from the same cycle) has given occasion, much as have Kafka's stories, to the most divergent, even contradictory, interpretations. All of them find some form of support in the text, but few of them do justice to the poem's anti-doctrinal refusal to speak for any point of view, whether religious, philosophical, psychological, political, historical or whatever. The poem reinforces nothing outside itself, but its own multivalent meaning has accumulated all these extrinsic significations and has, so to speak, negated them as its own position. It speaks as a silent reminder only for itself.

This nonpartisan reserve is not to be mistaken for a lack of solidarity with those who share Celan's experiences and concerns. But it is necessary to emphasize his insistence on this freedom of "uncommitted" solitude, because he had come to be gravely disturbed by the popularity of the one poem that had made him famous. This is the

"Death Fugue" of 1945, which was first published as the third and concluding section of his first volume of verse, *Der Sand aus den Urnen* (1948, The Sand from the Urns). It is probably the most frequently anthologized and interpreted poem in German postwar literature and the one often cited to refute Adorno's dictum about the impossibility of poetry after Auschwitz. There is no doubt that this intricate poem had a strong emotional effect on many readers. Perhaps it even brought about, not unlike Brecht's *Mutter Courage* (*Mother Courage*), a more than fleeting catharsis in some of them. But in the course of time it has been abused too often in the interest of legitimating the many pretensions of German-Jewish conciliation. This "false" reception aggravated also the sincere concern that Celan had used an imaged language too melodious, too harmoniously balanced, and too seductively mannered, even fascinating, to express appropriately the real experienced horror from which it takes its cues.

Celan often came back to this poem, and in the end he did not permit its republication in anthologies. But he also recalled it in his poetry in the form of slightly altered and sometimes cryptic self-quotes. These partial reformulations do not so much refute the poem as they denounce the compensatory functions and the apologetic misuse to which it was often subjected. One of its dominant fugal themes that had become a kind of slogan ("Death is a master from Germany") reappears in the following poem from the volume *Atemwende* (1967, Breath Turning):[9]

> NO MORE SANDART, no sandbook, no masters.
>
> No gain from dice. What sum of
> silents?
> Seventen.
>
> Your question-your answer,
> Your song, what's its wit?
>
> Deepinsnow,
> Eepinow,
> E-i-o.

A nonsense poem which in a mood of profound disillusionment slides into meaningless babble where it suffocates from its own frustration? A negative reaction of this sort may be premature and in need of rethinking for the German reader at least should have no difficulty equating the numbers on dice with "eyes" (*Augen*). These "eyes" are to be counted, and they should add up to a specific sum, just as eyes should see, and this seeing should be close to understanding. It may be more demanding to recognize the association of these two interdependent implications with Mallarmé's poem, "Coup des Dés" (Throw of Dice), which uses the topos of the throw of dice as an emblem of *fortuna* and as a symbolist image for human destiny. Celan alludes to this tradition of poetic signification, but he denies its continued credibility because in his "game" the numbers do not add up. Thus they say and mean nothing. Question and answer have become identical, and a radically exposed language reduced as it is to its elementary particles can be made to yield new crystallizations only on its own terms. Its terminology employs ever more often the "esoteric" and "antipoetic" idiom of the "pure" scientific disciplines (physics, medicine, geology, botany, etc.) in a precarious attempt to overcome an impasse of poetic communication. This impasse does not end in a deadlock, but, as a stretto ("Engführung"),[10] it provides the impetus for altogether unexpected interplays between language and reality, for new cognitive structures and new semantic densities. Their provenance and distinct character may be definable in psychoanalytical categories ("cumulative traumatization," "schizoid withdrawal after a breakdown of defense mechanisms"), but their impact is of more than private and individual relevance. Despite their intensely personal immediacy Celan's experiences have a very broad and deep social significance. For this reason a summary of his biography should not be misunderstood as providing the kind of personal information that seems prerequisite to an explanation of his poetic style. Knowledge of such details may help to clarify possibly obscure points of reference in an *oeuvre* that abounds with "autobiographical" signals and that always wanted to be accepted as an urgent invitation to inquiry and exploration, as a plea that readers should find out as much as possible for themselves. But the facts of Celan's life, about which he was very protective, do not allow us to act as though they enable us to understand why he wrote the way he did. Poetic authenticity is neither dependent on nor identical with the sum and truth of biography.

Paul Antschel was born on 23 November 1920 in Czernowitz, the capital of northern Bukovina, which had been a crownland of the Hapsburg Monarchy. The city was proud of its reputation as "Little Vienna," cherished its status as a regional center of Austro-German traditions, and had retained much of its cultural autonomy when it became the northernmost province of Romania after the Treaty of Saint-Germain

(1919). It was a prosperous city with an ethnically mixed population of 110,000, of whom nearly half were Jews. The poet's parents came from solid lower-middle-class families with roots in the country and ties to the professional bourgeoisie. His father worked as a broker in the firewood business with less than solid success. He observed the laws of his faith dutifully, had Zionist ambitions, insisted on rigorous discipline, and often resorted to strict punishment. His son suffered under his rigid sense of duty and came to detest him for it. Celan's mother, though often intimidated by her husband's claim to superior authority, was very kind, considerate, and loving to her only child and encouraged his artistic talents. He in turn adored his mother. His father sent him to a Zionist grade school. This became a traumatic experience because he was forced to learn Hebrew and to accept an often brutal regimen. The ten-year-old appears to have been a lonely child, often withdrawn and without friends when in the fall of 1930 he entered a state *Gymnasium* (Liceul Ortodoy de Băeţi), the traditional high school for the Romanian élite. It tolerated but did not encourage the attendance of Jewish pupils, who were required to become proficient in the official state language. After four years of anti-Semitic pressure Paul was transferred to a formerly Jewish institution, the Fourth Ukrainian Gymnasium, a traditionally liberal school from which he graduated in 1938 with the "Baccalaureat"-diploma. His later years as a student were more pleasant than his childhood, especially since he had completely separated himself from his father and found the friendship of kindred companions. He had also become an avid reader of literature, most congenially perhaps of Rilke, Hölderlin, Trakl, and Nietzsche. He had also started to write his own poetry and to recite it to small groups of appreciative friends. Upon graduation he took his father's advice to prepare for a career as a medical doctor even though political conditions forced him to enroll in a French university. Paul and other students from Czernowitz favored the "École preparatoire de médicine" in Tours. He went to France by way of Cracow, Berlin—where he arrived on November 10, the night after the *Kristallnacht*—and Brussels, spent an apparently uneventful year, and went back to his hometown in July 1939 for summer vacation. After the outbreak of war had made his return to France impossible, he matriculated at the local university to study Romance philology. When northern Bukovina was incorporated into the Soviet Union in June 1940, he also learned Russian in a very short time and took the obligatory courses in Marxism-Leninism and in the history of the Communist Party. The following year, during the Ger-

man occupation of the area, his parents were deported to an SS-concen-
tration camp in Transnistria, where they were forced to work in a
quarry ("Cariera de Piatră") near the Bug river. They and thousands of
other Jews were murdered there. Paul managed to hide during the
roundup and survived precariously in a Romanian labor camp, from
which he was released in February 1944. In the fall, after the Red
Army had reconquered Czernowitz, he resumed his university studies,
this time as a student of English literature. In April 1945, to avoid becoming a Soviet citizen, he fled to Bucharest, where he found work in a
publishing house as a reader and translator of Russian literature. During
his two-and-a-half years in Romania he maintained contacts with a
small group of modernist *litterati* and returned to writing poetry. For
his first publication (three poems in a journal, *Agora,* which was dis-
continued after its initial issue), he used the anagram of his family name
in Romanian orthography: Celan. When it was obvious that his native
country would soon become a satellite state of the Soviet Union, he
fled to Vienna in December 1947. There he was introduced on the
recommendation of the poet Alfred Margul-Sperber to a number of
young Austrian artists, among them Edgar Jené and the poet Ingeborg
Bachmann, who was to memorialize their friendship in her novel
Malina (1971). He wrote his first volume of poetry, *Der Sand aus den
Urnen,* after he had left Vienna for Paris in July 1948. This edition of
500 copies was so full of misprints, however, that he had it withdrawn.
Half of the original number of poems was included in his first "author-
ized" book of poems, *Mohn und Gedächtnis* (1952, Poppy and Remembrance). In Paris he began to study German literature and linguistics
formally, obtaining his Licence ès Lettres in 1950 and the position of
lecturer at the École Normale Supérieur in the Rue d'Ulm in 1959.
Before his academic appointments he had earned his living as a language
tutor, freelance writer, and translator. In May 1952 he read some of
his poems at the annual meeting of Group 47 in Niendorf on the Baltic
Sea, which brought him to the attention of the German literary avant-
garde. Later that year he married the artist Gisèle Lestrange. Their son
Francois died a few hours after birth and their second son Eric was
born in 1955, the year his new volume of poems *Von Schwelle zu
Schwelle* (1955, From Threshold to Threshold), was published. The
award of the Literature Prize of the Free Hansa City of Bremen in 1958
signaled the beginning of Celan's public reputation, which was further
enhanced by the award of the Georg-Büchner-Prize by the German
Academy for Language and Poetry (Darmstadt) in 1960. But he also

had to endure a painful controversy when the widow of the surrealist poet Yvan Goll (1891–1950), whose acquaintance Celan had made in November 1949, accused him of plagiarism, a totally unfounded charge that gained widespread notoriety. After *Sprachgitter* (1959, Speech Grill), a title that uses the *fenestra locutaria,* the small window in the parlatorium of convents, as its central metaphor, Celan published his most acclaimed volume, *Die Niemandsrose* (1963). During his last seven years he wrote almost 300 poems, which in addition to five private bibliophile printings were collected in the following volumes: *Atemwende* (1967), *Fadensonnen* (1968, Thread Suns), *Lichtzwang* (1970, Force of Light), *Schneepart* (1971), and *Zeitgehöft* (1976, Farmhouse of Time), a posthumous edition of his last poems.

In 1961 the Academy of Arts in West Berlin elected Celan to its membership, and he used this occasion for a trip to Germany, which was followed by brief stays in other European countries. These visits were usually of a private nature, though they sometimes coincided with invited readings before university audiences. Therefore no such activities should be considered a matter of an active participation in the public cultural life of either Germany or France. Still a reclusive outsider, Celan became in 1968 coeditor of a journal of experimental writing, *L'Ephémère.* In 1969 he went almost secretly to Israel to find out whether he might live there. He decided against immigration and returned to Paris, where he took his life, probably on 20 April 1970, the last possible way to express the true self. He is buried in the suburban cemetery of Thiais under the name of Paul Antschel.

Celan was a poet first and foremost. His prose writings include no more than one short narrative, "Gespräch im Gebirg" (1959, Conversation in the Mountains); an introduction to a catalogue of lithographs, *Edgar Jené und der Traum vom Traume* (1948, Edgar Jené – the Dream of the Dream); *Gegenlicht* (1949, Counter Light); and four very concise answers to requests for statements on issues of poetry and politics. His acceptance speeches for the Bremen and Darmstadt prizes, the latter entitled "Der Meridian" (1960, The Meridian), are important poetological reflections. Equally important are his translations, which add up to well over a third of his total *oeuvre.* They include selections of modernist French and Russian poetry, but also sonnets of Shakespeare as well as American, Italian, and Romanian verse and a small sampling of David Rokeah's Hebrew lyrics. Despite his proficiency in six languages Celan did not translate from German into these languages and used only German for his own writing.

Celan's beginnings as a poet are no longer subject to speculation. Extensive quotations from the carefully copied manuscripts of his years in Czernowitz are included in Israel Chalfen's biography of his youth;[11] a two-volume facsimile edition of ninety-seven poems from the years 1938 through 1944, which Celan had copied in minuscule calligraphic handwriting on the pages of an old black, leather-bound advertising calendar for his friend, the actress Ruth Lackner, has just been published.[12] These sources and the corrected republication of his first book make possible a reasonably accurate estimate of his early themes and style. The examples of Rilke and of symbolist imagery were a strong precept. Long mellifluous lines with a carefully balanced interplay of rhythmic and sound qualities predominate. They use suggestively expressive variations of metric pacing and subtle techniques of rhetorical persuasion with an abundance of nature imagery alternating between urgency and expansiveness, setting up word clusters through repetition and accumulation and juxtaposing them with an open-ended melodious form of declamation. A tone of impatient sadness, of constrained accusation and of bitter memory comes to the fore and is counteracted by a drive for liberating self-assertion. Many poems seek to find some form of mastery over an outside world that is suffused with a multitude of images. Celan's early language is seldom direct, and only in rare moments is it simply declarative. It is often heavily garnished with the fluid splendor of surrealist metaphors, and it is sustained by a lavish evasive symbolism. Its dreamlike blending of clear perception with the distortions of fantasy and the kaleidoscopic constellations of reconstructive memory produce a sometimes excessively ornate style, a mannered aestheticism. It is a distinctive language, however, rich in its sonorities and in its imaged sensual impressions. It contrasts markedly with the terse factual quality of much poetry that was written during the immediate postwar years, but its tendency to let inventive wordiness circumvent the controls demanded by experienced reality makes it also somehow inappropriate for its objective task. Its themes are, after all, the experience of horror and death, the feeling of loss and isolation, the sense of guilt and despair, as well as the temptation to forget and the search for compassionate responses.

There is no doubt that Celan began to write poetry out of an overwhelming need to subordinate all aspects of life past and present to an order of beauty. This need allowed him to expand his expressive abilities to the limits of their inherent legitimacy, but it also seduced him more than occasionally into extending too far the boundaries that stand between brutal reality and the transcending process of its sublimation through the metaphors of art. Celan was intensely conscious of this danger and accepted its risks in the belief that there are no preferable alternatives. The poem "Spät und Tief" (Late and Deep)[13] is an early formulation of this conflict. It begins with two opposite attitudes toward language: "Spiteful as aureate speech is the start of this night. / We eat the apples of the mute. / We do a work that one likes to pass on to one's star." Then it develops and sustains this contrast in which Celan includes himself among those who have chosen the more difficult task of unobtrusive simplicity. Thereafter it restates this difference in the central antithesis: "You grind 'neath the millstone of death the white flower of promise, / You place it before our brothers and sisters — // We brandish the white hair of time . . ." and affirms its right against the charge of "blasphemy" with the (at first sarcastic) invocation:

> We know very well,
> let guilt come upon us.
> Let guilt come upon us with signs of every warning.
> Let the gurgling sea come,
> the up-in-arms gust of reversal,
> the day with midnight at noon.
>
> Let come what was never before!
>
> Let a man come from his grave.

The poem also refutes the suggestion that faith in human resurrection and in the promise of an afterlife is anything more than the work of pious deception. At the same time Celan expresses a self-conscious dissatisfaction with his need for emphatic circumlocution. He develops a style of greater restraint and concentration and the awareness that "a changing key" is needed to "unlock the house in which the snow of what is being kept silent drifts."[14] This style is fully achieved in his third collection, Sprachgitter, after the somewhat hesitant and, as it were, transitional innovations of the Threshold poems. The persuasive intent of the later book is predicated to a remarkable degree on the realization that, so much else being said, discussed, described, and postulated, it may be the poet's duty to plead for and practice utter self-control if not commemorative silence:[15]

> Whichever stone you lift —
> you lay bare

those who need the protection of stones:
naked
they renew the entanglement.

Whichever tree you fell —
you construct
the bedstead on which
the souls once again jam up,
as if this aeon had not
its own tremors.

Whichever word you speak —
you thank
perdition.

This reserve also means an undoing and a gradual reconstitution of the narrative connections which had come with such apparent ease in Celan's early poetry. The return from the "too much of my speaking" to the "small crystal that is borne in your silence"[16] leads to "encounters again with / isolated words," words such as: snow, ice, crystal, eye, tear, light, earth, stone, ashes, shadow, and a small number of others that provide the frame for a new poetic construct.

With *Die Niemandsrose* Celan reached his greatest versatility and his most expressive precision. This subtly interacting cycle of fifty-three poems in four sections contains a release of seemingly boundless energy and shows the strength of that self-assurance which comes with a major poetic breakthrough. It is as though all the concentrated hesitation, which the exemplary poem "Stretto" ("Engführung") at the end of *Sprachgitter* upheld, was now allowed to burst forth and to find the appropriate direction for its multifarious voices. There is a full recapitulation and expansion of thematic concern including prominently the fate of poets who live under dictatorial regimes. The remembrance of an East European culture before the Soviet occupation, the realities of life in times of ideological warfare, and the search for indications of public morality find forceful and often direct expression. And so does above all the unsparing confrontation with what is now known as the Holocaust—a word Celan never uses—and with the contemporary evasions to which its "unspeakable" horror has given rise. *Die Niemandsrose* is also Celan's most distinctly Jewish poetry, thematically in its elegiac evocation of instances from a rich tradition that is forever destroyed and in its search for the redemptive recreation of the images and processes that define a meditative search for evidence of the divine and for possibilities of mystical communion.

Principal guides in this search were the writings of Martin Buber and the interpretations of the Kabbala by Gershom Sholem. It was for Celan the exploration of a path "upward and back," of a contemplative ascent toward "the heart-bright future" which, in the poem "Anabasis,"[17] is that of the liberating and perhaps even absolution-granting "tent-word: // Together." The attainment of this goal is envisioned ever more often in circular terms through the images, for example, of the meridian, the boomerang, and the dial on clock faces,[18] which mark the return to an origin after a course of projective probings. Frequent interruptions and deviations make a slow and gradual resumption of this journey necessary, a journey which is always also the search for words.

Often the encounters with the world outside with their tentative accumulation of contacts and experiences lead to pauses and moments of silence. Most characteristically these are overcome with a single word in Hebrew, which like an insular piece of firm ground becomes the poem's antithesis to the unsafe footing all around. Reliance on this kind of certainty permits also a greater measure of "narrative" complexity and progression. This may also indicate the possibility that the conflict between experience and its artistic transmutation has now been resolved in a manner that allows an attitude of aesthetic distance and even of freedom to absorb the facts of life and history in less directly personal ways than before.

From this vantage point Celan could imagine, against the overwhelming burden of contrary evidence and only in one poem, that a situation might exist in which the accustomed course of human history has reversed itself:

> THE CHIMNEY SWALLOW stood at her zenith, the arrow-sister,
>
> the One on the airdial
> flew toward the hour hand,
> deep into the chimes,
>
> the shark
> spat out the living Inca,
>
> it was landrush-time
> in humanland,

all things
turned around,
unsealed like us.[19]

This poem attempts the utopian evocation of a new beginning, of a New World with a future that has come to terms with and has reversed the practices of its ever-present past. There is full cognizance at this timeless moment of those whose lives went up in smoke and dissolved into the air. The arrow of Sagittarius, under whose sign Celan was born, suggests self-identification. It points in the direction of the sisterly swallow, an erotic hint as much as a sign of spiritual affinity. Under this constellation the normal manner of measuring time has been turned around. Time is told now by the airdial ("Luft-Uhr")—a word formed in analogy to sundial ("Sonnenuhr") but avoiding its association with sunlight. From this perspective a time of colonization is imagined in which the seemingly indestructible concatenation of the cultural claims of the Siglo de Oro, for example, with the murderous greed of the Conquista is broken. The poem refers to a past (which, in itself, was the beginning of the modern era) in totally revolutionary terms and with the assurances of complete liberation.

But it would be misleading to conclude this discussion on such an optimistic note. Celan's last two years were a time of almost crippling anxieties and phobias rather than of cautious hope. His marriage had come to an end, fears of Neonazism and a revival of anti-Semitism haunted him, the disillusionment over Israel's (but not only Israel's) patriotic militarism was a heavy burden, the fear that his readers were beginning to desert him grew ever stronger, the obsession with guilt over his parents' death became unbearable. Yet he continued to write poems, introspective verse with a strong tendency to recapitulate earlier images in the context of aphoristic abbreviations. His poetry had become a form of expression that defies comparison and that remains a challenge to its readers in its open-ended though unerring sense of direction. His last poem dated 13 April 1970[20] may testify to this sense in exemplary manner:

Rebleute graben	Vinegrowers dig up
die dunkelstündige Uhr um,	the darkhoured clock, turning
Tiefe um Tiefe,	depth upon depth,
du liest,	you read,

es fordert	the Invisible
der Unsichtbare den Wind	challenges the wind
in die Schranken,	to a joust,
du liest,	you read,
die Offenen tragen	the open ones bear
den Stein hinterm Aug,	the stone behind the eye,
der erkennt dich,	it will recognize you,
am Sabbath.	come Sabbath.

Notes

1. The most complete and reliable edition of Paul Celan's works to date is the five-volume *Gesammelte Werke* edited by Beda Allemann and Stefan Reichert, with the assistance of Rudolf Bücher (Frankfurt am Main: Suhrkamp, 1983). I have used it exclusively in preparing the translations for this essay. All quotes from Celan are therefore identified with reference to the originals and with standard abbreviations. The German text for the first quote can be verified in volume II, page 398, i.e., II, p. 398.

2. Paul Celan, *Gesammelte Werke,* vol. III, p. 193.

3. Ibid., p. 199.

4. Ibid., p. 190.

5. This is the fourth poem in section IV of Paul Celan's *Fadensonnen* II, p. 192.

6. This is poem 13 in part I of Paul Celan's *Atemwende* II, p. 23.

7. This is poem 14 in part I of Paul Celan's *Die Niemandsrose* I, p. 235.

8. Rose, oh reiner Widerspruch, Lust, / Niemandes Schlaf zu sein unter soviel / Lidern. Cf. Rainer Maria Rilke, *Sämtliche Werke. Sechs Bände,* ed. Ernst Zinn (Frankfurt am Main: Insel, 1955–1966); II (1956), p. 185.

9. This is the fifth poem in section II, p. 39.

10. "Engführung" is the unnumbered concluding section of Paul Celan's *Sprachgitter* I, pp. 195–204.

11. Israel Chalfen, *Paul Celan. Eine Biographie seiner Jugend* (Frankfurt am Main: Insel, 1979). The information on Celan's youth in the present essay derives almost exclusively from this book.

12. Paul Celan, *Gedichte 1938–1944;* with a foreword and annotations by Ruth Kraft (Frankfurt am Main: Suhrkamp, 1985).

13. Paul Celan, *Gesammelte Werke* I, pp. 35–36. This poem, entitled "Deukalion and Pyrrha" in the first edition of *Der Sand aus den Urnen* (III, 58), had different punctuation and a different last line: "Es komme der Mann mit der Nelke" (Let the man with the carnation come), as compared with: "Es komme ein Mensch aus dem Grabe." It is more easily apparent from the original title that the allusions are primarily to the son of Prometheus and to his wife, the daughter of Epimetheus and Pandora, who were saved in an ark after Zeus had decreed the destruction of the earth in a flood and who became the progenitors of a new human race.

14. This is a quote from the poem "Mit wechselndem Schlüssel" (With a Changing Key) from the middle section with the same title of Paul Celan's *Von Schwelle zu Schwelle* I, p. 112.

15. This is the fourth poem in the third and final section "Inselhin" (Toward the Island) of Ibid., p. 129.

16. "Und das Zuviel meiner Rede: / angelagert dem kleinen / Kristall in der Tracht deines Schweigens." This is the third stanza of Paul Celan's "Unten" (Below), Ibid., p. 157.

17. Ibid., p. 256.

18. Most characteristically perhaps in the poem "EIN WURFHOLZ, auf Atemwegen," Ibid., p. 258.

19. Ibid., p. 216.

20. My reading of this poem is indebted to the interpretive translation of John Felsteiner, "Translating Celan's Last Poem," *American Poetry Review* XI, no. 4 (1982), 21-27.

Bibliography

I. Works by Paul Celan in German

Der Sand aus den Urnen. Wien: A. Sexl, 1948.
Mohn und Gedächtnis. Stuttgart: Deutsche Verlags-Anstalt, 1952.
Von Schwelle zu Schwelle. Stuttgart: Deutsche Verlags-Anstalt, 1955.
Sprachgitter. Frankfurt am Main: S. Fischer, 1959.
Die Niemandsrose. Frankfurt am Main: S. Fischer, 1963.
Atemwende. Frankfurt am Main: Suhrkamp, 1967.
Fadensonnen. Frankfurt am Main: Suhrkamp, 1968.
Lichtzwang. Frankfurt am Main: Suhrkamp, 1970.
Schneepart. Frankfurt am Main: Suhrkamp, 1971.

Gedichte in zwei Bänden. Frankfurt am Main: Suhrkamp, 1975.
Zeitgehöft. Frankfurt am Main: Suhrkamp, 1976.
Gesammelte Werke in fünf Bänden. Frankfurt am Main: Suhrkamp 1983.
Gedichte 1938–1944. Frankfurt am Main: Suhrkamp, 1985.

II. Works in English Translation

Speech-Grill and Selected Poems, trans. Joachim Neugroschel. New
   York: Dutton, 1971.
Selected Poems, trans. Michael Hamburger and Christopher Middleton.
   Harmondsworth: Penguin, 1972.
Prose Writings and Selected Poems, trans. Walter Billeter and Jerry
   Glenn. Carlton (Vic.): Paper Castle, 1977.
Poems, trans. Michael Hamburger. New York: Persea and Manchester
   (UK): Carcanet, 1980.
Last Poems, trans. Katherine Washburn and Margret Guillemin. San
   Francisco: North Point, 1986.

III. Secondary Works in English

Cameron, Beatrice A. *Anticomputer: An Essay on the Work of Paul
   Celan, Followed by Selected Poems in Translation.* Dissertation,
   University of California, Berkeley, 1973.
Colin, Amy D., ed. *Argumentum e Silentio. International Paul Celan
   Symposium – Internationales Paul Celan-Symposium.* Berlin,
   New York: de Gruyter, 1987.
Foot, Robert. *The Phenomenon of Speechlessness in the Poetry of
   Marie Luise Kaschnitz, Günter Eich, Nelly Sachs and Paul Celan.*
   Bonn: Bouvier, 1982.
Glenn, Jerry. *Paul Celan.* New York: Twayne, 1973.
———. "Paul Celan in English: A Bibliography of Primary and Second-
   ary Literature," *Studies in 20th Century Literature* VIII, no. 1
(Fall 1983), 129–150 and "Paul Celan: A Selected Bibliography
   of Recent Secondary Literature," ibid., pp. 131–150.
Lyon, James K. *"Nature": Its Idea and Use in the Poetic Imagery of
   Ingeborg Bachmann, Paul Celan, and Karl Krolow.* Dissertation,
   Harvard University, 1962.

Robinson, Donna. *Paul Celan's Ich-Du Dilemma: Its Relationship to the Themes of Poetic Language and the Holocaust.* Dissertation, University of Cincinnati, 1977.

IV. Major Studies in German

Janz, Marlies. *Vom Engagement absoluter Poesie: Zur Lyrik und Ästhetik Paul Celans.* Frankfurt am Main: Syndikat, 1976.
Schulz, Georg-Michael. *Negativität in der Dichtung Paul Celans.* Tübingen: Niemeyer, 1977.
Voswinckel, Klaus. *Paul Celan. Verweigerte Poetisierung der Welt: Versuch einer Deutung.* Heidelberg: Stiehm, 1974.
Wiedemann-Wolf, Barbara. *Antschel Paul — Paul Celan. Studien zum Frühwerk.* Tübingen: Niemeyer, 1985.

Franz Theodor Csokor

Michael R. Mitchell

Franz Theodor Csokor is known primarily as a dramatist with some forty plays to his name as well as four volumes of poetry plus two of short stories and two longer prose works. He was born in 1885 and brought up in Vienna in a middle-class family—his father was a doctor and professor of veterinary medicine—which was a typically Austro-Hungarian blend (Csokor himself uses the English word) of Serbian, Croat, German, Czech, and Hungarian ancestors. He describes how his origins in a multinational empire and more particularly in the racial melting pot of Vienna were a key factor in the formation of the ideal of a humanism beyond race and nation which is at the heart of his outlook.

The start of his literary career had an international flavor: his first volume of poetry was published in 1912 in Berlin while in the same year his first play was performed in Budapest in Hungarian; in 1913–1914 he spent two months in St. Petersburg with a theater group that was performing two of his plays. After the outbreak of war he enlisted in the infantry in 1915, and after an illness he was transferred to the war archives. By the early twenties he had made a reputation as an avant-garde dramatist. Wider public acclaim came towards the end of that decade with *Gesellschaft der Menschenrechte* (1926, Society for the Rights of Man) and *Besetztes Gebiet* (1930, Occupied Zone),[1] which were performed with great success throughout Germany. But just as he was making a name for himself his career was interrupted by the coming to power of the Nazis. He recognized the evil nature of Hitler very early and consistently rejected the Third Reich and all it stood for. At the P.E.N. conference in Dubrovnik in the summer of 1933 he signed a protest against the persecution of writers in Germany. The result was the proscription of his work inside Germany, and his plays were immediately withdrawn from the repertory. In spite of approaches from Germany he stood by his convictions; it was a case of "principle versus profit" (*Zeuge,* 24) and Csokor steadfastly chose the former.

He maintained his total rejection of Nazism when Hitler occupied Austria: over fifty years old, he chose the uncertainty of voluntary exile, although being neither Jewish nor a socialist he could have stayed there unmolested had he remained silent on public issues. He went to Poland, a country that had recently honored him for his translation and adaptation of a nineteenth-century Polish classic, Z. Krasiński's *Ungöttliche Komödie* (1929, Profane Comedy). He was granted Polish citizenship and had started work on film and theater projects when Germany invaded Poland. He fled to Bucharest, where he had a short respite before the increase in German influence there forced him to flee once more, this time to Yugoslavia, where he experienced the German bombing of Belgrade. He eventually reached the island of Korcula, which was under Italian occupation; after the collapse of Mussolini's rule he just managed to escape ahead of the Germans to the liberated south of Italy and spent the rest of the war working for the Allies. He returned to Vienna in 1946 as a British officer and finally settled there in 1947.

After his return he never recaptured the success of the early thirties, but be became one of the key figures in postwar Austrian literary life, a highly respected elder statesman whose role in the reestablishment of a democratic literary order cannot be underestimated. He was the obvious choice as president of the reconstituted Austrian P.E.N. and steered it through the difficult period of denazification and the cold war when sniping from the right and left and the traditional infighting of Austrian cultural politics combined to put him under intense pressure. It is a tribute to his integrity that he stayed in office and kept the respect, if not always the agreement, of all sides.[2]

Csokor was a man for whom friendship meant more than money or office, and his circle of friends included a veritable academy of Austrian literature; in particular one should mention his fellow dramatists Ödön von Horváth and Ferdinand Bruckner and those of the younger generation, Carl Zuckmayer and Fritz Hochwälder. In spite of a number of relationships with women Csokor never married; indeed, he never settled down to a comfortable staid existence but remained to the end, as one obituary was entitled, the "Grandseigneur der Wiener Bohême." [3]

Csokor's first play to be performed was the five-scene one-acter *Eine Partie Schach* (1912, A Game of Chess), later published as *Thermi-*

dor (1978). It was performed with success in April 1912 in Budapest, where the theater specialized in operetta and risqué French farce. While *Thermidor* is neither of these, its dramatically engrossing presentation of daemonic woman was not unsuited to the location. Its theme of the woman who brings all the arts of her sex into play to arouse and subjugate men is close to the treatment of women in other works of the period such as Wedekind's *Erdgeist* (Earth Spirit) or even Weininger's *Geschlecht und Charakter* (Sex and Character). The scene takes place on the ninth of Thermidor in year four of the revolution in a Paris prison where a group of aristocrats is awaiting execution. Among them is the central figure, Thérèse Cabarrus, not an aristocrat but a bourgeoise who is the mistress of one of Robespierre's enemies, Tallien. She is totally lacking in the *tenue* the aristocrats maintain and sits there slumped in apathetic despair. Her antagonist, the jailer Herté, is something of a minor Robespierre, basically decent but with a fanatical belief in the rightness of what he is doing, even if it involves mann executions. Besides being an "incorruptible" he is also rather innocent: his wife died after six months of marriage, and he has avoided women since; also he is not used to alcohol. Thérèse, warned by her lover that Robespierre is likely to be toppled that afternoon, delays her execution by getting Herté to play a game of chess with her, during the course of which she bombards him with the whole range of femininity from the frail woman who swoons at his feet to the courtesan flaunting her charms. Although she is deliberately playing him like a fish, it is not merely play-acting, for it does represent something in her own nature. For Csokor it is the fate of women to arouse the animal side of man, and for some women this is their destiny. Like one of the *Gewalten* (1912, Powers) from the volume of poems of that title published in the same year, Thérèse is an elemental force, amoral and irresistible, and as such she overwhelms Herté. When she thinks Tallien's coup has failed, she betrays her lover without compunction and persuades Herté to flee with her; but at that moment Tallien arrives and Thérèse immediately betrays Herté to the mob. The play does not condemn her but portrays her as a force beyond good and evil. Variations on this type appear in other plays, for example, the *Weib* (woman) of *Baum der Erkenntnis* (1916, The Tree of Knowledge), Paula in *Die Sünde wider den Geist* (1918, The Sin against the Spirit), and Gerda in *Treibholz* (1959, Flotsam).

The play *Der große Kampf* (The Great Battle), which he wrote in the autumn of 1914, is a reaction to the First World War, but he later withdrew it from circulation with the agreement of the publishers because he felt it might be misunderstood as expressing uncritical approval of the war. After the Second World War when Hans Weigel attacked him for being a communist stooge, he used *Der große Kampf* against Csokor: "One cannot understand how Karl Kraus missed this orgy of jingoism."[4] Although the work was written under the immediate impression of the outbreak of war and not after the years of death and destruction, an "orgy of jingoism" is an unfair description. There are, it is true, weak passages where one hears "echoes of what one might call officially approved War Ministry jargon,"[5] but there is no glorification of war nor vilification of the enemy.[6] What Csokor presents in this "mystery play," which often transcends the immediate context of the war, is the conflict between selfishness and the acceptance of duty to something beyond the individual, to the community.

Its structure with seven "stations" and its abstract characterizations reflect the influence of Strindberg on the drama of the Expressionist period. In an opening scene recalling the "Prologue in Heaven" in Goethe's *Faust,* Ego reviles God for allowing the destruction of war. He is then given license to go out into the world seven times to try to find someone who will put self before duty. In the seven scenes of the play, then, Ego appears in different guises, playing a Mephistophelean role by trying to seduce men from their duty. Although sorely tempted, often with seemingly valid reasons, to follow Ego, they all accept the idea that they must submit their own well-being to the needs of the community. But none does so with jingoistic enthusiasm; the dominant tone is rather one of a sober and often melancholy recognition of "Thy will be done" (*Kampf,* 105). In the final scene Ego, who has failed to find a single witness to his cause, almost involuntarily helps one of the sick in the hospital and is transformed by this unthinking participation in "the great love" (*Kampf,* 125). The conclusion leaves the jingoism of autumn 1914 far behind and heralds one of Csokor's abiding themes, the Christian humanism that attempts to apply "love one another" to social reality. It is a message that even here is not confined to the "fatherland" but open to humanity in general.

The plays Csokor wrote in the decade after the outbreak of the First World War are generally characterized by commentators as Expressionist dramas. Like *Der große Kampf, Die rote Straße* (1918, The Red Street), *Der Feuerofen* (The Furnace) and *Ballade von der Stadt* (1928, Ballad of the City) employ the "station" technique and the abstract characterization of Expressionism, the figures being deliberately restricted to types, for example, Ego, der Sohn (the son), der Vater (the father), der Arbeiter (the worker), Er (He), Sie (She), der gelbe Mann (the Yellow Man). Csokor is seeking to portray the typical, in some cases the archetypical. The main themes are also those of Expressionism: suffering, man-woman relationships seen as a tragic conflict, the power of money, of eros, the metropolis as the incarnation of all that is degenerate in modern society, and the need for spiritual renewal. In *Die rote Straße* there are some passages in the exaggeratedly declamatory style of many Expressionist works, but otherwise Csokor at this period tends to combine rhythmic prose with alliteration, concentrated syntax, and imagery used directly and not as ornament to produce a pithy density of language which helps to create the mythical mode in which he treats his themes. Although his plays have many features of Expressionism, Csokor's use of language and dramatic structure always reveals a consciousness of form that avoids the worst excesses of some of his contemporaries.

The best known of Csokor's plays of this period and the one which established his reputation as an Expressionist dramatist is *Die rote Straße,* written in 1916-1917 but not published until 1918. It consists of fourteen scenes corresponding to the fourteen stations of the cross. This is not a matter of mere external form, since the image of Christ, the suffering man, is central to this as it is to other Expressionist plays; for example, it is found in *Von morgens bis mitternachts* by Georg Kaiser, to whom Csokor dedicated *Die rote Straße.* The form of *Die rote Straße* is a variant on the quest which is also found in *Der große Kampf* and other plays of the period.

The play opens with the bringing together of an archetypal couple on the "Mount of Judgment," "He" and "She," who are then sent out into the world on the journey of life. They search for and repeatedly find each other to try to fulfill the love they were created for but end up each time tormenting and losing one another. What separates them is partly within them, the compulsive urges of the flesh that overwhelm their love, and partly the hostile world represented by the figure of the Yellow Man, whose wealth gives him a power over the woman that her love cannot withstand. The play ends where it began, on the "Mount of Judgment" with the next pair about to begin its journey into the world. The transformation by love with which *Der große Kampf* ends is here replaced by a pessimistic Nietzschean eternal recurrence, which is emphasized by the circular imagery abounding in the play: the stage directions set it "everywhere and again and again," and one of the final scenes is a circular maze around a statue of Christ the Man. In the most celebrated and much anthologized third scene He waits outside the house too timid to knock, as we hear the voices of the houses "like an echo of the hallucinations they trigger off in the waiting man" (*Straße,* 19).

Written in 1916 shortly before *Die rote Straße, Der Baum der Erkenntnis* is a myth going back, as the title suggests, to the original couple and original sin. The play is in six scenes and has a monumental simplicity of structure and language. The Fall is not the result of temptation by the woman but of a split in man bringing both sex and self-consciousness into the world. The primeval harmony of the existence of "Man" and "Woman" is interrupted by the arrival of the "Shadow" to whom the woman succumbs with a mixture of hate and desire and by whom she is then abandoned when she becomes pregnant. After the birth of her child some unity of Man/Woman/Shadow is restored but not the primeval harmony of the opening.

Another play that can be counted part of Csokor's Expressionist period is *Die Stunde des Absterbens* (The Hour of Dying), subtitled "A Journey into Hell," which is an E.T.A. Hoffmannesque study in evil: the self-centered Archivar destroys the lives of all around him but is unrepentant even in death. It has a dark and brooding atmosphere, an enclosed setting in one gloomy room, and supernatural apparitions reminiscent of the atmosphere of early Expressionist films.

Definitely not Expressionist, however, is the play *Die Sünde wider den Geist,* written before *Die rote Straße,* which examines the figure of the artist. The sin against the Holy Ghost of the title is the artist's betrayal of his calling because he is in thrall to a woman who, like Thérèse in *Thermidor,* uses the whole range of feminine moods to keep him in subjection. The female vampire who sucks men emotionally dry is Paula Rumol-Hauser, an opera singer whose husband has abandoned his ambition to compose and is now *Kapellmeister* at the opera house. The movement of the action depends on the deployment of Paula's moods as men flutter helplessly around her like moths around a flame. The style of this traditionally constructed five-act play has little of Expressionism and looks back, if anything, to Ibsen rather than Strindberg.

The final and best play of Csokor's Expressionist period is the unjustly forgotten "dramatic fresco," *Ballade von der Stadt.* It was inspired by a series of pictures by his friend Carry Hauser depicting the city as the incarnation of the degradation of modern life with its squalor and show, prostitutes and starving children, profiteers and beggars. Both the themes and the cross-fertilization of visual and literary arts are typical of the period. A close parallel can be seen, for example, in Frans Masereel's contemporary series of woodcuts called *Die Stadt,* one of what he called "novels in pictures."

Csokor's play, which he called a "collective drama" (*Ballade,* preface), contains nineteen short scenes recording the growth of an archetypical city. It presents in microcosm the historical development of social forms from the mythical unity of man with nature down to the oppression, exploitation, and alienation felt to be characteristic of modern times. This "kind of tragic revue" (preface) recalls *Der Baum der Erkenntnis* in its use of an archaizing style, but its analysis of the development of society owes much to Marx, though without any call to class consciousness or class warfare.

The primeval harmony of the opening is disrupted by the discovery of gold, from which all the evils of society spring. Here Csokor uses once again the myth of the Fall of Man: gold is the motive and sex the means, as the woman, overcome with the desire for gold, arouses sexual passion in the man and they embrace with the lump of gold pressed between them. Csokor shows how the discovery of gold leads to the introduction of slavery, the division of labor, the institution of kingship and its perversion into tyranny, the transformation of *Gemeinschaft* (community) into *Gesellschaft* (society), the invention of paper money as a new instrument of slavery, and alienation. Contemporary events are evoked as the authorities turn to war against an external enemy to divert their subjects from revolution; when the revolution does come, the two opposing parties reveal themselves to be mirror images of each other, both seeking to enslave the people in the name of ideology. Money dominates the ensuing peace as the Merchant (cf. the Yellow Man of *Die rote Straße*) buys everything, including the arts which are prostituted in support of the system. The play ends with a prophetic vision of the destruction of the city and the liberation of mankind. All the figures reappear at the end in a massive tirade against the city, which causes the walls to crumble like those of Jericho and reestablishes the triple harmony of man within himself, with other men, and with the forces of nature.

The short scenes limited to the essential, the language of pregnant brevity and shorn of ornament, the compressed and concrete imagery all combine to allow the presentation of a modern analysis of history in the mode of archaic myth, making *Die Ballade der Stadt* the most powerful of Csokor's works of the years 1914–1922.

Throughout his career Csokor also wrote poetry, "primarily poems in balladesque form, for it was the ballad that led me to drama, which takes up almost the whole of my creative energies today" (*Immer ist Anfang,* preface). By ballad Csokor means both poems which narrate events and others which portray character; many of the themes and figures of his plays also appear in the poems. The verse forms vary from the traditional four-line ballad stanza to terza rima and even to sonnets that sound like a pastiche of Rilke ("Karl Stuarts Todesgang"). The Expressionism that influenced his plays is totally absent from his verse, which is always characterized by an economy and precision of language and never falls into facile rhythm. His most intense are probably the austere poems written in exile, in which the dominant tone is a questioning voice meditating on the uncertainty of existence: *Wo wird dein Bett sein* (Where will the bed be) / *darin du verendest?* (in which you expire?) / *Und ob es ein Bett ist?* (And will it be a bed at all?) ("Flucht," *Immer ist Anfang,* 127).

The link between the earlier plays and those of the later twenties and the thirties is provided by Csokor's interest in the early nineteenth-century dramatist Georg Büchner, whose *Woyzeck* was a work of seminal importance for the Expressionist drama. The new critical edition published by Bergemann in 1922 stimulated Csokor, who was working as *Dramaturg* (play selector) at the time, to attempt to complete it. As an excellent analysis by Margaret Jacobs shows, the adaptation demonstrates precisely those qualities that distinguish Csokor's early work from the mass of Expressionist drama: his clarity and concern for effective dramatic structure. Her final comment that "Csokor . . . is clearly at home with a more traditional dramatic method in dialogue and structure"[7] would seem to be at odds with his career in the preceding decade as an Expressionist dramatist. And yet, in one sense she is right; Csokor's early plays, even when they adopt the contemporary fashion, are always carefully written and well composed with none of the extreme dislocation of structure and syntax which was supposedly justified by the model of *Woyzeck.* Except for passages in *Die rote Straße* he avoided the declamatory pathos so common in Expressionist drama, which was what he singled out in his preface to the 1960 publication of his *Woyzeck* version, as being at the root of his dissatisfaction with Bergemann's analysis.

In his play on the life of Büchner, *Gesellschaft der Menschenrechte* completed in 1927, the excited pathos of some of the language might seem to echo Expressionism, but here it is a historical characteristic of the 1830s. It is a feature of the liberals around Pastor Weidig that the political and literary realist Büchner castigates. The language which Csokor puts into the mouth of his hero catches much of Büchner's own use of imagery: his anger at the sufferings of the oppressed comes out in violent language of a very earthy physicality, for example, "Naked flesh twitches at the lash of the bull-whip! And you gawp after a long-dead emperor! ... Have you daintier flesh round your bones? Does your dung smell better than his?" (*Gesellschaft,* 10-11).[8]

Csokor's Büchner believes that only the cool unemotional man of action can bring about political change, and he is the first of a series of figures in Csokor's dramas who, filled with necessity of action, have either never possessed or have cut out of their lives the emotion that clouds the vision. Fanatics of reason rather than of feeling, they are portrayed by Csokor with understanding, but he sees them ultimately as yet another of the destructive forces in the world. Some of them see this too but believe they must even destroy themselves before they can rebuild, an attitude their creator did not share. Examples are Latter in *Besetztes Gebiet,* Kacziuk in *3. November 1918* (1936), and Stipe in *Der verlorene Sohn* (1946, The Prodigal Son).

Csokor portrays Büchner's dedication to action as proceeding from a personal inadequacy for, as his enemy points out, he can embrace humanity but not feel real love for an individual. Warmth of emotion is replaced by intensity of activity. Did Csokor see something of himself in Büchner? At one point Büchner comments that his life is a "perpetual departure" (*Gesellschaft,* 86); *Ewiger Aufbruch* (Perpetual Departure) is the title of a volume of poems Csokor published in 1926, and the same idea appears twenty-six years later in the title of his collected poems: *Immer ist Anfang* (1952, Beginning Is Always). The poem he chose as epilogue to this collection expresses the same idea of restless activity: "You must continue on and on, / for no place will ever be your place" (153).

The precise historical setting of the Büchner play indicates the move away from Expressionism, and the plays that follow all center on either a contemporary or a historical theme. *Besetztes Gebiet* deals with the French occupation of the Ruhr in the years 1923 to 1925. Its five main acts focus on a single event modeled on an incident in the Krupp factory in Essen that led to the death of thirteen Germans. Most of the action takes place offstage, the play being set in confined spaces, mostly in or near the city council chambers. The claustrophobic stage setting contrasts with the hectic external events to provide the play with considerable tension. Csokor concentrates on the attitudes that the state of emergency throws into high relief.

In the council of the industrial town where the play is set all the colors of the German political spectrum are represented from the conservative nationalism of the industrialists to socialism and communism. The central figure, Mayor Monk, represents both the political moderation of the government's "policy of fulfillment" (of the Versailles treaty) and the moral moderation that tries to avoid extremes of action. The council's deliberations are interrupted by the arrival of a right-wing terrorist group intending to fight the French occupation through sabotage. Monk and the communist Latter are the only two who clearly recognize the danger the group represents. Latter is willing to let the parties to the right of him fight it out until the field is clear for him, even though he recognizes the human suffering it will cost and does not dismiss it lightly. Monk's sphere of action is limited by two things: on the one hand by his desire (not unlike that of the Emperor Rudolf in Grillparzer's *Bruderzwist in Habsburg*) to avoid decisive action in order not to precipitate a sequence of events he would no longer be able to control. On the other hand by political weakness, which Csokor sees as inherent in the moderate position: for all his moderation Monk is at heart a German patriot and cannot bring himself to hand over the terrorists to the French until it is too late, and his action turns the leader into a martyr for the nationalist cause. Csokor clearly had the case of Schlageter in mind. It was a prophetic portrayal; for Chancellor Schuschnigg's feeling that he could not order his troops to fire on "fellow Germans" contributed to his refusal to resist the Nazi invasion of Austria in 1938.

Characteristic of Csokor's humanist rather than narrowly political approach is that all of the figures are portrayed with understanding, even those proto-Nazis whose actions are decisively rejected. There is no ideal figure, but in the naively nonpolitical composer Malte there is a glimpse of a better, though at the time impossible, world. In spite of the tense situation he goes ahead with the first performance of his music, which the French commandant attends. Malte is characterized as naive. He gives the concert because he assumes that music is above politics, but he is taught a brutal lesson by the terrorists who murder him as a traitor to Germany. Malte gives expression to the idea of a common humanity beyond national differences, which is echoed by the nurse Christina at the end of the later play *3. November 1918.*

This idea is not a program for political action: it would betray its own nature if it tried to become one. It is, however, a testimony to the possibility of a world different than the divided Europe of the twenties and thirties.

In *3. November 1918* this world "that consists of human beings and not of nations and frontiers" (*3. November,* 77) is symbolized by the Austro-Hungarian empire. This play was Csokor's greatest success on the Austrian stage and is still performed today. It is set in an officers' convalescent home in the Carinthian mountains, cut off from the outside world for weeks by snowstorms and containing eight officers from various nations, a microcosm of the empire. By using this setting Csokor is able to concentrate into this small group and the two days of the action a picture of the empire before, during, and after its dissolution. As the play opens the officers do not know of the collapse and are unified by their sense of belonging to the multinational army, their occasional bickering not yet threatening the basic unity. This is reflected in the language—they all speak the same officers' jargon, colored in each case by their mother tongue. Their national feelings, which initially are absorbed in the higher unity of the empire, come to the surface with the arrival of the news of the collapse. In spite of an emotional appeal by the senior officer Radosin each decides to return to his new national homeland. Radosin, whose home is the multinational army, commits suicide, and two other officers, the German and the Slovene, are left to begin a new war over their common Carinthian home.

The officers—Czech, German, Hungarian, Italian, Polish, and Slovene—are not themselves the representatives of nationalism but rather the ground over which the battle between nationalism and supra-nationalism is fought. For them the empire is their *Vaterland* of which their own nation, their *Heimat* (homeland) is a part. They are bound to their *Heimat* by ties of feeling, blood, and language. The ideal of *Vaterland* developed by Csokor does not seek to deny these feelings but to subsume them in something higher. The appeal of such an ideal is less immediate and strong than that of a combination of home, blood, and language ties. Once political systems based on the individual nations have been established, the officers, although with a sense of loss, feel they have no choice but to join them. For Colonel Radosin this is a return to a dark and barbarous past, and the officers discover that nationalism, far from allowing them self-determination, submerges their individual humanity. They are all now prisoners of their own nations. Csokor's attack on the use of the racial principle as the basis of states is directed not so much at those founded in 1918–1919 as at their totalitarian successors that emerged in the twenties and thirties.

In *3. November 1918* Csokor is attempting not a precise reconstruction of Austria-Hungary's historical role but the formulation of an ideal based on the possibility it represented. According to a term Csokor himself used (*Zeuge,* 25), most commentators describe it as a requiem for the monarchy and see it as an exercise in nostalgia, an interpretation that can easily infect stage productions, especially in Austria. But the context of Csokor's own description of the play as a requiem is a discussion of postwar political extremism which he sees as resulting from the disappearance of the empire.

3. November 1918 is not only Csokor's best-known play, but also his best play. The concentration of the essence of an important historical moment into a small spatial and temporal compass is much more effective than the theatrical but ultimately lumbering large-scale historical plays which were his method of trying to deal with the events of the thirties. In showing fascism rising from the ashes of the empire the play has a theme that ensures it continued interest. The officers' jargon gives the language a specific color, lacking in many of his later plays in which all characters tend to speak with a similar voice. Finally, the natural congruence between the specific historical theme of extreme nationalism versus supranationalism and Csokor's general humanist concern for the individual give both an extra dimension lacking in his postwar plays, which often seem too obviously composed with a message in mind.

Two other plays from the thirties similarly reflect events through the microcosm of a small group of characters. *Die Erweckung des Zosimir* (The Awakening of Zosimir) was conceived after the Austrian civil war in February 1934 but completed only in 1960. Through the contrast of two political refugees, one an intellectual, the other a man of action, it shows the creation of a totalitarian power structure based on artificially induced national feeling. In the other, *Nicht da nicht dort* (Neither Here nor There), Csokor tried to repeat the formula of *3. November 1918* with a similar play on the Russian revolution, using as the focus a group of upper-class liberals who find that the movement they have helped to bring about is threatening to consume them. The approach is remarkably similar to the almost exactly contemporary monumental novel by R. C. Hutchinson, *Testament.*

Chronologically interwoven with these plays are the three large-

scale historical works through which Csokor tried to deal with the
question of fascism: *Der tausendjährige Traum* (1963, The Millennial
Dream), *Gottes General* (1938, God's General), and *Jadwiga* (1963).
In the first Csokor found in the Münster of the Anabaptists a historical
parallel to Hitler's Third Reich. In the other two, following a suggestion
of his friend Ödön von Horváth, he attempts to beat fascist literature at
its own game, to deny the Nazis a monopoly on the heroic. The heroic
figures Csokor chose were two "warriors for peace," Saint Ignatius and
a Polish queen Jadwiga, "an eastern Joan of Arc who, however, struck
the sword out of men's hands" (*Zeuge*, 175).

More than one writer has seen the parallel that struck Csokor between Münster and the Third Reich and more particularly between the
charismatic leader Jan Bockelsen and Hitler.[9] The parallels to 1933
abound from the burning of the cathedral library to the role of women
"to conceive, to bear, to suckle, men for Münster, warriors for Sion"
(*Traum*, 63). Csokor adds occasional formulations with echoes of
Nazism such as the cry of "One faith, one will, one King"[10] (*Traum*,
52) when Bockelsen is crowned king.

Like Nazism, Anabaptism was a movement which gave an illusory
hope to thousands of the poor and oppressed with its radical attack on
the established order, its promise of a role in a new system, and its
chiliastic message. In Csokor's play the rule of the Anabaptists opens
with a sense of joy, hope, and liberation expressed in the carnival cele-
brations, though their whirling frenzy portends future irrational violence. The worse the material situation becomes, the more exaggerated
the leaders' claims, the more splendid the illusion they present to the
people until at the end, with all food gone and no hope of victory, they
play out a magnificent pageant of the judgment of the world, executing
their enemies in effigy and dividing up the empire that is about to destroy them. The inflation of illusion until it is burst by the sharp edge
of reality reflects Csokor's hope of an early collapse of Hitler's regime.

The play ends almost on a note of despair; the victorious enemies
of Münster are as coldly cruel and calculating as the Anabaptists are
wildly careless of human life. The sybaritic Bishop destroys them not
for their heresy or their violence but for the threat they pose to the
established order. As a small counterweight to the picture of cruelty
and destruction Csokor adds a final image of suffering humanity similar
in function to Malte in *Besetztes Gebiet*. A painter in the Bishop's
retinue uses the body of his dead son, a convinced Anabaptist, as a
model for the figure of Christ in a picture of the entombment. It is a

quiet and poignant coda that Csokor spoils somewhat by allowing the Bishop to recognize the suffering it symbolizes in a trance-like but sententious speech. Csokor also used the material of the play for his only novel, *Der Schlüssel zum Abgrund, Roman einer Zeit* (1955, The Key to the Abyss, Novel of an Age). By extending the plot and interspersing it with twelve intermezzi set in different political and cultural centers he made it into a spiritual portrait of an epoch.

Gottes General portrays Saint Ignatius as the Christian soldier, the Spanish nobleman who learns to sacrifice his own honor to God's, the administrator who seeks to bring divine order into this world. But the crux of the figure is his ability to change other people and, even more importantly, himself. This applies not only to his conversion, but also to his whole life; he does not allow achievement to become a dead weight but constantly sees himself with new understanding. When at the end he renounces the generalship to become a simple brother of the order, his intention to join "the lowest of the low, the nameless multitude" (*General,* 150) smacks of inverted pride; but he overcomes this last temptation and leaves the stage following God's will, not his own. This theme of the transformation of the individual was to become more and more important in Csokor's plays after this time.

Loyola is a worthy subject, but dramatically the play is overloaded with character and detail. This is even more true of the other play in this group, *Jadwiga,* which is in the epigonic monumentalizing style of nineteenth-century historical drama. Fortunately, he did not return to this style. Later plays such as *Pilatus* (1954, Pilate), which are set at times of significant historical events, employ the technique of reflecting them through a small group of characters and concentrating on the interplay of reaction to the events rather than on the events themselves.

Csokor continued to write plays during his exile even though the prospect of seeing them performed must have seemed remote. He also wrote two volumes of prose on his experiences in exile. *Als Zivilist im polnischen Krieg* (1940, As a Civilian in the Polish War) and *Als Zivilist im Balkankrieg* (1955, As a Civilian in the Balkan War), which show the origin of much of the material in these plays. But they are more important than just source books for his works or biography; they stand in their own right and *Als Zivilist im Balkenkrieg* is one of the most moving and impressive of all Csokor's works. In characteristic fashion he largely ignores what he did or what happened to him preferring to record what he observed around him, the suffering, sorrow, heroism, guilt, and occasional cruelty in the people he encountered. It is not the record of a detached observer but of one who shares the suffering and guilt of others, of one who because of his talent with words can bear witness to what he has experienced. The book opens with a "Dedication to the Village of Borodin," a Yugoslav village which voluntarily undertook a two-month fast in expiation for the murder of a Jewish peddler by the mayor's son, the first serious crime there for decades. This capacity of *Mitgefühl* (empathy), for feeling part of humanity in guilt as well as in joy or sorrow, is shared by Csokor, who ends his description of the bombing of Belgrade: "Can man inflict such evil on their fellow men? 'Tat tvam asi' is written on the door of the Buddhist temple.—'That is you!'" (*Zeuge*, 60).

The figure of Odysseus became an important symbol for a whole generation of writers who suffered exile, but in Csokor's *Kalypso* (1946) he is not the refugee but the man of action who cannot accept the peace the woman (in this case represented by Kalypso) longs to bring him. The action of the play is minimal—Odysseus loves Kalypso and leaves her—and Csokor has padded it out with extra characters, Hermes, a mincing androgyne, and Galathea, an empty-headed society goddess, who seem to have strayed in by mistake out of Giraudoux' *Amphitryon 38* or Thorne Smith's *The Night Life of the Gods.* Their contrast with the high pathos of the Homer-figure, who insists on explaining the significance of what is going on, and with the passion of the protagonists is jarring, to say the least. Kalypso is typical of the majority of Csokor's female characters, who tend to be either angels of peace or calculating vampires arousing the beast in men; sometimes they are both at once but seldom something in between. It is interesting, therefore, that two other plays from the exile period offer a different view of women, presenting them as rounded characters with gradations of light and shade, as initiators of action and the equals of men. One of these, *Wenn sie zurückkommen* (When They Return) is an unusual play in any context. It consists of twelve scenes, usually containing two female characters. In each scene one of them has just come from making love to a man—a kind of inversion of Schnitzler's *Reigen* (*Round Dance*) for postcoital women. The purpose of these twelve variations on women's attitudes toward themselves, men, and their role in society, is to show "the woman of yesterday, of today, and of tomorrow" (*Wenn,* III) with a suggestion that the woman of tomorrow will be considerably more independent than the woman of yesterday.

The heroine of *Medea postbellica* (n.d., Postwar Medea) is one of these new women the guerrilla war in the Balkans has created; the tragedy arises from her role when along with peace many old attitudes return. She and her husband met as fellow soldiers and married during the partisan war. She is now pregnant, but with the return of peace her husband feels that something is lacking in their relationship which is still based on comradeship: he is seduced by the first "feminine" woman he encounters. His wife takes grisly revenge: she has an abortion and deliberately arranges for the other woman to become infected with leprosy. The end resolves the complex situation in a way that moderates the stark tones of ancient tragedy. Instead of being utterly destroyed the characters look forward to a life not of fulfillment but of usefulness as the wife devotes herself to surrogate children in the kindergarten and the husband is dissuaded from suicide to seek some similarly useful task.

Another play from the exile period which is much more successful in evoking the fatalistic overtones of Greek tragedy is *Der verlorene Sohn*. Using an incident from the partisan war, Csokor has created a tragic dilemma where both alternatives lead to guilt and death. The sense of antiquity is reinforced by the use of the pagan religious customs Csokor observed in Dalmatia alongside a Christianity which offers no solution to the moral dilemma. After the occupation the youngest son of a farmer has gone into the hills to join the resistance. He returns to ask his two elder brothers to join him and, when they refuse, kills them to avoid the betrayal of himself and his comrades. For him this is a harsh but clear necessity imposed by the code he has embraced in response to the political situation, but his father is placed in an insoluble dilemma. The situation is so arranged that if he warns the elder sons the younger will be captured and executed but if he does not warn them they will be killed. He lets them go; they are the "fatted calf" he slaughters for his "prodigal" son, but he himself is crushed by the inner conflict. As in other plays Csokor ends with a ray of light in the birth of the child of the middle son. In spite of the echoes of the birth of Christ it is not a symbol of change or of salvation but of the sober fact that life will continue.

Religious imagery, in particular the figure of Christ, was common in Csokor's early plays. It was part of the language of a whole generation as much as Csokor's own, and although it never disappeared entirely from his writing, it receded in importance in the more socially oriented works of the years between the wars. In the plays written in exile it reappeared to become a central concern of his postwar plays, so much so that the question of Csokor's own belief is raised. But here again it seems that he is using religion as a cipher for human values rather than expressing his own faith. He wrote in 1937 that he had given Loyola the faith he himself did not possess (see *Zeuge*, 145), and in a contribution to a book published in 1968 he made it clear that his beliefs did not have their focus in any transcendental reality. He wrote, "The meaning of life is something we must create ourselves—through our work and what we achieve in it. Existence thus becomes true being."[11] "Christian humanism," the commonest formula used to describe his outlook, fits very well as long as one bears in mind that "Christian" refers to a tradition and a morality, not to a faith.

The plays *Pilatus, Die Kaiser zwischen den Zeiten* (1965, The Emperors between the Epochs), and *Caesars Witwe* (1954, Caesar's Widow), to which one could add *Kalypso* (1946), in which the birth of Christ is foreshadowed, are all set around the point of change from the classical world to the Christian era. For Csokor the key factor in the change lies not in the new articles of faith themselves but in their ability to transform man, especially in the respect for human life and rights that he sees at the heart of Christ's message. In *Pilatus* this message emerges from the reactions of Pilate and the Romans, of the disciples, of Barabbas, and of those who believe in armed resistance. Christ is seen as a man, not as the Son of God but as a unique man who is the perfect incarnation of a humanity which ordinary humans can only aspire to or reject, as does Judas, who betrays him "because no man can be allowed to be as Christ is. Otherwise we are all in the wrong" (*Pilatus*, 29). Pilate, who is attracted by the personality of Jesus, especially in contrast to the emperor who has just declared himself divine, withdraws when he learns that Christ seeks not to convince but to transform the lives of his disciples. The theme of the play is this transforming power of what the centurion calls "the miracle of example" (*Pilatus*, 67) which, as Csokor states in his preface, is more important than the tenets of belief. The one article of faith that Csokor does emphasize can only be lived, not merely believed in, namely the command to love one another. Csokor sees this not as some vague brotherly love but as a revolutionary force that attacks barriers between classes, nations, and races to lay the basis on which human rights rest. And this is what the old order cannot accept. As the Roman commander says, "If we should ever begin to respect the lives of those whose place it is to serve us, then our world will collapse" (*Pilatus*, 16).

This conquest of Rome by a "Messiah of suffering and not of action" (*Kaiser,* 3) is the subject of *Die Kaiser zwischen den Zeiten.* The central scene of this "dramatic diptych" is a discussion between the Emperors Diocletian and Constantine about their treatment of the Christians. The irony is that, although the one persecuted and the other set himelf as their protector, they both acted from the same motive. They both wanted to counter the revolutionary force within Christ's teaching: Diocletian by trying to extirpate it, Constantine by making it the established religion. An epilogue shows that Constantine's calculation is wrong. Far from taking the sting from Christ's message, the emperors are still subject to its power to transform them. The historical development of the church as a power structure is reflected in the interview between Constantine and Athanasius, in whom the teaching that transforms men has already become a rigid dogma.

Caesars Witwe also has this combination of a Roman setting, portents of the coming of a Messiah who will be an example to the world, and parallels to our own century with show trials and government-inspired demonstrations. The theme is the question of the individual versus the state, elaborated through a dispute between Augustus and Calpurnia. Augustus wants to use her as a figurehead for his new order; she rejects the idea and reproaches him for the 2,000 murders on which his reign is founded. But she has no answer to his justification in terms of a "raison d'état": "Augustus: I had 2,000 politicians killed – and for twenty years we have enjoyed peace" (*Witwe,* 44). Not until she is on her deathbed twenty years later does she see the answer in a visionary moment that takes the belief in the supreme value of the individual out of the political sphere, where it can be misused like any other ideology, and transposes it into a general human ideal finding expression in religion. This is her recognition that "just as all blessings on earth can come only from individuals, so there can be only one single true one amongst those we have chosen as our gods" (*Witwe,* 71).

Caesars Witwe is a play full of an intensely felt humanism but one in which the dramatic expression of that humanism does not always match its intensity. The overall structure remains too subservient to the abstract argument and does not have sufficient life of its own to provide a vivid incarnation of the theme. An argument conducted at intervals of twenty years lacks dramatic force, especially as there is nothing in the action to motivate Calpurnia's final vision. The characters are similarly pale reflections of the ideas of the play; as Brygida Brandys points out, Csokor's "ideas are often stronger than his figures."[12]

These criticisms apply in varying degrees to Csokor's postwar work as a whole. The abstract themes, however noble or significant, tend to dominate language, plot, and characterization and often stifle their dramatic effect in spite of a use of the physical resources of the stage, which reveals the practiced man of the theater because these again relate too directly to the themes. This abstraction is, of course, a feature of his Expressionist plays, where it is taken to an extreme degree without weakening the impact because there is no pretense that the characters are specific individuals in a specific social and historical context. Their impact comes precisely from their passionate abstraction. His very best plays such as *Gesellschaft der Menschenrechte, Der tausendjährige Traum,* and *3. November 1918* have a subject which is strong enough to engage the audience's interest in its own right and one that imposes its own specific and distinctive language.

Hebt den Stein ab! (1957, Take away the Stone), *Das Zeichen an der Wand* (1962, The Writing on the Wall), and *Treibholz* (1959, Flotsam) are three of the postwar plays that so nearly succeed in forcing the audience to face up to awkward questions about the nature of man but ultimately fail to rise above the level of well-made and well-intentioned works. All three reflect Csokor's interest towards the end of his life in what he called "problems of a more eschatological nature."[13] *Hebt den Stein ab!,* subtitled a "comedy on the last things," examines the situation that develops when a man, and not one particularly deserving of such a distinction, rises from the dead. The whole of society, including the church, is concerned to see that this event, which overturns the assumptions on which they are based, shall have as little effect as possible on their outlook and activities. Some of the sting of the satirical possibilities Csokor develops from the situation is taken by the conciliatory ending in which the hero sacrifices himself to save lives in an accident similar to one caused by his negligence before his first "death."

Behind both *Treibholz* and *Das Zeichen an der Wand* is the suggestion that human society is reaching a self-destructiveness that will bring about its doomsday. In *Treibholz* it is the new atomic science, in *Das Zeichen an der Wand* the Nazi holocaust which is the trigger of the apocalyptic vision. The "driftwood" of the former is a family of extreme depravity: Gerda, a former dancer, vain, self-centered, and cruel; her alcoholic sister; her second husband, the opera singer Gregor, weak and lustful; and his cousin, who exploits people emotionally for his own diversion. They are confronted by a scientist, Herbert, who not unreasonably wants to rescue Edith, Gerda's daughter, from this situation. She finally rejects him for reasons that connect his personality with his role as a scientist. In contrast to his icy arrogance, which sees the whole world as material for his experiments, her family, "base and mean as they appear, yet live nearer to God through their tortured consciences" (*Treibholz*, 55).

The portrait of this "human dung-heap" (*Treibholz*, 57) is devastating, and the final confrontation between Gregor and Herbert has a theatricality which is well motivated by Gregor's profession. But Herbert, whose characterization is minimal and comes from what he says rather than from the way he behaves, as is the case with Edith's family, never has enough weight to act as a dramatic counterpart to the family.

In *Das Zeichen an der Wand* the figure parallel to Herbert is Mazza, a former Nazi (based on Eichmann) who has escaped to South America and is now a wealthy businessman. Whereas Herbert is posited as "the Scientist" and stands as a cipher for modern science, Mazza's inhumanity is motivated as stemming from a loss of faith in God so that the atrocities he committed were a kind of despairing challenge flung at Him. Such a character is open to doubt and uncertainty which betray the faintest stirrings of conscience. Although he never admits regret, he walks half knowingly and half willingly into the trap set by the Israeli Nazi hunter almost as if it were a relief to give up the life he has had to lead. It is typical of Csokor that the figure in the limelight reveals some humanity, even if it is largely submerged. The incurable Nazis are shown in two secondary characters, the totally cynical Baumer and the fanatically committed *Landesinspektor*.

Csokor's final play, *Alexander* (1969), completed a month before his death, is a suitable work to set as his poetic testament, combining as it does themes, types, and structures from all periods but also seeking to mold them into a new unity, not just to recreate a past model. There is in particular a new quality to the language. *Alexander* seems to have been originally conceived as a verse play, and this origin has left its mark on the prose, which displays an elevated idiom, sparse and austere, without ornament and rhetorical flourishes but with a subcutaneous rhythm that binds it together. The structure is the episodic series of the Expressionist *Stationendrama* (station drama) showing nine scenes from the life of Alexander from the death of his father to his own death in India. One of the main themes is the ideal of a world without barriers between nations and races, an idea that goes back to Csokor's *3. November 1918*.

The other theme that came to the fore in the plays written during and after exile is man's need to transform himself. The central figure is similar to that of Georg Büchner: Alexander too has an inner coolness which makes it impossible for him to give himself fully to another person. As Csokor's nephew Heinz Rieder points out in his preface, Alexander plunges into a career first of military conquest and then of social engineering on a grandiose and idealistic scale as a "flight from his own self" (*Alexander*, 5). His failure would then leave him with nothing to mask his inner emptiness. But Csokor here avoids the tragic disillusionment in which his Büchner dies. With a startling coup de théâtre he allows his hero to die a merely symbolic death—on the pyre is Praxiteles' statue of him—to be born again as the adopted son and disciple of an Indian philosopher king from whom he learns that true power lies in service, not to the gods he no longer believes in but to mankind.

"Service to mankind" would also be an apt description of Csokor's attitude throughout his literary career. Whether in his unjustly neglected Expressionist plays, in the more socially and politically orientated ones of the thirties, or in his postwar works that confront man with ultimate questions on his destiny, at the center is always a humanism beyond class, nation, race, or creed which he saw as the finest legacy of the multinational community he grew up in and of which his life is an outstanding example.

Notes

1. A translation of the titles of Csokor's works will, where necessary, be given in parentheses after the first occurrence in the text. Page references will be given in parentheses at the end of quotations with an abbreviated form of the title. For example, *Zeuge einer Zeit* = *Zeuge.*

2. For his role in P.E.N. see K. Amann, *P.E.N. Politik, Emigration, Nationalsozialismus: Ein österreichischer Schriftstellerclub* (Wien: Böhlau, 1984).

3. H. P. Anderle in *Der Literat,* Vol. 11 (1969), 30-31.

4. Hans Weigel, "The Jolly Csokor oder Als Zivilist im Kalten Krieg," in *Morgen, Monatsschrift freier Akademiker,* Vol. 5 (1953), 9-10, quoted in B. Brandys, "Das dramatische Werk von Franz Theodor Csokor," in *Kwartalnik Neofilologiczny,* Vol. 28 (1981), 411.

5. Theodor Sapper, *Alle Glocken der Erde. Expressionistische Dichtung aus dem Donauraum* (Wien: Europaverlag, 1974), p. 90.

6. One can compare this with what was clearly a result of his work in the War Archives, an essay on the history of art in Dalmatia in *Vom Isonzo zum Balkan,* ed. Col. A. Veltzé (München: Piper, 1917), pp. 10-20), which does contain some obligatory but mild sideswipes at the Italians, e.g., "... the testimony of ruins from Aquileia, laid waste by the Huns, to the most recent vandalism of the Italian 'saviors' in neighboring Gorizia" (p. 11).

7. M. Jacobs, "Franz Theodor Csokor: Büchners 'Woyzeck'—Versuch einer Vollendung," in *Oxford German Studies,* Vol. 1 (1966), 31-52.

8. The dactylic rhythm and accentuating alliteration of the German (e.g., "Habt ihr feineres Fleisch um die Knochen? Euer Kot riecht er besser als seiner?") is part of Csokor's linguistic signature. In his verse he is sparing in his use of this insistent rhythm but it appears in his prose whenever it becomes emphatic. The following example is from a *descriptive* passage in his novel *Der Schlüssel zum Abgrund:* "Und die eben noch zürnenden Züge entspannten sich sanft zur Verzückung" (p. 58). It is particularly frequent in his final play, *Alexander.*

9. E.g., R. Reck-Malleczewen, *Bockelsen. Geschichte eines Massenwahns* (Berlin: Schützen-Verlag, 1937).

10. Cf. the coin inscription "One King over all. One God, One Faith, One Baptism." Quoted in N. Cohn, *The Pursuit of the Millennium* (London: Paladin, 1970).

11. *Wozu leben wir,* ed. H. P. Richter (Freiburg/Colmar/Paris, 1968), p. 13.

12. B. Brandys, "Das dramatische Werk von Franz Theodor Csokor," p. 417.

13. Franz Theodor Csokor, "Blick über mich," *Welt und Wort,* 13 (1958), 301 f.

Bibliography

I. Works by Franz Theodor Csokor in German

Die Gewalten. Ein Band Balladen. Berlin: Axel Juncker, 1912.
Eine Partie Schach, published as *Thermidor.* Wien/München: T. Sessler, n.d. (Nachwort dated 1978).

Der große Kampf. Ein Mysterienspiel in acht Bildern. Berlin: S. Fischer, 1915.

Der Baum der Erkenntnis. Ein Mythos. Wien: Amalthea, 1916.

Die Sünde wider den Geist. Wien: Amalthea, 1918.

Die rote Straße. Ein dramatisches Werk in 14 Bildern. Weimar: Kiepenheuer, 1918.

Der Dolch und die Wunde. Gedichte. Wien: Deutschösterreichischer Verlag, 1918.

N-N. Evreinhoff (trans. F. T. Csokor). *Die Kulissen der Seele. Monodrama.* Wien: Verlag der graphischen Werkstätte, 1920.

Schuß ins Geschçft. Berlin: Schmiede, 1925.

Gesellschaft der Menschenrechte. Wien: Zsolnay, 1926.

Ballade von der Stadt. Ein dramatisches Fresko. Wien: Zsolnay, 1928.

Z. Drasinski (trans. and adapt. F. T. Csokor). *Ungöttliche Komödie.* Berlin: Kiepenheuer, 1929.

Besetztes Gebiet. Wien: Zsolnay, 1930.

Die Weibermühle. Zauberstück in fünf Vorgängen. Wien: Zsolnay, 1932.

Gewesene Menschen. Wien: Zsolnay, 1932.

Das Thüringer Spiel von den zehn Jungfrauen (adaptation). Berlin: Volkschaftsverlag, 1933.

3. November 1918. Wien: Zsolnay, 1936.

Über die Schwelle. Erzählungen. Prag/Wien: Prasser, 1936.

Gottes General. Bilthoven: Verlag De Gemeenschap, 1938.

Als Zivilist im Polenkrieg. Amsterdam: A. de Lange, 1940; collected with *Als Zivilist im Balkandrieg* in *Auf fremden Straßen.* München: Desch, 1955.

Der verlorene Sohn. Wien: Ullstein, 1946.

Das schwarze Schiff. Jerusalem: W. Verkauf, 1946.

Kalypso. Wien: published by author in 1946; also in *Olymp und Golgotha.* Wien: 1954.

Als Zivilist im Balkankrieg. Wien: Ullstein, 1947.

Immer ist Anfang. Gedichte von 1912-1952. Innsbruck: Österreichische Verlags-Anstalt, 1952.

Caesars Witwe. Wien: Zsolnay, 1954.

Pilatus. Wien: Zsolnay, 1954.

Der Schlüssel zum Abgrund. Roman einer Zeit. Wien: Zsolnay, 1955.

Der zweite Hahnenschrei. Sechs Erzählungen. Wien: Zsolnay, 1955.

Hebt den Stein ab!. Wien: Zsolnay, 1957.

Treibholz. Wien: Zsolnay, 1959.

Die Erweckung des Zosimir. Wien: Bergland, 1960.

184   Michael R. Mitchell

Das Zeichen an der Wand. Wien: Zsolnay, 1962.
"Büchners 'Woyzeck.' Versuch einer Vollendung," in *Forum,* Vol. 10
   (1963), 90–95; also in *Oxford German Studies,* Vol. 1 (1966),
   40–57.
"Der tausendjährige Traum," in *Der Mensch und die Macht.* Wien: Zsol-
   nay, 1963.
"Jadwiga" in *Der Mensch und die Macht.* Wien: Zsolnay, 1963.
Zeuge einer Zeit. Briefe aus dem Exil. München/Wien: Langen-Müller,
   1964.
*Die Kaiser zwischen den Zeiten. Ein dramatisches Diptychon mit einem
   Prolog und einem Epilog.* Wien: Zsolnay, 1965.
Alexander. Wien: Zsolnay, 1969.

A number of works have been published only as typed stage scripts by
the Thomas Sessler Verlag, Wien: most are also lodged in the Vienna
City Library. Among them are *Der Feuerofen, Die Stunde des Absterbens, Nicht da nicht dort, Wenn sie zurückkommen, Medea postbellica.*

The following collections have been published; quotations are taken
from these editions:

Europäische Trilogie. Wien: Zsolnay, 1952. Contains *3. November
   1918, Besetztes Gebiet, Der verlorene Sohn.*
Olymp und Golgotha. Wien: Zsolnay, 1954. Contains *Kalypso, Caesars
   Witwe, Pilatus.*
Der Mensch und die Macht. Wien: Zsolnay, 1963. Contains *Jadwiga,
   Der tausendjährige Traum, Gesellschaft der Menschenrechte.*
Zwischen den Zeiten. Wien: Österreichische Verlagsanstalt, 1970.
   Contains *Die Kaiser zwischen den Zeiten, Gottes General, 3. No-
   vember 1918.* This edition has been used for quotations from the
   first two of these plays.

II. Works in English Translation

As a Civilian in the Polish War, trans. P. Owens. London: Secker and
   Warburg, 1940.
K. M. Lichliter, "A Critical Edition and Translation of Franz Theodor
   Csokor's *'Europäische Trilogie,'*" Ph.D. dissertation, Brandeis
   University, 1979.

III. Secondary Works in English

Bithell, Jethro. "Franz Theodor Csokor." *German Life and Letters.*
NS 8 (1954-1955), 37-44.
Branscombe, Peter. "Some Depictions of the First World War in Aus-
trian Drama." *Studies in Modern Austrian Literature,* eds. B. O.
Murdoch and M. G. Ward. Glasgow: University Press, 1981,
pp. 74-86.
Mitchell, Michael R. "Aus der hellen Wohnung zurück in den Zucht-
stall: An Examination of F. T. Csokor's *3. November 1918.*"
Modern Austrian Literature 16, no. 1 (1983), 37-52.
Zohn, Harry. "Franz Theodor Csokor's *3. November 1918.*" *Modern
Austrian Literature* 11, no. 1 (1978), 95-102.

IV. Major Studies in German

Amann, Klaus. *P.E.N. Politik, Emigration, Nationalismus: Ein österreichischer Schriftstellerclub.* Wien: Böhlau, 1984.
Brandys, B. "Das dramatische Werk von Franz Theodor Csokor."
Kwartalnik Neofilologiczny 28 (1981), 407-427.
Goltschnigg, Dietmar. "Csokors Drama, *Gesellschaft der Menschen-
rechte.*" *Jahrbuch des freien deutschen Hochstifts* (1974), 344-
361.
Graf-Blauhut, Heidrun. *Sprache: Traum und Wirklichkeit: Österreichi-
sche Kurzprosa des 20. Jahrhunderts.* Wien: Braumüller, 1983.
Jacobs, M. "Franz Theodor Csokor: Büchners 'Woyzeck'—Versuch
einer Vollendung."*Oxford German Studies* 1 (1966), 31-52.
Lehner, Friedrich. "Literatur im Exil: Franz Theodor Csokor." *German
Quarterly* 20 (1947), 209-213.
Vogelsang, Hans. *Österreichische Dramatik des 20. Jahrhunderts. Spiel
mit Welten, Worten, Wesen.* Wien: Braumüller, 1981.
Wimmer, Paul. *Der Dramatiker Franz Theodor Csokor.* Innsbruck:
Wagner, 1981.

Heimito von Doderer

Bruno Hannemann

Heimito von Doderer has to this day remained a controversial writer. Some rank him with Musil and Broch; and Peter Demetz, for instance, acclaims Doderer as "the legitimate heir to Thomas Mann" and thinks that some of his novels are an "indubitable contribution to world literature."[1] Michael Hamburger praises Doderer's ability to write good and lively realistic novels, a rarity in German literature of any period. Like Demetz he also notes Doderer's passion for life and his humanistic psychology.[2] According to Herbert Eisenreich, the Austrian writer and critic, Doderer is "the greatest novelist of the epoch."[3] Heinz Politzer, on the other hand, while lauding his ability as a story-teller in the traditional sense, maintains that Doderer possesses "no style but only a cadence (*Tonfall*)."[4] Other critics, among them George Steiner and Hans J. Schröder, are even harsher. George Steiner, bluntly voicing his general dislike of Doderer and Vienna, has called his *Demons* "fantastically parochial."[5] The *advocatus diaboli* of Doderer criticism, H. J. Schröder, takes Doderer to task for being a reactionary totally divorced from political and social reality. Rebuking most of the lauda-tory criticism, he accuses Doderer of prejudice, intellectual dishonesty, and anachronistic narrowness, and he claims that Doderer stops think-ing where Musil begins.[6] How this writer will eventually be judged, once critics gain a greater perspective, remains to be seen.

Doderer was born in Weidlingau (Hadersdort) near Vienna on 5 September 1896 into a well-to-do middle class family. His ancestors, proficient architects and engineers, came from Austria, Germany, France, and Hungary. One of his more famous distant relatives was the nineteenth-century poet Nikolaus Lenau, with whom he shared bouts of depression. Doderer's father, who had come from Germany, was a construction engineer, a builder of railroads. Young Heimito spent his childhood in the third district of Vienna and at Prein near Vienna. Both locations left a lasting impression on him, and in many of his works he evoked them with considerable nostalgia. As a somewhat less than average student he passed his high-school examination (*Abitur*) only after extensive private tutoring. His *Abitur* in hand, he enrolled at the University of Vienna to study administrative law, but he was soon called to arms to fight in World War I as a dragoon officer on the Eastern Front. He was soon captured by the Russians and spent the years from 1916 to 1920 in various POW camps in Siberia. During his imprisonment he read works of Homer, Otto Weininger, and A. P. Gütersloh, and he also began to write fiction. Having had a most trenchant experience, he finally fled the camp, crossing the Kirghiz Steppe on foot. Upon his return to Vienna he studied history, particularly of the Middle Ages, and psychology. He completed a doctorate in history but found history too limiting and started to work as a critic and journalist before becoming an independent writer.

Like Gottfried Benn, Doderer too had a brief flirtation with Nazism, and in 1933 he even joined the illegal Austrian National Socialist Party, an action many of his critics will not easily forget. By 1937, while living in Dachau, he had already grown disillusioned, and one year later he officially withdrew. He converted to Catholicism in 1940. During World War II he was a captain in the German Air Force. Upon returning from a British POW camp he established himself principally in Vienna, but after 1952 he also lived frequently in Landshut, Bavaria, the home of his second wife. Although he continued his study of history and even became a member of the exclusive Institute of Historical Studies in Vienna, shortly after the war he felt called to become a writer of fiction.

In December 1944 he entered in his diary: "I look forward for that life that escapes the historian, that solemn fellow, that life which exists in spite of and alongside and between all of history as the only real one, which is the only decisive one."[7] Not that he had stopped writing fiction. On the contrary, he completed several lengthy novels before the war. In 1937 he had almost finished the epic novel *Die Dämonen* (*The Demons*), his longest and perhaps best prose work, but it was not published until 1956, mainly for political reasons. His first published novels were *Ein Mord, den jeder begeht* (*Every Man a Murderer*), and *Ein Umweg* (*A Detour*). As promising as these works were, they brought him only temporary fame. Goaded by his friend and mentor, the painter-writer Albert Paris Gütersloh,[8] he stubbornly continued to write fiction. Even his novel *Die erleuchteten Fenster oder die Menschwerdung des Amtsrates Julius Zihal* (The Illuminated Windows, or the Humanization of Councilor Julius Zihal), completed in 1939 but not published until 1950, failed to establish him as a writer. Indeed, not until 1951 after his voluminous novel *Die Strudlhofstiege* (The Strudlhof Stairway) had appeared, did Doderer, now fifty-five, experience his first breakthrough. Subsequently, *Die Dämonen* helped to further solidify his position as a storyteller of the highest caliber. He was awarded the prize of the Federation of German Industry (1954) and finally the Austrian State Prize for Literature (1958). In his last years he surprised his readers with two more ambitious works *Die Merowinger oder die totale Familie* (The Merovingians or The Total Family), his "reservation for the grotesque" (C, 35),[9] and the *Roman Nr. 7, Erster Teil: Die Wasserfälle von Slunj* (*Novel No. 7. First Part: The Waterfalls of Slunj*).

Although we have a fair grasp of Doderer, the writer, Doderer, the man, is still shrouded in mystery. Hiding forever behind his Viennese mask, this "great histrio"[10] had no intention of revealing himself to the public. In his sparse and short autobiographical statements as well as in his extensive diaries he remained rather detached, divulging little that would provide a clue to his personality. Even the friends with whom he hobnobbed in the Café Hawelka knew him only superficially. This "extrovert with a hidden soul"[11] is known to have been very courteous, a dashing cavalier with an exceptionally well-groomed appearance. Being modest and unassuming, he preferred to stay out of the limelight, and even his late fame never tempted him to play the Olympian. He was an outstanding conversationalist full of wit, irony, and humor, but Doderer's personality would be incomplete if we were to overlook his whims and vexatious moods. Heinz Politzer aimed in the right direction when he ascribed to him the double role of a "Viennese rascal and an archaic storyteller."[12] In a rare confessional passage he once answered the question of what he would like "to have and wish: . . . lots of money in order to perish finally and conclusively as a result of the most extreme sexual excesses, senseless drinking bouts, and corresponding violent acts" (C, 79).

Since the appearance of *Die Dämonen* Doderer has been hailed as the literary executor of the Hapsburg Empire. He depicts the "climate and rhythm of the old Austria,"[13] wrote Claudio Magris, who sees in him a typical representative of the Hapsburg myth in Austrian literature.[14] Doderer no doubt looks back and tries to fathom, as a subtitle

of *Die Strudlhofstiege* suggests, "the depth of the years." Like Marcel
Proust, whose art he once flippantly characterized as the "powerful
dynamics of boredom,"[15] he is constantly in search of the lost past. In
fact, on reading his diaries one gets the impression that the present is
being lived and perceived not so much for its own sake but rather for
the purpose of being remembered and reborn in the mind at a future
time. "Such a journal as this, sensibly written, should produce a kind of
retrospective autobiography" (C, 69), Doderer writes in his diary
Commentarii. It is astonishing how little space his two voluminous
diaries devote to the immediate environment or the sociopolitical
reality. Apparently he saw little need to confront the turbulent times
he lived through. Unlike many of his German counterparts after World
War II, he was not very much attuned to contemporary history. Somehow he acted as if he were outside the flow of time. "I will have to
think again about our world situation . . . . One does not get around it.
It is idiotic . . . to live beside the abyss without taking notice of it,"
(C, 72), he writes once in a self-accusatory manner. Even though he
repeatedly claims that the only important task for a writer is to perceive the "here and now" and to understand that the "depth is outside," Doderer does not always succeed in venturing outside of his own
inner self. Absorbed by his own writing, his state of mind, his dreams,
and his aspirations, contemporary, objective reality often takes on the
quality of a projection.

A close look at his diaries allows us to presume that the goal to
reach objectivity is more of a personal challenge than an accomplished
fact. "The tension between the passionate struggle for objectivity and
the equally passionate yielding of subjectivity determines the total
picture of Doderer's personality as well as his complete narrative
work,"[16] Dietrich Weber writes. It is a paradox that Doderer, the realist
and historian, actually lacks, in the words of Magris, an "interest in
history."[17] Rooted in a static psychological world view, he has developed few sensibilities to understand the inner dynamics of a society or
to perceive historical change. Leaving contemporary history to the
historian and sociologist, Doderer is primarily concerned with probing
the ahistorical realm of memory and perception. Writing is for him first
and foremost a tool in the personal struggle against his own subjective
mind and the disorders associated with it. "I became a writer because I
felt I could thus come to terms with life. This is the meaning of literature for me,"[18] Doderer once said in an interview. He submits to the
tortuous act of writing (C, 10) because by sharpening his cognition and

perception it can help him to gain a semblance of objectivity and to create order out of chaos.

Doderer's massive and highly complex work is concerned with essentially one theme: the process of humanization (*Menschwerdung*). This ethical goal was part of the *Zeitgeist* in the years after World War I. The expressionistic generation seldom grew tired of depicting this longing for a moral rebirth of mankind. But unlike the expressionists who wanted to change the whole society, Doderer limited himself strictly to the individual. To achieve this goal of *Menschwerdung* (literally becoming human) one must, as he outlined it once in an "Autobiographical Epilogue," shun the direct path at any cost in favor of "the indirect way; that of thinking according to life" instead of "living according to thinking . . ."[19] This is precisely the concern of Doderer's first major novels, *Ein Mord, den jeder begeht* and *Ein Umweg. Ein Mord, den jeder begeht,* which appeared in 1938 and was translated into English in 1964, focuses on a fifteen-year-old boy who unintentionally and unknowingly commits a murder while participating in a youthful prank. Feeling free of guilt, he leads a perfectly normal life and becomes a successful businessman. Seven years after the murder he marries a well-to-do girl whose parents happen to have a picture of their other, already deceased, daughter hanging on the wall. It is a portrait of the woman Conrad had murdered. For the hero this picture contains some magic qualities; it begins to move and haunt him. The woman acquires the quality of a saint, and Conrad becomes so enamored that he starts to woo her. Subsequently he takes it upon himself to search for the murderer and soon finds his trail. Finally, while playing a game with an old mirror he has a notion that the reflection in it is staring at him with black perforated eyes. It is he himself. When he also sees a reflection of a skull, he comes to know that he is the murderer of this woman.

By discovering the events and actions of his own past, Conrad gradually goes through a process of humanization. He gains insight into his childhood and adolescence and recognizes the determining factors in his life: "Everyone has his childhood dumped over his head like a bucket. Later we find out what was in it. But it runs down for an entire lifetime. . . ."[20] Adhering to an analytic structure, the author takes great care to show in detail what fate has "dumped" over Conrad's head while he was still a child. He tells us of his father's flaws, of Conrad's experiences in school and out in nature. While superbly recapturing Conrad's past, especially his boyhood and the influence of the outside world on him, this early work suffers from a number of flaws. The plot often appears contrived, particularly in regard to the strange sequence of events. Even one of the key scenes, the murder of Louison Veik, is too consciously constructed to appear totally convincing. And so is the accident that causes Conrad's death.[21]

This death, as accidental as it may seem, is fraught with meaning. As Conrad is opening his eyes for the last time and contemplating his past, he experiences a decisive change in his attitude towards life: "It was like a flash of grace, illuminating everything with a surpassing clarity."[22] Conrad is dying, but he is not doomed. Quite the contrary: like the hero of a baroque drama he experiences his death as the climax of his life. Besides adopting a new language he acquires a feeling of lightness which serves as a signal that he has surpassed the tragic stage.[23]

Doderer's second short novel, *Ein Umweg,* published in 1940, is set in the Thirty Years War. The action centers on Paul Brandter, a professional soldier, who is about to face the gallows for having violated the code of ethics by mistreating the civilian population. Being struck with utter fear, this mercenary pleads for his life. As custom has it, a condemned man can be saved if a woman declares herself willing to marry him. Hanna readily responds and, thanks to the prompt action of the officer of the Spanish guard, Manuel Cuendias, Brandter is soon pardoned by the emperor. But this newly won freedom seems only to compound his problems. His marriage to Hanna is a failure; he is unable to establish a meaningful relationship with her. His life becomes filled with routine and boredom in sharp contrast to the life of his mercenary days. Feeling miserable, Brandter is taken back into his past to retrace in detail his previous life, which is becoming increasingly more attractive to him. He particularly values the vitality and freedom of his former life style, even though he is fully aware that it led him to his sentence of execution.

In the meantime the other protagonist of the novel, Count Cuendias, who had aided in the rescue of Brandter, falls in love with Hanna, because Hanna's liveliness and spontaneity present a refreshing contrast to the cold and calculating noblewomen of his circles. The count is gradually lured away from his proper sphere, the Spanish court life with all its formalities, rituals, and regimentations. Hanna makes him stray from the destiny that fate had provided for him, and he too, like Brandter, eventually faces doom, but not until he has found new freedom. Ironically, he is killed by no other than Brandter, who suspects him of being his wife's lover. Brandter is subsequently executed for having killed the man who saved his life. His actual execution is a a signal to him that his death is part of his life's fate which he should have quietly accepted the first time instead of circumventing it. Viewing it from that perspective, Hanna does not actually save Brandter but in a sense seduces him by instilling in him the false belief that he can somehow avoid his fate. This, according to Doderer, will lead to an unfulfilled life, to misery and a loss of freedom. In the end Brandter fully perceives this, for his stepping onto the gallows does indeed, as Michael Bachem suggests, contain "hints of liberation and peace."[24] By taking a detour Brandter gains insight into his own life and what has determined it. This knowledge liberates him and lets him embrace life as it is. The beginning and end may be fixed, but in between, in the twists, turns, and diversions, life acquires a richness and fullness that can, according to Doderer, never be gained in any other way, least of all in the direct way. Unlike *Ein Mord, den jeder begeht* or *Ein Umweg* the short novel *Die erleuchteten Fenster oder die Menschwerdung des Amtsrates Julius Zihal,* which was completed in 1939 but not published until 1950, is Doderer's first longer work that is solidly anchored in Vienna. In this humorous story Doderer takes considerable care to capture the peculiar atmosphere, the habits, and the traditions of the Hapsburg Monarchy represented constantly by the double-headed eagle. Councillor Zihal, his mentality, and his world are so typically Austrian that this novel is virtually untranslatable.

As the subtitle indicates, Doderer is once again concerned with the question of *Menschwerdung,* this time of the civil servant Julius Zihal. However, even though Zihal does indeed metamorphose from a "troglodyte" or "worm" into a full-fledged human being, the theme of humanization often appears peripheral. What captures the imagination of the reader is the masterful depiction of Zihal's bureaucratic pedantry and stiffness, his peculiar obsessions and whimsies.

At first we meet Zihal as a stiff and dignified bureaucrat who is thoroughly caught up in a rigid order of government rules and regulations. Having internalized these rules to the point of becoming an allegory, this pedant lives in a grotesquely funny atmosphere. According to him, a person does not gain the status of a human being until he has become a file (*Aktwerdung*). Zihal is the satiric object *par excellence* but Doderer chooses to treat him with humor, understanding, and tolerance, calling him affectionately "our" Zihal. Yet, for all his sympathetic qualities, we should not forget that Zihal, in worshiping absolute order, has the potential viciousness of a Nazi leader. The foils to his whimsies are the brownshirts who happened to goose step through the streets of Vienna while Doderer was writing the novel.

When Zihal retires, he moves into a new apartment and, having no purpose, becomes a Peeping Tom. Opera glasses in hand he sits at his dark window and watches nude women and girls in the "illuminated windows" facing him. However, just as important as his voyeurism is his need to classify and order. With exceptional thoroughness he records, numbers, labels, and catalogues his visual experiences in an "Observation Book." The apex of humor is reached when, upon focusing his telescope on a window, he notices other binoculars staring at him. Doderer likens this visual confrontation to a naval battle in which Zihal is hit. He sinks to the ground and breaks his telescope. His submergence however turns out to be positive; it lets him experience "a primordial chaotic state" which propels him toward his "final humanization."[25] A little later, after recovering from a slight illness, Zihal becomes a different man. He gradually discards his old bureaucratic habits and his obsessive need for order. His stiff and formal manner of speech yields to a graceful rhythm and suppleness. He finally falls in love with Rosl Oplatek, a fleshy attractive lady whom he had the occasion to watch for some time from afar. The touch of her roundness helps to cure him of his old obsessions and manias. When Julius joins Rosl for a performance of Mozart's *Magic Flute,* that musical glorification of harmony, love, and marriage, his metamorphosis is nearly completed. The struggle between a rigid barren order and creative chaos associated with human contact, warmth, and light has clearly been decided in favor of the latter.

Zihal's story is particularly refreshing because of its stylistic elegance and its abundant humor, qualities not easily found in German literature. It is full of exuberance, hyperboles and countless grotesqueries. Doderer is truly masterful in displaying stylistic virtuosity and freedom that remind one of the German original Jean Paul. Not bound by many conventions, the narrator frequently takes the liberty of addressing the reader ironically and looks closely over Zihal's shoulder to point out humorous habits, ludicrous contortions, and obsessions.

If *Die erleuchteten Fenster* is appreciated for its grace and lightness, then *Die Strudlhofstiege* and *Die Dämonen* are known for their sheer weight and massiveness. Together they fill over 2,500 pages, demonstrating not only Doderer's iron discipline, but also his masterful control and inexhaustible creativity. The key to *Die Strudlhofstiege oder Melzer und die Tiefe der Jahre* lies only partially in its title. It is by any judgment an immensely complex novel, combining an expansive horizon with a lengthy time frame. Besides Melzer, who is only one of the principal characters, the reader is summoned to participate in the fate of about twenty major characters in a time span ranging from 1910 to 1925. Nearly all the representatives of Vienna's highly stratified society vie for appearance here, and Herbert Eisenreich may have exaggerated only slightly when he claimed that this epic work fulfills "historiographic functions."[26]

Die Strudlhofstiege has rightly been called "Doderer's most successful *Bildungsroman.*"[27] As in his previous works the focus is again on the transformation of characters who lead unfulfilled lives into true human beings. The two principal ones are the soldier Melzer and Mary K. Melzer. He is an ordinary lieutenant before and after World War I, but later he becomes a civil servant in a state tax office. Doderer introduces him as an awkward military-minded man slightly out of touch with the real world. This "modern Parsifal"[28] leads the life of a withdrawn bachelor too inhibited to accept love. Being shy and hesitant, he distinguishes himself by avoiding all involvement. Doderer aptly characterizes him and his wondrous habits with the image of a crayfish who is partially buried in the mud at the bottom of a stream. It is suggested that he dig out, crack his shell, and open himself up to meaningful human relationships. To achieve this goal Doderer exposes him to a shocking experience. He forces him to become a witness to a brutal streetcar accident in which Mary K., a woman he was once engaged to, loses one of her legs above the knee. Facing the blood, this ordinarily passive character suddenly becomes involved; he kneels down, puts on a tourniquet, and so keeps Mary from bleeding to death.

Mary K., who has lived a normal, contented, if slightly boring life before, is aroused by her accident. Showing remarkable resilience and psychological strength, she mobilizes her energies and develops into a radiant and beautiful woman. Melzer, also thoroughly shaken by the accident, begins to contemplate his life. Lying on a bear rug, he lulls himself into a semiconscious *Denkschlaf* (meditative slumber) by sipping Turkish coffee and smoking a chibouk. There he fathoms the "depth of the years" and comes to a living awareness of his own past. By conjuring up detailed images and smells from his youth he realizes his true potential and is gradually initiated into a life of increased sensitivity and regard for others. He readily embraces such Christian values as humility, self-sacrifice, and charity, and in the end he achieves a high degree of human dignity. Having successfully broken his shell, this bachelor is also ready to commit himself to a woman.

Behind the slowly moving action reigns the mysterious Strudlhof Stairway, the "central actor" of the novel.[29] This architectural master-piece with its complicated terraces, elaborate ramps and corners, orna-mented lamps, and sculptures connects and separates two Vienna districts, the aristocratic one above and the bourgeois one below. It links two different social and intellectual levels; but since it also serves as a bridge between the districts, people living in the area cannot avoid it. For Stangeler, the intellectual and one of Doderer's spokesmen, it is the "stage" of life where the Viennese characters play out their con-flicts, scandals, and intrigues, where they love, kiss, and exchange memories. It is a secret but friendly *genius loci* that reminds people of a living past. It too, like Melzer, perhaps even more so, is a (material) witness to "the depth of the years." Besides being functional it is a complex petrified actor, a true synthesis of life and art. People who walk on it do so devoutly and attentively with the awareness of the richness and color in its shapes and history. They momentarily forget their goals and surrender to a leisurely experience, as they see, feel, and take pleasure in every turn. In the stairway Doderer found a striking metaphor for his indirect way where art, memory, life, and beauty are harmoniously united, where in the words of Michael Bachem "the path is more than the goal."[30]

What is true of the stairway is equally true of the novel as a whole: the path is more important than its destination. Since the stair-way is the novel *in nuce,* the goal, more often than is good for the novel, falls by the wayside. An abundance of sensuous detail usually drowns any linear action or dramatic tension. The anecdotal individual scenes reign supreme. As in life itself there are many focal points, and several threads of action run side by side or crisscross each other to weave a most intricate tapestry. The technique of shuttling back and forth between different time planes complicates things further. The structural model that Doderer tried to imitate was the "big sym-phony,"[31] notably that of Beethoven.

Since Doderer is more than convinced that the "reality is out-side"—a refreshing reversal of the German tradition of placing it inside —he spares no effort to capture it in all its polychromatic diversity and multiplicity. The reader is faced with an astonishing accumulation of detail and sense impressions. Subscribing to the values of pre-industrial leisure, Doderer takes the time to tell us about specific smells such as that of stagnant water or tanbark, but he is equally sensitive to the various shades of light and color. "The final things that matter in narration are always sensuous data without commentary" (C, 85), he once claimed. But even Doderer does not subscribe to such an attitude with impunity. Sometimes he becomes stuck in chatting about banal and tedious detail, and his "baroque realism"[32] comes dangerously close to fulfilling the concept of *l'art pour l'art*. But this is precisely where Doderer's strength also lies. His style is highly digressive, parenthetical, even colloquial and gossipy but it shows an astonishing virtuosity. Metaphors, similes, oxymora, and other rhetorical devices abound, lending an ornamental, or "baroque" quality. There are passages of great lyrical beauty, but Doderer can also be fresh, bold, and direct, and can display striking images when necessary. And he knows how to inject humor ranging from the simple pun and belly laugh to the highly witty aphorism.

In describing a novel of the scope of *Die Strudlhofstiege* we inevitably commit an injustice regardless of how honest and fair we would like to be, because such a complex work of art simply defies a short description and easy classification. What is lost is the very essence of the novel, its great complexity, its unique character, its description of detail, its style, wit, humor, and lyrical quality. Drawing the limits of our critical efforts, Doderer once wrote: "A work of narrative art is all the weightier the less a summary is able to give an idea of it."[33] This is even more true of his next work, *Die Dämonen,* which is perhaps his most important, certainly most ambitious novel. Chronologically the novel is a sequel to the *Strudlhofstiege;* it starts where the other leaves off. But in reality *Die Dämonen* is the older of the two because the greater part of it was already written between 1931 and 1937.

Die Dämonen (translated into English in 1961) is a "total novel," which, according to Dietrich Weber, means "a novel without a theme."[34] In the words of Michael Bachem it is "one of the most kaleidoscopic novels written in German."[35] About thirty major characters and many centers of action allow Doderer to explore in detail even the periphery and fringe (often lunatic) of Viennese society. The main theme of the novel is the general decline of Viennese society in the twenties ending in the "Cannae of Austrian freedom" (Th. D., 1311).[36] By looking into the minds of many representatives of Viennese society Doderer tries to show how and why Austrian society skidded into dictatorship. Through the concrete examples of certain individuals rather than through abstract political events, Doderer tries to show how dangerous ideologies take root. The action of this virtually actionless novel culminates in the burning of the Palace of Justice in 1927 by an angry mob of demonstrating workers. Police and demonstrators clash and kill each other. This incident is symbolic and foreshadows the more ominous takeover of Austria by the Nazis in 1938.

One of the most intriguing aspects of *Die Dämonen* is its immensely complex structure. Doderer, paying little attention to the average reader, narrates the events on three different time levels. First he introduces the chronicle of Councillor Geyrenhoff, who observed and recorded the activities of a certain group of people from 1926 through the burning of the Palace of Justice. This chronicle remains unfinished because Geyrenhoff falls in love. It is taken up again in 1955, when he is temporally much further removed from the actual events. The third time plane is occupied by the author-editor of the whole novel who, becoming impatient with Geyrenhoff and his limitations, frequently intercedes to tell the events from his perspective. Thus, following the technique used in Dostoyevsky's *Possessed,* which served Doderer as a model, *Die Dämonen* is written in the first person singular. However, in order to accommodate various narrative perspectives Doderer, like Dostoyevsky, acts as an editor who presents the whole work as a composite of contributions from several characters in the novel. To add to the complexity *Die Dämonen* is not only written "according to the chronicle of Councillor Geyrenhoff," as the subtitle suggests, but Geyrenhoff, being aware of his limited horizon, accepts reports from some of his friends. He diligently edits and integrates them into his own chronicle. Since each writer has a different narrative mode and perspective, the reader has the illusion of looking at a multifarious picture of Viennese reality.

The chronicler Geyrenhoff is a retired bachelor who leads a comfortable and leisurely existence residing in a painter's studio above the roofs of Vienna. He is kind, concerned, and mature, a man well qualified for his task. As Doderer's Zeitblom (the narrator in Thomas Mann's *Doktor Faustus*) he is primarily a spectator who watches the events with relative detachment. To him Vienna is a city situated on the crossroads between the East and the West. Because of its unique location it is open to the influences of both cultural spheres. The East, which has always exerted a special fascination on Doderer reminiscent of that experienced by Rilke or Werfel, is presented as a flat expanse with infinite horizons and a lack of distinct lines. It is the land of the soul, of feeling. In contradistinction the West with its limited and defined space connotes rationality, individuality, and self-assertion.

Not unlike Proust, Joyce, and Musil, all of whom he once unconvincingly dispatched with a few disparaging remarks,[37] Doderer was deeply interested in the perception of reality and in experience. According to him, people live in either of two realities, the first or the second. Those living in the first are in tune with life as it is; they "think," as we noted before, "according to life" and accept the course fate has charted out for them, whether it be the loss of a leg, going to war, or even being killed. Flatly rejecting all utopian or idealistic philosophies, they are always eager to discover a complex reality free of any prejudices, ideologies, obsessions, or manias.

Unfortunately, most people, including nearly all of the characters at the beginning of *Die Dämonen,* happen to be trapped in the second reality, the "pseudological" world of nonperception. Opposed to those living in the first reality, they live more "according to thinking" and perceive the world not as it is but as it ought to be. Such an attitude can refer to any aspect of reality, to the political as well as racial, ethical, religious, sexual, and linguistic. Among those dominated by this "second reality" are all ideologues, revolutionaries, maniacs, and fanatics. They wear blinders that limit their horizon and are known for transporting the energy generated by their individual dissatisfaction into revolutionary action. In *Die Dämonen* Herzka, Gyurkicz, Schlaggenberg, and Meisgeier belong above all to this category. The wealthy businessman Herzka, for instance, is obsessed with the trial and punishment of witches and wants all middle-aged women to be tortured. Gyurkicz, a talented artist, sees reality only in terms of political action, a compulsion which eventually causes his death. The brilliant writer Schlaggenberg, on the other hand, fanatically pursues his ideal of "fat ladies" and writes a treatise on his search for them and how to classify the ideal type. Meisgeier, the most demonic of them, imposes his thinking on others by thieving and murdering. This thug, who is eventually caught and killed in the sewers of Vienna, had all the qualifications to become a perfect Nazi bully.

Doderer does not claim that all these characters who live in their own "pseudological" world are destructive. They can, as the example of Schlaggenberg demonstrates, be quite harmless and pleasant to live and associate with. But in one way or another they are still ideologues, and their own blindness or whims multiplied a thousandfold can potentially lead to movements that tend to impose their will on the people as a whole.

Doderer believes and takes great care to show that psychological makeup rather than political events is responsible for totalitarian regimes, for dictatorships on the right or left, and for the creation of racial stereotypes. Unlike the ordinary historian he prefers to explore the rise of ideologies with the aid of ahistorical principles, with psychology and the phenomenology of the mind. On this concrete human level of the minute depiction of individual weaknesses and shortcomings Doderer also explains the rise of the Nazi dictatorship. Thus in the eyes of Doderer the demons that cause the big conflagrations are all too human; they are ubiquitous and belong to the banal world of everyday life. In contrast to Thomas Mann's *Doktor Faustus,* which demonizes the rise of Nazism, Doderer actually "de-demonizes it by making it understandable."[38]

Perhaps the most important figure in *Die Dämonen* is the factory worker Leonhard Kakabsa. A "kind of proletarian Wilhelm Meister,"[39] he embarks on an autodidactic program, educates and thereby frees himself from the shackles of his narrow and stifling world. As curious as it may seem, not an intellectual exercise but rather the sense of smell triggers Kakabsa's educational development. As he lies on a leather sofa he draws in the odors of the Danube and its boats, and suddenly he is overcome by a trenchant mystical experience of exceptional well-being which in turn opens up his past. Knowing that he has not lived up to his human potential, he buys a Latin grammar and begins to study it. In addition he learns proper German, reads Renaissance philosophy, and is on his way to becoming an emancipated self-reliant person with an open and autonomous mind. He eventually leaves his old job and becomes the librarian of a rich count.

Kakabsa is a living example of Doderer's moral maxim that individual dissatisfaction can and should be solved only on a subjective level and not by revolutionary action. By changing himself Kakabsa involuntarily changes the conditions that determine his life.[40] It is worth noting that language enables Kakabsa to escape from the stifling world of his past.

Underlying his insistence on opening himself up to reality, to the here and now, is Doderer's axiom that the phenomenal world is not merely a symbol or cipher but is genuine, highly authentic, a revelation of God. Consequently it should neither be transcended for the sake of some other so-called higher reality as in the German tradition of the "trans-real" novel, nor should it be changed. "Every phenomenon is a position of the creator, his material language, and it should for that reason remain unopposed" (T, 727), Doderer once wrote in his diaries, combining a religious justification for his deterministic realism with an antirevolutionary attitude.

Doderer, though a highly original writer, is rather traditional in his literary technique. He is a "realist" who has synthesized and expanded the literary forms of the nineteenth-century novel, claiming that the empirical approach is the best method to capture reality as it is. Besides it also "helps to suspend again the harmful separation between art and science" (T, 374). As his diary entries show, he never grew tired in his struggle to reach exactitude and scientific objectivity because "the path toward objectivity is the actual arena of the writer," his "goal and reward, indeed, happiness" (C, 38). His novel shows that he took this goal seriously. For instance, when he worked on *Die Dämonen* he stayed in close touch with the Vienna Central Office for Meteorology because he felt he had to know precisely whether, how much, and when it rained on a certain day in the Vienna of the twenties. Adhering to the naturalistic rather than realistic technique, some days are told from hour to hour with an enormous accumulation of banal detail and a corresponding slowness of action that tests the patience of the reader to the utmost.

The world of Doderer's novels is in his own words a "fruitful chaos"[41] but, lest we forget, a carefully calculated one, designed on the drawing board. Despite its realistic details his composition reflects not so much an objective reality, as has been frequently claimed, but a reality that is carefully selected and directed to serve a moral purpose, namely, that of humanization. Since humanization can be achieved only by traveling an indirect meandering path, the course charted out for Doderer's figures has all the qualities of an intricate maze. It is characterized by unexpected turns, sudden accidents, random actions, and irrational events, all for the sake of creating a detour in space as well as in time. Once his figures have finally made their way through this labyrinthine reality, they are usually rewarded with a "happy ending" not unlike the one in traditional comedy. Doderer, obviously influenced more by his wish to harmonize than by depicting reality as it is, frequently, perhaps too frequently, lets the wedding bells ring at the end of his novels.

These structural peculiarities based on moral premises will inevitably introduce a certain "artificiality"[42] into Doderer's work, a feeling that the characters and events are too consciously manipulated in advance.[43] Henry Hatfield has remarked that Doderer's figures move "like dancers in an elaborate ballet."[44] The reader cannot help but anticipate many actions and reactions of Doderer's characters with a resultant weakening of the elements of surprise and dramatic tension.

Yet for all his faults and shortcomings we should not be blind to the fact that Doderer has created an immensely rich canvas that bubbles with life, sensuousness, and adventurousness. His monumental work presents nothing less than a declaration of love toward life and people, which save for his conservatism is relatively free from social messages. Being as suspicious of contemporary ideologies as he is humble about himself, Doderer is careful not to show that he knows better than others; he feels no urge to teach, much less heal, save, or improve anyone. According to him, social criticism is valid only if directed against oneself. If indeed there is any extra-literary purpose emanating from his momentous work, it is the subtle invitation to participate in the richness of experience, in his colorful and artistic detour. He summons us to join the pedestrians crossing the Strudlhof Stairway and to take the time to see, feel, hear, smell, and contemplate every turn of a world so rich in artistic detail.

Notes

1.   Peter Demetz, *Postwar German Literature: A Critical Introduction* (New York: Western Publishing, 1970), p. 229.

2.   Michael Hamburger, *From Prophecy to Exorcism. The Premises of Modern German Literature* (London: Longmans, 1965), pp. 132 and 139.

3.   Herbert Eisenreich, *Reaktionen. Essays zur Literatur* (Gütersloh: Bertelsmann, 1964), p. 166.

4.   Heinz Politzer, *Das Schweigen der Sirenen* (Stuttgart: Metzler, 1968), p. 74.

5.   George Steiner, "The Brown Danube," *Reporter,* 12 October 1961, p. 60.

6.   Hans-Joachim Schröder, *Apperzeption und Vorurteil: Untersuchungen zur Reflexion Heimito von Doderers* (Heidelberg: Winter 1976), esp. p. 444ff.

7.   Heimito von Doderer, *Tangenten. Tagebuch eines Schriftstellers 1940–1950* (München: Biederstein, 1964), p. 269 (henceforth cited in text as T with page number).

8.   For an analysis of their interesting relationship see Peter Karl Pabisch and Alan Best, "The Total Novel: Heimito von Doderer and Albert Paris Gütersloh," *Modern Austrian Writing. Literature*

and Society after 1945, ed. Alan Best and Hans Wolfschütz (London: Oswald Wolff, 1980), pp. 63–78.

9. Heimito von Doderer, *Commentarii 1951 bis 1956: Tagebücher aus dem Nachlaß*, ed. Wendelin Schmidt-Dengler (München: Biederstein, 1976) (henceforth cited in text as C with page number.

10. Hans Flesch-Brunningen, "Heimito," *BooksAbroad* 42(1968),360.

11. Ibid.

12. Heinz Politzer, *Schweigen,* p. 74.

13. Claudio Magris, *Der habsburgische Mythos in der österreichischen Literatur* (Salzburg: Otto Müller, 1966), p. 297. This myth is characterized by a patriarchal conservatism, the praise of non-action, resignation, a devotional narrowness, a static, anti-progressive world view and a love for tangible detail. Concepts such as freedom and democracy are rejected.

14. Ibid.

15. Heimito von Doderer, "Grundlagen und Funktion des Romans." *Die Wiederkehr der Drachen. Aufsätze/Traktate/Reden,* ed. Wendelin Schmidt-Dengler, introd. Wolfgang H. Fleischer (München: Biederstein, 1970), p. 165.

16. Dietrich Weber, "Heimito von Doderer," *Deutsche Literatur seit 1945,* ed. Dietrich Weber (Stuttgart: Kröner, 1968), p. 79.

17. Claudio Magris, *Mythos,* p. 297.

18. "Interview with Palma Caetano," *Erinnerungen an Heimito von Doderer,* ed. Xaver Schaffgotsch (München: Biederstein, 1972), p. 33.

19. Heimito von Doderer, "Autobiographisches Nachwort," *Das letzte Abenteuer* (Stuttgart: Reclam, 1953), p. 121.

20. Heimito von Doderer, *Every Man a Murderer,* trans. Richard and Clara Winston (New York: Knopf, 1964), p. 5.

21. Sensitive to the criticism that his plots lack credibility, Doderer in his "Autobiographical Epilog" (1953) refers to an identical accident that took place in Düsseldorf at the very day this novel appeared. Doderer proudly announces that this is "solid evidence" that Conrad's accident happened in accordance with the laws of life. See H.v.D., "Autobiographisches Nachwort," *Letztes Abenteuer,* p. 125.

22. Heimito von Doderer, *Every Man a Murderer,* p. 361.

23. See Herbert Eisenreich, "Heimito von Doderer," *Deutsche Dichter der Gegenwart,* ed. Benno von Wiese (Berlin: Schmidt, 1973), p. 54f.

24. Michael Bachem, *Heimito von Doderer* (Boston: Twayne, 1981), p. 67.

25. Heimito von Doderer, *Die erleuchteten Fenster oder die Menschwerdung des Amtsrates Julius Zihal* (München: Biederstein, 1950), p. 181.

26. Herbert Eisenreich, "Heimito von Doderer," p. 50.

27. Henry Hatfield, *Crisis and Continuity in Modern German Fiction* (Ithaca/London: Cornell, 1969), p. 102.

28. Ibid., p. 94.

29. Peter Demetz, *Postwar German Literature*, p. 234.

30. Michael Bachem, *Heimito von Doderer*, p. 86.

31. Heimito von Doderer, "Grundlagen und Funktion des Romans," p. 163.

32. Ivar Ivask, "A Winter with Heimito," *Books Abroad* 42 (Summer 1968), 345. It should be added that Ivar Ivask actually praises Doderer's style as a "most welcome antidote to the flood of abstract allegories unleashed upon modern literature by another great Austrian, Franz Kafka."

33. Heimito von Doderer, *Repertorium. Ein Begreifbuch von höheren und niederen Lebens-Sachen,* ed. Dietrich Weber (München: Biederstein, 1969), p. 72.

34. Dietrich Weber, *Heimito von Doderer. Studien zu seinem Romanwerk* (München: Beck, 1963), p. 181.

35. Michael Bachem, *Heimito von Doderer*, p. 93.

36. Heimito von Doderer, *The Demons* (2 vols.), trans. Richard and Clara Winston (New York: Knopf, 1961), p. 1311.

37. See Heimito von Doderer, "Grundlagen und Funktion des Romans," p. 165 f.

38. Michael Hamburger, *From Prophecy to Exorcism*, p. 139.

39. Peter Demetz, *Postwar German Literature*, p. 237.

40. See Anton Reininger, "'Die Dämonen': totaler Roman und antirevolutionärer Traktat," *Literatur und Kritik* 80 (December 1973), 604 f.

41. Heimito von Doderer, "Grundlagen und Funktion des Romans," p. 163.

42. Dietrich Weber, "Heimito von Doderer," p. 94.

43. See Martin W. Swales, "The Narrator in the Novels of Heimito von Doderer," *Modern Language Review* 61 (1966), 85-95, esp. 86.

44. Henry Hatfield, *Crisis and Continuity*, p. 107.

Bibliography

I. Works by Heimito von Doderer in German

Gassen und Landschaft. Wien: Haybach, 1923. A collection of twenty-seven poems written mostly in Siberian POW camps.

Die Bresche. Ein Vorgang in vierundzwanzig Stunden. Novel. Wien: Haybach, 1924.

Das Geheimnis des Reichs. Roman aus dem russischen Bfgerkrieg. Wien: Saturn, 1930.

Der Fall Gütersloh. Ein Schicksal und seine Deutung. Wien: Haybach, 1930.

Ein Mord den jeder begeht. München: Biederstein, 1938.

Ein Umweg. München: Biederstein, 1940.

Die erleuchteten Fenster oder die Menschwerdung des Amtsrates Julius Zihal. München: Biederstein, 1950.

Die Strudlhofstiege oder Melzer und die Tiefe der Jahre. München: Biederstein, 1951.

Die Dämonen. Nach der Chronik des Sektionsrates Geyrenhoff. München: Biederstein, 1956.

Ein Weg im Dunklen: Gedichte und epigrammatische Verse. München: Biederstein, 1957.

Die Posaunen von Jericho. Neues Divertimento. Zürich: Arche, 1958.

Die Merowinger oder die totale Familie. München: Biederstein, 1962.

Roman Nr. 7, Erster Teil: Die Wasserfälle von Slunj. München: Biederstein, 1963.

Das letzte Abenteuer. Stuttgart: Reclam, 1964.

Tangenten: Tagebuch eines Schriftstellers 1940-1950. München: Biederstein, 1964.

Meine neunzehn Lebensläufe und neun andere Geschichten. (Mit neunzehn Photographien und einer Schallplatte.) München: Biederstein, 1966.

Roman Nr. 7, Zweiter Teil: Der Grenzwald (Fragment) (Nachwort von Dietrich Weber.) München: Biederstein, 1967.

Frühe Prosa: Die Bresche/Jutta Bamberger/Das Geheimnis des Reiches, ed. Hans Flesch-Brunningen. München: Biederstein, 1968.

Repertorium: Ein Begreifbuch von höheren und niederen Lebens-Sachen, ed. Dietrich Weber. München: Biederstein, 1969.

Die Wiederkehr der Drachen: Aufsätze/Traktate/Reden, ed. Wendelin Schmidt-Dengler, introd. Wolfgang H. Fleischer. München: Biederstein, 1970.

Die Erzählungen, ed. Wendelin Schmidt-Dengler. München: Biederstein, 1972.

Das Doderer-Buch: Eine Auswahl aus seinem Werk, ed. Karl Heinz Kramberg. München: Biederstein, 1976.

Commentarii 1951 bis 1956: Tagebücher aus dem Nachlaß, ed. Wendelin Schmidt-Dengler. München: Biederstein, 1976.

II. Works in English Translation

"Foundation and Function of the Novel," *P.E.N.* XXX. Kongress der Internationalen P.E.N. in Frankfurt am Main, 1959, Berlin/Frankfurt am Main/Vienna, 1960.

The Demons (2 vols.), trans. Richard and Clara Winston. New York: Knopf, 1961.

"The Magician's Art," trans. Astrid Ivask. *Literary Review* 5 (1961), 5–17.

"Two Short Stories: Stepfield and Sonatina," trans. Astrid Ivask. *Literary Review* 6 (1961–1963), 176–180.

"The Torment of the Leather Pouches," trans. Robert S. Rosen. *Odyssey Review* 3 (March 1963), 219–232.

Every Man a Murderer, trans. Richard and Clara Winston. New York: Knopf, 1964.

The Waterfalls of Slunj, trans. Eithne Wilkins and Ernst Kaiser. New York: Harcourt, Brace, 1966.

"The Trumpets of Jericho," "Under Black Stars," "A Person Made of Porcelain," "My Nineteen *Curricula Vitae,*" "Two Lies of Classical Tragedy in a Village," "From *The Strudlhof Steps,*" trans. Vincent Kling. *Chicago Review* 26 (1974), 5–138.

III. Secondary Works in English

Anon. "The Austrian Scene," *Times Literary Supplement* (16 August 1957), x.

Bachem, Michael. "Chaos, Order and Humanization in Doderer's Early Works." *Modern Language Studies* 5/2 (1975), 68–77.

–––. *Heimito von Doderer.* Boston: Twayne, 1981. Excellent introduction to Doderer for the English-speaking reader.

Bithell, Jethro. *Modern German Literature 1880–1950* (London: Methuen, [2] 1959), pp. 504–513.

Boelceskvy, Andrew. "Spatial Form and Moral Ambiguity: A Note on Heimito von Doderer's Narrative Technique." *German Quarterly* 47 (1974), 55-59.

Demetz, Peter. *Postwar German Literature. A Critical Introduction* (New York: Western Publishing, 1970), pp. 229-241. Good, sympathetic introduction to Doderer.

Fleischmann, Wolfgang B. "A New Look at Austrian Literature." *America* (17 September 1960), 644-647.

Hamburger, Michael. *From Prophecy to Exorcism* (London: Longmans, 1965), pp. 131-139. Very sympathetic introduction to Doderer.

Hatfield, Henry. *Crisis and Continuity in Modern German Fiction* (Ithaca/London: Cornell University Press, 1969), pp. 90-108.

Hayward-Jones, Sylvia. "Fate, Guilt and Freedom in Heimito von Doderer's *Ein Mord* and *Ein Umweg.*" *German Life and Letters* 14 (April 1961), 160-164.

Hesson, Elizabeth C., "Bibliography of Secondary Material on Heimito von Doderer." *Modern Austrian Literature* 19/2 (June 1986), 47-60.

Ivask, Ivar. "Heimito von Doderer: An Introduction." *Wisconsin Studies in Contemporary Literature* 8 (Autumn 1967), 528-547.

———, ed. "An International Symposium in Memory of Heimito von Doderer (1896-1966)." *Books Abroad* 42/3 (Summer 1968), 343-384.

Jones, David L. "Proust and Doderer as Historical Novelists." *Comparative Literature Studies* 10/1 (1973), 9-23.

Larsen, M. Dean. "Heimito von Doderer: The Elusive Realist." *Chicago Review* 26/2 (1974), 55-69.

Pabisch, Peter Karl. "The Uniqueness of Austrian Literature: An Introductory Contemplation of Heimito von Doderer." *Chicago Review* 26/2 (1974), 86-96.

Politzer, Heinz. "Heimito von Doderer's *Demons* and the Modern Kakanian Novel." *The Contemporary Novel in German,* ed. Robert H. Heitner (Austin/London: University of Texas Press, 1967), pp. 37-62.

Shaw, Michael. "Doderer's *Posaunen von Jericho.*" *Symposium* 21/2 (Summer 1967), 141-154.

Swales, Martin. "The Narrator in the Novels of Heimito von Doderer." *Modern Language Review* 61 (1966), 85-95.

IV. Major Studies in German

Fischer, Roswitha. *Studien zur Entstehungsgeschichte und zum Aufbau der 'Strudlhofstiege' Heimito von Doderers* (Wien: Braumüller, 1975). (Dissertation, Wien, 1971).
Reininger, Anton. *Die Erlösung des Bürgers: Eine ideologiekritische Studie zum Werk Heimito von Doderers* (Bonn: Bouvier, 1975).
Schmidt-Dengler, Wendelin. "Bibliographie. Sekundärliteratur zu Heimito von Doderer." *Literatur und Kritik* 80 (1973), 615–620.
Schröder, Hans Joachim. *Apperzeption und Vorurteil: Untersuchungen zur Reflexion Heimito von Doderers* (Heidelberg: Winter, 1976).
Weber, Dietrich. *Heimito von Doderer. Studien zu seinem Romanwerk* (München: Beck, 1963).

Albert Paris Gütersloh

Ludwig Fischer

When Albert Paris Gütersloh's magnum opus *Sonne und Mond* (Sun and Moon) appeared in 1962 as the long-awaited masterpiece and universal chronicle of Austrian history, the eminent literary critic Walter Jens reviewed the novel in the newspaper *Die Zeit* with a statement that can serve as a motto for the author's complete oeuvre: "This novel has neither a beginning nor an end but a thousand midpoints."[1]

Albert Conrad Kiehtreiber assumed the pen name Albert Paris Gütersloh out of his love for the city of Paris and for a girlfriend of his youth who came from the city of Gütersloh in Germany. The author was born on 5 February 1887 in Vienna and received his early education at a Benedictine boarding school in Melk, an experience which Gütersloh did not remember kindly. He then continued school in Bozen, Southern Tyrolia under the direction of Franciscan monks. The religious focus of Catholic theology to which Gütersloh was exposed in his formative years served the author as the foundation of his world view throughout his life. He did not realize his intent of becoming a Catholic priest but instead took acting lessons in Vienna from W. Popp and studied painting on his own, developing a strong interest in the group of painters which formed around Gustav Klimt. In 1907 Gütersloh, by that time a student of Klimt, was recommended by his teacher to Max Reinhardt in Berlin, where Gütersloh began working as a stage designer and director.

Between 1911 and 1913 the author spent much of his time as an art correspondent for the magazine *Budapester Blätter*. He also began to publish literary essays in the journal *Die Aktion* (Berlin). In 1915 during World War I Gütersloh volunteered for medical service at the front. After a serious illness the writer Robert Musil intervened, and Gütersloh received a position at the headquarters of the war informa-

tion office in Vienna. A year later, in 1916, his wife, the dancer Emma
Berger, whom he had married three years earlier, died after giving birth
to a daughter. The turmoil and confusion accompanying the end of the
Austro-Hungarian Empire found their parallels in difficult experiences
affecting Gütersloh's personal life.

While working at the war information office Gütersloh made the
acquaintance of Hermann Bahr and Hugo von Hofmannsthal, and also
of Franz Blei, with whom he coedited the journal *Die Rettung* directly
after the war. From 1920 until 1921 Gütersloh held the position of
stage director at the Schauspielhaus in Munich. He remarried in 1921
and published four volumes in quick succession with Jakob Hegner in
Hellerau near Dresden, among them *Der Lügner unter Bürgern* (The
Liar among Burghers), for which he received the Fontane Prize in 1923.
During this same year Gütersloh traveled to Rome and wrote what he
called an autobiography, *Die Bekenntnisse eines modernen Malers.
Meine große und kleine Geschichte. Lebensbeschreibung quasi un'
alegoria* (Confessions of a Modern Painter. My Personal History on a
Big and Small Scale. Depiction of a Life as an Allegory). Returning
from the Villa Aldobrandini in Frascati near Rome, which was a monastery of the Oratorians, Gütersloh soon moved again to take up a longer
residence in Cagnes-sur-Mer in Southern France, where he stayed from
1924 until 1929. In 1928 he received a Grand Prix in Paris for Gobelin
design, a prize which he was awarded again in 1937. During the years
1929 to 1938 Gütersloh was a professor at the Academy of Applied
Arts in Vienna, but after the *Anschluß* the Nazis, who considered him a
member of what they classified as decadent art, dismissed him from
office. Gütersloh was forced to work in the airplane factory Fischam-
end and later in an office. In 1945, after the end of World War II, the
author was reinstated as a professor at the State Academy of Fine Arts
in Vienna, where he served as director from 1954 to 1955. Gütersloh
was awarded the Austrian State Prize for painting in 1952 and received
the same high honor for literature in 1961. He died on 16 May 1973 in
Baden near Vienna.

Gütersloh played a very influential role in Austrian culture of the
twentieth century, not only as a writer but also as a painter; and yet
his reputation and position as a cultural figure, the critical acclaim of
his work, which listed Goethe, Jean Paul, Swift, Sterne, Thackeray, and
Joyce as his literary compatriots and contemporary writers such as
Musil, Broch, and Roth as his equals, is hardly reflected in his reception
by the general public. His highly complex, intricately sophisticated,

difficult, and often extremely abstract novels found only a small audience among readers. His contribution as teacher, mentor, founder, catalyst, and innovator to the development of Austrian painting in this century—he was vice-president of the Secession, contributed to the Viennese "Art Club," and provided theoretical advocacy of the Viennese school of Fantastic Realism—was undisputably recognized. However, the reception of his paintings was limited to a relatively small circle of people.

Gütersloh was far from being an accessible author and repeatedly expressed his lack of interest in writing for the masses. He went so far as to write in his novel *Sonne und Mond:* "Who cares about the ordinary person? Do we write or paint for him?"[2] In a speech that he gave at the Viennese Academy of Fine Arts in 1948 entitled "Concerning Modern Art," he justified his position as an artist whose work challenges the reader's ability to follow the artist's intentions: "You know that I am a writer and not one who is easy to understand. I speak from the perspective of a humanistic education which has become rare in our days. I ask you not to be discouraged by the effort it takes to listen to me. Consider the fact that a speaker who places high expectations on his audience honors his listeners."[3] The painter Ernst Fuchs confirms Gütersloh's demands on the audience for his paintings, and these are equally true for his expectations from his readers. Fuchs heard Gütersloh after World War II, when Gütersloh was president of the Austrian section of the International Art Club: "Each of his opening speeches was a widely recognized event. Most of the time we did not understand a single word. Everything he said sounded so educated. We stood around somewhat embarrassed and were hardly aware that we became a moving force because of his influence."[4] Much later Ernst Fuchs found the novel *Eine sagenhafte Figur* (A Legendary Figure) in a used bookstore in Paris and became an avid Gütersloh reader. Not too many people transferred their respect for Gütersloh as an authority on art into an appreciation of his works.

Gütersloh remained an aristocrat of the mind and an elitist concerning quality and purity in art throughout his life. His intellectual roots were the educational values of a humanistic education in the nineteenth century, a strong belief in Thomistic, scholastic Catholicism, and a close association with the world view of the nobility in the declining Austro-Hungarian Empire. Gütersloh is "Catholic" in the original sense of the word and at the same time very critical of the church and the established attitudes of the clergy. He is an untiring seeker of new artistic forms and literary styles, experiments extensively with language and new narrative modes of expression, sometimes almost excessively to the degree of becoming incomprehensible. Yet he never departs from traditional positions in regard to content, and his views on political issues and social change are far from what could be termed "progressive." Gütersloh struggles with his relationship with the bourgeoisie, not to mention with the working class. In 1913 he wrote in *Der Ruf:*

> The only, but terrible creation of the bourgeois soul, the idiot of reason, is the monstrous jungle of customs, uncertain rumors, and intentionally obscure theories about the process called culture, by which an artist is taken aback, but behind which happiness is supposed to be found, according to the geographical ideas of the folksongs.[5]

On the occasion of Franz Blei's fiftieth birthday Gütersloh published his famous *Rede über Blei* (1922, Speech Concerning Blei), subtitled, "The Writer in Catholicism," in which he scorns simplifying social criticism, but also warns against the pure aesthetic approach he sees embodied in the poet Rainer Maria Rilke. In the speech concerning Blei, which rarely mentions Blei and reads more like a manifesto of Gütersloh's ideas on the subject of a writer's role in society, he outlines the dangers and pitfalls of writing in a secular society. For him an author is an advocate of truth who needs to understand his relationship with God and has to go beyond doubt and logical rationalism; yet he also must avoid naive unreflected devotion. Gütersloh describes the immense difficulties faced by a writer who is committed to expressing what he truly knows without compromise either because of politics, satisfying the demands of the readers' taste, or selfish interests in fame and fortune. An author suffers from the limitations of language, and his subjective understanding is always far greater than what can be conveyed. Therefore to write means actually to miss the truth continuously, yet the writer must be totally dedicated to penetrate deeper and deeper into what needs to be understood: "A writer's medium is the word. And you have to take him literally, whether the words are adequate or inadequate, whether they have been crystalized into clarity or are still obscured by interpretation: the words are his prison."[6]

Opposed to the hubris of romantic creative imagination, Gütersloh dislikes the demands of the bourgeoisie in art as much as he frowns upon art in the service of an ideology. He extends his critical attitude to all sides and approaches every subject as a myriad of possibilities which he presents from a seemingly objective point of view. He then suggests *and* negates many perspectives in an intricately woven interplay of often mutually contradicting actions but finally concludes the complex chaos of reason by showing the necessity of Christian faith as the source of truth and clarity: "Real development is possible only through religiousness, through the path of grace; and real meaning arises when something does not stand for itself but refers to another."[7] It is to be expected that Gütersloh's views on painting show evidence of the same philosophy. In his *Bekenntnisse eines modernen Malers* (1926, Confessions of a Modern Painter) he lashed out against irresponsible attitudes in painting and literature, condemning the lack of spirituality and the cheapening of all values. He pleads for an intellectual elite of responsible artists and writers: some of his ideas are close to the concerns of the satirist Karl Kraus, while others resemble more the vision of the poet Stefan George. Although the time span of Gütersloh's life suggests that he was certainly a witness to more political, social, and artistic changes in Europe from the beginning of this century until the 1970s, his basic criteria and *Weltanschauung* actually remained amazingly unchanged.

Already in his first novel, *Die tanzende Törin* (The Dancing Fool), presumably written in 1909 when Gütersloh was barely twenty-two years old, many elements of the style, language, and narrative structure which later became his trademark are already present. More than in his later works the plot of *Die tanzende Törin* develops chronologically. Ruth Herzenstein, the main protagonist, comes from a wealthy family of bankers in Berlin. The status-conscious parents find in Mr. Senius an acceptable groom for their daughter, but she invents a story about her lost virginity in order to free herself from him and meets the rich painter, Mr. Welser. Ruth, now suddenly in Vienna—change of locations and time gaps never present a problem for Gütersloh—plays the role of an eccentric seductive dancer who enjoys the ardent pursuit of several artists. Tonio Faustiner, one of her suitors, turns from love to religion and is determined to find an expression of divine revelation in his paintings. Ruth encounters severe financial problems when Welser discontinues his support. She is desperately waiting for an original composition which the homosexual composer Livland was supposed to write for her. Livland's composition would secure her success as a dancer, but the artist is in love with the boy Elias and neglects his promise. Finally, Ruth tries to work in a variety show and meets a man with a mask in a very dubious entertainment establishment. The man behind the mask of a Pierrot is pretending to be blind when in fact he is actually blind. When Ruth destroys his illusion, he kills himself.

Fast-changing scenes without transitions are characteristic of this first novel of Gütersloh. Berlin, Vienna, and the family background of the protagonists are only points of departure. Soon we find ourselves in an intricate net of rapidly changing situations, unable to connect the threads of the narrative to the gradually developing story line. The characters do not interact with any kind of consistent motivation or intention. There is an arbitrary time gap of a whole year in the narrative. Often it is difficult to determine who is narrating or whose point of view is being presented. Gütersloh moves from very detailed descriptions of profane activities to ecstatic monologues to lyrical passages concerned mainly with descriptive accuracy in the style and tone of his language. The author projects images on a screen which leave the reader with impressions, but the images change too fast to allow room for interpretation. In a kaleidoscope of metaphors he creates a world so full of alternating stimuli that neither the reader nor the protagonists are able to develop analytical strategies which give them the opportunity to evaluate the experiences which happen to them. Considerable theological, philosophical, and aesthetic speculation along with highly abstract thoughts never connect into a value system or provide a perspective which would serve as a rational model of understanding.

There is a definite element of optic art in Gütersloh's writing. Often one senses a cameraman at work, shooting scenes for a film, someone who is interested mainly in the accuracy of depicted details but has very little interest in the plot. Gütersloh's words paint pictures, always with astonishing unexpected particularities, always surprising, frequently startling, never predictable or monotonous. The author changes the narrative perspective at will, switches tenses, and discontinues main characters like Roland, Ruth's brother, in the middle of the novel. There is no suspense or deliberately built-up culmination of the action in *Die tanzende Törin*. The characters move around each other in continuously changing constellations. Individuals and circumstances interact as a series of situations which follow each other without any structural, psychologically plausible, or motivated necessity. The protagonists do not have a clear sense of identity of themselves, no center point from which they look at and relate to the world. They are thrown into a whirlpool of events which leave them disoriented and unable to act according to logical and rational categories. *Die tanzende*

Törin does not have a theme or a topic or a fundamental auctorial message.

Young people discover the world in this novel and are completely overwhelmed by the immense complexity and the vast contradictions of a life in which parental guidance and educational goals can no longer serve as models of conduct and behavior. The young people feel different about their time and the purpose of their life. The generation gap, which becomes a significant focal point for Expressionist literature, is well established as an important factor here. The younger generation longs for change, but the abundant ideas and many possibilities do not yet connect into a sense of direction or orientation. They are lost in the fullness of adult life, forced to make decisions without knowing how to build the bridge between their ideas, insights, and the reality around them. Gütersloh offers many vignettes, short, very accurately depicted incidents which add up to a gigantic chaos.

In *Die tanzende Törin* the author is almost equally involved with mutually exclusive views and writes about incest with the same fervor he uses when writing about the Catholic priesthood. The young Gütersloh is, like his characters, swept away by the seemingly unlimited possibilities they are able to imagine. Life in the worldly affairs outside the security of faith is an all-consuming dance of excitement with no real center. It is an experiment with unknown parameters and uncertain conclusions. Gütersloh's young protagonists—we find no heroes in his work—reject the old and demand something new, whatever this might be. In order to shed the constrictions of society, the individuals, above all Ruth, move freely into the emotional expression of their desires and defend them against the priorities of socially acceptable behavior. *Épater le bourgeois* is the slogan, and neither lies nor narcissistic indulgences are considered excessive. In a manner resembling Expressionism they act according to the maxim: reality is what I feel inside.

Gütersloh shortened *Die tanzende Törin* in 1913 while living in Berlin. The first version contained a more dramatic and mystical ending, in which Ruth dies after losing her virginity in an encounter with an old man. The novel becomes an allegory of a girl who loses her soul by assuming the power of a woman and of motherhood. Ruth then identifies with the Virgin Mary, and her partners become God and the Devil. The first version was dedicated to August Strindberg. Franz Blei considered *Die tanzende Törin* as one of the few incunabula of Expressionism,[8] and Gütersloh affirms his association with the Expressionist movement in an article for the journal *Die Rettung,* in which he wrote in 1918: "The word is expression, not meaning."[9]

Revolutions take place in the heart in this author's work. The political and economic dimensions are certainly the cause of suffering and despair, intrigues and jealousies, but they do not raise the social consciousness of the people involved. *Die tanzende Törin* was very much an avant-garde novel within the literary society of Vienna and Berlin before 1918. A sense of an old order breaking down without a new vision promising a better future is always present. Gütersloh lives in the world of a Musil and Broch, of George and Josef Hoffmann, the famous *Jugendstil* architect whom Gütersloh in 1950 still called "the creator of the image of a world epoch."[10] Wolfdietrich Rasch, in an epilogue to the novel, traced the main character to Ruth St. Denis, an American dancer, who toured Europe between 1906 and 1908 and was deeply admired by Hofmannsthal. There are many parallels between the life of Ruth St. Denis and that of Ruth Herzenstein in *Die tanzende Törin*.

The following example illustrates Gütersloh's style of writing in this first novel. He describes spring in the city, and ordinary expectations, subject-verb-object relations, semantic patterns of established sentence structure, and conventions of meaning are violated:

> The blue ceiling of the sky makes the space below so intimate. All conversations can hardly be heard and reach only those who move very close. Nobody tries to push a smile like a huge box through the rows of people. Each smile is oval. Smiling turns the eyes into an oval form, and everything glides along this most personal of all curves. This hour loosens all bonds quietly: the wife does not truly belong to the husband anymore, the lover not to the lover, and the children only feel the shape of the mother's hand. The silent awareness of a word almost spoken is in all of them. Everyone is ready to surrender to the first person who offers the most. Nothing must remain the same. Spring has them all in its hands, shakes them around, and gives to some and to others. Behind every woman appears the idea of the bedroom, the idea of her naked body.[11]

Unusual connections, fleeting perceptions, a foreground of thoughts without a background to which experience could relate; these are the characteristic features of Gütersloh's first novel.

Soon the author turns away from Expressionism and develops a peculiar style which could be characterized as a fluid meandering baroque factuality, a style which won him much critical acclaim. His novel *Der Lügner unter Bürgern* (The Liar Among Burghers), which appeared in 1922, was awarded the Fontane Prize. With some effort we can follow a progressively unfolding story line and a narrative sequence of actions in this work. Rosette Piou, the daughter of a merchant, is about to leave the house one evening to go to a formal dance, when she finds a young man lying unconscious in the street right in front of her parents' house. Rosette, dressed for the occasion, is angry about missing her carriage. Her father appears on the scene, and both are at a loss about what to do with the elegantly dressed young gentleman. Father and daughter engage in a dispute about calling the police. Madame Piou hears them arguing and joins them. A noble lady dressed in black stops in passing and suggests that the unconscious young man should be taken in to the living room of Mr. Piou's house. Madame Piou recognizes the opportunity of finding a husband for her daughter and orders her husband to dress up while Rosette is trying to revive the young man with cold packs on his forehead. When Thomas Pasteur finally regains consciousness, he is full of gratitude and praise for the charity and compassion of the bourgeois family. He plays the role of an aristocratic exotic guest, disillusioned with the decadence of nobility but enchanted with the warmth and virtuousness of bourgeois life. After elaborate excursions into a world of fantasy and imagination Thomas interprets the event before the house more and more as a fortunate coincidence and finally realizes that it is his destiny to marry Rosette. The parents leave the two young people alone, but Rosette's mother becomes suspicious and sees a confidence man in Thomas. When she returns to the room to end the dishonest pursuit of Thomas, the room is empty. Shortly afterwards Rosette returns in a state of utter confusion and emotional turmoil. She feels dishonored and leaves her parents' house.

Der Lügner unter Bürgern was written between 1913 and 1915. Gütersloh ignored the outbreak of World War I and the political reality of his time in his literary efforts, but certainly responded to the contemporary artistic movements, in this case Expressionism. He saw *Der Lügner unter Bürgern* "in the middle of a literary vogue of egomania as a classical-realistic description of a 'natural' event."[12] His use of critical terminology: classical, realistic, and naturalistic, is highly idiosyncratic and should not be interpreted within the context of these various literary movements as normally defined. The characters in this novel are not individuals but types, representatives of different social classes.

The class differences are not reflected as political or economic realities but as sources of psychological motivations, as a backdrop to illustrate ambition, jealousy, conceitedness, deceit, and greed. Gütersloh is a master at illuminating the motives behind actions. The behavior of the characters and the course of events as they unfold as a sequence of decisions leading to changes and conclusions are not his major interest. He sees the role of the writer as an observer who shows the inner conflict, the personal intentions before they surface on the scene and have consequence. The reader often feels lost in a labyrinth of descriptive adjectives, appositions, and extremely complex sentence structures which lead deeper and deeper into specific details or into the hidden layers of a person's pretense. Often one does not know who is acting in the present as a consequence of what previous event and for what purpose.

The entire story takes place on one evening in Paris towards the end of the nineteenth century. Yet with the exception of a few names there is hardly any reference to the city which Gütersloh knew very well from many extended visits and from his years as a student there. The author wrote *Der Lügner unter Bürgern* like a psychological case study; none of the circumstances or previous experiences leading to the situation of Thomas Pasteur's suddenly lying unconscious before Piou's house are revealed. The reader receives a segment of the characters' lives like the middle part of a film. The novel has no real end. The characters fade, and Rosette, leaving the house, screams again that someone is lying in front of the house, referring back to the beginning. Gütersloh refrains from taking sides in the conflict and leaves the evaluation of the whole event to the reader. He shows people who are caught in their norms, their prejudices, their hopes, and their guilt. The characters are not in control of their lives; they move in a circle of frustrations, anger, and pretense, reacting continuously to outside pressures. They undergo a psychoanalysis on the author's literary couch but receive no prescription or advice for positive changes. Gütersloh diagnoses: "They have a very vague, general sense of guilt because they are unable to break through to the clarity of specific insights."[13] *Der Lügner unter Bürgern* was published together with two other novels by Gütersloh in a new edition by Piper in Munich in 1984, possibly an indication of a renewed interest in Gütersloh sparked by the one-hundredth anniversary of his birth in 1987.

Love and passion in opposition to faith and truth as a theme plays a significant role in Gütersloh's life and work. The polarity of innocence and experience, purity and desire as a personal tension and as a source of literary, creative endeavor found its expression in *Innozenz oder Sinn und Fluch der Unschuld* (1922, Innozenz or the Meaning and the Curse of Innocence). Theological questions are central to this novel, which was written as an allegorical fantasy in 1914, the year after Gütersloh married. We find no person by the name of Innozenz in the book. None of the characters actually have individual names. They are called "monk," "saint," "boy," "young man," "bishop," "sage." In this work we follow the biography of a religious person for over three-hundred years. A noble boy is first raised by a hermit and visits in his dreams the girls of the village, who become pregnant. Since he is unaware of his actions in his waking state, the young man is shocked when he meets a child who addresses him as "father." We are told that he has to learn how to love in order to be able to die, because in love angels and animals meet through human beings. The young man finally falls in love with a woman who is a nun. She declares him to be a seducer and wants him imprisoned, but the young man is freed by a sage and transformed into an old man who enters a monastery. The nun and the monk, both now considered to be holy people, meet in the castle of the king, where she seduces him and turns him into a young man again. At this point chaos befalls the people. The earth trembles, the palace crumbles, and the saint withdraws with a mirror into his cell to await the completion of his rejuvenation. God now sentences all men to live eternally and all people to continue their present activity forever. The saint before the mirror becomes a symbol for Narcissus.

Gütersloh uses the narrative techniques of legends in this novel. He writes in a biblical style and connects the individual events through mystical and supernatural transitions. The Devil and demons appear, and a part of the narrative takes place in heaven. Apocalyptic visions and the total breakdown of human order add to the dreamlike quality and the surreal atmosphere of the novel. In the spotlight of Gütersloh's descriptions we find people in situations without context. We see sharp contrasts without detecting any linear progression of movement in the action of the protagonists. Although the author has very little trust in the ethical competence of man, in the ability of human beings to establish a truly valid moral and meaningful existence, he sees a unity behind the dualism and the contradictions in human action. The sage responds to the young man in the novel:

... because everything in the universe is unlimited, therefore

the senses too are unlimited. Because everything grows continuously, the senses grow too. What was red today changes to
yellow tomorrow, and black slowly turns into white. Nothing
is fixed to one place. Therefore, if you contemplate for a long
time and live with your senses, your senses will begin to transcend into the spiritual realm and see much more than is
known by the angel who has returned to the world of the
senses because everything always changes.[14]

Human destiny from a religious perspective in conflict with
secular interpretations of life, the relationship between God, nature,
and man, the appropriate paths towards spiritual truth, the role of trust
and doubt, the difficulties of man to understand the will of God, and
the almost impossible task of realizing religious truth in a world full of
error and sin, these are questions Gütersloh wrestles with again in *Kain
und Abel* (1924) a short volume containing his own lithographs inter-
preting the biblical legend in a new way. Eve begs God for one of
her sons to be in harmony with God and not be affected by the primordial sin. Abel is that symbol of purity, and his sister Lilith is portrayed as the lascivious, sensuous, earthbound woman who, according
to Adam, will bring paradise on earth. Kain, the coarse, uncouth,
obedient brother, who wants to succeed in this world and believes in
authority, one Sunday accompanies his brother Abel to the forest,
where Abel listens to God. Kain feels that Abel's love of God constitutes a betrayal of the father, of all authority both of the state and of
the community. Both come to a house in the forest, the house of God.
Abel celebrates a Mass-like ritual on the altar in the house, is tempted
by doubt since there is no evidence of God but overcomes the doubt
through faith. At this point in the legend the temptation of Adam by
Eve is retold, showing Eve as the doubting woman who wants to see
God as the mighty ruler and authority on earth. God's presence in
human beings is interpreted as the divine will to experience the transitoriness of existence and the transcendence of the eternity of God
through human life: "As in the woman the birth of the children, so the
birth of God is continuously repeated in Man."[15] Kain complains to
God that He has revealed himself to Abel but has condemned Eve: "My
brother whom I love, You have turned into a being who is above me
because You talked to him. My mother You have turned into a being
who is below me because You have cursed her. You have destroyed the
unity among Man by creating the chosen and the condemned."[16] Kain

challenges God to reveal Himself clearly to all men. He wants to know how to contact God, but Abel now confesses that he never really saw God. Kain slays Abel who lied about God. He feels that he saved parents and children from an invisible God. The categories of experience through mind and sensual perception are reestablished. Kain killed the uncertainty and reestablished the order of nature. He returns home and questions Adam and Eve about God but receives no answer. The author feels that spiritual truth cannot be penetrated by rational thought. The act of revelation takes place on a different level of understanding: "The union between truth and its manifestation lasts only a moment. The rest is history, the history of misunderstanding which is weighed by a higher scale of balance and rejected."[17] For Gütersloh human beings are still spiritual dwarfs, highly ignorant of truth and hanging on to solutions expected to result from illusions of reason. He sees God developing in Man: ". . . God is still growing. A pair of oxen still provides his power, where he would like to see fast horses. And so for God too there is the greatness in a miracle. . . . God jumped on the back of Man to be carried faster and faster through all of His possibilities."[18]

These possibilities, when not viewed from the distance of theological speculation or moved into the remote past of biblical times, present themselves as moral and ethical decisions in an individual's life. While living in Cagnes-sur-Mer in Southern France from 1924 until 1929, Gütersloh wrote the novel *Eine sagenhafte Figur* (A Legendary Figure), which was not published until 1946. In this novel he returns to the theme of passionate love versus human compassion which had been a major issue in *Innozenz*. In spite of the author's introduction placing the events into the far-distant past, we find much more reference to actual historical events and real people. Some critics see in the main protagonist a portrait of Franz Blei, as we are used to from Gütersloh:

> The story I am now beginning to record happened a long time ago. The place where it occurred has been destroyed along with the generations of people who lived there. . . . I was born in this city, became an orphan very early but found new parents and two new sisters soon thereafter. I lost one sister, not through death, which would have separated us in purity, but when we both crossed the bridge to maturity at the same age.[19]

The novel evolves around one central figure, the nobleman Kirill, who after having been adopted, grows up with his stepsisters Laura and Bettina. When Kirill becomes of age, he is informed that he is to be engaged to Laura, who returns the engagement ring and becomes seriously ill: her legs become paralyzed. War then breaks out in the country, and Kirill decides to volunteer and sacrifice his life as a soldier in order to heal Laura, but he is declared unfit for service. The opportunity for love presents itself in the form of the woman Tamila, but Kirill out of feelings of loyalty towards Laura leaves Tamila. Laura is unable to accept her brother as a lover. Her fear of incest is not affected by the reality that they are not blood relatives. However, Kirill's decision to become a soldier to die for her changes her mind. She begins to feel love for him, but there is no lasting resolution to the conflict between the love of passion and love as loyalty and friendship. In a very confusing and rather abstruse epilogue, which the author added to the novel when it was finally published, we find Kirill as a misanthropic painter living in isolation, disappointment, and bitterness in Cagnes-sur-Mer. Kirill has failed to resolve the archetypal conflict between wife and mother and has nothing to look forward to except to carry his failure, his "vie manqué," to its bitter end.

Eine sagenhafte Figur is again a novel of ideas, of constellations, of situations, this time around Kirill, who acts as a reflecting mirror for the author. Gütersloh is testing his own commitment to truth, to self-realization against the chaos of diversity in countless confrontations with a world which must be structured according to a consistent, absolutely reliable set of values. He attempts to find orientation in a flood of contradicting situations and new impressions for which none of the established criteria seem to have answers. Gütersloh and his character Kirill are indefatigable seekers of truth: but truth and the need to act in life with integrity as an individual who must participate in a reality not determined by his inner convictions are in constant contradiction to outside pressures, which force the seeker to move in a world full of lies, pretenses, and temptations.

More than in other novels we recognize historical events in the background of *Eine sagenhafte Figur*. World War I serves as a catalyst to solve personal problems. The author portrays the irresponsible arrogance of those in power as well as the blind enthusiasm and the fanaticism of those who are ready to give their blood in the war. War appears as an opportunity to get even, as an outbreak of many suppressed and unresolved problems. Subconscious feelings of failure, anger, and hostility surface as an armed struggle on the conscious level. Kirill expresses the analogy between individual strife and collective combat through a direct equation: "Somehow one has to become a man. If not through woman, where I have failed, then in battle, where I will succeed. And the bloodier the action, the more it will resemble the encounter which I could not have."[20] An in-depth Freudian analysis of this statement would be very revealing. What is more relevant for an understanding of this novel in a literary context is that war here becomes a violent outbreak of a conflict which individuals do not dare to resolve in a peaceful way. It is easier to follow the law requiring bravery or the moral code requiring virtue than it is to take on the responsibility of truly facing the limitations and shortcomings of one's own behavior. Personal courage in the service of self-realization, the rebellion against decadent norms and restrictions usually end with the defeat, the failure, and the destruction of the individual in Gütersloh's works.

The tenacious clinging to outdated meaningless traditions brings frustration and creates a world of illusions and lies for Gütersloh's protagonists, but also brings a certain security, which, when abandoned and when living at risk outside of the old structure, turns into a dangerous all-destroying chaos. The writer always portrays extraordinary persons who suffer from the limitations of their environment. They reject those restrictions but are unable to rise completely above them. Their idealism, their clarity and understanding, their inner aristocracy represent a rare and a brief encounter with truth in solitude and even rarer in moments of brotherly love for another person. For the most part, for the thousands of small incidents and situations which make up their daily lives, this noble truth is a nagging longing, like a distant memory of another realm of existence which is continuously attacked and destroyed by the necessities of a dualistic, competitive, and essentially hostile world. This secular world without a fundamental grasp of the true reality, which is only comprehensible through religion, is an amorphous mass of confusion. It is almost as if the author is trying to exhaust our efforts to establish valid criteria on a secular basis. Once we see the futility of our intentions, which move us in circles, we might abandon our faith in a profane world view and break through to divine truth. If a reader has not given up on his expectations concerning structure, purpose, plot, direction, plausibility, logical progression, and orientation in any of the previous novels, he certainly has underestimated Gütersloh's insistence on portraying the world as a "perpetuum mobile" of digressions.

For twenty-seven years the author worked on a novel of gigantic dimensions. From 1935 until 1962 Gütersloh's "universal chronicle," as he himself called it, was in the making. On almost 900 pages he presented his own form of the novel, for which he coined the term "materiology." Gütersloh's "materiology" cannot be defined through conventional language. It is essentially a narrative mode, in which, as Hansjörg Graf phrases it, "The situation is not developed as a consequence of the character's action, but the protagonists illustrate an insight, like the innocent tragic heroes exemplify the incomprehensible psychology of the Gods."[21] *Sonne und Mond* (1962, Sun and Moon) is the title of Gütersloh's *grand oeuvre,* and it is indeed a literary work of extraordinary dimensions. It is virtually impossible to outline more than the very basic narrative skeleton of this novel. There are more than fifty characters in *Sonne und Mond,* and the time span covered extends from the beginning of the thirteenth century until the 1930s. With this universal chronicle Gütersloh presented his ultimate challenge to the reader and the literary critic. A curiously precise historical date, 27 July 1933, is set as the narrated present from which this encyclopedia of digressions evolves. For readers who absolutely insist on a plot and an introduction to the events about to take place, Gütersloh essentially provides the whole story line in the first sentence.

Count Lunarin inherits a ramshackle castle from Baron Enguerrand, who wants to force the wandering Count into a more stable life. The Count, always in debt, returns and claims his inheritance, falls in love again with his former girlfriend, Bettina, and leaves again after handing over the castle to the rich and capable farmer, Till Adelseher, who will act as a caretaker of the castle for three days. Adelseher renovates the castle during the prolonged absence of Lunarin and falls in love with Melitta Rudigier, the eternally escaping woman. They live together in a mysterious tower. Count Lunarin returns after one year, generously presents the completely renovated castle to Adelseher as a gift, and leaves again with Adelseher's lover, Melitta. If the reader insists on a story line, this is all he will find, well-hidden and interspersed in almost 900 pages.

Besides Count Lunarin and Till Adelseher several other characters have larger roles in the novel, although they are introduced and abandoned with an abruptness and arbitrariness which violate every single rule of the conventional novel. Adelseher is in conflict with the pre-fascist clan of the anti-Semitic Ariovist von Wissensdrum; Mullmann, a representative of bureaucracy, acts as the prophet of the past; the

painter Andree and his patrons, Baruch and Genia Mendelsinger, portray the conflict between art and business; Strumpf is the architect and
builder who renovates the castle. Then there is Colonel von Rudigier,
the militarist, the butler Murmelsteg, the Jewish rare bookseller Brom-
beer, Obdetürkis, another painter who acts at times as the voice of
Gütersloh, and too many more to even mention.

The author most appropriately selected a sentence by Heraclitus
as the motto preceding the text: "A pile of things hurled without
intention is the most beautiful world order." History is certainly not a
Hegelian movement towards inevitable progress for Gütersloh. He is
closer to Theodor Lessing's verdict on history as a sea of blood and
tears. And yet Gütersloh unleashes his literary chaos for a purpose. The
author definitely did not write to entertain or to describe existential
hopelessness, but to teach; and he teaches in a way which makes it
almost impossible for the student/reader to know what the curriculum
is, what he is supposed to learn. The extremely complex associations,
the highly sophisticated reflections, and the barrage of unconnected
images require a reader who is willing to meet the author completely
on his terms. Gütersloh makes no concessions: he is the authority who
preaches from the pulpit of complexity and depth of experience.

Scholasticism, Catholicism, and the humanistic education of
nineteenth-century Austria are without doubt Gütersloh's philosophical
reference system, but he is as far from orthodoxy or dogmatism as his
characters are from establishing consistency, continuity, and clearly
identifiable goals. The chaos which unfolds in Gütersloh's work is the
chaos of human reason, behind which the divine plan of a world in the
hands of incomprehensible providence charts its courses. Existential
nothingness, life as an absurd search for meaning, are not Gütersloh's
philosophical parameters. Once the reader carries the confusing, rapidly
changing events above the level of direct actions and responses, he will
see on a more abstract level representational roles and structures in the
main figures. For example Count Lunarin and the rich farmer Adelseher
stand as symbols for the decline of the aristocracy and the rise of the
bourgeoisie. Many critics saw in *Sonne und Mond* a portrait of Austria
itself after 1918, but Gütersloh avoids direct references and statements
about history.

The novel unravels according to a very subjective inner concept of
time and takes place in locations which serve as stage decorations for
reflections and psychological observations. Vienna and several small
towns in the vicinity are mentioned but are not recognizable as actual

historical places. On a very abstract level the central issue of *Sonne und Mond* appears as the question of succession, the idea of monarchy, reliable authority, and the contradicting concepts of nobility by birth versus the claim to power by virtue of ability. Seen from this perspective, the novel becomes more of an allegorical parable, in which the legal caretakers, the aristocracy in the form of Count Lunarin, abandon the castle, i.e., Austria decays without leadership until the advocate of the republic, Till Adelseher, renovates the castle. The old order should be restored by the new caretakers. This is a very accurate metaphor for Gütersloh's own world view: "The poor castle stood on the hill and waited. And is still waiting today for its real owner because it only has a caretaker."[22] Kafka's castle is an authority which is inaccessible to the people, but Gütersloh's castle is an abandoned structure, a destroyed hierarchy, with no new order truly capable of replacing it. Something has been lost for Gütersloh, an unquestioned order which did not have to justify itself. In the dictionary of terms which the author wrote for *Sonne und Mond* he defines aristocracy as "a set of qualities which blend into each other like the tones and shades between the major colors of the spectrum, the halftones actually are the major scale, and the purpose and results of the actions are irrelevant."[23] The secular rational approach, the reality of the democratic consensus with its goals of technological improvement are a naive illusion in Gütersloh's view.

He argues that man without religion and tradition is separated from himself:

> Can anyone today truly distinguish with the clarity that is more necessary than ever between what he thinks and what his ancestors thought? Can anyone say with certainty that he found the God he prays to in the solitude of his room and not in the estate of his father? And can anyone say that the woman he loves is not an image of his mother? And the newly founded state, does it not grow out of the debris of the foundations which built the old state?[24]

Shortly after this statement, which he wrote as an aphorism in the dictionary of terms for *Sonne und Mond,* Gütersloh concludes: "Man separated can only portray what separates."[25] The digressions of language, the labyrinth of observations become the limitations of reason. Gütersloh's works, then, would have to be interpreted as textbooks which deal with the anatomy of alienation through lack of faith.

The critics often felt very ambivalent about and at times became impatient with Gütersloh's narrative eccentricities. Claus Pack called *Sonne und Mond* "The most circumstantial excesses and digressions ever committed with loving persistence by any author writing in the German language. . . . Gütersloh offers us not an all-penetrating humor but witticisms based upon ideas carefully prepared, sharpened, and served."[26] Heinz Rieder chose a more poetic description when he called the novel "a maze full of lush vines growing across all the paths, behind which there is hidden a plot that is a mere nothing, to be told in three sentences. . . . The whole thing is a seemingly unsystematic system of digressions swollen by the continuous addition of material."[27] Particularly strenuous for the reader are the constant interruptions and explanatory comments by the narrator. Friedrich Knilli, who in an article entitled "Detour as a Shortcut" sees influences of the psychologist Alfred Adler and the medieval alchemists in *Sonne und Mond,* excuses the auctorial interruptions and characterizes them as "a poetizing device to transform what could be easily understood into complex, hard-to-understand situations, to change simplicity into universality, and to add superfluous elements to necessities."[28] In a similar vein the poet Helmut Heissenbüttel interprets the novel as a "radically phenomenological description of man through an intricately allegorical ambiguity."[29] In a reply to the predominantly negative reactions to his style Gütersloh justifies his way of writing:

> I would like to take the opportunity to respond to some of my critics, who almost always benevolently accuse me of interpreting the narrative in *Sonne und Mond* again and again, almost on every page, much to the detriment of the novel, with materiological reflections. It seemed more important to me to show the unfathomable swamp through which we all wade than to point at the firm ground which we think we stand on.[30]

Gütersloh takes it for granted that the reader prefers the unfathomable swamp to the firm ground. One passage from *Sonne und Mond* may serve as an example of the author's restless prose and convoluted sentence structure for which the English reader would even have significantly less tolerance than his German counterpart:

> Assuming the agreement of the reader, who does not want to stay in one place just as little as we want to, neither in the

> comfort of love, nor in the pain of the sinner (even though the world wants us to believe we have to decide for one or the other), who through the help of a constant restlessness wants to suffer or enjoy the deeply felt completeness of life in its fevering, sparkling, everflowing, and mingling—both approaches lead to the same goal—we now leave a description, which actually never was one but rather a commentary on a description, in order to move ahead nine months.[31]

The author stands way above the reader, confirmed by the novelist Heimito von Doderer, who considered himself a student of Gütersloh. In his introduction to "Gewaltig staunt der Mensch" (To the Utter Amazement of Human Beings), a collection of excerpts from major works published on the occasion of Gütersloh's seventy-fifth birthday in 1962, Doderer simply states: "The reader will never be able to possess the fundamental knowledge which is characteristic of the author."[32] In the same year appeared *Laßt uns den Menschen machen* (Let us Create the Human Being), a collection of twenty-two novellas and short stories, one of which, *Der Henker* (The Hangman), was written in Viennese dialect.

Approaching eighty, Gütersloh saw the publication of his major work *Sonne und Mond* and witnessed the reedition of many of his earlier works. However, like almost every German writer he had carried the Faust theme with him, and in 1969 Gütersloh presented a Socratic novel, *Die Fabel von der Freundschaft* (The Fable of Friendship) to his audience. It is a novel about Faust's pact with the devil, beginning with a professor of Hebrew, then focusing on theological conversations in a school for young boys, after which we find ourselves in a monastery where the prior dies. We are then led back in time to witness medieval knightly rivalries over a woman named Mechthild; in between we meet Mephistopheles who argues with Faust about the fulfillment of the pact. Gütersloh shows Faust and the devil condemned to a mutual dependency, in which Mephistopheles has great difficulty in keeping up with the clever professor. The author is again master of complex intrigues and impenetrable complications. Gütersloh conducts a linguistic jungle expedition into the realm of allegory and mythology. His usual fireworks of brilliant thoughts and observations leave the reader breathless and disoriented and make it impossible to organize and categorize the events according to notations of familiarity and plausibility. Faust and Mephistopheles actually appear at three places in the book, twice for thirty pages and once for four pages, which amounts to less than one-third of the novel. The remainder is made up of reflections, diversions, episodes, and what Hartmut Scheible called "a soup of metaphors." The following paragraph from the novel illustrates the narrator's position, which remains unchanged from what we saw in *Sonne und Mond*. Gütersloh lectures to the reader in *Die Fabel von der Freundschaft:*

> So finally we can continue with our exciting tale. The educational discourse was as little fun for us as it was for the reader, but it was necessary; strangely enough, now that we enter the main topic, we actually present what is superfluous. We only expose what would be before everyone's eyes, if he could look through the layers of words in which we wrap things. (No matter how sharp the lenses of art are, they should not be necessary.) We finish the abandoned abstract painting with more sensual colors after the student has disappeared.[33]

Many critics and certainly many more readers lost patience with Gütersloh's labyrinth of images and abstract mosaic of reflections and left the classroom before the professor finished his lectures. On the other hand, Wilhelm Hock expresses the view of the majority of critics when he praises "the rhythmic-syntactic balance of Gütersloh's narrative prose and the poetic acuity of the author." It is rather surprising to learn that Gütersloh disliked superlatives, considered exaggeration as a real terminal disease, and advocated "moving along the shortest road, which involves true asceticism and real modesty."[34]

Gütersloh's importance for Austrian literature in the twentieth century is determined by his contribution as an innovator in language, by the precision of his observations, and by his commitment to push this "vehicle of thinking," as Wittgenstein called language, to its outermost limits of expression. As an author Gütersloh shows that he was very much aware of the dangers inherent in his emphasis on accuracy of detail over continuity in action when he wrote, "I walk the tightrope of the utmost precision in words, at the edge of being incomprehensible, in the phantom ice of passion, in the fervor of cold reason, in order to give at least a somewhat comprehensive example of your completeness."[35]

Notes

1. Walter Jens, "Noch einmal die ganze Welt," *Die Zeit* 49 (7 December 1962).

2. Albert Paris Gütersloh, *Sonne und Mond. Ein historischer Roman aus der Gegenwart* (München: Piper, 1962), p. 173.

3. Albert Paris Gütersloh, "Die heutige Situation der modernen Kunst," *Forum* (Wien, 1962), p. 20.

4. Ernst Fuchs, "Über Gütersloh," *Literatur und Kritik* 68 (1972), 481.

5. Albert Paris Gütersloh, "Bewertung der Nacht," *Der Ruf* (Mai 1913), 5.

6. Albert Paris Gütersloh, "Rede über Blei" (Hellerau: Hegner, 1922), p. 46.

7. Ibid., p. 40.

8. Cf. Wolfdietrich Rasch, "Nachwort zu *Die tanzende Törin*" (München: Langen Müller, 1973), p. 463.

9. Albert Paris Gütersloh, "Rede über Blei," p. 463.

10. Ibid., p. 467.

11. Albert Paris Gütersloh, "Die tanzende Törin," in *Gewaltig staunt der Mensch*, (Auszug aus dem Roman) (Graz: Stiasny, 1963), p. 29.

12. Albert Paris Gütersloh, in Heimito von Doderer, *Der Fall Gütersloh* (Wien: Haybach, 1930), pp. 105-106.

13. Albert Paris Gütersloh, *Der Lügner unter Bürgern.*

14. Albert Paris Gütersloh, *Innozenz oder Sinn und Fluch der Unschuld* (Hellerau: Hegner, 1922), p. 24.

15. Albert Paris Gütersloh, *Kain und Abel* (Wien: Haybach, 1924), p. 44.

16. Ibid., p. 48.

17. Ibid., p. 35.

18. Albert Paris Gütersloh, *Gewaltig staunt der Mensch* (Wien: Stiasny, 1963), p. 58.

19. Albert Paris Gütersloh, *Eine sagenhafte Figur. Ein platonischer Roman mit einem Nachwort in usum delphini* (Wien: Luckmann, 1946), p. 7.

20. Ibid., p. 309.

21. Hans-Jörg Graf, "Die Schlüssel zum Schloss," in *Albert Paris Gütersloh, Autor und Werk* (München: Piper, 1962), p. 51.

22. Albert Paris Gütersloh, *Sonne und Mond.* p. 551.

23.   Hans-Jörg Graf, *Albert Paris Gütersloh, Autor und Werk,* p. 41.
24.   Albert Paris Gütersloh, *Der innere Erdteil. Aus den Wörter-büchern.* (München: Piper, 1966), p. 179.
25.   Ibid., p. 180.
26.   Claus Pack, "Parturiunt montes," *Wort und Wahrheit* 4 (1963), 227.
27.   Heinz Reider, "A. P. Gütersloh, Sonne und Mond," *Neue deutsche Hefte,* Jg. 10, Heft 98 (1964), 233-234.
28.   "Knilli, Der Umweg als kurzester Weg," *Sprache im technischen Zeitalter* (1963), 577.
29.   Helmut Heissenbüttel, "Zu A. P. Gütersloh *Sonne und Mond,*" in *Albert Paris Gütersloh, Autor und Werk,* p. 32.
30.   Albert Paris Gütersloh, quoted by Peter von Tramin, "Unterwegs zum totalen Roman," in *Albert Paris Gütersloh, Autor und Werk,* pp. 62-63.
31.   Albert Paris Gütersloh, quoted by Helmut Heissenbüttel (note 29), p. 34.
32.   Heimito von Doderer, from Introduction to Albert Paris Gütersloh, *Gewaltig staunt der Mensch,* (Graz: Stiasny, 1963), p. 8.
33.   Albert Paris Gütersloh, *Die Fabel von der Freundschaft. Ein sokratischer Roman* (München: Piper, 1969), p. 40.
34.   Albert Paris Gütersloh, quoted by Hans-Jörg Graf, "Die Schlüssel zum Schloss," in *Albert Paris Gütersloh, Autor und Werk,* p. 25.
35.   Albert P. Gütersloh, quoted by Alfred Focke, "Versuch über A. P. Güterslohs Materiologie," *Literatur und Kritik* 68 (1972), 466.

Bibliography

I. Works by Albert Paris Gütersloh in German

Die tanzende Törin. Ein Roman des Märchens. Berlin: Baumhauer, 1910; Neuausgabe: München: G. Müller, 1913; München: Langen-Müller, 1973; Pocket book edition: München: Heyne, 1979.
Egon Schiele. Versuch einer Vorrede. Wien: Rosenbaum, 1911.
"Die Vision vom Alten und vom Neuen." Prose tale. Hellerau: Hegner, 1921.
Die Rede über Franz Blei oder Der Schriftsteller in der Katholizität. Hellerau: Hegner, 1922.
Innozenz oder Sinn und Fluch der Unschuld. Novel. Hellerau: Hegner, 1922.

Der Lügner unter Bürgern. Novel. Hellerau: Hegner, 1922; Pocketbook editions: Frankfurt am Main: Fischer, 1969; München: Piper, 1984.

Kain und Abel. Eine Legende. Wien: Haybach, 1924; New edition: München: Piper, 1963.

Die Bekenntnisse eines modern Malers (= *Meine große und kleine Geschichte. Lebensbeschreibung quasi un' allegoria*). Wien/Leipzig: Zahn und Diamant, 1926.

Der Maler Alexander Gartenberg. Monograph. Wien: Haybach, 1928.

Eine sagenhafte Figur. Ein platonischer Roman mit einem Nachwort in usum delphini. Novel. Wien: Luckmann, 1946; Pocketbook edition: München: Piper, 1985.

Die Fabeln vom Dros. Prosa tales. Wien: Luckmann, 1947.

Musik zu einem Lebenslauf. Poems. (=*Neue Dichtung aus Österreich* 27), Wien: Bergland, 1957.

Laßt uns den Menschen machen. Prose tales. Wien: Luckmann, 1947.

Sonne und Mond. Ein historischer Roman aus der Gegenwart. Novel. München: Piper, 1962; Pocket book edition: München: Piper, 1984.

Zur Situation der modernen Kunst. Aufsätze und Reden. Essays. Wien/Hannover/Berlin: Forum-Verlag, 1963.

Gewaltig staunt der Mensch. Prose and Poetry. Introduced by Heimito von Doderer. Graz/Wien: Stiasny, 1963.

Der innere Erdteil. Aus den Wörterbüchern. München: Piper, 1966.

Die Fabel von der Freundschaft. Ein sokratischer Roman. Novel. München: Piper, 1969.

Miniaturen zur Schöpfung. Eine kleine Zeitgeschichte. Essays. Salzburg: Residenz-Verlag, 1970.

Treppe ohne Haus oder Seele ohne Leib. Späte Gedichte. Mit einer Grabrede für Gütersloh von Alfred Focke. Poems. Eisenstadt: Roetzer, 1974.

Works Edited

Der Knockabout. Journal edited by Karl Adler and Albert Paris Gütersloh. Wien, 1914. Only one issue appeared.

Die Rettung. Blätter zur Erkenntnis der Zeit. Journal edited by Franz Blei and Albert Paris Gütersloh. Wien: Harbauer, 1918/1919. Jg. 1, Hefte 1-12/14; Hellerau: Hegner, 1919, Jg. 2, Hefte 1-4/5.

Albert Paris Gütersloh   233

Franz Blei. Schriften in Auswahl, edited and with a postscript by Albert Paris Gütersloh. München: Biederstein, 1960.

Letters

Albert Paris Gütersloh. "Briefe an einen imaginären Empfänger." *Jahresring* 63/64, 7-11.

Franz Blei. "An Gütersloh (1926-1939)." *Agathon.* Almanach a.d.J. 46 (1945), 301-308.

Reinhard Tötschinger, ed. "Albert Paris Gütersloh: Briefe an Milena (1932-1970)," mit einem Essay von Herbert Hutter, St. Pölten, Herbert Eisenreich. "Offener Brief an A. P. Gütersloh, 1957." In H. E., *Reaktionen.* 1964. pp. 253-260.

Contributions to Journals

"Wo steht die Dichtung heute?" *Literatur und Kritik* 68 (1972), 449-450.

"Kurzgefaßter Prolog zu meinen Schriften." *Literatur und Kritik* 68 (1972), 450-452.

"Der Roman und die Materiologie." *Literatur und Kritik* 68 (1972), 452-456.

"Dr. Doderer an seinem Schreibtisch." Poem. *Literatur und Kritik* 80 (1973), 577.

"Tandaradei." Novel fragment. *Literatur und Kritik* 118 (1977), 134-139.

II. Works in English Translation

None

III. Secondary Works in English

Pabisch, Peter and Alan Best. "The 'total novel': Heimito von Doderer and Albert Paris Gütersloh," in *Modern Austrian Writing,* edited by Alan Best and Hans Wolfschütz. London: Oswald Wolff, 1980, pp. 63-78.

234   Ludwig Fischer

Eisenreich, Herbert. "Albert Paris Gütersloh," in *Handbook of Austrian Literature,* edited by Frederick Ungar. New York: Ungar, 1973, pp. 105-107.

IV. Major Studies in German

Bielefeld, Michael. "Bibliographie zu Albert Paris Gütersloh," in *Kritisches Lexikon zur deutschsprachigen Gegenwartsliteratur,* edited by Heinz Ludwig Arnold. München: Text und Kritik, 20. Nlg.

Doderer, Heimito von. *Der Fall Gütersloh. Ein Schicksal und seine Bedeutung.* Wien: Haybach, 1930; Neudruck München: Biederstein, 1961.

Doderer, Heimito von. "Gütersloh," in *Albert Paris Gütersloh. Autor und Werk.* München: Piper, 1962, pp. 7-18.

Focke, Alfred. "Versuch über A. P. Güterslohs Materiologie." *Literatur und Kritik* 68 (1972), 466-472.

Fröhlich, Hans Jürgen. "Albert Paris Gütersloh. 5. Februar 1887 in Wien, 16. Mai 1973 in Wien." *Jahresring* 73-75 (1974), 193-276.

Graf, Hans-Jörg. "Die Schlüssel zum Schloss. Notizen zu A. P. Güterslohs *Sonne und Mond,*" in *Albert Paris Gütersloh. Zum 75. Geburtstag.* München: Piper, 1962, pp. 40-45.

Albert Paris Gütersloh. Zum 75. Geburtstag. München: Piper, 1962.

Albert Paris Gütersloh. Autor und Werk. München: Piper, 1962.

Hartl, Edwin. "Gütersloh—den gibt es wirklich." *Wort in der Zeit* 3 (1963), 36-39 (zu: *Sonne und Mond*).

Hutter, Heribert. *Albert Paris Gütersloh.* Wien: Rosenbaum, 1977.

Prokop, Hans F. "Albert Paris von Gütersloh: Bibliographie," *Literatur und Kritik* 68 (1972), 483-492.

Rieder, Heinz. "Jenseits des Romans: Albert Paris Güterslohs 'Sonne und Mond,'" in H. R., *Österreichische Moderne.* Bonn: Bouvier, 1968, pp. 109-117.

Rieder, Heinz. "A. P. Gütersloh, 'Sonne und Mond,'" in *Neue deutsche Hefte* 10/98 (1964), pp. 133-139.

Rieser, Hannes. "Doderer und Gütersloh. Metaphorik und 'totaler' Roman." Maschinenschriftliche Dissertation, Salzburg, 1968.

Schmidt-Dengler, Wendelin. "Die Anfänge des 'Falles Gütersloh.'" *Literatur und Kritik* 68 (1972), 473-479.

Thurner, Felix. *Albert Paris Gütersloh. Studien zu seinem Romanwerk.*
    Bern: Herbert Lang, 1970.
Tramin, Peter von. "Unterwegs zum totalen Roman." *Forum* 9 (1962),
    103-104; also in *Albert Paris Gütersloh. Autor und Werk.* Mün-
    chen: Piper 1962, pp. 62-69.

Fritz Hochwälder

Donald G. Daviau

In the chaotic aftermath of World War II, when the theater in Austria was attempting to revive itself, two plays touched the sensibilities of audiences more than all others: *Draußen vor der Tür* (1947, Outside before the Door) by the German dramatist Wolfgang Borchert and *Das heilige Experiment* (1947, *Lonely Are the Brave*), by the Austrian playwright Fritz Hochwälder. The success of the latter drama at the prestigious Burgtheater in Vienna in 1947 propelled Hochwälder into the front rank of Austrian dramatists, and the progression of theatrically successful plays that followed has kept his name prominent to the present day. Even though his works were no longer performed as frequently as earlier because of the changing tastes of theater directors, his reputation as a major literary figure remained undiminished as he continued to ignore popular trends and follow his own solidly conservative direction. In one sense he holds a unique position among contemporary Austrian writers, for his serious career as a dramatist began only out of necessity while in exile in Switzerland, where he spent his life after 1938, refusing to return to Austria after the war. Following his death on 9 October 1986 his body was returned to Vienna for burial in an *Ehrengrab* (grave of honor) in the Zentralfriedhof.

Hochwälder was surprised at the vagaries of fate that led to his later development as a dramatist, for little in his early life would have suggested such a future. He was born in Vienna on 28 May 1911, the son of a master upholsterer. His mother ran a small secondhand store in the house in which they lived. He grew up in the Seventh District in Vienna with the streets around the Schottenkirche as his playground. He considered himself a city person, and claimed that he would not be able to live permanently in the country.[1] His memories of school con-

sisted mainly of the "unforgettable impressions" of theater perform-
ances of Ferdinand Raimund's *Der Bauer als Millionçr* (The Farmer as
Millionaire) and *Der Verschwender* (The Profligate), to which his class
was taken, and the recitals of fairy tales and ballads by the actress
Melanie Gnad on Saturday afternoons in the Cosmos movie house.
Another lasting memory was the death of Emperor Franz Joseph I in
November 1916, an event which made him realize that he felt closer to
the Czechs and Hungarians of the old Monarchy than to the Germans.

When he entered high school (*Realgymnasium*) Hochwälder also
became an apprentice in his father's upholstery shop. He passed his
journeyman test in 1929 and the master's examination in 1936. He
then opened his own shop, and it appeared that the future course of his
life was set. These were hard years of depression and unemployment in
Vienna following the burning of the Palace of Justice on 15 July 1927.
Despite the difficult social and political conditions in Vienna during
those years Hochwälder remained a devoted Austrian; if the choice had
been his, he would never have left his native country. But after the
Anschluß he was forced to flee in August 1938 "like a thief in the
night" across the border into Switzerland, where he settled in Zürich
until his death. The tragedy of his parents' execution in the concentration camp at Treblinka kept Hochwälder from returning to Austria
despite his deep-rooted affinity and obvious love for his former homeland: "I was and am Austrian through and through, more precisely
Viennese."[2] He had always felt like a stranger in Switzerland.

Since Hochwälder was permitted to stay in Switzerland but was
not allowed to work for a living, he had abundant time on his hands
and began to write. He had belonged to a literary group in Vienna while
attending night school and had already tried his hand at playwriting in
1927. In 1932 he wrote a radio play entitled *Trommler* (Drummers),
a highly derivative piece dealing with the theme of the returning soldier.
In the same year under the influence of Expressionism he wrote his first
play for the theater, the three-act drama "Jehr," which was performed
at the Kammerspiele in Vienna on 1 March 1933. Other early dramas
and radio plays, several in the tradition of the Vienna folk plays of
Nestroy and Raimund, include *Weinsberger Ostern 1525* (Weinsberg
Easter 1525), *Der liebe Augustin* (Dear Augustine), *Liebe in Florenz*
(Love in Florence), *Kaufmann und Künstler* (Merchant and Artist), *Der
Prozeß* (The Trial), and *Eulenspiegels Erdreich* (Eulenspiegel's Earthly
Realm).[3] Besides "Jehr" only *Liebe in Florenz* was performed, initially
in 1936 in the Theater für Neunundvierzig and in a revival of 1985. Of

all these works *Liebe in Florenz* is the only one he considered worthy of including in the four-volume edition of his collected works.

"Out of inner necessity" during what Hochwälder called the oppressive summer of 1940 he wrote the first of his major dramas, *Esther,* a "serious persiflage of the biblical tale."[4] Hochwälder considered this work not his best but one of his boldest plays. It is the only one of his mature dramas that has not yet been performed, because Hochwälder claimed he wrote this "old fairy tale" for himself and had never released it for the stage. At the time he wrote the play he was in his Marxist phase and believed that society could resolve the Jewish question. Later he was less optimistic, but he showed no inclination to revise the play accordingly.

In *Esther* Hochwälder treats the fundamental conflict of good and evil that remains the basic theme of all his works. It is the first of six plays which superimposes contemporary relevance on a setting in the past. The play is "historical" in the sense that Hochwälder bases it on the biblical tale, which is freely modified to accommodate allusions to recent events. It is well known today that Hitler, following the lead of Georg Ritter von Schönerer, the founder and leader of the German National Party in Austria in the 1880s,[5] and "handsome" Karl Lueger ("der schöne Karl"), three-time Mayor of Vienna,[6] capitalized on the idea of using the Jews as scapegoats to consolidate his power and carry out his political plans. Hochwälder incorporates this idea in the biblical story of Esther. The King, whose throne is in jeopardy, shamelessly admits his plan to sacrifice the Jews to Esther's father, Mordechai, who represents his moral opposite. With his power threatened by Hamann, a young radical modeled on Hitler, the King turns into a pragmatic politician who follows the expedient policy that might makes right. He argues that he is justified in his action because he is thereby averting revolution and saving his crown. As a thorough materialist he is not concerned about his immortal soul after death but only with holding on to his power in this life. He transforms into a man without conscience, character, or soul, an empty shell maintaining his power for its own sake at the cost of his humanity.

Esther, who had initially concealed her Jewishness in order to gratify her selfish ego as the King's mistress, now transforms into a mature responsible human being who proudly acknowledges her Jewish heritage. She had helped the King entrap Hamann, and in gratitude he plans to make her his queen. However, when she learns of the impending fate of her people, she renounces the King and joins her father in whatever fate may await them. She recognizes that her sacrifice will not accomplish any purpose, but she must follow her conscience and preserve her integrity regardless of the consequences. The play is a well-crafted powerful work, and it is difficult to understand why Hochwälder continued to withhold it from performance, for as a study of corrupt power as well as a message of idealistic courage its relevance remains undiminished.

Hochwälder spent the year 1941 in a work camp at Tessin, until he could be released by finding a sponsor who was willing to guarantee his livelihood, although this was only a formality and involved no real financial support. This friendly gesture enabled Hochwälder to lead a more normal life. He lived in his own apartment, married, and had a child. During the spring of 1942 friends made available to him a small house in Ascona, where in two months of relative isolation he wrote *Das heilige Experiment,* which became his greatest success and remains his finest play. Initially, the play was declined by the Schauspielhaus in Zürich, and its première was held on 24 March 1943 at the Städtebund Theater Biel-Solothurn. However, not until the performance of the play in the Burgtheater in Vienna in 1947 on the recommendation of the dramatist Franz Theodor Csokor, one of Hochwälder's closest friends, was his reputation as dramatist really launched.

Because *Das heilige Experiment* treats the Jesuit social experiment in Paraguay, Hochwälder was sometimes mistaken for a Catholic author, a view he attempted to correct: "I am anything but a Catholic author. This error of taking me for such occurred without my doing, primarily because one of my plays, *Das heilige Experiment,* treats the Jesuit colony and therefore had to be presented in Catholic dress. None of my other plays reveals an orthodox Catholic outlook."[7]

Hochwälder explicitly identified the roots of his kind of dramatic production as deriving from his Viennese background:

> The theater impressions that I received in my youth were in the best sense of the word Viennese. They are the factors that determine my efforts as a stage writer again and again, whether in foreign material, in foreign dress, in foreign places. The tradition to which I feel I belong is that of the Viennese folk theater. And nothing, neither being hostile to one's time nor being exiled, can drive out and replace a tradition which one has absorbed into himself. The Viennese air has given me something inestimable: clarity of thought, sensible form,

theater blood. To be sure, I do not necessarily designate myself as a writer. With pleasure I remain an illiterate (*Analphabet*), in order to put plays on the stage in my own way—unliterary, unpretentious, popular national works.[8]

In adamantly insisting on distinguishing between theater and literary works Hochwälder perceptively described his dramatic outlook and characterized the nature of his plays:

> Theater is by no means literature. It can become literature. From the viewpoint of the stage, literature is only the noble patina which the products of great theatrical periods acquire with age. From its beginning and in the periods of its highest flowering genuine theater was always closer to the circus and to clownery than to university seminars and the scholar's study. Sometimes theater works will eventually become literature; but when plays begin as literature, they will usually not live long as theater.[9]

One of Hochwälder's closest friends in Zürich was the exiled German writer Georg Kaiser, one of the leading dramatists of Expressionism. They shared many ideas about the theater: both are rationalists who believe in the well-made, logically constructed play (*Denkspiel*) using the Aristotelian unities, and both emphasize conflicts of ideas, usually unresolvable moral and ethical problems. However, their resemblance is a case of affinity, not influence. Hochwälder always staunchly preserved his literary and intellectual independence. In any event he had little actual background in Expressionism like Kaiser; that very influential movement in Berlin between 1910 and 1925 was too early for Hochwälder and made little impact in Vienna.

In addition to maintaining traditional form Hochwälder showed himself to be a maverick, one of the few dramatists of the postwar era not influenced by the dramatic theories of Bertolt Brecht. Instead, although he respected Brecht as a writer, Hochwälder considered Brecht's concept of epic theater useful only to Brecht, and his plays represent the very kind of entertaining theater that Brecht referred to deprecatingly as culinary theater, although he does deal with issues intended to make audiences think. Hochwälder was even more intolerant of the theater of the absurd, which he repudiated along with all other postwar experiments, theatrical gimmickry, and foreign imitation.

He steadfastly clung to his traditional form; like the master artisan that he was, he pointed with pride to the excellent craftsmanship of his dramas.

Although the first six of Hochwälder's dramas make use of historical settings to gain perspective on contemporary problems, they are not historical plays in the conventional sense of the term, nor can Hochwälder be considered a historical writer. The particular historical period was not chosen for itself but rather as the background that best allows Hochwälder to illustrate his major themes, which in that phase of his career were all relevant to World War II: the awakening of man's conscience under the pressure of adversity and criminality, the problem of achieving justice in the world, the corruption of power in the belief that might makes right, and the conflict between personal inclination and obedience to authority, or in other terms the conflict between conscience and following orders. Hochwälder had no qualms about using poetic license and playing freely with history. It was permissible to change events to suit his purposes, he felt, since it was never his intention to write a historically accurate version of events but merely to illustrate a burning question of the day.

As a conservative in the sense of defending traditional humanistic values Hochwälder is a strict moralist, and all of his protagonists regardless of the period in which the plays are set become embroiled in a moral conflict of timeless relevance. In treating conflicts of ideas or values he presents the evidence on both sides fairly, but as seen in *Esther* he usually indicates clearly what he considers to be the proper resolution to the moral dilemma. In his hands the theater remains a moral institution with an obligation to entertain and also to edify and instruct. Writing in the tradition of the Viennese folk theater as he does, Hochwälder is usually less interested in the psychological development of his characters than in illustrating the central problem per se. As is appropriate to the entertaining plays he wished to produce, his characters are usually stereotpyes who enunciate a fixed position and undergo little psychological change or development in the course of the action. In his best plays, which do involve growth and transformation as in *Esther, Das heilige Experiment, Der Flüchtling* (The Fugitive), and *Der Befehl* (The Order), the situation ends tragically for the characters involved.

An example that best typifies his dramatic technique is *Das heilige Experiment,* the only one of Hochwälder's plays destined to take its place as a classic. Here he uses the Jesuit experiment in communal living in Paraguay in the seventeenth and eighteenth centuries to

Christianize and improve the lot of the Indians as a metaphor for such fundamental questions as the role of Christianity in achieving social improvement, and the problem of conscience versus duty or following orders. In the period between 1609 and 1767 Spanish Jesuits founded a series of thirty missions in Paraguay which ultimately contained about 150,000 Indians. The natives were treated benevolently by the Jesuits and enjoyed prosperity and happiness. The contrast between the enlightened benevolent rule of the Jesuits and the cruelty of the other landowners was so great that other Indians fled their enslavement to seek refuge in the Jesuit colonies. When the landowners complained about this problem to the Spanish King, the Jesuits were forced to withdraw from Paraguay in 1767, ending a noble social experiment that was sacrificed paradoxically not because it failed but because it was too successful. It is this paradox that forms the climax of the action and the pivotal point on which Hochwälder's play reverses itself.

Hochwälder has telescoped the ending of this 150-year struggle into a matter of hours; in the play stage time and real time are almost equivalent. Yet the action of the play does not seem forced into this intensified time span. The play deals with the dilemma of the sympathetic idealistic protagonist, the Father Provincial, who as head of the Jesuit mission in Paraguay is extremely proud of the humanitarian achievement of the Jesuit experiment. He dreams of expanding his mission to rescue all the Indians from the enslavement of the cruel wealthy landowners. Although he knows that his policies have been denounced to the King, he is confident that the success of the missions will vindicate them and him.

Don Pedro de Miura, the King's emissary, arrives to examine the allegations against the Jesuits. Although the Father Provincial disproves all of the charges, Don Pedro reveals that the King has already ordered the dissolution of the colony. The Jesuits are not guilty of being wrong in their social experiment: "No, you are guilty of much worse than that. You are guilty of being right. Don't you see how unpardonable that is? It is because you are right that your state must be destroyed — ruthlessly destroyed."[10] The Jesuit success is considered dangerous for Spain, and therefore it is in the best interest of the state to end the experiment. As in *Esther* might again makes right, expediency again triumphs over conscience and justice.

The Father Provincial and his loyal friend Oros, who commands the armed garrison, are prepared to fight against what they consider an unfair decision of the King. But a Jesuit superior from Spain intervenes; after reminding the Father Provincial of his oath of strict obedience, he orders him to comply. He must personally oversee the disbandment of the colony to prevent any attempt at rebellion. If he fails to fulfill the King's edict, the Jesuit order will be repressed in Spain. When the situation is viewed in this perspective, the Father Provincial, although deeply frustrated and aggrieved, finds strength in a picture of Francis Xavier, the Jesuit founder, and resolves to keep his sworn oath of allegiance. Oros, however, tries to resist with military force, and the Father Provincial in trying to bring him to reason is mortally wounded. In his final moments he remains convinced about the value of the colonies as a successful social endeavor, but he nevertheless feels that he was right to obey even what seemed like an unjust order that will sacrifice all the Indians who trusted him. In his mind the preservation of the Jesuit order takes precedence over any other consideration. The Father Provincial thus resolves his inner conflict and does not die a broken man but full of confidence about the future vindication of his life's work. He considers his setback analogous to that of Francis Xavier, who likewise suffered reversals in carrying out his mission to improve the world. The Father Provincial dies as a victor in defeat, the closest Hochwälder ever came to creating a tragic character. The conviction with which he delivers his final triumphant speech is so compelling that even the coldhearted cynic and opportunist Don Pedro is overwhelmed and moved to the words that close the play: "I confess, I confess."

This powerful play, which develops great tension in the conflicts between church and state, ideal and reality, and the temporal and eternal, aroused an enthusiastic response in postwar Austria and Germany particularly because of the relevance of the theme of following orders. What makes the play so moving is that most of the principals are basically good men acting under higher orders with which they do not necessarily agree. Unlike the impulsive Oros the Father Provincial could not bring himself to use force against his own leaders and become both a heretic to the Church and a traitor to his country, even for the good cause of protecting the Indians. He is placed in the impossible situation of not having a correct choice, for he will be implicated in guilt whichever path he chooses. However, he is able to assuage his conscience with respect to the Indians by believing that he is serving the greater good by preserving the existence of the Jesuit Order. The Father Provincial's hope for the future turns to irony when one looks ahead in history and discovers that the Jesuits' acquiescence in Paraguay did not accomplish its purpose after all. In 1773, a mere six years later, the Pope dissolved the entire Order.

In the years following the writing of *Das heilige Experiment* but before its triumph in Vienna Hochwälder completed three plays dealing with the topic of exile: "Casa Speranza," *Hôtel du Commerce*, and *Der Flüchtling*. The five-act play "Casa Speranza" (1943) has never been published or performed, although Wilhelm Bortenschlager feels that it is "not only an interesting, but also the most ethical emigrant play that has been written."[11] It deals with a group of fugitives living in a pension after the occupation of France. Hochwälder has created a wide variety of characters to show a cross section of the spectrum of people affected by exile. Like *Erdbeben in Chili* (*Earthquake in Chile*) by Heinrich von Kleist, the writer Hochwälder most admired, this play is intended to show that people do not necessarily become better human beings under the pressure of adverse experience. The individuals in "Casa Speranza" remain concerned only with their own petty feelings and are not able to rise to the great demands of the day. This view reinforces the idea of Heimito von Doderer, who shows in *Die Dämonen* that people are more affected by the small events in their everyday lives than they are by major historical happenings.

Following this "interlude work," as Hochwälder designated it, he wrote *Hôtel du Commerce* (1944, Hotel Commerce), adapting the plot of Maupassant's early novella *Boule de suif*. This comedy in five acts was first performed on 1 February 1946 in the Theater des ersten Mai (Theater of the First of May) in Prague. The play takes place during the Franco-Prussian War of 1870–1871 and deals with a group of refugees fleeing to England to find refuge from the German occupation. For the most part they are wealthy opportunists more concerned about protecting their fortunes and themselves than they are about their country. The group also includes two nuns, who are carrying a badly needed serum to a French military hospital, and finally a prostitute, Elisabeth, who is fleeing because, outraged by the Prussian occupation, she declined to serve a German officer and instead drove him out of her bedroom.

The conflict arises when the Prussian officer in charge stipulates a night with Elisabeth as a condition for approving their continued travel. She refuses for the same reasons of patriotism, and the group remains imprisoned for the next three days. Her companions reveal their corrupt natures by the various means they use to try to persuade her to change her mind. However, only when the nuns appeal to her conscience by citing the number of soldiers dying for lack of the serum they are carrying does she capitulate. After she has saved the situation by her action the group is initially grateful, but the next morning all of the good intentions are forgotten and they snub her totally. When they depart she must ride up front with the driver because they will not permit her with them inside the carriage. At the end she shows the sense of humor and indomitable spirit that will sustain her.

With the changes he has introduced Hochwälder has turned Maupassant's poignant tale of a young maiden's traumatic experience into a boisterous comedy with well-drawn if clichéd characters and sharp dialogue. Not surprisingly, in the simplified black-and-white technique used here the upper-class characters, French and German, are without redeeming qualities, while the prostitute Elisabeth and the proletarian coachman display integrity and human sensibilities. Although this lightweight comedy is one of Hochwälder's lesser works, it is still successful as a theatrically effective play with value as a portrayal of character and human nature.

In 1944 Hochwälder began work on *Der Flüchtling,* another interlude work based on a sketch given to him by his friend Georg Kaiser. The play was performed on 5 September 1945 in the Städtebundtheater Biel-Solothurn and then revised in 1955 at Kaiser's request. The imprint of the Expressionist dramatist can be seen in the theme of transformation and in the lean construction of the drama, which is limited to three people who are designated only as Man, Wife, and Fugitive. The unity of time is observed, the setting could be any border between a fascist and a free country, and the theme is the universal conflict between loyalty to one's conscience and humanity and duty to an oppressive unjust state. Although Hochwälder considered this melodramatic play only a secondary work, it became one of his more popular productions because of its relevant theme.

Der Flüchtling presents the conflict of conscience and duty from a somewhat different perspective than *Das heilige Experiment;* namely, should a border guard who has sworn an oath of duty follow his orders, even if he knows that as a result innocent people will be killed, or should he follow his humanitarian instincts to help the persecuted escape to safety? Although he has maintained his loyalty by closing his eyes to the oppressiveness of the dictatorship in his country, the Man, a border guard, is finally forced to confront the cruel fate of the fugitives he captures when an escaped fugitive takes refuge in his house. The sympathy of his wife for this victim of persecution and her decision to help him regardless of the consequences transforms the attitude of the Man. He is brought to the recognition that in actuality he himself is the fugitive, for he has always avoided his individual responsibility by taking refuge in the excuse of following orders. Once circumstances force him to recognize that he is not the honorable man he pretended to be, he seeks to expiate his former failure as a human being by sacrificing his life so that his wife and the fugitive can escape to a new life together.

Hochwälder seems to be saying that in a time of moral crisis one must not remain neutral, a criticism possibly leveled against Switzerland. The play's problem is a serious one — caught up in tyranny, at what point does an individual know when he should defy orders or in effect become a traitor to his country to avoid crimes against humanity —but the execution fails to do it justice, producing melodrama instead of tragedy. *Der Flüchtling* is constructed in overly simplistic fashion, a *pièce à thèse* using again a starkly black-and-white technique. In the beginning the guard announces how happily married and what a decent loyal civil servant he is, only to have this false veneer stripped away by the following events until he is forced to confront his real nature and the fact that his life is a fraud. Even his wife, who he thought loved him, is now prepared to leave him. His death is therefore a humanitarian gesture not only to save the fugitive, but also to make up for his former officious behavior toward his fellow citizens, and in no little part because he has lost his wife. The play, which exemplifies the earlier Expressionist shibboleth that "man is good," is intended to glorify resistance to tyranny with a reminder that one's humanitarian duty supersedes loyalty to a tyrannical government.

Since Hochwälder fled over the border to Switzerland illegally, the play has autobiographical overtones. But the central idea is troublesome, for it is not so much an anti-fascist play as it is a portrayal of a corruptible human being who sought only his own advantage at the expense of others. All Jesuit priests who truly believe in their calling would have had to act exactly like the Father Provincial, but not all border guards are corrupt or corruptible and thus would not face the same situation as Hochwälder's character. The play would have been stronger if the guard had been the good man he claimed to be, for then Hochwälder would have confronted the real dilemma of choosing between conscience and duty. As it is he begged the serious problem and contributed only to publicizing the question, not presenting the answer. Recognition of this deficiency is most probably why Hochwälder did not rank *Der Flüchtling* among his best works.

In the same period between 1946 and 1951 Hochwälder wrote four additional plays, which have never been published, although one has been performed: "Die verschleierte Frau" (1946, The Veiled Woman), which deals with a situation blending the plots of *Hôtel du Commerce* and *Der Flüchtling:* a border guard at a remote mountain post propositions a woman only to discover that she is his wife who had been imprisoned and is returning home; "Virginia" (1948), performed in 1951 in the Deutsche Schauspielhaus under the direction of Erwin Piscator; a radio play entitled "Vier Paragraphen" (1951, Four Paragraphs), the text of which has been lost; and "Der gestohlene Mond" (1951, The Stolen Moon), a play in two acts set in Paris. Whether any of these or a number of other plays in manuscript will ever be finished is impossible to determine at this point.

Hochwälder's technique in his early plays was to find an idea or plot and then search for an appropriate historical setting in which to place it. This led him in 1946 to the fourteenth-century rogue's novel *Meier Helmbrecht* by Wernher der Gärtner. The play follows the medieval novel closely, and in three acts, which take place in the spring, summer, and winter, shows the rise and fall of Meier Helmbrecht, who thought he was too good to be a farmer and instead became a dangerous criminal, robbing, plundering, and killing until he was brought to justice.

The plot turns on the question of guilt and punishment but differs widely in this respect from the original, where the son must pay for his crimes. In his version, however, Hochwälder blames the father for tolerating the behavior of his son instead of trying to stop him, even though it probably would have cost the parent his life. The wronged farmers seeking vengeance take everything from the father—his wife, his daughter, and his farm—but let him live. The son, who has been blinded and has had his right hand cut off, passes by. The father chases him away and then constructs a tool with which he begins to hack at the earth in an attempt to start over. The guilt of the son is unpardonable, but that of the father can at least be expiated.

The play is written in a starkly realistic manner, as is the original story, and the dialogue maintains its intensity. The theme was timely in 1947, when the world was seeking answers to the questions of how Nazism could have happened and who was responsible. Hochwälder's idea of the parents' responsibility was not a view that was widely accepted and may have detracted from the play's acceptance by the public. This work has not been revived since its initial production.

Succumbing to complicity in guilt is also the theme of the three-act play *Der öffentliche Ankläger* (1947-1948, The Public Prosecutor), a dramatic tour de force portraying a corrupt public prosecutor who is tricked into prosecuting himself and making a persuasive case for his own execution. Again using the perspective of the historical past—in this case the French Revolution—Hochwälder examines a highly relevant postwar issue: the validity of the defense offered by former Nazis accused of war crimes that they were not guilty because they were only following orders. Fouquier-Tocville, the zealous public prosecutor at the end of a reign of terror, considers himself only a servant of the state: "I was only the axe. Does one guillotine an axe?"[12] He insists that he is simply carrying out his assigned duties, for which he has no personal responsibility, and cannot see that he has become an unfeeling monster without conscience or scruple: "Me frightening? Not in the least.—Give me a good law and proper orders—and you have in me a conscientious official who does not deviate a hair's breadth from them. Give me orders that lead to bloodshed, and I become Satan."[13]

Despite his protestations of objectivity in carrying out his duty Fouquier is not simply an unfortunate individual trapped by circumstances in an unpleasant job. The enthusiasm that he displays for his cruel and bloody orders carries him beyond duty into guilt, for to expedite "justice" he blackmails witnesses to give false testimony and fabricates cases against innocent victims. On the surface he masquerades as the epitome of a dedicated public servant while in his heart he is totally corrupt and capable of any atrocity. He enjoys the power over helpless people and the personal advantages that his position gives him. It is not even a matter of his overcoming his conscience and following orders simply to survive; he has become a vicious criminal out of desire for personal gain. His ambition and greed finally entrap him and bring his downfall; with the end of the reign of terror Fouquier is a liability to the new government. The offer of a political position leads him to ignore his normal caution and to prosecute a high-ranking victim whose name is to be revealed only at the trial when it is too late for help. Fouquier falls into his own trap and is executed. Although the plot may sound far-fetched in the telling, it works beautifully on the stage and remains convincing and suspenseful until the end.

Unlike Helmbrecht, a good but weak man forced into evil against his wishes and therefore salvageable, Fouquier, who is absolutely corrupted by his absolute power, experiences no catharsis and no inner transformation. He has no conscience and is completely amoral. The characters of Theresa Tallien, who entraps Fouquier, and of her husband are similar, as Hochwälder portrays the insidious effects of revolution on the people involved in it, provided that they are capable of evil to begin with.

That one can display integrity even in a criminal state is shown by Montane, the only honorable person in the play, who has resigned his position as judge rather than become an accomplice of the injustice and general corruption. This willingness to withdraw rather than compromise is a course of action that not many of Hochwälder's characters follow. When Fouquier blackmails him into sitting on the bench one more time for this special case, Montane accepts the task with a heavy heart: "I will be content when our day can purchase freedom with this crime—that is my first."[14] Actually the case is such that Montane can retain his integrity, for Fouquier is clearly guilty. Not only justice, but also a higher poetic justice is served, when the criminal public prosecutor convicts himself by his own unscrupulous methods.

As in all of the preceding plays Fouquier illustrates how a man can be caught up in criminal circumstances beyond his control. The test that determines the quality of his character is whether, given the opportunity, the individual succumbs to evil or remains moral, whether he follows the path of Fouquier or Montane. In short, it is a question of whether the individual has a conscience that will not allow him to violate his integrity. At this point Hochwälder still believes that there are incorruptible individuals, for, as we have seen, he does depict characters who refuse to compromise themselves. Later, however, he changes his view, arguing that it is all a matter of luck and circumstances as to whether one can maintain his integrity and honor.

Donadieu (1953), which had its première on 1 October 1953 in the Vienna Burgtheater, is also set in the time of the French Revolution and deals with the issue of punishing war crimes. Hochwälder based the play loosely on Conrad Ferdinand Meyer's poem "Die Füße im Feuer" (Feet in the Fire) and sets the action at the end of the Huguenot rebellion in 1726 when the King had defeated the Protestants and was willing to grant freedom and religious tolerance to those who would surrender without further resistance. The situation is not precisely analogous to that after World War II, but the issue of judging former war criminals is the same.

By chance the protagonist, Donadieu, whose castle was pillaged while he was away at war, finds the killer of his wife and most of his followers delivered into his hands. He is, however, prevented from taking revenge, because by killing the war criminal Du Bosc, a messenger of the King, he will break the King's amnesty and bring down retaliation on all Protestants. Lavalette promises Donadieu that Du Bosc will be tried and punished for his war crimes. When Du Bosc tries to goad Donadieu into a duel, so that he can kill him and not have to worry about his testimony, Lavalette intercedes and kills his fellow officer to keep Donadieu from breaking the amnesty. Thus the play displays Hochwälder's ethical concerns even though he again vitiates the problem and avoids confronting it by having Du Bosc killed without being tried. It is also one of his most optimistic works, for it demonstrates that justice and truth can prevail in this world. Typically the play is tautly constructed and theatrically effective, but in literary terms it loses much of its effectiveness by an ending that leaves the problem not only unresolved but also virtually untouched. However, this drama does make clear that at this time Hochwälder felt war criminals should be punished.

After setting the preceding six plays in the historical past Hochwälder reached a turning point in his approach, setting his next play, *Die Herberge* (1955/1956, The Inn), a dramatic legend in three acts, in the present. This work also represents an important departure in terms of Hochwälder's point of view,[15] for whereas he had argued for justice and for punishing war criminals, he now expresses his new idea that harmony and order are greater values to society than justice. In his mature view it is preferable to forget the past for the sake of restoring harmony in the present.

The action, which takes place in an inn called "Die Herberge" located in a mountain village, is more ambitious and complicated than in most of Hochwälder's plays. Here he strives for that multilevel complexity that makes a great drama more than the sum of its parts. There is an attempt to use symbolism to suggest the realm of the inexpressible, to create an ambiguous mystical atmosphere in which instinctive feeling predominates over logic. However, despite the serious effort the play fails to coalesce into a tightly knit unity as *Das heilige Experiment* does, and it does not rise above the explicit level.

The cast of characters includes a young couple who steal money so that they can marry, a corrupt speculator with a driver who has a record for sex crimes, an avaricious innkeeper, a coffin maker, a vagrant who turns out to be the only whole person in the play, and finally a cynical official who solves the crime by chance. Like Azdak in Brecht's *Kaukasischer Kreidekreis* (*Caucasian Chalk Circle*) the official, Smalejus, judges people according to his intuitive estimate of their character rather than by the legal statutes, as the narrow-minded policeman does. He believes that the sense of order transcends the strict application of the law. In his plays to this point Hochwälder has deplored instances of justice brutalized by power. Now he modifies his outlook and shows authority invoking a higher sense of divine justice to achieve a greater good for society than would be accomplished by a strict application of the law. In general Hochwälder henceforth defends what he considers to be best for society rather than what best serves society's rules and laws. Although the complicated plot is unraveled and the play concludes happily with justice done, Hochwälder makes clear through the ending that this is only a rare instance. The world remains a complicated and nasty place.

The only character who emerges from the play unsullied, free, and untainted is the vagrant Schimke, who resembles Akki in Friedrich Dürrenmatt's drama *Ein Engel kommt nach Babylon* (An Angel Comes to Babylon).[16] Schimke believes in God and His justice and is not tempted by power, position, or money. He serves as the foil for the official Smalejus, who has no faith in human justice or in human nature and disputes Schimke's view: "God's justice is contained in the midst of injustice—like the pit in a piece of fruit."[17] The skeptical Smalejus sees little hope for achieving justice, earthly or divine, even though occasionally right may triumph. The ending portrays symbolically how this lack of faith weakens man; Smalejus must call on the idealistic Schimke to support him, for he is too weak to walk home without assistance. Hochwälder insists that to prevail in life man needs the support of love, faith, and hope, adumbrating a theme that he will use shortly in *Donnerstag* (Thursday).

Hochwälder uses Schimke as the spokesman for his personal view of divine justice, as he made clear in his commentary on *Die Herberge:*

> The symbolic happenings in *Die Herberge* correspond to the plot in the dialectical [*Das heilige*] *Experiment;* certainly our world is filled with injustice that shrieks to heaven, but just as certainly in the hour of reconciliation everyone will reap what he has sown in the course of his life. The moral: whoever is granted the probability of spending his earthly days in external

freedom receives a higher justice out of all the injustice that he has committed, and no ideal state can remove this guilt from our own breast."[18]

This is an important expression of the Weltanschauung operative in all of Hochwälder's remaining works and helps explain the reason for his shift of outlook.

Understanding Hochwälder's concept of poetic justice is helpful in approaching *Der Unschuldige* (The Innocent Man), which he originally wrote in 1948 and completed in its definitive version in 1958, for it helps to clarify the ambiguous ending bordering on black humor. Hochwälder varies here the idea presented in *Der Flüchtling* and *Die Herberge,* that a chance occurrence can plunge a calm organized life into chaos. In this comedy set in the peaceful world of 1911 skeletons literally come out of the closet to reawaken a long forgotten past. The successful businessman, Christian Erdmann, who in his younger years was known for his violent temper that brought him into trouble with the law, is suspected of a murder, when by chance the sewer lines being dug through his garden uncover a skeleton. Suddenly people remember that some thirty years earlier Erdmann had had an altercation with a rival suitor for his wife's hand, after which the man suddenly disappeared without a trace. Because of his reputation and the fact that he was opposed to the sewer lines, everyone, including his family and friends, believes that he is guilty. After his innocence has been proven, Erdmann confuses the issue by suggesting that he might have killed his rival after all, describing how he might have done it. He concludes the play with a loud resounding laugh at the consternation this announcement causes, and "amid this infernal laughter the curtain falls."[19]

This lightweight comedy involves two thematic lines: one, the eternal question of appearance and reality, and the other, the psychological exploration of character when confronted with such a bizarre occurrence. According to Bortenschlager, this work was based on an incident that took place in Vienna in 1928.[20] Whereas in the original situation the merchant Christof Bauer killed himself because his friends turned away from him even though he was judged innocent, here Hochwälder has created a much stronger character in Erdmann, who is capable of defending himself and even enjoys the situation.

Der Unschuldige ends on a note of ambiguity that is not usually present in Hochwälder's plays. The audience can continue to ponder whether Erdmann is really guilty and the discovery of the French skeleton has enabled him to be absolved of his crime or whether his confession at the end is merely his way of taunting his friends who had doubts about him earlier. His laughter is likewise ambiguous, either ironical laughter at having fooled society and flaunted justice or bitter laughter about how quick the world is to believe accusations. The central image symbolizes Hochwälder's view that chance could put anyone into a similar situation. Ultimately this comedy strikes the new theme that will recur in the later works: evil wears the same face as all men and can be identified only under particular circumstances.

This concept of man's relationship to evil became the subject explored in two of Hochwälder's most unusual and most experimental works. In 1959 Hochwälder was commissioned to write a play for the Salzburg Festival, and in keeping with the spirit of the baroque theater tradition created *Donnerstag,* a modern mystery play, which premièred in Salzburg on 29 July 1959. The result is a blend of elements from the Faust legend and Hofmannsthal's *Jedermann* (Everyman),[21] the play for which the Salzburg Festival was originally designed. Hochwälder had always insisted that his origins were in the Viennese Folk Theater, and *Donnerstag* more than any other play confirms this judgment. It contains a number of elements common to folk tradition such as the use of magic and the faithful servant who speaks in Viennese dialect and has a healthy common-sensical attitude toward the sometimes irrational behavior of his superiors. Despite the change of form this play still fits well into the progression of his works, for ultimately it deals with the basic question of the conflict of good and evil, the central theme of all his works, only from a different perspective than used previously.

Donnerstag is a modern parable written to address the major contemporary problem of the drift of society into soulless materialism. As expected in a morality play the moral is clear: one can sacrifice one's soul to find release from suffering, from conscience, and from despair, but the cost is high, for the result is the loss of one's humanity. *Donnerstag* is thematically one of Hochwälder's most important plays, for he escalates the conflict of good and evil to its ultimate possibility, showing that such moral values will have no validity in a dehumanized, materialistic, and amoral society. By demonstrating that faith can be generated out of nothing Hochwälder emphasizes that the situation of modern man is not hopeless, for each individual has not only the possibility but also the burden of responsibility to determine his own fate. Although he was a Catholic, Hochwälder, a child of the twentieth century, indicates that man, who now controls his own destiny, is also his own problem and must provide his own solution, that is, he must decide whether he wishes to remain human or not in the traditional definition of the term. He has the possibility of changing his present harmful course of action at any time.

Through the concern of two altruistic individuals, both of whom still believe in love and miracles, the protagonist Pomfrit, a questioning Faust figure, is restored to an understanding of life's promise and possibilities that are always available to anyone who opens his heart to them. Through his discovery of the love and concern of his fellow man Pomfrit becomes a human being again. He rejects Wondrak's (read Mephistopheles) offer for success, preferring to continue the search for human happiness even with the suffering that human existence involves. He still does not believe in God, but he would like to believe and hopes that he will find the way to do so.

The positive, optimistic message of the play is that, although faith has waned in the twentieth century, it can be rekindled from nothing as Death informs Pomfrit: "Don't worry about despairing, man: belief comes from nothing—a summons along the way, a tremendous light—and didn't creation spring from nothing?"[22] Pomfrit learns that all of the qualities that he needs to live a happy life as a human being are within him and do not depend on outside factors. By giving of oneself to others one will reap benefits in return. The play suggests a way to combat the growing soullessness of the twentieth century and to restore the notion of God. As a universal parable of our time in a universal form the play must be considered one of Hochwälder's most important works, even though critics and audiences have been cool to it thus far. *Donnerstag* is also significant in Hochwälder's development, for it marks another thematic turning point. Up to this time he has always presented the conflict of good and evil in terms of man and society or man afflicted by chance circumstances. Now he has escalated the struggle into an internal personal one between the human being (*Mensch*) and the non-human being (*Nicht-Mensch*).

In the years 1961–1963 Hochwälder continued this theme in a sequel to *Donnerstag, 1003,* a play in three acts, which was first performed on 7 January 1964 in the Theater in der Josefstadt in Vienna. The play contains only two characters, the writer Ulrich Valmont and his alter ego representing respectively the *Mensch* and the *Nicht-Mensch*. This play is intended to show what Pomfrit would have become if he had exchanged his soul for permanent relief from suffering.

Valmont is suffering from writer's block, and one of the questions of the play is whether, if man has become impossible, drama, which is the study of man in the world, may also have become impossible. Hochwälder again borrows the Faustian concept of the divided soul in a general way: Valmont struggling to dictate his latest work, begins talking to the tape recorder, i.e., his alter ego, which then materializes in the form of Bloner, the *Nicht-Mensch,* who represents the values of the contemporary materialistic world.

Bloner has no scruples to impede his desire to succeed. Moral values have no meaning for him, and he is unconcerned about death, for he does not believe in the soul. He is a creature of prosperity, the successful manager of lucrative but not quite honest businesses, a hedonist who has everything because he can buy everything, and a man who pursues every temptation. He is the modern version of Don Juan, hence the title *1003,* an allusion to Mozart's opera *Don Giovanni,* where this figure represented the number of his conquests. Here it represents the license plate of Bloner's fancy car. Bloner, "the projection of Valmont's own worst elements," has the kind of mentality that made mass murder possible and that if continued will lead to the destruction of mankind. Hochwälder intends the parable as another warning that man is surrendering to his darkest instincts and threatening his own existence. No arguments are effective to change Bloner, and Valmont recognizes that the only way he can rid himself of this representation of the evil side of his own nature is to kill himself. The problem is not outside in the world but in his own mind: "The non-human: projection of my own despicable side! Hans Bloner a phantom that flees from the morning light!—Not the world, the brain is sick!—"[23] Valmont finally causes Bloner to disappear and then feels reassured that his pessimistic vision of man was only a nightmare. However, when he answers the door to meet his new neighbor, it is Hans Bloner! The nightmare is not fantasy but the new reality.

Donnerstag and *1003* are linked together thematically like Goethe's *Faust I* and *Faust II* and must be viewed together to see the full implications of the idea of the non-human's gaining supremacy in the world. Although the critics, accustomed to Hochwälder as the writer of well-made traditional plays, resented the novelty of form found in these two works, the latter should be considered among his most important contributions, for they represent the culmination of his thinking about the duality of man and about the nature of evil in the world today. The progression from *Esther* to *1003* is thematically a straight line of development. The subsequent dramas continue to play additional variations on these ideas but do not go beyond them.

Rebuffed by the lack of success of his two experimental plays, Hochwälder returned to his earlier successful form and themes. In the comedy *Der Himbeerpflücker* (1964, The Raspberry Picker) Hochwälder revived the theme of *Der Unschuldige* — guilt concealed beneath the surface of respectability — and made it relevant to contemporary circumstances by illustrating it in terms of present-day Nazis hiding secrets of a war-criminal past while serving as respectable members and leaders of the community.

This play was written to address a contemporary problem that disturbed Hochwälder greatly: the fact that the Nazi spirit was still so strong in provincial Austria. The plot, "which is unfortunately not invention but reporting . . . ,"[24] is set in contemporary Bad Brauning (read Braunau) and takes place in the "Inn at the Sign of the White Lamb," a name chosen for its obvious irony. The innkeeper and mayor, Konrad Steißhäuptl, and the other leading citizens of the town are all former Nazis, who have built the prosperity of the community with gold taken from the teeth of the victims at a nearby concentration camp during the war. This sordid past has been forgotten until suddenly, as in *Der Unschuldige,* a chance happening revives it unexpectedly. It is reported that "the raspberry picker," the former commandant of the concentration camp whose specialty was shooting prisoners he had taken into the canyon to pick raspberries, has been seen in town. The group around Steißhäuptl assumes that their former leader has returned to claim his share of the gold. Through their jubilant discussions of the past all of the figures reveal their true character, which is only shallowly concealed beneath the façade of respectability. They still remain as loyal as ever to Nazism, the only time they really felt alive: "What was one then, and what is one now? Rich but from the standpoint of ideals, a nothing."[25] To complete his perversion of values Steißhäuptl calls the raspberry picker a hero. There is a total absence of conscience here, and no feeling of guilt or remorse. The characters have not undergone any transformation or experienced any inner growth: "We all know that nothing has changed in our breasts, we can elect whomever we want, inwardly we have remained what we were. . . ."[26]

This satirical comedy culminates in the discovery that the alleged notorious war criminal is only a petty thief named Kerz who turns out to be a Jew to the disgust of the Nazi group. The play ends with the reading of a notice from a newspaper that the raspberry picker had been captured and has hanged himself in his cell. This announcement unmasks the hollowness of these characters, for despite all the talk of "Treue" (fidelity) Steißhäuptl is relieved at the news because now he does not have to share the gold.

After the severe satiric criticism of former Nazis in *Der Himbeer-pflücker* it is surprising to find the tone considerably muted and the attitude radically changed in *Der Befehl* (1966/1967, The Order), written as a television play and revised as a three-act drama for its première on 3 March 1968 in the Burgtheater in Vienna. This work also shows a radical shift in Hochwälder's attitude toward war criminals: whereas in earlier plays he had always insisted that they should be punished, here his attitude is one of tolerance and reconciliation, rationalizing their behavior simply as a manifestation of the times. Just as in *Der Unschuldige* he indicated that everyone could uncover a skeleton from the past, he now argues that anyone who was not forced into guilt by the fascist system should count himself lucky. This debatable thesis makes the play controversial, for Hochwälder's suddenly altered view of former Nazis as decent people who were forced into guilt by the circumstances of the time is not widely shared.

The play, one of Hochwälder's most serious works, utilizes a variation of the clever idea in *Der öffentliche Ankläger*. A happily married successful detective named Mittermayer in Vienna is assigned to find the SS officer who murdered a young girl in Holland in 1942, only to discover that he himself committed the crime. Excessive drinking leading to a nervous breakdown at the end of the war enabled him to repress the past until the reopening of this case now forces him to face it again. Whereas in *Donadieu* twenty years earlier Hochwälder had espoused punishment of war criminals and in *Der Himbeerpflücker* had shown that Nazis were still alive and unchanged in their attitude, he now describes this play as "the tragedy of the little functionary who must follow orders."[27]

As an illustration of how the Nazi network is still in operation Mittermayer's colleagues, who have retained their old Nazi efficiency and zealousness, offer to find a victim to use as a scapegoat, but he will not permit this erosion of responsibility. Neither will he accept the platitude that those were different times and they were different people than they are now. His colleague Dwornik, who was with him in Holland, recommends that he admit his past guilt by saying "I was the one, but I am not the one."[28] Mittermayer, however, disputes this view: "No, Dwornik, I was the one, and I am the one."[29] To the view, "It was the time," Mittermayer responds, "It was the people." He refuses to accept the facile whitewashing of the past by blaming everything on the events of the time. He is a decent man who does not understand how he could have done the things that he has on his conscience, but he refuses to try to evade his personal responsibility. Faced with the truth of his guilt in a way that he had never confronted it earlier, he expiates his crime by letting himself be killed by a criminal in a case in which he was not even supposed to be involved. He illustrates Hochwälder's view that the potential for bestiality exists in all men and can surface under the right provocation, but that a man of integrity will accept the responsibility for his actions.

The conscience of Dwornik, however, is more malleable. He is a survivor who has never experienced a crisis of conscience because he is able to blame everything on circumstances and assume none of the blame himself. He meets the murdered girl's father and rationalizes that, although he did not kill the daughter, he could have been the criminal if chance had so decreed: "The man who has the crime on his conscience looks no different than I do. . . . A beast then, unquestionably . . . and today in everyday civilian life an ordinary average man whom no one would suspect of anything evil. The only lesson to be learned is to make sure that such times never return."[30] Thus Hochwälder, continuing the idea of *Die Herberge* that order and stability in society are more important than justice, advocates overcoming the past in order to establish harmony in the present. In the contrast between Mittermayer, the *Mensch* who possesses a conscience and the capacity for suffering and inner growth, and Dwornik, the *Nicht-Mensch,* Hochwälder continues the theme of *Donnerstag* and *1003.*

In his next play *Lazaretti oder der Säbeltiger* (*Lazaretti or the Saber-Toothed Tiger*), written in 1968/1973 and performed on 29 July 1975 at the Salzburg Festival he continues the same themes which he regards as very important: that the low, the mean, the evil slumbers in all of us and can break out at any time,[31] and that the *Nicht-Menschen* are becoming increasingly prevalent. The play concerns Lazaretti, who has come to the conclusion that the world must take desperate steps to protect itself from the *Nicht-Menschen* who are threatening to take over society. After a lifetime of defending the values of justice, order, and humanitarianism Lazaretti under the attack of his enemies has come to the depressing conclusion in his final book that "The good do not stand to the right, the bad are not on the left, the lukewarm are not in the middle; man is simply a beast, a scoundrel, mean, low, deluded, unteachable, incorrigible and bloodthirsty as a giant leech."[32] To combat this trend he wants to establish an international secret society to intercede with whatever means may be necessary wherever the law and humanity are threatened.

Despite his plan to save man from himself Lazaretti wonders whether he might be wrong about the possibility of saving mankind and society as we know it. Possibly the problem is not one of guilt or innocence at all. What if *Homo sapiens* is nothing other than a genial error of creation, he muses, a grandiose miscarriage that must sooner or later be canceled into nothingness? As an example he cites the saber-toothed tiger, which was equipped with extra-long teeth for the purpose of ensuring its survival. Instead, the unwieldy tusks became the very liability that caused its extinction. He thinks that possibly man's brain is his version of the saber tooth, designed as a means of survival, but carried to an extreme, it brings the opposite result: "What if we can't speak about good and evil but only about a broken-down masterpiece of creation, destined for miserable extinction like the saber-toothed tiger? Then what's the purpose of my frantic mission . . . my merciless fight for the true, the noble, the good."[33]

Lazaretti is surrounded by his trusted colleague Camenisch, a ruthless professor who is suffering from writer's block and unable to meet his publisher's deadline, by Dr. Fließ, an unscrupulous psychiatrist, and by ex-Nazis, who are only too happy to have an occasion to reactivate their old skills. He feels that he is being pursued, which may be true or may be paranoia, and seeks sanctuary with his friend. Camenisch demonstrates the basic corruption of the *Nicht-Menschen* by advising Lazaretti to incarcerate himself for life in Dr. Fließ's clinic while leaving his manuscript with him. The play concludes with Camenisch calling his publisher to say that the manuscript is almost finished and that he will be able to make the deadline after all. This lightweight but so relevant play brims with action and with elements of the detective thriller along with its extremely serious message.

Hochwälder's final play, *Die Prinzessin von Chimay* (The Princess of Chimay), also in three acts, appeared in 1983 to poor reviews. This work, possibly Hochwälder's weakest published play, is a sequel of *Der öffentliche Ankläger* and represents Hochwälder's strongest plea for dropping the pursuit and prosecution of war criminals. The central character, the Princess of Chimay, formerly Terese Thalien, who outwitted the public prosecutor, is now over sixty years old a generation after the French Revolution; she has been a widow for five years and depends greatly on her private secretary George von Maergesse. She still suffers from the feeling that a revolutionary zealot is trying to kill her and hires Valprès, the famous hunter of war criminals (the allusion to Simon Wiesenthal is obviously intentional), to find him so that she can dispel her fear. Without much effort Valprès discovers that the potential assassin is Maergesse, who insists that he is now a completely changed person. The Princess dismisses him but misses his companionship so much that when he returns for his things she takes him back. The first version of the play ends with their playing cards and giggling uncontrollably. In the latest version the laughter has been omitted.

The central conflict is stated explicitly when Valprès insists: "We have to show the world that the demand for justice never relents."[34] But opposed to that point of view comes the clear message of the play: "What good does revenge do us after a generation?"[35] Hochwälder insists once more that order and tranquility are more important to society than justice, particularly when the criminals are people of advanced age whose crimes lie more than a generation in the past. He no longer believes the view of Valprès he once shared, the Dürrenmattian view that injustice must be fought wherever it occurs and that there is no statute of limitation on justice. This weak comedy was not well received and did his reputation more harm than good.

In recent years Hochwälder added two new experimental plays to his oeuvre: the fairy-tale play *Der verschwundene Mond* (1982, The Moon that Disappeared), a revised version of an earlier work "Der gestohlene Mond" (1951, The Stolen Moon). According to Hochwälder, the rediscovery in the meantime of the vagrant poet Jakob Haringer (1898–1948) enabled him to recast and complete this work to his satisfaction. It is a short two-act play, incorporating Haringer's poems and seemingly written to express the idea of the importance of the moon—and of literature: "Without the moon, no poetry—and without poetry no love, no life, . . ."[36] And reminiscent of Georg Kaiser's drama *Von morgens bis mitternachts* (1915, *From Morn to Midnight*) the protagonist Gustav, who has sold the moon for a million dollars, adds on the basis of his experience: "What good is money? Money is the most pitiful thing. One can't buy anything of any real value with it."[37]

Die Bürgschaft (1977–1984, Word of Honor), a three-act contemporary satire set in classical antiquity but intended to be performed in timeless dress, shows how the old fable of keeping one's word of honor would work out in contemporary society. The original idea used both by Gaius Julius Hyginus (60 B.C.–10 A.D.) and Friedrich Schiller

(1759–1819), both of whose versions are included for comparison, has been radically changed. In the earlier form a man convicted of trying to execute a tyrant is allowed three days before his execution to arrange his sister's wedding. A friend serves as hostage while he is gone. When the man returns on time, the tyrant is so moved that he releases them both with the request that they include him in their friendship. Hochwälder's protagonist requests three days to foment a revolution. In the interim his substitute, the philosopher Agathon, advises the tyrant Dionys to escape with his treasure before he is executed. As a result Agathon's life is forfeited along with that of Heloris, whose revolutionary bid has failed. Hochwälder's version has only minimal similarity with the idea and intent of the original. His plan was apparently to show again how low man had sunk so that there is no longer any room for idealism, but neither the play nor the idea is convincing.

In addition to his dramas Hochwälder published a volume of autobiographical sketches and essays entitled *Im Wechsel der Zeit* (1980, In the Change of Time), in which he provides a brief sketch of his youth in Vienna and his early exile in Switzerland as well as a few theoretical essays conveying his views about literature and particularly about the nature of drama, his own as well as that of his contemporaries. In "Über mein Theater" he discusses his own type of Aristotelian theater and provides illuminating comments on the intent of each of his plays. He first wrote this essay in 1956 and revised it in 1966 to soften it after he was criticized for some of his outspoken views about his colleagues. His main point, as mentioned earlier, is that he writes plays for the theater and has no pretensions of writing literature. Dramatists, in his view, have a primary obligation to produce effective plays for the stage that audiences can enjoy as entertainment. If they are solidly crafted and endure as literature, that is another matter. Clearly he hoped that at least some of his plays would fall into that category.

In the essay "Vom Versagen des Dramas in unserer Zeit" (1961, On the Failure of Drama in Our Time) Hochwälder defends his kind of traditional drama against the innovations of his contemporaries, arguing that the theater is being ruined by a loss of language, conscience, and naiveté. He blames the philosophers for the loss of language, the recent wars for the loss of conscience, and the direction pursued by writers for the loss of naiveté. In his view, when the theater loses its sense for the naive which has been intrinsic to the stage from its origins, it becomes a showcase for intellectual charlatans.

In the final essay entitled "Kann die Freiheit überleben?" (1976, Can Freedom Survive?) Hochwälder addresses the question of whether freedom can survive equality. The essay is an outgrowth of his study of the French Revolution. After citing a number of examples throughout history showing that freedom and equality are polar opposites Hochwälder describes a play that he intended to write to illustrate the idea that freedom is a higher value than equality. Whether it will be completed remains to be seen, but to date there has been no further mention of it. He believed that freedom can survive, although he added that we not only should believe this, we must also hope for it, for without this hope we are already in our graves.[38]

Like his plays the essays reveal Hochwälder as an individual who refused to follow trends or fashions of any kind. Perhaps this defense of tradition as much as his allegiance to the techniques of the Viennese folk theater characterize him as an arch-Austrian. He has stood fast as a bulwark of conservative thinking and traditional dramatic production while his contemporaries have explored a variety of new techniques and forms. It is noteworthy that the representatives of avant-garde thinking in the 1960s and 1970s, for example Bernhard and Handke, are now also returning to more traditional ways of thinking and linking their works to the heritage that they had neglected. Hochwälder, acerbic, outspoken, and never in doubt about the correctness of his chosen course, would have seen this phenomenon only as a confirmation that he had been right all along. He has enriched the theater with more than a dozen rewarding and successful theatrical plays. The only remaining question is how many of them beyond *Das heilige Experiment* will survive as literary works, a matter that only time will decide.

Notes

1. Fritz Hochwälder, *Im Wechsel der Zeit* (Graz: Verlag Styria, 1980), p. 19. Unless otherwise indicated all works cited are by Hochwälder.
2. "Als Bühnenschriftsteller im Exil," in ibid., p. 27.
3. For more information on these and other unpublished plays see Wilhelm Bortenschlager, *Der Dramatiker Fritz Hochwälder* (Innsbruck: Universitätsverlag Wagner, 1979).
4. "Als Bühnenschriftsteller im Exil," pp. 27–28.
5. Cf. Andrew G. Whiteside, *The Socialism of Fools* (Berkeley: University of California Press, 1975).

264   Donald G. Daviau

6.   Johannes Hawlik, *Der Bürgerkaiser. Karl Lueger und seine Zeit* (Wien/München: Herold, 1985).
7.   "Über mein Theater," *Im Wechsel der Zeit,* p. 89.
8.   Ibid., p. 61.
9.   Fritz Hochwälder, "Über mein Theater," *German Life and Letters* 12, no. 2 (January 1959), 110.
10.   *Das heilige Experiment,* in *Dramen I* (Graz: Verlag Styria, 1975), p. 116.
11.   Wilhelm Bortenschlager, *Der Dramatiker Fritz Hochwälder,* p. 73.
12.   *Der öffentliche Ankläger,* in *Dramen I,* p. 266.
13.   Ibid., p. 267.
14.   Ibid., p. 303.
15.   "Über mein Theater," in *Im Wechsel der Zeit,* p. 94.
16.   There are a number of other parallels in the play to works of Dürrenmatt. The motif of the psychotic child murderer Andusz is analogous to *Das Versprechen* (The Pledge), Smalejus's belief in justice through chance is one of Dürenmatt's favorite ideas used in *Das Versprechen* and many other works, and the passing on of guilt by the conversion of one character, Berullis, to honesty, while another, Karolius, takes over his corruption is similar to *Der Besuch der alten Dame,* as is the theme that one sells one's soul to materialism at the cost of one's humanity.
17.   *Die Herberge,* in *Dramen III,* p. 137.
18.   Ibid., p. 86.
19.   *Der Unschuldige,* in *Dramen II,* p. 209.
20.   Wilhelm Bortenschlager, *Der Dramatiker Fritz Hochwälder,* p. 120.
21.   Cf. "Marginalien zu Hugo von Hofmannsthal," in *Im Wechsel der Zeit,* pp. 51-53.
22.   *Donnerstag,* in *Dramen III,* pp. 197-198.
23.   *1003,* in *Dramen III,* p. 245.
24.   "Über mein Theater," in *Im Wechsel der Zeit,* p. 100.
25.   *Der Himbeerpflücker,* in *Dramen II,* p. 234.
26.   Ibid., p. 257.
27.   "Über mein Theater," in *Im Wechsel der Zeit,* p. 101.
28.   *Der Befehl,* in *Dramen II,* p. 331.
29.   Ibid.
30.   Ibid., p. 334.
31.   *Lazaretti* was performed in English at Rockwell College, Illinois in 1986 in the translation of James Schmitt.

32. *Lazaretti oder der Säbeltiger,* in *Dramen III,* p. 261.
33. Ibid., p. 292.
34. *Die Prinzessin von Chimay,* in *Dramen IV,* p. 23.
35. Ibid., p. 19.
36. *Der verschwundene Mond,* in *Dramen IV,* p. 74.
37. Ibid.
38. "Kann die Freiheit überleben?" in *Im Wechsel der Zeit,* p. 131.

Bibliography

I. Works by Fritz Hochwälder in German

Collected Works

Dramen I. Graz: Verlag Styria, 1975.
Dramen II. Graz: Verlag Styria, 1975.
Dramen III. Graz: Verlag Styria, 1979.
Dramen IV. Graz: Verlag Styria, 1985.
Im Wechsel der Zeit. Autobiographische Skizzen und Essays. Graz/
     Wien/Köln: Verlag Styria, 1980.

Works by Date of Completion

Jehr, 1932.
Liebe in Florenz, 1935.
Esther, 1940.
Das heilige Experiment, 1941/1942.
Der Flüchtling, 1944.
Hôtel du Commerce, 1944.
Die verschleierte Frau, 1946.
Meier Helmbrecht, 1946.
Der öffentliche Ankläger, 1947/1948.
Virginia, 1951.
Donadieu, 1953.
Die Herberge, 1954/1955.
Der Unschuldige, 1948.
Donnerstag, 1958/1959.

266   Donald G. Daviau

Works by Fritz Hochwälder in German (*continued*)

Schicksalskomödie, 1960.
Der Himbeerpflücker, 1964.
Der Befehl, 1965.
Lazaretti oder der Säbeltiger, 1974.
Die Prinzessin von Chimay, 1981.
Der verschwundene Mond, 1982.
Die Bürgschaft, 1984.

II. Works in English

The Public Prosecutor and Other Plays. New York: Frederick Ungar,
    1980. Contains: *The Public Prosecutor, The Strong Are Lonely,
    The Raspberry Picker,* and *Lazaretti or the Saber-Toothed Tiger.*
The Strong Are Lonely. London: Heinemann, 1962.

III. Secondary Works in English

Best, Alan D. and Hans Wolfschtz, ed. "Shadows of the past: the
    drama of Fritz Hochwälder." *Modern Austrian Writing: Litera-
    ture and Society after 1945.* Festschrift, pp. 41-62. London:
    Wolf; Totwa, New Jersey: Barnes and Noble, 1980.
Chandler, Elwood Venton, Jr. "Fritz Hochwälder as Heir to the Vien-
    nese *Hanswurst* Tradition with a Hochwälder Bibliography."
    Dissertation, Abstracts International, 39:6787A.
Coenen, F. E. "Modern German Drama." *Studies in German Literature.*
    Carl Hammer, ed. Baton Rouge: Louisiana State University,
    1963, pp. 107-129.
Daviau, Donald G. "Fritz Hochwälder's Range of Theme and Form."
    Modern Austrian Literature, 18/2 (1985), 31-45.
Haley, Thomas D. "A Translation and Analysis of 'Der Unschuldige' by
    Fritz Hochwälder." Unpublished Master's dissertation, University
    of Denver, 1969.
Hayes, Richard. "The Strong Are Lonely." *Commonweal,* 10 October
    1953, p. 60.
Holdman, M. Paula. *The Concept of Order in the Drama of Fritz Hoch-
    wälder.* Dissertation, City University of New York, 1976.

Secondary Works in English (*continued*)

Loram, Ian. "Fritz Hochwälder." *Monatshefte* 57 (1965), 8-16.

Schmitt, James. *The Theme of Responsibility and Its Presentation in the Dramas of Fritz Hochwälder from 1943-1965*. Dissertation, University of Iowa, 1973.

———. "The Theater of Fritz Hochwälder: Its Background and Development." *Modern Austrian Literature* 11/1 (1979), 49-61.

———. "Fritz Hochwälder Bibliography." *Modern Austrian Literature* 11/1 (1979), 63-73.

Theobald, Erika. "An Austrian Playwright Confronts the Past." *American-German Review* 33 (1966), 9-10.

Wellwarth, George. "Fritz Hochwälder: The Drama within the Self." *Quarterly Journal of Speech* 49 (1963), 274-281.

———. *The Theater of Protest and Paradox*. New York: New York University Press, 1971, pp. 207-221.

IV. Major Studies in German

Bortenschlager, Wilhelm von. *Der Dramatiker Fritz Hochwälder*. Innsbruck: Universitätsverlag Wagner, 1979.

———. Österreichische Dramatiker der Gegenwart." *Kreativlexikon*. Wien: Osterreichische Verlaganstalt, 1976, pp. 252-260.

———. "Theaterspiegel." Band 4: *Autoren aus Österreich und der Schweiz*. München, Wels: Welsermühl, 1972, pp. 261-271.

Gerlach, U. Henry. "Unterdrücktes Gewissen als Zentralmotiv in Fritz Hochwälders 'Heiligem Experiment.'" *Österreich in Geschichte und Literatur* 24 (1980), 360-366.

Langer, Norbert. *Dichter aus Österreich*. Vienna: Österreicher Bundesverlag, 1958, pp. 28-33.

Meister, Richard. "Religiöse Problematik in den Dramen Hochwälders." *Maske und Kothurn* 2 (1956), 60-65.

Thieberger, Richard. "Macht und Recht in den Dramen Fritz Hochwälders." *Deutsche Rundschau* 83 (1957), 1147-1152.

Vogelsang, Hans. "Fritz Hochwälders klassizistisches Ideendrama." *Österreich in Geschichte und Literatur* 2 (1958), 224-232.

———. *Österreichische Dramatik des 20. Jahrhunderts*. Vienna: Braumüller, 1963.

Christine Lavant

Bernhardt Blumenthal

Christine Lavant (pen name of Christine Habernig, née Thonhauser), born in Großedling/Carinthia in 1915, has written verses and stories that invoke the spirit of her Austrian homeland, in particular the landscape of Carinthia, recount the hard life of the poor and infirm in mountain villages, and recall in style and substance the writings of her countrymen Adalbert Stifter and Theodor Kramer. In her work she pursues Stifter's goal announced in *Der Nachsommer* (*Indian Summer*) to become a describer of things, especially those things that inhabit her nocturnal landscape: wind, moon, and stars. With Stifter she stands before open windows and climbs mountaintops to survey better the world about her. Unlike her great predecessor, however, this almost blind and deaf poet is unable in her writings to focus on an ordered universe radiant with sunshine and flowers; she is confronted rather by a capricious and often disorderly night world from which she retreats:

> The passage of the earth is unfathomable
> Again and again perhaps only the heart of an angel
> crosses it, who himself is still looking
> and never finds the right path
> to make the moment bearable.[1]

She shares Theodor Kramer's concern for the disenfranchised in life: the physically and mentally handicapped, old people, children born with birth defects, mendicants, alcoholics, and the working poor. The language, style, and imagery of her verse recall Kramer's direct poetic statements and his imagery drawn from the fields and meadows of the Austrian countryside and the home life of the Austrian peasant.

In contrast to most twentieth-century writers Christine Lavant completely ignores modern technology, city life, and such major events of her time as wars, political change, and space exploration. Unlike much of modern literature her works do not provide commentary upon the artistic or literary productions of others, nor do they contribute to contemporary efforts to refine a language that could give expression to the mass culture of our times. In fact, these things are quite inimical to her writings, Of the possibility of composing poetry in an urban setting she states simply: "I will certainly not write poetry in Berlin."[2] Her work is entirely a portrait of her soul. It records impressions of interior turmoil, in particular her incessant efforts alternately to invoke and to reject the God of Christian tradition. The search for religious truth was always a difficult chapter in her life: "Creatures like me are very far from the heart of God."[3] Christine Lavant's poems and her largely autobiographical stories are a dialogue between herself and the external environment, a mythical construct of healing and destructive forces. Her work reflects the almost total isolation in which she lived and records the sleeplessness that always plagued her and made her a night person. Her stories and verse are laced with references to her faithful companions: moon and stars, spirits of the wood, herbs, roots, crickets, spiders, the night, the water, and the wind. They are filled with elements of Carinthian village life: domestic, farm, and wild animals, flowers, fields, children and, curiously, windows great and small from which she interacts with a frequently hostile environment: "My sleep has gone into the water. / Its coat and its shoes / were thrown through the window to me by the night, / tied to a stone (*DB*, 89).

Christine Lavant is gradually being recognized as a lyric talent of considerable significance. Wieland Schmied states the case very simply: "Christine Lavant's word holds up: it is genuine."[4] Helmut Scharf in reviewing her lyric poetry speaks of "the honesty of expression,"[5] and Heinz Politzer sets her work against a background of the tradition of modern German literature: "Her verse collections mark the point where the restoration of modern German literature meets with the genuine tradition of its creative genius."[6] Harald Weinrich appraises Lavant's lyric talent most highly: "Some, indeed many of Christine Lavant's poems are among the most beautiful texts in the German language."[7] Her work has also attracted numerous literary prizes: the Georg Trakl prize in 1954 together with Christine Busta and again in 1964, the Austrian prize for the promotion of lyric poetry (1956 and 1961), the second prize for lyric poetry from the *Neue Deutsche Hefte* (1956), the

Anton Wildgans prize (1964), and the Austrian national prize for literature (1970). From 1966 to her death in 1973 Carinthia provided her with substantial financial support in recognition of her extraordinary contribution to the cultural life of the region, but these accolades have not inspired a great deal of scholarly interest in her. On this point Johann Strutz observes in a monograph on Christine Lavant's lyric poetry in 1979 that hers is "the work of a lyric poetess with whom literary criticism has had only marginal contact,"[8] and Wolfgang Nehring in a recent issue of *Modern Austrian Literature* notes that "very little scholarly research has been done to date on Christine Lavant's lyric poetry."[9] To Nehring's statement can only be added that nothing whatsoever has been done critically about her numerous prose works.

The early secondary literature on Christine Lavant consists largely of nonanalytical reminiscences of literary acquaintances. The groundwork for a critical evaluation of Christine Lavant was laid by Grete Lübbe-Grothues in her careful study of imagery in Lavant's verse "Zur Gedichtsprache der Christine Lavant"[10] (1968, The Poetic Language of Christine Lavant) and by Strutz in his recent monograph. Encouraging short studies on specific themes are also beginning to appear, notably August Stahl's "Das Bild des geschundenen Menschen in der Lyrik der Christine Lavant"[11] (1981, The Image of the Abused Human Being in Christine Lavant's Lyric Poetry). Stahl provides the reader with a catalog of spiritual and physical ills short of death and dying evident in Lavant's lyric poetry.

Much of Christine Lavant's writing centers around her dead mother and generally seeks a return to some protected warm shelter: "because all who live here are afraid" (*KWM*, 214). Her stories especially are attempts to communicate the felt presence in her life of a magical realm of childhood, a safe zone before and beyond fear. Christine Lavant's poetic homeland is the world of the child, the realm of naive relationships with nature and God. "I was a star and am a child" (*DB*, 166), she explains as she traces in her heart and in her verse the imprint of a child. The poet knows that only in the perceptions of a child would she be able to find lost innocence and the security of the womb which she everywhere and so ardently seeks. Therefore, she desires once again those magical games of childhood. "Straw, stones, leaf, and wind" (*DB*, 21) fill this world that is accessible only to the open heart which loves without compromise and without qualification. Only children dwell here: adults remain intruders.

Children have long discovered what adults have long forgotten, namely, the omnipresence of God in things. In a child's hand all things come to life. Every child knows what the fabled velveteen rabbit learns when he questions another toy about the nature of reality: "Real isn't how you are made. . . . It's a thing that happens to you. When a child loves you for a long, long time, not just to play with, but REALLY loves you, then you become Real."[12] The things that inhabit a child's world become real upon contact. Through the tactile sense children gain knowledge of the inner nature of things. Christine Lavant seeks a return to the world of the child to regain authenticity and to hold once again pulsating life in her hands.

None of this should be surprising. The poet earned her living by knitting. It was her practice while knitting to read; thought and feeling were activated by tactile perceptions. She reports that the knitting and reading produced a constant stream of undifferentiated images in her mind. She also painted in watercolors, drew with a felt pen, did chalk sketches, and made prints by cutting designs on mounted linoleum. She had a fine sense of size, shape, and distance in her hand. Because of her partial blindness and deafness from earliest childhood she became dependent upon her sense of touch to audit the world: "He who talks to me tenderly from above, / runs around with my eyesight, / He who entreats me from down below, / stole my ear which no longer hears" (*DB*, 13). Touch became the poet's most immediate and most intimate contact with realities. In fact, her stories about children and the rich imagery of her verse evidence a highly developed kinaesthetic consciousness.

Christine Lavant's poems and visionary stories recreate the perceptions of children. Much like stories told by children, they are often passionate dreamlike vignettes that intertwine real and imagined events. In fact, they are kneaded and molded as if pressed from hand to hand with the motions of the child who learns by grasping and reaching, who perceives by weighing, feeling, and measuring objects in his hand. The objects filtering through her touch — most frequently bread, onions, leeks, fountains, stones, and candles — become a part of her safe world. They take on magical properties, share her dreams of childhood, and exist before and beyond death.

A major characteristic of Christine Lavant's perspective is the continual interchange between external and internal realities, between the world as experienced and the world as imagined. Her poetic landscape, anchored in the perceptions of a child, obliterates accustomed distinctions between the things of the world themselves and thoughts about these things. Johann Strutz recognizes in Christine Lavant's world view a childlike, naive relationship of the self to nature: "The attitude of the I corresponds to that of fairy-tale figures who also do not distinguish categorically among human beings and animals, plants or natural phenomena."[13] All external reality is interpreted and understood only in terms of the poet's inner life, where there is a continual interchange between the powers of light and darkness.

In the hearts of children death finds fertile soil, and this is the grist that Christine Lavant mills: "In my heart are child and death / the two most sublime signs / over which the grass never grows" (*DB*, 158). Christine Lavant's writings make frequent reference to the dead, especially deceased family members. Several poems as well as the story *Die Verschüttete* (1978, Buried Alive) recall the circumstances of her mother's death and lament her passing and the separation from her. The terminally ill, both children and adults, are also frequent subjects of her attention. Cancer is a special matter of concern in her writings. *Nell* (1969), for example, is the story of a woman dying of breast cancer. The blind and the deaf are also referred to very frequently in her writings. This death of the senses is treated most sympathetically by her—undoubtedly a reflection of her own situation. Suicides are dealt with most indulgently by Christine Lavant: "To do such a thing one must have some greatness within oneself and mettle."[14] Most frequently children terminate their own lives in her stories. Death by drowning is the method of choice, although Maria Katharina of the story of the same name (1969) throws herself in front of an auto, and others speculate on the possibility of leaping from church towers.

Death cuts a wide swath here. Christine Lavant's writing is filled with the accouterments of death. There are burials, cemeteries, cemetery lanterns, graves, gravestones, crypts and coffins. There are runes etched in marble slabs and many dark cold places. Mining terminology suggestive of burials abounds in her writings—no doubt a reflection of her father's occupation. There are pits and shafts and a continual process of shoveling, digging, and burying. There are even murderers, bodies, and blood. Christine Lavant is most productive in developing the vocabulary of death. Individuals and things are frequently "gestorben" (dead), "abgestorben" (perished), "ausgestorben" (extinct), "erstorben" (expired) or "verstorben" (deceased), if not "aufgefressen" (devoured), "durchfroren" (frozen through), "enthauptet" (decapitated), "erschlagen" (slain) or "zerfleischt" (torn to pieces). There is no limit as to what can happen to someone or something once the poet has armed herself with a "ver-" compound. The unfortunates are variously "verbrannt" (cremated), "vergraben" (buried), "verkalkt" (calcinated), "verlöscht" (extinguished), "vernagelt" (nailed up), "vernesselt" (nettled), "verraucht" (vaporized), "verschüttet" (buried alive), "vertilgt" (annihilated) and "verzehrt" (consumed). Needless to say, after this their lives are "verdorben" (ruined), "verkommen" (wrecked), "verpfuscht" (botched) and "verweht" (blown away). It is no wonder then that the individuals described in her verse and stories are most frequently "blaß" (pale) and "bleich" (wan). She is most creative in combining death with objects from life, thus "Totenäpfel"[15] (apples of the dead), "Todesrose" (*SIM*, 114, rose of death), "Honig-Tod" (*SIM*, 156, honey death) and "Totenwein" (*DB*, 95, wine of the dead). The ability to toy creatively with word compounds is an obvious stylistic feature of her work not restricted to the realm of death, thus "Sternenbruderschaft" (*SIM*, 16, brotherhood of the stars), "Sonnenspindel" (*SIM*, 17, sun spindle), "Nachtnelken"[16] (night carnations) and "wurzelabwärts" (*DP*, 72, root-downwards). In fact, the numerous and unusual moon compounds, e.g., "Mondkork" (*SIM*, 146, moon cork), "Mondkuh" (*SIM*, 27, moon cow), "Mondzehe" (*DP*, 87, moon toe), and "mondelang" (*DP*, 54, moon-long) have been frequently observed in Lavant criticism. These cute compounds and appellations such as "Zähmer aller wilden Wölfe" (*DB*, 104, tamer of all wild wolves) and "Herr der Zauberei" (*DB*, 104, master of magic) represent her childlike toying with nocturnal demonic forces in an effort to render elemental powers harmless.

Transcendental notions about death, so much a part of Lavant's early work, give way in her mature writings to a sense of the immanent presence of death in life. Her views on death shift as her ideas change on the nature of God and the ultimate sense of life. Early Catholic views of God as a providential father who seeks to enhance man's salvation wane before the image of a God who has absconded from this world, abandoning man to the arbitrariness of his own fate: "To whom as an elixir have we been offered? / Wild herbs, none entirely safe, / so much poison only a penitent consumes, / Our father, I am completely scandalized" (*SIM*, 146). As her own misfortunes increase, her later verse intensifies her railing at the absent God and reassesses her conceptions of life and death.

The events of a childhood destroyed by illness (scrofula, ear infections, severe loss of sight and hearing, lung tuberculosis, insomnia) and poverty, memories of deceased parents, of ailing brothers and sisters, and deep depression inform Christine Lavant's writings. Not surprisingly, the image of the child occurs frequently in a negative context: "through the entire evil new year / and through its child" (*DB,* 45), "a child, / a little cripple" (*DB,* 48), "perhaps a child, perhaps a dumb fool" (*DB,* 92), "child and fool" (*DB,* 92). It is a melancholy observation that with increasing years and distance from her dream of motherhood the image of the child in the poet's work tarnishes.[17] This occurs at the same time that references to an unfruitful womb, still-birth, and feelings of general bitterness increase.

With age Christine Lavant suffered from increased loneliness; her letters and reminiscences continuously lament her growing isolation. The more renowned she became, in fact, the less able she was to deal with the public. Official ceremonies designed to honor her and her work were particularly odious to her. Because of her inability to see and hear well and because of her physical appearance – Christine Lavant's several disorders and diseases had aged her well beyond her years – she retreated more and more into herself: "The only thing that can perhaps save me for a little while from a total breakdown is a life completely withdrawn, the withholding of all imaginative powers, the renunciation of all hope for help from the outside, and the simple return to childhood" (*B,* 152).

Christine Lavant's search for a child and the unfulfilled expectations which result from this permeate her work. She laments: "Have no little child, no animals, / and the stem on which I freeze, / does not bear fruit" (*DB,* 11). When considerations arise as to what under different circumstances might have occurred in her life, the poet denounces the stars which have failed to light up her sky, and tells melancholy tales about the pillaged and the shorn.

The poet sees the distant planets, particularly the moon and the stars, through a child's eyes as companions in life's journey that determine fate. The moon occupies a special position in Lavant lore. It is the gathering place for departed souls, a notion the poet may have picked up from her readings of P. D. Ouspensky's *Auf der Suche nach dem Wunderbaren* (1949, *In Search of the Miraculous*). Upon death souls are set free from the body and gravitate to the moon. The moon grows and warms by feeding on this released energy. "And a soul, which was perhaps mine, / goes estranged to the moon, / poor as an orphan" (*KWM,* 182). When a soul passes from one plane to another, the energy released at death is conserved. The souls inhabiting the moon still possess a certain amount of consciousness and memory. These are tormented souls alienated from all that still matters to them on earth. At this point Christine Lavant's penchant for eastern occultism and her attachment to the legends of her Carinthian homeland merge. The dead in her writings are restless; they are dependent upon the living to perform some specific task to free them. They are night creatures who return to the earth as lights on a field or the gleam in someone's eye to find salvation or to vent their anger. The poet offers the soul of an unborn child to these moon spirits: "Determined I offer what was most dear to me / to the moon" (*DB*, 23).

Frequently the dead along with sundry spirits pursue the living at night by entering their homes in the light of the moon through window or door. Most often the image of the dead mother appears to the poet at her window, although not infrequently death itself comes calling: "Once again he broke in at the neighbor's / and I had my door and windows wide open" (*DB*, 161). Internal doors, especially glass doors, serve the same function for children in Christine Lavant's writings as windows and external doors do for adults. Great mysteries and emissaries from other worlds lurk behind the pane. A child's glance through a doorway is a passage to an alien world.

The night that drives away the light particularly endangers children. The evil spirits that customarily frighten children perform their mischief at night, menacing those who have lost their way or become confused. The poet seeks to protect them from the spirits of the night by toying creatively with nocturnal demonic forces, but in this nightmare of death and children there is no safe harbor. It may be that the unfortunate children much like their poet-creator must learn to love the dark before they may experience the light. Certainly Lavant's world provides them with ample opportunity to learn to love the dark.

Although Lavant is generally recognized as a lyric talent and quite neglected as a writer of short stories, the latter works comprise the great volume of her oeuvre. They are dark tales, visionary vignettes about deeply troubled lives. The largely autobiographical stories revolve around events in Austrian village life and principally relate occurrences in the lives of impoverished and abused children.

The children of these stories exist in a very sterile atmosphere that induces internal decay. They mature beyond their years while their souls atrophy. They rapidly become callous in their treatment of each other, unreceptive to love, indifferent to life, and enchanted with death and with suicide. The vacillating image of the child in Christine

Lavant's writings—on the one hand naive, innocent; on the other cunning, uncaring—should not surprise the reader. The poet's emotional scale, which knows only extremes, tolerates very divergent images of the child. Nehring underscores this polarity of feeling: "The basic attitude of Christine Lavant's thinking and writing is evident in the contrast between city and orchis, between up and down, between the world of the sacred and the ciphers of nature."[18]

Das Kind (1948, The Child), Christine Lavant's earliest published story, relates events in a children's hospital. While being cared for by pale nurses and a glassy-eyed doctor, a child contemplates death and the spiritual implications of suicide. In *Das Krüglein* (1949, The Little Jug) a child avenges the death of his dog at the hands of his cousins by having the dog served up to his unsuspecting relatives as the main course at a family dinner. The disenchanted children console themselves by chanting a song about a mother who nails down the coffin on her only living child to enhance her own chances at remarriage. In *Der Messer-Mooth* (1961, Mooth, the Knife) a mother imparts the wisdom to her violent son that everything dies when its time comes. In fits of depression the boy, skilled in using and throwing knives, seeks to work out his own timetable for death; he kills a tree, drinks up his mother's savings, and threatens everyone with whom he comes into contact. Later on he pins his young wife to a tree with knives, leaving her to die there so that he may run off with a whore. As he throws the sharpest knives he sings a song to the effect that a woman's suffering gives a man pleasure.

Not all of Christine Lavant's sad stories concern children or adolescents. The title story of her late collection *Nell* relates the frustrations of a woman who struggles in vain against the church hierarchy and bureaucracy in an effort to provide her impoverished family with a modicum of peace and dignity. The bitterness of a life of hardship petrifies the spirit of the old as well as the young. *Maria Katharina* in the same collection retraces familiar ground. A poor orphan mistreated by nuns who cater to the well-to-do is abandoned to the wiles of uncaring and unfeeling relatives, is sexually abused by them, and eventually commits suicide by throwing herself in front of a car.

All of this notwithstanding, the poet strives to reconstruct the world of her lost childhood, a protected place where the deceased mother, the unborn child, and the runaway lover of her verse and stories dwell. Christine Lavant became increasingly attracted to untarnished objects from her childoood (her table, her stove) and to children generally, although she had none of her own. The children of her stories suffer loneliness without fear and without need for adult escape mechanisms: "We all live in fear. The active ones cover it up with good or bad performances; the others bear it with drugs or simply out of inertia. Children, still pure, are brave whatever the danger. And above all: they bear up under loneliness" (*B*, 154/155). Christine Lavant lived out her entire life in the familiar surroundings of her childhood. A trip to Istanbul in 1957, her only extended journey, merely intensified her loneliness, and an attempt to settle in the provincial capital, Klagenfurt, failed (1966-1968). She returned homesick to her village and the Lavant Valley, from which incidentally she took her pen name.

Christine Lavant's childlike perception of the world makes it possible even for this poet to find joy in life—something that she terms "a very crystalline, hard joy / from the innermost strength of the earth."[19] Because of the preponderance of the imagery of suffering and death in Christine Lavant's writings, her sense of joy is obscured and generally overlooked in the literature.[20] The warmth of the sun, the growth of plants, the rain and the wind, however, are strong and positive impulses in the life of the poet. Nell, a woman dying of cancer who struggles in vain against the church hierarchy and bureaucracy, sees it this way:

> It suddenly seemed to her that it were good fortune enough for every life to be able to see, smell, and hear and at some point to do something that would so quickly change the heart in one's body, as if one had come free from oneself with a single bound and partaken of a greater and more important fate (*N*, 193).

Lavant's verse expresses pleasure in the simple things of the earth, in tracing the warmth of the sun on rough wood, in sensing the power of the nettles as they grow, in feeling the rain on her cheeks and the wind as it passes through the leaves. A return to the earth for Christine Lavant means a return to the herbs, beets, and roots of her Carinthian homeland: "I will walk in the woods / and dig out roots" (*SIM*, 149). Onions, turnips, and garlic are the recurrent symbols *par excellence* in her verse for this rootedness in her native soil. She likes to depict herself as a humble gardener who prepares bowls from these gifts of the earth for the poor and the disenfranchised. Life itself, the poet concludes, is the greatest glory: "Life is so holy" (*KWM*, 234), and the difficult death, the death without transcendence, is something that must be learned. "I must learn here how to die" (*SIM*, 53), she announces as she seeks to nurture a consciousness of death that matures within the individual human being. Each one must work out his own destiny. "Everyone has a different likeness of God within himself" (*N*, 9), she observes: no one lives another's life; no one dies another's death. There is no collective immortality; each individual has to work on the death growing within himself—place himself, as it were, in the service of this death.

Christine Lavant seeks to bring the knowledge of death into life. Death is immanent in the eternal values that comprise life: "Oh, we will consume them with delight, / Death and apple and the black pits" (*DB*, 47). The succulent earth with its fruits and flowers represents fulfilled being, the sought-after saturated plentitude of reality: "From today on, but forever, / I know: the earth is truly warm" (*DP*, 95). In all of this chthonic delight the poet knows that with life death too matures. Death in this context is the ultimate expression of existence: it is real, not just appearance, not just a rite of passage into another more glorious existence.

There is little joy to be found in Lavant's verse and stories. There is almost no mention of happiness or joy. The vocabulary of suffering, misery, terror, loneliness, and despair predominates. Christine Lavant married (1939) an impoverished, divorced, and ailing painter—thirty-six years her senior—to increase her own misery, suffered lifelong from depression, committed herself briefly in 1963 to a sanatorium for treatment of this illness, and aggravated her already poor health with smoking and drugs. In this context even her carefully couched underscorings of her own happiness in letters to Gerhard Dessen are surprising: "There are times when I am happy for no reason at all" (*B*, 135), "I am not particularly unhappy . . . ," "I feel as happy as a pig in slop" (*B*, 140), "There is so much sweet, gentle bliss in me" (*B*, 141), "immutable happiness . . . ," "warmly happy . . . ," and "delighted" (*B*, 142). It is conceivable Lavant found a measure of satisfaction in her sad fate. The toil and struggle of life itself, particularly under difficult circumstances, is enough to fill the heart. We should imagine her happy.

In the simple tones of a child's prayer she acknowledges beneficent gifts:

> Everything is very beautiful, indeed, dear Father, indeed . . .
> The earth makes me only a little sad, because I am not an
> animal that can feel this differently: the pollen, the rain, a
> reed stalk and the sound of the wind in the leaves—and then
> above all and everything: Your Sun (*DB*, 149).

The poetic heart is moved by the very simple things of the earth. Even
the ever-present sense of death in her writings is suggestive of a return
to gentler, simpler, humbler beginnings. There is an aura of a gentle
falling in her verse, particularly in the early collection *Die unvollendete
Liebe* (1949, The Incomplete Love), reminiscent of her great poet-
mentor Rilke: "And that in the last analysis / I am absolutely nothing
but a weight which falls."[21] Although she sheds much of Rilke's
influence in subsequent collections of verse, notably *Die Bettlerschale*
(1956, The Beggar's Cup), *Spindel im Mond* (1959, Spindle in the
Moon), and *Der Pfauenschrei* (1962, The Shriek of the Peacock), the
gentleness and stillness of death that she encountered in his verse—
above all death's greatness—persist.

This gentleness of soul, according to her essay *Die Stille als
Eingang des Geistigen* (1961, Quietude, the Entry of the Spiritual) is to
be achieved everywhere. It is not simply given but must be acquired
through great effort over a sustained period of time—thus the frequency of reference to "üben" (practice) and "arbeiten" (work) in her
writings. A store of accumulated grace or depth of soul is required, as
Lavant observes, to free the individual from the distractions of everyday life. During hours of knitting and reading she came closest to
recovering these quiet moments. Stillness is a matter of developing
composure of spirit by renouncing desire, by engendering love and compassion. This quietude of soul radiates spirituality, "because now that I
am so light, fear and care avoid me" (*KWM*, 164).

Quietude of soul is the ultimate source of the conception of
death coextensive with life that matures in the poet's middle and late
writings. It is the irony of death in these verses that it has the characteristics simultaneously of harshness and gentleness. Death's compromise
between harshness on the one hand and gentleness on the other is
consistent, however, with the ambiguities of life's uneasy middle
position: "Below roots, above stars, / fearful I stand in the middle"
(*DB*, 123), or as she variously expressed it: between "bird and carnation" (*DP*, 27), "clouds and roots" (*KWM*, 97), "simplicity and wisdom" (*KWM*, 217). The quietude of death, however, resolves life's

ambiguities, tames violence, and makes heavy things light.

The immediate and intuitive grasp of realities that the poet sought, however, is a very difficult assignment and distant goal for us: "We are in-between beings, plunged into immoderation, capable neither of simplicity nor of wisdom" (*KWM*, 217). We have somehow strayed from paradise, lost our innocence, have an impoverished existence, and are homeless and stateless. Only the experience of the immanent transcendental in life, only a knowledge of death in life saves us. Rilke said it all many years before: "Only in the dual realm / do the voices become / eternal and mild."[22] The poet who experiences reality with the perceptions of a child learns to accept his own mortality and finds at least temporarily that middle ground in the dual realm where all life is as well as death.

Notes

1. *Die Bettlerschale: Gedichte* (Salzburg: Müller, 1956), p. 15. The initials *DB* refer henceforth in this text to this edition.
2. "Briefe an Gerhard Dessen," in *Ensemble* 5 (1974), 150. The initial *B* refers henceforth in this text to this edition.
3. *Kunst wie meine ist nur verstümmeltes Leben: Nachgelassene und verstreut veröffentlichte Gedichte-Prosa-Briefe* (Salzburg: Müller, 1978), p. 223. The citation is from a letter of July 1955 to Ludwig von Ficker. The initials *KWM* refer henceforth in this text to this edition.
4. Wieland Schmied, "Sonnenvogel: Gedichte von Christine Lavant," in *Wort in der Zeit* 6/8 (1960), 53.
5. Helmut Scharf, *Kärntner Literaturspiegel 1960–1965: Autoren – Werke – Würdigungen* (Klagenfurt: Kärntner Druck and Verlagsgesellschaft, 1966), p. 56.
6. Heinz Politzer, "Literary Germany and Austria 1958/1959: A Progress Report," in *The German Quarterly* 33/2 (1960), 124.
7. Harald Weinrich, "Christine Lavant oder Die Poesie im Leibe" in *Über Christine Lavant: Leseerfahrungen, Interpretationen, Selbstdeutungen,* ed. Grete Lübbe-Grothues (Salzburg: Müller, 1984), p. 67.
8. Johann Strutz, *Poetik und Existenzproblematik: Zur Lyrik Christine Lavants* (Salzburg: Müller, 1979), p. 7.
9. Wolfgang Nehring, "Zur Wandlung des lyrischen Bildes bei Christine Lavant," in *Modern Austrian Literature* 12/3-4 (1979), 170.

10.   *Zeitschrift für deutsche Philologie* 87/4 (1968), 613-631.
11.   *Literatur und Kritik* 16/152 (1981), 77-93.
12.   Margery Williams, *The Velveteen Rabbit or How Toys Become Real* (Philadelphia: Running Press, 1981), p. 14.
13.   Johann Strutz, *Poetik und Existenzproblematik,* p. 19.
14.   *Nell: Vier Geschichten* (Salzburg: Müller, 1969), p. 170. The initial *N* refers henceforth in this text to this edition.
15.   *Spindel im Mond: Gedichte* (Salzburg: Müller, 1959), p. 100. The initials *SIM* refer henceforth in this text to this edition.
16.   *Der Pfauenschrei: Gedichte* (Salzburg: Müller, 1962), p. 87. The initials *DP* refer henceforth in this text to this edition.
17.   Paola Schulze Belli in *Index zu Christine Lavants Dichtungen* (Milano: Dott A. Giuffrè, 1980), p. 311 observes that the word "Kind" (child) occurs eighteen times in *Die Bettlerschale* (1956), thirteen times in *Spindel im Mond* (1959), and twice in *Der Pfauenschrei* (1962).
18.   Wolfgang Nehring, "Zur Wandlung des lyrischen Bildes bei Christine Lavant," p. 170.
19.   *Wirf ab den Lehm* (Graz/Wien: Stiasny, 1961), p. 39.
20.   Cf. Kornelius Fleischmann, "Mystisches und Magisches bei Christine Lavant: Versuch einer Deutung der Sammlung 'Die Bettlerschale,'" in *Literatur und Kritik* 109 (1976), 524-541 ("Lavant's lyric poetry in its totality presents a landscape of suffering," p. 524). August Stahl, "Das Bild des geschundenen Menschen in der Lyrik der Christine Lavant," pp. 77-93 ("This poetry essentially and rather thoroughly depicts the valley of tears after the fall in which even the promise of salvation becomes a source of torment," p. 83).
21.   *Die unvollendete Liebe* (Stuttgart: Brentano, 1949), p. 12.
22.   Rainer Maria Rilke, *Sämtliche Werke* 1 (Wiesbaden/Frankfurt am Main: Insel, 1955-1966), p. 736.

Bibliography

I. Works by Christine Lavant in German

Das Kind. Stuttgart: Brentano, 1948.
Das Krüglein: Erzählung. Stuttgart: Brentano, 1949.
Die unvollendete Liebe. Stuttgart: Brentano, 1949.

Baruscha. Graz: Leykam, 1952.
Die Rosenkugel. Stuttgart: Brentano, 1956.
Die Bettlerschale: Gedichte. Salzburg: Müller, 1956.
Spindel im Mond: Gedichte. Salzburg: Müller, 1959.
Sonnenvogel: Gedichte. Wülfrath: Heiderhoff, 1960.
Wirf ab den Lehm, ed. Wieland Schmied. Graz/Wien: Stiasny, 1961.
Der Pfauenschrei: Gedichte. Salzburg: Müller, 1962.
Hälfte des Herzens, eds. Horst Heiderhoff and Dieter Leisegang. Darm-
    stadt: Bläschke, 1967.
Nell: Vier Geschichten. Salzburg: Müller, 1969.
Gedichte, ed. Grete Lübbe-Grothues. München: DTV, 1972.
*Kunst wie meine ist nur verstümmeltes Leben: Nachgelassene und
    verstreut veröffentlichte Gedichte – Prosa – Briefe,* eds. Armin
    Wigotschnig and Johann Strutz. Salzburg: Müller, 1978.

Letters of Christine Lavant in German

26 Letters to Gerhard Deesen, in *Ensemble* 5 (1974), 133-157.
 2 Letters to Otto Scrinzi, in *Die Brücke* 1/2 (1975/1976), 180; 2/3,
    p. 182.
 1 Letter to Hermann Lienhard, in *Die Brücke* 1/2, p. 170.
14 Letters to Hilde Domin, in *Über Christine Lavant: Leseerfahrungen,
    Interpretationen, Selbstdeutugen,* ed. Grete Lübbe-Grothues.
    Salzburg: Müller, 1984, pp. 142-166.

II. Works in English Translation

Two Poems, translated by Michael Hamburger, in *German Poetry
    1910-1975.* New York: Urizen, 1976, pp. 266-269.
Four Poems, translated by Deen Larsen and Soraya Wimmer, in *The
    Chicago Review* 29/3 (1978), 8-15.
Five Poems, translated by Beth Bjorklund, in *The Literary Review* 25/2
    (1982), 184-186.
Four Poems, translated by Milne Holton and Herbert Kuhner, in
    Austrian Poetry Today / Österreichische Lyrik heute. New York:
    Schocken, 1985, pp. 56-59.

III. Secondary Works in English

Mitgutsch, Waltraud. "Hermetic Language as Subversion: The Poetry of Christine Lavant," in *Modern Austrian Literature* 17/1 (1984), 79-107.

IV. Major Studies in German

Aichinger, Ingrid. "Alles geht im Schwermutkreise: Christine Lavant zum 50. Geburtstag," in *Österreich in Geschichte und Literatur* 9/8 (1965), 429-447.

Lübbe-Grothues, Grete. "Zur Gedichtsprache der Christine Lavant," in *Zeitschrift für deutsche Philologie* 87/4 (1968), 613-631.

———. "'Schlange'–'Schlüssel'–'Schlüsselschlange': Zu den Substantiven und deren Kompositionen in der Gedichtsprache Christine Lavants," in *Untersuchungen zum 'Brenner': Festschrift für Ignaz Zangerle zum 75. Geburtstag*, ed. Walter Methlagl. Salzburg: Müller, 1981, pp. 460-478.

Nehring, Wolfgang. "Zur Wandlung des lyrischen Bildes bei Christine Lavant," in *Modern Austrian Literature* 12/3-4 (1979), 147-170.

Scharf, Helmut. "Christine Lavant: Dichtung mit gutem Gewissen," in *Wort in der Zeit* 7/2 (1961), 7-11.

Schulze-Belli, Paola: *Index zu Christine Lavants Dichtungen: (Die Bettlerschale, Spindel im Mond, Der Pfauenschrei)*. Milano: Dott A. Giuffrè, 1980.

Stahl, August. "Das Bild des geschundenen Menschen in der Lyrik der Christine Lavant," in *Literatur und Kritik* 16/152 (1981), 77-93.

Strutz, Johann. *Poetik und Existenzproblematik: Zur Lyrik Christine Lavants*. Salzburg: Müller, 1979.

Weinrich, Harald. "Christine Lavant oder Die Poesie im Leibe," in *Über Christine Lavant: Leseerfahrungen, Interpretationen, Selbstdeutungen*, ed. Grete Lübbe-Grothues. Salzburg: Müller, 1984, pp. 63-76.

Alexander Lernet-Holenia

Hugo Schmidt

Few writers have elicited such a wide range of positive and negative criticism as Alexander Lernet-Holenia (1897–1976). He has received the highest praise from the likes of Rainer Maria Rilke and Hugo
von Hofmannsthal, not to mention later critics who had the opportunity to witness his literary career beyond the 1920s, and he was
lambasted by Karl Kraus (who, to be sure, also pounded Hofmannsthal)
and many others, the most severe criticism coming from reviewers who
chose to ignore his books altogether. He produced so easily that his
facility at writing was suspect to some. When his friend, the dramatist
Carl Zuckmayer, mentioned that he never spent less than half a year or
even a year writing a play, Lernet-Holenia replied that it should not
take a playwright longer than a rainy weekend to finish one.[1]

He wrote nearly thirty stage plays, some two dozen novels, many
poems, short stories and essays, numerous translations from the English, French, Italian and Spanish, two biographies, and several radio and
television plays. Five of his novels and short stories were made into
films. He had little respect for the literary establishment, and his disparaging remarks about the literary production of his time included
some of his own writings, justly or unjustly. In 1930, when accused of
having borrowed the plot of one of his light comedies from a minor
playwright, he countered in two published letters that too much ado
was being made about nothing, that borrowing plots was a time-
honored custom, that he wrote his plays only for the royalties they
afforded him, and that any author who did likewise and did not admit
it should be ashamed. The two plays in question, he continued, his own
and the one from which he may have borrowed, were both trash and
had nothing to do with real literature.[2] When these two missives appeared in print, he was called an embarrassment to the world of Ger-

man letters, a reproach he no doubt relished.

He figured prominently in Viennese society, yet he snubbed his social peers with gusto in some of his plays, novels, and essays, and attacked many of the myths dear to the select circles in which he moved with such ease. His attitude to his literary peers was equally critical. As president of the Austrian P.E.N. Club from 1969 to 1972 he kept young authors whose writings he considered offensive from joining. He called himself a "conservative revolutionary" and acquired the reputation of being a "difficult gentleman" as he grew older. In 1972 he resigned from the presidency of the P.E.N. Club in protest against Heinrich Böll's winning the Nobel Prize in literature and more generally, as he put it, against the interference of certain Swedish circles in Central European affairs.

Some of the praise Lernet-Holenia has received from critics is mitigated by a display of exasperation at his nonchalant attitude, by friendly words of admonition, and by an encouraging pat on the back. This treatment raised his ire more than outright criticism. He has been called the cavalier of the pen, the knightly poet, the grandseigneur and the Lord Privy Seal of German literature, epithets that carry a number of associations: conservatism, shying away from literary innovation, adherence to an antiquated value system, and perhaps an all too gentlemanly attitude toward the arts. That he spoke disparagingly of some of his own works made critics assume a patronizing attitude, even if they approved of him on the whole. Even the friendliest among them, like Hilde Spiel, have chided him for what they call the uneven quality of his writings.[3] It is true that the scope of his vast oeuvre reaches from sophisticated entertainment to subtle works of classical beauty and purity. However, contrary to what Lernet-Holenia may have said, none of it is worthless trash, "kitsch."

A wide gamut in the intent and purpose of his writings need not make those on the lighter end appear frivolous and inferior. Everything that he wrote was subjected to his own crucible of good taste and sound judgment. His facility in both inventing fascinating plots and using and creating language allowed him to reconcile felicitously content and form in all of his writings, making each one of them a perfect representative of its kind. Even in his lightest plays and novels he never offends the most discriminating reader through what is the characteristic of inferior art: a discrepancy of content and form and the use of inadequate means in trying to achieve a superior effect. While his purely entertaining titles, some of which can be compared to Oscar Wilde's, delight the reader by their brilliance and wit, his more subtle and searching works do what one can expect of the finest literary creations: they bring about their own poetic world and lead the reader to the frontier of all possible inner experiences. Through their imagery they raise questions about man's identity, about life and death, not in an abstract philosophical fashion but through powerful symbolic representation. While active in every literary genre Lernet-Holenia ranked his lyric poetry highest and tended to look upon his novels and stories as secondary in his claim to literary fame. Paradoxically, his critics, possibly with some reason, are prone to reverse this order. They look upon his works of prose fiction as his finest achievements and tend to de-emphasize the importance of his poetry.

The themes of Lernet-Holenia's works, at least those of the first half of his literary career, are rooted in his background and early experiences. He was born in Vienna in 1897 into a family of military officers, with some of his ancestors having come from Spain and Lorraine. His father, Alexander Lernet, a lieutenant commander in the Austrian navy—prior to 1918 Austria did indeed have a navy—left his spouse early, and young Alexander was adopted by his mother's family, Holenia, a legal arrangement that gave him the double name Lernet-Holenia. He was raised both in Vienna and on his mother's family estate Schloss Wasserleonburg in the Austrian province of Carinthia, in an environment of landed gentry, secure in their ways and traditions. Loving descriptions of these surroundings can be found in some of his novels. After attending secondary school he enlisted as a cadet in a dragoon regiment and, like Heimito von Doderer, experienced as a very young man the first World War on the Eastern Front. The Austrian cavalry, a branch of the armed forces with a great tradition and reputation and, 150 years earlier, superior even to the cavalry of Frederick the Great of Prussia, had become, like the cavalry of other European nations, an anachronistic institution. With their officers still recruited mostly from the ranks of the nobility and still wearing, in the early years of the war, their colorful uniforms, sparkling tall helmets and, in some cases, even lances, they made perfect targets for Russian machine-gunners whenever they launched one of their noble but doomed attacks.

Having survived the war miraculously, Lernet-Holenia looked back upon his service years as an experience of frustration and futility before a background of faded splendor. The end of the Austro-Hungarian monarchy in 1918 affected him as it did many of his contemporaries: although the end was unavoidable and had been brought about by both inescapable political developments and the failing of the monarchical government, it was experienced as a deep shock from which some never recovered emotionally. Lernet-Holenia's works show an ever-recurring ambiguity toward the vanished glory of the Austro-Hungarian monarchy: on the one hand he criticized the inefficiency and pretenses of a moribund society, on the other he made it explicit that his own roots reached deeply into what was bound to collapse and that he was fatefully attached to it. For his poetic imagination the personal experience of the awe-inspiring cataclysm became a fertile ground that produced literary symbols central to the purport of his work.

Shortly after the war, having returned to what was left of Austria, Lernet-Holenia began to write poetry, the medium, as he felt from then on and for the rest of his life, in which he could convey what moved him most deeply and in which he could offer his best. In his first collections of poems, *Pastorale* (1921) and *Kanzonnair* (1923), although he followed in the footsteps of Rilke and Hofmannsthal, he proved himself immediately as a master of words, form, and style. There is no fermentation, no struggling for a mode of expression in Lernet-Holenia's earliest literary efforts. Like Hofmannsthal twenty-five years before him, he had supreme command over his medium from the very outset. Hermann Bahr called him an incomparable goldsmith of words, Rilke referred to him as the only hope for the future of German letters, and Hofmannsthal commented, with ever so gentle a stab at this newcomer's facility but surely not without a touch of envy, that Lernet-Holenia was able to do anything he wanted.

It is characteristic of his unpredictability that in the mid-twenties Lernet-Holenia turned to an entirely different genre, baffling his readers and admirers: he composed a number of spicy social comedies that became immediate successes on the Viennese stage. Although he continued to regard the lyric genre as his true domain, he stated that the contemplative art of lyrical poetry was defunct in our age of activism. Since modern man is activist, the art appropriate to him must be the same. He expressed his conviction that the collapse of the contemplative genre of poetry was not a temporary phenomenon but a permanent state.[4] No doubt he felt that he was not willing to follow Rilke faithfully in terms of his outer existence. It was not his desire to be coddled for the rest of his life as a devoted and spiritualized lyrical seer at the country estates of aristocratic ladies, a fate that Rilke had come to embrace. Lernet-Holenia was not averse to considering writing a vocation that should provide a livelihood. But to complicate matters further, his efforts for the stage were not limited to comedies. During the same period he wrote a number of searching and subtle tragedies. Within the span of two years there appeared the comedies *Ollapotrida* (1926) and *Österreichische Komödie* (1927, Austrian Comedy), and also the tragedies *Demetrius* (1926), *Alkestis* (1926), and *Saul* (1927).

In both types of stage plays the sure hand of the master was evident from the very beginning. The one-act play *Saul* shows the king of Israel on the eve of his defeat by the Philistines, according to its biblical source, Samuel I:28. The scene is transposed into a rural area in Austria or Bavaria, and the biblical Witch of Endor is a young local woman known for her gift of prophecy. Saul is depicted as haunted and tormented. He feels that he has been abandoned by God, whose existence he now denies in the strongest terms. The woman conjures up from the realm of the dead the specter of Samuel, who rejects Saul's pleas for help and accuses him of being a demon in the shape of the king. Samuel advises Saul not to think of such matters as victory and defeat when his end is near. Instead Saul should eat a meal and get a night's sleep. After this confrontation Saul appears stunned and beaten and willingly eats from the dish of plain peasant food the young woman places in his lap. The short play with its wide range of passions is masterfully composed and affects the reader deeply. The author presented the reduction of a powerful yet torn individual to a state of defeat and resignation, and at the same time the metamorphosis of a tyrannical ruler into a helpless human being who solicits our compassion.

In 1968 Lernet-Holenia published an expanded version of the play under the title *Die Hexe von Endor* (The Witch of Endor) with a new first act preceding the action of the original *Saul*. Characters from the second act, among them Saul, his field marshals, and his son Jonathan, appear as members of a present-day commission of medical examiners sent to investigate the hallucinations and the alleged psychic powers of a young local woman. They become engaged in a debate among themselves and with the local priest (who subsequently appears as Samuel) about the reality of psychic phenomena, a debate in which materialistic and spiritualistic views are brilliantly posed against each other. Through the new first act Lernet-Holenia placed the main action into our own time, thereby giving it a new profile and adding a dimension of contemporary social criticism. At the same time the immediacy of the original scene is somewhat diminished in the new version.

In *Alkestis,* while preserving the splendor of the myth, the play-wright added to the story an aspect of human motivation and made it a vehicle for a penetrating psychological study of man's fear of death and the viciousness of which he is capable in trying to escape it. Admetus's father Pheres is a pompous pathetic buffoon trying to gloss over un-pleasantries interfering with his plans, for example, the appearance of a gruesome clump of snakes on the bridal bed. His mother is a shrew, and Admetus himself a loving but ineffectual young man. When he tries to induce another to die in his stead, both his parents shrink back in horror. When Alcestis volunteers, Admetus appears reluctant to dis-suade her. Behind a veneer of remote and divine dispassion Apollo is portrayed as fluctuating between capriciousness and indifference, with an added touch of jealousy. The comic element that emerges here and there is counterbalanced by the truly majestic figure of Alcestis, free of all petty concerns and completely filled by her love, a character that will recur frequently in Lernet-Holenia's works.

Despite their striking qualities the early serious plays have not enjoyed much success on the stage. *Demetrius* was produced only once in Leipzig, *Alkestis* and *Saul* a few more times, but none of them in the playwright's native Vienna. On the other hand his social comedies, which he must have composed concurrently with the serious plays, quickly became favorites on the stage. The aspect in which they truly excel is their consistently brilliant dialogue. Lernet-Holenia had an uncannily fine ear for the nuances and the intonation of the idiom used in the upper social strata, and he managed to reproduce their conver-sational style so faithfully that his dialogues draw part of their comic quality from their very degree of realism. He rendered the speech of this social group even more precisely than Arthur Schnitzler, who was in this situation more of an outside observer. Lernet-Holenia's plots are cleverly invented, and the situations invariably irresistible. *Ollapotrida,* for example, starts out as a farce of extramarital relations with several couples, married or unmarried, in the same apartment and trying to hide from each other in a scenario reminiscent of Nestroy but definitely with the ambience of the twentieth century. The second act offers a surprise: When the curtain rises, the spectator sees the stage from behind, with an imaginary audience in the back of the new arrange-ment. The main action presented in the first act is now given the function of a play within a play in the nature of *I Pagliacci.* Behind the scene, i.e., on the present front stage, a passionate private quarrel takes place between the hero and the leading lady of the play. They are lovers, but he is about to leave her, and she berates and threatens him. The theater manager, the director, stagehands, and propmen are drawn into the incidental personal drama. Basically we are faced with a familiar theater situation of reality interfering and eventually becoming identical with playacting, but done with much charm and imagination. The end, of course, is not the tragic one of Leoncavallo's opera. The actress, now on stage again with the audience still watching from the back, waves under her lover's nose a pistol that was loaded with live ammunition by mistake, and he surrenders and promises to marry her, in both the inner and the outer plots.

Lernet-Holenia wrote several plays in a similar vein and quickly became known as the author of comedies. When he received the coveted Kleist Prize in 1926, it was not certain whether he was rewarded for his unperformed tragedies or his acclaimed comedies. Certainly the latter were more in the public eye. Altogether he wrote some eighteen light comedies, some in collaboration with other playwrights, others as stage versions of his own novels, and one as an adaptation from the Italian. In his later comedies he poked fun at various social and political phenomena, among them the Austrian internal revenue service (*Das Goldkabinett,* 1957, The Gold Store Room), and the succession to the Spanish throne (*Die Thronprätendenten,* 1965, The Pretenders to the Throne).

One play, *Glastüren* (1939, Glass Doors), occupies a special place among Lernet-Holenia's comedies. It contains so many serious elements that it can barely be classified a comedy, and its early stage history makes it memorable for another reason. It concerns the love between a young Austrian woman of noble lineage and a gentleman from America. The wedding has been arranged, but the groom believes — erroneously or at least not as he imagines—to have discovered in his fiancée's past a dubious episode, and now he cannot decide whether to go through with the wedding ceremony. On a deeper level the play is about trust and the strength of feelings but also about the conflict between two attitudes: an innocent but destructive naiveté on the one side and on the other the nobility's unapproachable composure that often has to hide the seamier side of their faded glory. Yet the composure reveals itself in this case to be genuine, and the play ends on a positive note. *Glastüren,* reminiscent of Hofmannsthal's sophisticated comedies, grants deep insights into human nature and the complexity of man's motivations. The play was produced, even before it appeared in print, in Vienna's prestigious Josefstadt theater in 1938 to great public acclaim but closed very quickly, supposedly upon the personal intervention of Hitler's propaganda minister, Dr. Josef Goebbels. This is not surprising, for the play, although it does not touch on any political issues, concentrates on the fine nuances and intellectual differentiations that are characteristic of a complex society and therefore anathema to the socially equalizing efforts of a totalitarian regime bent on controlling all aspects of public life, including the arts.

While writing comedies Lernet-Holenia also pursued his interest in serious plays and tragedies, among them most notably *Die Lützowschen Reiter. Ein Festspiel* (1932, Lützow's Riders: A Festival Play). It is set against the background of the Napoleonic Wars of Liberation, but when this political "festival play" appeared it would have been difficult to find a stage to produce it. In the early 1930s, in Austria as in Germany, the political dichotomy between liberalism and nationalism had reached a new extreme, and a play with a political theme would have been expected to espouse one of the two orientations. Lernet-Holenia refused to take either stand. His protagonist Herbeck (in the original printing of 1932 his name was Holenia) is drawn into the political turmoil against his will. He rejects those who serve Napoleon's cause for selfish reasons, but also the German patriots eager to sacrifice themselves and countless others in fighting the French. He subscribes to a supranational European dimension in political thought which could be found, if anywhere, in Napoleon's rather than in the other camp. In a dialogue with Theodor Körner, historically a poet and a member of Major Lützow's volunteer corps of irregulars, Herbeck opposes the patriotic fervor that inspires the others and criticizes those who let themselves become part of an unthinking mass, swayed by meaningless but dangerous slogans. He doubts whether Germany's injured pride is important enough to start new wars and set the world ablaze. Surely these sentiments, which foreshadowed disastrous events to come, did not endear Lernet-Holenia to the nationalistic majority of 1932, be it in Germany or in Austria.

Despite his gloomy predictions about the future of lyric poetry Lernet-Holenia did continue to write poems. They appeared in several volumes published before and after the second World War: *Die goldene Horde* (1935, The Golden Horde), *Die Titanen* (1935, The Titans), *Die Trophäe* (1946), and *Das Feuer* (1949, The Fire). These collections no longer show the overwhelming influence of Rilke. Although reflections of Pindar's and Friedrich Hölderlin's poetry have been found in them, the poet's voice essentially has become his own. The poems continue to excel through their formal polish and beauty. Lernet-Holenia had a predilection for classical models such as the ode and the sonnet, but also frequently used free verse. His preferred themes were not always strictly lyrical but often had a narrarive quality with lyrical overtones. For example, the long title poem in *Die goldene Horde* describes an abortive attempt on the part of the last descendants of the "Golden Horde," Mongolian tribes in medieval Russia, to free the czar from his captors in 1918. Yet the poem derives its strong impact not so much from the description of the external events as from certain atmospheric excursions such as a brief stay of the imperial prisoners at an abandoned estate where they seem to hear the voices and sounds of the long-absent occupants of these rooms and their guests. The czar and his family listen to these sounds and take a step into an overgrown garden, as if in search of something, until a flock of small birds, titmice, circles overhead and two of the birds light on the czar's shoulder. But whatever they sing into his ear he misses because the prisoners are again loaded on trucks, to meet their death shortly. In poems such as this Lernet-Holenia followed an approach similar to the one taken in his finest prose narrations: the foremost concern is an inner spiritual dimension, with the narrator's introspection giving the external events their true meaning.

In another poem, "Der Bethlehemitische Kindermord" (The Massacre of the Innocents), the poet subtly transferred the scene of the massacre into a timeless realm vaguely reminiscent of Brueghel's painting: The captain in charge is clothed in a brick-red cape, the soldiers wear cuirasses, but also rifle shots are heard, removing the episode into a later era. There is repeated mention that the massacre takes place under the "lofty banner, the eagle of the empire." The captain tries to ignore the scene taking place before him and sits on his horse "leaning forward slightly because the screaming annoyed him." When he hears someone report to him that they were done, he has a path cut through the lamenting crowd by blows with the flat of the sabres. With a few masterful strokes the poet rendered what he saw as essential in the scene: the horror of it enhanced through the remoteness of the commander who will not soil his hands needlessly and ironically even avoids "unnecessary violence" by having the troops use the flat of their sabers upon leaving the scene. Themes that recur in his prose fiction frequently appear in Lernet-Holenia's poems, such as the relationship between life and death or the nature of the realm between the two.

In "Todesfahrt" (Journey into Death), for example, he describes a person's departure from this world: how he equips himself, what type of horses he takes, which supplies and which weapons. Those who loved him and are now left behind are not crying; the sounds he hears are caused by the wind. Leaving his house he looks for certain wagon tracks he must follow, and he is last seen entering a narrow ravine leading north.

In 1946 Lernet-Holenia published a long poem, "Germanien" (Germany), in which he describes the fall of Hitler's Germany before the background of the Roman and other empires that fell in an aura of tragedy or even glory. The poet shows how the present disaster bears no sign of greatness and is a mere caricature of other downfalls. Now there is no one, he writes, who, when beaten with a cane, would not hope to wield a cane himself one day to beat others; there are none who did not break an oath when swearing allegiance to a new master; none who receive praise and rewards from hands that are not vile. But since these men are no longer free, they fear worse than death those who rule but are not natural masters. The poem, written in a powerful classical idiom, is a devastating indictment of the last travesty of an imperial idea. Three years later, in 1949, Lernet-Holenia published his last collection of poems, *Das Feuer*, printed in a facsimile edition of his own handwritten manuscript. It includes two "Olympian Hymns" and other hymns, among them "Aetna" and "Lazarus." In the latter the poet raises once more the question of where life and death begin and end, wondering whether he dreamed of something in an earlier life that he can no longer remember, and asking whether life did not begin in this fashion; but if so, then death does likewise and one does not know that it has begun.

Surely Lernet-Holenia approaches in these later poems a realm that, even for a poet, borders on silence. Comparisons between this group of poems and those of Hölderlin have been drawn conclusively.[5] Yet in evaluating Lernet-Holenia's poems one does finally miss that element of creative intensity that lends the finest poems in world literature their unforgettable quality. It is not a negative critical statement to say that some of his poems could have been written by Schiller or Hölderlin, but it does imply that the innovative element, especially in terms of Lernet-Holenia's exquisite language, is often missing. He was not wrong when he called his poems his purest accomplishments and the genre in which he could express himself most directly, unencumbered by the unnecessary baggage of the epic narrative genre. Yet one cannot help seeing in some of that baggage a quality that gave Lernet-Holenia his unique voice in literature. The sensitivity of his observations as they appear in his poems is also present in his prose fiction, but the latter also includes an element that had to be barred from his poems: the sovereign yet humorous quality of his style, and his skill and imagination in inventing and developing plots. One is tempted to look upon his poems despite their undisputed excellence as a training ground that helped him bring his art to its finest perfection in some of his prose.

There is no doubt that Lernet-Holenia's statements about his narrative fiction were not always fair. He spoke in unflattering terms of his early prose, and the deprecating term "military novels" that he applied to his most successful and widely read works is anything but kind, for it embraces, aside from the charming early romances *Die Abenteuer eines jungen Herrn in Polen* (1931, *The Adventures of a Young Gentleman in Poland*) and *Ljubas Zobel* (1932, Luba's Sable Coat), masterpieces such as *Die Standarte* (1934, *The Glory Is Departed*) and the novella "Der Baron Bagge" (1936, "Baron Bagge"). All of these are set in the first World War and surely are war novels or stories, although the war merely serves as a background. In addition there is *Beide Sizilien* (1942, Two Sicilies), which is set after World War I but has as its characters mostly former officers and makes constant reference to the war. One would also have to include in this group *Mars im Widder* (1941, Mars in Aries), which is likewise a military novel, although it takes place not in the first but during the early months of the second World War. These books surely constitute the main body of the author's accomplishments.

Lernet-Holenia was in his mid-thirties when he turned to prose fiction, the genre that was to predominate in his remaining literary career. To simplify matters one could say that the three traditional genres, poetry, drama, and epic prose, appear in this order in his oeuvre. He started with poetry in 1921, turned to drama in 1926, and to prose in 1930. However, he did not cease writing in the preceding genres when he turned to a new one but merely concentrated in each instance on the newly embraced form, although his lyrical output seems to have come to a stop after 1949. His prose style immediately captivates the reader: It has an urbane elegant quality about it, it is polished and intellectually brilliant, while at the same time displaying charm and making the reader feel that he is being taken along on a fascinating narrative course by a most able and pleasant guide. Indeed, it is difficult to put down any of Lernet-Holenia's books. The preponderance of "military novels" for about ten years is not accidental. In his choice of topics the author turned to what he knew best: Austrian society and the historical events before, during, and after World War I, and his own experience of the war that played a predominant role in his most formative years. He wrote mostly about the social circles he was familiar with, aristocrats and military officers, but his attitude toward his characters is by no means uncritical and later on even became polemical.

His first novel other than a narrative version of one of his plays, *Die nächtliche Hochzeit* (1930, The Nocturnal Wedding), was *Die Abenteuer eines jungen Herrn in Polen.* Although it includes gruesome war scenes, it is a light, charming book. On the surface it is a classical war story following the familiar pattern "one man alone wins the war." But the novel quickly reveals its true qualities that remove it from such clichés. During the Russian Kerenski offensive in the summer of 1917 a very young officer finds himself caught behind enemy lines after taking part in an unsuccessful cavalry attack. He tries to hide, disguising himself as a girl, and finds employment as a milkmaid on an estate. He manages to do a little snooping among staff officers billeted at the estate and is finally freed by his own troops and celebrated as a hero. However, he is altogether unaware of his great service to the fatherland and appears dumbfounded when a high military decoration is bestowed upon him. The tone of the novel is ironical, and the author takes relish in exposing stupidity wherever it can be found, especially in the area of military incompetence on both sides. Commanders distinguish themselves mostly through vanity and do little beyond trying to save face. Yet these observations are not made angrily but rendered humorously and even lovingly.

One highpoint of the novel occurs early in the action: an ill-fated cavalry attack which Lernet-Holenia describes with the unrelenting realism derived from personal experience without abandoning his ironical stance. He shows how the attack is launched for no good reason, how the commanding officers—in this case a German and an Austrian cavalry brigade are fighting jointly—vie with each other for the greater glory but less dangerous positions, what goes on in the minds of the soldiers as the charge proceeds, how they are cut down in droves and how the survivors continue, partly in a state of mad inertia and partly because by then the horses are out of control, and how the commanders justify having ordered the charge after it failed. There are a few details underscoring the inanity of the situation. For example, several military bands play frisky marches in an effort to inspire the troops to greater heroic deeds; and during the attack the entire division, consisting of the two brigades, was under the command of an officer who did not know that he was in charge: he automatically and unknowingly moved into the position upon the death of the commanding general. Nothing but chance determines the course of events, and an individual's fate depends not on his own volition but on accidental circumstances.

Lernet-Holenia conveyed these and other observations without ever resorting to the abstract and always retaining his graceful narrative style. Purely through symbolic representation he imparted to the reader and aroused in him subtle impressions, such as the futility of man's striving. If Lernet-Holenia referred to this book as one of his military novels, this reference in itself must have been made tongue in cheek. The greatest part of the action consists of hilarious thwarted love stories brought about by the protagonist's disguised identity—a number of men, fooled by his disguise, fall in love with him, and he in turn falls in love with several young ladies—and wherever the military element does appear, it is shown in a negative light and characterized by pretenses and futility. No doubt Lernet-Holenia had set out to write an entertaining novel, but inadvertently motifs entered into the plot that pressed themselves upon him out of his personal experiences, adding a dimension of poetic truth and significance to an otherwise clever but inconsequential plot. It is characteristic of the author's great skill that he succeeded in fusing these disparate elements into an organic whole.

Much of what has been said also applies to another of his early novels, *Ljubas Zobel* (1932). A "military novel" like the preceding one, it is set in Russia toward the end of World War I and interweaves descriptions of the collapsing frontline with a love story: a young officer rescues a Russian girl from marauders. The love story is brought to a happy end, and the two of them get married upon their arrival in the rescuer's homeland. But again there are scenes that run almost contrary to the perfunctory love story and underscore the vanity of human efforts and the frustrations experienced in trying to achieve a goal. Mutinous soldiers, belonging to Austria's Slavic minorities and refusing to fight when the collapse of the multinational empire is imminent, serve as such a symbol and show the ineffectual attempts to come to terms with them. An officer, infected with influenza—it is the worldwide epidemic of 1918—in a never ending downpour tries to prevail over his sickness as well as over the unruly soldiers while facing the enemy, is seized by attacks of helpless rage, and is finally killed in hand-to-hand combat. Such descriptions leave an indelible impression because of their simple truthfulness inspired by experience and observation. Although they are not necessarily part of the main story line, they give the novel its unique import. A soldier seized by illness in combat while having to face mutinous troops is not part of the literary stockpile of war stories; he is a symbol of frustration and defeat in the face of overwhelming odds. Uncertainty and confusion prevail throughout the action. In one scene an Austrian cavalry division encounters a large unit of Mongol horsemen. Uncertain as to whether they should consider each other friend or foe, the two columns gallop side by side while trying to decide on a course of action. After a brief period of guarded reserve there is an outburst of violence over the Mongols' attempt to abuse civilian travelers they encounter, and the two large units become engaged in a ferocious battle. Such close combat scenes, frequent in Lernet-Holenia's writings, are made all the more horrid by virtue of the author's informed dispassionate account.

A third novel dealing with the war's end and the dissolution of the empire is one of Lernet-Holenia's acknowledged masterpieces, *Die Standarte.* It was a critical as well as a popular success and was included in the selections of no less than five book clubs. The scenario is similar to that of the two novels discussed above: an officer experiences the collapse of the armed forces and manages to make his way home while rescuing a young woman. The plot is richer and even more colorful than in the earlier works, and the author's compelling narrative style reaches its highest level. But again the plot, exciting though it is, does not tell enough about the novel's significance. Here it even includes a few burlesque elements (such as the protagonist's comic servant) that merely attest to the author's narrative exuberance.

On a more essential level the novel is about foiled efforts, useless sacrifices, and their lasting effect on man. As in a good many of Lernet-Holenia's prose works the action is told to the author by the person who experienced it, and the novel is set in a narrative frame with its ending left open. The narrator, now a successful young businessman, was a junior officer and the last standard-bearer of a distinguished dragoon regiment that experienced a most ignominious fate at the end of the war. Now he seeks out beggars in the streets of Vienna apparently in search of former members of the regiment in need of help. In this situation he is observed by the author, is greatly embarrassed, and tells him his story. Upon crossing the Danube near Belgrade the enlisted men of the regiment refuse to take orders. The officers, unable to handle the situation, eventually ask that the mutinous regiment be fired upon by another unit. In the process not only the mutinous enlisted men but also their officers are struck down by the bullets, something they had counted on when the order was issued. They considered themselves as guilty as the soldiers, not of mutiny but of not being able to avert it. The commander, hit several times and dying, leads the remainder of his regiment away from the scene as long as he can support himself in his saddle. This experience, if anything, ties the surviving men and officers together more closely, and in its pathos determines the rest of the action. Under enormous difficulties and with the additional loss of several lives the narrator carries the regimental standard, hidden under his uniform, back to the capital in order to return it symbolically to the emperor to whom he had sworn an oath to protect it with his life. In the meantime the empire has ceased to exist, and upon arriving at the imperial palace the narrator witnesses the emperor's disgraceful stealthy departure. Unimpeded he wanders into a hall where several sergeants burn stacks of regimental banners in a fireplace, and he throws his into the flames too.

Again the author conveyed the sense of futility through powerful moving symbols. The concurrent love story appears almost out of place in a setting of destruction and collapse. The protagonist, although an impetuous determined lover, is at the same time emotionally remote from his beloved, and this situation does not change when they are married after the war. They are considered a happily married couple but do not seem to communicate with each other. In terms of literary motifs the young man has his place in the tradition of the returnee whose experiences in the war overshadow the remaining years of his life and do not allow him to adjust to a normal civilian existence. In the figure of the young woman the author has created a character that recurs several times in his writings. She is the dreamlike ethereal representation of an ideal image, strangely disembodied from reality and removed from the concerns that occupy those around her. She impresses the reader not so much as a real person but as a projection of the protagonist's yearning for a realm of purity and permanence. His inability to become part of the realm in which she exists and to extricate himself from a world of stubbornly male concerns has far-reaching implications. He seems to be excluded from a state of metaphysical grace.

The motif of the unattainable glorious woman and the concerns of the "military novels" are blended most skillfully in what is generally considered Lernet-Holenia's masterpiece, the novella "Der Baron Bagge." Its characters are the officers and men of a cavalry squadron, and the action takes place during the Russian campaign early in World War I. The story's poetic impact has a source different than that of military adventure and lies in an area that henceforth captured the author's imagination again and again: the realm between life and death. On a reconnaissance mission in Hungary the captain of the squadron issues the insane order to attack a heavily defended bridge. During the charge, amid chunks of flying ice and frozen dirt, the protagonist Bagge feels that he is hit by two pebbles. Miraculously the attack is successful, the squadron meets no resistance on its further advance, and, even more strangely, it never finds another trace of the enemy whose positions it is to scout.

In a small town that appears to be untouched by the war and filled with crowds of happy people, Bagge meets a young woman of unearthly beauty and disposition, the daughter of friends of the family, and within a few days the two get married. The captain, still obsessed with the desire to find the enemy, has the squadron continue on its mission although it has advanced far beyond expectations. They live through experiences that are situated more and more in the realm of the fantastic, but no one except Bagge seems to notice. As they follow the course of a river through a dark ravine,

> from the bed of the river a strange glow rose up to us, something like the ocean's phosphorescence, and now the ground itself began to shine as if it were strewn with phosphorus; even the riders and horses emanated an unnatural light, or rather they were surrounded by a luminous mist as though a candle were burning behind each man.

Soon they approach a bridge that gleams metallically from afar. "There was a tremendous roaring, as from heavenly waterfalls of glass, and steam, as if from intensely hot waters, rose in all colors of the rainbow from the deep cleft."[6] When the squadron draws closer, the bridge turns out to be made of gold. At this point Bagge perceives that he must be dreaming, although he cannot tell when the dream had started. Frantically he pulls his horse aside, as it is about to step on the bridge which all the others are crossing quietly—and awakens, lying on the wooden bridge which the squadron had tried to take. The pebbles he had felt were bullets, the charge had ended disastrously, and the entire squadron, all 120 men except for three or four survivors, were killed. What Lernet-Holenia had described in such detail was, as he puts it, the interval between dying and death, represented here in the mythological tradition through a nine-day ride to the north, ending with the crossing of a bridge.

Bagge's further life is under the spell of the other reality he has experienced. He cannot get married because he feels that in his more essential existence he is married already. After the war he travels through the area covered in his dream as if in search for his lost other life. The personages he had met, including his imagined wife, had really existed but had died by the time they appeared in his dream. Nothing he comes across resembles closely what he remembers, even his celestial beloved was, as he discovers, plain-looking in reality. He begins to question the reality of both his existences. If death is a dream, life may be one as well. He feels that "between these dreams bridges lead back and forth," and asks "who may truly say what is death and what life, or where the space and time between them begin and end?"[7] The story excels through its fascinating subject matter as well as through the classical purity of its form and style.

The nature of the no man's land between life and death continued to fascinate Lernet-Holenia, and often it is connected, as in "Der Baron Bagge," with the motif of a journey into death or of entering subterranean areas. The above-mentioned poem "Todesfahrt" treats the same subject matter but without the return described in the novella; and the motif recurs in several novels. When buried during an air attack in *Mars im Widder,* the protagonist loses consciousness, but not altogether, for, according to the author, in such a state of semiconsciousness we merely advance from one realm into another. At times small particles break loose from the one and float into the other "like driftwood from unknown continents."[8] In *Beide Sizilien* one character dying from unknown causes describes in great detail and in very concrete terms his inner experiences as he approaches the realm of the dead. The novels *Der Mann im Hut* (1937, Man with Hat), *Die Standarte* and *Der Graf Luna* (1955, *Count Luna*) contain scenes of individuals entering subterranean areas such as tombs and catacombs.

In *Der Graf Luna* the protagonist Jessiersky perishes while trying to find an exit from catacombs under Rome, and the author depicts with splendid imagery his hovering between life and death. Jessiersky sees himself leave the catacombs and enter a wintery landscape with a sleigh waiting for him and driving him to the estate of his ancestors in

Poland. Even in his fantasies Jessiersky knows that he is dying, but he experiences the ride to the estate with great curiosity. He is received and feted by many of his ancestors, but he is so tired that he can think only of lying down to rest. Lernet-Holenia's lasting enchantment with the realm between life and death is one, and surely the most subtle, aspect of his interest in the mysterious and supernatural. Other aspects of this interest can be found in the frequently recurring motif of the loss or exchange of one's identity, in the author's predilection for motifs from detective stories, and the occurrence of dubious characters and confidence men in his novels.

In fact some of his books are neatly woven mystery novels. The motif of exchanged identities is central to *Ich war Jack Mortimer* (1933, I Was Jack Mortimer), *Beide Sizilien, Die Inseln unter dem Winde* (1952, The Windward Islands), and *Die weiße Dame* (1965, The White Lady), but it occurs more marginally in other books as well and occupied Lernet-Holenia's imagination as much as the question of life and death. One character in *Beide Sizilien*, a police inspector who comments on the uncertainty of people's identity may well express the author's views (notwithstanding Lernet-Holenia's strong dislike for the police). People do not remain the same throughout their lives, he says, but change so much that they seem to be playing the roles of others. Napoleon surely did not remain the insignificant artillery officer he had been, and Friedrich Schiller did not remain a surgeon. Man's perpetual change, he comments sarcastically, is his only excuse for his existence.

The "military novels" discussed so far were completed while the Austro-Hungarian empire was still in the forefront of public memory. Nostalgia surely played a great part in making them so successful and popular. The author even felt that the empire had not vanished altogether at the end of World War I but somehow survived in spirit and in the climate of the age up to the absorption of Austria into Germany in 1938 and to the outbreak of World War II. Between the wars Lernet-Holenia lived mostly in Vienna and played a prominent role in Viennese society, but he also traveled widely, especially in the Americas, staying in South America for a long period. Several of his novels, for example *Ich war Jack Mortimer* and *Die Inseln unter dem Winde,* reflect his Spanish-American experiences.

At the outbreak of World War II he was drafted immediately and fought in the Polish campaign. After being wounded he served for a short time in the military film office ("Heeresbildstelle") in Berlin. In 1941 he published *Mars im Widder,* a novel dealing with the war against

Poland. Newly off the press, the entire edition was confiscated before it could be distributed, upon the order of the censorship office. It was hidden away, apparently illegally, in a warehouse in Leipzig, only to be destroyed in an air raid. In 1947 it was reissued from the only copy the author had saved. Naturally the book did not contain any material directly critical of Hitlerian Germany—if it had, no publisher would have dared to even consider it. It must have been rather the mysterious complexity of the novel that displeased the authorities, the very non-military attitude of the author and his protagonist.

Lernet-Holenia was obviously describing his own experiences, but he showed them in a bewildering, at times supernatural, context—characteristics that had no place in the eyes of the censorship office in a novel that was after all about a victorious campaign. Many scenes in the book are open to a wide range of interpretations. The protagonist becomes acquainted with a group of mysterious characters in Vienna, volunteers to deliver confidential letters, and meets a woman who is not who she claims to be. He receives vague admonitions not to associate with certain personages and, like the reader, has no explanation for all these occurrences. Possibly he may have become acquainted with a resistance group. While in Poland he witnesses a strange phenomenon that the author leaves for the reader to interpret: Thousands of crayfish move across a road from east to west in an inexplicable mass migration, shunning various creeks that would have been for them a more natural travel route. Inexplicably they suddenly vanish as mysteriously as they had appeared. Scenes such as this give the book a puzzling but captivating quality.

During the remaining war years, which Lernet-Holenia spent mostly in his summer home in St. Wolfgang near Salzburg, he published only one additional book, *Beide Sizilien*. His plays were not performed and none of his older books reprinted. *Beide Sizilien*, although it is set in Vienna a few years after the end of World War I, can still be classified as a late military novel. Its characters are the remaining officers of a dragoon regiment named "Ferdinand I, King of the Two Sicilies,"— significantly after a kingdom long vanished even when the Austrian empire still existed—and the action has its origin in the war years. In this novel, often called his most subtle and successful work, Lernet-Holenia uses lyrical means to convey his intent: the demise of a cultural era, a mode of existence. Given this theme, which applies in the context of the novel to the destruction of an empire whose memory was anathema to the new rulers of Germany, it is not surprising that the novel passed through the censorship office with no problems.

In its outer shell *Beide Sizilien* can be called a mystery novel. The few surviving officers of the regiment feel called to duty one more time, although the war is over, the empire dismantled, and the armed forces demobilized. They come to the aid of their former colonel, whose daughter is by all appearances implicated in the murder of one of their comrades. Trying to investigate the crime and to exonerate the young lady, some of them, including the colonel himself, disappear mysteriously, die in strange accidents, or are crippled in duels. The perpetrator, whose identity is a complex issue, is discovered eventually. What the author tried to express under the guise of a detective story was an inner experience that would be more appropriate to the medium of lyric poetry than to prose, and yet he succeeded admirably in recreating the ambience of a slow fading away, a gradual cessation of life. As one character observes, the various deaths occurring throughout the action, although they are often unrelated or truly accidental, do have an inexplicable interconnection that transcends the realm of empirical actuality. They are part of the symbolic aura that characterizes the book. Large sections of it could be called successful prose poems; here in the tangible realm of a plot Lernet-Holenia's lyrical genius manifests itself most markedly.

Especially the end of Silverstolpe, the man who dies without a medical cause, occupies the center of the author's intentions. When Silverstolpe feels that death is approaching, he takes refuge with two relatives, elderly ladies who live on an estate in Carinthia, the province so dear to the author. From there he writes a long letter to a friend, expressing in arresting images his inner experiences. His friend and former fellow officer comes to visit him in his last days. But even here the futility of human efforts is underscored by a frustrating detail: sitting at the dying man's bedside, the friend leaves for a moment to take away a barking dog. When he returns moments later, Silverstolpe is dead. His funeral is attended by a rural association of army veterans who carry with them an old flag. In describing it the author once more sums up in one image the transience and futility of worldly things, recalling similar trends in the tradition of Baroque literature that remained alive in Austria: "When the cloth moved, the embroidered eagle gleamed in the sun. It reached with its talons for kingdoms that no longer existed."[9]

Of the prose works written between the two wars and not dealing with military matters, mention should be made of the very successful detective novel *Ich war Jack Mortimer,* of which no less than three film versions exist. It is the story of a taxi driver who discovers that a passenger in his cab was murdered and now makes desperate attempts to escape being accused of the crime, including changing his identity. Also there is *Die Auferstehung des Maltravers* (1936, Maltravers' Resurrection), the story of a nobleman engaged in criminal activities, and *Der Mann im Hut,* a spellbinding rendition of a search for evidence of the conflict between the Huns and Germanic tribes in the early middle ages, which is also the subject of the thirteenth-century Middle High German epic poem about the end of the Nibelungs.

With *Der Graf von Saint Germain* (1948, The Count of St. Germain) and *Der Graf Luna* Lernet-Holenia began a series of novels with more recent or current themes, although their characters in origin, life style, and values are still rooted in the Austria of pre-World War I. *Der Graf von Saint Germain* is the loosely knit story of an industrialist who becomes less and less able to cope with the modern world and comes to a frightful end: prevented from proceeding in his car by a fanatical crowd (significantly including two policemen) taking part in a pro-Nazi rally in Vienna two days before the German takeover, he is seized by a fit of fury, drives into the crowd, and is killed by them. The theme of death, violent or otherwise, prevails throughout the book. The mysterious figure of an eighteenth-century adventurer, the Count of St. Germain, who had predicted the decline of the modern world, lends an element of unity to the book, which otherwise consists mostly of long excursions, including an ingenious interpretation of Hofmannsthal's novella "Das Märchen der 672. Nacht" (The Tale of the 672nd Night) as a representation of death.

Der Graf Luna is set in post-World War II Austria and deals with the themes of crime, persecution, and punishment during the Hitler era. Alexander Jessiersky, a well-to-do businessman and owner of a large transportation and shipping agency, has to blame himself for the incarceration of one Count Luna in a concentration camp and for his surmised death, although this happens against Jessiersky's will and only through his inaction. His subsequent attempts to have Luna discharged are unsuccessful, and he loses track of him. After the war Jessiersky comes to believe that Luna has survived and is bent on taking revenge. He feels pursued by Luna and in trying to defend himself and his family against these imagined persecutions, becomes guilty of several murders. In desperation and still trying to escape Luna, he plans to feign his own death by disappearing into one of Rome's unexplored catacombs, leaving them through an exit he imagines to have found on an ancient map, and sailing for South America under a false identity. The plan fails, and he perishes in the catacombs. The character of Jessiersky was to the author a vehicle for the portrayal of contemporary issues: guilt by default and inaction, a tortured conscience, fear, and rage brought on by fear.

In his later novels Lernet-Holenia continued and deepened a technique that he had used previously in many of his longer works: to inject excursions into the plot, mostly contemplative sections indirectly related to the theme and lending it added significance. One of the most striking examples occurs in *Beide Sizilien* in Silverstolpe's powerful rendition of a dream he has about the end of the world.[10] The cataclysm is caused by a solar nova and the metamorphosis of its benign light into a catastrophic emanation of unimaginable heat that sets on fire all the planets and satellites of the solar system. The novel *Der Graf von Saint Germain* consists mostly of excursions held together tenuously by the thin thread of the plot, a structure that has no bearing on the excellence of the book. While such excursions often have special poetic intensity in the novels of the 1940s and 1950s, in his later works Lernet-Holenia preferred to use them for essayistic reflections of widely ranging themes. Both *Die weiße Dame* and *Die Hexen* (1969, The Witches) deal vaguely with a subject that the author presented amusingly on several occasions: the fate of some of the crown jewels of the Austrian and Russian empires that appear to have been removed illegally and sold hastily by departing members of the ruling houses or their agents. But the various excursions give these books their charm and interest. For example, in *Die weiße Dame* the author comes to speak of the Iron Curtain and mentions another significant demarcation line, the Roman *limes* of 2,000 years ago, which ran in a mostly east-westerly direction through central Europe following the Rhine and the Danube and delineating the extent of the Roman Empire. The author pinpoints the geographic location where the two borders would have intersected and adds a brilliant comparison of the cultural and political situations on either side of these heavily guarded borders, with amusing sociological implications.[11]

In addition to his novels, which never exceed 300 pages in length, Lernet-Holenia also wrote a large number of novellas and short stories gathered in nine collections between the years 1935 and 1972. Some of his finest prose works such as "Der Baron Bagge" are in this category. Most of them have historical settings from classical antiquity and earlier to the present. At times he presents ingenious fictionalized elaborations of scant historical data, as in "Hildebrands Lied" (The Lay of Hildebrand), a tragicomic account of how this early German poem may have come to be recorded. "Mona Lisa" is the story of a young man so infatuated with Leonardo's painting that he is determined to find the young woman portrayed despite assurances by the artist and others that she has died. During his pursuit he becomes guilty of various crimes and is executed. The novella is another exposition of one of Lernet-Holenia's dominant themes: the desperate pursuit of something that no longer exists. "Maresi," about the fate of a man and his horse, represents symbolically and on a small scale what the author described so often with a more panoramic view: the decline of a cultural era and its society with attempts by individuals to retain their personal dignity and integrity amid the chaos. "Der 20. Juli" (The 20th of July) pictures a similar situation during the unsuccessful plot against Hitler in 1944. In 1940 during World War II Lernet-Holenia published in Stockholm a story "Die Heiligen Drei Könige von Totenleben" (The Three Magi of Totenleben), a moving recreation of the Biblical story set toward the end of the Thirty Years' War, with three leaders of the fighting nations having a vision of peace instilled in their hearts while witnessing the birth of a child. Again a story about peace published in 1940 could not have endeared Lernet-Holenia to the authorities.

There are a good many essays in Lernet-Holenia's oeuvre, some of them coming out of his historical studies, others more in the vein of fictionalized investigations of cultural-historical questions. Definitely within the essay genre are such scholarly investigations as the attitude of Manzoni to the Christian religion (Lernet-Holenia had translated Manzoni's *I promessi sposi* into German) and his exchange of letters with Gottfried Benn on the nature of modern art. Other essay topics were drawn from various cultures, among them classical antiquity (he assumed that his readers had a humanistic background and often included in his books lengthy passages in Latin), Asia, and America, but he also wrote about such contemporary issues as Hitler's family roots.[12] Themes dominating in his fiction also recur in his essays. In "Die Eroberung von Peru" (The Conquest of Peru) he gave a fascinating description of an excavated sculptured head of an Inca noble whose smile he found captivating. It is a simile both mild and imperious, secure in its supremacy. When Peru was destroyed, all the accomplishments that the Inca dynasties were destined to achieve had reached their culmination, and the smile expresses the calm self-confidence of an ancient culture. If such perfection is doomed in the end, the enchanting smile prevails. The vulgar ordinary world cannot reach it.[13]

History was more than a hobby to Lernet-Holenia. His historical knowledge was formidable and not limited to the western world. His expertise in such specialized areas as genealogy and gemmology was impressive and elicited the respect of professional connoisseurs in these areas. Various essays and biographies show the extent of his research into lesser-known areas and periods, and yet he carried the burden of his scholarship lightly. *Prinz Eugen* (1960) deals with the life of one of the great military geniuses of all times, and *Naundorff* (1961) is about one of the adventurers who claimed to be the legitimate French King Louis XVII during and after the Napoleonic era. *Pilatus. Ein Komplex* (1967) grew out of an excursion in *Der Graf von Saint Germain.* It tackles subtle questions of religious faith by examining the role Pontius Pilate played in the life and death of Christ. The theme is treated in an ingenious way: Upon being asked for a proof of the existence of God that would go beyond the banalities usually offered in such a situation, an erudite and socially eminent canon relates an event from his student days in a seminary. In their leisure hours the young clerics had planned to investigate a very similar question, the veracity of Jesus Christ's claim to be the Son of God, by performing an impromptu stage play, set after Christ's death with the now aging Pontius Pilate having to defend himself against the accusation of deicide. The brilliantly composed narration is set against a rich background of ancient philosophy and history of religion.

Although his own roots were firmly planted in the pre-World War I Austrian society whose conservative social views and values he espoused, the arrogance of some of the scions of an aristocracy long defunct never ceased to annoy Lernet-Holenia and did not escape his scorn, in his personal life as well as in his writings. In his early *Österreichische Komödie* he captured admirably the ways and manners of aristocratic circles. The play is a riotous rendition of the events during a riding and hunting (and mostly drinking) party at a country estate with revelations about the dubious extracurricular activities of some of the people present. It did not contribute to the author's popularity in this milieu. Upon the invitation of a prominent periodical, he wrote a sarcastic essay in 1957, "Adel und Gesellschaft in Österreich" (Nobility and Society in Austria),[14] which he opened by stating that as far as the Republic of Austria was concerned there existed neither nobility nor society. He poked fun at the pretenses of a long noble lineage—he related that attempts have been made to trace the House of Habsburg back to the kings of Troy — and reminded the reader where one ends up, biologically speaking, if one goes back too far in the search of ancestors.

Shortly thereafter he published a novel, *Die vertauschten Briefe* (1958, The Switched Letters), a hilarious story of fraud committed in socially prominent circles and including so many real persons and events that it has been called a *roman à clef*. Five years before his death in 1976 he published a book of partially fictionalized essays, *Die Geheimnisse des Hauses Österreich. Roman einer Dynastie* (1971, The Secrets of the House of Austria: Story of a Dynasty), where he played the *enfant terrible* once more: with much relish he debunked some of the myths dear to many conservative or sentimental Austrians such as the sad love story of Mayerling (as a potential rebel Crown Prince Rudolph was almost certainly murdered), the kindly figure of old Emperor Francis Joseph (the author shows him as incapable of true emotions), the tragedy of Königgrätz, and the fate of some of the archdukes and of several illegitimate offspring of the ruling house. In other essays in this collection he confronted more contemporary issues such as the never-ending to-do about the past pretender to the Austro-Hungarian crown, Dr. Otto Habsburg. Thus Lernet-Holenia horrified two prominent groups in contemporary Austria and owing to his outspoken honesty gathered few friends as he grew older. He turned against the conservatives, not because they were conservative but because he was angered by their sentimental pretenses, and he had little appreciation for progressive groups, especially certain literary rebels, not because of their innovative ambitions but because of their bad manners.

In the end a writer's significance must be sought in his artistic achievement rather than his social and political orientation or engagement. Lernet-Holenia's claim to lasting fame is supported to a lesser degree by his masterful narrative skill and the beauty and perfection of his language, but to a greater degree by his ability to give voice to timeless human experiences that are ineffable except in the imagination and expressive power of great artists.

Notes

1. Cf. Carl Zuckmayer, "Die Siegel des Dichters," *Alexander Lernet-Holenia. Festschrift zum 70. Geburtstag des Dichters* (Wien: Zsolnay, 1967), p. 11.

2. In *Die Literatur* 32 (1930), 679-680, and 33 (1930), 58.
3. Hilde Spiel, "Alexander Lernet-Holenia," *In meinem Garten schlendernd. Essays* (München: Nymphenburger, 1981), pp. 91-105.
4. Lernet-Holenia in *Der Morgen,* 31 January 1927, p. 6.
5. For a fuller discussion of Lernet-Holenia's poetry see Hilde Spiel (note 3).
6. "Baron Bagge." *Count Luna* (New York: Criterion Books, 1956), pp. 78-79.
7. Ibid., p. 81.
8. *Mars im Widder* (Stockholm: Bermann-Fischer, 1947), p. 211.
9. *Beide Sizilien* (Amsterdam: Bermann-Fischer, 1950), p. 241.
10. Ibid., pp. 221-233.
11. *Die weiße Dame* (Wien: Zsolnay, 1965), pp. 102-105.
12. "Hitlers Herkunft." *Götter und Menschen* (Wien: Zsolnay, 1964), pp. 106-121.
13. "Die Eroberung von Peru." Ibid., pp. 51-54.
14. In *Der Monat,* 9/101 (February 1957), 33-43.

Bibliography

I. Works by Lernet-Holenia in German (Selection)

Books of Poetry

Pastorale. Wien: Wiener Literarische Anstalt, 1921.
Kanzonnair. Leipzig: Insel, 1923.
Das Geheimnis Sankt Michaels. Berlin: Fischer, 1927.
Die goldene Horde. Gedichte und Szenen. Wien: Reichner, 1935.
Die Titanen. Wien: Amandus, 1945.
Die Trophäe. Vol. 1: *Gedichte.* Zürich: Pegasus, 1946.
Germanien. Stockholm: Bermann-Fischer, 1946.
Das Feuer. Wien: Erasmus, 1949.

Plays

Demetrius. Berlin: Fischer, 1926.
Ollapotrida. Stage manuscript. Berlin: Fischer, 1926.
Alkestis. Stage manuscript. Berlin: Fischer, 1926.

Saul. Alkestis. In *Die Neue Rundschau,* 1927.
Österreichische Komödie. Berlin: Fischer, 1927.
Kavaliere. Berlin: Fischer, 1930.
Die Lützowschen Reiter. Berlin: Kiepenheuer, 1932.
Die Frau des Potiphar. Berlin: Fischer, 1934.
Glastüren. Berlin: Fischer, 1939.
Spanische Komödie. Wien: Bermann-Fischer, 1948.
Radetzky. Frankfurt am Main: Fischer, 1956.
Die Schwäger des Königs. Wien: Zsolnay, 1958.
Die Thronprätendenten. Wien: Zsolnay, 1965.
Die Hexe von Endor. Stage manuscript. Wien: Zsolnay, 1968. (Expanded version of *Saul.*)

Novels

Die Abenteuer eines jungen Herrn in Polen. Berlin: Kiepenheuer, 1931.
Ljubas Zobel. Berlin: Kiepenheuer, 1932.
Jo und der Herr zu Pferde. Berlin: Kiepenheuer, 1933.
Ich war Jack Mortimer. Berlin: Fischer, 1933.
Die Standarte. Berlin: Fischer, 1934.
Die Auferstehung des Maltravers. Wien: Reichner, 1936.
Der Mann im Hut. Berlin: Fischer, 1937.
Ein Traum in Rot. Berlin: Fischer, 1939.
Mars im Widder. Berlin: Fischer, 1941. Edition confiscated and destroyed. Reissued by Bermann-Fischer in Stockholm in 1947.
Beide Sizilien. Berlin: Suhrkamp, 1942.
Der Graf von Saint Germain. Zürich: Morgarten, 1948.
Die Inseln unter dem Winde. Frankfurt am Main: Fischer, 1952.
Der Graf Luna. Wien: Zsolnay, 1955.
Die vertauschten Briefe. Wien: Zsolnay, 1958.
Die weiße Dame. Wien: Zsolnay, 1965.
Pilatus. Ein Komplex. Wien: Zsolnay, 1967.
Die Hexen. Wien: Zsolnay, 1969.

Short Stories and Essays
(Only collections of stories and the most important
individual stories are cited)

"Der Herr von Paris." *Philobiblon* 8, 1935.
Die neue Atlantis. Nine stories. Berlin: Fischer, 1935.

"Der Baron Bagge." Berlin: Fischer, 1936.

"Mona Lisa." Wien: Höger, 1937.

"Die Heiligen Drei Könige von Totenleben." Stockholm: Fritze, 1940.

"Der 20. Juli." *Die Neue Rundschau,* 1946.

Spangenberg. Ten stories. Wien: Bellaria, 1946.

Der siebenundzwanzigste November. Eight stories. Wien: Amandus, 1946.

Stimmen der Völker. Five stories. München: Bavaria, 1948.

Die Wege der Welt. Seventeen stories. Wien: Herold, 1952.

Monologische Kunst? Ein Briefwechsel zwischen Lernet-Holenia und Gottfried Benn. Wiesbaden: Limes, 1953.

"Adel und Gesellschaft in Österreich." *Der Monat* 9/101, February 1957.

Mayerling. Seven stories. Wien: Zsolnay, 1960.

Das Bad an der belgischen Küste. Twenty stories and essays. Wien: Zsolnay, 1963.

Götter und Menschen. Fifteen stories and essays and one novel. Wien: Zsolnay, 1964.

Die Geheimnisse des Hauses Österreich. Roman einer Dynastie. Nineteen essays. Zürich: Flamberg, 1971.

Pendelschläge. Three stories. Wien: Zsolnay, 1972.

Biographies

Prinz Eugen. Wien: Zsolnay, 1960.

Naundorff. Wien: Zsolnay, 1961.

II. Works in English Translation

Saul, trans. anon. *Contemporary One-Act Plays,* ed. Percival Wilde. Boston: Little, 1936.

The Standard, trans. Alan Harris. London: Heinemann, 1936.

A Young Gentleman in Poland, trans. Alan Harris. London: Duckworth, 1933.

The Glory Is Departed, trans. Alan Harris. New York: Harper, 1936. Also under the title *The Standard.* London: Heinemann, 1936.

Count Luna, trans. Jane B. Greene. New York: Criterion Books, 1956. Also contains "Baron Bagge," trans. Richard and Clara Winston.

"Mona Lisa," trans. Jane B. Greene. *German Stories and Tales,* ed. Robert Pick. New York: Knopf, 1954.

III. Secondary Works in English

Schneditz, Wolfgang, "Alexander Lernet-Holenia," *Books Abroad* 22 (1948), 229–232.

IV. Major Studies in German

Ackermann, Friedrich. "Alexander Lernet-Holenias Gedicht 'Der beth-lehemitische Kindermord.'" *Wirkendes Wort* 11 (1961), 334–344.
Alexander Lernet-Holenia. Festschrift zum 70. Geburtstag des Dich-ters. Wien: Zsolnay, 1967. Contains contributions about Lernet-Holenia: Carl Zuckmayer, "Die Siegel des Dichters"; Friedrich Torberg, "Ein schwieriger Herr"; Siegfried Melchinger, "Poeta Seigneur"; György Sebastyén, "Vermutungen über Lernet-Holenia"; and W. E. Süskind, "Pilatus im Spiegelkabinett."
Ayren, Armin. "Alexander Lernet-Holenia 70 Jahre." *Neue deutsche Hefte* 14 (1967), 118–130.
–––. "Der Helweg. Zu einem zentralen Motiv im erzählerischen Werk Alexander Lernet-Holenia," appended to *Der Mann im Hut.* Wien: Zsolnay, 1976, pp. 289–300.
Brunkhorst, Ingeborg. *Studien zu Alexander Lernet-Holenias Roman 'Die Standarte.'* Dissertation, Stockholm, 1963.
Müller-Widmer, Franziska. *Alexander Lernet-Holenia. Grundzüge seines Prosawerkes dargestellt am Roman 'Mars im Widder.' Ein Beitrag zur neueren österreichischen Literaturgeschichte.* Bonn: Bouvier, 1980. (Studien zur Germanistik, Anglistik und Komparatistik, ed. Arnim Arnold et al., vol. 94).
Pott, Peter. *Alexander Lernet-Holenia. Gestalt, dramatisches Werk und Bühnengeschichte.* Wien: Braumüller, 1972. Wiener Forschungen zur Theater- und Medienwissenschaft, ed. Institut für Theater-wissenschaft an der Universität Wien, vol. 2.
Spiel, Hilde. "Alexander Lernet-Holenia." *In meinem Garten schlen-dernd. Essays.* München: Nymphenburger, 1981, pp. 91–105.

Robert Musil

Michael W. Jennings

When Robert Musil in the essay of 1934 "Der Dichter und diese Zeit" (The Poet and These Times) offered a programmatic definition of the modern author and his place and function in his age, he was at the height of his European renown. Musil had achieved a preeminent position as a German-language author starting with his first novel, *Die Verwirrungen des Zöglings Törleß* (*Young Törless*) of 1906, and enhanced his reputation through a series of brilliant short prose texts and dramas written in the teens and twenties. He had in 1930 published the first volume of his *magnum opus, Der Mann ohne Eigenschaften* (*The Man Without Qualities*), to universal acclaim and had every prospect of quickly bringing the novel to its conclusion. He could not know that the remaining years of his life would lead him into exile, poverty, and near oblivion, nor could he foresee his failure to finish the great novel or indeed any other major work.

Yet Robert Musil belongs to that small group of twentieth-century novelists who successfully captured in fictional form a lasting image of their age. His early work includes unsurpassed examples of an innovative, modernist prose style suited to the investigation of complex psychological states. Like his contemporaries Joyce, Mann, and Proust, Musil gradually moved away from this intense concentration on the individual subject and broadened the scope of his literary investigations to include an entire society. Musil in *Der Mann ohne Eigenschaften* points the modern novel on its path beyond narrative. His novel stages the confrontation of the modern individual with a set of competing yet tragically intertwined ideologies. In the novel Musil emerges as the twentieth century's greatest ironist and one of its premier writers.

The story of Musil's family contains not a single chapter that hints at his aesthetic proclivities.[1] His father, Alfred Musil (1846–1924), a prominent professor of engineering, was an ambitious scholar and administrator. He clearly regarded family life and in particular attention to Robert as impediments to his research. If his son later accused him of provinciality and pettiness, Alfred Musil furnished a model for certain prominent characteristics in the son: not merely the exactitude with which he analyzed even the most apparently marginal of his insights and observations, but the compulsive necessity to be at work and to write.

The father was balanced by a mother who was passionate, emoional, and often willful. Very early in her marriage she entered into a relationship with another engineer, Heinrich Reiter, which was unusual even in the open atmosphere of late imperial Austria. A constant presence in the Musil household, Reiter accompanied the family on their vacations and finally in 1900 moved in with the Musils. It is hardly surprising, having grown up in a household dominated by a ménage à trois, that Musil's writings consistently reflect not only the family tensions that resulted, but especially the atmosphere of illicit eroticism that must have dominated the household.

In his early youth Musil revealed the energy and intelligence of his mature production; he also fell early prey to the nervous disorders that plagued his maturity. For the most part he distinguished himself from his fellows both in the classroom and on the athletic field; he was given, though, to lapses into lethargy. When he was about ten he began to display an independence that defined itself largely through rejection of his parents' values.

His mother solved the problem by convincing Alfred Musil to send Robert to a series of military academies, first at Eisenstadt from 1892 to 1894, and then to Mährisch-Weisskirchen from 1894 to 1897. These five years saw an unbroken series of academic successes, but also a growing impatience with the intellectual limits of the military. His dissatisfaction with a military life had not yet achieved enough definition, though, to prevent his taking the next orderly step toward a military career: he enrolled in September 1897 in the Technical Military Academy in Vienna, where he intended to study ballistics.

The first decisive shift in the pattern of Musil's life came in early 1898, not to a career as an author but to the study of mechanical engineering: Musil transferred to his father's institution, the Technical Institute in Brünn, becoming a certified engineer in 1901. It was during his study at Brünn that Musil began to show the first tentative signs of interest in literature. He attended lectures on literature and the arts at the university in Brünn and began to write for himself in 1897. These sketches, along with poetological pronouncements, reflections on his own experiences, and excerpts from his reading, began to fill the pages of a series of notebooks, a practice Musil would continue for the rest of his life.

Musil's initial literary efforts were colored by his reading of local authors such as Peter Altenberg and Richard Schaukal, but also by his enthusiasm for Mallarmé, Emerson, and above all Nietzsche. In fact it is Musil's reception of Nietzsche that leaps out from these pages and reveals the nucleus from which the mature writer will develop. Musil's reading of Nietzsche is one of the most radical of his time, distinguished from that, for example, of Mann with its fixation on the early Nietzsche of *Die Geburt der Tragödie* (*The Birth of Tragedy*) and its emphasis upon the Dionysian/Apollonian dichotomy. Musil emphasizes in the notebooks Nietzsche's attack on a timeless truth, his perspectivism and radical relativism, and above all his critique of the subject.

The problem of possibility, in some ways the key category of Musil's mature work, derives quite clearly from his reading of Nietzsche:

> It is characteristic of Nietzsche that he says this could be so and that could be so. And one could build one thing on one assumption, something else on the latter. In short, he speaks of pure possibilities, pure combinations, without showing us how any one could be carried out.[2]

Musil begins very early to grope toward a new conception of the self predicated upon Nietzsche's attack on the notion of subjectivity. Musil stresses the discontinuous, random aspects of human thought and action, anticipating the later promulgation of the notion of a man wholly without salient or defining characteristics.

Musil was aware that these ideas could eventuate in a new understanding of literary form: he defines naturalism as one of many possible "systems of coordinates,"[3] remarking that no one has yet found the form to capture the essentially random nature of life, its structurelessness, while still representing it as beautiful. In the Diaries Musil in fact styles himself "Monsieur le vivisecteur," a Nietzschean "brainman" who dissects contemporary culture.

Yet this cold modernism is tempered in Musil's early years by a form of the neo-Romanticism so prevalent in Austria at the turn of the century. Even while thinking of himself as a remorseless vivisectionist,

Musil portrays himself at a window, observing the change from day to night. This is the classical Romantic figure for a voyage beyond reason and into the depths of the unconscious. The diaries contain excerpts from Eduard von Hartmann's pioneering study of the unconscious, from Ricarda Huch, Novalis, and Franz von Baader, one of the central figures in the importation of mystical motifs into German Romantic thought.

Musil's fascination with Romanticism finally took a turn somewhat different from that of other writers of his generation, though. Whereas for Hugo von Hofmannsthal the heady mixture of a repertory of hermetic symbols derived from French symbolism and German Romantic thinking on the possibilities dormant in the unconscious was of primary interest, for Musil it was precisely the more radical fringe of Romanticism, the direct line to the German mystical tradition which was of concern. "The Cartesian 'ego' is the last firm point in epistemological train of thought, it is the certain momentary unity. The 'I' of which the mystics speak is the complex I."[4] Here we border on Musil's specific concentration in these matters. Often portrayed as a dualist who inexorably opposed mystical cognition to discursive reason, Musil was actually concerned to explore the relation between reason itself and those aspects of our lives not yet penetrated by reason. He thus recurs again and again to the word "senti-mental," in which the hyphen stands for the complex of forces which define the economy of thought and feeling. Convinced of the importance of a form of mystical experience in all human life, Musil was equally concerned to discover a rational faculty capable of defining and articulating that experience. His wariness vis-à-vis instrumental reason is characteristic of many of the best minds of his generation.

A year of compulsory military service (1901–1902) also left its mark on Musil. He retained throughout his life something of the posture and dress of the young officer who is also a dandy. The officer's ethos had one other effect: Musil for the first time plunged headlong into a series of sexual adventures. One of the key themes of his diaries would from now on be sensuality.

With the help of his father, Musil in 1902 attained a position as an assistant in one of the leading mechanical engineering laboratories in Europe, that of Julius Carl von Bach in Stuttgart. Ironically enough, it was here, at the height of his intended career as an engineer, that Musil made the final turn from science and toward his humanistic leanings. He felt wholly isolated in the provinces of Wilhelmine Germany; it took this isolation from friends, family, and indeed anything familiar to lend Musil the certainty that the life of an engineer was not for him. In the winter in Stuttgart he formulated a plan to study philosophy and psychology in Berlin. He also began writing a novel.

That novel, *Die Verwirrungen des Zöglings Törleß* (*Young Törless*) is one of the great first novels in German. *Törleß* is nominally a portrait of adolescent life in a military academy. Yet this generic description hardly does justice to Musil's work. While *Törleß* does depict the coming to adolescent consciousness of the young cadet Törleß, with the attendant and painful experiences of awakening sexuality and the struggle for independent critical intelligence, the significance of the concepts and problems with which Törleß — and indeed Musil — struggles far exceed those normally confronted in a novel of puberty.

Sent to an exclusive academy, Törleß enters into a difficult relationship with two classmates, Beineberg and Reiting. The three friends discover that a third classmate, Basini, has stolen from his peers, and they turn this knowledge into a form of brute power over Basini. Humiliated, subjected to a series of homoerotic episodes, and finally tortured, Basini confesses to the theft in order to escape Beineberg and Reiting.

Törleß occupies an ambivalent position in all of this. He is frequently present while Basini is tortured and in fact has his own homosexual encounters with him in the absence of Beineberg and Reiting. Yet Törleß remains removed from his fellows and their activities. He is separated from them by his confusions, by a pervasive sense that the world before him *and* the world within himself somehow remain inaccessible to him: "No, I wasn't wrong when I spoke of a second, secret unnoticed life in things! . . . There is something dark in me, beneath all thoughts, that I can't measure with thoughts, a life that can't be expressed in words and yet is still my life."[5] When Törleß, late in the novel, flees from the academy, he flees less his role in the Basini affair than the intensity and complexity of his attempt to regulate the economy of his thoughts and feelings. This problem has often been characterized as a dualistic incommensurable relation between thought and feeling. Yet Törleß's problem is not the anxiety or impotence which would arise from an irreparable division of our rational and affective capabilities; his confusions stem rather from the attempt to describe the relations between the two realms. He realizes that his two worlds — that which is "bright" and "everyday" and that which is "passionate, naked, and destructive"[6] — intermingle, that he must search "for a bridge, a context, a comparison—between himself and that which stood word-lessly before his spirit."[7]

A good deal of the book's power stems from the carefully main-tained tension between the naturalistic description of milieu and action on the one hand and the infinitely variegated portrayal of Törleß's inner life. The novel's narrative frequently verges on essayism in its attempts to describe the relations between thought and feeling; the narrative impulse all but disappears, the narration spreads out into a morass of description, the formal counterpart to Törleß's own reaction. Thus Törleß's particular way of torturing Basini consists in forcing him to *narrate* his reaction to what has happened, to name his sensations. Yet the world around Törleß is evoked in a way that is convincing and occasionally frightening. When Musil remarked late in life that Basini and Reiting were "proto-dictators" who anticipated the course of Ger-man and Austrian history in the twentieth century, he pointed accu-rately to the effect of his earliest portrayal of a society in crisis.

For all its originality Musil's novel is very much a product of its age. The intensive preoccupation with eroticism ties it closely to the work of Freud, Schnitzler, Klimt, and Schiele. And its exploration of the limits of language's ability to give shape to interiority points to the more general "crisis of language" perceived in turn-of-the-century Austria, a crisis best described in Hofmannsthal's "Ein Brief" (Letter to Lord Chandos). This mixture of innovation and tradition led to an im-mediately enthusiastic critical response. Alfred Kerr's long review in the 21 December 1906 issue of the Berlin journal *Der Tag* was only the first—and in some ways most acute—of a long series of positive evalua-tions. Volker Schlöndorff's 1965 film adaptation (with a musical fantasy for six strings by Hans Werner Henze) attests to the staying power of Musil's first work.

When *Törleß* was published in 1906, Musil had already been studying in Berlin for three years. His teacher was the philosopher and psychologist Carl Stumpf, whose early integration of experimental psychology and phenomenology paved the way for the foundation of the school now known as "Gestalt" psychology. Musil concluded his studies in Berlin with a dissertation on the Austrian physicist and philosopher Ernst Mach.

The years in Berlin were the richest in Musil's life in terms of his personal contacts. One of his earliest Berlin acquaintances, Johannes von Allesch (1882-1967), was also a student of Stumpf's. Allesch proved to be a lifelong friend, one Musil valued not only for his loyalty, but for qualities of mind and sensitivity which Musil would seldom encounter later. Outside his academic work Musil also began to move in Berlin's literary circles. Through his contact with Alfred Kerr he came to know the writers associated with the journals *Hyperion,* whose editors were Franz Blei and Carl Sternheim, and *Die neue Rundschau,* of which he himself would later become an editor. It was also through Kerr that Musil met Martha Marcovaldi.

After his long and often painful affair with a young woman of proletarian origins, Herma Dietz, Musil had longed for a partner with whom to share his life and ideas. Martha Heimann Marcovaldi had been raised in an assimilated Jewish family in Berlin. Her artistic leanings were evident early; she eventually studied with Lovis Corinth and attracted considerable attention in the Italian artistic community. When Musil met her in 1907 at the Baltic resort town of Graal, she had been married twice. Seven years older than Musil, Martha in many ways represented a particular sort of German modernist: she was an outspoken feminist and advocate of sexual freedom, an accomplished painter, in short, in her situation, dress, and bearing a member of the avant-garde. Musil's letters home and to Allesch were soon full of references to Martha as his "married sister." Sexual relations that transcended the bourgeois norm certainly played a large role in solidifying their bond; Musil spoke often of their "strong, inward directed sexuality." They were married in April of 1911 in Vienna.

More than two years passed between the completion of the dissertation and the publication of Musil's next works, the novellas *Die Vollendung der Liebe* (The Perfection of Love) and *Die Versuchung der stillen Veronika* (The Temptation of the Quiet Veronika), which were published together in 1910 under the title *Vereinigungen* (Unions). The long gestation of these short texts points to Musil's struggle to discover a formal vocabulary adequate to the expression of his ideas on psychology. After the writing of *Törleß* he had recognized that realism represented only one possible "coordinate system," and indeed one which too often excluded the realm of the sentimental. In the two novellas Musil sought a formal vocabulary capable not so much of the *representation* as the *exploration* of those states of consciousness in which the boundary between affectivity and rationality becomes indiscernible. The thematic center of the two works, the problem of infidelity and *Fernliebe* (love directed towards an absent or nonexistent object, i.e., a form of what Rilke called intransitive love) as they relate to the establishment of identity, is well suited to this sort of exploration. The result was two of the most radically experimental of all modernist texts.

The tendency in *Törleß* toward the abandonment of the linear narrative impulse is intensified here: the "plots" of the two novellas consist of little more than the evocation of interpersonal situations that are in themselves quite banal. In *Die Vollendung der Liebe* a woman travels by train to a distant town and there betrays her husband. In *Die Versuchung der stillen Veronika* a woman rejects the advances of the more spiritual of two brothers in favor of his animalistic sibling; ultimately even this temptation is rejected in favor of an autoeroticism of an astonishing intensity. In place of action and indeed even of character the reader encounters an attempt to make transparent the awakening self-consciousness of the protagonists. The stream of traditional narrative is allowed to come to a standstill, to spread out in pools of a unique combination of figurative language and philosophical reflection on the psyche:

> She no longer knew what she thought; a desire for being alone with alien experiences quietly took hold of her. It was like the play of the lightest, most incomprehensible disturbances and of great, shadowy movements of the soul grasping for them. She tried to remember her husband, but she found of her almost past love only a curious image, like that of a room with long-shut windows.[8]

In *Vereinigungen* Musil experiments with the possibilities of the simile as a stylistic analog to this theme, a device that accurately portrays the neither/nor, both/and character of certain moments of being. In *Die Vollendung der Liebe* alone Musil employs 337 similes; this elaborate refusal to opt for either psychic reality or its imagined description is reinforced by 151 subjunctive constructions.[9] The combination of this thicket of similes and the static patient narrative representation of consciousness lends to these novellas a unique oneiric quality. *Die Versuchung der stillen Veronika* and *Die Vollendung der Liebe* are not easy to read: they have the density, complexity, and angularity of other classic works of high modernism, qualities reminiscent of Schönberg's music or Picasso's cubist canvases. They stand as two of the most daring formal experiments in the German language.

In 1910, at the age of thirty and the author of two books, Musil was still supported by his parents. Now, contemplating marriage and seeing for the moment no possibility of earning a living through literary activity in Berlin, Musil returned, with extreme reluctance, to Vienna. His father had arranged through friends for a position in the library of the Technical Institute (Technische Hochschule). Musil began work in January 1911; what was to have been a brief return home turned into three years of well-paid but exhausting and frustrating employment. The period during which he worked at the library is marked not only by repeated serious illness but especially the almost total failure to write. There are, for example, almost no journal entries for the year 1912. Musil's isolation and resentment were not only exacerbated by his work; he found the intellectual life in Vienna stifling. The efflorescence of the arts that Vienna had enjoyed at the turn of the century was now on the wane; the important strands of German-language modernism were tied increasingly to Berlin.

Between 1911, the year of the publication of *Vereinigungen,* and 1921, when his drama *Die Schwärmer* (The Enthusiasts) appeared, Musil completed not a single work of imaginative literature. This is not to say that he was not productive: after the lacuna referred to above, the notebooks again swelled, as drafts and materials for an array of later works filled their pages. In addition these years saw the highpoint of Musil's essayistic production. In 1913 alone Musil published eleven important essays in Franz Blei's journal *Der lose Vogel* and in *Die neue Rundschau.* These essays show Musil moving away from the fascination with decadence and aestheticism that had characterized too much of his early work and indeed that of his generation. The relentless introspection of *Törleß* and the novellas in *Vereinigungen* would be supplanted in years to come with a highly developed sense for the dialectical relationship between the individual and his society. In an essay like "Moralische Fruchtbarkeit" (Moral Fruitfulness) Musil hints at a new understanding of literature as a tool of *moral* and not simply psychological analysis.

Musil had visited Berlin whenever possible in the years before the war, and the chance to return for what promised to be an extended stay came in late 1913. Samuel Fischer, the publisher of *Die neue Rundschau,* the leading literary journal of the period, offered Musil a position as editor. The journal, which espoused a moderate democratic liberalism, had built its reputation primarily upon its literary offerings. An emergent German modernism, with authors such as Thomas Mann and Hesse, appeared in its pages alongside the work of established foreign models such as Hofmannsthal, Wilde, Maeterlinck, and Ibsen.

Musil immediately resigned from the Austrian civil service and returned to Berlin in December 1913. He saw the new post as a real opportunity to further his career, as it offered him not only a congenial atmosphere for his own writing, but also contact with other similarly inclined artists, something he had sorely missed in Vienna. The change of venue and profession proved short-lived.

Musil, a reserve officer since 1911, was called up immediately on the outbreak of World War I. Musil served with distinction, first in command of a company and then as a battalion adjutant, on the war's southwestern front in southern Tyrolia. The diary entries for these years alternate between a sober recounting of the routine of military service and the highly conscious reworking of individual observations for subsequent use in literary works: the novellas "Grigia" and "Die Portugiesin" are deeply colored by Musil's war experience. In March 1916 Musil's active service was brought to an end by a serious stomach ulcer; after six weeks in various hospitals he was reassigned to the headquarters of the southwestern army group in Bozen, Austria.

Musil's new assignment was as editor of the *Soldaten-Zeitung* (Soldier's Newspaper) of the southwest front. Under Musil's direction and at the express wish of the general staff the publication took shape as a professional and highly sophisticated organ for the dissemination of information and propaganda. Musil's own contributions to the newspaper are notable largely for the first appearance of that mode of literature that was to characterize so much of his later production: satire. The command to discontinue the paper, which came in March 1917, meant for Musil a series of transfers, first to Adelsberg near Trieste, and then to Vienna, where he served on the staff of the propaganda journal *Heimat* (Homeland).

As the director of the propaganda unit of the military press headquarters in 1918, Musil found himself reporting on the defeat and collapse of an empire. He remained in his position as an imperial functionary until December 1918 and transferred his services to the new Austrian Republic in January 1919. His work in the press section of the Austrian Foreign Office consisted in collecting and indexing newspaper reports relevant to the foreign policy of the new nation. Musil found considerable cause for humorous irony in his new situation: he styled himself the "archivist of newspaper cuttings," a vocation that found its way, like so much else, into *Der Mann ohne Eigenschaften*.

The end of the war, the dissolution of the empire, and the creation of the new Austrian Republic prompted a rapid series of essays from Musil. These essays, "Skizze der Erkenntnis des Dichters" (1918, Sketch of the Poet's Cognition), "Der Ánschluß an Deutschland" (1919, The *Anschluß* with Germany), and especially "Die Nation als Ideal und als Wirklichkeit" (1921, The Nation as Ideal and as Reality), are only in a limited sense political essays. They deal, to be sure, with the contemporary problems confronting Europe—with the peace of Versailles, with the establishment of a new identity for an Austria shorn of its empire, and with the nature of the state under democracy—but Musil's approach remains that of a humanist concerned primarily with cultural issues. The state and with it political life emerge here as more than the ghostly presence they had remained in Musil's early art and essays, yet the state and political life remain clearly marked out as the *horizon* against which the individual and his development takes place and can be measured. For Musil the questions of European direction remain radically individual questions: what will the new European person be like? Individuals, not collectives and certainly not states, which are for Musil little more than abstract categories invested with a brutal power, will determine the shape of the new civilization. Behind these positions lie, of course, a self-understanding as the heir of Emerson and Nietzsche, the advocate of the strong self-reliant individual; the repeated insistence upon the absolute uniqueness of each human, however, points to a Kierkegaardian element in Musil's thinking that is too seldom acknowledged. In differentiating the poet from the man of reason, Musil points precisely to the ability to recognize the radically individual, the exception to the rule of regularity and law. In his famous distinction, articulated in "Skizze der Erkenntnis des Dichters," between the "ratioïd" and the "non-ratioïd," that is, the distinction between that which is susceptible to rational understanding due to its facticity or regularity and that which eludes rational comprehension because of its endlessly variable and individual character, Musil attempts to delineate the sphere in which literature plays a leading role. The poet must above all else be sensitive to that aspect of life which is essentially reactive: human reactions to the world and to other humans. "The task is: to discover ever newer solutions, contexts, constellations, variables, to suggest prototypes of courses of events, to *invent* the inner man, tempting models of how to be human."[10] Literature becomes in Musil's hands a powerful tool of moral analysis. Throughout the essays of the immediate postwar period Musil develops the central aspect of his mature thought, the tendency which the title of his novel attempts to define. Musil was intensely aware of the complexity of moral action and especially of the tendency of western high capitalism to reduce this complexity, to conceptualize and finally reify it. The new European must thus be without qualities, that is, he must be eternally plastic, undefined, variable, if he is to resist the dehumanizing forces around him.

The astonishing outpouring of new literary work in the years 1921 to 1924 represents Musil's answer to his own challenge. In the dramas *Die Schwärmer* (1921, The Enthusiasts) and *Vinzenz und die Freundin bedeutender Männer* (1923, Vinzenz and the Girlfriend of Important Men), and especially in the novella collection *Drei Frauen* (1924, Three Women), Musil not only establishes several of the experimental, prototypical forms of life called for in the essays, he also for the first time allows for the interaction of these inventions and a sociopolitical environment.

Die Schwärmer is Musil's imaginative exploration of those same issues with which he wrestled in the essays. Like the plots of the novellas in *Vereinigungen,* the dramatic action of the play turns on a banal, almost clichéd situation: seduction and the breakup of a marriage. Anselm, a philosophical seducer, has torn Regina away from her husband, the professor Josef. They have sought refuge in the home of Regina's sister Marie and her husband Thomas. Thomas, the protagonist, is that typical Musilian hero: pure possibility, unpredictability, the refusal to be frozen by concepts or ideals. "Ideals," says Thomas, "are dead Idealism."[11] Interestingly enough, many of these same qualities, or rather lack of qualities, apply to his opponent, Anselm. The two figures are finally differentiated by their language. Thomas emerges as the champion of an intellect intensely, indeed almost morbidly, aware of the complexity of human ethical behavior and of the difficulty of finding linguistic forms adequate to this complexity; Anselm shows himself in his speech to be less fluid than simply unstable, less distanced from the convention and repression of society than compulsively driven to destroy it. Thomas's language retains a beautifully unfixed quality that stands in stark contrast to the increasingly debased because inauthentic language of the seducer Anselm.

The contemporary situation is presented in the play through Musil's use of types and, more generally, in the portrayal of all human action as inevitably compromised. In Josef Musil caricatures the unthinking bourgeois adherence to moral norms and ideals. Josef is the twentieth-century man of reason who applies tools appropriate to the ratioïd realm to aspects of non-ratioïd forms of life, that is, to morals. Stringent moral judgments as to right and wrong blind him to the complexity and nuance which characterize the relationships in the house in which the play takes place. Stader, the detective hired by Josef to unmask Anselm as a fraud and thus to bring Regine back, represents an ever more extreme example of the dangers arising from the false application of rationality. A "scientific" detective, Stader believes that the marriages and the lives they contain can be sorted out through the amassing and analysis of factual evidence. The judgmental hubris of Josef and Stader contrasts sharply with Thomas's absolute refusal to judge. Even as Anselm gradually tears Maria, Thomas's wife, away from him, Thomas proves incapable of stopping or condemning him.

Musil's comedy stands alongside Hofmannsthal's *Der Schwierige* as one of the great German-language comic dramas of the century. Like Hofmannsthal, Musil examines the position of the outsider in a society increasingly unwilling to address the changes necessitated by new political, social, and economic conditions, a society content to fall back on the mores and, more damningly, the language of the fallen empire. The challenges presented by Musil's drama to theatrical performance are considerable; the almost total absence of action, the extreme subtlety of the language, and the play's resolutely cerebral nature represent genuine obstacles. The first performance in Berlin in 1929 was a bowdlerization, with the play cut in half. Musil, who was in attendance, afterwards stormed through the Berlin streets and could be calmed only as morning approached. More recently, however, the play has found its place in the repertory of Germany's and Austria's major houses.

Although the volume *Drei Frauen* appeared a year later than *Die Schwärmer,* the three novellas that it contains reached far back into Musil's past. "Tonka," the account of a young man's epistemological crisis, makes use of notebook entries from as early as 1903, while sketches for "Grigia" and "Die Portugiesin" (The Portuguese Lady) appear in the notebooks from the war years. The novellas are tied by common themes: in each a strong male protagonist discovers in the encounter with the titular female figure what Musil calls "the other condition," the dimension of life which is "mobile, singular, irrational." In each case eroticism is the trigger for this turn inward to an epiphanic mystical experience. The three novels can be seen as Musil's answer to his own challenge, expressed in the essay "Skizze der Erkenntnis des Dichters," to "invent the inner human"; the protagonists of the three novellas represent three radically different experimental instantiations of the "other condition." In search of a firm sense of identity each of the three emerges instead with a deep sense of the shifting deeply un-settling character of that identity.

The protagonist of "Grigia," Homo, the modern engineer at work in an Italian valley so remote that its inhabitants preserve primitive cultural and social practices, satisfies his longing for his wife through sexual encounters with Grigia, a peasant woman of the valley. The con-stellation of an eroticism both real and imagined indeed opens him to a mystical experience: "He sank to his knees between the trees with the poison-green beards, spread out his arms, and he felt as if someone had at that moment taken him out of his own arms. He felt the hand of his lover in his, her voice in his ear, it was as if every place on his body had just been touched for the first time, he sensed himself as a form shaped by another body."[12] As the subtly negative description of Homo's nat-ural surroundings indicate, though, the preconditions for a productive encounter with the irrational are wholly absent: a parallel is established between the capitalistic exploitation of the valley and its inhabitants on the one hand and Homo's sexual subjugation of Grigia on the other. Homo understands his epiphanic insight as a revelation to him alone, and his messianic pretensions lead directly to a form of solipsistic amor-ality and death. In Homo Musil experiments with a life that shows that a mere openness to the irrational is insufficient and dangerous.

At the other pole in *Drei Frauen* stands the nameless protagonist in "Tonka"; strongly autobiographical, the novella is a reworking of Musil's accounts in his diaries of his relationship with Herma Dietz be-tween 1905 and 1907. The protagonist, a young engineering student, is confronted with a stark and apparently insoluble contradiction: the young woman from the proletariat with whom he lives has contracted a venereal disease for which he cannot be responsible, yet she adamantly insists never to have betrayed him. The contradiction between the evi-dence against Tonka, which from a scientific point of view is decisive, and the protagonist's growing conviction of Tonka's own deeply rooted simplicity and honesty leads him to call into question the general applicability of a rational explanation of his world. He discovers, as will Ulrich in *Der Mann ohne Eigenschaften,* that another world exists, "which we don't merely carry in our heart or in our head, but which stands out there exactly as real as the world in force."[13] He is able to transcend, if only temporarily, the rational limits set to knowledge and to perceive something of that "other world" behind appearances.

At the center of the triptych that is *Drei Frauen* stands "Die Portugiesin" with its powerful evocation of Lord von Ketten, a medieval robber knight engaged in an endless and draining war with the neighboring bishop. Having won his wife after an assiduous courtship in her native Portugal, von Ketten returns home to his former existence, spending all but one day and night of each year away at war. Only the unexpected death of the bishop changes this pattern: von Ketten's sense of the purpose and meaning of his life had been defined against the negative horizon offered by the bishop. The loss of this meaning is symbolized in the novella as von Ketten is bitten by a fly and contracts an apparently fatal illness. While he attempts to recover in his own castle, the pitiful nature of his now faded existence is brought home to him as a friend of his wife recently arrived from Portugal seems gradually to usurp his place. He comes to feel that only a miracle can save him, and that miracle indeed occurs in the novella, albeit in highly ironic form: a small cat, similarly afflicted with a wasting sickness, enters the castle and draws the sympathy of all the major figures. Unable to watch the cat suffer further, von Ketten has it killed. In an apparent attempt to avoid the fate of the cat, von Ketten rises from his bed to try to scale the exterior wall of the castle, a superhuman task. When he arrives safely at the top, he finds his strength and will restored to him; sensing that the stranger may be in his wife's room, he finds her instead sleeping alone. Von Ketten's return to ascendancy is signaled by the departure of the stranger the next morning.

It is surely no accident that "Die Portugiesin" mediates between the negative experiment of Homo and the largely positive experience of the protagonist of "Tonka." The key feature of the central novella is its undecidability. Musil's irony cuts through the lush exotic quality of the tale, weighing against the unequivocal interpretation of any of the story's elements, and in particular of the value assigned to von Ketten's encounter with the "other condition." Of all Musil's texts, *Die Portugiesin* conforms most closely to his own demand for fluidity and lack of definition; the novella stubbornly resists assimilation to a unified—and unifying—interpretation.

In August 1920 Musil gave up his job in the Foreign Ministry and returned to Berlin, hoping to find an editorial position similar to the one he had occupied so briefly at *Die neue Rundschau* before the war. He met with a total lack of success. Neither Samuel Fischer at *Die neue Rundschau* nor any other publisher was in a financial position to add to his staff. When Musil this time turned back to Vienna in September

1920 it was an all but final return. With the exception of visits abroad and a brief period of residence in Berlin in the early 1930s, he lived in Vienna until 1938. Upon his reutrn he assumed a position in the War Ministry, charged with the reeducation and integration of Austrian officers into the ways of a peacetime democratic army. This well-paid position had a singular advantage for Musil: it made relatively few demands on his time. The great outpouring of literary production in these years is attributable in part simply to the amount of free time at Musil's disposal. The new freedom was, however, to be short-lived. Musil's position was eliminated for budgetary reasons in December 1922.

Musil's estimation of himself as outsider, as someone who found his work "contested, misunderstood, or undervalued as something alien,"[14] stems from more than his self-understanding as a European writer destined to live out his life in a provincial capital. The year 1923 marks a turn inward in Musil, the all-consuming turn to his vocation as writer. There is, properly speaking, very little "biography" to be written of Robert Musil after 1923. In contrast to the war and the period immediately following it, when Musil's engagement with his society and culture were intensive, after 1923 his life became synonymous with the writing of his one great novel. The story of this period is largely the story of Musil sitting at his desk in his apartment in the Rasumofskygasse, wrestling with the enormous amount of material he had assembled for the novel. The only significant breaks in this routine were periodic difficulties with Ernst Rowohlt, his publisher. Rowohlt had, with the appearance of *Vinzenz* in 1923, become Musil's publisher. *Drei Frauen* appeared in 1924; soon afterwards Rowohlt reissued *Törleß*, *Vereinigungen*, and *Die Schwärmer*. And most importantly for Musil, he agreed to pay him a monthly stipend against the eventual completion of the great novel, then without a name or definite shape. The late 1920s offer the repeated dance of Musil promising the first volume of the novel, his dissatisfaction with the finished material, the decision to work on, and Rowohlt's threats to suspend his payments.

The struggle with the novel and his economic circumstances took a terrible toll on Musil; the year 1929 saw a nervous breakdown complicated by a nicotine infection from which he recovered only slowly. His difficulties were of course more than physical; unable to continue wrestling with his materials in 1928, Musil had accepted the advice of his friend Béla Balázs to consult a therapist. Hugo Lukács, an Adlerian analyst, apparently had some effect, since the novel began to move forward again.

Even as he neared the end of the first volume, Musil despaired that his novel would ever be completed. It finally appeared in November 1930 to immediate and unanimous critical acclaim. The widespread recognition that *Der Mann ohne Eigenschaften* was in many ways the definitive modern German novel and Musil its leading practitioner led rapidly to the improvement of his financial and emotional situation. The year 1931 saw the creation of the Robert Musil Society, led by Professor Kurt Glaser, the director of the State Art Library in Berlin, and charged specifically with the provision of an ongoing stipend intended to make possible Musil's undisturbed work on his novel. The possibility of support and sympathy in Berlin was more than enough incentive to induce another move. Musil and Martha arrived in Berlin in November 1931 and remained there until 1933. Residence in Berlin, for all its positive aspects, also led to more direct pressure from Rowohlt. The second volume of Musil's novel was published, not without some reservation on the part of the author, in March 1933.

In *Der Mann ohne Eigenschaften* Musil attempted to write the representative novel of his era, an all-encompassing account of the situation of the European intellectual in the new social, political, cultural, and especially scientific and technological conditions that accompanied the end of the war. Although the action of the novel takes place in the years 1912 to 1914, and although the 1914 mobilization was intended to coincide with the novel's conclusion, it is nonetheless clear that nothing less than the fate of the individual in twentieth-century Europe is the focus of the novel. Ulrich, the protagonist, is that modern individual whose identity and behavior are in constant flux, with no apparent defining traits and no discernible permanent core. In contrast to those other great encyclopedic novels that represent a certain defining moment within high modernism—I am thinking here of novels such as *Ulysses, À la récherche du temps perdu,* and *Der Zauberberg*—Musil's novel conceives this erasure of identity, this lack of definition, as something positive, indeed as something very difficult to attain. Ulrich comes to the realization that the maintenance of *possibility* outweighs any possible involvement with (and inevitably fixedness within) the real.

At the textual level the primary sign of the essential fluidity and lack of definition that characterize Ulrich is the device of essayism. Ulrich is finally nothing more than a shifting textual construction, a momentary nexus in a larger field made up of the prevalent ideas in western philosophy, politics, psychology, and literature. "Essayism" in Musil is thus much more than a narrative mode; it is the constructive principle of characterization in the novel. "[Ulrich] believed it was best to regard and treat the world and one's own life approximately as an essay, which examines, in the sequence of its sections, a thing from many sides, without wholly comprehending it—for a wholly comprehended thing instantly loses its contours and melts into a concept."[15]

Any discussion of *Der Mann ohne Eigenschaften* must begin with the acknowledgement that the novel remains a fragment. The first volume of 1930 contains two parts. The first, "Eine Art Einleitung" (A Sort of an Introduction), comprises a relatively brief account of Ulrich's development—the early attempt to become a man of significance by beginning, successively, careers as a soldier, an engineer, and a mathematician—and his situation in life. The justification for Ulrich's flight from a fixed identity and a fixed system of beliefs occurs, however, not at that level of the novel that depicts Ulrich himself, but rather in the satirical, epic depiction of Austrian (or rather Kakanien, the name Musil uses for Austria under the monarchy) society.

The second section is entitled "Seinesgleichen Geschieht." The title of this section is central to an understanding of its subject: the German words mean, first of all, "something like it happens," but also "something like *him,* i.e., Ulrich, happens." The society, in other words, is in search of that same identity and definition that had been of such importance to the young Ulrich. The 600-page second section narrates the foundation and activities of the "Parallel Action," a committee attempting to organize a celebration of the jubilee of Franz Josef's rule. Conceived as a "parallel" to the similar celebration of the German Kaiser's reign, the parallel action figures as Musil's typological analysis of the upper strata of Austrian society, including representative types from the bourgeois bureaucracy upward. Musil depicts a society and a culture that is not so much exhausted as ossified, locked by a rigid structure of beliefs, approaches to the world, and *idées fixes* onto a path toward defeat and war.

The most prominent figure on this vast stage is Ulrich's primary opponent, Arnheim. Like Anselm in *Die Schwärmer,* Arnheim bears a striking resemblance to the protagonist. Like Ulrich, he is concerned with questions of the balance of "rationality and soul" in human affairs. Unlike Ulrich, though, Arnheim claims to have *found* that mystical balance; based loosely upon the figure of Walther Rathenau, Arnheim becomes the prophet of a new European order. Ulrich's call for the establishment of a secretariat for "Exactitude and Soul" is intended as a rebuttal to Arnheim, as an assertion that these matters admit of no definitive resolution.

Ulrich's infrequent attempts to imbue the parallel action with his own principles, or rather careful lack of principles, do not constitute the only suggested alternatives in the novel to the present course of society. Moosbrugger, an apparently insane sex murderer, figures in some ways as the window onto another possible form of reality; he exists at "the edge of possibility." Yet all attempts to open the parallel action to new courses of action meet with defeat. Having called, in that half earnest, half ironic tone that characterizes so much of the narrative, for the creation of a Secretariat for Exactitude and Soul, and having found no echo, Ulrich withdraws from the movement and into a dangerous and provocative liaison with his own sister, Agathe. The novel's third section, which recounts this relationship, is entitled "Ins tausendjährige Reich" (Into the Thousand Year Empire). It is not altogether a matter of historical coincidence that this volume and Adolf Hitler appeared to the world simultaneously.

Ulrich and Agathe form in the course of part two an intimate union. They voyage together toward a state—the "other condition" which had been so important to Musil's work since the early 1920s—in which exteriority and interiority might be bridged. The other condition is more than mystical ecstasy, it is a form of self-love open to infinite possibility and variation. Ulrich and Agathe are brother and sister, in fact twins, spiritual siamese twins, in whom the separations between individual identities become increasingly blurred. Like Moosbrugger, they journey to and beyond the border of that held to be morally permissible. But their action itself is less important than their linguistic attempts to get at the essence of their actions. It is indeed by no means clear whether the novel would have included a portrayal of the consummation of their union.

The "meaning" of Musil's novel turns on the manner in which the reader constructs the connection between the parallel action and Ulrich and Agathe's intensely felt form of love. Both are marked by an intense though always frustrated longing for wholeness and unity, whether these qualities inhere in the individual, the family (Ulrich and Agathe are, after all, a family), a society, or the state. Both stand as possible modes through which to experience the world, to bridge the gap between feeling and perception. Georg Lukács's characterization of the path of the European novel from the nineteenth century "big world" of society and its complicated net of relationships toward the "small world" of the individual and his subjectivity is rendered proleptically in Musil's novel. Whereas the consequences of this movement are for Lukács unambiguously negative, the connection is more problematic for Musil.

He labored in his final years to complete the novel. His papers contain hundreds of pages of fragments and entire sections of the novel that would have gone into the completion of part three and into the conclusion, "Eine Art Ende" (A Sort of an Ending). But the resistance to closure so evident at every level of the novel—in Ulrich's very incompleteness, in the open, ultimately destabilizing effect of the narrator's ironic voice, and especially in the characteristic eschewal of linear narrative, "plot," in favor of "essayism," the tendency toward reflection and analysis that dominates the novel—strongly suggests that even a completed *Mann ohne Eigenschaften* would have remained radically open. Musil once said that he wanted the novel to end in the middle of a sentence, with a comma.

Hitler's ascent in Germany was followed immediately, in early summer 1933, by Musil's voluntary return to Vienna and to renewed financial worries. With Hitler's accession to power the Berlin Musil Society ceased to exist, its members either in exile or unable to continue their financial contributions. The publication of the novel had made a difference, though. Voices—among them that of Thomas Mann—were immediately raised in support of Musil, and Bruno Fürst was able to form a new Musil society in Vienna in spring 1934.

The mid-1930s saw Musil ensconced again in the Rasumofsky-gasse, at work on the second half of his novel. In 1935 appeared Musil's last significant publication, *Nachlaß zu Lebzeiten* (Pre-posthumous Legacy), a collection of short prose pieces most of which had appeared in newspapers and journals. Best known for its inclusion of the novella "Die Amsel" (The Blackbird), *Nachlaß zu Lebzeiten* has been consistently undervalued by Musil's critics and readers. His mastery of this form, the very short prose piece, in such texts as "Das Fliegenpapier" (Flypaper) and "Triedere" places him alongside Kafka as that author who has best opened the short, almost fragmentary, sketch to the possibilities of modernity.

In these years Musil was again beset with problems with his health and his psychological state. Dr. Lukács was again able to help him overcome his inhibitions regarding his work, but Musil in 1936 suffered a stroke. Although he was able to recover to a large extent, he never again felt that his health could support the work he needed to accomplish.

Musil in 1937 delivered two of the best known of his speeches, "Der Dichter in dieser Zeit" (The Poet in These Times) and "Über die Dummheit" (On Stupidity), further attempts to define the character of the age and to awaken Europe to the threat posed to its culture. "Über die Dummheit" in particular aroused considerable interest as a definitive characterization of the age; Musil repeated it several times in Vienna, and the Bermann-Fischer Verlag, which had purchased the rights to Musil's works from Rowohlt, published it that same year.

The *Anschluß* of Austria into the Third Reich in March 1938 marked another break in Musil's pattern of residence. Following a visit from a representative of the Propaganda Ministry, who requested Musil's services, Musil quietly left Vienna, much as he had left Berlin five years before. Traveling in summer to Italy, purportedly to restore himself to health, he turned next to Switzerland in September 1938 and established himself in a small hotel in Zurich. Musil and Martha spent ten months in Zurich, continuing to labor over the continuation of the novel, maintaining correspondence with that circle of readers and friends without whose intellectual sustenance Musil was unable to work, and, as always, seeking financial support. Of Musil's Zurich acquaintances, the friendship with Pastor Robert LeJeune stands out. LeJeune's aesthetic proclivities and critical insight replaced some part of the intellectual and cultural stimulation the Musils had left behind.

Yet the letters and notebooks of the period record Musil's increasing feeling of isolation. Like the other great German literary figures living in exile, Musil found himself deprived of publishers and readership alike; his situation was in many ways worse, though, than that of a Mann or a Brecht. Musil's readership, and especially that of the great novel, had even in the best of times been limited to a narrowly defined segment of the intelligentsia. Now from his vantage in Zurich Musil saw his peers such as Mann establish themselves, however tenuously, in such a way as to continue as German intellectuals and writers. Musil's reaction shows his increasing desperation: he moved again after only ten months in Zurich, this time to Geneva, definitively severing the tie to German-language culture. In Geneva he moved four times in two years, always in search of the ideal working conditions for the completion of the novel. In Zurich there had been at least some echo from the community; in Geneva Musil found himself alone and unknown. He emerged from his retreat only once more, to read from his works at a reading organized by LeJeune in Winterthur. One of the greatest living German-language authors of his age found fifteen listeners awaiting him. One last hope, for emigration to America, was shattered in 1940. Einstein and Mann attempted to persuade the Rockefeller Foundation to grant Musil a stipend, but without scholarly credentials nothing could be done.

Martha Musil found her husband collapsed on the floor of the bathroom on 15 April 1942, the victim of a massive stroke. Eight friends appeared at the funeral, after which Musil was cremated. Martha retained his ashes until her departure for America, when she scattered them in the woods near Geneva.

Musil left behind him thousands of pages of notes and drafts for the novel. He had worked feverishly to the very end, leaving behind whole chapters which, in their polish and complexity, approximate the published sections of the novel. What is missing, however, is any sense of how the various drafts and completed chapters were to be ordered. Martha published a tentative reconstruction of the continuation of the story of Ulrich and Agathe in 1943. In 1952 Rowohlt published the novel as edited by Adolf Frisé. This edition, which contains a new ordering of the posthumous material, met with violent criticism from Musil's critics. A third edition, also edited by Frisé, appeared in 1978; it contains a much larger, but by no means complete, selection from the posthumous papers and still another tentative ordering of the more polished material. A historical-critical edition of Musil's text remains a *desideratum*. The uncertain textual status of Musil's masterpiece has not, however, detracted from its acknowledged position as a major monument of twentieth-century European culture. And the very openness of his novel in its final form will continue to remind Musil's readers that he was the author of the possible.

Notes

1. The biographical information in the essay is based on Karl Dinklage, "Musils Herkunft und Lebensgeschichte" in K.D., ed., *Robert Musil. Leben, Werk, Wirkung* (Hamburg: Rowohlt, 1960), pp. 187-264 and on David S. Luft, *Robert Musil and the Crisis of European Culture, 1880-1942* (Berkeley: University of California Press, 1980).
2. Robert Musil, *Tagebücher* (Hamburg: Rowohlt, 1976), p. 19.
3. Ibid., p. 118.
4. Ibid., p. 138.

5. Robert Musil, *Gesammelte Werke* (Hamburg: Rowohlt, 1978), vol. 6, p. 137.
6. Ibid., p. 46.
7. Ibid., p. 65.
8. Ibid., p. 167.
9. Jürgen Schröder, "Am Grenzwert der Sprache," *Euphorion* 60 (1966), 316.
10. Robert Musil, *Gesammelte Werke,* vol. 8, p. 1029.
11. Robert Musil, *Gesammelte Werke,* vol. 6, p. 313.
12. Ibid., p. 240.
13. Ibid., p. 298.
14. Robert Musil, *Tagebücher,* p. 665.
15. Robert Musil, *Gesammelte Werke,* vol. 2, p. 250.

Bibliography

I. Works by Robert Musil in German

Die Verwirrungen des Zöglings Törleß. Wien: Wiener Verlag, 1906.
Vereinigungen. München: George Müller, 1911. Contains "Die Vollendung der Liebe" and "Die Versuchung der stillen Veronika."
Die Schwärmer. Dresden: Sibyllen, 1921.
Vinzenz und die Freundin bedeutender Männer. Berlin: Ernst Rowohlt, 1924.
Drei Frauen. Berlin: Ernst Rowohlt, 1924.
Der Mann ohne Eigenschaften. Berlin: Ernst Rowohlt, vol. I (1930) and vol. II (1931).
Nachlaß zu Lebzeiten. Zürich: Humanitas, 1936.
Der Mann ohne Eigenschaften, vol. III, ed. Martha Musil. Lausanne: Imprimerie centrale, 1943.
Briefe, 2 vols., ed. Adolf Frisé and Murray G. Hall. Reinbek bei Hamburg: Rowohlt, 1981.
Tagebücher, 2 vols., ed. Adolf Frisé. Reinbek bei Hamburg: Rowohlt, 1976.
Gesammelte Werke, 2 vols., ed. Adolf Frisé. Reinbek bei Hamburg: Rowohlt, 1978. I. *Der Mann ohne Eigenschaften*. II. *Prosa und Stücke, Kleine Prosa, Aphorismen, Autobiographisches, Essays und Reden, Kritik*.

II. Works in English Translation

Young Törless, trans. Ernst Kaiser and Eithne Wilkins. London: Secker and Warburg, 1955. Also New York: New American Library, Signet Classic, 1964.

Tonka and Other Stories, trans. Ernst Kaiser and Eithne Wilkins. London: Secker and Warburg, 1965. Also as *Five Women.* New York: Delacorte Press, Delata Paperback, 1966.

The Man Without Qualities, 3 vols., trans. Ernst Kaiser and Eithne Wilkins. London: Secker and Warburg, 1953-1960. Also New York: Putnam Capricorn Paperback, 1965.

III. Secondary Works in English

Cohn, Dorrit. "Psyche and Space in Musil's 'Die Vollendung der Liebe,'" in *Germanic Review* 49 (1974), 154-168.

Luft, David S. *Robert Musil and the Crisis of European Culture 1880-1942.* Berkeley: University of California Press, 1980.

Peters, Frederick G. *Robert Musil: Master of the Hovering Life.* New York: Columbia University Press, 1978.

Pike, Burton. *Robert Musil: An Introduction to His Work.* Ithaca: Cornell University Press, 1961.

IV. Major Studies in German

Baumann, Gerhard. *Robert Musil. Zur Erkenntnis der Dichtung.* Bern: Francke, 1965.

Corino, Karl. "Ödipus oder Orest? Robert Musil und die Psychoanalyse," *Musil-Studien* 4 (1973), 123-235.

Dinklage, Karl, ed. *Robert Musil. Leben, Werk, Wirkung.* Hamburg: Rowohlt, 1960, pp. 187-264.

Henninger, Peter. *Der Buchstabe und der Geist. Unbewußte Determinierung im Schreiben Robert Musils.* Frankfurt am Main: Peter Lang, 1980.

Kühne, Jörg. *Das Gleichnis. Studien zur inneren Form von Robert Musils Roman "Der Mann ohne Eigenschaften."* Tübingen: Niemayer, 1968.

Reniers-Servranckx, Annie. *Robert Musil. Konstanz und Entwicklung von Themen, Motiven und Strukturen in den Dichtungen.* Bonn: Bouvier, 1972.

Roth, Marie-Louise. *Robert Musil. Ethik und Ästhetik.* München: Paul List, 1972.

Joseph Roth

Sidney Rosenfeld

The Austrian novelist Joseph Roth had just won major acclaim with the novels *Hiob* (1930, *Job*) and *Radetzkymarsch* (1932, *The Radetzky March*) when Hitler's rise to power drove him into exile and denied him his German publishers and readers. Thereafter, until his death in Paris in 1939—before the end of his forty-fifth year—he lived precariously on advances from his Dutch publishers and with the aid of friends. After the defeat of Nazi Germany he remained for over ten years a virtually forgotten writer, unknown to a whole generation of readers who had grown to maturity during the Third Reich. Although a collection of appreciative essays and reminiscences commemorating his life and work appeared in 1949 (*Joseph Roth, Leben und Werk: Ein Gedächtnisbuch*), followed the next year by new editions of *Radetzkymarsch* and *Die Kapuzinergruft* (*The Emperor's Tomb*), it was not until 1956, when Roth's friend Hermann Kesten edited his *Werke* (Works), that he was rediscovered for a new audience.

Further landmarks on Roth's posthumous return from exile were the publication in 1964 of a one-volume selection of novels, tales, and essays, which made him accessible to a larger audience, and in 1966 of the fragmentary novel *Der stumme Prophet* (*The Silent Prophet*), reconstructed from variant manuscripts found among the author's literary remains. In a full-page review the critic Marcel Reich-Ranicki attributed Roth's neglect by the literary critics and historians on the one hand to his traditional narrative style and on the other to the near impossibility of defining the "unobtrusive as well as incomparable beauty of his prose."[1] By the time Roth's *Werke* appeared again in 1976, now in an expanded four-volume edition which included a much larger sampling of his journalistic work, the situation had changed once more. Numerous printings, including paperbacks, of individual novels and story collections, a much-reviewed volume of letters (1970, *Briefe 1911-1939*), and of essays (1970, *Der Neue Tag,* [The New Day]) along with a monumental biography by the American Germanist David Bronsen (1974, *Joseph Roth: Eine Biographie*), had helped to secure Roth the critical attention that had been lacking. He was now recognized as one of the most accomplished prose stylists in twentieth-century German literature, as a master storyteller in the tradition of Flaubert and Stendhal, and as a poetic chronicler of the lost worlds of both Eastern European Jewry and Hapsburg Austria. Meanwhile, English translations, mainly reissues of older ones from the 1930s, sometimes revised but also new ones, have introduced Roth to readers in Great Britain and America.

In a letter of 10 June 1930 to his publisher Gustav Kiepenheuer, Joseph Roth described his origins as follows:

> I was born in a tiny hamlet in Volhynia on the second of September 1894 under the sign of Virgo, to which my given name Joseph has some sort of vague relationship. My mother was a Jewess, a strong earthy Slavic type . . . [My father] must have been an odd person, an Austrian kind of ne'er-do-well. He squandered a great deal, probably drank, and died in madness when I was sixteen years old.[2]

This is but one pronouncement among many that confirms the correctness of Hermann Kesten's characterization of his friend Roth as a "Maskenspieler," a player of many roles. While the birthdate is indeed correct, Roth was not born in Volhynia, which at that time formed a part of the Western Ukraine in Czarist Russia; rather, he was born in Austrian Galicia. But because this most easterly of the Hapsburg crown lands was also the most backward and disparaged, he denied it as his birthplace. Nor was he born in "a tiny nest" or, as he was also apt to claim, in the "German colony" of Szwaby (or Schwabendorf) but in Brody, an ethnically diverse town of some 17,500 souls, two-thirds of them Jewish. However, to admit this truth would have likewise revealed the Galician-Jewish origins he was intent on hiding. Thus he also endowed his mother, Maria (or Miriam), née Grübel, a withdrawn anxious woman of orthodox Jewish upbringing, with Slavic characteristics and, so it would seem, hoped to reduce his Jewish identity still further by relating his name, which in reality was Moses Joseph Roth, to the Holy Family.

Roth's father was Jewish too (and not the Austrian as Roth vaguely defines him here, nor as he claimed in still other versions, a Polish count, an Austrian state official, or a Viennese munitions manufacturer). Nachum Roth, who was likewise born in Galicia, was an unsuccessful trading agent. On a business trip shortly before the boy's birth he became deranged and, according to a report, died in 1910 at the court of a Hassidic rabbi in Russian Poland. Roth never saw him and knew little of his fate. He was raised by his mother in the orthodox home of his grandfather Jechiel Grübel. From 1901 to 1905 he attended the Baron-Hirsch-Schule, a German-language elementary school maintained by the Jewish community of Brody. The curriculum included instruction in Jewish religion, Hebrew, and Polish. Roth then attended the Royal-Imperial Crownprince Rudolf Gymnasium and graduated with honors in 1913. Here too the official language of instruction was German, but classes in Polish literature and history were conducted in Polish. The language of Roth's home was German, but along with Polish he also learned some Yiddish and Ukrainian, both of which he heard daily in his native town.

Despite the large Jewish majority in Brody Roth's surroundings confronted him from his boyhood with questions of personal and national identity. For the nationalities problems that were endemic to the vast multi-ethnic Hapsburg empire and finally led to its downfall were a potent force in Galicia too and posed constant challenges to individual and group interests. Thus the political conflicts between Poles and Ruthenians, as the indigenous Ukrainians were termed in Austria, could only aggravate the always insecure situation of the Jews. Although the Jewish masses in Galicia, particularly in the small towns and villages, led a largely separate folk existence, they too were caught up in the conflicts of nineteenth-century nationalist revival and compelled more and more to choose either to assimilate if possible to the predominant ethnic group among which they lived, or to declare their loyalty as Austrians to Hapsburg. This meant in effect that they become Austrians of German language and culture and thus uphold, if only tacitly, the hegemonic policies of the imperial government, which pitted the national interests of one ethnic community against those of the other's. Given this critical constellation of ethnic, cultural, and political forces, it is not surprising that Zionism, the movement for Jewish national renewal, gained powerful impetus among Roth's Galician brethren, just as the drive to establish an officially recognized Jewish nationality with political rights found ever more adherents.

In this context it appears telling for the Jewish quandary that Roth's gymnasium German teacher, Max Landau, was a Polish assimilationist. While he encouraged his pupil's early literary ambitions, he also warned him that the future of Brody was not German but Polish.[3] Two of Roth's Galician-Jewish contemporaries, Bruno Schulz (1892-1942) and Jozef Wittlin (1896-1976), later became major Polish authors. But Joseph Roth rejected both Polish and Jewish national aspirations. Already as a pupil in the gymnasium he aimed to become an assimilated Austrian and a German writer.

Although Roth's stay in the Galician capital of Lemberg, where he attended the university for a semester in 1913, is but scantily documented, one must assume that there too he experienced the same tensions of identity with which he had been faced in Brody. The fact that Lemberg's Polish university had some Ruthenian chairs did little to ameliorate the ethnic conflicts in the city, which in the latter half of the nineteenth century had witnessed not only a blossoming of Polish learning and the arts but had also become the center of Ukrainian national culture, thanks to the emigration of Ukrainian intellectuals fleeing Russian chauvinism. Unlike both groups, however, the Jews, who constituted some twenty-eight percent of the city's population, could make no claims to a national identity and certainly none to a national territory. Thus, in order to secure their own economic and social interests, they had to affiliate politically with one or the other of the two vying groups. This was not an environment in which a young aspiring German writer could envision his future.

When Joseph Roth left Brody and Galicia for Vienna in 1914, his move signified an escape from the national tensions in which he as a Jew was unavoidably caught; because his goal was assimilation as an Austrian, it also meant the departure from the world of his forbears, not only from a place but from a culture and tradition as well. Sentiments and emotions that were profounder than he could know bound him to that world. When he later set some of his most typical novels and stories in the Slavic and Jewish East of the Austrian monarchy, it was inevitably Brody and Galicia from which he drew the inspiration for the tone and color of his figures. "Only there, where he came from, was he not completely torn apart inside," stressed the novelist Irmgard Keun, recalling a trip with Roth to Galicia in 1937.[4] Nonetheless, when the young Roth arrived in Vienna in 1914 to begin university studies in German literature and pursue a literary career, he was determined to shed his Galician-Jewish identity and with it the stigma of squalor and backwardness that it bore.

During his university years from 1914 to 1916 Roth published mainly poems but also short stories and essays, all quite unexceptional, in a popular illustrated newspaper, *Österreichs Illustrierte Zeitung.* In 1916 he broke off his studies and enlisted for military service (a step that may testify to the declared pacifist's fervent wish to become a full-fledged Austrian). While serving in the press corps in his native Galicia, he contributed feuilletons and poems to newspapers in Vienna and Prague. In December 1918, after his discharge, he returned briefly to Vienna and from there traveled to Brody to visit his mother. Then, after an adventurous flight from Brody through the Carpathians and Hungary, he returned once more to Vienna in March 1919. (Roth's claim that he had fought at the front and had been held in Russia as a war prisoner also belongs among the many disparate legends that he wove into his biography.)

For the next five years, until 1924, Roth's writing was almost exclusively journalistic, mainly for socialist or socialist-oriented newspapers in Vienna, Prague, and Berlin. During this time he also published his first novel, *Das Spinnennetz* (The Spider's Web), which appeared serially in the Berlin *Arbeiter-Zeitung* in 1923 but not in book form until 1967. It depicts the rise of its protagonist Theodor Lohse from his petty bourgeois origins through the ranks of the outlawed fascist Right to secret-police chief in the strife-ridden Weimar Republic. In his sweeping portrait of Berlin in the early twenties, Roth reveals both the political-economic forces and the mechanisms of personal psychology that fostered the early Nazi movement under Hitler and Ludendorff, both of whom appear in the book. In the end Lohse is trapped in the web of his own base ambitions, cabals, and debauchery.

The second part of the stylistically and structurally uneven novel is dominated by the figure of Benjamin Lenz, a rootless, opaque, and cunning Eastern European Jewish anarchist bent on the downfall of decadent western postwar society. The double agent Lenz, who humiliates the Jew-hating Lohse in a clash of will and wit, describes his prey in images that evidence Roth's strikingly prescient view of the later Nazi upheaval: "He will beget sons, who will kill in turn. They will be Europeans, murderers, bloodthirsty and cowardly, warlike and nationalistic, bloody churchgoers, the faithful of the European God who guided politics. Theodor will beget children, dueling-fraternity students. They will populate schools and barracks."[5]

Despite his keen insight into the origins and workings of political criminality Roth was not a political thinker. As "Der rote Joseph"—with this sobriquet he sometimes signed articles for the Berlin *Vorwärts*—he sympathized with the outsiders and disadvantaged of Central European bourgeois society and polemicized against their exploiters, but in this early period he abstained from political activism entirely. The "socialist engagement" that has sometimes been ascribed to him appears to have been largely a matter of humane inclination, sincere but without ideological commitment or concrete political result. Rather, Joseph Roth was an acute but essentially impressionistic observer of the human condition and everyday events in both the public and private realms. He was neither an E. E. Kisch nor a Kurt Tucholsky, but he was indebted rather to the inherently conservative Viennese feuilleton tradition of Peter Altenberg and Alfred Polgar, both of whom he extolled in literary portraits. When he did involve himself politically during his exile years in Paris, his basically conservative bent manifested itself in an ardent but thoroughly unrealistic Austrian monarchism.

Between 1924 and 1929 Roth published another five novels, all of which depict the efforts of a war returnee to secure his identity and personal existence in a postwar society undermined by the loss of traditional values. The first two of these, *Hotel Savoy* (*Hotel Savoy*) and *Die Rebellion* (The Rebellion) appeared in 1924 and, like *Das Spinnennetz*, were originally printed serially in newspapers. *Hotel Savoy* appeared in the prestigious *Frankfurter Zeitung,* whose Berlin staff Roth had joined in 1923 and for which he wrote prolifically until 1932, except for a break over salary matters in 1929–1930, and *Die Rebellion* in *Vorwärts,* the Berlin paper of the German Social Democratic Party. Gabriel Dan, the protagonist and first-person narrator of *Hotel Savoy,* wends his way back to Vienna after three years in Siberia as a war prisoner and takes up quarters in the Hotel Savoy in an unnamed city at "the gates of Europe." Dan's encounters and observations in the town and particularly in the hotel are intended to mirror the decay of the economic and social order after the World War. The hotel reflects a vertical scale of human values set according to the guest's ability to pay. The moneyed and respectable guests occupy the elegant lower floors; the top floors house a motley community of dispossessed figures into which Dan is introduced by the vaudeville dancer Stasia. But despite Roth's attempt at symbolic portrayal the microcosm of the hotel does not yield a universal model of social corruption and decay. For this purpose the novel is too confined by the particularity of its setting and the majority of its figures. Both the hotel and the town, which has been identified as Lodz in central Poland, embody specific- ally the spiritually corrupting material aspects of Jewish existence as they persisted in Eastern Europe well after the Western emancipation. In fact, almost the whole gamut of hapless persons who populate the novel are *Ostjuden*. It is their world, not one that could validly reflect postwar Western European society, that Gabriel Dan encounters and describes.

The annual return to this world by Henry Bloomfield, a chari- table native son grown rich in America, and a violent protest by the town's exploited workers and jobless war veterans inject the only move- ment into the otherwise static plot. While prospects of Bloomfield's beneficence stir hopes and schemes among the town's beggars and would-be entrepreneurs, the workers' revolt foreshadows the threat from below to the order of wealth and privilege against which Roth directs his criticism. However, the hotel's destruction by fire is less effective as a symbol of social conflagration than as a narrative device meant to free Gabriel Dan from his role as a passive observer of events, to allow him to move on, and thus to conclude the story.

Roth's next work, *Die Rebellion,* like *Hotel Savoy,* also decries social injustice, but he now depicts its consequences in the misfortunes of an individual existence rather than in the deformations of a collec- tive fate. Andreas Pum, a crippled war veteran, renounces his naive faith in the justice of the state when a legal system biased toward those with title, office, and capital rescinds the organ grinder's license with which a "just fate" had rewarded his civic virtue. Shorn of his illusory belief in the rectitude of the law, before which, as he discovers, all are not equal, in the end he rebels against God—in the name of suffering mankind. In reality, however, Pum's rebellion achieves nothing, since his indictment of God takes place as he is dying in a coffeehouse toilet. Nevertheless, his rejection of divine grace, even though pronounced in a feverish delirium, does rescue his own human dignity from the debasement to which his job as toilet attendant had subjected him. But this does not suffice to offset the profane pessimistic thrust of the novel. At its conclusion exploitation and immorality in the person of Pum's em- ployer, the small-time criminal Willi, prevail.

In 1924 and again in 1926 Roth traveled to Eastern Europe, to his native Galicia, which now lay in Poland, and to the Soviet Union, each time on assignment for the *Frankfurter Zeitung.* The first trip resulted in a series of three articles entitled "Reise in Galizien" (Travels in Galicia). The second trip, meant to placate him after the paper had terminated his coveted assignment to Paris, was considerably more consequential. In seventeen articles published as "Reise in Rußland" (Russian Journey) he described the gains of the Russian revolution, but he also lamented its bourgeois transformation. He found in the Soviet Union a spiritual and intellectual vacuum that he attributed to blind admiration for American material progress. Roth never recovered from this disillusionment. With it began the estrangement from his earlier socialist sympathies, and his political writing and other pronouncements of the 1930s found more and more radical expression.

When Roth's book-essay *Juden auf Wanderschaft* (Jews on Their Migrations) appeared in 1927 in Berlin, it joined a number of similar works of the period on the life of the *Ostjuden*. In 1920, for example, Arnold Zweig published *Das ostjüdische Antlitz* (The Face of East European Jewry) and in 1925 Alfred Döblin his *Reise in Polen* (Polish Journey), to name but two works by major writers, who like many other German Jews had encountered the folk life of their Eastern European brethren for the first time either during war service on the eastern front or through the widely noted performances of Yiddish theater troupes in the West both before and shortly after the war. Joseph Roth, however, wrote from his own deepest and most intimate experience. In his impassioned portrayal of the sorely maligned *Ostjuden* he espouses their traditions and values, opposing them to the spiritual emptiness, as he saw it, of assimilationist western Jewry. With inspired eloquence he depicts the life of the *Ostjuden* both in the "shtetl," the small mainly Jewish towns of Eastern Europe, and in the large western centers of Jewish immigration such as Vienna, Berlin, Paris, and Amsterdam. In a final section he describes the situation of the Jews in the Soviet Union with an overflowing optimism that was not to be borne out by the history of his own century. Ten years later, however, in a new foreword to a planned reissue of the book he proved to have striking discernment. Writing in 1937, still a year before the "Kristallnacht," he says of the Jews who had remained in Hitler's Germany: "The believing Jews have the consolation of heaven. As for the others: 'vae victis'" (III, 369).

Above all through his contributions as feuilleton correspondent of the *Frankfurter Zeitung* Roth had established his journalistic reputation within a fairly short time among a wide audience as a lucid, original, and stylistically brilliant portrayer of people, places, and events. Then in 1927 the publication of *Die Flucht ohne Ende (Flight*

without End) brought his first real success as a novelist. This work together with the two that followed, *Zipper und sein Vater* (1928, Zipper
and His Father) and *Rechts und Links* (1929, Right and Left), led some
critics to regard him as a leading writer of the literary movement *Neue
Sachlichkeit* (new factualism). Originating in the early 1920s, in part as
a countermovement to Expressionism with its excesses of subjectivity,
Neue Sachlichkeit urged a new realism of firsthand observation. It
championed the documentary and biographical or autobiographical
novel and "eye-witness" accounts of social conditions as the sole
adequate means for depicting the problems of the day. As a literature
of social criticism it focused with deep skepticism or irony on such contemporary themes as the World War, industrialization and technology,
reemerging militarism, fascism, and social decay and corruption. In a
piece dedicated to the "living spirit of Emile Zola" Joseph Roth expressly called upon German authors to abandon their desks, as it were,
and confront the political problems of their time. If his praise of Zola
was a summons to respect for historical reality as the thematic material
of literature, the preface to his novel *Die Flucht ohne Ende* was com-
monly read as a statement of aesthetic principle for the movement:

> In what follows I tell the story of my friend and comrade
> Franz Tunda, a man whose views I share. In part I am follow-
> ing his own notes, in part his oral accounts. I have invented
> nothing, composed nothing. "Dreaming things up" is no
> longer what counts. Most important is what one has observed.
> Paris, March 1927   Joseph Roth (I, 317)

Three years later Roth seemed to reject these tenets. In an often cited
article of 1930 aggressively titled "Schluß mit der 'Neuen Sachlichkeit'!" (Enough of "Neue Sachlichkeit!"), he decries the confusion
common among German readers and critics between report and event,
that is, the accepted claim of the writer-reporter to pure objectivity,
and rejects the dictum that true literature can arise only from factual
depiction. The "facts," Roth argues, are merely the material of writing,
and as such they must be formed by language; observations must be
filtered through, and conveyed by, a poetic temperament. Indeed, his
own novels of this period often enough witness the very narrative subjectivity that the movement programmatically shunned. Nonetheless,
both their realism and thematic content legitimately link Roth's name
to the literature of Neue Sachlichkeit as it was represented by its

outstanding exponents (among them Heinrich Mann, Alfred Döblin, Arnold Zweig, Erich Kästner).

Following the pattern of his earliest works the novels *Die Flucht ohne Ende, Zipper und sein Vater,* and *Rechts und Links* again depict Austrian and German society in the period of inflation and the later economic recovery after the World War. Like Gabriel Dan and Andreas Pum, the protagonists are war veterans who discover that they are outsiders and superfluous in the materialistic peacetime world to which they have returned. They reject, or are unable to uphold, the false ideal of bourgeois respectability and success that society imposes on them and succumb to hopelessness or become entrapped in the conformist role into which they have fallen. Franz Tunda's "flight without end" leads him from Siberian war captivity through European Russia, where as a Red Guard he fights in the revolution and discovers its failings, back to Austria. After a short stay in his native Vienna he moves on to Germany. There he visits his brother, a successful orchestra conductor in a Rhenish provincial city, and is repelled by the pretense and shallowness of the bourgeois upper crust. Neither is his disillusionment relieved in Paris, the "capital city of the world." At the end of the novel he stands alone on the plaza before the Madeleine, faced with boundless uncertainty: "He had no profession, no love, no desire, no hope, no ambition, and even no egoism. No one in the world was as superfluous as he" (I, 421).

In a long letter to the protagonist of *Zipper und sein Vater,* which the author-narrator Roth appended to the novel and signed with his own name ("Brief des Autors an Arnold Zipper"), he expressly states his theme: the homelessness of the war generation, embodied by Arnold Zipper, in a world molded by the beliefs and values of its fathers, of whom the memorably portrayed elder Zipper is likewise representative. Although the letter follows the "last" page of the novel, it forms part of it, a narrative device intended not only to declare the exemplary character of the story, but also in the spirit of the "new factualism" to authenticate it as biography. Beyond this, however, Roth sees in Zipper's fate a reflection of his own isolation and impotence as a writer. For he must fear the misapprehension of his novel as an indiscreet "private report on two private lives," whereas he attempted to portray in it the momentous differences and similarities between two generations. Thus *Zipper und sein Vater* also underscores the problems attendant on its reception as a work of Neue Sachlichkeit. Like Franz Tunda in *Die Flucht ohne Ende* Arnold Zipper is an outsider. This condition is movingly underscored at the end of the novel when, after attempts at a career fail and his humiliating marriage ends, Zipper joins a vaudeville act as a violin-playing clown. In brotherly sympathy Roth tells Zipper of the helplessness that they share alike: "Your profession ... is symbolic of our generation of war veterans, who are prevented from performing a role, a deed, a piece on the violin" (I, 528). By closely depicting Zipper's petty-bourgeois Viennese background and his social environment before and after the war Roth shows him both as a victim of his society and, in his weakness and failures, as its helpless accuser.

The unexpected success of Roth's next work, *Rechts und Links,* in 1929 — it was reprinted that same year — prompted its author to suggest that his novel had been misconstrued. Writing in the Berlin journal *Literarische Welt,* he argued that "right and left" did not describe real political positions and at most his book only touched on questions of "primitive politics." The greater part of his discussion, which Roth ironically titled "Selbstverriß" (Panning Myself), goes on to deal in general with the contemporary reader's false notion of literature as a reproduction of "life" and with the false reading of *Rechts und Links* in particular. But his rather strained arguments fail to explain away the discrepancy between the book's title and its conspicuously disparate plot. In fact the brothers Paul and Theodor Bernheim, on whom the novel initially centers, both pursue their goals on the political right and have no antagonist on the left. Paul, to be sure, involves himself for a time in pacifist and revolutionary activities but without binding commitment. Once he returns from the war, he zealously strives after greater wealth and social status than his parvenu father had bestowed on him. His marriage to the niece of the industrialist Enders binds him to a woman he is unable to love and makes him a puppet of her powerful opportunistic uncle.

Theodor Bernheim, like Theodor Lohse in *Das Spinnennetz,* enmeshes himself in the radical right, but Roth falls short of his intent to typify in this younger brother the revanchist generation that spawned the assassins of the German foreign minister Walther Rathenau. Theodor betrays whatever convictions he has by entering the employ of a Jewish-owned liberal newspaper. He does this, moreover, with the scornful patronage of Nikolai Brandeis, an inscrutable Russian-Jewish financial adventurer who comes upon the scene unannounced, so to speak, and thereafter dominates it almost completely. The reader cannot but feel that Roth was unsure of his theme and that the design of the novel had escaped his grip. His biographer David Bronsen concluded that by 1929 a combination of political disillusionment, financial and personal setbacks, and health problems worsened by excessive drinking had brought Roth to a crisis of artistic uncertainty and self-alienation.

In 1922 Roth married Friederike Reichler, a young Viennese. In the same year she joined him in Berlin, where for the only time they shared quarters of their own; otherwise they lived in hotel rooms. While Roth sometimes took his overly sensitive and shy wife along on his assignments, he often left her behind while he traveled extensively. Friederike was but twenty-two when they married, and it has been suggested that Roth's attempts to sophisticate the charming but basically naive young woman may have quickened the onset of the schizophrenia that befell her in 1928. Although there had been early signs of mental illness, Roth blamed himself for her tragedy. For a time he resisted committing her to a mental hospital, but the severity of the disease finally left him no choice. Friederike spent the last ten years of her life in asylums in Austria before she was murdered by the Nazis in 1940.

Roth's financial straits steadily worsened, and writing itself became a trial. Starting in 1929, his letters document more and more the agonies of guilt and despair that scourged him until his death. On 2 September 1929 he wrote to his friend Stefan Zweig:

> I have been living for weeks without being able to write a word, and painfully I force from myself the lines for newspapers that I need so that I can live. I will spare you a detailed description of my condition. The word torment has suddenly gained a terrible content, and the feeling that I am beset by misfortune . . . does not leave me for a second.[6]

Roth was convinced, moreover, that his sufferings were a punishment by God.

To probe the questions of personal suffering and guilt that were harrowing his existence Roth returned in his next novel to the East European Jewish world of his origins. Postwar western society, which he condemned for its idolatrous materialism, could not provide him with the setting for a novel whose theme transcended the social criticism that lay at the heart of his earlier work. In *Hiob: Die Geschichte eines einfachen Mannes* he clothed the biblical legend in the story of a "simple man," the poor Russian-Jewish "children's teacher" Mendel Singer. Whereas in *Hotel Savoy* with its almost exclusively Jewish milieu Roth had only hinted at a positive Jewish content, in his new work the themes of lost and regained faith, suffering and redemption, remembrance and continuity assume prime significance. Though the sorrows of Mendel Singer—estrangement, sickness, and death among his nearest kin—are universal, Roth casts them firmly in the frame of Jewish history in Eastern Europe. What spurs the family's emigration to America is not that Mendel's daughter Mirjam cannot tame her sexual urgings but rather that she indulges her lust in trysts with the soldiers of the nearby garrison, thereby alienating herself from her family and people. Similarly, Mendel's younger son Jonas joins the Czar's army and thus lives by choice outside the pale of Jewish law and tradition. His older son Schemarjah, who has preceded the family to America and is later killed in the World War, Americanizes not only his dress but also his name. As Sam Singer he is no longer entirely his father's son. Menuchim, the youngest son, left behind in Russia as a retarded cripple, is believed dead. Thus Mendel can grieve by the body of his wife Deborah, who has died of heartbreak: "It is a pity that you have left no son behind. I myself have to say the mourner's prayer. But soon I will die, and there will be no one to mourn for us" (I, 940).

The sorrow of Mendel Singer that no son will remain after him to recite the Jewish mourner's prayer is grounded not in fear for his soul's redemption, something that is suggested by neither the prayer nor the story, but in the unspoken concern that with his passing the last bond of his family with the House of Israel will be torn. The ethos that this prayer expresses and the theme that Roth shaped from it describe the principle of Jewish peoplehood that Martin Buber metaphorized as the "chain of generations." In defining the relationship of the individual Jew to his people Buber wrote in his essay "Judaism and the Jews": "The past of his people is his personal memory, the future of his people his personal task."[7] This ethos lends the "miracle" in which Roth's modern Job story culminates, the return of Mendel's son Menuchim, long thought dead, its full meaning. Inherent in Singer's overflowing joy is renewed faith in the continuity of life and the unbroken link between the living and the dead.

Roth's commentators have pointedly noted the flaws of his novel, citing above all the disparity between novel and legend, which is already inherent in the book's title, along with the author's uninformed depiction of America in the story's second part, and finally the somewhat contrived ending. But even if Mendel Singer is unable to regain faith in the God against whom he rebelled without the help of a "miracle," his humanity, as Roth tenderly portrays it, remains unimpaired in its depth and purity. Beyond its merit as a modern legend of renewed faith and love in a world that obscures transcendent vision Roth's *Hiob* now projects new meaning as a memorial to the life and spirit of Eastern European Jewry, which was destroyed in the Holocaust.

If in *Hiob* Roth had paid loving tribute to his Jewish heritage, in *Radetzkymarsch* (1932) he no less passionately declared his faith as an Austrian. In his foreword to the serialized preprint of the novel, which appeared in the *Frankfurter Zeitung* in 1932, he wrote:

> A cruel wish of history destroyed my old fatherland, the Austro-Hungarian monarchy. I loved this fatherland. It permitted me to be a patriot and a citizen of the world at the same time, among all the Austrian people also a German. I loved the virtues and merits of this fatherland, and today, when it is dead and gone, I love even its flaws and weaknesses (IV, 405).

In the fate of his protagonist, the young lieutenant Carl Joseph von Trotta, Roth mirrored the decline and end of this fatherland, which he once called the only one that he had ever had. For Trotta's grandfather, the fabled "hero of Solferino," Austria was a boundless all-embracing homeland, for which he intrepidly risked life and limb when he saved the Emperor Franz Joseph from enemy fire during the Battle of Solferino. Only when Trotta's father, the quintessence of the Old Austrian civil servant, is forced to recognize that the empire is not secure but threatened from within by the centrifugal forces of nationalism, is his belief in Austria's vitality shaken. For the son Carl Joseph, however, Austria is no longer a homeland to whose destiny he can bind his life and yearnings. It has diminished to a name without content, present only in wistful memories of the Radetzky March, played on Sundays by a military band in the Moravian province of his boyhood, and in the slowly darkening portrait of his grandfather, which hangs in his father's house and tells of deeds that he can not emulate.

Trotta's quest for a homeland that could be for him, the pensive irresolute officer without a war, what the empire had been for his grandfather and remained, if uncertainly, for his father, symbolizes Austria's dissolution. It leads him—unawares—to negate the principle of supranationalism upon which the existence of Austria historically rested. His petition for transfer to Slovenia, the home of his peasant forebears, threatens to reverse the full assimilation of his family as Austrians that had been achieved only two generations earlier by his grandfather; that is, in sublimated form it expresses the same nationalism that threatens to undo Austria itself. Thus the elder Trotta admonishes his son when he learns of his request for transfer: "Fate made Austrians of our family of borderland peasants. We want to remain Austrians" (II, 127).

Through the ennoblement of Carl Joseph's grandfather, the hero of Solferino, the Emperor Franz Joseph had taken the Trottas into a new covenant. This covenant is broken by the last Trotta in a personal crisis that in its essence illuminates the actual political crisis that hastened the end of the monarchy. One of the novel's many colorfully drawn figures, the Polish landowner Count Chojnicki, laments the betrayal of the Austrian idea, i.e., the transcendent faith in a multinational homeland, with these words:

> The people no longer believe in God. Their new religion is nationalism. The nations don't go to church. They go to national clubs. The monarchy, our monarchy, is founded on piety, on the belief that God chose the Hapsburgs to rule over so-and-so-many Christian peoples. . . . The Emperor of Austro-Hungary must not be forsaken by God. But now God has forsaken him (II, 161).

Despite the severity of this pronouncement, spoken without doubt in the author's name, Roth's compassionate portrayal of Carl Joseph von Trotta's unfulfilled life and tragic end suggests that he deeply sympathized with what one may regard as a spiritual transformation of the same nationalist tendencies that he adamantly rejected, both in the novel and polemically in numerous articles and essays.

To the end Trotta seeks a return to the home and ways of his Slovenian ancestors. Transferred by the army to Galicia, which he wishfully regards as the "northern sister" of Slovenia, he eventually quits the service and lives for a time among the Ukrainian peasants, but he is unable to return to his family's ethnic past. When the World War breaks out, he rejoins the army in the illusory hope that he can relive the glory of his grandfather. Instead he falls in a rain of bullets while fetching water for his troops. Neither his pedantic unresponsive father nor his elusive fatherland nor the military had been able to nourish his existence. He dies unfulfilled. The elder Trotta, bereft of his only child, dies too—on the day of his Emperor's burial. At the novel's end the wise physician Dr. Skowronnek tells the major of W., the Trottas' provincial home: "I think that neither of them could survive Austria" (II, 323).

Thus does the history of the Trottas reflect the Austrian historical theme: not as a concrete exemplification of the forces that hastened Austria's decline but rather as an intrinsically related phenomenon whose tragic character poetically illumines the tragedy of Austria. By drawing the new national boundaries that dissolved the empire its peoples succeeded where the last Trotta had failed: to return to their forebears.

Radetzkymarsch won Roth lasting esteem as a modern German novelist and, thanks to its memorable treatment of the Hapsburg theme, renown as an eminently *Austrian* writer. In fact Roth's devotion to the Emperor and monarchy, so glowingly evidenced in the novel, soon intensified to an unqualified veneration of the Hapsburgs with inordinate hopes for their restoration in the threatened First Republic. Various friends and colleagues who shared his exile years in Paris have described his politically unrealistic, even bizarre, schemes centered on Otto von Hapsburg and the Catholic Church to save Austria and Europe from Nazism. Roth's fervent espousal of the monarchist cause and his apotheosis of Old Austria as a lost paradise had little to do with political insight. It was rather the ever growing bleakness of his personal and artistic existence that led him to take flight from a hopeless present and to seek consolation in an idealized past. Less than a year after *Radetzkymarsch* had won him widespread critical acclaim without relieving his financial distress, Hitler's ascent to rule robbed him of his major source of income. Despite his later contrary claim evidence shows that his books were among those burned in Germany in May 1933. Considerably before Austria was annexed to the Third Reich his position had become untenable there too. In September 1934 he wrote to his friend and benefactor Stefan Zweig: "Since Hitler the Austrian papers treat me as if I didn't exist. I also no longer have any friends in the editorial offices."[8]

In the years from 1933 until his death in 1939 Roth contributed political articles to exile journals in Paris, Prague, Brussels, and elsewhere. Starting in 1934, his books appeared in Holland with Albert de Lange and Querido, both of whom had created a division for German exile literature. But he soon exhausted the limited income that these writings brought him, and the help of publishers and friends did not save him from constant debt. He was burdened not only by the costs for Friederike's care in various mental hospitals, but during the years from 1931 to 1936 he also helped to support the children of his intimate companion Andrea Manga Bell. In Paris he lived in a single hotel room and was a familiar sight at the café table, where he regularly wrote, drank heavily, and met with friends. For the most part, however, he led a nomadic life. Depending on need and circumstances, he journeyed for longer or shorter stays to Marseille, Nice, Zurich, Amsterdam, Brussels, Salzburg, and other European cities.

All the while he was racked by guilt feelings, and alcoholism was steadily eroding his health. To his ever concerned friend Stefan Zweig he wrote despondently in a letter believed to date from February 1936:

> Humiliated, dishonored, in debt, smiling with clenched teeth. So that the hotel proprietor does not catch on—it's an acrobatic feat—I cling desperately to my pen, keeping rein on the thought that just came to me, because otherwise it will gallop off. At times, I am also hungry, nodding off in my seat after three sentences. What do you want of me, how can you demand patience from a person who is half corpse, half mad?[9]

Despite his extreme personal straits Roth was able to write prolifically during these years. In 1934 alone he published, in addition to his journalistic work, a novel, *Tarabas: Ein Gast auf dieser Erde* (*Tarabas: A Guest on Earth*); two short stories, both of which appeared originally in French, "Le buste de l'empereur" (Die Büste des Kaisers) and "Le triomphe de la beauté" (Triumph der Schönheit), and an apocalyptic essay *Der Antichrist*. This latter work, which Roth called a novel, is a curious hybrid of religious vision, cultural criticism, and political polemic. In rhapsodic cadences, Roth damns the "Antichrist" in his modern-day manifestations as Nazism, communism, anti-Semitism, and the corruptive civilization of technology, for which Hollywood (*Höllewut,* that is, the Hades of modern man) was his prime example. In addition he denounced the signs of the "Antichrist" among Western European Jewry, to whose materialism and assimilationist strivings he had always opposed the spiritual values of the *Ostjuden,* and, because of the Vatican's 1933 Concordat with Hitler, such signs within the Church itself.

Der Antichrist starkly evidences Roth's tendency during his exile years to view historical events metaphysically, to replace reason with belief, and concrete analysis, which had never been his hallmark, with diffuse condemnation. The consequences of this tendency for his narrative prose become especially clear in the Napoleon novel *Die hundert Tage* (1935, *The Ballad of the Hundred Days*). Set in France, it depicts with great poetic license the period in Napoleon's career from his triumphant return from banishment to his final defeat at Waterloo. In a letter of 17 November 1934 to his French translator, Blanche Gidon, Roth delineated his narrative aims: "Je voudrais faire un *'humble'* d'un 'grand.' C'est visiblement la *punition de Dieu*, la première fois dans l'histoire moderne. Napoléon abaissé: voilà le symbole d'une âme humaine absolument terrestre qui s'abaisse et qui s'élève à même temps."[10] Written at a time when Roth's Catholic leanings had become decidedly more pronounced, *Die hundert Tage* seems to have been inspired by religious emotions that blurred the author's sense for narrative scale and conjuration. The wholly personal tale of Napoleon's transformation from a demigod to a God-seeker, who gives up his scepter for a cross, strains to define itself within the novel's broad historical setting. Too often Roth resorts to an over-blown lyricism in order to lend epic quality to the private turns of his protagonist's fate. He had lamented his recourse to history in *Radetzky-marsch,* but in that work he had convincingly portrayed a historical epoch in the individual, or generational, story of a family. In *Die hundert Tage* history becomes a mere backdrop to the intimate story of Napoleon's conversion. Inasmuch as Roth too was disappointed with the novel, he concurred with its general reception by the critics. But aside from his renewed regret at having drawn on historical material his self-criticism reflects the same penchant that contributed to the novel's failings. He called his undertaking "gottlos" (impious) and declared that the Antichrist had lured him to it.

With varying intensity the religious themes of evil and righteous-ness, hubris and fall, penance and forgiveness are likewise central to the three other novels that Roth published between 1934 and 1937: *Tarabas, Beichte eines Mörders, erzählt in einer Nacht* (1936, *The Confession of a Murderer, Told in One Night*), and *Das falsche Gewicht: Die Geschichte eines Eichmeisters* (1937, *Weights and Measures*). Unlike *Die hundert Tage,* all three draw their central figure (or those who surround him) and their setting fully or in part from the Slavic borderlands of Imperial Austria whose life and peoples the author knew from boyhood.

Like a whole series of figures in Roth's earlier novels Nikolaus Tarabas, the protagonist of *Tarabas,* has no home or personal ties. A Czarist officer during the World War and the Revolution, he finds a "great, bloody home" in the army. The new, peacetime army assigns him to Koropta, a tiny town in an unnamed republic, where he is to set up a new regiment. Restive and insecure without license for violence, he feels himself "betrayed" by an uneventful peace. Paper work unnerves him, his ragtag recruits lack discipline, soldiers desert him. One of them, a certain Ramsin, satanically incites Tarabas's drunken soldiers and the peasants who have come to Koropta for the market to a pogrom against the town's defenseless Jews. Tarabas's guilt is indirect: he had failed to uphold order. He vents his exasperation by brutally ripping out the beard of a frail Jew, Schemarjah, upon whom he chances after the pogrom. He himself recognizes this desecration as his real guilt. The man of violence now becomes a humble wanderer. He can find peace only after he is able to beg and receive forgiveness from Schemarjah, the most helpless of his victims. Therewith a gypsy's prophecy at the start of the novel that Tarabas "will sin and do penance" is fulfilled. Despite asymmetries of plot—the pogrom episode, for one, partly displaces the main story line in interest and thematic import—Roth's balladesque narration of Tarabas's religious-moral awakening surpasses his treatment of the same theme in *Die hundert Tage.* Tarabas's turn to faith in its earthly simplicity is more touching and convincing than Napoleon's somewhat melodramatic conversion.

The nocturnal "confession" of Semjon Golubtschik, the first-person narrator in Roth's 1935 novel *Die Beichte eines Mörders,* resembles the tale of Nikolaus Tarabas in several ways. In both the plot is set before the World War and partly in Russia. Also both central figures live for a time in the belief that they committed a murder. Just as Tarabas later learns that the barkeeper in New York, whom he had left for dead, survived his violent attack, Golubtschik discovers that he had killed neither his calculating mistress Lutetia nor his rival and half-brother, the young Prince Krapotkin, whom he had found together as lovers. Further still, like Tarabas, Golubtschik first experiences remorse for his misdeeds after he has claimed a Jewish victim. As an agent of the Czarist secret police in Paris he betrays the Russian-Jewish revolutionary Chana Lea Rifkin, whose nobility of character had won his love. His overwhelming drive to rid himself of his comical surname—figuratively Golubtschik means "darling" or "sweetheart"—

and claim his birthright as the natural son of the wealthy Prince Krapotkin had made of him "a hard-hearted servant of hell," but unlike
Tarabas he experiences no conversion. Thus the drama of his fate
dissolves into banality. After attempting vainly to expiate his crimes
by risking death in the World War he returns to Paris and ends up as the
henpecked husband of his former mistress, now an embittered hag.

In *Das falsche Gewicht*, too, Roth once again narrates the trials of
a private fate. At the same time the novel's ambiguous conclusion
hints that its author took pains to reconcile his theme of desolation
and self-alienation with the concepts of sin and repentance that occupied him so intensely at this time. At the end of the novel its central
figure, the Austrian weights inspector Anselm Eibenschütz, hallucinates
while dying that the Great Weights Inspector has come to test *his*
"weights": "All of your weights are false, and yet all of them are
correct. So we will not report you. We believe that all of your weights
are correct" (II, 861). Eibenschütz is astonished to hear this judgment.
The former army man assigned as an Austrian official to Zlotogrod, a
backwater in distant Galicia, had fallen prey to the dreariness and
crude temptations of his surroundings. Despite his deeper and more
humane feelings he was unable to temper his rigid honesty with compassion for the indigent Jewish traders of the town. Thus they feared
and detested him. His loveless marriage—Roth's novels contain no
happy ones—was ruined when his wife bore his assistant's child. Later
both wife and child succumb to a cholera outbreak. His lust for the
seductive gypsy Euphemia Nikitsch had undermined his moral self, and
he gave way to drink and dissoluteness. In the end he is murdered by
Euphemia's earlier lover, the brutal smuggler Jadlowker, who thus
avenges himself for the prison sentence that Eibenschütz had contrived in order to remove him as a rival.

Andreas Pum in *Die Rebellion* refuses God's grace as a protest
against the injustice of the social order. Eibenschütz, on the other hand,
has no right to accept it. The weights of the poor traders of Zlotogrod
were indeed false, but theirs is a daily struggle for existence amid
pervasive poverty without prospect of a better lot. Even if Eibenschütz
was not driven by evil intent but rather by urges he could not fathom,
Roth's moral equation still breaks down in quasi-religious sentimentality. Possibly, however, a kinder consideration might be offered to
help resolve the story's questionable end. In his memoirs the Russian
writer Ilya Ehrenburg recalls a conversation with Roth about the novel,
in which Roth told him that the Great Weights Inspector himself denied

the existence of "exact scales."[11] Perhaps this expresses the measure by which Roth wished to judge the "sinners" who populate his later novels and stories: as poor human beings they, like all of us, are prone to err, and thus they merit our understanding.

In February 1938 Roth visited Vienna for the last time. As an emissary of the legitimist supporters of Otto von Hapsburg he sought an audience with Chancellor Schuschnigg in the extravagant hope of averting the *Anschluß* through a return to Hapsburg rule. However, he got only as far as the Vienna police chief, who urged him to leave the country without delay. Three days after his departure Hitler annexed Austria to the Third Reich. That same year Roth returned to the Austrian theme in *Die Kapuzinergruft,* a kind of sequel to *Radetzkymarsch,* his masterwork of six years earlier. In it he traces the fate of Franz Ferdinand Trotta, an untitled cousin of Carl Joseph von Trotta, from his days as a young Viennese would-be bohemian just before the outbreak of World War I to his despair at the fall of the Austrian government in March 1938.

Die Kapuzinergruft combines a number of themes and motifs that figure typically in several of Roth's earlier novels. Trotta, his protagonist, serves at the front as an Austrian lieutenant, returns from Russian war imprisonment to a postwar Viennese society in which he feels alien, marries a woman who deserts him for a lesbian lover and a film career, and finally seeks nightly refuge in a Viennese coffeehouse as an "extraterritorial person . . . among the living" (II, 979). Above all, like his cousin in *Radetzkymarsch,* he finds himself unequal to the challenge of his family heritage. But there are also essential differences. Carl Joseph's longing to return to the Trottas' unrestorable past defines his entire existence and, because it embodies the denial of Austria's sustaining principle of multinationalism, projects meaning for the novel's overarching historical theme. Franz Ferdinand's search for *Heimat,* on the other hand, is less deeply rooted and woven only loosely into the novel's thematic design. Stirred by a vague feeling of homelessness, he vainly and superficially seeks some source of warmth or permanence, whether in friendship, love, or the security of his mother's home. His wish to return to Sipolje, the family village in Slovenia, is the sentimental urge of a confessed romantic for what seems to him both vital and exotic. To be sure, he has not forgotten his father's dream of a Slavic kingdom under Hapsburg rule, but he lacks the inner conviction that could turn this ideal into a political mission. As in *Radetzkymarsch,* in *Die Kapuzinergruft* too   Count

Chojnicki voices the novel's "political" message. Now, however, it is no longer the nationalities of the crown lands that he censures for the empire's decline but rather the Germans of Austria with their Pan-Germanic ambitions. "Austria's essence," he declares, "is not at its center but at its periphery.... Austria's substance is nourished and constantly replenished by the crown lands" (I, 323).

Roth intended his story to illumine Austria's undoing beyond the dissolution of the monarchy to the *Anschluß* in 1938, but Chojnicki's broadly expressed conviction is as close as he comes to a concrete understanding of the historical process. At the novel's end Trotta stands forlorn in the heart of Vienna before his emperor's tomb, the Capuchin Crypt, from which the novel takes its title, and asks hopelessly: "Where can I go now, I, a Trotta?" (II, 982). His impasse suggests Roth's own. Hitler had destroyed his livelihood in Germany and with it his dream of assimilation as a German writer. Now he had lost his Austrian homeland too and was driven permanently into exile. Like Trotta he could only look backward into an idealized past.

After the *Anschluß* Roth intensified his journalistic and public protests against Hitlerism. But despite the growing Nazi threat to the entire European continent he clung to his quixotic legitimist notions and professed a more and more devout Catholicism that some among his friends claimed to be authentic, while others regarded it with equal certainty as a masquerade. By then alcoholism had irreversibly ruined his health. His liver was diseased, and in 1938 he suffered a heart attack. Yet during this time he was able to complete still another novel, *Die Geschichte von der 1002. Nacht* (1939, The Story of the Thousand-and-Second Night). Composed before *Die Kapuzinergruft* but published a year later, it stands alongside his finest works in the glow and persuasiveness of its artistry. All of the narrative qualities that distinguish *Hiob* and *Radetzkymarsch* and account for Roth's eminence in German literature are once more vividly present: the graceful sweep of his prose rhythms, the captivating legendary tone, the precision and color of his descriptions, the poetic evocation of atmosphere and mood in their finest shadings, the nostalgic recollection tempered with subtle irony of the lost world of the Danubian monarchy.

While *Die Geschichte von der 1002. Nacht* is set before the turn of the century, when the troubles that were to overtake Austria were heard only as distant rumblings, the darkness of the 1930s in Central Europe hovers over the novel. In the course of its telling the three main figures—the ne'er-do-well cavalry captain Baron Taittinger, the aging brothel keeper Frau Matzner, and the naive prostitute Mizzi Schinagl — fall victim to the unexpected rewards they had reaped from a visit to Vienna by the Persian Shah. Not long after the Shah's departure the "story of the thousand-and-second night," i.e., the Shah's brothel adventure with Schinagl (told with delectable humor in the "Arabian Nights" framework plot) brings to grief the three who had helped to contrive it. Their good fortune proves both short-lived and treacherous. Inexorably its consequences confront them with the falsity and hollowness of their lives. Shorn of their sustaining illusions, they lose their former "innocence" and give way to hopelessness. Mizzi Schinagl's powers of discernment are too slight to save her from her exploiters once she abandons the security of the brothel for the world outside. Deserted by Taittinger, the father of her illegitimate son, she literally becomes a puppet, the "Favorite Wife of the Schah," in a sideshow travesty of her own fate. Frau Matzner too grows helpless and disoriented after she retires from her profession for the illusory comforts of a private life. Consumed by her stinginess, she dies as a fearful freakish old woman. Similarly Taittinger loses his last foothold in life when the exposure of his role in the Shah's long-past brothel visit forces him to leave the army, his only real home. Unable to master the complexities of his fate — life had once seemed far simpler — he shoots himself. Although Roth drew his three central characters and their world with empathy and affection, the novel probes and condemns the moral languor, callousness, and self-deception that lay below the surface of Gay Vienna and were to erupt in barbarism in the author's final year.

In the spring of 1939 Roth let pass an invitation from Eleanor Roosevelt that would have gained him entry to the United States and thus escape from the Nazi threat. Likewise he disregarded an invitation from Dorothy Thompson, the president of the American P.E.N. Club, to attend the International P.E.N. Congress in New York that May. As his letters grippingly testify, he had lost all hope for himself and was waiting only to die. His final work, the novella *Die Legende vom heiligen Trinker* (1939, The Legend of the Holy Drinker), superbly transforms the vain dreams and bottomless despair of the poet and drinker Roth into the charmingly ambiguous story of the Paris *clochard* Andreas Kartak. After a prison term for murder Kartak, a coal miner from Polish Silesia, who lives aimlessly under the bridges of the Seine, is set on the path of virtue through an unlikely chain of "miracles," but he succumbs time and again to worldly temptations. In the end he dies blissfully in the chapel of Sainte Marie des Batignolles, believing that he has finally redeemed his pledge to an unknown benefactor to give two hundred francs as a tribute to Sainte Thérèse de Lisieux. In truth, however, he has mistaken a young angelic onlooker of the same name for the saint. In his simplicity he expires with the sigh "Fräulein Therese!" Wherewith Roth's gently ironic narrator comments: "May God grant all of us drinkers such an easy and beautiful death!" (III, 257).

Roth's death was not blissful. After learning that his dramatist friend Ernst Toller had hanged himself in New York exile he collapsed in the Café Tournon in Paris and was taken to the Hôpital Necker. On 27 May 1939 he died of delirium tremens and pneumonia after four tormenting days. The little masterpiece *Die Legende vom heiligen Trinker* appeared posthumously in the same year, a poetic transfiguration of his woeful end.

ECRIVAIN AUTRICHIEN / MORT A PARIS EN EXILE are the words inscribed on his gravestone. What they tell us goes beyond the purely biographical fact that Joseph Roth was born an Austrian subject, had lived for a time as a citizen of the First Austrian Republic, and had carried an Austrian passport. Their content also transcends the historical fact of Austria's annexation in March 1938 to Nazi Germany, after which all thought of return to his homeland became doubly impossible for the Jewish writer and relentless foe of the Third Reich. To grasp adequately Joseph Roth's fate and work one must view both his Austrianism and exile in a sense deeper than the merely factual. From the start his Austrian identity had been molded by the national and political conflicts that finally led to the dissolution of the Empire, and its character had been compounded by the singular strains that attached generally to Jewish identity in Central Europe in the post-emancipation period.

As a Galician Jew who aspired to become a German writer Roth was compelled to abandon his native Brody for the promise of Imperial Vienna. There he launched his literary career, but it would be mistaken to regard him as a Viennese writer or as an assimilated Viennese. In fact he became neither, nor did he acquire a distinct Austrian identity, something the First Republic by its nature was unable to provide. In Germany he won prominence as a writer, but Nazism cut the ground from under his feet. He lost his place in the present and could hope for no future. Thus his sole dimension became the past. Therein lay the futility of his retrogressive political activism. But therein lies too the magic of his finest books and most especially of *Radetzkymarsch*, the work that above all others defines him as an *Austrian* writer. In its pages the tensions between deepest personal longing and inexorable reality are resolved in a humane vision that for Joseph Roth, the "wanderer on a flight without end," bore the name Austria.

Notes

1. Marcel Reich-Ranicki, "Joseph Roth: barmherzig und unerbittlich" *Die Zeit,* 17 June 1966, p. 23. (All translations are my own.)
2. Joseph Roth, *Briefe 1911-1939,* ed. Herman Kesten (Köln: Kiepenheuer & Witsch, 1970), p. 165.
3. David Bronsen, *Joseph Roth: Eine Biographie* (Köln: Kiepenheuer & Witsch, 1974), p. 85.
4. Ibid., p. 492.
5. Joseph Roth, *Werke,* ed. Herman Kesten (Köln: Kiepenheuer & Witsch, 1975-1976), vol. I, p. 115. Henceforth volume and page numbers will follow in the text and will refer to this edition.
6. Joseph Roth, *Briefe 1911-1939,* p. 154.
7. Martin Buber, *On Judaism,* ed. Nahum N. Glatzer (New York: Schocken Books, 1967), p. 16.
8. Joseph Roth, *Briefe 1911-1939,* p. 381.
9. Ibid., p. 451.
10. Ibid., p. 395.
11. Quoted in David Bronsen, *Joseph Roth: Eine Biographie,* p. 577.

Bibliography

I. Works by Joseph Roth in German

Hotel Savoy. Berlin: Die Schmiede, 1924.
Die Rebellion. Berlin: Die Schmiede, 1924.
Die Geschichte einer Liebe. Berlin: J.H.W. Dietz Nachf., 1925.
Der blinde Spiegel. Berlin: J.H.W. Dietz Nachf., 1925.
Juden auf Wanderschaft. Berlin: Die Schmiede, 1927.
Die Flucht ohne Ende. München: Wolff, 1927.
Zipper und sein Vater. München: Wolff, 1928.
Rechts und Links. Berlin: Kiepenheuer, 1929.

366   Sidney Rosenfeld

Hiob: Roman eines einfachen Mannes. Berlin: Kiepenheuer, 1930.
Panoptikum: Gestalten und Kulissen. München: Knorr & Hirth, 1930.
Radetzkymarsch. Berlin: Kiepenheuer, 1932.
Tarabas: Ein Gast auf dieser Erde. Amsterdam: Querido, 1934.
Der Antichrist. Amsterdam: Allert de Lange, 1934.
Beichte eines Mörders, erzählt in einer Nacht. Amsterdam: Allert de Lange, 1936.
Die hundert Tage. Amsterdam: Allert de Lange, 1936.
Das falsche Gewicht: Die Geschichte eines Eichmeisters. Amsterdam: Querido, 1937.
Die Kapuzinergruft. Bilthoven: De Gemeenschap, 1938.
Die Geschichte von der 1002. Nacht. Bilthoven: De Gemeenschap, 1939.
Die Legende vom heiligen Trinker. Amsterdam: Allert de Lange, 1939.
Werke in drei Bçnden. Ed. Hermann Kesten. Köln: Kiepenheuer & Witsch, 1956.
Romane, Erzählungen, Aufsätze. Köln: Kiepenheuer & Witsch, 1964.
Der stumme Prophet. Köln: Kiepenheuer & Witsch, 1966.
Das Spinnennetz. Köln: Kiepenheuer & Witsch, 1967.
Briefe 1911-1939. Ed. Hermann Kesten. Köln: Kiepenheuer & Witsch, 1970.
Der Neue Tag. Unbekannte politische Arbeiten 1919 bis 1927, Wien, Berlin, Moskau. Ed. Ingeborg Sültemeyer. Köln: Kiepenheuer & Witsch, 1970.
Werke: Neue erweiterte Ausgabe in vier Bänden. Ed. Hermann Kesten. Köln: Kiepenheuer & Witsch, 1975-1976.
Perlefter. Ed. Friedemann Berger. Köln: Kiepenheuer & Witsch, 1978.
Romane und Erzählungen. Köln: Kiepenheuer & Witsch, 1982.
Berliner Saisonbericht: Reportagen und journalistische Arbeiten 1920-1939. Ed. Klaus Westermann. Köln: Kiepenheuer & Witsch, 1984.

II. Works in English Translation

Hotel Savoy. Trans. John Hoare. London: Chatto and Windus, 1986.
Flight without End. Trans. Ida Zeitlin. New York: Doubleday, 1930.
Flight without End. Trans. David Le Vay. London: Dent, 1984.
Job: The Story of a Simple Man. Trans. Dorothy Thompson. New York: Viking, 1931; Woodstock: Overlook Press, 1983; London: Chatto & Windus, Hogarth Press, 1983.

Radetzky March. Trans. Geoffrey Dunlop. New York: Viking, 1932.

The Radetzky March. Trans. Eva Tucker. Woodstock: Overlook, 1983;
Penguin, 1984.

Tarabas: A Guest on Earth. Trans. Winifried Katzin. New York: Viking,
1934; Woodstock: Overlook, 1987.

Antichrist. Trans. Moray Firth. New York: Viking, 1935.

The Confession of a Murderer, Told in One Night. Trans. D. L. Vesey.
London: Hale, 1937; London: Hogarth, 1985; Woodstock:
Overlook, 1985.

The Ballad of the Hundred Days. Trans. Moray Firth. New York:
Viking, 1936.

Weights and Measures. Trans. David Le Vay. London: Dent, 1982.

The Emperor's Tomb. Trans. John Hoare. London: Hogarth, 1984;
Woodstock: Overlook, 1984.

"The Legend of the Holy Drinker." In *Heart of Europe.* Eds. Klaus
Mann and Hermann Kesten. Trans. Ashton. New York: L. B.
Fischer, 1943.

The Silent Prophet. Trans. David Le Vay. Woodstock: Overlook, 1980.

III. Secondary Works in English

Bronsen, David. "Austrian versus Jew: The Torn Identity of Joseph
Roth." In *Leo Baeck Institute Yearbook XVIII.* Ed. Robert
Weltsch. London: Secker & Warburg, 1973, pp. 219-226.

———. "The Jew in Search of a Fatherland: The Relationship of Joseph
Roth to the Habsburg Monarchy." *Germanic Review* 54 (1979),
54-61.

Browning, B. W. "Joseph Roth's *Legende vom heiligen Trinker:* Essence
and Elixir." In *Protest–Form–Tradition: Essays on German
Exile Literature.* Ed. J. P. Strekla et al. n.p.: University of Alabama Press, 1979, pp. 81-95.

Rosenfeld, Sidney. "Joseph Roth and Austria: A Search for Identity."
In *Leo Baeck Institute Yearbook XXXI.* Ed. Arnold Paucker.
London: Secker & Warburg, 1986, pp. 455-464.

Williams, Cedric E. "Joseph Roth: A Time out of Joint." In *The
Broken Eagle: The Politics of Austrian Literature from Empire to
Anschluß.* New York: Barnes and Noble, 1974, pp. 91-112.

IV. Major Studies in German

Arnold, Heinz L., ed. *Joseph Roth.* München: Edition Text + Kritik, 1974.

Bronsen, David. *Joseph Roth: Eine Biographie.* Köln: Kiepenheuer & Witsch, 1974.

———, ed. *Joseph Roth und die Tradition.* Darmstadt: Agora, 1974.

Koester, Rudolf. *Joseph Roth.* Berlin: Colloquium, 1982.

Linden, Hermann, ed. *Joseph Roth: Leben und Werk.* Köln: Kiepenheuer, 1949.

Magris, Claudio. *Weit von wo: Verlorene Welt des Ostjudentums.* Trans. Jutta Prasse. Wien: Europaverlag, 1974.

Nürnberger, Helmuth. *Joseph Roth in Selbstzeugnissen und Bilddokumenten.* Reinbek bei Hamburg: Rowohlt Taschenbuch, 1981.

Pflug, Günther, ed. *Joseph Roth, 1894–1939: Eine Ausstellung der Deutschen Bibliothek Frankfurt am Main.* 2nd rev. ed. Frankfurt am Main: Buchhändlervereinigung, 1979.

Sültemeyer, Ingeborg. *Das Frühwerk Joseph Roths: 1915–1926.* Wien: Herder, 1976.

George Saiko

Friedrich Achberger

The relatively small oeuvre of George Saiko—two novels, a volume of short prose, scattered essays on modern art and the twentieth-century novel—contains a highly complex literary world in which the scrutiny of recent history is inextricably bound up with the exploration of the unconscious realm, a world that is both unmistakably unique and yet closely related to the cosmos of the modern Western novel. Like the major novels of Robert Musil, Hermann Broch, and Heimito von Doderer, Saiko's novels thematize the experience of historic change in Central Europe, in particular the breakup of the multinational Austrian state in 1918. Saiko's attempt to capture the totality of society is akin to Musil's rendition of social totality in *Der Mann ohne Eigenschaften* (*The Man Without Qualities*) or that of Doderer in *Die Dämonen* (*The Demons*), and he participates equally in the modernist project pursued by writers such as Joyce, Woolf, Musil, Broch, and Faulkner, namely to push the frontier of the "sayable" far beyond the conventional limits of the novel. Saiko's entire oeuvre is as specifically Austrian in content and concern as it is international in its experimental thrust—and it is decidedly underrated in both respects.

Given the complexity of Saiko's prose, his lack of popular success does not come as a surprise. But the uneven critical response raises several questions. Is the experimental quality of his work too radical for general acceptance, as exemplified by the charge of obscurity (rejection by a publisher),[1] or is Saiko continuing a project of the 1920s and 1930s that was already abandoned by the 1950s? Is the novelist's emphasis on subjective psychological reality to be read as a tendency to evade historical reality,[2] or is it to be read as a calculated challenge to conventional concepts of what is real? Is the theatrical, somewhat stiff quality of the character configuration a sign of hackneyed plot lines,[3] or is it an aspect of the allegorical structure of the novels? The ambiguous status of Saiko's work—it undoubtedly belongs to the mainstream of Austrian literature, yet stands apart—raises many such questions, but this brilliant and provocative literary world clearly deserves a fresh reading.

George Saiko was born on 5 February 1892 in the northern Bohemian town of Seestadtl (now Czechoslovakia) and died at the age of 70 on 23 December 1962 in Rekawinkel near Vienna. His life span parallels that of Heimito von Doderer (1896–1966) and that of the North German author Hans Henny Jahnn (1894–1959), with whose work there is a stronger kinship than with Doderer's. In terms of generations Saiko is a decisive few years younger than Robert Musil (1880–1942) and Hermann Broch (1886–1951), who was Saiko's lifelong friend. Though he published a major short story in 1913, it was not until 1948 that his first novel appeared, so that his oeuvre must be considered as following the work of Musil, Broch, and possibly Jahnn. After forsaking the option of an officer's career, Saiko spent his formative years in Vienna with the study of art history, archeology, psychology, and philosophy, especially under the prominent art historian Max Dvořák (1874–1921). During the 1920s and 1930s he spent many years abroad, particularly in Paris, studying modern art and publishing several articles on that subject in English journals. The anglophile Saiko also turned his first name "Georg" into the English "George." As a literary author Saiko had a belated start. Doderer's tongue-in-cheek claim that "Musil was successful for many years in preventing the excellent Austrian novelist G.S. from writing"[4] may not fully explain Saiko's late start; but there is evidence in his writing of at least a dual talent, and it seems that the writer of fiction was dominated by the art historian through the early 1930s. By the time he had finished his first novel, it was 1938 or even 1939 and too late for publication in Germany or Austria. Hermann Broch wrote a touching letter on 10 July 1937 to Peter Suhrkamp, who was then editor of Fischer's *Die Neue Rundschau,* in which he tried to place a chapter of Saiko's novel *Auf dem Floß,* making specific reference to Saiko's non-Jewish status ("The person Dr. Saiko conforms to your publication regulations"),[5] a status Broch himself, who did not publish in Nazi Germany after 1933, did not have. Broch's effort failed; *Auf dem Floß,* like so many other works of the 1930s,[6] was not published until after the war (1948).

During the war, Saiko held a crucial position at the Albertina in Vienna, the museum of graphic arts, where he prevented the pillage of this major collection by issuing counterfeits to greedy Nazi officials and after the liberation of Vienna to similarly inclined Soviet officers. He was not rewarded for his services but instead quit his post in a dispute with the state which was not finally settled until 1951.[7] He remained in disillusioned retirement until his death. During the 1950s he developed a theoretical framework for his fiction, which has become known as "magic realism," published his second novel, albeit in a slightly abridged version, and several short stories. The bitter irony of this writer's career came in 1962, when he saw two volumes of short stories published, of which *Der Opferblock* rivals the novels in importance. In the same year he also received his first major recognition in the form of the Great Austrian State Prize but was prevented from enjoying its fruits by an untimely death. The posthumous works include only an unfinished short story and the fragment of a novel.

While a discussion of Saiko's oeuvre will necessarily focus on the two novels, an introductory detour through his stories, all but one of which appeared after the novels, will provide a useful approach, since they present the writer's concerns in stark, concise pictorial form. One group of stories, collected in 1962 under the title *Giraffe unter Palmen* (Giraffe under Palm Trees), is linked by the Mediterranean, i.e., Italian, themes. The title could be the caption of a painting, and indeed it refers to the tattoo on the left upper arm of Brogio, an Italian fisherman. This four-page title story is seemingly static, yet possesses the graphic quality of a painting imbued with the tension of opposing forces. Brogio's wife Betta, terminally ill, has been refusing to die for weeks, and her friend Letizia has been taking care of the household. Betta's clinging to life and to her hold over her husband is subverted by the vital attraction between Brogio and Letizia, so that the raw energy of sex—the neck of the giraffe on Brogio's muscular arm turns phallic in Letizia's eyes—breaks the barrier of social convention, and Betta dies in the moment of that realization. Saiko stages the conflict in "Giraffe unter Palmen" on two levels, of which the first, that of conscious, conventional reality, is sketched with a bare minimum of strokes, whereas the other level, that of subliminal, spontaneously perceived reality, comes under close scrutiny: the bodily movement of Brogio's washing himself brings to life the images on his body, and Letizia reads their irresistible sign language as she dries him off. The forces of life are associated with the power of desire, whereas the realm of convention, here associated with the death of the wife, are swept aside in this story with singular deftness. Whatever one may and should find problematic about the vitalistic assumption beneath this story is another matter (and will be discussed below).

In "Die Geburt des Lammes" (The Birth of the Lamb), another story from this collection, the narrative pits a pair of tourists against the Italian landscape and pits the male and the female against each other. On the surface Paul and Gerda visit an ancient fertility temple on a sightseeing tour, but beneath that conventional experience Gerda "reads" the signs of the country, the temple, the flock of sheep on its grounds, and comes to challenge the rules governing her life up to that point, particularly Paul's position that it would be "inconvenient" to have a child together. Gerda, who is pregnant without Paul's knowledge, begins to recognize her link to the enactment of birth all around her, whereas Paul refuses to participate, stays on the tourist level ("There you have it again, architecture is nothing but proportion."), and talks about abortion in an offhanded manner. As the two witness the birth of a lamb, Gerda's realization of their incompatibility takes the shape of a rupture like that of the amniotic sac just prior to birth. Gerda gives birth, however, to an intense anger, and she nearly pushes Paul over the precipice to his certain death. This story, too, subverts and discredits the daylight realm of conventional behavior—Paul is a caricature of smug instrumental rationality—by juxtaposing a rich realm in which the nonrational rules: the realm of instinct, *genius loci*, myth. Of course, this separation of realms mirrors the Freudian separation of conscious and unconscious, but the story's power cannot be explained away by reducing it to its Freudian basis, which Saiko would also acknowledge. "Die Geburt des Lammes" is a vividly concrete exploration of modern alienated life. Saiko uses spatial imagery to let the setting "speak" its silent language against the dwarfed creatures of civilization: there is the symbiosis of architecture and landscape, of the ancient Roman temple and the timeless flock of sheep; there is the deep abyss, above which Paul and Gerda walk perilously; and by implication, there is the big city, the world of convention that loses its validity in Gerda's mind as she experiences the other realm.

Saiko's writing, as we have seen, is characterized by several unique features that border on the experimental while observing the limits of realistic and plausible prose. Exposition is kept to a minimum, just enough to construct a frame of surface reality, whereas the reality of subjective perception is explored to its fullest. The two realms are opposed but not irreconcilably; the text's movement usually involves a disillusionment and thus a new beginning stemming from the experience of the nonrational—Gerda may start a new life with a child and without Paul, and Letizia joins Brogio directly after Betta's funeral with the approval of the community. The opposition conscious/unconscious is often linked with the opposition self-deception/truth, and similar dualistic configurations abound throughout Saiko's work: mind/body, civilization/nature, North/South, etc. There is, however, nothing simplistic in these texts, because they do not reach black/white conclusions but rather explore the tension between the poles. In the story "Das andere Leben" (The Other Life), for instance, Harold's desire to stay in the primitive fishing village he considers "un paradiso" is met with the scornful laughter of the local schoolteacher who calls it a prison. Of the two perceptions, the tourist view is clearly demolished— in the eyes of the reader—by the authentic bitterness of the teacher's perception, who is, however, also an outsider. In characteristic fashion this text, not unlike a painting, develops contrasts but does not spell out a resolution.

The intensely visual quality of Saiko's work is connected to this feature, but also to the Freudian imagery the author uses to present the drama of the unconscious realm. If the text's overall gesture is often a critique of conventional rationality, of abstraction and alienation from immediate experience, then it follows that the other realm features radiant but silent images, corporality, and immediacy. Certainly Saiko's emphasis on the visual is as much connected to his work as an art historian as it is to his psychological studies: both involve the "reading" of symbols and allegories. His writing is therefore also situated in the characteristic dilemma between word and image, reason and non-reason: just like the art historian approaches a painting with words, i.e., a medium avoided by the work itself, and the psychoanalyst attempts to grasp the night's dream images with daylight analytical tools, Saiko, the novelist, captures his vision of the unconscious realm in realistic prose, a contradictory, potentially self-defeating proposition. Saiko steadfastly maintained the concept of realism, albeit a "magic" one, and never tired of disavowing the surrealist approach as inadequate and unproductive.[8] His writing hovers between the intellectual mode, in which the unconscious realm is presented in analytical terms (for which he names Musil as a contemporary instance),[9] and the surrealist mode, in which the unconscious is recreated in its own terms, namely "automatic writing," a-logical discourse, etc.

Taking up the image of his earliest theoretical statement, "Die Wirklichkeit hat doppelten Boden" (Reality Has a Double Bottom), we can describe the movement of a typical Saiko text as coming from the realms of rational discourse (conventional realism), dipping into the largely uncharted space "below" or beyond conscious perception, exploring the tension between the two, and then integrating the fruits of that excursion to the nether world into a precisely structured text, that is, in the final analysis he composed a well wrought rational discourse. The ambitiousness, but also the potential weakness, of Saiko's writing lies in the attempt to hover between image and word, dream and analysis, between the hermetic and chaotic realm of the first-person interior monologue and the orderly instance of the third-person omniscient narrator. Appropriately enough the tightrope figures as another prominent image in this same theoretical statement, for we can see the author on just such a tightrope, attempting to do justice on the one hand to that which resists capture by rational discourse and on the other hand to the readers' need for clarification. This brings to mind the concluding proposition of Wittgenstein's *Tractatus logico-philosophicus:* "What we cannot speak about we must pass over in silence."[10] Overtly, Saiko's writing seems to negate Wittgenstein's maxim, but in the sense that Wittgenstein was concerned with the borderline between the sayable and the ineffable and that his investigative thrust was indeed directed at the latter,[11] Saiko's attempt to reach beyond that border falls into line not only with Wittgenstein but also with a whole Austrian tradition from Hofmannsthal to Musil, Bachmann, and Aichinger.

A brief look at Saiko's first story, published in 1913 in Ludwig von Ficker's celebrated but decidedly marginal journal *Der Brenner* will round out and complement our preliminary view. "Das letzte Ziel" (The Last Goal) is thoroughly expressionist in theme and to a lesser degree in style, and very Austrian in its thematization of the civil servant. A modest promotion revives the middle-aged clerk Schneider's hope of becoming a father, but his plan, announced suddenly after years of pennypinching and denial, meets with his wife's incomprehension. Schneider's belated embrace of life can only cause a catastrophe in their narrow, deadened lower-middle class existence, so that the vital energy unleashed in a lavish feast causes not the beginning of new life but the death of the wife: Schneider tramples on her because she represents the prison that he had built for himself. Here we see the battle of instinct and desire against convention just as in the Italian stories; the conflict is framed in sexual terms, even though the implications point toward social criticism. The human is pictured strung out between the opposite demands of career (here caricatured in the pettiness of bureaucratic distinctions) and inner self, the archetypal struggle of civilized humankind. This early story already shows two of the major strains in Saiko's oeuvre: his skepticism towards the veneer of civilization—here in the form of an expressionist attack strongly reminiscent of Carl Sternheim—upon petty bourgeois conventions and the Freudian concept of the self, here presented in a pessimistic vision emphasizing the irreconcilability of its contradictory aspects. Given the unusual time lapse of twenty-five years or more between this story and the first novel, there is a remarkable continuity in Saiko's work; at the same time there are also major developments, which will be addressed subsequently.

The novel *Auf dem Floß* (On the Raft), which was published in 1948, a decade after its completion, takes place on a large country estate somewhere in Eastern Austria sometime after 1918, a setting seemingly sheltered from history, yet pervaded by the uncertainty and the subterranean struggle that characterized Austria between the Wars. The time frame given in the novel ("since the disssolution of the Monarchy")[12] is specific enough to guide the reader's perception, yet vague enough to evoke an atmosphere of transition, as if the national boundaries of 1918 were not yet firmly in place (as indeed Hitler's War was to erase them once more).[13] The indeterminacies of time and place themselves contribute to the atmosphere of being "adrift" that is signaled in the novel's title. The country estate of Alexander, Prince Fenckh, serves as a would-be refuge on which he attempts to shape his existence without interference from his elder brother, Bishop Nico, and against the resistance of those who would form part of his existence. Alexander is pictured as an anachronism: not only had all titles of nobility been abolished by one of the first laws of the First Austrian Republic (3 April 1919), but Alexander's rule over his estate and subjects is ineffectual in most respects, and the consistently ironic portrayal by the narrative voice robs this figure of all outward stature. Yet in spite of his weaknesses and failures, this figure commands our sympathy through his very struggle.

Besides Alexander the novel's cast falls into two groups, corresponding to the structural division into twelve chapters entitled "Joschko I" to "Joschko XII" and twenty-two individually titled chapters (such as "Sainte Anne," "The Hand") which form eleven pairs between the Joschko-chapters. The Joschko-plot with Alexander, his brother, his gigantic coachman Joschko, his gypsy ex-lover Marischka, his Hungarian chauffeur Imre, the valet Franz, and all the estate personnel and peasants forms the structural backbone of the novel, where-as the more diffuse plot of the titled chapters develops Alexander's interaction with his peers: his neighbor Mary, whom he courts, her children Mick (16) and Gise (18), and his guest Eugen, who eventually wins Mary. With its intricate construction and the large cast of charac-ters, *Auf dem Floß* rivals the major novels of Saiko's contemporaries Musil, Broch, and Doderer, but in spite of marked similarities it follows a different agenda. Read in visual terms like a painting, the vertical axis developed in the twelve Joschko-chapters deals with the problem of domination/subversion; the horizontal axis explores the problem of communication. The center is formed by the anti-hero Alexander in his effort to command the raft, namely, his attempt to evade tutelage from above (the Bishop), to appropriate Joschko below, and to define him-self in relation to a partner (Mary, and later her daughter Gise) or to a friend (Eugen). Dynamic tensions similar to those between left and right and above and below in a painting inform the novel throughout, as when Alexander appears suspended between the sexual partner Ma-rischka and the unattainable Mary ("at the other pole, precisely oppo-site Marischka," 32), or disoriented between his firm social function of the past and his apparent functionlessness in the present. Countless recurrent images structure the narrative, such as the swamp that seals the fate of both Joschko and Imre, or the mirror into which the broth-ers look instead of facing each other. Spatial relations always carry significance, such as the shifting relations between castle, village, and church as they are viewed from different perspectives,[14] or the islands in the river as the goal of Mary's and Eugen's desire, or the prison courtyards in which Eugen faces execution by the Reds and the Whites respectively. The pervasive structural signals tend to evoke the readers' response that the novel is contrived, but the actual root of reservations against Saiko's work lies probably in its profoundly allegorical orienta-tion that is at odds with most contemporary reading habits.[15] But this is the point where the existing interpretations are most in need of reevaluation.

The twelve Joschko-chapters tell the strange tale of the relation-ship between Alexander and his coachman (later doorman) Joschko, "a huge and powerful cowherd whom he had met on a hunting trip some-where in the Tatra mountains" (9), i.e., in Slovakia. Joschko is intro-duced in terms of both an extension of his master—performing feats of strength and virility—and of a hunting trophy; in the latter respect he forms the culmination of a series ranging from rare minerals and stuffed animals to shrunken Indio heads and live rare animals. Alexander's original intent is to assimilate Joschko into an "organic" (7) symbiosis with mutual benefits, where intelligence and brawn, master and servant, would complement each other in mutual loyalty, and where Joschko would make up Alexander's perceived deficiencies. This is problematized from the start by the image of the hunting trophies (Alexander "did not understand that every animal is the enemy of the hunter and that owning the corpse is less than half ownership and probably none at all," 14), and the hoped-for symbiosis must end in Joschko's death. The relationship between prince and doorman is in fact characterized by possession in the dual sense of the word: Alexander is possessed by the idea of Joschko ("his favorite fantasy: to speak of Joschko as if he were a bear, not yet quite tamed," 130), and Joschko as a possession turns into an object and thus literally loses his life. The outward cause of Joschko's death is that Alexander marries him off to Marischka, the gypsy woman Alexander had to relinquish under pressure from his brother, who still retains some authority over Alexander due to his status as the first-born son and as Bishop. In retaliation, Marischka gradually poisons and finally suffocates Joschko, while Alexander plots to have the prized doorman stuffed after his death and exhibited in the great hall; but even that project fails when Marischka and her accomplice Imre sink the corpse in the swamp and flee. In the last brotherly confrontation after the Joschko-project has failed, Alexander is able to assert his independence by announcing his plan to marry.

Woven into this relatively linear plot are the individual histories of and current relationships between Mary, her children, and Eugen, as they bear on Alexander. The widowed Mary Countess Tremblaye has returned from years abroad and a life style not considered respectable by her peers; her son Mick fantasizes and acts out his adolescent aggressions while ostensibly preparing for the priesthood; her daughter Gise is going through the initiation into womanhood and will possibly become Alexander's wife. Eugen, an exile from the Russian Revolution teaching in France, is using Alexander's rural estate for a writer's retreat but finds a future partner in Mary. While the figures in the Joschko-plot form a spectrum of social and national types, these other figures form a spectrum of psychological types: Eugen contrasts with Alexander in that he does not feel "adrift" (552), Mick acts out the Oedipal phase, Mary has the maturity Alexander lacks, and Gise has the self-sacrificing fervor (cf. chapter "The Sacrifice") that may be needed to redeem Alexander.

The plot lines weave a fascinating tale of flesh and blood, energized by such traditional themes as love and rivalry, and concretized by some Austrian local color (the near-pagan rural atmosphere, the gypsy element, the tension between church and castle, etc.). *Auf dem Floß*, however, endeavors to grasp the human experience not only on the outer level of *what* happened, but also on the subliminal level, the "double bottom" of feelings, associations, miscarried intentions, and repressions. Thus the novel's primary focus is on *how* actions are imbedded in a whole apparatus of psychic events. In his theoretical statements Saiko repeatedly acknowledges his debt to Joyce and Faulkner and proposes to surpass their work in his project of "Magic Realism": "to explore the realm of what can be said in the direction of the pre- and unconscious, of the irrational in every sense, the depiction of those forces and attitudes—generally not acknowledged—which belong to the realm of the animistic and magic, which are anchored in the depths of the soul and whose power emanates from there."[16] In this endeavor *Auf dem Floß* must be considered a major breakthrough for the Austrian novel of this century, and it is by the same token a victim of its delayed publication. In the late 1930s Saiko's radical experiment in psychological verism would possibly have been received as a continuation of the line from Schnitzler to Musil and Broch, but the culturally as well as politically regressive era of the Corporate State and the *Anschluß* years brought that tradition to an abrupt halt, and the postwar climate did not favor experiments.

Saiko's writing builds upon the techniques of the interior monologue and stream-of-consciousness as developed in Schnitzler's *Leutnant Gustl* and Joyce's *Ulysses,* where the level of unconscious mental activity is represented as speech. An entirely different model may be found in the figure of the murderer Moosbrugger in Musil's *The Man Without Qualities,* of whom Ulrich says: "If humankind as a whole could dream, the result would have to be Moosbrugger."[17] Moosbrugger, as a disenfranchised figure who is both appealing in his naiveté and fear-inspiring in his strength, has much in common with the gentle giant Joschko, and both figures serve as externalizations of the unconscious. Sometimes the level of the unconscious takes over the narrative of *Auf dem Floß* in the form of a sudden onslaught of memory, as in the passage where Alexander's hunt for a mountain cock is superseded by the memory of a defloration scene in the East Indies and then by memories of Marischka, thus mimicking the unconscious activity by

multiple layers of scenes which are tied together by Alexander's identification of the hunt with sex. When Alexander confronts his brother,
his outward action resembles that of Hans Karl Bühl, the protagonist of
Hofmannsthal's *Der Schwierige,* who shies away from utterance as an
act of "indecency" and would rather speak through gestures and
silences. Saiko's narrator, however, lifts the veil of silence and records
the unspoken dialogue.

Saiko's singleminded determination to commit to language previously uncharted layers of communcation creates a text of unparalleled density that puts high demands on the reader. The novel abounds
with intricately detailed scenes that attempt to capture the totality of a
fictional figure's experience, such as Gise's initiation in "The Sacrifice."
Ostensibly this chapter narrates how Gise goes to the would-be lover of
her best friend at boarding school and manages to be seduced by him.
This "content," however, is framed as Gise's recollection and her insistent attempts to understand her own motivation, which are in turn
mediated and augmented by the narrative voice. The emerging picture
shows Gise wishing to hurt her friend Claire, wanting the sexual initiation for its own sake, but also performing it as a vicarious union with
Alexander, while the Italian jockey performs the role of a pawn even
though he pictures himself as the irresistible seducer. Strategies of
deception, manipulation, and self-delusion surface in this chapter in a
way that compels the reader into the investigative process. Yet this
passage and similar ones can leave a bitter aftertaste, when the author
behind the narrator seems nothing more than a skeptical, even cynical,
manipulator of a puppet show in which one puppet after another strips
off the layer of conventional appearance in order to reveal a more or
less miserable "true self." In this respect Saiko's writing depends to an
unusual degree on the readers' "willing suspension of disbelief." On the
other hand, the figures of *Auf dem Floß* are not mere wretches but frail
human beings on their tortuous way towards redemption, though not
in a narrowly religious sense (the questionable figure of the Bishop
would forbid such a view), so that the disillusioning operation of the
narrative is still imbedded in an overall hopeful quest.

Auf dem Floß has been treated to a thorough and valid reading
along the lines of a "search for identity," which pays particular attention to the technical characteristics of the novel and reads figures like
Alexander and Mary as realistically depicted characters.[18] This reading
is to the point but far from exhaustive. If Saiko pictures "reality" with
a "double bottom," this feature characterizes also his work, in the sense

that *Auf dem Floß* operates on several allegorical levels beneath the realistic level of an individual's self-definition. If chapters like "The Sacrifice" stage and analyze the conscious and unconscious levels of interaction between two specific individuals, providing the micro-structure of the novel, an encompassing macrostructure is to be found in the staging of all the major figures as components of the human psyche, as players in the psychological drama that forms an allegory of the modern condition. Alexander is clearly cast as the frail ego, with the Bishop as the superego and Joschko as the id, while the women form a constellation within which the male ego acts out his desire, and Eugen and Mick are contrastive ego-figures, Eugen mature, Mick infantile. Far from a schematic or reductionist construction, this allegory comes alive through the vivid and specific characterization of each fictional figure. Read as an allegory the Joschko-plot acquires a sharp critical thrust that questions the "civilizing process."[19] The price to be paid for dominating and attempting to civilize the id (Joschko) is described as the id's slow death, which is also linked to the repression of sexuality (Marischka). As Joschko increasingly becomes an object, an empty shell of his former vitality, civilization is pictured as a costly process, and the final truce between superego and ego, with the en-visaged marriage of rank (Gise), seems pale in comparison to its cost. The staging of the theoretical problem—however forcefully it may actually develop in the plot—reveals the author's disposition: the domestication of the id is depicted in terms of a Pyrrhic victory, since the price to be paid for social status (Bishop) and power is alienation and impoverishment of the senses.

Given the fact that Saiko, like most of his contemporaries, re-flected upon the breakup of the Austrian empire, it is not surprising that *Auf dem Floß* invites another allegorical reading focussed on the question of Austrian identity in a time of transition. A trenchant analysis of the three-way ideological split (Catholic-Austrian, German-Nationalist, Socialist) that dominated the 1920s and 1930s documents Saiko's deep concern with the political and national Austrian self-definition (1957, "Behind the Face of the Austrian").[20] Read along these lines, Alexander with the programmatic name who fails in his attempts at conquering and mastering, would represent an Austrian ruling elite cut off from its traditional purpose. The figure of the Bishop who had abadoned a military career (cf. Saiko's biography, 95!) and had abdicated his rights as the firstborn (93) graphically captures the role of the Catholic church in Austria, especially after 1918. The

1918. The various nationalities represented in the novel (Hungarian, Slovak, gypsy, Austrian) merely hint at the problem of the nationalities involved in the dissolution of the empire. The feudal regime appears in the process of failure, Joschko, like the gigantic mass of potential subjects, can be retained only in the form of a trophy, and the effort to retain him reveals itself as an idea as groteque as the attempts to revive the Habsburg rule after 1918.[21] The uneven master-servant relationship mirrors that between a thin aristocracy and the vast number of politically and economically underdeveloped non-German nations in the old Austro-Hungarian empire, a relationship that is nevertheless described in the novel as interdependence. The project of stuffing Joschko after his death may be read as an image for the "Austrian Idea" that was propagated during and after the dissolution of the empire in an attempt to reaffirm a multinational "mission" for Austria.[22] As a project framed in futility, it also resembles the "parallel plan" in Musil's *The Man Without Qualities,* in which a celebration of the year 1918 is envisaged in 1913 as a means of commemorating the projected seventieth anniversary of Franz Joseph's reign and the thirtieth anniversary of Wilhelm II in 1918.

The fact that an allegory of the self and one of the state are pictured in the same plot is a problematic aspect but not surprising if we consider that the crisis of the Austrian state was an influential mental image in the conception of Freud's model of the self. The allegorical imagination unfolding in this novel is not a oneway process, however, and while this novel is open to the charge of obscuring history by neglecting some economic and political specifics, its distinct advantage over other forms of discourse lies in imagining a totality of interaction larger than the merely political forces. If the "Habsburg Myth"[23] in literature relied on picturing the state as a family with the emperor as a benevolent father (as in the identity of Franz von Trotta and Franz Joseph I in Roth's *Radetzkymarsch*), *Auf dem Floß* decidedly does not belong in this tradition, for there is no nostalgia for paternal relations. The picture of feudal relations in this novel is complex, nevertheless: it stresses the anachronistic quality of the Prince and treats his rule with irony, but it also captures the social intimacy of feudal relations in contrast to alienated and anonymous relations in modern society and thus contains the seed of a social utopia. It is a unique feature of *Auf dem Floß* that it juxtaposes in stark terms the symbiotic with the internecine aspects of the hierarchical and multinational old Austrian order.

Saiko's second novel, *Der Mann im Schilf* (1955 abridged, 1971 complete, The Man in the Reeds), centers on a more concrete subject matter than the first but is more elusive in its overall gesture. Its focus is the failed *Putsch* of 25 July 1934, in which the illegal Austrian National Socialists assassinated the Austrian Chancellor Dollfuss but were almost comically inept at linking up with the rest of Austria and with Nazi Germany. Saiko takes a well-known, if somewhat obscure, event from the twilight years of Austria and tackles it from a startling angle: the offbeat locale of *Der Mann im Schilf* is a lakeside resort in rural Salzburg, far away from the decisive action in Vienna; the governing perspective is that of an outsider, the Austrian archeologist Robert who is returning after two years' absence and ready to leave again; and the central activity of digging/searching is countered by the impenetrability, the murkiness, of the matter at hand, be it reeds, politics, or Austrian psyche. "Failure" may be the subscription of this work, since everything fails, the lovers' communication as well as the political projects, but the disillusionment resulting from this failure contains the skeptic's truth which we may assume as this novel's telos.

Sir Gerald, Loraine, and Robert, on their way from an archeological site in Crete to London, are interrupting their trip in Salzburg, because Robert plans to meet his lover Hanna once more. Gerald has not found the large statues from the late-Minoan period he had hoped for, but he plans to write the book on their expedition with Robert. Loraine, outwardly Gerald's companion, makes their relationship a triangle in her desire for Robert. The muddled NS-*Putsch* is witnessed by Robert and Hanna at the rural resort, where state artillery is blasting supposed insurgent positions and the militia scours the countryside without tangible results. The attention of all parties is focussed on an alleged escapee in the reeds who serves as a convenient scapegoat. As the reunion with Robert goes awry, Hanna adopts the project of rescuing the fugitive, not for political reasons—she sees National Socialism abusing the idealism of the German-speaking peoples[24]—but out of an antipolitical and humane motivation that is depicted in irrational terms. Loraine and Gerald participate in her scheme to transport the fugitive to safety in the rolled-up sail of their boat, but Hanna, as the driver of the getaway car, is shot by the militia, and the roll of sailcloth in her car is found empty.

Der Mann im Schilf is divided into two types of chapters, not unlike the first novel, and into two spheres of action which partly overlap. Three titled chapters frame the novel, while two groups of five numbered chapters each provide the substance: chapters I-V between "Kleon" and "Gerald," chapters VI-X between "Gerald" and "Robert."

Loraine, "a constant swing of the pendulum" (292) between Gerald and Robert, uses the Cretan Kleon to arouse jeaousy in Robert and coerce a commitment from him. Her effort to come to terms with past events carries the Cretan plot of the novel in which archeology and psychoanalysis appear fused. Robert on the other hand establishes the connection to the Austrian plot, and the triangle created with Hanna mirrors the earlier triangle. The incongruences are part of a narrative strategy that aims to subvert conventional notions of separate private/public realms and of clear cut subject matters: this is neither a novel about the Nazi *Putsch,* nor is it a love intrigue; rather it is concerned with the intersection of violence and sexuality and with the everyday consequences of political processes. Saiko's choice of locale betrays his stance: in the backwaters of the rural setting, political lines inevitably get muddled and the result is often absurd. The choice of this particular incident does not allow for sharply defined issues and positions, for the differences between the authoritarian Dollfuss regime and the adherents of German fascism (*Anschluß* or not) were less significant than their commonalities, their similarly negative views on democracy, socialism, Jews, etc. Given the–historically correct–lack of political clarity of July 1934 (the opposition had been silenced with the suppression of the Socialist revolt in February 1934), Saiko's novel situates the questions: what does it mean and what is it worth to be Austrian? at the seemingly least promising point. Saiko eliminates any harmonizing or idealizing retrospection but captures Austria at one of its darkest moments.

Even though the central narrative perspective is that of the detached Robert and his friends Hanna, Loraine, and Gerald, the novel also provides extensive views from the inside, in particular four detailed character sketches that flesh out the context of the political choice within Austria. Robert's elder half-brother Felix, a cavalry captain of meager means who had been eclipsed by Robert in every respect, opts for the Nazi camp because of the money and power involved, but also because it appeals to his officer past. A similar power struggle determines the choices of the brothers Florian and Cölestin, where the elder Florian had inherited the family farm, whereas Cölestin has overcome a humiliating youth and is now in a power position in the Corporate State. As a cabinet member with vested interest in the Dollfuss regime he is now in the position to take bribes, to buy the homestead he has always dreamed of and thus to triumph over Florian, which drives Florian into the insurgent camp. Lastly, the high-ranking civil servant (*Ministerialrat*) Mostbaumer uses the volatile situation by playing both hands in his bid for power in cynical disregard for the content of the political choice.[25] The extended portrait of the sinister Mostbaumer includes a childhood scene in which he kills a bird in order to impress his mother, repeated attempts to rape a woman on his staff, and his need to prove to himself that he has the courage to kill. Whereas Felix operates with strict moral precepts, Mostbaumer adheres to a nihilistic philosophy of action ("To act, to take steps— that's what counts!" 281). He decrees himself "the highest instance of his own actions" (283) and shoots Felix; he also betrays the rescue plan and is thus responsible for Hanna's death.

Der Mann im Schilf clearly does not aim to make a statement about the Austrian events through its relatively straightforward if inconclusive plot. Its primary gesture is not telling a story but exploring a configuration, which involves a scrutiny of the actors in terms of their past and in their mutual relations. Whereas the ostensible action (digging for sculptures, searching for *Putschists*) yields no result, it is the juxtaposition of figures (Gerald-Loraine-Kleon; Loraine-Robert-olive-skinned woman, etc.) that fuels the novel. The search is fruitful only in the one respect that the past of some figures reveals some of their motivation, as is the case with the four major Austrian figures Felix, Cölestin, Florian, and Mostbaumer. While these are mostly defined vertically (tension between present and past), the other four major figures, Gerald, Loraine, Robert, and Hanna, are defined in terms of their horizontal (present) relationships. The tension-filled configurations as main characteristics point to the canvas-like quality of this novel and its ostentatious neglect of the historical dimension, but this should not be misread as a deliberate evasion. The novel is rather built on the assumption that the reader is well-versed in the historical situation (otherwise the veiled references to the salt-mine workers and the socialist uprising of February 1934 [56] would be lost). It addresses, in appropriately static configurations, the essential *aporia,* the stalemate of 1934–1938, when Austria was in the grip of the Depression, had abandoned parliamentary democracy, had outlawed the socialists, and was torn between a lackluster independence and a union with the appealing/abhorrent Nazi Germany. The fact that Saiko addressed the topic "1934" at all is evidence of history-mindedness at a time when that topic was repressed on the whole, and the seemingly opaque presentation may be attributed to both the topic and the era in which the novel was published.

While the first novel, when read as a "quest for Austria" (significantly identified with the idea of Europe in the penultimate chapter "Where Is Europe?"), is still carried by an optimistic undercurrent, the quest for Austria is hopelessly mired in *Der Mann im Schilf,* and Saiko can be read as Thomas Bernhard's forerunner in this respect. Though Robert is in a situation similar to that of Alexander—haunted by an older brother, suspended between exile and homecoming and between two women—he is eventually relegated to the fringe of Austrian society, not only physically (beaten up in the streets of Salzburg), but also in his existence as a middle-class intellectual. Such is his verdict of the Austrian people:

> He hated their attitude, which congealed flexibly around anything solid and sharp, this attitude that was the product of a government that had broken every last bit of resistance. He knew the other face of the feudal order with its centuries' worth of patina: the inability to rise to an idea, not even the idea of one's own self; and the reckless opportunism. And now he also hated these miserable mountain folk, half small farmers, half salt-mine workers; he hated them for their denseness, for the eruptions of their strength to which no one lent shape and which were thus so easy to choke. But most of all he hated himself (76f.).

With that realization, Robert's definition of Austria as "Heimat" specifically excludes its people, i.e., society, and affirms only its landscape. Robert's last sentence can be read as characteristic of Saiko's attitude which never excludes the self from the bitter scrutiny: "most of all he hated himself."

The other sympathetic Austrian figure, Hanna, does not clarify the impenetrability of the Austrian scene, but she cuts through it by refusing to accept the political terms, refusing even to enter into the intellectual debate with which Robert attempts to grasp the situation. Her mission is to rescue the mirage of the "human being" in the reeds— and the novel leaves open to doubt whether that being is there anymore—and literally becomes a martyr in the process. A recent appreciation of the novel sees Hanna's project affirmed in the image of the Resurrection by reading the empty roll of sailcloth as "a symbolic shroud from which the fugitive seems to have escaped."[26] The life-affirming impulse of this reading, which points to pagan rites of the ritual killing and rebirth of the Alpine "wild man" or scapegoat, can be construed, together with the redeeming function of Hanna's martyrdom, as the novel's mythical answer to a deadlocked historical situation. In contrast to the Italian stories, there is no luminous and liberating southern landscape, the center of the action is a lake "which reflected the height of the sky in its dark green mirror" (63), a lake that is as impenetrable as the thick growth of reeds around its rim, murderous and lifesaving at once.

Der Mann im Schilf goes beyond an abstract anti-political stance, however. The text is laden with the experience of the body and with psychoanalytical matter (the homophony with "Saiko-analytical" may have not been lost on the anglophile author), both of which are not anti-political in themselves but significantly enlarge the realm of what is conventionally deemed political. The politics of Felix, Mostbaumer, etc., are depicted in terms that include their bodily and psychological needs and functions, which means that the emerging picture is anything but clear cut, but does not mean that the author "obscures the events."[27] The fact that hunger plays such an important —and irrational—part in the depiction of politics in this novel (Hanna phrases it in fairy tale, i.e., mythical, terms: the yearning for the "magic pot," 57) is not only literally correct for the 1930s but also symbolizes the hunger for identity in the ambivalent Austrian/German situation. Far from advocating the irrationalism it depicts, this novel constitutes a scathing and encompassing critique of 1930s mentalities; yet it has been misunderstood along the same lines as Broch's unfinished novel Die Verzauberung (The Bewitchment).[28] Figures like Felix and Mostbaumer and his idol, the "man in the grey-green mackintosh," are apt to let us grasp the problem of an entire society flirting with fascism precisely because these portraits reach into the realm of the irrational that is not accessible to scientific scrutiny of social behavior. Most characteristic of Saiko's approach is the mixture of compassionate proximity and horror felt by Robert as he meets his brother Felix, who has turned Nazi since Robert last saw him, and whose unhappiness belies his name as much as Alexander is a failure at conquests. As in the touching and bitter poem "Requiem for a Fascist" by Theodor Kramer,[29] it is the ambivalence between closeness and distance to "the fascist brother" that makes this early attempt at coming to terms with the past ring particularly true.

If the above assessment is valid, we can conclude that the backbone of Saiko's writing project—to explore previously uncharted realms of the unconscious and to integrate them into the narrative—is more than an aim in itself, more than a technical innovation. In the praxis of *Der Mann im Schilf* in particular, the theory of "magic realism" turns what could be a merely psychological narrative into a novel of social criticism of extraordinary incisiveness. In taking the scrutiny of the unconscious to its application in the social and political realm, Saiko is, we might say, taking the step from Freud to Wilhelm Reich (1933, *Mass Psychology of Fascism*). On another level, however, Saiko is not going beyond Freud but rather regressing to Otto Weininger's *Geschlecht und Charakter* (1903, Sex and Character), namely in the dualistic conception of sex roles, and this is where Saiko's oeuvre is likely to irritate many contemporary readers. Since Saiko's critique of modern (alienated) consciousness is rarely formulated explicitly, it relies on the juxtaposition of the conscious with the unconscious, or civilization with nature, or male with female. However sophisticated the rendition of human communication in Saiko's texts, each text operates on a basically dualistic, allegorical scheme, and since the narratorial perspective is close to the central male figure, women figures can only be the "Other" and play subservient roles in the iconographic scheme. Not unlike the allegorical Christian in John Bunyan's *Pilgrim's Progress* (1678), Alexander picks his way to a secular redemption by choosing between women, between the saintliness of Mary and the merely sexual entity Marischka. In a characteristic ironic operation (i.e., secularization), *Auf dem Floß* casts Mary as the holy one (by virtue of her name but also of Alexander's adoration) only to undercut her status by references to her earlier loose life style; similarly her daughter Gise turns her religious fervor into the sexual adventure of the "Sacrifice." The irony betrays the writer's cognizance of the problem, but the mythical/allegorical male-female relationships nevertheless operate on the unreflected premises that female existence can be defined only in relation to the male and that it is always diametrically opposed to the male. In the scheme of "magic realism," it is thus the intersection of the "magic" and the "realistic" that proves troubling, in some cases downright offensive, as with the figure Marischka, whose allegorical function disavows the credibility of the realistic figure. The characterization of this gypsy woman exclusively in terms of sexuality, odor, bodily function, obsession, basic speechlessness, etc., might pass for racism if it were not for her predominantly allegorical function and the fact that the reader sees her largely through Alexander's subjective perception ("subjektive Symbolbildung," Saiko).

The term "Magic Realism," incidentally, is not Saiko's original coinage. The art historian must have encountered Franz Roh's anti-Expressionist definition of Magic Realism in 1924 or the 1925 Mannheim exhibit of Magic Realism in painting that has since become known as "Neue Sachlichkeit" (New Objectivity). Forerunners of that predominantly German school are the Italian Metaphysical Painters, especially Chirico. Since the 1920s, Magic Realism has meant alternately a return to the verifiable, often provocatively banal, object world (as from the peaks of emotion in Expressionism), and a projection of mythical magical dimensions onto the everyday reality. Thus the industrial cityscapes of Franz Radziwill are perforated by glimpses of another, menacing world; the triptychs of Max Beckmann reveal an allegorical structure beneath the everyday quality of the figures. The novel *Perrudja* (1929) by Hans Henny Jahnn explores the tension between myth and realism in literary terms, and Jahnn's novel *Das Holzschiff* (1949, The Wooden Ship) may be read along lines similar to Saiko's *Auf dem Floß*, namely as an allegory of the psyche. Whereas Jahnn's texts, however, tend to affirm the mythical as an end in itself, Saiko tends into the other direction, namely to reclaim the mythical as an integral and integrated part of the modern novel. In this respect the "magic" in Saiko's realism is a misleading label, especially when identified with the Vienna School of "Fantastic Realism" in painting (since 1956), which is also referred to as "Magic Realism."[30] In the final analysis, Saiko stands firmly in the Enlightenment tradition. Even though he repeatedly criticized Musil for his intellectualization of the novel and probably shuddered at Musil's aim in writing *Der Mann ohne Eigenschaften* ("I want to contribute to our intellectual grasp of the world."),[31] his aims are fundamentally similar. The critique of instrumental rationality, the unmasking of rational delusions at the hand of the unconscious, the renewed attention to the mythical realm— all these tendencies in Saiko's work fold back into the overriding aim, "to penetrate our existence with consciousness."[32]

The last story published during his lifetime may demonstrate most convincingly to what a high degree Saiko's writing is fueled by critical and also self-critical reflection. Surprisingly, both of the stories in *Der Opferblock* (1962, The Sacrificial Stone) have been largely overlooked, even though these stories from the two world wars are superbly crafted and almost explosive in their social criticism. The second of the two, "Die Badewanne"(The Bathtub), concerns itself not only with a hefty tale—the grotesque capture of a bathtub during

the Nazi armies' retreat from the Soviet Union—but it also thematizes
the mediation of that tale—and shows that the cost of writing about
an atrocity is to be drawn into it and to be tainted by it. The anecdotal
incident with the bathtub is pieced together by the vacationing government official Rubiczka von Felsenwehr, who overhears the swashbuckling tales of a nameless first lieutenant in the barroom of his hostel.
Rubiczka, henceforth nameless like the other officer and distinguished
only by an italicized *he* whenever necessary, feels revolted by the
swashbuckling officer who nevertheless seems kin ("again and again the
man, unknown before and never seen, echo and rebirth out of *himself*").[33] *He* challenges the other's boasting and is in turn confronted
with the fact that *he* did not see active service. Rubiczka, whose perspective governs the narrative, attempts to get more information about
the ex-officer's exploits against the hostility of the men surrounding
the latter, who are either dependent on him or who share his unchanged
supremacist (Nazi) views. The picture reconstructed by Rubiczka—
vacationing presumably in the late 1940s or early 1950s—shows a
German army going through the futile motions of retreat in Russia
circa 1943, commanded by a pleasure-seeking general whose only need
is a bathtub so that he might persuade a woman to stay with him. The
lieutenant seizes this as his chance for promotion and distinction and
finally "conquers" a tub in a foray that costs seventeen of his men
and an equal number of partisans their lives.

Grotesque as this anecdote may be in itself, it acquires its raw
edge only in the beer- and pork-saturated barroom context of its retelling and in the prevailing attitude that nothing needed to be re-
thought. Years after the Second World War has come to its disastrous
end, neither teller nor listeners see a need to change their view—this is
also the thrust of Ingeborg Bachmann's equally scathing story "Unter
Mördern und Irren" (Among Murderers and Madmen), published only
a year earlier than Saiko's. "As though not a day had passed," laments
the observer of an ex-servicemen's reunion in Bachmann's text before
he becomes a martyr.[34] In Saiko's text the conclusion is the same
but implicit; the startling aspect of "Die Badewanne" is the "intimacy"
felt by the observer towards the officer, albeit an "intimacy of hate
and contempt" (263).

In this problematization of the observer stance Saiko goes far
beyond the standard of "coming to terms with the past" in German
and Austrian literature,[35] because he acknowledges that an author
cannot presume to recreate the horror of the war and the abyss of the

mentality that supported it without becoming in some sense part of that horror himself. The text juxtaposes the identification between the lieutenant and the general with Rubiczka's obsessive quest for the whole story of the lieutenant, which in turn mirrors the writer's task. With this operation "Die Badewanne" radically calls into question the notion of an unassailable critical stance, while it fervently affirms at the same time that critical work. Here again the narrator/author is looking "behind the face/façade of the Austrian" and recognizes some of his own features. The irritating, confusing closeness of *"he"* and "he" in this text might pass for "deliberate obscurity"[36] upon superficial reading; in truth it may contain the text's most significant political statement. The secret identity between critic and object of critique repeats the relationship between Saiko and Austria, an "intimacy of hate and contempt."

Notes

1.   Jeannie Ebner, "Hermann Broch und George Saiko," *Literatur und Kritik* 54/55 (1971), 264.

2.   Wendelin Schmidt-Dengler, "Die Strudlhofstiege. Literatur zwischen Anarchie und Ordnung," in *Das größere Österreich,* ed. Kristian Sotriffer (Wien: Edition Tusch, 1982), p. 391.

3.   C. E. Williams, "George Saiko: Worlds within World," *Modern Austrian Writing,* ed. Alan Best and Hans Wolfschütz (London: Wolff, 1980), p. 99.

4.   Heimito von Doderer, "Nicht alle zogen nach Berlin," *Magnum* 35 (1961), 53.

5.   Hermann Broch, *Briefe 1 (1913-1938),* ed. Paul Michael Lützeler (Frankfurt am Main: Suhrkamp, 1981), p. 448.

6.   A representative list, far from complete: Broch, *Der Versucher* (= *Die Verzauberung*) (1953); Brunngraber, *Der Weg durch das Labyrinth* (1947); Canetti, *Komödie der Eitelkeit* (1949); Doderer, *Die Dämonen* (1956); Gütersloh, *Eine sagenhafte Figur* (1946); Kraus, *Die Dritte Walpurgisnacht* (1952).

7.   Hermann Broch, *Briefe 3,* p. 544.

8.   George Saiko, "Die Wirklichkeit hat doppelten Boden. Gedanken zum 'magischen Realismus' in der Literatur," *Wiener Bücherbriefe* no. 1 (1959), 1.

9.   Ibid., p. 1f.

10. Ludwig Wittgenstein, *Tractatus logico-philosophicus* in *Schriften* (Frankfurt am Main: Suhrkamp, 1963), p. 83.

11. Cf. Allan Janik and Stephen Toulmin, *Wittgenstein's Vienna* (New York: Simon and Schuster, 1973), p. 191.

12. George Saiko, *Auf dem Floß. Roman* (Wien: Gutenberg: 1968), p. 35. Page numbers indicated in text refer to this edition.

13. Only one date gives a precise clue: Eugen's escape from the Russian Civil War 1917/1918 and his subsequent twenty years of émigré life in France (129) would date the novel's events as taking place during the summer of 1937.

14. Cf. Carol Lewis, *Search for Identity: Theme and Structure in George Saiko's 'Auf dem Floß'* (Ph.D. dissertation, Indiana University, 1977), p. 164.

15. For an exemplary reintroduction of allegory, cf. Heinz Schlaffer, *Faust Zweiter Teil. Die Allegorie des 19. Jahrhunderts* (Stuttgart: Metzler, 1981).

16. George Saiko, "Zur Erneuerung des Romans," *Wiener Bücherbriefe* 3 (1955), 1.

17. Robert Musil, *Gesammelte Werke 1. Der Mann ohne Eigenschaften* (Reinbek: Rowohlt, 1978), p. 76.

18. Carol Lewis, *Search for Identity*, p. 164.

19. Cf. Norbert Elias, *The Civilizing Process* (1936) (New York: Urizen Books, 1978).

20. George Saiko, "Hinter dem Gesicht des Österreichers," *Comprendre* 17/18 (1957), 141-148.

21. Cf. the two attempts by Karl, the last Habsburg emperor, to regain the Hungarian throne, March and October 1921.

22. Cf. Hugo von Hofmannsthal, "Die österreichische Idee" (1917), *Reden und Aufsätze 2* (Frankfurt am Main: Fischer, 1979), pp. 453-458, and similar texts. Cf. also Leopold von Andrian, *Österreich im Prisma der Idee* (Graz: Schmidt-Dengler, 1937).

23. Claudio Magris, *Der habsburgische Mythos in der österreichischen Literatur* (Salzburg: Otto Müller, 1966).

24. George Saiko, *Der Mann im Schilf. Roman* (Zürich: Benziger, 1971), p. 57. Page numbers indicated in text refer to this edition.

25. Saiko did not intend a *roman à clef*. The volatile behavior exhibited by Mostbaumer was, however, widespread among high-ranking civil servants and exemplified by cabinet member Emil Fey. Cf. Hellmut Andics, *Der Staat, den keiner wollte* (enlarged edition München: W. Goldmann, 1980), pp. 201 ff.

26.   C. E. Williams, see note 3, p. 106.
27.   Wendelin Schmidt-Dengler, see note 2, p. 381.
28.   Readings of Broch's novel as endorsing irrationalism have been refuted by Paul Michael Lützeler, "Hermann Brochs *Die Verzauberung* als politischer Roman," *Neophilologus* 61 (1977), 111-126.
29.   "Requiem für einen Faschisten" (1946), on the suicide of Josef Weinheber: "Du warst in allem einer ihrer Besten, / erschrocken fühl ich heut mich dir verwandt"; Theodor Kramer, *Orgel aus Staub. Gesammelte Gedichte,* ed. Erwin Chvojka (München: Hanser, 1983), p. 65 f.
30.   Cf. Alessandra Comini, *The Fantastic Art of Vienna* (New York: Knopf, 1978), p. 25.
31.   "Was arbeiten Sie? Gespräch mit Robert Musil" (1926), in R.M. *Gesammelte Werke 7* (Reinbek: Rowohlt, 1978), p. 942.
32.   George Saiko, *Erzählungen* (Zürich: Benziger, 1972), p. 213. Page numbers indicated in text refer to this edition.
33.   George Saiko, "Zur Erneuerung des Romans," p. 3.
34.   Ingeborg Bachmann, *The Thirtieth Year* (New York: Knopf, 1964), p. 109.
35.   Cf. Hamida Bosmajian, *Metaphors of Evil. Contemporary German Literature and the Shadow of Nazism* (Iowa City: University of Iowa Press, 1979); Judith Ryan, *The Uncompleted Past. Postwar German Novels and the Third Reich* (Detroit: Wayne State Press, 1983).
36.   Rejection of *Auf dem Floß* by Houghton Mifflin quoted in Ebner, see note 1.

Bibliography

I. Works by George Saiko in German

Auf dem Floß. Zürich: Carl Posen, Lizensausbage für Deutschland. Wiesbaden: Limes, 1948. Also Hamburg: Marion von Schröder, 1954; Wien: Gutenberg, 1968; Zürich: Benziger, 1970; Zürich: Ex Libris, 1976; Frankfurt am Main: Fischer, 1980.
"Aus der Korrespondenz über das gestrichene Kapitel im Roman *Der Mann im Schilf.*" *Protokolle* 2 (1970), 153-154.
Die dunkelste Nacht. Ed. Ferdinand Wernigg. Graz:Stiasny, 1961.

Die erste und die letzte Erzählung. Dichtung aus Österreich 145. Wien: Bergland, 1968.

Erzählungen. Zürich: Benziger, 1972.

"Europa als Wunsch und Wirklichkeit." *Lebendige Stadt: Literarischer Almanach der Stadt Wien.* Wien: Amt für Kultur, Volksbildung und Schulverwaltung, 1960, pp. 11-18.

Giraffe unter Palmen: Geschichten vom Mittelmeer. Wien: Deutsch, 1962.

"Die gnadenlose Stadt." *Die Muskete: Humoristische Wochenzeitung* 458 (1914), 115-118.

"Hinter dem Gesicht des Österreichers." *Comprendre, Société Européenne de Culture* 17-18 (1957), 141-148.

"Das letzte Ziel." *Der Brenner* 15 (1913, 675-693 (in reprint edition [Innsbruck: Brenner, 1969], vol. 6), unter dem Namen Markus Saiko.

Der Mann im Schilf. Hamburg: Marion von Schröder, 1955. Also Wien: Gutenberg, 1968; Zürich: Benziger, 1971; Frankfurt am Main: Fischer, 1979.

Der Opferblock. Wien: Deutsch, 1962.

"Der Roman: heute und morgen." *Wort in der Zeit* 9/2 (1963), 37-40.

"Roman und Film: Die Formen unserer Weltinterpretation." *Literatur und Kritik* 54/55 (1971), 271-282.

"Die Rückkehr aus dem Unbewußten: Das Facit des Surrealismus." *Wort in der Zeit* 5/4 (1959), 15-18.

"Surrealismus und Realität: Aus den Prinzipien einer neuen Ästhetik." *Kontinente* 11/12 (1955), 35-40. Also *Wiener Bücherbrief* 3 (1959), 4-10.

"Ein unveröffentlichtes Kapitel aus dem Roman *Der Mann im Schilf.*" *Protokolle* 2 (1970), 148-152.

"Vorwort" zu *Der Zauberwald: Deutsche Märchen.* Ed. Georg Ebert. Wien: Verlag der Wiener Graphischen Werkstätte, 1922, pp. 5-7.

"Die Wirklichkeit hat doppelten Boden: Gedanken zum magischen Realismus in der Literatur." *Aktion* 19 (1952), 80-82. Also *Wiener Bücherbrief* 1 (1959), 1-4.

"Zur 'Entschlüsselung' der Symbolik in zwei Kurzgeschichten." *Literatur und Kritik* 14 (1967), 213-215.

"Zur Entstehung des modernen Landschaftsgefühls." *Die Schönen Künste* 1 (1947), 20-25.

"Zur Erneuerung des Romans." *Wiener Bücherbriefe* 3 (1955), 1-3.

"Zur Situation der erzählenden Prosa." *Wiener Bücherbrief* 1 (1969), 1-5.

II. Works in English Translation

"La letteratura austriaca." *Almanaco letterario*. Milan: Bompiana, 1961, pp. 181-184.

"The Meaning of Cubism: 'Cubist' Drawings of the Sixteenth Century." Trans. Arthur Oakey. *The Studio* 100 (1930), 206-213.

"The Possibility of Symbolism in Modern Painting." Trans. Arthur Oakey. *Creative Art* 9 (1931), 467-474.

"The Tragic Position of Abstract Art." Trans. Arthur Oakey. *The Studio* 105 (1933), 43-48.

"Why Modern Art Is Primitive." Trans. Arthur Oakey. *The Studio* 108 (1934), 274-277.

III. Secondary Works in English

Lewis, Carol. "Search for Identity: Theme and Structure in George Saiko's *Auf dem Floß*." Dissertation, Indiana University, 1977.

Schoolfield, George C. "Exercises in Brotherhood: The Recent Austrian Novel." *German Quarterly* 26 (1953), 228.

Schuschnigg, Maria D. "George Saiko: An Austrian Writer of Transition." M.A. thesis, Washington University, St. Louis, 1965.

Williams, Cedric E. "George Saiko: Worlds within World." *Modern Austrian Writing. Literature and Society after 1945*. Ed. Alan Best and Hans Wolfschütz. London: Wolff, 1980, pp. 97-107.

IV. Major Studies in German

Alker, Ernst. "George Saiko." *Schweizer Monatshefte* 6 (1971), 443-446.

Blauhut, Robert. "George Saiko." *Österreichische Novellistik des 20. Jahrhunderts*. Wien: Braumüller, 1966, pp. 244-248.

Doppler, Alfred. *Wirklichkeit im Spiegel der Sprache: Aufsätze zur Literatur des 20. Jahrhunderts in Österreich*. Wien: Europa, 1975, pp. 172-196.

Ebner, Jeannie. "Hermann Broch und George Saiko." *Literatur und Kritik* 54/55 (1971), 262-270.

Heger, Roland. "George Saiko." *Der österreichische Roman des 20. Jahrhunderts*. Vol. 1. Wien: Braumüller, 1971, pp. 82-85.

Mayr, Christina. "Historisch-zeitkritische und psychoanalytische Dimensionen im Werk von George Saiko, unter besonderer Berücksichtigung seines Romans *Der Mann im Schilf.*" Dissertation, Innsbruck, 1978.

Musulin, Janko von. "George Saiko." *Schriftsteller der Gegenwart.* Ed. Klaus Nonnemann. Olten: Walter, 1963, pp. 267-274.

Rieder, Heinz. "George Saiko." *Österreichische Moderne: Studien zum Weltbild und Menschenbild in ihrer Epik und Lyrik.* Abhandlungen zur Kunst, Musik- und Literaturwissenschaft 60. Bonn: Bouvier, 1968, pp. 94-108.

Roček, Roman. "Bewußtsein aus dem Konflikt: George Saiko." *Neue Akzente: Essays für Liebhaber der Literatur.* Wien: Herold, 1984, pp. 163-173.

Széll, Zsuzsa. "George Saikos Wirklichkeit." *Literatur und Kritik* 99 (1975), 553-561.

Friedrich Torberg

Laurence Rickels

> "But Papa, I don't want to be no
> cantor . . . I want to be a singer in
> a theayter."   — *The Jazz Singer*

> Wherever I go, the dark garments
> of the dead flutter about me.
>   — Torberg, "The Return"

Der Schüler Gerber hat absolviert (1930, The Pupil Gerber Has Graduated) instantly made a name for Friedrich Torberg, who would never sign this new name to another work that equaled his first novel's impact and success. This "work of hatred," as Torberg put it,[1] issued from his own sense of betrayal and victimization within the educational institution. The novel was conceived when in a single week of winter 1929 the newspaper reports of ten student suicides penetrated to Torberg, who was brooding over a recent humiliation at the hands of school authorities. What culminates in the writing of *Der Schüler Gerber hat absolviert* can already be read into the changes Torberg introduced into his life upon graduating from secondary school; these range from the reversal of his daily routine — going to bed, for example, when as a pupil he had gotten up — to changing his patronymic Kantor to the pseudonym Torberg, the name under which his publications, beginning with *Der Schüler Gerber hat absolviert*, would appear.[2]

By referring all who seek out his works under the name Torberg to the name Kantor-Berg, that archival guardian of the proper name, the card catalogue, exceeds its duties to the point of perpetuating a confusion. According to the card catalogue, Torberg arrived at his pseudonym by merging the patronym of his father with that of his mother's line, though the resulting Kantor-Berg was evidently subsequently truncated to Torberg. This original surname, which never existed, a marriage of patronyms which, however, never actually took place, serves to obscure the origin of the name Torberg, which lies in the mutilation of the father's name.

The relationship between father and son, which predominates in Torberg's works to the extent that the mother remains out of the picture, is accordingly one of ambivalence framed by worship, rebellion, and guilt. Torberg's inability to sign his patronym to his works invokes, to the full extent of its ineluctable transgression, the Old Testament injunction to commemorate the father god without naming or representing him. According to this ambivalent program, the father issues a commandment that can be followed only by transgressing against it, because commemoration always issues and inheres in naming. The Tower of Babel, which corresponds to the people's desire to circumvent dispersion by assimilating themselves into a collective, was itself the monument to and transgression against the father god's injunction. In Kantor's works this commemorative construction yields Torberg, just as every move described in his works toward assimilation within a collective, be it through sports or show business, is attended by transgression against family traditions guarded by the father.

Born on 16 September 1908, Friedrich Kantor was raised in Vienna but completed his secondary education in Prague, where in 1930 he brought out *Der Schüler Gerber hat absolviert* under his new name. By the time he was required by the encroachment of Nazi Germany to flee to Switzerland in 1938, Torberg had written and published three additional novels: *–und glauben, es wäre die Liebe* (1932, –and think it might be love), *Die Mannschaft* (1935, The Team), and *Abschied* (1937, Farewell).

After his flight to Switzerland, Torberg enlisted in the short-lived Czech national army operating in France. During this period of uncertainty, while he was searching for a place of refuge and a means of defense, Torberg composed the novel *Auch das war Wien* (That Too Was Vienna), which he commenced writing in Vienna in May 1938, continued in Prague, and completed one year later in Paris. Occluded by forgetfulness until its publication in 1984, five years after Torberg's death, the novel organizes its depiction and analysis of the Nazi takeover of Austria around a love affair between a Jewish playwright and a non-Jewish actress. As we know from a note appended to the recently discovered manuscript, Torberg had planned in 1941 to continue the central love story through two additional volumes, one devoted to Prague, the other to Paris, and to publish all three together under the title *Trilogie des Untergangs* (Trilogy of the Downfall).

With the assistance of the International P.E.N. Club and Warner Brothers Torberg was able to enter the United States, where first in Hollywood and then in New York he awaited the end of the war. During his exile in the United States Torberg composed his most important works: the novella *Mein ist die Rache* (1943, Revenge Is Mine) and the novel *Hier bin ich, mein Vater* (1946, Here I Am, My Father).

In 1951 Torberg returned to Vienna with his wife Marietta, whom he had met and married in the United States. But first he published and dedicated to his wife *Die zweite Begegnung* (1950, The Second Encounter), a novel highly critical of communism, which Torberg on one occasion deemed "the most ghastly masturbation of world history."[3] Back in Vienna Torberg conducted a polemic within his own journal *Forum* against such prominent communist writers as Brecht. He reserved his most severe criticism, however, for the flawed language of those who would occupy positions of authority and responsibility and whose dislodgment on grounds of moral and intellectual deficiency Torberg relentlessly demanded. In this stance he has invited comparison with Karl Kraus.

After twelve years of such anti-journalistic journalism Torberg began again to write literature, bringing out in 1968 a collection of novellas entitled *Golems Wiederkehr* (The Golem's Return). This collection, which includes his 1943 novella *Mein ist die Rache* and addresses in the title story conditions in Prague under the Nazis, marks Torberg's return to questions raised by the Nazi persecution of the Jews. The work he considered to be his masterpiece and testament, *Süsskind von Trimberg* (1972), recasts and forecasts the final destination of German-speaking Jewry in terms of the destiny of the first German-Jewish poet, the minstrel von Trimberg.

In 1963 Torberg edited and arranged for the publication of the collected works of the Austrian-Jewish writer Fritz von Herzmanovsky-Orlando, whom he had first met in 1931. To make them more accessible to the belated recognition they deserved, Torberg also revised and shortened the works he collected. The charge made by certain scholars that this rescue operation was but a shortcut to popular acclaim for works Torberg had counterfeited in the process confirmed

Torberg's reservations about the institutional destiny or destination of literature. These reservations had already prompted him to ally himself with the culture industry which, he trusted, was less open than educational institutions to exclusion.

Until his death in Vienna on 10 November 1979 Torberg continued to write theater criticism, translated into German various joke books by the Israeli humorist Kishon, and compiled two volumes of humorous anecdotes rescued from the annihilation of prewar Jewish culture in Vienna and Prague. The first volume, *Tante Jolesch* (Aunt Jolesch), became in 1975 his only work after *Der Schüler Gerber hat absolviert* to attain best-seller status, even summoning a sequel, *Die Erben der Tante Jolesch* (1978, The Heirs of Aunt Jolesch). Both *Aunt Jolesch* collections juxtapose humorous accounts—for example, of name changes made by Jews to enhance their careers—with melancholy reflections on the disappearance of such veritable Jewish institutions as the coffeehouse. According to Torberg, what has thus vanished lives on only in and as the perpetual exile that is now Aunt Jolesch's sole legacy.[4]

For Torberg this exile or banishment had begun out of phase with political developments but already within structures of thought that are properly institutional. *Der Schüler Gerber hat absolviert* charts the suicide of the bright and independent pupil Gerber back to his dread fear that failure on the final examination, which his instructor's taunts appear to guarantee, would fatally affect his father's weak heart. And yet the altercation between Gerber and his instructor, who, much to his satisfaction, was fully named by the pupils "God Kupfer," would have remained imaginary if the pressure Kupfer applied to Gerber, in lieu of actually failing him, had not, right from the start, condemned the boy in the name of his father. According to Torberg, such parasitism is a typical production of the educational institution, which can conceive power only in alliance with Oedipal structures belonging in the home. God Kupfer, also a casualty of the institution, transmits to his pupils a disturbed relationship to knowledge, which is in fact replaced according to a certain logic of overcompensation and impotence by the exhibition of power. In this exhibition or show students merely pretend for the duration of the game to play along in the production they in fact attend as spectators of the professor's solo performance.

This exhibition can be enacted only by hiding the one side, which vacation otherwise reveals, of the inside/outside polarity that governs institutions. Because vacation evacuates his charges to the outside, where they occupy with their families positions of social prominence beyond an instructor's reach, it is for Kupfer a vacant space of time in which his own circulation systems run empty in the absence of access to the *curriculum vitae* of each student. As Kupfer reflects:

> After the empty summer months—empty since he had circulated simply as a person among persons and not as a God among pupils, since he could make no one shudder before his omnipotence, since the many things he saw could not be coerced to conform to his need for power— after this banishment he threw himself heart and soul into his resurrected empire.[5]

From the other end of this perspective the students recognize that institutional vampirism is limited to the extent that retirement is for the professor tantamount to being put to rest. "It is fine and appropriate," the students reason, "that at the end of this year a gate could close behind us. But behind him as well, for whom unlike us no other gate will open?"[6] And yet, awaiting each student's return home from school is according to Torberg the vampire king, the father, on whose behalf the institution illegitimately demands sacrifice to its circulation system of library books and blood.

Looking back on *Der Schüler Gerber hat absolviert,* Jean Améry recalled that "Torberg's novel literally detonated like a bomb" though, noting that it appears more dated than earlier works on the casualties of the educational institution, including those of Mann, Musil, Wedekind, or Hesse, he accords it no enduring status.[7] Yet Torberg's first novel did in fact bring him the support and approbation of such leading writers as Musil and Brod. Repeating the function he had served for Kafka, Brod had secured publication of *Der Schüler Gerber hat absolviert* without consulting Torberg. According to Torberg, Brod was his "'Jewish' father":[8] Brod had previously encouraged Torberg, then Fritz Kantor, to abandon his focus on parody, indeed, journalism, in favor of poetry and literature, a shift in focus that brought with it the change in his name. Among the various manuscripts given to Brod were a couple of love poems which Torberg had never dared to submit for publication because they were not consistent with the body of writing he considered his trademark and which he saw as comparable to the cabaret, as a part, that is, of the entertainment industry. His curiosity aroused by these love poems, Brod questioned Torberg as to what really motivated his writing, to which Torberg, in thinking about this question perhaps for the first time, responded that it was evidently such serious subjects as love, sports, Judaism, and school reform that had incited him to write.[9]

Améry stresses that adolescent sexual confusion, which *Der Schüler Gerber hat absolviert* also depicts and displays, blurs the contours of Torberg's critique of educational institutions also to the extent that neither sublimation nor sex but only a certain "erotic sultriness" pervades what cannot come into focus. For several years after publication of his first work Torberg was in fact preoccupied solely with scenarios of "erotic sultriness," so much so that he sought out Alfred Adler in the hope of preventing this obsession from obstructing his writing.[10] Perhaps influenced by Adler Torberg was able to inject between his two love stories – *und glauben, es wäre die Liebe* and *Abschied* a story about sports, his sports novel *Die Mannschaft* (1935, The Team). Now able to push aside his concern with adolescent sexual confusion and initiation, he focused instead on the virtues of team sports, virtues ranging from cooperation to reciprocity and comradeship. To the extent that *Abschied* represents ultimately a leave-taking from adolescent sentimentality, *Die Mannschaft* may well mark a new beginning in Torberg's writing rather than some momentary respite in the safety zone of sports from that sultriness otherwise guiding his pen. In *Abschied* the protagonist decides by the end of the novel to pursue single-mindedly his training and career as concert pianist rather than consummate and protract in an adult relationship a love affair that ended with adolescence.

Torberg's appreciation of sports was such that, when asked in later years what had been the most glorious day of his life, he could not decide whether it was the day he heard that both Karl Kraus and Alfred Polgar had expressed their high opinion of him or the day he shot both the goals that won the game for his team during the Czech waterball championship games. The older he gets, Torberg muses at the close of "Lieben Sie Sport?" (Do You Love Sports?), the more he tends to single out as his paramount achievement the day he twice scored the winning goal (*Tor*).[11] By the time he composed *Die Mannschaft*, which he declared to be his favorite work, Torberg's central concern was no longer the individual and his tribulations but rather the group, seen by the end of the novel as a means whereby a team member can live on after his own death as an integral part of that group to which he contributes. Unlike the institution depicted in *Der Schüler Gerber hat absolviert,* which periodically fails, graduates, or discharges its constituents, the team gains and maintains its continuity through the gradual assimilation of new members:

> Now something crumbles, now something takes its place. The old remains and the new is already there; they absorb and assimilate each other, stream onwards, change and form anew as if unexpected and unnoticed . . . and so it goes and streams on and continues developing and takes the former team players along into the ever new generation.[12]

The hero's name, Baumeister (architect), points again to that dominant aspiration in Torberg's writing to build a new tower of Babel, in this case the collective of the team. As his 1954 essay on soccer and progress makes clear, Torberg's conception of the collectivity constituted by team sports was never meant to bear any specific political or ideological affiliation:

> A soccer player may unceasingly serve progress–however, from the moment he enters the game till the instant he leaves it again he is a soccer player and nothing else, serves the rules of the soccer game and no other rules. And he serves not so much these rules as that inner law which inheres in soccer as in all team sports and which at the same time links together all teams around the world.[13]

But this collective governed by an "inner law" is no more apolitical than had been the construction of the tower of Babel. Torberg's own involvement in sports had, for example, aimed to reverse anti-Semitic charges that Jews were too weak or cowardly for physical competition,[14] and yet the commitment to assimilation within some towering collective, represented in Torberg's works by team sports and the culture industry, can be achieved only by abandoning Jewish identity.

Acknowledged by Torberg to be the first Jewish poet to write in German, the *Minnesänger* Süsskind von Trimberg was actually the very first subject that inspired Torberg to write.[15] Yet it was not until the end of his career that Torberg finally produced his novel *Süsskind von Trimberg,* his last major work. Abraham Tobias has noted the proximity of the name Trimberg to Torberg which, like an omen, rehearses and repeats a more far-reaching similarity between the two artists: Torberg indeed saw himself as the last exponent of what Trimberg had initiated, namely, the Jews' adoption and enrichment of German as their mother tongue.[16] Torberg once noted: "For me Süsskind von Trimberg embodies—and anticipates by seven hundred years—that which we had viewed optimistically as German-Jewish cultural symbiosis, and which in our day is irrevocably coming to an end." By describing, for example, Süsskind's sitting for his portrait under coercion and contrary to the tenets of his faith Torberg calls attention to the specific relation of Jew to Christian within this symbiosis as being literally one of assimilatory exchange whereby text is transferred to image, and image to text. In a television interview Torberg identified the specifically Jewish contribution to this literary symbiosis that Trimberg initiated. The contribution "lies in the verbal responsibility and the special rapport of the Jew—as a member of an imageless faith—to the word. . . ."[17]

According to Tobias, Torberg identified with Trimberg to the point of mirroring and reversing his achievements: Torberg conceived himself to be the last representative of the "German-Jewish cultural symbiosis," while at the same time he set himself up as the first author to rhyme a Hebrew word with a German word within a German text. And yet as a latecomer Torberg could contemplate this cultural symbiosis only in terms of the charges the Jewish guest covered for the host culture. Or, in the words of Torberg's inspirational figure Martin Buber: "Every symbiosis the Jew enters upon is treacherous. Every alliance in his history contains an invisible terminating clause, every union with other civilizations is informed with a secret divisive force."[18]

In the wake of the pogrom murder of his parents Süsskind von Trimberg—or, as he is called in Hebrew, Mordechai ben Jehuda—pursued an always divided allegiance to the language in which he had elected to sing:

> The attempt to negotiate an adjustment between the two languages that are his own, to establish and demarcate German as "mother tongue" and Hebrew as "father tongue" did not help him along—even though it appeared enticing. For in fact he felt bound to his father in all the Hebrew he knew. . . . From his mother, on the other hand, he had never heard any language other than German. . . .[19]

German corresponds to a certain sensation of "sweetness" instilled in him by tranquil nature[20] which inheres in his German name Süsskind (sweet child). Though this name sounded effeminate to his peers, his Hebrew first name Mordechai, Süsskind reflected, would have resounded in German ears with the more dreadful charge of *Mord* (murder). To write or sing in this mother tongue the first Jewish writer had to replace with a changed or feminized name the Hebrew name that doubled within German as murder, as death. In the German-Jewish symbiosis the Jewish guest is always also a ghost.

During his exile in Hollywood Torberg conceived and began writing what are generally considered to be his major works, which in contrast to earlier projects addressed the fragile status of Jewish identity. Torberg addressed these issues during the reign of Nazi persecution, which was to claim the lives of his mother and sister. In these narratives Torberg was concerned primarily with what he saw as "religious" issues confronting those subject to persecution: whether to resist, flee, or simply submit.[21] All these narratives include, moreover, consideration of the end of such persecution in terms of the work of mourning for the dead.

Torberg, like so many other European Jewish intellectuals, had in fact been rescued by Warner Brothers Studio, which along with other Hollywood studios offered film contracts to those otherwise unable to emigrate to the United States. Though he viewed the film industry, especially its Hollywood milieu, with contempt, in his third year at the studio he composed a *Casablanca*-like film, *Voice in the Wind*, about the plight of people fleeing the forces of Nazi Germany. This movie, which enjoyed considerable box office success, is set in Nazi-occupied Prague, where in defiance of a certain decree a Czech pianist plays a Czech song with nationalistic appeal. After his arrest by the Nazis he escapes to the French colony of Guadeloupe, where together with his fellow refugees he secures entry into the United States with the help of gangsters.

Entry into the culture of assimilation capitalized on by Hollywood, which in turn served as its capital, had already been memorialized in *The Jazz Singer*, which lapsed Jews produced to commemorate and cover their own assimilation into a kind of nondenominational yet essentially Christian American society. Jakie Rabinowitz, the son in Hollywood's first sound film, abandons Jewish family traditions when he ignores his father's wish that he too should serve as cantor. Instead Jakie changes his name to Jack Robins just as he exchanges his patrimony for a career as jazz singer. *The Jazz Singer* thus marks a descent from *Gesang* to *Gerede,* from silent films with musical scores to "talkies," from the voice to the vitaphone used to record that other voice in the wind called jazz. Jack Robins becomes a successful mammy singer. When he returns home he injures his father by babbling on about having made a name for himself. The mortally ill father must be replaced as temple cantor on the Day of Atonement. Jack accepts this invitation to identify with his father by canceling his Broadway première; as he receives his dying father's blessing, Jack sings the Kol Nidre.

Jack's show of piety remains, however, a one-time stint as cantor, a brief delay injected into his career as jazz singer. The culture of assimilation represented by Broadway and Hollywood thus prevails to the point of securing the blessing of that which it then eradicates. The seductive alternative to the Jewish patrimony, which Jack's mother Sarah "understands," consists of a series of "Marys," including Mary Dale, whom Jack Robins hopes to marry, and the injunction to assimilate through intermarriage, which "America" harbors. Despite these seductions that Hollywood continued to transmit Torberg saw Hollywood as a place haunted by those European casualties of the drive to assimilate for whom the name alone now circulated as product and producer of phantom assimilation. If he were ever to write a book about his Hollywood experience, Torberg later reflected, he would entitle it "Sons, Widows, and Ghosts": "Whenever ... one encountered the name of a European celebrity, nine times out of ten it concerned the son or widow of someone long since deceased; if it did turn out to be the name bearer himself, then one was invariably brought face to face with a ghost."[22]

According to Torberg, "modern man's susceptibility to dictatorship" is "a religious problem" that renders his "relation to God" the "'true' question."[23] Torberg first addressed these problems and questions in California under the Biblical titles *Revenge Is Mine* and *Here I Am My Father.* Hailed by Robert Neumann as the "most stirring émigré novel,"[24] *Here I Am My Father* is the confession of a young Viennese Jew, the unemployed jazz pianist Otto Maier, who becomes an agent for the Gestapo in exchange for the promise of safety for his father in Dachau. When Otto discovers that he has been duped by his former classmate, who blackmailed him with the father's death that had already transpired, he attempts to turn his espionage work in Paris into his cover as a double agent. But according to the French authorities who respond to his proposition by imprisoning him as a Jewish Nazi spy, Otto is already his own double agent. Before he concludes his double life with the suicide that doubling always calls for, Otto rejects the counsel of his former religion professor that morality and not force is the only form of resistance available to the Jews. Otto had always resisted the "defect" of Jewish identity, an identifying mark that had only prevented his being "treated like a normal person, that is, in the sense non-Jews give the word normal."[25] By rejecting his professor's view that Jews should resist their persecutors by answering to some higher moral standard Otto returns to the conflict that opened the novel when, rather than become a physician like his father, he decided to pursue a career as a jazz musician. The novel's closing pages project the conflict between father and son onto the struggle between Jew and Nazi: "Why do you say Jews? Why not sons? Why not: all those for whom it matters whether their fathers live or die? And why do you say: Nazis? Why not: all those for whom the lives of their fathers play no role? All those for whom the phantom of a leader replaced their proper fathers and the phantom of a higher community replaced their own morality?" And then with reference to Otto's plight: "No, of course one cannot spy for the other side . . . One cannot join forces with them, not even for the sake of one's own father. But to realize that one must have the strength to be a father oneself."[26]

These themes of responsibility and guilt already informed Torberg's earlier work *Revenge Is Mine,* which Hermann Broch praised for including in its depiction of Nazi persecution both the sadistic-homosexual component in the torture sessions and the silent pact of the Jews not to resist, so uncannily characteristic of the fate of the Jews.[27] The title *Revenge Is Mine* refers to that divine declaration, according to which the Lord alone has the right to avenge his chosen people. This declaration and its consequences are examined within a concentration camp, where the Jewish quarters are being decimated by the new commandant's seemingly random yet uninterrupted selection of individual Jews to be tortured to the point that they commit suicide. One exception to this series of provoked suicides, the secularized Jew Landauer characterized by his pride in his nationally acclaimed status as champion swimmer, unexpectedly volunteers to be the commandant's next victim. Inasmuch as Landauer refuses to kill himself and, before dying in the Jewish barracks, reveals his intention to assassinate the commandant, it is he who first raises the question of a choice for the Jews between compliance and resistance, to which the devoutly religious candidate for the office of Rabbi, Joseph Aschkenasy, counters that vengeance is God's exclusive right.

The anonymous narrator, who has survived to recall these events, is struck by the way in which Aschkenasy and the commandant Wagenseil would thus be unwitting accomplices rather than opponents within the holocaust:

> "That would imply that the Jew had the choice to be either good or bad. But the Jew has no choice."
>
> Yes, those were Wagenseil's words earlier today, and they confused me now just as much as they did then, when in resonance with Aschkenasy's nighttime invocation they seemed to ring in my ears. And were they not in fact the reverse—no, not even the reverse anymore but almost exactly the same thing as what Aschkenasy had meant? Aschkenasy, when he declared that we cannot escape dependence on divine vengeance? And that only for that reason were we still living? Only because we had no choice—that was it: no choice between our revenge and the revenge of the Lord? And therefore ceded revenge to the Lord and thus were "good" whether we wanted to be or not? If Wagenseil now calls "bad" what we cannot help but be, that made no difference anymore. What was crucial was the necessity. It was crucial that we were without choice or will, that we had to be—"good" from this standpoint, "bad" from that standpoint, but either way without choice . . .
>
> Yes, that is what I still wanted to tell my fellow inmates before I died. See, Aschkenasy is right, I wanted to tell them. We are chosen, and we have no choice. This is known even to those who persecute us. They do not know, however, just how pointless it is to persecute us. It is just as pointless as our seeking revenge would be pointless. Revenge is Mine, says the Lord—and that means: do not ruin My revenge. You, who have withstood persecution for centuries—you, whom I avenge on all who persecute you, since they persecute Me in you— you who are My revenge—do not ruin yourselves by attempting to avenge yourselves. That, mind you, that would finally be your death: if you were to take revenge from Me, if you were to take yourselves out of My hands.[28]

The narrator, who immediately succeeds Landauer as the commandant's next chosen victim, refuses to kill himself so that, like

Landauer, he may die in the Jewish barracks. Even when the commandant predicts that he will probably die before being able to return to
the barracks and that even his corpse may never be returned there, he
agrees to shoot himself, but inside the barracks. Confronted with having
to "choose" between suicide and being beaten to death, the narrator
determines that he must return to the barracks before dying now to tell
his fellow inmates that Aschkenasy is wrong, that there are times when
the Jews should take revenge in God's name, for this too is part of service and obedience. Picking up the revolver at his side, the intended
instrument of his suicide, he kills the commandant and even manages
to escape, thereby fulfilling Landauer's goal by discarding his own. In
the course of following with Aschkenasy the father god's injunction
against seeking revenge the narrator nevertheless returns to his most
fervent wish that he, like Landauer, be mourned in the barracks:

> For these—afterwards it returned ever more clearly to my
> recollection—these were my last clear thoughts, before I shot
> at Wagenseil: *I have the choice* and *revenge is Mine.* These
> were the two thoughts and they circled about this one image:
> the dismembered corpse of Landauer in our quarters—and we
> in the flickering candlelight around the corpse—and Gure-
> witsch, who says: "This one here had the choice"—and Asch-
> kenasy, who says: "We have no choice, for revenge is Mine,
> says the Lord!"—yes, that was it. That was the image I saw,
> and *I have the choice* and *revenge is Mine:* that was what I
> thought. And then I fired.[29]

His separation from the one place where mourning could tran-
spire produces the narrator's startling conclusion: "My name is Joseph
Aschkenasy."[30] This ambiguous conclusion has always been accepted as
the narrator's true confession of identity. However, if he divided himself into two figures in order to tell his story, he is also someone else.
The narrator's alleged identity, then, must be construed as identification with the deceased he has left behind unburied and unmourned.
The concentration camp survivor must identify with and carry the
corpses of loved ones who, never properly buried or mourned, are not
at rest. The concentration camp inflicts its most severe persecution
when it heightens feelings of ambivalence—the murder of another
always means deferral of one's own extinction—and deprives inmates of
the possibility of mourning their dead.[31] With regard to mournful

commemoration the Jew and the Nazi, father and son, take up their antagonistic positions.

Torberg's first work depicting a Jewish protagonist would also have been his last major work to focus on a love story. Because he was writing it while fleeing the Nazis, the book that would center on this love affair and the trilogy that would have extended it had become impossible for Torberg. *Auch das war Wien* commences with the lovers turning for assistance to the American film industry, which is credited with having been the first institution to pick up the signals of impending disaster before the Nazi advance.[32] But Hollywood assimilation is projected only by the interracial couple; the Jewish playwright ends up trapped in Nazi Austria, already deprived of passport and ontological status. An almost hallucinatory refusal to accept loss characterizes Nazi projections. In the chapter entitled "Im Zeichen des Zeichens" (In the Sign of the Sign) Torberg interprets the nihilistic "hell dance" into which Austria was transformed immediately upon Nazi annexation as having transpired, like the shouts that vied with the planes overhead, in the sign of the sign, and of nothing else. The sign that thus no longer served but only commanded the subject was nothing but an amplification of the senses, an amplification made possible by the internal shattering of the unity of the subject. Torberg links this secret disunity and the willingness to participate in its loud cover-up to the refusal to accept loss, the loss of empire as well as of the First World War. "Now I am powerful," the amplified Austrian proclaimed; ". . . I am a world power, a victorious world power. I have conquered territory, I have conquered myself, I have incorporated myself and incorporated for myself. I have doubled and risen above myself . . ."[33]

In his final reckoning with the National Socialists, *Golems Wiederkehr,* Torberg resurrects the golem, that legendary robot created to safeguard the Jewish people from oppressors, in Torberg's version a dimwitted laborer who in further contrast to the legendary golem "animates" himself by articulating the sacred words, "Holy, holy, holy, is the Lord God of hosts." In Torberg's novella the golem intervenes in the Nazi attempt to torch the Altneuschul temple in Prague in order to put an end to the 700-year-old legend of the temple's indestructibility.

This arson attempt contradicts while revealing the aim of that comprehensive documentation of the Jewish race Hitler had ordered to demonstrate that the annihilation of the Jews served humanitarian interests. *Golems Wiederkehr* describes the construction of that museum and archive of Jewish history which, as Hitler planned, would serve to represent or frame the race he had extinguished. In this way Hitler sought to make himself the guardian and curator of the artifacts of those whose existence he would confine to the past.

According to the golem legend, a rabbi—in the famous Prague legend Rabbi Löw—shapes a clay son and savior that he animates by imbuing it with one of God's names, *aemaeth*. The deactivation of the golem in turn requires the removal of the parchment on which the name of God has been inscribed, a task accomplished in other accounts of golem-making through the erasure of the letter aleph which renders the name *aemaeth*, literally "truth," simply *maeth*, "dead." On the one hand the golem requests deactivation—pointing out to his creator that golem-making implies the death of God—and on the other the creator, fearing for his own life or for the safety of the world, finds it necessary to destroy the golem gone awry.

Golem means unformed, amorphous, and, as Gershom Scholem suggests, perhaps embryo.[34] Adam was golem or "unformed mass" before the breath of God touched him. Thus a man who creates a golem is in some sense competing with God's creation of Adam. Like Adam, the golem is created out of the earth by the power of the father god's words, and the tellurian powers the golem thereby inherits are responsible for the dangerous aspect of this creation. Unlike the making of Adam, however, golem-making amounts to animation of the dead. Though animate, the golem cannot speak or reason, nor can he procreate. According to at least one account of golem-making, the golem first had to be buried in the earth before he could be animated. This legend, as in most accounts of monstrous creation including vampire and mummy legends, involves a fantasy of reproduction, even self-reproduction, which is carried out without the mediation of the womb. Only by circumventing the mother's role in the reproductive process can the undead or the unborn come into being.

In the many versions of the legend that precede Torberg's novella the golem is the product of a ghetto culture in which there is little room for the mother. For example, in Wegener's 1920 film *The Golem: How He Came into the World*, the golem is produced in a household without a mother. In Wegener's film the golem, the animated image, yearns to be more than a mere product of assimilation, yearns, that is, to be further assimilated into the Christian host culture of flower-gathering women, effeminate men, and children, a culture that also seduces Rabbi Löw's daughter Miriam. In response to the emperor's decree that all Jews be banished from the realm Miriam initiates negotiations, largely sexual in nature, with the Christian messenger from the emperor's court, while her father and his male assistant undertake the creation of a son to be the savior of his threatened people. According to the film, the guilty relationship to the mother associated with Judaism virtually creates Christianity, which is conceived as the introduction of the saving virgin mother and her child. At the end of the movie the animated golem, the artificial son, on the loose and out of control within the Jewish ghetto, knocks down the gates; now calmed and contented, he seeks to join Christian children as they pick flowers outside the ghetto walls. But one child who lingers unafraid to play with the golem innocently removes the label *aemaeth* that gives him life, thereby bringing about the death or perhaps the redemption of the golem. The Jewish ghetto culture, depicted in the film as a dead golem-like reading-and-writing tradition consisting entirely of male to male transmissions, is contrasted with the at once innocent and knowing child, that embodiment and invention of Christianity.

In contrast to most versions of the legend, including Wegener's film, *Golems Wiederkehr* does not center on oppositions between life and death, outside and inside, or speech and writing but rather elaborates the correspondence of two blocked relations to mourning. Torberg's golem defends the Jewish cemetery and the Altneuschul temple, itself a shrine of countless martyrs, at a time when the Jews are being effaced and made to disappear without mourning and proper burial. But does not the museum the Nazis are erecting in fact occupy, while refusing to occupy, the place of a tomb? When inspecting the crowded precincts of the ancient Jewish cemetery, one of the Nazi experts engaged in the Jewish museum project disdainfully comments that the Jews could not even bury their dead properly. Yet the vast archive he is working to complete is itself an empty tomb without survivors, without mourning. And without commemoration this collection of artifacts would be mere display, mere image and mere name, and hence would be that eidetic crisis that Judaism has ever sought to push back.

To safeguard against such crisis the Jews were granted, according to the golem legend, a single media support system, though under the constraint of numerous restricting clauses and terms. Golem-making exploits those powers of image-making and nomination otherwise interdicted by Old Testament law. Wegener's *The Golem* takes up this problem of image-making and extends it to the film medium through Rabbi Löw's conjuring of spirits from the past at the emperor's request. His magic show, represented as a film within the film *The Golem*, carries with it Löw's warnings of the dangers of the show, warnings which, unheeded, materialize in catastrophic fashion. To the extent that German Expressionist film's short-lived legacy—essentially carried on only by Hollywood's monstrosity films of the 1930s—includes a warning about the limits of image-making and film-making, this legacy, like golem-making, also bears a warning about the limits of assimilation. As demonstrated by those Expressionist films centering on the preservation of the dead or the composition of new life out of decomposition, the refusal to accept loss leads only to monstrous assimilation or image-making; those substitutive processes essential not only to proper mourning, but also to any individual's assimilation even into his own culture have thus been discarded. Hollywood monstrosity films continued to transmit these warnings at a time when the German film industry had from 1927 on come to be dominated by anti-Semitic nationalistic concerns. That is to say, the transfer of German-Jewish involvement in film-making preceded the Nazi takeover of the German state and amounted to a warning signal that only Hollywood could have received. Indeed, many of those who had left for Hollywood before 1933 were active in arranging the movie contracts that would save many imperiled Jewish intellectuals by granting them entry into the United States, specifically to the very capital of this state of assimilation, Hollywood, where largely secularized Jews were in control.

In the first half of the twentieth century two prominent popular discourses—Freudian psychoanalysis and film—momentarily place a certain Jewish need or desire to assimilate at the very controls of assimilation, including the assimilation of secularized Christians into their "own" culture. In his 1962 parody "The Complex Dances: From a Screenplay of an Impending Hollywood Film" Torberg addresses this convergence of psychoanalysis and film:

Voice of the Subego:	Terrible . . . terrible . . .
Voice of the Superego:	That's how it will be.
Voice of the Subego:	In America?
Voice of the Superego:	Not only in America.
Voice of the Subego:	In film?
Voice of the Superego:	Not only in film.
Voice of the Subego:	Can nothing be done about it?
Voice of the Superego:	At most a back projection (*Rückprojektion*).
Voice of the Subego:	Projection is my province. But what

<blockquote>
do you mean by "back"?

Voice of the Superego: A playback.[35]
</blockquote>

Though film in particular was active in getting Jews out of that ghastly museum of Jewish history planned by Hitler, it should be stressed—lest this Jewish indebtedness to film remain a screen memory—that Jews have always been pushed to assimilate and have been pushed into those positions that influence the assimilation of all persons within a given collective. The drive to assimilate, which for Jews has always entailed transgression against the father god, is not restricted to the first half of the twentieth century. This drive, which today traverses television and deconstruction, dates back to Marx, Spinoza, the picaro, all the way back in fact to Christ, who is the model of Jewish assimilation that springs from a transgression and creates a discourse at once esoteric, popular, and with great power over the host culture.

This programing of Jews to adopt or internalize the drive to assimilate may, according to Hannah Arendt, be traced back to the new eighteenth-century culture of *Bildung* (education), itself formulated as a response to the Jewish question. For, Arendt continues, it became the earliest proof of *Bildung* that the oriental in the midst of educated Europe, the Jew, could be shaped into a paragon of edification—the most famous example being Moses Mendelssohn in the eighteenth century, who was called the "Jewish Socrates." Specifically, the culture of *Bildung* instituted, Arendt points out, the "exceptional Jew," the Jew who would both be and yet not be a Jew, that is, never an "ordinary Jew" but one always educated, emancipated from Jewish "superstition" and yet, because Jewish, somehow extraordinary, exciting; that is, the Jew, formerly viewed exclusively as parasite, was transformed through this impossible demand into a "virtuoso," an actor, image-maker, or jazz musician.[36]

The new culture of *Bildung,* inaugurated in the Enlightenment to promote the assimilation of Jews into secular society, meets with its utter reversal and gruesome literalization in the so-called "Enlightenment Project" (*Aufklärungsreferat*) instituted and destined by the Nazis to build the largest museum of Jewish history on earth. As described in *Golems Wiederkehr,* what remains of German-Jewish cultural symbiosis is a project to which Jews, who are kept ignorant of the Nazis' motivation in archivizing Jewish history, contribute to the point of giving instruction in Jewish traditions to Nazis, who must remedy their ignorance of that which they aim to collect and discredit. As Sigrid Mayer notes:

> For to turn Jewish tradition against the Jews themselves, the Germans must indispensably acquire some knowledge of this tradition. Thus at the same time they must sit on the 'school bench of their victims,' where they then promptly try to outdo each other in knowledge of Jewish matters.[37]

The Jewish emigration precipitated during World War II must never, Torberg insisted, be reversed, not even after the war, lest the Jews become assimilated again as mere "stepchildren."[38] But his own return to Austria after the war marked a return to that "cabaret" with which he had earlier chosen to compare his first writings signed Fritz Kantor. Having decided that the novel form was no longer the most effective forum for his struggle against the resurgence of totalitarianism, Torberg turned to media publication ranging from parody to theater criticism.[39]

Torberg decided then to enter the media—which had been his first desire and which he had realized in part when he worked as a scriptwriter in Hollywood and as a journalist in New York—in order that he might tamper with the controls. In this way Torberg managed to keep Brecht off the Viennese stage for a full decade at a time when Brecht was elsewhere enjoying considerable acclaim. Though Torberg may be justified in designating himself the last representative of German-Jewish cultural symbiosis—if this symbiosis is understood as harmonious collaboration—to his credit he should be acknowledged as the late arrival of another symbiosis embodied both in the golem, who is as much a threat to assimilation as he is an amalgam of its aspirations, and in Christ. Ever since Christ broke with Jewish tradition not so much to become assimilated into any extant non-Jewish society as to control and reroute the drive to assimilate, the media in the broadest sense of the term have proffered Jews an alternative to that museum of history that Hitler sought to realize.

Torberg saw his own survival as the most appropriate opposition to the Nazi threat. His 1942 poem "Terza Rimas of Life that Has Fled," conceived in response to Stefan Zweig's suicide, culminates in the line: "I want to outlive the great butcher." And though in his Hollywood Holocaust works, for example, this fervent wish to outlive appears to reside within his sister's and mother's crypts, in his turn to the media, his return to cabaret and athletic team, Torberg secured survival to the full extent of accepting substitution and restitution for loss. Torberg was content to influence his assimilation within that collective to which he himself had contributed.

Notes

1. Cited in Erwin Ringel, "Die Bedeutung von Torbergs *Schüler Gerber* für die moderne Selbstmordprophylaxe," *Das Pult* XII, 57 (1980), 73. All translations in this essay are my own. Torberg had in fact failed his first attempt to pass the secondary school exam.

2. See Edwin Hartl, "Der verlorene Wortführer Friedrich Torberg," *Literatur und Kritik* 141 (1980), 2-3. Cornelius Schnauber informed me about this turnaround in Torberg's daily schedule following Torberg's release from secondary school.

3. Cited in Roland Heger, *Der österreichische Roman des 20. Jahrhunderts* (Wien: Wilhelm Braumüller, 1971), I, p. 197.

4. Friedrich Torberg, *Die Erben der Tante Jolesch* (München: Langen-Müller, 1978), pp. 259-261.

5. Friedrich Torberg, *Der Schüler Gerber hat absolviert* (Mährisch-Ostrau: Julius Kittls, 1938), p. 19.

6. Ibid., p. 40.

7. Jean Améry, *Bücher aus der Jugend unseres Jahrhunderts* (Stuttgart: Klett-Cotta, 1981), p. 63.

8. Friedrich Torberg, "Am Anfang war Max Brod," *Max Brod. Ein Gedenkbuch. 1884-1968,* ed. Hugo Gold (Tel Aviv: Olamenu, 1969), pp. 20-22.

9. Friedrich Torberg, "Die Entdeckung," *Apropos. Nachgelassenes – Kritisches – Bleibendes* (München: Langen Müller, 1981), p. 410ff.

10. Jean Améry, p. 63 and Erwin Ringel, p. 75. Torberg gives a humorous account of his interview with Adler in *Die Erben der Tante Jolesch.*

11. Ibid., p. 183.

12. Friedrich Torberg, *Die Mannschaft. Roman eines Sport-Lebens* (Wien: Fritz Molden, 1968), p. 601.

13. Friedrich Torberg, *Apropos. Nachgelassenes – Kritisches – Bleibendes,* pp. 352-353.

14. Friedrich Torberg, *Die Erben der Tante Jolesch,* pp. 159-160.

15. Franz-Heinrich Hackel, "In der Sprache der Verfolger schreiben? Friedrich Torberg befragt Süßkind von Trimberg," *Emuna/Israel Forum* III (1977), p. 29.

16. Abraham Tobias, "Torbergs *Süsskind:* Seine Confessio judaica," *Bulletin des Leo Baeck Instituts* 56/57, 19 (1980), p. 169.

17. Torberg's remarks on German-Jewish cultural symbiosis are cited and discussed in Guy Stern, "Biographischer Roman als Selbstzeugnis aus dem Exil: Friedrich Torbergs *Süßkind von Trimberg*," *Preis der Vernunft. Literatur und Kunst zwischen Aufklärung, Widerstand und Anpassung. Festschrift für Walter Huder,* ed. Klaus Siebenhaar and Hermann Haarmann (Berlin: Medusa, 1982), p. 170ff. Though Marcel Reich-Ranicki in his review of *Süsskind von Trimberg,* in his *Über Ruhestörer: Juden in der deutschen Literatur* (München: Piper, 1973), p. 75ff., rightly points to the difficulties in equating anti-Semitism in medieval Christian society with the anti-Semitism of the Nazis, where the former derived principally from religious bigotry and the latter from racial prejudice, he fails to take cognizance of that generalization that appears to underlie Torberg's novel, namely, that the entire admittedly changing and shifting chronicle of anti-Semitism underscores from the Jewish perspective one and the same thing, the questionable efficacy of assimilation.

18. Martin Buber, "Der Jude in der Welt," *Der Jude und sein Judentum* (Köln: Joseph Metzer, 1963), p. 216.

19. Friedrich Torberg, *Süsskind von Trimberg* (Frankfurt am Main: S. Fischer, 1972), p. 93.

20. Ibid., p. 44.

21. See Cornelius Schnauber's various articles on this period of Torberg's life, for example, "Werk und Leben Friedrich Torbergs im amerikanischen Exil," *Literatur und Kritik* 181/182 (1984), 60–67.

22. Friedrich Torberg, *Die Tante Jolesch oder Der Untergang des Abendlandes in Anekdoten* (München: Deutscher Taschenbuch-Verlag, 1977), p. 208.

23. Cited in Joseph Strelka, "Friedrich Torberg," *Deutsche Exilliteratur seit 1933* I, ed. John M. Spalek (Bern: Francke, 1976), p. 624.

24. Cited in Roland Heger, *Der österreiche Roman des 20. Jahrhunderts,* p. 197.

25. Friedrich Torberg, *Hier bin ich, mein Vater* (München: Langen-Müller, 1974), p. 314.

26. Ibid., p. 337.

27. Referred to in Joseph P. Strelka, "Friedrich Torberg," p. 625.

28. Friedrich Torberg, *Mein ist die Rache* in *Golems Wiederkehr und andere Erzählungen* (Frankfurt am Main: S. Fischer, 1968), pp. 56–57.

29. Ibid., p. 73.

30. Ibid., p. 76.

31. See Joost A.M. Meerloo, "Delayed Mourning in Victims of Extermination Camps," *Journal of Hillside Hospital* XII (1963), p. 2 ff.

32. Friedrich Torberg, *Auch das war Wien* (München: Langen-Müller, 1984), p. 209 ff.

33. Ibid., p. 317.

34. See Gershom Scholem's chapter on the golem in his *Zur Kabbala und ihrer Symbolik* (Zürich: Rhein, 1960).

35. *PPP. Pamphlete, Parodien, Post Scripta* (München: Langen-Müller, 1964), pp. 250–251.

36. Hannah Arendt, *The Origins of Totalitarianism* (New York: Harcourt, Brace, 1951), pp. 56–67.

37. Sigrid Mayer, *Golem: Die literarische Rezeption eines Stoffes* (Bern: Herbert Lang, 1975), p. 189.

38. In his "Friedrich Torberg in den USA," *Der Weg war schon das Ziel: Festschrift für Friedrich Torberg zum 70. Geburtstag*, ed. Joseph Strelka (München: Langen-Müller, 1978), p. 205, Cornelius Schnauber refers to Torberg's essay, which first appeared in English, "Whose Stepchildren?" in which Torberg points to the ruin of all Jewish writers who sought assimilation through denial of their Jewishness.

39. See "Blaugrau karierte Berufung zum Dichter: Ein Nachruf zu Lebzeiten" (1968) in Friedrich Torberg, *Apropos*, p. 19.

Bibliography

I. Works by Friedrich Torberg in German

Der Schüler Gerber hat absolviert. Roman. Wien: Paul Zsolnay, 1930.
—und glauben, es wäre die Liebe. Ein Roman unter jungen Menschen.
Wien: Paul Zsolnay, 1932. (= Band X, *Gesammelte Werke in Einzelausgaben*).
Die Mannschaft: Roman eines Sport-Lebens. Mährisch-Ostrau: Julius
Kittls, 1935.
Abschied. Roman einer ersten Liebe. Zürich: Humanitas, 1937.
Mein ist die Rache. Los Angeles: Pazifische Presse, 1943.
Hier bin ich, mein Vater. Roman. Stockholm: Bermann-Fischer, 1948.
(= Band I, *Gesammelte Werke in Einzelausgaben*).
Die zweite Begegnung. Roman. Frankfurt am Main: S. Fischer, 1950.
(= Band II, *Gesammelte Werke in Einzelausgaben*).
Golems Wiederkehr und andere Erzählungen. Frankfurt am Main:
S. Fischer, 1968. (= Band VI, *Gesammelte Werke in Einzelausgaben*).
Süsskind von Trimberg. Roman. Frankfurt am Main: S. Fischer, 1972.
(= Band VII, *Gesammelte Werke in Einzelausgaben*).
Auch das war Wien. Roman. München: Langen Müller, 1984. (= Band
XV, *Gesammelte Werke in Einzelausgaben*).

Poetry

Der ewige Refrain. Lieder einer Alltagsliebe. Wien: Saturn, 1929.
Lebenslied. Gedichte aus 25 Jahren. München: Langen-Müller, 1958.
Mit der Zeit, gegen die Zeit. Graz: Stiasny, 1965.

Anecdotes, Articles, Essays, Parodies

PPP. Pamphlete, Parodien, Post Scripta. München: Langen-Müller, 1964.
(= Band III, *Gesammelte Werke in Einzelausgaben*).
Das fünfte Rad am Thespiskarren. Theaterkritiken. München: Langen-
Müller, 1966. (= Bände IV-V, *Gesammelte Werke in Einzelausgaben*).
Die Tante Jolesch oder Der Untergang des Abendlandes in Anekdoten.
München: Langen-Müller, 1975. (= Band VIII, *Gesammelte Werke in Einzelausgaben*).

Die Erben der Tante Jolesch. München: Langen-Müller, 1978. (= Band IX, *Gesammelte Werke in Einzelausgaben*).
Apropos. Nachgelassenes – Kritisches – Bleibendes. München: Langen-Müller, 1981. (= Band XI, *Gesammelte Werke in Einzelausgaben*).

Correspondence

In diesem Sinne . . . Briefe an Freunde und Zeitgenossen. Ed. David Axmann, Marietta Torberg, and Hans Weigel. München: Langen-Müller, 1981. (= Band XII, *Gesammelte Werke in Einzelausgaben*).
Kaffeehaus war überall. Briefwechsel mit Käuzen und Originalen. Ed. David Axmann and Marietta Torberg. München: Langen-Müller, 1982. (= Band XIII, *Gesammelte Werke in Einzelausgaben*).
Pegasus im Joch. Briefwechsel mit Verlegern und Redakteuren. Ed. David Axmann and Marietta Torberg. München: Langen-Müller, 1983. (= Band XIV, *Gesammelte Werke in Einzelausgaben*).

II. Works in English

None

III. Secondary Works in English

Moore, Erna. "Friedrich Torberg's *Mein ist die Rache* as a Literary Work of Art." *Protest – Form – Tradition: Essays on German Exile Literature.* Ed. Joseph P. Strelka, Robert F. Bell, and Eugene Dobson. University, Alabama: The University of Alabama Press, 1979, pp. 111–121.
Mornin, Edward. "Taking Games Seriously: Observations on the German Sports-Novel." *Germanic Review* 51 (1976), 278–295.

IV. Major Studies in German

Ahl, Herbert. "Emigranten des Daseins: Friedrich Torberg." In *Literarische Portraits.* München: Langen Müller, 1962, pp. 93–100.
Améry, Jean. "Sie lernten nicht für das Leben." In *Bücher aus der Jugend unseres Jahrhunderts: Schülertragödien von Emil Strauss, Hermann Hesse, Friedrich Torberg.* Stuttgart: Klett-Cotta, 1981, pp. 51–64.

Beer, Otto F. "Zur Polemik B. Grunert-Bronnens und F. Torbergs (Heft 5 und 6)." *Literatur und Kritik* 8 (1967), 60-64.

Hackel, Franz-Heinrich. "In der Sprache der Verfolger schreiben? Friedrich Torberg befragt Süsskind von Trimberg." *Emuna* 3 (1977), 29-33.

Hartl, Edwin. "Der verlorene Wortführer: Friedrich Torberg." *Literatur und Kritik* 15 (1980), 1-5.

Heger, Roland. *Der österreichische Roman des 20. Jahrhunderts*, vol. 1. Wien: Wilhelm Braumüller, 1971, pp. 194-197.

Kaiser, Joachim. "Heißer Krieg gegen kühle Dramen: Zu Torbergs Anti-Brecht-Thesen." *Der Monat* XIV (1962), 60-64.

Lennartz, Franz. "Friedrich Torberg." *Deutsche Dichter und Schriftsteller unserer Zeit.* Stuttgart: Kröner, 1963, pp. 698-699.

Mayer, Sigrid. *Golem: Die literarische Rezeption eines Stoffes.* Bern: Herbert Lang, 1975, pp. 186-192.

Neumann, Robert. "Ich warte auf Torbergs Roman." *Tribune* 7 (1968), 3055-3056.

Reich-Ranicki, Marcel. "Friedrich Torbergs Gleichnis vom Juden." *Über Ruhestörer: Juden in der deutschen Literatur.* München: E. Piper & Co., 1973, pp. 73-80.

Ringel, Erwin. "Die Bedeutung von Torbergs *Schüler Gerber* für die moderne Selbstmordprophylaxe." *Das Pult* 57 (1980), 66-78.

Schnauber, Cornelius. "Torberg und Kesten: Die Emigration in Los Angeles und New York." *Das Exilerlebnis: Verhandlungen des vierten Symposium über deutsche und österreische Exilliteratur.* Ed. Donald G. Daviau and Ludwig M. Fischer. Columbia, South Carolina: Camden House, 1982, pp. 56-63.

Schneider, Rolf. "Die Wiener Institution Friedrich Torberg: Zu seinem 70. Geburtstag." *Musil-Forum* 4 (1978), 309-314.

Schönwiese, Ernst. "Die chassidische Seele singt: Der Lyriker Friedrich Torberg (1908-1979)." *Literatur in Wien zwischen 1930 und 1980.* Wien: Amalthea, 1980, pp. 159-165.

Sperber, Manès. "Friedrich Torberg (1908-1979)." *Jahrbuch. Deutsche Akademie für Sprache und Dichtung* 2 (1980), 115-118.

Stern, Guy. "Biographischer Roman als Selbstzeugnis aus dem Exil: Friedrich Torbergs Süsskind von Trimberg." In *Preis der Vernunft: Literatur und Kunst zwischen Aufklärung, Widerstand und Anpassung.* Festschrift for Walter Huder. Ed. Klaus Siebenhaar and Hermann Haarmann. Berlin: Medusa, 1982, pp. 167-181.

Strelka, Joseph. "Friedrich Torberg." In *Deutsche Exilliteratur seit 1933*, vol. 1. Ed. John M. Spalek. Bern: Francke, 1976, pp. 616-632.

Tobias, Abraham. "Torbergs *Süsskind:* Seine Confessio judaica— Bemerkungen zu den hebräischen und judaistischen Elementen des Romans." *Bulletin des Leo Baeck Instituts* 19 (1980), 169- 173.

Weigel, Hans. "Beruf: Zeitgenosse; zur Erstausgabe von Briefen Friedrich Torbergs." *Literatur und Kritik* 16 (1981), 257-258.

Wenzel, Edith. "Friedrich Torberg: *Süsskind von Trimberg.* Jüdische Identitätsuche in Deutschland." In *Mittelalter-Rezeption.* Ed. Jürgen Kühnel. Göppingen: Kümmerle, 1982, vol. 1, 367-381.

Zohn, Harry. *Wiener Juden in der deutschen Literatur.* Tel-Aviv: Olamenu, 1964, pp. 101-105.

Franz Werfel

Lionel B. Steiman

Franz Werfel was born in 1890 in Prague, where he lived until the First World War, after which he lived in Vienna until the Nazi annexation of Austria in 1938. His first place of refuge in exile was France, and in the fall of 1940 he reached the United States. The last five years of his life were spent in California. He died at home in Beverly Hills in 1945.

Fame had come to Werfel at an early age. Before 1914 his poetry established him as the leading voice of Expressionism. Success as a playwright followed quickly, and after the war his fame reached new heights with novels and short stories. *Die vierzig Tage des Musa Dagh* (1933, *The Forty Days of Musa Dagh*), a historical novel depicting the Turkish massacre of Armenians during World War I, made its author a hero to Armenians throughout the world.[1] In 1941 *Das Lied von Bernadette* (*The Song of Bernadette*) won the hearts of Americans, both as a best selling novel and two years later as an academy award winning film. Today thousands of Americans over forty remember *The Song of Bernadette,* but few remember or ever knew the name of its creator.

Werfel was a most authentic representative of a world that disappeared in the First World War, the world of the Austro-Hungarian Monarchy with its multitude of peoples, languages, and religions coexisting in tense and ambiguous symbiosis ever erupting in political and social conflict. He embodied the most humane qualities of this world of old Austria: tolerance, compassion, and an open, loving, and joyous disposition. He was remarkably free of one of its worst qualities, that almost toxic sentimentality that could fill Austrian eyes with tears of nostalgia while leaving them blind to brutal realities. Werfel loved this world and its rich culture deeply rooted in a past that was as Spanish and Italian as its present was Slavic and Germanic. The Gothic and Baroque architecture, the Catholic Mass and the music of Mozart, Beethoven, and Bruckner united the Austria north of the Alps with her Italian remnant and the world of the Mediterannean and of Verdi. Werfel drank deeply from this well fed by so many springs; and what combined all these elements in his perception and his growing love for them was the Church of Rome in her most sensuous and her most mystical manifestations. The German language that was the vehicle of his creativity carried a multifaceted heritage of human experience but was neither defined nor bounded by that of any national group.

Werfel was a Jew like such other important literary representatives of old Austria as Franz Kafka, Joseph Roth, and Stefan Zweig. Living in a world of multiple antipathies as a minority within minorities, the Jews placed their hope and loyalty on the head of the Imperial and Royal House of Habsburg, Emperor Franz Joseph. This *Kaisertreue,* a fidelity to the person of the ruler that transcended ethnic, linguistic, and religious divisions, was an indispensable bond in the armed forces, where nationalist hostilities might otherwise have undermined the effectiveness of this essential base of Austrian unity.

Throughout his life Franz Werfel retained a quiet pride in having served in the army of Franz Joseph. His great-grandfather had been a staff courier in Russia during the Napoleonic Wars; his grandfather Nathan, a wholesale merchant in a small Bohemian town, was a sergeant in the imperial army. Around mid-century he moved to Prague, where his son Rudolf founded a glove manufacturing concern. The firm of Werfel and Böhm had factories in Prague and Tuschkau and offices in London, Glasgow, Paris, Brussels, and Berlin. Its gloves took gold medals at Brussels and at Melbourne in 1888 and other honors in London in 1906 and in Prague in 1908. In addition to his skill and industry in business Rudolf Werfel was a cultured man. He played the piano, spoke a number of foreign languages fluently, and often amazed Franz with the range of his knowledge. Werfel's maternal ancestors were mill owners in the area around Pilsen. At his grandfather's hundredth birthday party in 1932 Franz Werfel asked the old gentleman what had made the greatest impression on him during his lifetime and received the reply "the abolition of serfdom." After publicly attributing his longevity to regular beer drinking the centenarian received a large quantity of free beer from a local brewery but lived for only three more months.[2]

As the only son of one of the Monarchy's most prominent industrialists Werfel enjoyed every advantage of his parents' position and favor. He grew up with the firm but quite unself-conscious conviction that what he thought mattered and should be taken seriously. His mother combined a motherly overprotectiveness with that detachment common to contemporaries of her class, preoccupied as they were with maintaining a home and appearances proper to their station. The great need for maternal nurture that she initially instilled in him was met increasingly by the family's Czech nurserymaid Babi. Through her the very young Werfel first consciously experienced what later became the key values and motifs of his work. Above all it was her simple, accepting, and loving attitude toward all creation that became the basis of Werfel's concept of "piety," so important in his later writing.[3]

Babi began taking Franz to Mass with her when he was only four, thus planting in him a reverence and fascination for Roman Catholicism that continued to grow. Meanwhile his parents observed at least the formalities of their Jewish faith, taking Franz to synagogue on high holidays and preparing him for his bar mitzvah. But in synagogue only the elements that resembled those of Catholicism – the candles and the air of otherworldly mystery – made a lasting impression on the boy. The rest filled him with a combination of fear and repugnance. Having fulfilled his obligation to his father's faith, he resolved to have nothing further to do with it.[4]

Werfel attended the most exclusive school in Prague, the *Piaristenkollegium.* The school was run by a Catholic order with instruction in German, and the majority of its pupils were from middle class Jewish families. Later he attended the *Stefansgymnasium,* where he met Willy Haas, who was to remain his lifelong friend. At the university he studied law and philosophy and then had a brief stint at business school. In 1910 he was sent to Hamburg to gain experience working for an export firm. He completed the apprenticeship requirement with the secret assistance of a friendly foreman but soon became bored and got himself fired by flushing bills of lading down a toilet. Werfel's father was disappointed but doubtless found some consolation in his son's growing literary renown. Yet Franz never forgot this incident and possibly other disappointments to his father. The fact that the father-son conflict was prominent in Werfel's early plays was due not merely to its being a fashionable theme of Expressionist drama[5] but also to its deep roots in personal experience. In the spring of 1939 Werfel's still living father appeared to him in a dream. Exposing his penis admonishingly to his terrified son, the elder man became young and strong and fell upon the dreamer, punishing him with blows.[6]

The city of Werfel's birth was synonymous with mysticism, a tradition centuries old popularized and capitalized on by Gustav Meyrink in his highly successful novel *Der Golem* (1915, *The Golem*). Prague's skyline was a thicket of spires, and its streets and byways were haunted by the ghosts of alchemists and miracle rabbis. Franz Werfel grew up amidst a wide range of religious and intellectual forces, fads, and fashions. Czech nationalism and Czech anti-Semitism were both on the rise, compounding the isolation of Prague's Jews and the hostility they had traditionally incurred by virtue of their cultural identification with the city's German minority. Zionism and various streams of social- ism and Judaism were flowing in from all directions. Werfel sampled and discussed them but never attached himself to any group or figure because they all clashed in some way with his growing lyric orientation that combined a quasi-anarchism with a deeply ethical sense of human equality.

In the company of Max Brod, Franz Kafka, and other members of the Prague literary circle he attended seances and table levitations. Kafka remained skeptical, as he would of everything; Werfel responded with open wonder, as he did to everything. There were countless eve- ning hours spent in the Café Arco, one of those inimitable cultural institutions of central Europe. These coffeehouses were hothouses of intellectual and literary life. In them one not only drank coffee, ate whipped cream, and smoked, but also received mail, read an inter- national array of newspapers and magazines, slept, discussed, argued, held court, and wrote.

Werfel had published poems and made something of a name for himself locally while still in school, but it was Max Brod who really launched his literary career. On a visit to Berlin in 1911 he read samples of Werfel's poetry before an expressionist literary circle. Within a month Brod's Berlin publisher, Axel Juncker, who was also the first publisher of Rainer Maria Rilke, brought out the first collection of poems by Franz Werfel, *Der Weltfreund* (The World Friend). His repu- tation was established almost overnight. Meanwhile he had left Ham- burg, served his one-year voluntary term of military service, and spent the following year, 1912, in Leipzig working as a reader for the newly established publishing house of Kurt Wolff.

The poems of *Der Weltfreund* and the volumes that followed in quick succession established Franz Werfel as the leading voice in early expressionism. "Mein einziger Wunsch ist Dir, O Mensch, verwandt zu sein!"[7] (My one and only wish, O Man, is to be thy brother!) became the motto of a movement and expressed a primary impulse that continued to power Werfel's creativity all his life. It was a purely human cry, but one that would be choked if channeled toward some political or dogmatically religious goal. Only when his friends and contemporaries made their choices political and opted for one of the various streams of literary activism did Werfel elaborate his own philosophical outlook and its concomitant conception of the function of artistic creativity. This was done in a series of polemics against activists like Kurt Hiller and Alfred Kurella, who in later years was to hold a ministerial post in the government of the communist German Democratic Republic.

Werfel advanced the view that the functions of poet and politician were fundamentally different and that writers in politics invariably ended by doing more harm than good. The writer's outlook was and had to remain universal, fixed on the larger entities of humanity and transcending the concerns of necessarily biased politicians and statesmen. Max Brod, then evolving a Jewish-humanist-Zionism, had pointed out that love of humanity, which inspired the lyric of Werfel's immensely successful *Der Weltfreund* and its successor *Wir sind* (1913, We Are), required a corresponding plan of political and social action. But for Werfel any such plan could only involve a monstrous bureaucracy staffed by poets and intellectuals, an utter travesty of the true creative imagination whose purpose was to transform into words a consciousness of the tragically flawed reality of human life.

In Werfel the notion of "tragic" links a convention of classical drama with a central dogma of Christianity, a linkage not surprising in the light of his nurserymaid's crucial influence and his education in a system that emphasized almost exclusively the literature of the ancient world. Not surprising again is the fact that Werfel tailored his conception of Christianity to suit his aesthetic and humanist predilections and implicitly his political purpose. The institutions of Christianity already assure conditions that provide for maximum development of the human potential of every individual, he argued, so there is no need for intellectuals to engage in political activism to secure what we already have.

But the Christianity that Werfel had in mind is obviously the product of a Jewish poet whose aesthetic orientation was defined in a culture of baroque Catholicism. Christianity, Werfel wrote, affirms rather than denies the self; it celebrates rather than denies the world; it rejects abstraction in favor of the concrete; and far from being ascetic it is the only genuine hedonism. Christianity is thus the very opposite of what it is usually thought to be, at least for Werfel, trying as he was to convince people that the humanistic goals of activism could be achieved in Christianity. Political activism on the part of intellectuals was the real enemy of humanism because it invariably dealt in "abstraction," a process violently inimical to the integrity of being.

Werfel equated sin with this process of analytical thought he called abstraction. Activism was thus sinful, a collective flight into abstraction. Christianity remained a force working from within individual consciousness; activism imposed terrifying abstractions from without. Activism demanded that the individual deny himself for the sake of a higher good; Christianity invited him to live.[8] However world-affirming this vision of Christianity, the foundation on which it rested was Werfel's conviction that what is inaccessible to reason and the senses is far more real than what is not. True reality and genuine values are metaphysical, and materialism can only lead us dangerously astray. He believed this for the rest of his life.

It was not in ivory tower isolation that Werfel defined these ideas but amidst the dislocation of the first years of World War I. Still it does not seem that the war itself significantly influenced them. His duties on active service involved monitoring a telephone and adjusting the sights on artillery. Neither gave him a view of combat, though he did see seriously wounded men. His correspondence of the period shows a preoccupation with the deadening routine of military life and its effect on his ability to carry on his literary work. Many of his companions had become machines. Books, the spirit, love, joy, tears, and all the other springs from which he had drunk before the war had no place in this society of sluggards and automatons. Werfel scorned his semiliterate companions but felt guilty about enjoying a security that they lacked. He dealt with this guilt by attributing his security to God's loving care for the lilies of the field and the birds of the air, a care in which he felt "as one of the few, genuine *born Christians.*" But then he asked himself whether his faith was not primarily an expression of egotism.[9] This suspicion of self remained a source of psychic tension throughout Werfel's life, one that he could resolve only in deepening faith, yet a faith whose origins were in emotional needs and whose elements continued to be more human and aesthetic than theological. Still he came to know and love both testaments of the Bible and the writings of the Church fathers. To the end of his life he carried a well thumbed small catechism, which he loved as much as the great *Summa* of Thomas Aquinas—in fact probably more.

It is often asserted that Franz Werfel was a pacifist or at least that he wrote antiwar poems and plays during the war. It is true that a volume of his verse aroused the suspicion of the military authorities and caused him to be summoned for a hearing, which may have resulted in his transfer to the eastern front as a disciplinary measure. But the themes of *Einander* (1915, One Another) are continuous with those of his prewar expressionist verse. Rather than attacking specific aspects of the war they treat the eternal ironies and tragedies that beset the human course, as does his adaptation of Euripides' *The Trojan Women,* first performed in Berlin in 1916. Although the themes here are antiwar in general, Werfel had completed the play before the outbreak of war, and it reflected the general cry for human brotherhood so characteristic of his early expressionist period. Other writings of his at this time were also strongly pacifist in general terms but lacked political content.

While not an antiwar poet, neither was Franz Werfel a war propagandist, an epithet often applied in connection with his work at the War Press Office in Vienna. Here he joined other prominent writers in work consisting largely in the polishing of military press releases. He also wrote an introduction to a volume of military songs for children but found it a painful task and avoided direct glorification of war or military virtue.[10] He wanted to encourage the human solidarity children felt with their brothers and fathers at the front without encouraging admiration for their military tasks or achievements. But of course it was difficult to separate the spirit of sacrifice that was to be admired from the goal for which the sacrifice was to be made.

Some saw a more direct propaganda purpose in the mission on which he was sent to Switzerland early in 1918. He was to give a series of ten lectures and readings, which might be seen more as a gesture of goodwill than as propaganda. On one occasion, however, he departed from his scheduled program to recite a poem parodying the diplomatic establishment when the town's entire German and Austrian diplomatic mission was in his audience. And during his appearance at the Workers' Education Society of the Swiss Social Democratic Party he preceded the reading of his poems with a political harangue. In it Werfel denounced bourgeois culture as a parasitic swindle, addressed his listeners as "comrades," and proclaimed that his greatest happiness would be to make some contribution "to the dissolution of the bourgeois world and to the renewal of socialism." Contemporary culture was a fraud, he claimed, and the task of the artist must be redefined to meet the needs of real people: workers, soldiers, miners, everyone. One had only to look to Russia to see what wonderful possibilities awaited the efforts of those who would awaken to their responsibilities.[11]

Was all this a contradiction of Werfel's anti-activist Christian stance? Was it an expression of hitherto submerged radicalism? Was it impelled by a need to identify with a particular audience? It was all three. Moreover, this notorious address to the workers of Davos was in tune with the temper of the times. By 1918 war weariness reigned everywhere; pacifism of some sort was becoming the fashion even in high places. In Germany industrial strikes and the parliamentary peace resolution, in Austria secret peace initiatives and worsening structural cracks in the monarchy, and everywhere increasing human suffering and its attendant political disaffection had created an atmosphere in which an apparently dissident voice was no longer exceptional. Switzerland, where internationally minded pacifist writers from many countries had established themselves and their publications, was a hothouse of free minds that doubtless had its effect on "the World Friend" after years of stultifying military routine. Then too the newborn revolution in Russia was in the first flush of its victory, and to many western intellectuals, disillusioned by their own societies' many failures, it appeared to be the answer.

All this notwithstanding, Werfel's fraternal words to Swiss workers raised many an Austrian eyebrow, especially when the famous poet and dramatist mounted the stage of revolution a few months later at home. Together with other café intellectuals he participated in the formation of a Red Guard, got involved in an attempt to found a journal whose object was the union of Catholicism and Communism, and harangued a crowd gathered outside the financial houses at the *Schottentor*. Arrested on suspicion of being a communist, Werfel insisted that he was a Tolstoyan Christian anarchist, a term which deflected the "communist" charge while still explaining his apparently seditious deeds. He was released and taken more seriously in the literary sections of Vienna newspapers than by either the authorities or serious revolutionists.[12]

What really had brought an end to Werfel's brief excursion into revolutionary activism was the disapproval of his lover. In 1917 he had met and fallen passionately in love with Alma, widow of the composer Gustav Mahler and until 1922 legal wife of the architect Walter Gropius. Alma was eleven years Werfel's senior, a practicing Catholic, politically and socially conservative, a knowledgeable music lover, and a patroness of the arts with a wide circle of distinguished friends. Their love was instant but lasting.

In January 1918 Alma became pregnant and seven months later gave birth by caesarian section. Only days earlier Werfel had visited Alma at her summer home. Despite her uncertain condition and his conviction that its cause was their sin, he deepened his sense of guilt by succumbing to what he regarded as selfish physical lust. After an encounter in which he "did not spare her" Alma required emergency medical attention. Having sex with a pregnant woman, he told his diary, was the same as kicking her in the stomach. When their infant son died ten months later, Werfel felt utterly worthless[13] and ever after regarded this death as a divine punishment.

His letters to Alma during these months are filled with effusive, adoring submissiveness. He vowed to bring all his values strictly into accord with hers, promised to cut off all friends and acquaintances of whom she did not approve, and proclaimed that he was seeing life and the world "with her nerves."[14] On the night that climaxed his revolutionary activity, when their son was just over three months old, he approached Alma for "her blessing," which she reluctantly gave but disdainfully withdrew when he returned a few hours later filthy and reeking of cheap tobacco and liquor. "If you had done something beautiful, you would be beautiful now," she told him, and thus ended Franz Werfel's brief career as a political activist.[15] Alma's displeasure combined with the guilt he felt in relation to her reinforced the antipolitical, quasi-conservative tendency in Werfel's thought and work.

This is evident in the pattern of his postwar writing. His vision of human transformation focused increasingly on the individual rather than on society, on moral regeneration rather than social revolution. Werfel's prewar plays were generally pacifist but nonpolitical. Those of the immediate postwar period were by contrast antipolitical or conservative. *Spiegelmensch* (1920, Mirrorman), portrays political activism as an expression of egomania disguised as messianism. In *Bockgesang* (1921, *Goat Song*) the son of a prostitute grows to adulthood filled with resentment and assumes the leadership of a group of rebels, which he leads ultimately to destruction.[16] *Schweiger* (1922) similarly exposes nihilism behind the idealistic mask of a political messiah. Here and in other writings Werfel advanced his view of political activism as the expression of warped fanatical minds without any positive goals. Its proponents were impelled by feelings of personal inadequacy transformed into delusions of grandeur and monomaniacal aggressiveness. The ultimate evil from which all this sprang was "materialism."

The targets of these and other antipolitical dramas, however, were never conservatives. The latter might appear incompetent or foolish but not evil. Werfel wanted to demonstrate the folly of attempting to implement any ideal. The protagonists of *Juarez und Maximilian* (1924) and *Das Reich Gottes in Böhmen* (1930, The Kingdom of God in Bohemia) both attempt to establish utopian societies, and both end in tragedy. Again and again the lesson is clear: attempts to transform an ideal into reality by means of revolution end in disaster, revealing only the selfish and hypocritical egotism of human nature.

In Werfel's first important prose work, *Nicht der Mörder, der Ermordete ist schuldig* (1920, *Not the Murderer*), the problem of authority is indeed the theme, but it is explored in the personal and psychological terms of generational conflict. Political institutions form the background – the old monarchy, the state, and the military – but they are larger personifications of an authority still conceived in individual rather than political terms. The father-son conflict, a favorite theme in expressionism, recurred frequently in Werfel's writing to the end. He also continued to employ an early dramatic technique throughout his work, namely to elucidate the various aspects of ideas by embodying them in antithetical individual characters. He continued to abhor collectivities as "abstractions," dangerous by definition.

As Werfel's writing thus became more tendentious, he lost some of his earlier admirers such as Karl Kraus and Franz Kafka. In the case of Kraus the feud was based on personal and literary disagreements dating back to the early days of the war,[17] but both he and Kafka felt that Werfel had betrayed the pure poetic gift he had displayed in his early verse. Kafka loved to hear Werfel read his poems and evinced an admiration bordering on the erotic. Even after Kraus and others such as Robet Musil had made it fashionable to deprecate and even ridicule Werfel, Kafka's affection and admiration for him continued to grow. But a turning point came with the publication of Werfel's postwar plays, and after *Schweiger* he concluded that Werfel had forfeited the leadership of his generation.[18]

Verdi. Roman der Oper (1924, *Verdi. A Novel of the Opera*) was Werfel's first full-length novel and his greatest success of the postwar decade. Ever since childhood music and especially opera had been his love. Every spring the stars of Italy – Caruso, Tetrazzini, Toscanini – would come to Prague for the May Festival, the highlight of Werfel's year. At a time when Wagner's popularity was dominant he preferred Verdi and even memorized entire libretti. A frequent sight and sound in Prague cafés and streets was young Werfel singing an aria in a tenor that earned him the nickname "Caruso." He also sang along during performances and probably annoyed some in the audience but moved others to good-humored jibes. "Come into our loge," called a lady on one such occasion, "we haven't yet heard you in Rigoletto!" This love of music continued to the end. The day before he died Werfel was singing, accompanied by Bruno Walter, his neighbor in Beverly Hills.[19]

In *Verdi. Roman der Oper* artistic inspiration and the creative process are embodied in two great rivals of genius, Verdi and Wagner. Verdi was pure melody, Wagner was abstract structure; Verdi was humanity in all its fullness, Wagner was disembodied intellect and dissatisfied soul. In Wagner were all the worst aspects of a romanticism that had destroyed the noble and much scorned ideals of the liberalism of 1848. Historical themes and conflicts figure in the subplots and secondary characters as well. Verdi had chosen Venice as the place in which to attempt to overcome his ten-year composer's block. His host's son turns out to be a materialist infected by political currents in Rome and as a result believes that music can be understood only in its socioeconomic context. He also affected the dress and mannerisms of political revolutionaries. Significantly, his mother had died in giving birth to him, a fact that echoes Werfel's guilt for having caused Alma's life-threatening pregnancy at a time when he himself was busy playing at revolution.

Here as in later works Werfel was struggling to subdue earlier tendencies in himself and was heaping scorn upon those in whom they still lived. Here and in later works there are biographical parallels and characters modeled on real life counterparts, which suggests that Werfel was still dealing with a guilt conceived early in life and repeatedly compounded, as in his affair with Alma. Thus another son of Verdi's host impregnates a woman nine years his senior. *Her* feeling is depicted as genuine sexual passion, but *his* is no more than trivial pleasure seeking. But the emotional makeup of Werfel's characters and their interrelations are complex, and analysis does not always yield neat parallels with corresponding figures and episodes in his life. Werfel took situations and experiences from his own life and explored them with his creative imagination guided but uninhibited by the parameters of biographical reality. For example, in one character he suggests an identity between sexual and musical passion. Was this in order to elevate the one by association with the other and by implication to mitigate the guilt he felt over Alma? Or was it rather to devalue Wagner by associating his appeal with animal passion? Again the heroines in *Verdi* are all figures of suffering and sacrifice, constantly reenacting the eternal drama of woman's painful life-giving act of birth. Was Alma the inspiration here?

The answer to all the above is a very qualified yes and no. Werfel made such associations because he saw life as a whole. This fundamental imaginative perception of reality influenced his judgment of the conduct of real individuals as much as the other way around. There was, in other words, a reciprocal interaction of imaginative and empirical perception in Werfel's process of creative literary transformation. One has only to read the verses in *Der Weltfreund* and *Wir sind* to see that his vision of woman was established in his youth. Again the dramatic structure of *Verdi* as of many of Werfel's subsequent works with their antithetically drawn characters, overdrawn contrasts, melodramatic climaxes, and often unlikely resolutions are all highly operatic. Was this because Werfel had absorbed so much opera in his formative years? Possibly, but then what had made him such a passionate opera lover in his youth? The elements in a creative personality might be delineated but they cannot easily be derived from one another or from any ultimate source.

For *Verdi* Werfel found a new publisher. The postwar inflation in Germany made it financially impossible to continue with Kurt Wolff of Leipzig, with whom Werfel parted professional company while remaining on close personal terms. Paul von Zsolnay, wealthy Viennese heir to the former supplier of the Imperial Austrian tobacco monopoly, was interested in founding a publishing house. He offered Werfel an attractive advance in Swiss francs, and in the spring of 1924 *Verdi* appeared under the imprint that was to remain on Werfel's books until the Nazi takeover of Austria fourteen years later.

During these years Franz Werfel and Alma Mahler Gropius, who became his legal wife in 1929, led an idyllic life. Working alternately in resort hotels on the Italian Riviera or in Capri, in Alma's homes in Vienna, in Breitenstein on the Semmering to the south, or in her town house in Venice and retreats in Locarno or Ischl, Werfel produced a steady flow of stories, plays, and novels. By 1926 his popularity had outstripped that of such giants as Gerhart Hauptmann and Stefan George according to some accounts. In that year he was awarded the Grillparzer Prize for *Juarez und Maximilian* and was made a member of the literary section of the Prussian Academy of the Arts, founded in the same year. He shared the Schiller Prize with Hermann Burte and Fritz von Unruh in 1927, when he also received the Czechoslovakian State Prize. The award he valued most, however, came just a year before he lost his home and was forced into exile: in 1937 Franz Werfel was awarded the Austrian Cross of Merit for Art and Science from federal chancellor Kurt von Schuschnigg.[20]

In Vienna the Werfels lived in the old Mahler house on Elisabethstrasse 22, less than five minutes from the Opera. In 1931 they moved to a villa in Vienna's exclusive *Hohe Warte* district near the lovely suburb of Grinzing, famous for its "heuriger" wine gardens and still a popular tourist attraction today. (These houses were still standing in the late seventies, although the first had been subdivided, the villa had become the seat of the Saudi Arabian legation, and the summer home on the Semmering a rest home for workers of a nearby industrial concern.) Alma conducted a glittering salon from which Werfel was able to retreat to his spacious top floor study or to seek out old friends from Prague in the Café Central in the Herrengasse or in the Café Herrenhof, his later favorite. He preferred to work through the nights, sustained only by tobacco and coffee, a practice that worried Alma. He loved food, delighted in fine restaurants, old Czech dishes, and was a child again when dessert came. He never liked alcohol and sometimes irritated Alma by his indifference to fine wines, but he loved big cigars of all kinds. Alma tried in vain to get him to moderate his smoking or at least to choose less ferocious-looking forms.[21]

There were frequent lecture tours through Germany. After appearances in twenty cities in 1925 Werfel visited Paris for the first time.[22] Earlier that year he and Alma had taken a two-month trip to the Middle East. In Cairo he was moved and often repelled by the human misery amidst luxury, but in Palestine he was unable to deal with the emotional conflicts stirred in his depths by this encounter with the land of his fathers.[23] Instead he set out to transform them creatively and wrote *Paulus unter den Juden* (1926, Paul among the Jews). The central focus of this drama is the historical moment in which Christianity definitively parted from Judaism. Werfel discussed his view with Freud during a brief visit in 1926 and elaborated it in subsequent letters to him (Werfel Collection, University of Pennsylvania) which make concessions surprising in the light of his later attacks on psychoanalysis. A second trip to the Middle East in 1929 provided the stimulus for *Die vierzig Tage des Musa Dagh*. The sight of half-starved Armenian orphans in a Damascus factory sparked Werfel's interest in the history of their people and its recent tragedy.

The year 1929 also saw the marriage of Franz and Alma and the publication of Werfel's most ambitious novel thus far, *Barbara oder die Frömmigkeit (The Pure in Heart)*. It presents a panorama of central Europe before, during, and immediately following World War I. In it Werfel rendered his vision of that past he seemed increasingly to despise, the world of political activism, especially as it erupted at the end of the war when scores of literati appeared to be scrambling for positions in the revolution, whose waves were breaking over the capitals of Europe. It was also a final concession to Alma's conservatism and a celebration of the quasi-mystical piety embodied in his nurse Babi, who is the novel's heroine and who figures in its German title, *Barbara oder die Frömmigkeit*. Although Barbara herself plays almost no part in its action, her selfless love and innocence provide a rich spiritual resource for her former charge, young Ferdinand, as he leaves home to come of age in an alien world and to experience the violence of war, the collapse of the monarchy, and the subsequent turmoil. In the end it is her piety, this spiritual treasure, which alone is revealed to be of any value.

Barbara oder die Frömmigkeit is full of characters whose real-life models were still living when the book appeared and who were most unflatteringly portrayed and even caricatured in it. Werfel had a real penchant for revealing the selfishness, hypocritical cruelty, egotism, and downright dishonesty of the politically minded intellectuals of the time. Former Prague friends such as Egon Erwin Kisch, Franz Blei, and Otto Gross, with whom he had been involved during his period as would-be revolutionary, became inhabitants of the novel's "Shadow Realm," a world of ruthless hypocrites epitomized by Gebhart (Otto Gross), self-appointed herald of a new age of love who in the meantime brutalizes his own child. The book immediately aroused considerable controversy. Egon Erwin Kisch, who remained a left-wing journalist all his life, was asked by a newspaper interviewer whether he was going to sue Werfel for defamation of character for depicting him as the cynical and hateful Ronald Weiss. He would not, he said, because even though Werfel had changed his sympathies he had not misrepresented the actions and events of the time. What is more, he added, Werfel's astoundingly accurate memory made the book a significant document for that reason alone. Conversations Kisch had heard over ten years earlier were reproduced in the book "with the exactness of a gramophone."[24] *Barbara oder die Frömmigkeit* thus remains of considerable interest but was for a long time neglected, partly no doubt because its title gave no hint of its content.

The gifts that had served Werfel so well in *Barbara oder die Frömmigkeit* were equally displayed in his shorter prose works.[25] These usually lack the tendentious and polemical qualities of his plays and novels; they therefore recreate more directly and convincingly the world and character of old Austria. In *Der Tod des Kleinbürgers* (1931, *The Man Who Conquered Death*) the quintessential Viennese petit bourgeois Karl Fiala, mortally ill, summons the strength to hold death off long enough to enable him to pay up his insurance policy. In *Das Trauerhaus* (1927, *The House of Mourning*) a bordello is presented as a microcosm of the monarchy in its twilight years, its proprietor, personnel, and patrons all embodying in their own ways the vices and foibles, ideals and illusions of that larger world. Werfel's genuine sympathy with all these representatives of flawed humanity together with his gift of inventing fascinating plot make his writing irresistible. As the clouds began to gather a second time in the mid-thirties, Werfel published a collection of the best of these stories as a tribute to the world of old Austria with a preface containing a lengthy paean to the ideals Austria had embodied.[26]

But Werfel's response to the crisis of the time was not merely one of nostalgic flight to the past. In a number of lectures and essays he offered his solution to the current malaise. He defined the basic evil of the time as materialism, an evil that was responsible for the two dangerous ersatz religions of Communism and Nazism. The solution he offered was a return to a genuine spiritual belief in God, for without it even the noblest of purely human ideals was doomed.[27] Of course this faith was rooted in Werfel's pre-1914 expressionism, but in the thirties he developed it as a direct response to the evolving crisis of the time.

The first great literary fruit of this engagement, and a celebration of its faith, was *Die vierzig Tage des Musa Dagh*. This is such a rich work, and its genesis so closely parallel to the rise and triumph of Hitler, that it is impossible to reduce it to any clear equation with the historical crisis of the time. As has been noted, the initial stimulus was given in 1929, but Werfel waited two years before starting the project and, as he researched the tragic story of the Armenians in Turkey, the current threat to the Jews in Europe was becoming increasingly clear. Did he consciously intend his book about the one tragedy as a warning against another? Was it the rise of Nazism in Germany that impelled him to write a book about the Armenians? Alma said it was, but Werfel himself gave contradictory replies to this question at different times. The process at work was indeed complex.[28]

While the action of the book is about the siege of the Armenians on Musa Dagh—the mount of Moses—the relationships between the characters and the issues around which they revolve suggest parallels with the author's life and situation in Europe. The novel's protagonist is an Armenian assimilated to European culture with a French wife and a son raised in Paris. Historical accident forces their return to the Levant, where Gabriel Bagradian is compelled to choose between his people and his wife. Their son is torn between them, but where the father failed the son succeeds in completely identifying himself with the destiny of his people. Ultimately Stephan sacrifices his life for them. His mother has meanwhile shamed herself with a Greek, while his father's platonic affair with an Armenian girl has grown from a deeply latent conscious-ness of unity with her people. But he is not destined to experience the freedom to which his heroism has helped to lead them. Struck by a Turkish bullet, he dies upon the grave of his son as the remnant of the besieged community is picked up by a French cruiser below.

The estimates of the number of Armenians who were deliberately killed by the Turks in 1915 vary between one and two million. Werfel's was one of the very few books to publicize this awesome reality and to emphasize especially the role of the Turkish government and the failure of other powers to intervene or assist the victims in any way. In 1933, the year it was published, *Die vierzig Tage der Musa Dagh* was banned by Hitler, partly at the urging of officials at the Turkish Embassy in Berlin. (Later Hitler boasted that no one would bother about the Jews because no one had lifted a finger for the Armenians.) But the book was given a new lease on life in 1934, when it was published in New York by the Viking Press. In 1935 it was a Book-of-the-Month Club selection. Metro-Goldwyn-Mayer soon acquired the film rights, but the U.S. Department of State is said to have blocked all efforts to turn the book into a movie because of diplomatic considerations vis-à-vis Tur-key.[29] Meanwhile in Paris and New York in the thirties Werfel was mobbed and feted by Armenians; thirty years after his death his re-mains were transferred from Hollywood to Vienna with the financial assistance of the Armenian community in the United States, which in that year also helped finance a Werfel Symposium and the publication of the final volume of his collected works. The reason for such devotion was simple. As a prominent member of the Armenian community in the United States put it, "For Armenians, Franz Werfel embodies the con-science of European literature and its commitment to universal justice and dignity of man."[30]

It is ironic that the author of a book which was so tragically prophetic and which to this day is attacked by official Turkish denials of its truth was himself optimistic about Europe's future in the spring of 1933 when it was published. Werfel hoped that Hitler might turn out to be some kind of evil means to a good end, but within months the Nazi ban on his work cost him its largest German market. Max Reinhardt suggested he write a play with a biblical theme in response to events in Germany. The result was *Der Weg der Verheißung* (1935, *The Eternal Road*) performed two years later in New York with music composed by Kurt Weill. It was followed by a novel with another biblical theme, *Höret die Stimme. Jeremias* (1937, *Hearken unto the Voice*). Both works portray Jewish personalities and concerns, current and historical, and both epitomize Werfel's view of the Jewish predicament and a possible solution to it. Although Werfel made careful studies of both the Bible and the Midrash in attempting to provide his themes and characters with a historically authentic foundation, his Jewish types nevertheless tend to be rogues or simpletons, anti-Semitic caricatures, or idealized devotees of the spirit. *Der Weg der Verheißung* portrays unattractive, stereotypically "Jewish" behavior; *Höret die Stimme. Jeremias* tells Jews to behave more "spiritually." This message was in keeping with Werfel's general view of Christianity, Judaism, and the relationship between them. He saw Christianity as more "worldly" than in fact it was, and Judaism as more "spiritual," largely in order to rationalize the existence of two historically and theologically antagonistic principles, with both of which he strongly identified.[31]

Indeed all the major works he wrote from the midthirties on can be considered extended commentaries and explorations of this problem of two antagonistic but interdependent and (for Werfel) theologically indispensable peoples. *Der veruntreute Himmel* (1939, *Embezzled Heaven*), which he wrote in France almost immediately on his arrival there after the Nazi takeover of Austria,[32] explores the nature of Christian faith in its quest for heaven. The embodiment of this faith is Teta Linek, a simple Czech woman who invests her entire life savings in an effort to "secure" heaven for her soul. She finds her way to a genuine faith only after she discovers how her "broker" had systematically "embezzled" the funds entrusted to him over the years. (That her way to genuine faith is assisted by a Jewish convert hustling pilgrims to the Vatican is not only a typical Werfel touch, but it also related to his vision of the Jew's role in Christian salvation.) The model on whom Werfel based his heroine had been a cook in Alma's household for years. Hearing her story from Alma over lunch one day gave Werfel the idea for the story that became *Der veruntreute Himmel*. Given his curiosity and memory for detail, it is more than likely that he would have found out exactly where this woman had come from. The fact that in the book he gives as *her* place of origin the town from which *his own* forefathers had come is a good measure of the identity he felt with her.[33]

Werfel followed *Der veruntreute Himmel* immediately with a novel depicting the fate of Vienna's Jews at the time of the *Anschluß*. *Cella oder die Überwinder* (Cella or the Overcomers), a fragment unfortunately not yet translated, displays Werfel's talent for capturing in essence a wide range of fascinating human and historical types. Bodenheim, an Austrian Jew who remains proud of having served the Kaiser, has joined a totally inept conspiracy of monarchists whose solution to the Nazi threat is a Habsburg restoration. Their schemes are overtaken by events, and Bodenheim makes off through side streets in tears, his war medals clattering a taunting reminder of the fate of the ideals in whose service they had been earned. The cultured and wealthy Freudreich, arrested and subjected to gross indignities by the Nazis, keeps insisting that he couldn't possibly be the person they had in mind. To which Werfel as narrator responds sardonically: "They don't mean you Freudreich: They don't mean me. Then whom do they really mean? Israel is not a people. Israel is an order of the blood, which one enters involuntarily by birth."[34] Werfel's portrayal of Vienna during the *Anschluß* is unsparingly authentic but sympathetic and distinguished by psychological understanding.

But before the actual *Anschluß*, while Bodenheim was scheming with the monarchists, his gifted daughter Cella was being prepared for a grand benefit concert before high society. For Werfel this represented the cultural solution in which blind and politically inept Jews like Bodenheim had for so long placed their hopes. The concert's promoters include a dissipated aristocrat and a fawning academic led by an old school friend of Bodenheim's who turns out later to be a Nazi. In an unpublished draft Werfel has this friend, Zoltan Nagy, as Cella's real father but ruled out such heavy irony for the published version. Sufficient it was to have Nagy emerge as the Nazi *deus ex machina* who later secures Bodenheim's release from a train bound for Dachau. Cella had earlier fled with her mother to Paris, leaving her father to face the Nazis in Vienna alone. Bodenheim's refusal to leave Austria in time foreshadowed Werfel's own misplaced optimism which in 1940 almost landed him in the hands of the Gestapo in recently conquered France.

Franz and Alma Werfel lived in France from the summer of 1938 to the summer of 1940, alternating their residence between Paris and Sanary-sur-Mer, home of a colony of well-known German literary exiles. After the fall of France in June 1940 they embarked on a harrowing flight from the Gestapo. (At one point it was reported in Britain and America that Werfel had been caught and shot.) During a respite in the famous pilgrimage town of Lourdes Werfel conceived the idea for the book that was to take him to the pinnacle of his fame. He became interested in the story of the little girl whose vision of a beautiful lady in a grotto had produced a controversy that involved every level of church and state, which dragged on for decades before she was finally beatified. As Sainte Bernadette of Lourdes she made that town famous, attracting as pilgrims the afflicted from all over the world. During his three-week sojourn there Werfel devoured every available bit of information on the girl. Here was a simple little soul whose faith was in a direct line with that of Babi, Barbara, and Teta. It also struck a chord of the grief he had carried since the death of Alma's daughter Manon five years earlier. Werfel had loved this beautiful and gifted child of eighteen as his own, and nothing since the death of his son had touched him so deeply. By this time too his awareness of his own serious heart ailment sharpened his already keen sensitivity to human mortality and deepened his conviction that true reality was spiritual. So, in mortal danger from the Gestapo but with a regenerated faith, Franz Werfel made a sacred vow: if he reached America he would set aside all other work and would, as he put it, sing *Das Lied von Bernadette* (1941, *The Song of Bernadette*).[35]

In October 1940 the *Nea Hellas* docked at Hoboken, New Jersey, and the Werfels walked into freedom. Within six months Franz fulfilled his vow. Paradoxically, the work that he considered his most personal and most spiritual turned out to be his greatest commercial success. It was the Book-of-the-Month Club selection for June 1942 and an Academy-award winning film a year later. Overnight a central European Jew in flight from the Nazis had become a hero to the nation's Catholics and not just to Catholics. The hundreds of letters with which Werfel was inundated came from individuals and organizations representing a wide range of faiths and causes.[36]

In Lourdes Werfel had also met the Polish Jewish refugee he transferred into the protagonist of *Jacobowsky und der Oberst* (1944, Jacobowsky and the Colonel). Subtitled "*Komödie einer Tragödie*"

(The Comedy of a Tragedy), the original was worlds apart in tone and substance from the Broadway adaptation by S. N. Behrman, who had made a straight comedy of it. Furthermore, because material and situations that Americans might have found offensive or incomprehensible were taken out, little of what Werfel had wanted to convey was left. Not only were speeches implicating America in the plight of Europe's Jews removed,[37] but Werfel's subtlety of characterization was also reduced. He was greatly angered and became involved in lengthy haggling with agents and lawyers. The 1958 film adaptation *Me and the Colonel* departed even further from the original. While Danny Kaye portrayed a touchingly human and sympathetic Jacobowsky, what Werfel had in mind was an ordinary businessman with all the traits that are the stock jibes of anti-Semites, a character not only more true to life but essential to Werfel's scheme of the Jewish-Gentile relationship.[38]

Because the East had suited neither Werfel's taste nor his health, after ten weeks in New York he and Alma crossed the continent to California in December 1940. At first they lived in Hollywood in a small house at the edge of the Hollywood Bowl, which often provided a gentle musical background to their evening conversation. In this simple house without even a study Werfel wrote *Das Lied von Bernadette.* In 1942 the couple moved to 610 North Bedford Drive in Beverly Hills. There, with conductor Bruno Walter and writer Bruno Frank as neighbors, Thomas Mann, Lion Feuchtwanger and other members of the German emigré colony as frequent visitors, and his intimate friend Friedrich Torberg close by, Werfel led a pleasant life. In the fall of 1943 he suffered a series of nearly fatal heart attacks. His apparent recovery was considered miraculous. He spent his last eighteen months writing the posthumously published *Stern der Ungeborenen* (1946, *Star of the Unborn*). During the week he worked in a bungalow of the Hotel Mira Sol in Santa Barbara with his physician at hand, and he drove back to Beverly Hills for weekends.

Star of the Unborn is an antiutopian fantasy. The world a hundred thousand years hence is depicted as one where there is no work, class distinction, illness, distance, or death. Every conceivable material desire of the twentieth century has been met. And yet there is violence and other evil, all due to the very ideals—really illusions— that had produced this materialist utopia. The solution is to exorcise fully these seductive ideals of the Enlightenment from those of Voltaire and Kant to those of Marx and Freud, and to surrender to the creed of the Catholic Church. Werfel's research in dogma had been thorough; the priest who instructed him in the *Rituale Romanum,* the rite of exorcism, found it used in one of the most gripping scenes of the book.[39]

Regardless of whether one is attracted or repelled by the book—Henry Miller loved it, while Eric Bentley wrote that the only feeling it evoked in him was one of nausea—*Stern der Ungeborenen* remains an unparalleled source on the life and beliefs of Werfel. His astounding memory was put to even greater use here than in *Barbara oder die Frömmigkeit.* Willy Haas, Werfel's closest boyhood friend and a key figure in his last book, was amazed to read reproduced in it verbatim conversations he had had with its author over thirty years before. Haas thought that Werfel had completely forgotten him after going to America but was now convinced that he must have been thinking of no one else.[40] So it probably was also with others who read the book, but they may not have been as flattered. Again one meets Werfel's cronies from the cafés of Vienna, "motivated by the consuming ambition to outdo each other in absurdity."[41] But there are also passages reflecting Werfel's lasting obsession with his own guilt, a guilt superficially related to the lustful indulgence that he believed cost him his son but which doubtless ran to the very wellspring of his creativity.[42]

In spite of the precarious state of his health Werfel was surprisingly active on the intellectual front of the war effort,[43] but he was forced to reject far more offers and invitations than he could accept. He spent his time writing and in the company of close friends. That Roman Catholic clergy were numbered among the latter appeared to substantiate the widespread view that he had indeed converted despite his continued insistence to the contrary. He gave Jewish and Catholic circles alike clear explanations of his position. To convert would be a cowardly desertion of his people in their hour of greatest peril. Furthermore, the continuation of Israel as a separate historical entity was essential to the truth of Christianity and the fulfillment of its messianic gospel. The Jew was to be the eternal witness to the historical reality of Christ. Judaism and Catholicism were parallel: they would meet in infinity, but in finite time the role of the Jew in the Christian drama of salvation remained essential.[44]

Nevertheless, rumors of Werfel's conversion multiplied at the time of his death. He signed letters to senior clergy "Your obedient servant in Christ"; his body was secretly baptized; the archbishop of Los Angeles offered a dispensation allowing the author a Catholic burial; the funeral address was given by a Catholic priest; and a rosary was displayed in the casket between Werfel's hands. But the proffered

dispensation was declined; the baptism had been unsolicited; and
Father Moenius opened his eulogy by emphasizing that he spoke in
no official capacity but only as a friend, though from what followed
one might have assumed that Werfel had been a devout Catholic.[45]
The fact is that Werfel died what he had been born and remained
all his life, a Jew.

Franz Werfel had been a child of fortune. His success came early,
and he rose to fame steadily. Few of the German literary exiles enjoyed so quick and easy an adaptation to American culture and its ways
as he did. He never knew the alienation felt by so many other exiles,
nor did he ever express the disdain so many of them felt: he loved the
movies and other forms of American popular culture, and he loved the
company of film stars. Open and generous by nature, he was nevertheless extremely sensitive to any criticism of his work, so much so that
friendships were sometimes thereby broken.[46] Honest and loving, he
could also be duplicitous, as when he offered fulsome praise to Ludwig
Lewisohn for his translation of *Das Lied von Bernadette* but to others
denounced it as an atrocity.[47] Werfel had fervent friends and admirers,
just as he had detractors. Thomas Mann called him the most talented
writer of his generation. Erich Kahler called him a bad author but a
great poet.[48] More recently the reissue of his major prose works has
upgraded Werfel's stature as a novelist.[49] The great appeal of his writing, novels, and short stories lies in its characterization of individuals
and its authentic evocation of times and places now past and in danger
of being forgotten. It is true that the historian will always need the
storyteller. It is also true, however, that much of Werfel's writing has a
tendentious quality and is marred by signs of a "bad conscience." But
these weaknesses rarely interfere with the pleasure and instruction to be
gained from reading it. As to his person, so with his work, opinions are
divided. But then so was his own. Three days before his death on 26
August 1945 Werfel gave a close friend the just completed manuscript
of *Stern der Ungeborenen* with these words: "I could have made a nice
life for myself, but instead I slaved."[50]

Notes

1. In 1979 a group of West German writers visiting Soviet Armenia
    were met on arrival by an Armenian delegation that greeted
    them with the words: "We extend a hearty welcome to our

friends from the land of Franz Werfel!" For these Armenians the name Werfel rather than Goethe was synonymous with the world of German letters. Hans Christoph Buch, "Ein inoffizieller Völkermord," *Frankfurter Allgemeine Zeitung,* 31 July 1980, p. 19.

2. Notebooks of Adolf D. Klarmann, Folder 34, Franz Werfel Collection, University of Pennsylvania. See especially the page in the handwriting of Werfel's mother, prepared for Klarmann in 1936, and the latter's notes on an interview with Alma Mahler-Werfel dated 27 October 1945.

3. The novel *Barbara oder die Frömmigkeit,* whose heroine was directly inspired by Babi, is in many ways an exposition and celebration of what she meant to him. Its German title, which translates literally as "Barbara, or Piety," conveys this more directly than the English, *The Pure in Heart.*

4. "Erguß und Beichte," *Zwischen Oben und Unten. Prosa, Tagebücher, Aphorismen, literarische Nachträge* (München/Wien: Langen Müller, 1975), pp. 690-700 is an autobiographical account of Werfel's early years, especially good on his attitude toward his Jewishness and his attraction to German culture.

5. Herbert F. Wiese, "The Father-Son Conflict in Werfel's Early Works." *Symposium* 1/2 (1958), 160-167.

6. "Träume," *Zwischen Oben und Unten,* p. 749.

7. "An den Leser," *Der Weltfreund. Gedichte von Franz Werfel* (Berlin/Charlottenburg: Axel Juncker-Verlag, 1911), p. 110. On the background to its publication see Roy F. Allen, *Literary Life in German Expressionism and the Berlin Circles* (Ann Arbor: University of Michigan Research Press, 1983), p. 90.

8. "Die christliche Sendung. Ein offener Brief an Kurt Hiller von Franz Werfel," *Die Neue Rundschau* XXVIII (January 1917), 92-105; Max Brod, "Franz Werfels christliche Sendung," *Der Jude* I/2 (February 1917), 717-724; and Lionel B. Steiman, *Franz Werfel. The Faith of an Exile. From Prague to Beverly Hills* (Waterloo/Ontario: Wilfrid Laurier University Press, 1985), pp. 23-36.

9. Ibid., pp. 17-22. Werfel wrote regularly to Gertrude Spirk, his girlfriend in Prague. His letters to her are in the Schiller-Nationalmuseum in Marbach.

10. "Vorbemerkung zu 'Neue Bilderbogen und Soldatenlieder,'" reprinted in *Zwischen Oben und Unten,* p. 484ff.

11. "Rede an die Arbeiter von Davos," reprinted in *Zwischen Oben und Unten*, pp. 531–534.

12. For example, "Der Fall Franz Werfel," in the 'Theater, Kunst und Literatur' section of the *Neues Wiener Journal*, 21 November and 24 November 1918. For the Austrian socialists' view of these café intellectuals' attempts at revolution see Julius Braunthal, *Auf der Suche nach dem Millennium*, 2 vols (Nürnberg: Nest, 1948), vol. 1, p. 431.

13. See the account in Werfel's diary, reprinted in *Zwischen Oben und Unten*, p. 631 ff., and the autobiographical passages in *Star of the Unborn*, p. 364 f.: "I only knew that I felt like a murderer. . . . How could a person be so convinced of his own depravity as I was and still go on living?"

14. See the letter quoted in Lionel B. Steiman, *Franz Werfel. The Faith of an Exile. From Prague to Beverly Hills*, p. 203, n. 23.

15. Alma Mahler-Werfel, *Mein Leben* (Frankfurt am Main: Fischer, 1960), p. 122; Willy Haas, "Ein Dichter, nur ein Dichter. . . . ," *Die Welt*, 10 September 1970.

16. This was Werfel's first drama written in prose. The première was held in Vienna in 1922, and in January 1926 it was produced by The Theater Guild in New York, with leading roles played by Alfred Lunt and Lynn Fontanne.

17. See Roger Bauer, "Kraus contra Werfel. Eine nicht nur literarische Fehde," in *Laßt sie koaxen* (Wien: Europa, 1977), pp. 181–199.

18. See Roger Bauer, "K. und das Ungeheuer. Franz Kafka über Franz Werfel," *Neue Zürcher Zeitung* 107 (11 May 1979), 32, a discussion based on Kafka's diaries and letters.

19. Leo Brod, "Keinen Straßennamen bekommen. Deklamierend durch Prag: Unzertrennliche Schulfreunde Ernst Deutsch und Franz Werfel," *Sudetendeutsche Zeitung*, 29 October 1982, p. 7, and Willy Haas, *Die literarische Welt*, pp. 9–39. Bruno Walter had a very high regard for Werfel both as a man and as a writer, but he was especially impressed with Werfel's knowledge and understanding of music and by the sheer musicality of his nature. *Theme and Variations* (New York: Knopf, 1946), pp. 275 f., 338.

20. Lore B. Foltin, *Franz Werfel* (Stuttgart: Metzler, 1972, pp. 68 and 78.

21. On the Werfel residences see "Der wohlverdiente Himmel," *Die Presse*, Saturday/Sunday, 10/11 December 1977, pp. 17–19. On

their personalities and life style at the time. Joseph Wechsberg, "Franz Werfel's Vienna, *Saturday Review,* 11 March 1967, 62–65, and unpublished interview, Ben Huebsch Collection, Oral History Research Office, Butler Library, Columbia University. Contrary to Wechsberg, Huebsch says that Werfel did like to drink wine, but other accounts support Wechsberg.

22. Diary entry "Sommer 1925," *Zwischen Oben und Unten,* p. 689.

23. "Ägyptisches Tagebuch," ibid., pp. 705–742.

24. "Romane von gestern–heute gelesen. Der Weltfreund auf den Barrikaden. Ulrich Weinzierl über Franz Werfels 'Barbara oder die Frömmigkeit,'" *Frankfurter Allgemeine Zeitung* 17 (21 January 1983), 25.

25. *Erzählungen aus zwei Welten,* 3 vols., ed. Adolf D. Klarmann (Frankfurt am Main: S. Fischer, 1948–1954). (Vol. 1 was published in Stockholm by Bermann Fischer.)

26. *Twilight of a World* (New York: Viking, 1937). Roger Bauer makes the point that after World War I Werfel's concern shifted from humanity in general–"My one and only wish, O man, is to be thy brother"–to the representative types of the world that had collapsed, of which Karl Fiala was a prime example. "Ruhm und Nachruhm Franz Werfels," *Neue Zürcher Zeitung,* 15 July 1977 (Fernausgabe No. 163), p. 22.

27. "Realism and Inwardness" ("Realismus und Innerlichkeit"); "Can We Live without Faith in God?" ("Können wir ohne Gottesglauben leben?"); and "Of Man's True Happiness" ("Von der reinsten Glückseligkeit des Menschen") originated as lectures Werfel gave in 1931, 1932, and 1937 respectively. They were also published individually in book form at the time, and are reprinted in *Zwischen Oben und Unten,* pp. 16–109.

28. Lionel B. Steiman, *Franz Werfel. The Faith of an Exile,* pp. 75 and 209, n. 1. Always concerned with authenticity of detail, Werfel had visited an Armenian monastery in Vienna to seek instruction on historical and theological matters, and to have Armenian documents translated. Subsequently he asked the abbot to read the galley proofs of *Musa Dagh.* When His Excellency did so, however, Werfel refused to incorporate his suggestion, saying he was writing a novel, not a scholarly treatise. Adolf D. Klarmann interviewed the abbot on a visit to Vienna in 1952. See the typescript memoir of this visit, "Besuch bei der Mechitaristen-Congre-

gation in Wien," in the Franz Werfel Collection, University of Pennsylvania.

29.   "Ein inoffizieller Völkermord. Hans Christoph Buch über Franz Werfels 'Die vierzig Tage des Musa Dagh,'" *Frankfurter Allgemeine Zeitung* 175 (31 July 1980), 19; "Fremd sein und Opfer werden. Franz Werfel und der armenische Widerstand am Musa Dagh," *Neue Zürcher Zeitung* 155 (9 July 1982), 29; David Marshall Lang, *The Armenians: A People in Exile* (London: Allan and Unwin, 1981), p. 158f.

30.   Letter of 25 February 1974 from Vartan Gregorian to Adolf D. Klarmann, Franz Werfel Collection, University of Pennsylvania.

31.   In 1935 Werfel discussed various aspects of *The Eternal Road* with Albert Einstein. While deeply gratified that a writer he regarded so highly should have chosen so important a theme, Einstein nevertheless differed with Werfel on certain points in his treatment of it. See their exchange of letters, Albert Einstein Collection, Princeton University.

32.   Werfel was working on Capri at the time of the *Anschluß*, whence he traveled to Switzerland to meet Alma.

33.   "Der wohlverdiente Himmel," *Die Presse*, Saturday/Sunday, 10/11 December 1977, pp. 17-19. This is a prepublication discussion of Dietmar Grieser's *Sorbas, Piroschka & Co. Der Dichter und sein Modell* (Langen-Müller, 1978), which traces the roots and destiny of Teta Linek's real life counterpart, Anežka Hvižďová, who had died in 1933. Grieser finds it fitting that author and model came together thirty-eight years later when Werfel's remains were transferred to Vienna's *Zentralfriedhof*, just a few hundred paces from hers.

34.   "Sie meinen nicht dich Freudreich! Sie meinen nicht mich. Wen meinen sie eigentlich? Israel ist kein Volk. Israel ist ein Orden dem Blute nach, in den man durch Geburt eintritt, unfreiwillig." *Erzählungen aus zwei Welten*, vol 3, p. 275f.

35.   See Werfel's account in his preface to *The Song of Bernadette*.

36.   These letters are in the Werfel Collection at the University of California, Los Angeles. "Roman Catholic readers perceived in its worldly success something that might be called a secular beatification of their rare heroine...." B. W. Huebsch, "One Hundred Years of Lourdes. Werfel Remembered," *Saturday Review of Literature*, March 1958, p. 36.

37. See correspondence between Werfel and the New York Theater Guild, Folder 23, Franz Werfel Collection, University of Pennsylvania.

38. Lionel B. Steiman, *Franz Werfel. The Faith of an Exile*, pp. 174-178.

39. Georg Moenius, "Hollywooder Abende bei Franz Werfel," typescript of a 1952 talk on Bavarian Radio, Franz Werfel Collection, University of Pennsylvania, pp. 9-10.

40. Willy Haas, *Die literarische Welt*, p. 27; *Der junge Werfel. Erinnerungen von Willy Haas*, typescript dated January 1953, Franz Werfel Collection, University of Pennsylvania, p. 3.

41. *Star of the Unborn*, p. 154.

42. *Geheime Tagebücher,* unpublished notebook, Franz Werfel Collection, University of Pennsylvania, pp. 81-92; cf. Alma Mahler-Werfel, *Mein Leben*, p. 128, and *Star of the Unborn*, pp. 364f. and 366.

43. Lionel B. Steiman, *Franz Werfel. The Faith of an Exile*, pp. 123-126 and 144-149.

44. "My Profession of Faith," *Jewish Digest*, January 1941, pp. 1-4; Letter to Archbishop Rummel of New Orleans, 27 October 1942. German translation in *Zwischen Oben und Unten*, p. 892f.

45. Lore B. Foltin, *Franz Werfel*, p. 108. Werfel's secret posthumous baptism is reported in Adolf D. Klarmann's notes of an interview with Alma held on 27 October 1945. Folder 34, Franz Werfel Collection, University of Pennsylvania. According to Klarmann this baptism was performed through the efforts of Father Moenius and the archbishop of Los Angeles, John J. Cantwell. A typescript copy of Moenius's eulogy, "Denkrede auf Franz Werfel," is in Folder 43, Franz Werfel Collection, University of Pennsylvania.

46. Hubert Mittrowsky, "Erinnerungen an Franz Werfel – Zu seinem 20. Todestag," *Die Presse* 21/22. August 1965, 19, recalls an incident in which a 1936 review of his that offended Werfel was later followed by a warm reconciliation. But this was not always so. On Werfel's break with Ludwig Marcuse, see Lionel B. Steiman, *Franz Werfel. The Faith of an Exile*, p. 161f.

47. In a letter of 19 July 1943 Werfel told Lewisohn how happy he was that "the splendid English dress you gave my Bernadette is after fourteen months still like new and getting compliments everywhere." (Alma Mahler Werfel Collection, University of Pennsylvania.) Six weeks earlier he had complained to Felix

450   Lionel B. Steiman

Braun about "the horrible English translation" of *Das Lied von Bernadette,* which was like a "blurred photograph" of the original. Letter of 31 May 1943, Franz Werfel Collection, University of Pennsylvania.

48.   As quoted in Antal Madl and Judit Gyori, eds., *Thomas Mann und Ungarn. Essays, Dokumente, Bibliographie.* (Köln/Wien: Böhlau, 1977), pp. 5 and 380; Erich Kahler, "Franz Werfel's Poetry," *Commentary* 5 (1948), 186-188. A balanced recent assessment is Ronald Taylor, *Literature and Society in Germany 1918-1945,* pp. 169 and 314.

49.   The 1975 publication of the final volume of Werfel's Collected Works, made possible through the untiring devotion of their editor, Werfel's friend and disciple Adolf D. Klarmann, was followed by an undertaking by the S. Fischer Verlag to reissue his major titles. Fischer also commissioned Peter Jungk to write a biography of Werfel. Much of the reassessment of Werfel, overwhelmingly positive, has taken place in the series "Novels of Yesterday—Read Today," a regular feature in the *Frankfurter Allgemeine Zeitung.* The *Badische Neueste Nachrichten* of 5 June 1982 hailed *The Song of Bernadette* as especially timely in our present "spiritually exhausted" world. Other reviewers in various publications praised *The Forty Days of Musa Dagh, Embezzled Heaven,* and *The Pure in Heart* for both their historical authenticity and their moral and spiritual message; one attempted to settle the question whether Werfel had talent by asserting that, if anything, he was overendowed with it. *Frankfurter Allgemeine Zeitung,* 31 July 1980, p. 19; 2 April 1982, p. 25; 21 January 1983, p. 25; *Neue Zürcher Zeitung,* 9 July 1982, p. 29.

50.   "Ich hätte mir ein schönes Leben machen können, aber ich habe geschuftet!" Quoted in Georg Moenius, "Hollywooder Abende bei Franz Werfel," typescript of a 1952 talk on Bavarian Radio, Franz Werfel Collection, University of Pennsylvania, p. 10.

Bibliography

I. Works by Franz Werfel in German

    A. Collected Works. Edited by Adolf D. Klarmann, published by the S. Fischer Verlag of Frankfurt am Main

        i.   Poetry: *Das lyrische Werk,* 1967.
        ii. Stories: *Erzählungen aus zwei Welten.* 3 vols., 1948–1954. (Volume I was published in Stockholm by Bermann Fischer.)
        iii. Plays: *Meisternovellen,* 1974.
                      Die Dramen. 2 vols, 1959.
        iv. Essays, Diaries, Aphorisms, and other smaller pieces: *Zwischen Oben und Unten. Prosa. Tagebücher, Aphorismen. Literarische Nachträge.* Müchen/Wien: Langen Mller, 1975.

    B. Chronological list of individual major works

    Der Weltfreund. Gedichte. Berlin: Axel Juncker, 1911.
    Wir sind. Neue Gedichte. Leipzig: Kurt Wolff, 1913.
    Einander. Oden Lieder Gestalten. Leipzig: Kurt Wolff, 1915.
    Der Gerichtstag. In fünf Büchern. Leipzig: Kurt Wolff, 1919.
    Nicht der Mörder, der Ermordete ist schuldig. Eine Novelle. München: Kurt Wolff, 1920.
    Spiegelmensch. Magische Trilogie. München: Kurt Wolff, 1920.
    Bockgesang. München: Kurt Wolff, 1921.
    Schweiger. Ein Trauerspiel. München: Kurt Wolff, 1922.
    Verdi. Roman der Oper. Berlin/Wien/Leipzig: Paul Zsolnay, 1924.
    Juarez und Maximilian. Dramatische Historie. Berlin/Wien/Leipzig: Paul Zsolnay, 1924.
    Paulus unter den Juden. Berlin/Wien/Leipzig: Paul Zsolnay, 1926.
    Der Tod des Kleinbürgers. Novelle. Berlin/Wien/Leipzig: Paul Zsolnay, 1927.
    Geheimnis eines Menschen. Novellen. Berlin/Wien/Leipzig: Paul Zsolnay, 1927. (Contains *Die Entfremdung, Geheimnis eines Menschen, Die Hoteltreppe,* and *Das Trauerhaus.*)

452   Lionel B. Steiman

Der Abituriententag. Die Geschichte einer Jugendschuld. Berlin/Wien/Leipzig: Paul Zsolnay, 1927.

Barbara oder die Frömmigkeit. Berlin/Wien/Leipzig: Paul Zsolnay, 1929.

Das Reich Gottes in Böhmen. Tragödie eines Führers. Berlin/Wien/Leipzig: Paul Zsolnay, 1930.

Kleine Verhältnisse. Novelle. Berlin/Wien/Leipzig: Paul Zsolnay, 1931.

Die Geschwister von Neapel. Roman. Berlin/Wien/Leipzig: Paul Zsolnay, 1931.

Die vierzig Tage des Musa Dagh. Roman. 2 vols. Berlin/Wien/Leipzig: Paul Zsolnay, 1933.

Der Weg der Verheißung. Ein Bibelspiel. Wien: Paul Zsolnay, 1935.

Höret die Stimme. Jeremias. Roman. Wien: Paul Zsolnay, 1937.

Der veruntreute Himmel. Die Geschichte einer Magd. Roman. Stockholm: Bermann-Fischer, 1939.

Cella oder die Überwinder: Versuch eines Romans [1938]. First published in Adolf D. Klarmann, ed., *Franz Werfel. Erzählungen aus zwei Welten,* vol. 3, Frankfurt am Main: S. Fischer, 1954.

Das Lied von Bernadette. Roman. Stockholm: Bermann-Fischer, 1941.

Jacobowsky und der Oberst. Komödie einer Tragödie in drei Akten. New York: F. S. Crofts, 1945; Stockholm: Bermann-Fischer, 1944 [despite the dates, the New York edition was the first].

Stern der Ungeborenen. Ein Reiseroman. Stockholm: Bermann-Fischer, 1946.

Zwischen Oben und Unten. Stockholm: Bermann-Fischer, 1946. (Contains the essays "Realismus und Innerlichkeit," "Können wir ohne Gottesglauben leben?" and "Von der reinsten Glückseligkeit des Menschen," which were published individually in the early thirties).

II. Works in English, with German titles in parentheses

A. Poetry

Poems. Translated by Edith Abercrombie Snow. Princeton: Princeton University Press, 1945.

B. Stories

Twilight of a World. Translated by H. T. Lowe-Porter. New York: The Viking Press, 1937. This collection was prepared especially for The Viking Press by Franz Werfel and contains what he considered his best short stories as well as two short novels, and a lengthy introductory essay on the Austrian Imperial ideal.

Not the Murderer (Nicht der Mörder, Der Ermordete ist schuldig), 1920.

The House of Mourning (Das Trauerhaus), 1927.

Estrangement (Die Entfremdung), 1927.

The Staircase (Die Hoteltreppe), 1927.

Saverio's Secret (Geheimnis eines Menschen), 1927.

The Man Who Conquered Death (Der Tod des Kleinbürgers), 1928. *Class Reunion*

Class Reunion (Abituriententag), 1928.

Poor People (Kleine Verhältnisse), 1931.

C. Plays

The following are Werfel's major plays in translation. His early plays may be found in the complete German edition of his collected works above.

Goat Song (Bockgesang). Garden City, New York: Doubleday, Page and Co., 1926.

Juarez and Maximilian (Juarez und Maximilian). New York: Simon and Schuster, 1926.

Paul among the Jews (Paulus unter den Juden). London: Diocesan House, 1928.

The Eternal Road (Der Weg der Verheißung). New York: Viking Press, 1936.

Jacobowsky and the Colonel; comedy of a tragedy (*Jacobowsky und der Oberst. Komödie einer Tragödie in drei Akten*). New York: Viking, 1944.

D. Novels

Verdi. A Novel of the Opera (*Verdi, Roman der Oper*). New York: Simon & Schuster, 1925.

The Pure in Heart (*Barbara oder die Frömmigkeit*). New York: Book League of America, 1931. (Published in London in the same year by Jarrolds, Ltd., under the title "The Hidden Child.")

The Pascarella Family (*Die Geschwister von Neapel*). New York: Simon & Schuster, 1932.

The Forty Days of Musa Dagh (*Die Vierzig Tage des Musa Dagh*). New York: Viking, 1934.

Hearken unto the Voice (*Höret die Stimme. Jeremias*). New York: Viking, 1938.

Embezzled Heaven (*Der veruntreute Himmel*). New York: Viking, 1940.

Cella oder die Überwinder: Versuch eines Romans (untranslated). Adolf D. Klarmann, ed., *Erzählungen aus zwei Welten*, vol. 3. Frankfurt am Main: S. Fischer, 1954.

The Song of Bernadette (*Das Lied von Bernadette*). New York: Viking, 1942.

Star of the Unborn (*Stern der Ungeborenen: Ein Reiseroman*). New York: Viking, 1946.

E. Essays

Between Heaven and Earth. New York: Philosophical Library, 1944. Contains "Can We Live without Faith in God?" (Können wir ohne Gottesglauben leben?), "Of Man's True Happiness" (Von der reinsten Glückseligkeit des Menschen), "Realism and Inwardness" (Realismus und Innerlichkeit), as well as smaller theological pieces.

III. Secondary Works in English

Foltin, Lore B. *Franz Werfel*. Stuttgart: J. B. Metzlersche Verlags-buchhandlung, 1972. This is the most comprehensive bio-graphical and bibliographical survey available to date.

———. and John M. Spalek, "Franz Werfel's Essays: A Survey." *The German Quarterly* 42 (March 1969), 172-203.

Klarmann, Adolf D. "Franz Werfel's Eschatology and Cosmog-ony." *Modern Language Quarterly* 7 (1946), 385-410.

———. "Franz Werfel and the Stage." In Lore B. Foltin, ed., *Franz Werfel 1890-1945*. Pittsburgh: University of Pittsburgh Press, 1961.

Spalek, John M. *A Guide to the Archival Materials of the Ger-man-Speaking Emigration to the United States after 1933*. Charlottesville: University of Virginia Press, 1978.

Steiman, Lionel B. *Franz Werfel: The Faith of an Exile: from Prague to Beverly Hills*. Waterloo, Ontario: Wilfrid Laurier University Press, 1985.

Williams, C. E. *The Broken Eagle: The Politics of Austrian Literature from Empire to Anschluß*. London: Paul Elek, 1974. (Contains chapter on Werfel.)

A. Dissertations

Blumenthal, Werner. "Sin and Salvation in the Works of Franz Werfel." Dissertation, University of California, Los Angeles, 1967.

Brown, Albert Harrison Eayre. "Franz Werfel's Dramaturgy: Theory and Practice." Dissertation, University of Pennsyl-vania, 1976.

Davidheiser, James C. "Franz Werfel and the Historical Novel: An Analytical Study of *Verdi: Roman der Oper, Die vierzig Tage des Musa Dagh,* and *Das Lied von Bernadette.*" Disser-tation, University of Pittsburgh, 1972.

Krügel, Fred August. "Suffering and the Sacrificial Ethos in the Dramatic Works of Franz Werfel." Dissertation, Uni-versity of Minnesota, 1959.

Lea, Henry A. "The Unworldly Character in the Works of Franz Werfel." Dissertation, University of Pennsylvania, 1962.

Mitchell, Janis Diane. "Exile and Historical Existence in the Writings of Franz Werfel, Alfred Döblin and Hermann Broch." Dissertation, Pennsylvania State University, 1976.

Smith, Clyde Robert. "Karl Kraus and Franz Werfel: The Conflict between Sorcerer and Mystic." Dissertation, University of California, Los Angeles, 1970.

IV. Major Studies in German

Adams, Eleonora K. and Ursula Kuhlmann. "Perspektiven über Werfels dramatischen Schaffen." In Karl S. Weimar, ed., *Views and Reviews of Modern German Literature. Festschrift for Adolf D. Klarmann.* München: Delp, 1974.

Arnold, Martin. *Lyrisches Dasein und Erfahrung der Zeit im Frühwerk Franz Werfels.* Dissertation, Freiburg (Schweiz), 1961.

Bach, Anneliese. "Die Auffassung von Gemeinschaft und Kollektiv im Prosawerk Franz Werfels." *Zeitschrift für deutsche Philologie* 76 (1957), 187-202.

Bauer, Roger. "Werfel als Kritiker (Ein Nachwort zu allen Nachworten)." *Canadian Review of Comparative Literature* 5 (1978), 178-192.

Braselmann, Werner. *Franz Werfel.* Wuppertal-Barmen: Emil Müller, 1960.

Brunner, Robert. "Franz Werfels theologisches Vermächtnis." *Judaica* 2 (1946), 209-229.

Goldstücker, Eduard. "Rainer Maria Rilke und Franz Werfel. Zur Geschichte ihrer Beziehungen." *Acta Universitatis Carolinae, Philologica* 3 (1960), 37-71.

Guthke, Karl S. "Wunderkind und Impresario in eigener Sache: Franz Werfels Anfänge." In K.S.G. *Das Abenteuer der Literatur* (Bern/München: Francke, 1981), 295-309. Also in *Deutsche Vierteljahrschrift für Literaturwissenschaft und Geistesgeschichte* 52 (1978), 71-89.

Hempel, Johannes. *Vision und Offenbarung in Franz Werfels Romanen "Jeremias: Höret die Stimme" und "Das Lied von Bernadette": Ein Beitrag zur Frage nach einer evangelisch-theologischen Literaturkritik.* Dissertation, Leipzig, 1963.

Jungk, Peter Stephan. *Franz Werfel – Eine Lebensgeschichte.* Frankfurt am Main: Fischer, 1987.

Klarmann, Adolf D. "Das Weltbild Franz Werfels." *Wissenschaft und Weltbild* 1/2 (1954), 35-48.

Kuhlenkamp, Detlef. *Werfels späte Romane: Seine Kritik an der Rationalität.* Dissertation, Frankfurt am Main, 1971.

Maier, Bernhard. *Vater und Sohn: Zur Deutung der Dichtung Franz Werfels.* Dissertation, Freiburg im Breisgau, 1960.

Meister, Helga. *Franz Werfels Dramen und ihre Inszenierungen auf der deutschsprachigen Bühne.* Dissertation, Köln, 1964.

Mierendorff, Marta. "Spekulierende Einbildungskraft und historische Analyse. Franz Werfels Exilroman 'Stern der Ungeborenen.'" In Manfred Durzak, ed., *Die deutsche Exilliteratur 1933-1945.* Stuttgart: Philipp Reclam jun., 1973.

Politzer, Heinz. "Dieses Mütterchen hat Krallen. Prag und die Ursprünge Rilkes, Kafkas und Werfels." *Literatur und Kritik* 81 (1974), 15-33.

Puttkamer, Annemarie von. *Franz Werfel: Wort und Antwort.* Würzburg: Werkbund, 1952.

Rück, Herbert. *Werfel als Dramatiker.* Dissertation, Marburg, 1965.

Specht, Richard. *Franz Werfel: Versuch einer Zeitspiegelung.* Berlin: Paul Zsolnay, 1926.

Turrian, Marysia. *Dostojewski und Franz Werfel: vom östlichen zum westlichen Denken.* Bern: P. Haupt, 1950.

Urban, Bernd. "Franz Werfel, Freud, und die Psychoanalyse. Zu unveröffentlichten Dokumenten." *Deutsche Veierteljahresschrift* 47 (1973), 267-285.

Wimmer, Paul. *Franz Werfels dramatische Sendung.* Wien: Bergland, 1973.

Zahn, Leopold. *Franz Werfel.* Berlin: Colloquium, 1966.

Further listings of studies in German may be found in Lionel B. Steiman, *Franz Werfel: The Faith of an Exile,* and more especially in Lore B. Foltin's bio-bibliographical *Franz Werfel,* both in Section III above.

Name and Title Index